# POLITICAL SCIENCE: SCOPE AND THEORY

# HANDBOOK OF POLITICAL SCIENCE

Volume 1

# POLITICAL SCIENCE: SCOPE AND THEORY

Edited by
**FRED I. GREENSTEIN** Princeton University
**NELSON W. POLSBY** University of California, Berkeley

 **ADDISON-WESLEY PUBLISHING COMPANY**

Reading, Massachusetts
Menlo Park, California · London · Amsterdam · Don Mills, Ontario · Sydney

**ST. PHILIPS COLLEGE LIBRARY**

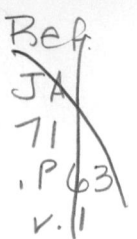

This book is in the
ADDISON-WESLEY SERIES IN POLITICAL SCIENCE

Copyright © 1975 by Addison-Wesley Publishing Company, Inc. Philippines copyright 1975 by Addison-Wesley Publishing Company, Inc.

All rights reserved. No part of this publication may be reproduced, stored in a retrieval system, or transmitted, in any form or by any means, electronic, mechanical, photocopying, recording, or otherwise, without the prior written permission of the publisher. Printed in the United States of America. Published simultaneously in Canada. Library of Congress Catalog Card No. 73-11886

ISBN 0-201-02601-5
ABCDEFGHIJ-HA-798765

# *PREFACE*

Early in his career, the fledgling political scientist learns that his discipline is ill-defined, amorphous, and heterogeneous. This perception will in no way be rebutted by the appearance of a presumably encyclopedic eight-volume work entitled *The Handbook of Political Science.* Indeed, the persistent amorphousness of our discipline has constituted a central challenge to the editors of the *Handbook* and has brought to its creation both hazards and opportunities. The opportunities were apparent enough to us when we took on the editorial duties of the *Handbook;* the hazards became clearer later on.

At the outset, it seemed to us a rare occasion when a publisher opens quite so large a canvas and invites a pair of editors to paint on it as they will—or can. We immediately saw that in order to do the job at all we would have to cajole a goodly number of our colleagues into the belief that our canvas was in reality Tom Sawyer's fence. We did not set out at the beginning, however, with a precise vision of the final product—i.e., a work that would be composed of these particular eight volumes, dealing with the present array and number of contributions and enlisting all the present contributors. Rather, the *Handbook* is the product of a long and in some ways accidental process. An account of this process is in order if only because, by describing the necessarily adventitious character of the "decisions" that produced this work, we can help the reader to see that the *Handbook* is not an attempt to make a collective pronouncement of Truth chiseled in stone, but rather an assembly of contributions, each an individual scholarly effort, whose overall purpose is to give a warts-and-all portrait of a discipline that is still in a process of becoming.

We first became involved in discussions about the project in 1965. Addison-Wesley had already discussed the possibility of a handbook with a number of other political scientists, encouraged by their happy experience with a two-volume compendium of highly respected review essays in social psychology (Lindzey, 1954), which has since been revised and expanded into a five-volume work (Lindzey and Aronson, 1968–69).

Of the various people to whom Addison-Wesley aired the handbook idea, we evidently were among the most persistent in encouraging such a project. No doubt the reason was that we were still close to our own graduate work in a department where a careful reading of many of the chapters in *The Handbook of Social Psychology* was in some ways more fundamental to learning our trade than a comparable exposure to many of the more conspicuous intellectual edifices of the political science of the time. Gardner Lindzey, in writing his introductory statement to the first edition of *The Handbook of Social Psychology* (reprinted in the second edition), described *our* needs as well as those of budding social psychologists in saying that

> the accelerating expansion of social psychology in the past two decades has led to an acute need for a source book more advanced than the ordinary textbook in the field but yet more focused than scattered periodical literature. . . . It was this state of affairs that led us to assemble a book that would represent the major areas of social psychology at a level of difficulty appropriate for graduate students. In addition to serving the needs of graduate instruction, we anticipate that the volumes will be useful in advanced undergraduate courses and as a reference book for professional psychologists.

With the substitution of "political science" in the appropriate places, Lindzey's description of his own purposes and audiences reflects precisely what we thought Addison-Wesley might most usefully seek to accomplish with a political science handbook.

In choosing a pair of editors, the publisher might well have followed a balancing strategy, looking for two political scientists who were poles apart in their background, training, and views of the discipline. The publisher might then have sought divine intervention, praying for the miracle that would bring the editors into sufficient agreement to make the planning of the *Handbook*—or *any* handbook—possible at all. Instead they found a pair of editors with complementary but basically similar and congenial perspectives. We were then both teaching at Wesleyan University and had been to graduate school together at Yale, at a time when the political science department there was making its widely recognized contribution to the modernization of the discipline. Each had recently spent a year in the interdisciplinary ambience of the Center for Advanced Study in the Behavioral Sciences. Moreover, we were both specialists in American politics, the "field" which in 1973 still accounted for three-quarters of the contributions to *The American Political Science Review*. There were also complementary divergencies. Within political science, Polsby's work and interests had been in national politics and policy-making, whereas Greenstein's were more in mass, extragovernmental aspects of political behavior. Outside political science, Polsby's interests were directed more toward sociology and law, and Greenstein's tended toward psychiatry and clinical and social psychology.

To begin with, neither we nor the publisher could be sure without first gathering evidence that the discipline of political science was "ready" for a handbook comparable to the Lindzey work. We were sure that, if it was at all possible for us to bring such a handbook into being, we would have to employ the Aristotelian tack of working within and building upon existing categories of endeavor, rather than the Platonic (or Procrustean) mode of inventing a coherent set of master categories and persuading contributors to use them. First, at our request the publisher inquired of a number of distinguished political scientists whether they felt a need would be served by a handbook of political science similar to *The Handbook of Social Psychology*. This inquiry went to political scientists who had themselves been involved in extensive editorial activities or who were especially known for their attention to political science as a discipline. The responses were quite uniform in favoring such a handbook. The particular suggestions about how such a handbook might be *organized,* however, were exceptionally varied. But fortunately we had asked one further question: What half-dozen or so individuals were so authoritative or original in their contributions on some topic as to make them prime candidates for inclusion in any political science handbook, no matter what its final overall shape? Here agreement reemerged; the consultants were remarkably unanimous in the individuals named.

Seizing the advantage provided by that consensus, we reached the following agreement with the publisher. We would write the individuals who constituted what we now saw as a prime list of candidates for inclusion as authors and ask whether they would be willing to contribute to a handbook of political science, given a long lead time and freedom to choose the topic of their essay. (We did suggest possible topics to each.) It was agreed that unless we were able to enlist most of those with whom we were corresponding as a core group of contributors, we would not proceed with a handbook. Since all but one of that group indicated willingness to contribute, we signed a publishing agreement (in September 1967) and proceeded to expand our core group to a full set of contributors to what we then envisaged as a three-volume handbook, drawing on our core contributors for advice. Our queries to the core contributors were a search not so much for structural and organizational suggestions as for concrete topics and specific contributors to add to the initial list.

The well-worn term "incremental" suggests itself as a summary of how the table of contents of *The Handbook of Political Science* then took shape. As the number of contributors increased, and as contributors themselves continued to make suggestions about possible rearrangements in the division of labor and to remark on gaps, the planned three volumes expanded to eight, most of which, however, were shorter than the originally intended three. Throughout, Addison-Wesley left it to us and the contributors, within the very broadest of boundaries, to define the overall length of the project and of the individual contributions. And throughout, we urged the contributors not to seek intellectual anonymity in the guise of being "merely" summarizers—or embalmers—of their fields but rather to endeavor to place a distinctive intellectual stamp on their contributions.

A necessary condition of enlisting the initial group of contributors was a production deadline so far in the future as to dissolve the concern of rational individuals about adding to their intellectual encumbrances. As it turned out, our "safely remote" initial deadline (1970) was in fact a drastic underestimation of the number of postponements and delays.* Along with delays there have been occasional withdrawals, as individual contributors recognized that even with a long fuse the task of preparing a handbook article would be a major one and would inevitably preempt time from other projects and interests. Departing contributors were often helpful in suggesting alternatives. Both through the late enlistment of such substitutes and through the addition of collaborators taken on by invited contributors, we feel we have been spared a table of contents that anachronistically represents only the cohort of those individuals who were responsible for the shape of political science circa 1967.

Whether one builds a handbook table of contents a priori or ex post facto, *some* basis of organization emerges. We might have organized a handbook around:

1. *"political things"* (e.g., the French bureaucracy, the U.S. Constitution, political parties);
2. *nodes or clusters in the literature* (community power, group theory, issue voting);
3. *subdisciplines* (public administration, public law, comparative government, political theory, international relations);
4. *functions* (planning, law-making, adjudication);
5. *geography* (the American Congress, the British Cabinet, the politicoeconomic institutions of the U.S.S.R.);
6. or any combination of the above and further possibilities.

Any of our colleagues who have tried to construct a curriculum in political science will sympathize with our dilemma. There is, quite simply, no

---

* For the comparable experience of *Handbook of Social Psychology* editors with delays, see Lindzey, 1954, p. vii, Lindzey and Aronson, 1968–69, p. ix.

sovereign way to organize our discipline. Although much of our knowledge is cumulative, there is no set beginning or end to political science. Apart from certain quite restricted subdisciplinary areas (notably the mathematical and statistical), political scientists do not have to learn a particular bit of information or master a particular technique at a particular stage as a prerequisite to further study. And the discipline lacks a single widely accepted frame of reference or principle of organization. Consequently, we evolved a table of contents that to some extent adopted nearly *all* the approaches above. (None of our chapter titles contains a geographical reference, but many of the chapters employ one or more explicitly specified political systems as data sources.)

The protean classifications of subspecialization within political science and the ups and downs in subspecialty interests over the years are extensively reviewed by Dwight Waldo in his essay in Volume 1 on political science as discipline and profession. A further way to recognize the diversity and change in our discipline—as well as the persisting elements—is to note the divisions of disciplinary interests used by the directories of the American Political Science Association, the membership of which constitutes the great bulk of all political scientists. A glance at the three successive directories which have been current during our editorial activities is instructive.

The 1961 *Biographical Directory of the American Political Science Association* (APSA, 1961) represents a last glimpse at a parsimonious, staid set of subdisciplinary categories that would have been readily recognizable at the 1930 Annual Meeting of the Association.

1. American National Government
2. Comparative Government
3. International Law and Relations
4. Political Parties
5. Political Theory
6. Public Administration
7. Public Law
8. State and Local Government

In the next *Biographical Directory* (APSA, 1968), there appeared a categorization that was at once pared down and much expanded from the 1961 classification. A mere three "general fields" were listed. The first was "Contemporary Political Systems." Members electing this general field were asked to specify the country or countries in which they were interested, and those countries were listed parenthetically after the members' names in the subdisciplinary listing, presumably out of a desire to play down the importance of "area studies" as an intellectual focus and to accentuate the importance of functional or analytic bases of intellectual endeavor. "International Law, Organization, and Politics" was the second general field, and "Political Theory and Philosophy" was the third. But the 26 categories in Table 1 were provided for the listing of "specialized fields." They included some venerable subdivisions, perhaps in slightly more fashionable phrasing, and other distinctly nonvenerable subdivisions, at least one of which (political socialization) did not even exist in the general vocabulary of political scientists ten years earlier. In this *Handbook*, the 1968 categories have many parallels, including the general principle of organization that excludes geography as a specialized field criterion while at the same time recognizing that political scientists can and should study and compare diverse political settings. Diplomatically avoiding the presentation of a structured classification, the editors of the 1968 *Directory* relied on the alphabet for their sequence of specialized fields.

TABLE 1 Subdisciplinary categories used in *Biographical Directory* of the American Political Science Association, 1968

1. Administrative law
2. Administration: organization, processes, behavior
3. Budget and fiscal management
4. Constitutional law
5. Executive: organization, processes, behavior
6. Foreign policy
7. Government regulation of business
8. International law
9. International organization and administration
10. International politics
11. Judiciary: organization, processes, behavior
12. Legislature: organization, processes, behavior
13. Methodology
14. Metropolitan and urban government and politics
15. National security policy
16. Personnel administration
17. Political and constitutional history
18. Political parties and elections: organizations and processes
19. Political psychology
20. Political socialization
21. Political theory and philosophy (empirical)
22. Political theory and philosophy (historical)
23. Political theory and philosophy (normative)
24. Public opinion
25. Revolutions and political violence
26. State and local government and politics
27. Voting behavior

Even with this burgeoning of options, many members of the discipline evidently felt that their interests were not adequately covered. Goodly numbers took advantage of an opportunity provided in the questionnaire to the APSA membership to list "other" specialties, referring, for example, to "political sociology," "political behavior," "political development," "policy studies," "communication," "federalism," and "interest groups."

The 1973 *Biographical Directory* (APSA, 1973) attempted still another basis of classification, a revised version of the classification used in the 1970 *National Science Foundation Register of Scientific and Technical Personnel.* Braving a structured rather than alphabetic classification, the authors of this taxonomy divided the discipline into nine major classes and a total of 60 specialized classifications, with a return to the antique dichotomy of foreign versus U.S. politics. The specifics of the 1973 listing are given in Table 2.

TABLE 2 Subdisciplinary categories used in *Biographical Directory* of the American Political Science Association, 1973

| | |
|---|---|
| I | Foreign and Cross-National Political Institutions and Behavior |
| 1. | Analyses of particular systems or subsystems |
| 2. | Decision-making processes |
| 3. | Elites and their oppositions |
| 4. | Mass participation and communications |
| 5. | Parties, mass movements, secondary associations |
| 6. | Political development and modernization |
| 7. | Politics of planning |
| 8. | Values, ideologies, belief systems, political culture |
| II | International Law, Organization, and Politics |
| 9. | International law |
| 10. | International organization and administration |
| 11. | International politics |
| III | Methodology |
| 12. | Computer techniques |
| 13. | Content analysis |
| 14. | Epistemology and philosophy of science |
| 15. | Experimental design |
| 16. | Field data collection |
| 17. | Measurement and index construction |
| 18. | Model building |
| 19. | Statistical analysis |
| 20. | Survey design and analysis |
| IV | Political Stability, Instability, and Change |
| 21. | Cultural modification and diffusion |
| 22. | Personality and motivation |
| 23. | Political leadership and recruitment |
| 24. | Political socialization |
| 25. | Revolution and violence |
| 26. | Schools and political education |
| 27. | Social and economic stratification |

(continued)

V Political Theory
28. Systems of political ideas in history
29. Ideology systems
30. Political philosophy (general)
31. Methodological and analytical systems

VI Public Policy: Formation and Content
32. Policy theory
33. Policy measurement
34. Economic policy and regulation
35. Science and technology
36. Natural resources and environment
37. Education
38. Poverty and welfare
39. Foreign and military policy

VII Public Administration
40. Bureaucracy
41. Comparative administration
42. Organization and management analysis
43. Organization theory and behavior
44. Personnel administration
45. Planning, programing, budgeting
46. Politics and administration
47. Systems analysis

VIII U.S. Political Institutions, Processes, and Behavior
48. Courts and judicial behavior
49. Elections and voting behavior
50. Ethnic politics
51. Executives
52. Interest groups
53. Intergovernmental relations
54. Legislatures
55. Political and constitutional history
56. Political parties
57. Public law
58. Public opinion
59. State, local, and metropolitan government
60. Urban politics

---

As will be evident, the present *Handbook* contains articles on topics that appear on neither of the two recent differentiated lists and omits topics on each. Some "omissions" were inadvertent. Others were deliberate, resulting from our conclusion either that the work on a particular topic did not appear ripe for review at this time or that the topic overlapped sufficiently with others already commissioned so that we might leave it out in the interests of preventing our rapidly expanding project from becoming hopelessly large. There also were instances in which we failed to find (or keep) authors on topics that we might otherwise have included. Hence readers should be forewarned about a feature of the *Handbook* that they should know without forewarning is bound to exist: incompleteness. Each reviewer will note "strange omissions." For us it is more extraordinary that so many able people were willing to invest so much effort in this enterprise.

It should be evident from our history of the project that we consider the rubrics under which scholarly work is classified to be less important than the caliber of the scholarship and that we recognize the incorrigible tendency of inquiry to overflow the pigeonholes to which it has been assigned, as well as the desirability that scholars rather than editors (or other administrators) define the boundaries of their endeavors. Therefore we have used rather simple principles for aggregating essays into their respective volumes and given them straightforward titles.

The essays in Volume 1 on the nature of political theory which follow Waldo's extensive discussion of the scope of political science are far from innocent of reference to empirical matters. This comports with the common observation that matters of theoretical interest are by no means removed from the concerns of the real world. And although we have used the titles *Micropolitical Theory* and *Macropolitical Theory* for Volumes 2 and 3, we have meant no more thereby than to identify the scale and mode of conceptualization typical of the topics in these volumes. Here again the reader will find selections that extensively review empirical findings.

Similarly, although the titles of Volumes 4, 5, and 6 on extragovernmental, governmental, and policy-output aspects of government and politics may appear to imply mere data compilations, the contents of these volumes are far from atheoretical. This is also emphatically true of Volume 8, which carries the title *International Politics*, a field that in recent decades has continuously raised difficult theoretical issues, including issues about the proper nature of theory. Volume 7 carries the title *Strategies of Inquiry* rather than *Methodology* to call attention to the fact that contributors to that volume have emphasized linking techniques of inquiry to substantive issues. In short, contributions to the eight volumes connect in many ways that can be only imperfectly suggested by the editors' table of contents or even by the comprehensive index at the end of Volume 8.

It can scarcely surprise readers of a multiple-authored work to learn that what is before them is a collective effort. It gives us pleasure to acknowledge obligations to five groups of people who helped to lighten our part of the load. First of all, to our contributors we owe a debt of gratitude for their patience, cooperation, and willingness to find the time in their exceedingly busy schedules to produce the essays that make up this *Handbook*. Second, we thank the many helpful Addison-Wesley staff members with whom we have worked for their good cheer toward us and for their optimism about this project. Third, the senior scholars who initially advised Addison-Wesley to undertake the project, and who may even have pointed the publishers in our direction, know who they are. We believe it would add still another burden to the things they must answer for in our profession if we named them publicly, but we want to record our rueful, belated appreciation to them. Fourth, Kathleen Peters and Barbara Kelly in Berkeley and Lee L. Messina, Catherine Smith, and Frances C. Root in Middletown kept the paper flowing back and forth across the country and helped us immeasurably in getting the job done. Finally, our love and gratitude to Barbara Greenstein and Linda Polsby. And we are happy to report to Michael, Amy, and Jessica Greenstein, and to Lisa, Emily, and Daniel Polsby that at long last their fathers are off the long-distance telephone.

Princeton, New Jersey F.I.G.
Berkeley, California N.W.P.

## REFERENCES

American Political Science Association (1961). *Biographical Directory of The American Political Science Association,* fourth edition. (Franklin L. Burdette, ed.) Washington, D.C.

American Political Science Association (1968). *Biographical Directory,* fifth edition. Washington, D.C.

American Political Science Association (1973). *Biographical Directory,* sixth edition. Washington, D.C.

Lindzey, Gardner, ed. (1954). *Handbook of Social Psychology,* 2 volumes. Cambridge, Mass.: Addison-Wesley.

Lindzey, Gardner, and Elliot Aronson, eds. (1968–69). *The Handbook of Social Psychology,* second edition, 5 volumes. Reading, Mass.: Addison-Wesley.

# CONTENTS

**Chapter 1** **Political Science: Tradition, Discipline, Profession, Science, Enterprise**   1
*Dwight Waldo, Syracuse University*

| | |
|---|---|
| Perspective on Perspectives: A Note on Method | 2 |
| The Tradition of Political Science | 4 |
| The Development of Political Science in the United States: Formation of the Matrix | 18 |
| Growth of Self-Consciousness and Search for Identity: Political Science before World War I | 23 |
| The Middle Period: Political Science from World War I to World War II | 41 |
| The Recent Period: Political Science since World War II | 50 |
| Centripetal and Centrifugal Tendencies | 73 |
| Fields and Foci | 80 |
| Political Science Viewed Internationally | 110 |
| Toward a Postbehavioral Political Science | 113 |
| The Faces of Political Science | 116 |

**Chapter 2** **The Logic of Political Inquiry: A Synthesis of Opposed Perspectives**   131
*J. Donald Moon, Wesleyan University*

| | |
|---|---|
| Introduction: Alternative Models of Political Inquiry | 131 |
| The "Scientific" Ideal | 134 |
| The Interpretation and Explanation of Political Action | 154 |
| Interpretation, Theory, and Models of Man | 182 |
| Explanation, Interpretation, and Political Inquiry: An Overview | 207 |

|  |  |  |
|---|---|---|
| | A Postscript on the Relationships among Political Theory, Political Philosophy, and Political Evaluation | 209 |
| | Bibliographical Note | 216 |
| **Chapter 3** | **The Contemporary Relevance of the Classics of Political Philosophy** | 229 |
| | *Dante Germino, University of Virginia* | |
| | Preface | 229 |
| | Introduction: On the "Uses" of Political Philosophy | 233 |
| | Political Philosophy as a Conversation of Many Voices | 236 |
| | The Classics as Touchstones of Political Philosophy | 237 |
| | What is Man? | 239 |
| | What is the Paradigmatic Society? | 243 |
| | What is History? | 248 |
| | Philosophy, Theory, and Nonnoetic Thought | 250 |
| | Conclusion: The Relevance of Political Philosophy | 256 |
| | Bibliographical Essay | 262 |
| **Chapter 4** | **The Language of Political Inquiry: Problems of Clarification** | 283 |
| | *Felix E. Oppenheim, University of Massachusetts* | |
| | Descriptive Political Concepts in General | 284 |
| | The Role of Explication | 289 |
| | Explicating Political Concepts | 297 |
| | Categorical and Comparative Concepts | 309 |
| | The Language of Normative Political Inquiry | 314 |
| | Conclusion: Unresolved Issues | 328 |
| **Chapter 5** | **Political Evaluation** | 337 |
| | *Brian Barry, Nuffield College, Oxford, England* | |
| | *Douglas W. Rae, Yale University* | |
| | Introduction | 337 |
| | Requirements of Evaluation | 340 |
| | Conflicts among Criteria | 349 |
| | Six Pure Criteria | 357 |
| | Coping with Complexity | 368 |
| | Five Political Principles | 377 |
| | Conclusion | 394 |

# CONTENTS OF OTHER VOLUMES IN THIS SERIES

**Volume 2** **MICROPOLITICAL THEORY**

1 *Fred I. Greenstein.* Personality and Politics
2 *David O. Sears.* Political Socialization
3 *Moshe M. Czudnowski.* Political Recruitment
4 *J. David Greenstone.* Group Theories
5 *Dennis J. Palumbo.* Organization Theory and Political Science

**Volume 3** **MACROPOLITICAL THEORY**

1 *Samuel P. Huntington and Jorge I. Domínguez.* Political Development
2 *Robert A. Dahl.* Governments and Political Oppositions
3 *Juan J. Linz.* Totalitarian and Authoritarian Regimes
4 *Michael Taylor.* The Theory of Collective Choice
5 *Charles Tilly.* Revolutions and Collective Violence
6 *Arthur L. Stinchcombe.* Social Structure and Politics

**Volume 4** **NONGOVERNMENTAL POLITICS**

1 *Sidney Verba and Norman H. Nie.* Political Participation
2 *Philip E. Converse.* Public Opinion and Voting Behavior
3 *Robert H. Salisbury.* Interest Groups
4 *Leon D. Epstein.* Political Parties

## Volume 5  GOVERNMENTAL INSTITUTIONS AND PROCESSES

1. *Harvey Wheeler.* Constitutionalism
2. *William H. Riker.* Federalism
3. *Anthony King.* Executives
4. *Nelson W. Polsby.* Legislatures
5. *Martin Shapiro.* Courts
6. *Mark Nadel and Francis Rourke.* Bureaucracies

## Volume 6  POLICIES AND POLICYMAKING

1. *Harold D. Lasswell.* Research in Policy Analysis: The Intelligence and Appraisal Functions
2. *Joseph A. Pechman.* Making Economic Policy: The Role of the Economist
3. *Harvey M. Sapolsky.* Science Policy
4. *Charles E. Gilbert.* Welfare Policy
5. *Duane Lockard.* Race Policy
6. *Robert C. Fried.* Comparative Urban Policy and Performance
7. *Bernard C. Cohen and Scott A. Harris.* Foreign Policy
8. *John G. Grumm.* The Analysis of Policy Impact

## Volume 7  STRATEGIES OF INQUIRY

1. *Clement E. Vose.* Sources for Political Inquiry: I Library Reference Materials and Manuscripts as Data for Political Science
2. *Jerome M. Clubb.* Sources for Political Inquiry: II Quantitative Data
3. *Harry Eckstein.* Case Study and Theory in Political Science
4. *Hayward R. Alker, Jr.* Polimetrics: Its Descriptive Foundations
5. *Richard A. Brody and Charles N. Brownstein.* Experimentation and Simulation
6. *Richard W. Boyd and Herbert H. Hyman.* Survey Research
7. *Gerald H. Kramer and Joseph Hertzberg.* Formal Theory
8. *Herman Kahn.* On Studying the Future

## Volume 8  INTERNATIONAL POLITICS

1. *Kenneth N. Waltz.* Theory of International Relations
2. *Dina Zinnes.* Research Frontiers in the Study of International Politics
3. *George H. Quester.* The World Political System
4. *Richard Smoke.* National Security Affairs
5. *Robert O. Keohane and Joseph S. Nye.* International Interdependence and Integration
6. *Leon Lipson.* International Law

# 1
# POLITICAL SCIENCE: TRADITION, DISCIPLINE, PROFESSION, SCIENCE, ENTERPRISE

*DWIGHT WALDO*

Political science is concerned centrally with matters indicated by such words as politics, government, state, society, policy, authority, and power. But *precisely* what matters it should be concerned with, with what ends in view, with the use of what means—these are subject to differing opinions. The differences in opinion are sometimes of no essential importance, and certainly there are large areas of consensus among contemporary political scientists. But sometimes the differences are profound. They cannot be ignored if the purpose is an understanding of political science.

In a widely cited and highly regarded formulation of recent years, that of David Easton, political science is the study of the authoritative allocation of values for a society. It focuses on the "political system," which is conceived as that behavior or set of interactions through which authoritative allocations ("binding decisions") are made and implemented for a society (Easton, 1953, 1965a, 1965b, 1968).

The wide acceptance of this formulation suggests that it is a useful, congenial formulation. Probably most political scientists would accept it as at least a good first approximation of what political science is about. However, some would find it unacceptable, some would insist on this or that amendment before acceptance, some would accept it only if permitted to define its key terms in their own way.

To appreciate the difficulties of definition it is necessary to understand that both the noun *science* and the adjective *political* are problematical, contentious. In its broadest construction, etymologically and historically legitimated, science is simply (though nothing here is simple) "knowledge." In its strictest construction science is only knowledge of a certain type, obtained

---

The author acknowledges with gratitude the assistance of Andrew Hegedus and Henry Muse.

and legitimated according to the canons of a specified methodology. Between the two extremes are a wide variety of possible constructions. *All* the possible constructions come entangled in a web of history and represent varied societal arrangements and philosophies. The selection of the "correct" (or most "useful") conception of science is itself something of an act of faith, not a scientific act.

The difficulties of the adjective *political* have already been suggested. From absolutist to anarchist no one doubts that a something, denoted by such terms as "government" or "the political," *exists* and is of major import for human life and destiny. "It" can be as real as a tax levy, a military draft, or an execution chamber; "its" presence is clear to the perceptive, even in so-called stateless societies. But what "it" is, is subject to varied interpretations and sometimes heated disputes. As with the noun science, the adjective political comes entangled in a web of history, with differing constructions representing differing societal arrangements and conflicting philosophies. Again, there is no authority (i.e., accepted by all political scientists) to which to appeal. As a practical matter, some solve the problem of defining political science, practically and operationally, by an appeal to science: Political *science* concerns only "political" phenomena that can be studied scientifically, according to a strict definition of science. This resolution is not unreasonable. Neither is it beyond reasonable objection.

In its conflicting interpretations of purpose and methods, political science is little different from the other social sciences; indeed, in this it is much less different from physics or biology than is customarily presumed. What unites political scientists is a great deal of agreement at the commonsense level on what constitutes the stuff of the "political," and a belief that the enterprise to which they address themselves is of central importance to human life, collective and individual.

There are limitations and dangers in all brief definitions of complex matters. In any case, the aim of this essay is to further an understanding of political science "in the round," not to attempt an authoritative definition. It is now time to set forth the terms and conditions of the attempt.

## PERSPECTIVE ON PERSPECTIVES: A NOTE ON METHOD

Honesty and fairness compel an attempt to speak for the whole of political science. But at best such an attempt must be limited and flawed. There is no unquestionable "objective" perspective: Personal opinion, selective perception, individual idiosyncrasy inevitably shape the product. So that the reader may understand and evaluate what follows, the author here sets forth the methods that will be employed and the points of view that will be adopted.

1. The primary method employed will be historical-interpretative. It is premised that to understand political science one must view it in its origins,

its development, and its environing circumstances. The author will not presume, however, that because political science patently bears the marks of its history and responds to its environment, it is wholly "explained," that it has no force or validity of its own.

2. The center of attention will be the contemporary United States; that is, the historical-interpretative approach will be used as a means of understanding contemporary political science in the United States, not for its own sake or "in general." Recent and contemporary political science outside the United States will be noted chiefly as it relates to political science in the United States.

3. Although the evolution of the "strict" interpretation of political science in the United States will be sketched and its rationale and methods delineated—this has been the central story of American political science for four generations—there will be a steady *intent* to maintain a spectrum-wide view, an "ecumenical" approach.

For the author an attempt at ecumenicism is a congenial labor. The drive to make political science a "genuine" science, after the model of the physical sciences, commands his respectful attention. On the other hand, he finds "softer" versions of political science intellectually respectable and sociopolitically useful: "true." For what is one to say of the large and complex politically organized societies of the past and present? That they did function or do function without political knowledge? By instinct and in ignorance of sociopolitical cause and effect? For the author this is an unacceptable presumption.

4. Political knowledge, that is to say political science, is cumulative. This premise is one of common sense. But it is not nonsense, on a reasonable interpretation of the historical record.

In the strict interpretation of science, "cumulative" knowledge must have certain strict theoretical qualities—else it is neither scientific knowledge nor cumulative. This is not the place to explicate the argument and to examine its rationale. Nor does one assert that this argument is "wrong"; on the contrary, for its purposes and within its limits, it is probably "right."

What *is* premised is that political science is an enterprise in which, through time and with experience and study, we gain more knowledge of things political. In the author's view, it is absurd to believe that the Greeks had no political science because they did not have a theoretical system analogous to models of scientific endeavor set forth in the twentieth century; that the Romans, whose political achievements still shape much of the world's politics, made no advances in political science beyond the Greeks; that the American Founding Fathers did not have more political knowledge available to them than to the Greeks and Romans; that in the latter third of the twentieth century we do not have, in the corpus of American political science, much more political science than was available to the Founding Fathers.

This is not to assert that everything that is written in political science is a "contribution" and every new political technique or institution is an "advance." It is to say, on the one hand to those who feel that the ancients already knew it all, and on the other hand to those who feel we yet know nothing truly scientific (but surely one day *will*): We have learned much political science and we are learning more.

## THE TRADITION OF POLITICAL SCIENCE

Whatever the outcome of ambitions to construct a science of politics of complete generality, political science is carried on in a particular tradition. This tradition ineluctably shapes the manner in which students of the political address their subject.

"Tradition" is used here broadly to refer to such matters as institutional forms, systems of thought, ideas of justice, perceptions of reality, and styles of argumentation. The position taken is that what has happened in history—more precisely (if still loosely) Western history—gives political science its purposes, its methodologies, its technologies; and that understanding of political science is impossible without knowledge of the unique history in which it is embedded and to which it is heir. Political science may well be in some senses a natural science. But that it is also in some senses a cultural science is wholly clear.

This is hardly the place to speak at length of the tradition of political science. In fact, there are no works in which the tradition, in the round and in full, is treated. Histories of political thought treat one aspect of the tradition at length but give scant attention to the development of political institutions. Other works are limited in other ways: e.g., Anderson (1964) gives a rounded account but only for the ancient period; Pollock (1960) provides an overall view but a patchy and imperfect one; Mackenzie (1967, introductory chapters) provides an excellent sketch but not a full discussion. The matter can perhaps be best treated in short compass not by trying to develop a history in which the various aspects of the tradition are seen to interrelate but by saying something about each of several of the more important aspects.

### *Political Institutions*

The essential points here are two. One is that Western history has provided for political science a certain repertoire or inventory of political institutions for comparative and illustrative purposes. The other is that certain of these political institutions proved, in one way and another, decisive for the values and techniques assumed by recent political science.

"Western" has been used as a limiting adjective. But an account or analysis must begin with experience that is general for civilized mankind; and it must be recognized that Western civilization only gradually and never entirely differentiated itself from a matrix of Near-Eastern experience.

The decisive first step was the neolithic revolution, leading to settled agriculture. This "simple" step was of enormous consequence. In a complex mesh of cause and effect it brought increased population, much greater occupational specialization, the growth of cities, technical (and in a loose sense, scientific) advance, the rise of traditions of learning, growing social differentiation and complexity. In the Near East, though there came to be important littoral and island civilizations, the first and decisive developments centered on the valleys of major rivers, particularly the Tigris-Euphrates and the Nile; and the crucial factor was the development of the "public works" which controlled and directed the river waters (Childe, 1946; Eisenstadt, 1963; McNeill, 1971).

Politically, an all-important transformation took place. The comparatively simple, familial-tribal arrangements for "governance," suitable to hunting and food-gathering cultures, were replaced by other political forms and styles. In general terms, the distinguishing characteristics of the new political arrangements were larger size, more definite boundaries, increased differentiation in political power as between groups or classes, the development of belief systems ("ideologies") to justify and sustain the exercise of strong power over wide areas, kingship as the central and uniting institution; and in the service of royal power, the growth of both a specialized military apparatus and a civilian bureaucracy of priests, scribes, clerks, and technicians.

These events are not simply "ancient history"; causal arrows fly from them into the present. To a significant degree this ancient experience (extending over millennia) has been determinative for all later political experience. The ancient empires were not "states" in the modern sense, even less nation-states. But they created certain patterns that have endured or recurred. The Roman experience, which is of undoubted importance for the political present, to a significant degree was built on and influenced by these ancient empires.

The Greek experience, which is also a living presence, was in part shaped by opposition to and in a dialectical interaction with the "barbarian" despotisms. Probably chiefly for geographical reasons (rugged terrain and many islands) Greek political development took a different turn: many small, independent political units—so-called city-states—instead of large unified kingdoms, through the classic period and until the Macedonian conquest and unification. Although many of the Greek city-states were despotic and much of their political experience was not unlike that of their larger and older neighbors, the many units made for diversity and experimentation. Of pre-eminent importance were the political history and the development of the civic culture of Athens. These led, in the fifth and fourth centuries B.C., to the birth of a tradition of political analysis and discussion that is very much a part of contemporary political science.

On that subject, more below. The present concern is with political institutions. In the Greek experience several factors are important for later political science, although their influence, rather than being direct and continuous, was mediated through later students of politics. One such factor was the development in Athens of a form of democratic government, which was to become not so much a model as an inspiration for subsequent generations. Another was the coexistence of many independent political units that were more or less equal; this "world" of city-states foreshadowed the modern world of nation-states and in some ways influenced its evolution. Another was the diversity in political development among the city-states, providing many "models" of the politically possible and stimulating comparative political analysis.

The Roman political experience extended over centuries and varied greatly—from small republic to "world" empire. The Romans were the heirs of their predecessors, and to some extent they adopted, adapted, and synthesized; but their political experience was unique and massively important for subsequent political development. Though Rome "fell" in the fifth century, the Eastern Empire survived till 1453, and the Holy Roman Empire launched by Charlemagne in 800 endured into the Napoleonic period. It is impossible to study the rise of the modern political system without being impressed with the fact that it is erected on foundations laid down in antiquity.

There would be general agreement that the main influence of the Roman experience has been on the legal component of modern political institutions: With the Romans law became and has remained centrally involved with the political. But the Roman influence is so vast and varied as to make even a brief summary impossible. Two further observations must suffice. One is that in the transition from the medieval to the modern, the Roman example was studied and invoked endlessly. That the "example" was complex and even sometimes contradictory, susceptible to use in varied and even opposing ways, complicates the story but in no way refutes the generalization. The other observation is that a review of the vocabulary of modern politics signifies the Roman association of many central concepts, including state, nation, government, republic, imperialism, constitution, citizen, and liberty.

The medieval influence on our political tradition certainly was not negligible, and it can be discerned, for example, in systems of representation and in legal procedures. But its main impact concerns a development that goes back to the later Roman Empire, namely, the introduction of a new type of religious complement and component: religion claiming universality and a validity sustained by an authority above and beyond the mundane political. For more than a millennium the proper articulation of the spiritual and the temporal "powers" was the central preoccupation of politics, both in practice and in political thought. In the secularization of thought that accompanied the rise of the modern state system, the problem, as such, receded—albeit after paroxysms of violence. But the resulting varied, pragmatic solutions to the problem of the "two powers" became a part of our political heritage. Nor should the secularly inclined presume that for a secular age the import of the matter ends with church-state relations. On the contrary, questions concerning such matters as civil rights and civic obligations, the origin, validity, and possible universality of moral norms, civil disobedience and revolution, are perhaps posed at all and certainly are posed in some of the styles they assume because of the Christian centuries.

The debt owed to the past by the modern state system in general and by its component states in varying degree and differing manner is obvious. But the modern state system is of course a new chapter in Western political experience. The modern states were created by powerful political actors, aided more or less by skillful political thinkers. Both took what they needed or wanted from the past and used it for contemporary purposes. New factors, pre-eminently the idea and sentiment of nationalism, evolved (or "happened") and became a part of the state system. Old ideas, preeminently democracy, were revived and (mingled with medieval survivals) became a part of the state system. But for all the qualifications that must be made and for all the complications that must be recognized, there is a discernible pattern: It is meaningful to speak of the modern state system. It is a recognizable stage in the succession of dominant political styles which constitute for political science its tradition.

The state system *exists*. Political science, as science or as discipline or profession, must recognize its institutional matrix or pay a price in irrelevance and futility. But this is not to say that the state system is permanent, the end of political change. On the contrary, the state system is patently under severe stress; perhaps we have begun a transition to a new political condition of man. A knowledge of our political tradition creates an awareness of change. It also creates an awareness of the continuity in change.

## *Political Thought*

From one point of view it is unrealistic to discuss political institutions and political thought separately; thought and action are clearly interwoven. At any time a political system is justified and sustained by a rationale—myth, ideology, philosophy, theory, or whatever; and political actions are normally related by some logic to ends thus justified. This is true even when the tribal level of human association has been attained. On the other hand, thought about political action can take many forms, and it can exist on varying levels.

When it attains a high level of sophistication, abstractness, and self-awareness, it gains a certain independence from immediate circumstances. A *tradition* of political thought gains self-consciousness, providing facts and ideas from the past against which the present can be assessed and from which, perhaps, a future can be projected.

In the West there is such a tradition of political thought. It is of course related to the history of Western political institutions. Political thinkers are characteristically concerned with solving existing problems, and even if they have ambitions to speak *sub specie aeternitatis*, later generations will discount the claim. But this tradition of political thought—it has been called the Great Dialogue—has a degree of independence. Study of it has sometimes constituted the main part of a formal education in "politics." It is a part of, or at least a background for, current curricula in political science.

**Development of the Great Dialogue.** The Great Dialogue in the West began in Athens, which was then at or just past its political apogee, as a part of one of the most remarkable cultural-intellectual flowerings in history. The older civilizations of the Near East had achieved notable successes in the building of political institutions. This had not been done through sheer instinct. Thought, often sustained or insightful, and will and force were all necessary to the achievement. But it was in classical Athens that thought about the political first reached what subsequent generations would regard as a high level. There, stimulated by difficult political problems and sustained by the generally high intellectual attainment, political thought reached levels of abstractness and generality far above those of the past and seldom to be reached in the future.

No attempt will be made, here or in the following discussions, to "tell the story" of even the major political thinkers or to summarize (much less analyze) their products. That is the aim of many books, including, among the better known of the general treatments, those of Catlin (1939), Sabine (1964), and Wolin (1960). Rather, the aim is the modest one of relating the tradition of political thought to the development of political institutions and, generally, to give a sense of the development of an intellectual tradition. (Here and elsewhere the use of "development" and "growth" are not meant necessarily to imply an upward movement—this is a complex question—but to signify change resulting in increasing complexity and options.)

The conditions that stimulated the Athenian Greeks to raise the level of political thought to new heights have been suggested. Defense against the "barbarian" empire of the Persians was not only a military exercise but a stimulus to inquiry into the question: What does it mean to be Greek? War between the Athenians and the authoritarian, militaristic—but Greek—Spartans likewise led to self-examination and introspection. Diversity among the city-states stimulated questions and provided a wealth of comparative experience, on a scale on which it could be observed and understood. The Athenian experiment with democracy opened a new phase in political life, and the generally high culture provided a favorable milieu for thought. But above all, it was a sense of trouble that challenged political thought to rise to a new level: Athens, weakened by war and troubled by domestic problems, was threatened with decay and decline.

The response of Athenian thinkers, notably Socrates (469?–397 B.C.), Plato (427–347 B.C.), and Aristotle (384–322 B.C.), did not preserve or restore Athens. But it was a truly remarkable product of the human intellect. The writings of Plato and Aristotle laid the foundations for a tradition of political inquiry which is still vital after almost two and a half millennia. The questions they asked are still asked. The political categories they established are still common coin. The modes of thought they exemplified—Plato more philosophical, speculative, "idealistic," Aristotle more factual, scientific, "sensible"—still have their followers and protagonists. To be sure, some regard the Greek-established tradition of discourse as more of a handicap than a help in building a genuine science of politics. But even of these, most would say that at least Aristotle pointed the study of politics in the correct direction.

Several aspects of the Greek achievement should be underscored. The first is hardly likely to be denigrated by any political scientist: The Greeks "created" the political, that is, delineated the political, differentiated it from—but also related it to—other aspects of individual and collective existence. This origin is appropriately signified by the fact that "political" and its cognates derive from the Greek word for city-state, *polis*. Second and related, the Greeks created political science in the sense of an activity, *conscious of itself as an activity*, devoted to a study of the political. Third, the Greeks created a lasting awareness of the problems inherent in the duality of individual-polity ("state"): Neither "is" the other, but each is meaningless without the other. What citizenship *is*, what obligations it entails, what benefits it confers, what (if any) "rights" are beyond and opposed to it—the discussion of such matters can hardly be free from Greek influence. Fourth, the Greeks first seriously addressed a central, baffling, recurring problem in political study, namely, the relationship of "what is" to "what ought to be." The paths they made in dealing with the problem of the relationship of the factual and the ethical have since provided points of departure, if not accepted routes, for subsequent political inquiry.

The philosophers of the Hellenic and early Roman periods, especially the Stoics, deserve notice. With only slight exaggeration it is said that classical Greeks could not imagine man apart from the *polis* that had nurtured him. But the *polis* fell victim to decay and destruction, and in the larger, more impersonal and troubled world following the Macedonian conquests, the Stoic philosophers found a distinction between the individual and his political community quite imaginable, in fact even desirable. They contributed to the tradition of political thought a sense of individuality, of personal importance and dignity, of essential human equality, existing apart from the political and perhaps in opposition to it. They contributed also to a related idea: that one's membership in some other community, perhaps a community of mankind in general, is more important than membership in a particular political community. They began the elaboration of the idea of a "state of nature" somehow preceding or opposed to civil society; and they developed the idea of "natural law," law God-given or somehow immanent in the universe, which provides norms of conduct to which a proper polity will conform. These ideas were to have importance in the development of the Roman Empire, in the development of the medieval political world, in the development of modern political thought.

The Romans were not, of course, given to speculation and philosophy, and no Roman stands among the "greats" in the history of political thought. Nevertheless, their pragmatic success, the power, depth, and longevity of the Roman political experience profoundly affect political thought down to the present (and probably into any imaginable future). There were three causative factors. One was magnitude: The Roman political experience was itself vast and varied, extending from primitive city-state to world empire. Given Rome's paradigm quality for subsequent centuries, political thinkers could and did search its history for precedents and ideas relevant to their purposes. Another was its "conduit" function: In one way or another, the Romans conveyed much of the political thought of antiquity into the medieval world and thus into the modern world. Indeed, they did not merely "convey" in a passive or accidental sense; they adopted much previous political thought, particularly that of the Hellenic period, as their own. Third, the Roman practical genius resulted in a great and overarching system of law. With the Romans the polity became a "creature of law." The importance of this circumstance for later institutional development can hardly be exaggerated, but its importance for political thought (to the extent that this is separable) is also profound. Much theorizing has proceeded in legal modes, and even those otherwise inclined have had to reckon with the force of the idea that the legal and political are closely conjoined. These three ways of influence, though separable for some purposes, were closely joined through Roman law. The great codifications that came in the twilight of the Roman experience summed the Roman political experience and embodied a repertoire of historically derived political ideas.

The political thought of the medieval period was in some ways rich, and certainly it was sometimes complex. Men of undoubted high talents, including Dante (1265–1321) and St. Thomas Aquinas (1225–1274), contributed to it. But because of the styles and idioms in which it was framed and the specific issues (such as the investiture of bishops) to which it was addressed, much of it seems more remote to contemporary sensibilities than the writings of either the classical Greeks or the Stoics. For present purposes, attention can be limited to two aspects.

The first is what Sabine (1964, p. 180) designates as "the most revolutionary event in the history of western Europe, in respect both to politics and to political philosophy." This event was the rise of the Christian church, with its claim of the right to govern spiritual concerns in independence of the political. Actually, the Christian church but climaxed and intensified a movement toward cleavage into two worlds. Pre-Christian philosophies, especially Stoicism, as well as other "eastern" religions of the Roman period, provided ideas and prepared the emotional climate. The conversion of Emperor Constantine to Christianity signifies that the problem of the relation between church and state was posed before the fall of Rome and the creation of a strong papacy; St. Augustine (354–430) explored the question in depth in his *City of God*. But it was in the medieval period, in contests between Pope and Holy Roman Emperor, and in the early modern period, when the modern state was forming, that the great intellectual battles were fought.

In part the significance of the great controversies concerning the two powers lies again in a "conduit" function. The past was a living presence to the debaters, and Stoic and Roman sources, as well as specifically Christian sources, were mined and developed; a tradition of thought was preserved and extended. But the central significance of the controversies lies in the idea that there is a realm of human experience properly beyond the power of government, that there is another institution of equal or greater stature, that the individual is at core "sacred" and is not merely a secular object. The force of these ideas survived the particular arguments and the particular beliefs that animated them. They "left a residuum without which modern ideas of individual privacy and liberty would be scarcely intelligible" (Sabine, 1964, p. 196).

The other matter warranting attention is the influence of feudalism. Some modern governmental institutions that limit or disperse political power, including constitutionalism, representation, and judicial independence, owe a debt to the evolution of feudal institutions and ideas in the medieval period. These in turn, however, owe some debt to earlier ideas and to the limitation on the political at the center of the debate over the two powers, church and state.

**The modern period.** The modern nation-state system is not the Greek city-state system writ large or a congeries of small Roman empires or, even less, a projection of medieval-feudal institutions. It is something different, historically unique. It has its own distinctive characteristics, some of which—above all nationalism—had no close equivalent in preceding eras. Yet it is inconceivable without the legacy of the past. The political past presents a vast inventory of ideas and institutions. So varied is the inventory that it can be drawn on to support positions quite opposed: to glorify citizenship or to denigrate it, to centralize power or to disperse it, to justify small political entities or large ones. It can be used to justify nearly all forms of regimes (at least in their "pure" as against "debased" form) and to suggest a precedent for nearly all types of arrangements. The conscious use of the past in argumentation, common through most of the modern period, is not currently in favor. But this does not mean that the influence of the past is ended. We write on a palimpsest on which the previous tracings can always be descried.

From one perspective the main and characteristic political thought of the modern period divides itself into three categories: that concerned with creating and justifying the modern state, that directed toward changing and improving the state, and that seeking to destroy or transcend the state. In the first category one would place Machiavelli (1469–1527), Bodin (1530?–1596), and Hobbes (1588–1679). Locke (1632–1704), Bentham (1748–1832), and John Stuart Mill (1806–1873) fit satisfactorily in the second. Marx (1818–1883), Bakunin (1814–1876), and Kropotkin (1842–1921) exemplify the third. Nor is it wholly accidental that when one seeks theorists to fit the categories, there is a chronological sequence in the names that come most easily to mind.

Of course no classificatory scheme does justice to the complexity of the facts. There are not three neat chronological periods. In any century, indeed in any generation, there has been a wide diversity of theory. Some theorists (Locke, for one) fit plausibly into two categories, and others fit only with violence into any (what shall be done with Rousseau?). Yet the scheme has a certain utility in understanding modern political thought. Three tendencies exist, and there is even a rough chronological ordering.

Other perspectives and classificatory schemes are not only possible but, for certain purposes, more useful: state authority versus private rights, interest in domestic affairs versus interest in relations among states, orientation toward past versus orientation toward future, regime preference, level of generality, influence of time and circumstance, style of argumentation. A perspective germane to present purposes is suggested by a question: What modern theorists have been most clearly in line with the recent drive toward a more empirical-analytical political science?

Relevant though it undoubtedly is, the question is not easy to answer. Those seeking a "hard" political science have differed significantly among themselves as to the implications of the quest. They have differed among themselves, for example, as to the relative emphasis to be placed on the empirical as against the rational, and on applied science as against pure science; and thus they honor different intellectual ancestors. Nevertheless, in a general way it is possible to indicate those whose work has most clearly foreshadowed or influenced political science, as that discipline has developed in the twentieth century.

Machiavelli is a convenient beginning, and some would argue the only proper one. His work—and here we focus on *The Prince*—was frankly secular in tone in a milieu still dominated by religious considerations. It stood outside the Stoic-Christian natural-law tradition, which was to remain prominent into the nineteenth century; it was "practical" in its concentration on political power as against political ethics; it sought frankly to discern cause and effect in the generation and maintenance of political power. Widely read and often cited, Machiavelli presumably had some influence in the creation of the modern state. (He sometimes has been credited with "inventing" the term—*lo stato*, from the Latin root *stare*.) Certainly he has served as reference point or model for subsequent students of the political whose bent has been pragmatic, realistic, applied.

Hobbes is another whose work was to appeal to later students interested in developing a scientific politics. His *Leviathan* shares with *The Prince* a driving interest in the power of the ruler. Despite much talk of religion it is hardly less secular in tone; almost as much as *The Prince* it stands outside the natural-law tradition; it too professes to see political man as he is rather than to speak to what political man ought to be. But there are distinct differences in tone and methodology. Hobbes had ambitions beyond his immediate interest in consolidating royal power; he was consciously trying to establish politics on a scientific base. There is an abstractness and a logical rigor, even an appeal to the authority of mathematics, that many later students seeking to establish a true science of politics were to find attractive. Many—but far from all. Some have found him too little the empiricist and too much the philosopher, too little given to careful observation and too much given to a geometrical-deductive method without genuine scientific roots.

A French writer of the sixteenth century, Bodin (1530?–1596), and a French writer of the eighteenth century, Montesquieu (1689–1755), contributed notably to the study of politics in the contemporary spirit—though the former and perhaps even the latter were less contemporary in some ways than either Machiavelli or Hobbes. Like Machiavelli and Hobbes, and for similar reasons, Bodin was interested in consolidating royal power, and his chief contribution to political thought was in the elucidation of the idea of *sovereignty*, the supreme power of the monarch (by extension of the state). But *Six Books Concerning the Republic*, in which he dealt with the concept of sovereignty, constituted a general and detailed treatment of politics in a more or less secular spirit. The ambition, in fact, was to do for modern politics what Aristotle had done for ancient politics. Today Bodin's *Republic* appears flawed and tedious. But it reintroduced factors into the stream of political study that had long been absent; above all, it reintroduced the historical-comparative method, and it sought to place the political in social and physical context (Franklin, 1963).

Montesquieu presents an interesting comparison with his compatriot, Bodin. Living two centuries later, he feared civil strife and anarchy considerably less, royal power much more, illustrating both the relevancy of political thought to context and the "progression" in theorizing about the state noted above. Like Bodin, he is noted in the history of political thought for one outstanding contribution: the elucidation of the theory of the separation of powers, a halter on political power rather than a spur to it. In *The Spirit of the Laws* he sought, as Bodin had done, though not so pretentiously, a general treatment of politics. Montesquieu's accomplishment, too, was seriously flawed and contains much that today is regarded as irrelevant and even superstitious. However, he surpassed Bodin considerably in seeking to place the political in total context: physical, cultural, psychological, sociological. It is this ambition that commends him to the twentieth century, however limited his accomplishment in this respect (Shackleton, 1961; Merry, 1970).

Another Frenchman, more immediately important for the contemporary study of politics, stands in the tradition of Bodin and Montesquieu. Alexis de Tocqueville (1805–1859) is the author of two major works, *The Old Regime and the French Revolution* and *Democracy in America*. Seen as a political philosopher, de Tocqueville is judged a careful expositor and sympathetic critic of democracy. Viewed as a political scientist, he is credited with seeking to place the study of politics (above all, democratic politics) in context. The man and his writings are wholly congenial to the contemporary spirit, whatever disagreement there may be with his conclusions. Not only did he treat contemporary themes, such as social stratification, industrialism, and mass culture; he did so with a penetration that still commands attention (Mayer, 1960).

This sketch of modern political thought from the perspective of the scientific ambitions of the current century is of course only suggestive. A thorough review would examine many more claims, including, for example, those of Jeremy Bentham (1748–1832) and John Stuart Mill (1806–1873) —though the latter perhaps more for his *Logic* than for his political essays. But even a brief review can hardly omit comment on Karl Marx (1818–1883).

Marx's influence on the scientific study of politics is unquestionably important—if only because it is widely judged to be important and men act and react accordingly. But it is exceedingly difficult to say in what precisely the importance lies; and any statement on the subject is open to challenge. The beginning point is to note that Marx, though undoubtedly an important political thinker (or some would say, an *anti*political thinker), was also more and other. His whole system of thought included elements from many realms of knowledge (economics, philosophy, and history, for example), it was very complex, and it changed significantly in the course of his intellectual life. Beyond that, he combined with a dedication to science as he interpreted it a reformist and revolutionary zeal that has seldom been equalled.

One can perhaps approach the truth of the matter by distinguishing between two things. One is the substantive contributions. Marx's findings and assertions about such matters as class phenomena and the relationship of thought, including political thought, to the historical circumstances in which it takes place—these are of such prima facie force and wide acceptance that they can hardly be ignored, whatever the conclusion as to their validity or the intellectual methods by which they were reached. They are an important component of contemporary political science (indeed of social science in general) because they have importantly determined its agenda. The second matter is Marx's "methods." Here differing, and contrary, opinions reign. At one extreme are those who would deny that, even in his laborious gathering of data in the British Museum, he was doing other than putting a cutting edge on preconceived opinions. At the other extreme are those who agree with his own view that the method of dialectical materialism is a uniquely useful tool for discovering sociopolitical truth, and that using it makes the reaching of socialist conclusions necessary and "scientific" (Averini, 1968; Lichtheim, 1964, 1971).

**The problem of categorization.** This is perhaps an appropriate place to take note of a matter that may or may not be obvious, but that in any case is important to the understanding and should not be neglected. Although it is customary to speak of "political thinkers," and this is for many purposes a legitimate usage, the category is by no means clear and exclusive—as the example of Marx signifies. Many of the so-called political theorists—Plato, Aristotle, St. Thomas, Hegel—have been, above all, philosophers, and their political thought has been but a part of a larger body of philosophic thought. Some have been "professional" men—legalists, clerics, journalists, bureaucrats—and their political thought represented an offshoot of their professional work or perhaps an avocation. Increasingly in the modern period, and culminating in the late nineteenth century and the early twentieth century, those who produced significant political theory might be designated as "general" or "undifferentiated" social scientists. Their political thought has been a part of study and thought spanning much of the range of the more specialized disciplines—such as economics, psychology, history, sociology—that occupy the terrain of the behavioral or social sciences in the contemporary university.

Probably few of those we designate "political theorists" became important in the history of political theory by saying to themselves: Now I will produce political theory. Rather, they addressed themselves to immediate and often urgent *problems*. The designation "political theory" is largely ex post facto, a judgment of subsequent times.

Thus it is that in attending to the development of political thought, perhaps in any sense but certainly with respect to the development of the scientific aspirations of recent political science, one must be aware of rigid categories, careful not to prejudge what is or is not political, and sensitive to the intimate involvement of the political with the whole human enterprise. One implication of this is that there are writers not ordinarily treated (or only mentioned) in the histories of political thought who may nevertheless have considerable significance for the development of contemporary political science. To illustrate: Francis Bacon's political writings, as such, earn him only minor mention in the histories. But it is certain that his *Novum Organum* (1620), his praise of science and his exegesis of scientific method (as he conceived it), had more influence on political writers of the nineteenth and twentieth centuries than his political writings. Another example is Giovanni Battista Vico (1668–1744), whose extraordinarily original work cannot be sensibly classified; but this work came eventually to influence work in many areas of social science (e.g., Marx and Engels acknowledged a debt to him).

As the nineteenth century advanced and the twentieth century opened, the concomitant growth of social science and its "intermixture"—as it seems retrospectively, following the subsequent separation of social science into a half-dozen academic disciplines—make the tracing of ideas and judgments of "influence" especially difficult. Certainly one needs to be aware that a number of major writers who are claimed (with considerable legitimacy) by other disciplines as their intellectual ancestors and founding fathers were also political writers, or at least that their ideas, given recent tendencies in political science, are now judged to be important for political science. In this connection one can mention, among the important names, Auguste Comte, Emile Durkheim, Robert Michels, Vilfredo Pareto, Georg Simmel, Ferdinand Tönnies, and Max Weber. If one is to understand current political science, an understanding of the ideas and influence of such figures is quite as important as an understanding of the ideas and influence of those (ancient or recent) recognized as "in the family." There are even some cases in which the influence of one "in the family" is mediated through the "outsiders"; thus it is probable that de Tocqueville has had influence on American political science more via European sociology than directly.

### The Languages of Politics

This brief summary of the tradition of political science can be concluded with some comment on the languages with which the political has been addressed. Certainly an awareness of the language factor is necessary not only for an understanding of the tradition, historically considered, but for an understanding of current trends and controversies. One perceives—or does not perceive—as languages provide categories and modes of relating and evaluating them.

"Language" is used here primarily in the sense of different idioms, specializations, realms of discourse; especially, for present purposes, the philosophical, the legal, the religious, the scientific. (But the subject is much broader. What is the import of the fact that, since the time of the ancient empires, the Western tradition of political science has developed within a single language family, the Indo-European?) At risk of oversimplification, one can say that each of the four main stages in the development of the polity in the West (i.e., following the ancient empires) was accompanied by the rise of a distinctive language for addressing the political. The language of the period of the Greek *polis* was philosophical; the language of the Roman world empire was legal; the language of the feudal period was religious; the language of the modern state is scientific.

Qualifications are immediately necessary. First, not only is there no sharp break between epochs; there is a cumulative effect: Later epochs inherit the languages of the past and continue to use them in addition to developing their new distinctive language. Second, although each of the languages undoubtedly has distinctive characteristics, there is nevertheless a tendency to merge at the peripheries: The historical association of philosophy and theology is not accidental; theology and law are sometimes stitched together; and science has its metaphysics, despite heroic efforts to free it of philosophical "taint." Indeed, the belief system of science can be reasonably argued to have important aspects of philosophy, of law, and even of religion. (Perhaps the different languages speak to many of the "same things" but in differing styles? But perhaps also each reveals a truth which the others conceal?)

Third, the fourfold classification takes no account of some "languages" more or less important in all four periods. The logic which Aristotle shaped and sharpened has had a profound and incalculable effect on the manner in which the Western mind perceives reality, forms categories, and directs action; and its influence is apparent in all four periods of Western politics, whatever the future may hold with reference to the development (or revival or "reception") of non-Aristotelian logics. And what is one to say of rhetoric, "persuasive" language? The study of rhetoric is closely connected with the political from the school of the Sophists to the Oxford Union; and anyone who fancies that rhetoric is absent from contemporary political science (even at its most "scientific") cannot have read its literature or attended its meetings.

Fourth, it is recognized that a full development of the subject would take account of the complexities already suggested but would be obliged to take account of the fact that each of the four main languages is itself complex—a language family, so to speak. Thus philosophy is divisible into such aspects as epistemology and ontology; law into natural and positive, civil and common, public and private; theology into apologetics, homiletics, and exegesis; science into applied and pure, experimental and theoretical (plus of course its specialization by field and its use of the languages of special logics, statistics, and mathematics).

All the complicated matters so summarily indicated would have to be explored if the significance of language for the enterprise of political science were to be fully understood. If contemporary political science had an Aristotle, he might well choose this approach to his subject.

## THE DEVELOPMENT OF POLITICAL SCIENCE IN THE UNITED STATES: FORMATION OF THE MATRIX

"The study of politics in the United States today is something in size, content and method unique in Western intellectual history." Thus a foreign observer introduces his study of political science in the United States (Crick, 1959, p. xi). In what follows the objective is to understand why and how this political science developed. Why, of the various Western countries, did the United States take the lead in developing political science in the twentieth century? What *kind* of political science did it develop? What was selected, what rejected, from the Western political tradition? To what extent has this political science been peculiarly American? To what extent and in what ways has it transcended its location in the America of the late nineteenth century and the twentieth century, becoming a generalized (or generalizable) political science? Such questions cannot be satisfactorily answered in brief compass. Indeed, they cannot be answered to the satisfaction of all who call themselves political scientists, whatever the length of the answers. Nevertheless they indicate the kind of knowledge that is sought.

### *Some Preliminary Observations: A Point of View Restated*

All societies, even the so-called stateless ones, may be said to have a political technology. That is, they have a set of institutional arrangements for making authoritative allocations of values for society, to use the language which has been most widely accepted in recent years to define the political. As civilization develops, that is, as size and complexity increase, the institutional arrangements for dealing with the political tend to become more formally differentiated, to become in some aspects (not necessarily in all, as anthropologists well know) more complicated. At some point what can be called political knowledge becomes formalized. The rules that govern political life are "codified"—perhaps reduced to written record if the culture has reached this stage; and knowledge of "cause and effect" with respect to the political becomes specialized, role-differentiated, and may also be codified.

Knowledge of cause and effect is not necessarily codified separately from the rules of political life; in fact, close intermingling—in the West in law—has been typical.

At some point in the development of a society, "political knowledge" may be said to exist: "What works" for that society is known. When the political knowledge reaches a certain level of complexity, sophistication, and self-consciousness, one can call it political science if he wishes to accept a soft definition of science. It may be observed that if one accepts the point of view that the findings of science are always contingent and falsifiable, *no* society can get beyond "what works," i.e., what is empirically demonstrable, however much its political science is improved and refined.

In the history of the West, codification of political knowledge has been sometimes fairly well advanced. This has been particularly true of the modern period. The state system did not simply "happen." It developed because political knowledge permitted it to develop; and it developed as it did because of the nature of the political knowledge it inherited and itself developed. This is not to assert the primacy of ideas over "facts." How can one understand the development of the state system apart from Henry IV, the Great Elector, Louis XIV, Napoleon, Bismark? It is to assert that political knowledge—or political science—played an important and in some respects decisive role.

The types of political knowledge that are accumulated and transmitted and the manner in which accumulation and transmission take place vary widely, according to culture, institutional arrangements, and circumstances: They are neither foreordained nor immutable. Certain general patterns may be discerned within an area that shares much of a culture and a history. Thus there has been a widespread Continental disposition—from Spain to Russia, from Scandinavia to Greece—to merge law and political knowledge in a single set of intellectual-institutional arrangements, a set which encompasses the functions of teaching, learning, and exercise. But to say that they "merged" the two is to put the matter from the viewpoint of an outsider: Why law and the political might seem so naturally the "same thing" should be clear from the foregoing discussion of the Western political tradition. More in need of explanation are the type and measure of separation that took place in England and, in addition, the rise of the American notion of a political science, which recognizes a distinction between legal and political knowledge and proposes to pattern the teaching and learning of political knowledge on the natural science model.

What is necessary if one is to *understand* political science in the United States is an awareness both of the patterns and possibilities presented by Western history and of the particular circumstances presented by the American experience. From the two, something "unique in Western intellectual history" indeed has been created. It is necessary to take some account, however brief, of some of the background and environing factors which led to the emergence of a discipline of political science and helped to give it the particular form that it assumed.

### The American Political Experience

American political science may achieve (or may already have achieved) some of its universalistic aspirations, but plainly in its origins and development it is related to American history in much the same fashion that a national literature, however much influenced by foreign sources and currents, is related to national experience. Paradoxically, even the idea of a political science rising above parochial circumstances is a product of a certain set of circumstances and is in that sense culture-bound.

The American political experience begins with well over two centuries of "Englishmen living in America," in which time certain English political institutions, such as the common law, were permanently implanted. But also in that period the ground was prepared for significant divergences. Notably, the "federal" pattern had already been developed in essentials by long experience of divided jurisdiction and rule between London and the colonies. The Revolution was made and the Constitution framed in the name of ideas derived from many British sources, as well as from Continental sources reaching back into antiquity. Nevertheless, "the first new nation" had been created, and its political experience was to be a significant departure from anything presented by the Western political past.

Important features of this political experience include: a written Constitution featuring the principle of popular sovereignty, a bill of rights, a territorial division of powers, and a functional separation of powers; the flourishing of the ideas and ethos of liberalism, largely derived from European sources, but freed of the restraining power of the European past; an experience-grounded feeling of individual independence and local self-rule; the development of an enduring two-party system and a luxuriant group life with political associations; the rise of a vigorous nationalism and a related notion of national "mission," susceptible, however, to varying and even conflicting interpretations; the growth of theories and practices of democracy superimposed on the original republican design; and a deep and pervasive sense that the American experience is or will become the *human* experience. Such matters are written deeply into American political science, so deeply that they may not be noticed by Americans who take them for granted.

### The Citizen Literature

An important aspect of American political development, arising from it and contributing to it, has been the so-called citizen literature. The United States, it appears, has not produced a great political philosopher. But in the course of its distinctive political development it has produced a rich stock of political writings, some of undoubtedly high literary, rhetorical, and expository merit. The Declaration of Independence and even the Constitution, from one point of view, can be so regarded. The *Federalist* papers, written to explain and justify the Constitution, are prominent in the literature. Included also are notable presidential addresses and state papers, opinions rendered in leading judicial decisions, famous speeches and letters of statesmen, editorials appearing in influential newspapers and journals, and so forth.

In the latter part of the twentieth century, when the Constitution may not even appear as an appendix in an introductory textbook, the reading and study of the citizen literature of American politics may be easily overlooked as an influence on political science. But in the post-Civil War formative period a student of politics might be required to memorize, recite, and construe the Constitution, as well as other literature deemed central to national experience. The influence of such training is readily apparent in early political science.

The influence of the citizen literature today is problematical. But to the extent that the spirit and concepts of the citizen literature remain diffused in the corpus of political learning, there is an influence—an influence which it is reasonable to presume is related to some of the strains and conflicts discussed below.

## *Industrialization, Urbanization, Specialization*

American economic and social life entered into sweeping transformations in the latter part of the nineteenth century. The fact that a self-conscious political science did arise, that it arose when it did, that when it arose it took the form it did take, must be understood as a part of these transformations. The victory of the North in the Civil War meant, of course, the victory of industrialism over agrarianism, and it was followed by a remarkable era of capitalist development and exploitation. The events and characteristics of that era—such as the closing of the frontier, the rapid growth of cities, the continued and increasing immigration, the rise of large commercial and industrial units, the spreading adulation of technology and of science understood in a vulgarized Baconian fashion as knowledge giving power and control, the shifting of class patterns and stresses, the emergence of the United States as a major world state—created new political needs and problems. Simultaneously, however, they created new opportunities and resources for responding. Increased wealth, for example, permitted the growth of new centers of learning. Respect for technology and science stimulated and licensed the rise of new types of knowledge, and expanding commerce and improved transportation facilitated the immigration of ideas as well as of people.

Implied in these developments and of great importance for our purposes was the advance of professionalization and of specialization in learned callings generally. A more varied and complex economy and a more complicated society had as correlates increasing—and increasingly varied and esoteric—knowledge and technologies: both "hard," such as engineering, and "soft," such as law. By midcentury there was already significant movement toward increased specialization and professionalization, notable even in the traditional callings of the law and the ministry; and it is clear—in retrospect—that old bases for the generation and transmission of knowledge would have to be transformed and new ones created. The rise of the "idea" of social science in its contemporary sense, and establishment of the several social science disciplines, were part of a larger societal adjustment to a changed mode of life.

### Rise of the New University and Reception of European Learning

American social science is not only heir to a millenia-old Western tradition; it cannot be understood apart from specific European influences and contributions of the nineteenth and twentieth centuries. The university in which social science has been nurtured is in many respects a comparatively recent "importation" (Veysey, 1965). And the flow of ideas and talent from European sources was crucial not only in the formative period of the several disciplines; it has continued to be of vital importance.

Institutions of higher education, known as "colleges," had of course existed from early colonial times, and mid-nineteenth-century America was sprinkled with a fairly large number. These institutions, originally modeled more or less on English (and Scottish) prototypes, offered "advanced" instruction—above all, preparation for the ministry. But no American institution was, by European standards, a strong or "true" university. Henry Adams's account of his Harvard years in his *Education* is indicative: The university taught neither very much nor very well. It was scarcely a place for the generation and diffusion of *new* knowledge.

A few ambitious or curious young Americans were finding their way into European universities before the Civil War, and significant numbers followed their example in the decades thereafter. Most went to Germany, whose universities were then the envy of the world. On their return they not only commanded knowledge and skills in advance of what could be imparted at home; they also brought new concepts of the proper nature of a university. These new concepts fitted the needs of an increasingly complex industrial society, and joined to native initiatives, particularly the Morrill Act of 1862, they worked a transformation in the American university system. Older institutions, such as Harvard and Columbia, vied with new ones, such as Johns Hopkins and Cornell, in becoming "genuine" universities.

For present purposes the central fact is that the university became the center of a new and intense learned specialization, of professionalism, and of research, i.e., of the creation of *new* knowledge. These developments chiefly affected instruction, methods, and arrangements at the graduate level. Indeed, they might be said to have had the effect of adding a new level: The Ph.D. was superimposed on the A.B. and M.A. and became the accepted criterion of preparation for research and teaching "at the highest level."

Although the United States has been preeminently the home of disciplinary specialization and professional organization in the social sciences since the late nineteenth century, contemporary European influence has been important from the beginning and remains so. That influence is exerted on American social science in several ways. It may occur through works and example (thus Bagehot, Durkheim, Marx, Michels, Pareto, Weber). It may come through American study abroad (thus, for political science, Burgess and Herbert Baxter Adams, Goodnow and Dunning). It may be exerted when European scholars lecture or teach briefly in the United States (thus, for political science, Bryce and Laski). It may result from the immigration to the United States of mature and highly trained scholars (thus, for political science, a distinguished roster from Lieber to Friedrich).

Especially in its origins and early development, political science owes a large and unmistakable debt to European influences. The stimulus and example of the German *Staatswissenschaft,* centered on the concept of the state, engrossed with the concept of sovereignty, and focused on law as the embodiment of state will and sovereign power, are evident in the majority of the seminal early works. French influence was less pervasive but important and much to the same effect; state, sovereignty, law—and history—were at the center of a general, western European approach to the political. British influence was also important. The impact of John Stuart Mill, Herbert Spencer, Walter Bagehot, and James Bryce is often conspicuous in the early works. Indeed, the British influence (speaking now to political science, not to social science in general) may be as important as the Continental. With passing time probably it becomes more important: Bryce is more relevant to contemporary political science than Bluntschli, Wallas than Wappaus. But the British influence is more difficult to assess; closeness in history, culture, and above all, language reduces visibility rather than enhances it.

## *GROWTH OF SELF-CONSCIOUSNESS AND SEARCH FOR IDENTITY: POLITICAL SCIENCE BEFORE WORLD WAR 1*

It is now clear that conscious concern for the political can vary in many dimensions, that search for the "stuff" of politics is both old and still continuing, that the idea of political *science* is complex and controversial, and that a sense of discipline or profession among those devoted to the study of political science is not in itself decisive with respect to significant results. But clearly also the emergence in the United States in the late nineteenth century and the early twentieth century of an academic discipline and a sense of profession was an important event in the history of the study of politics.

Reflecting in its origins a national experience, the "creation of political science" also interacts in the shaping of that experience as the twentieth century advances and, indeed, becomes a potent influence in the study of politics in much of the world. The objective now is knowledge of the main features of this development and understanding of some of the implications.

### Academic Political Science Prior to 1880

Much of importance for the future of political science took place in British North America, in the experiences of revolution and constitution-making, and in American history in the late eighteenth and nineteenth centuries. But the contribution of academic political science to what occurred was marginal. That contribution consisted of the perpetuation, through teaching, of the Western political tradition and, increasingly, the American strain of that tradition; and of the inculcation of that tradition in a relatively small number of citizens who were to occupy positions of more than average influence. In more than three centuries no important work of political thought was produced in the colleges, no significant political innovation was devised and launched, no research was conducted that resulted in what contemporary political scientists would regard as worthy political science.

The record of college teaching of political science from the beginning down to 1900 has been painstakingly researched and recorded in considerable detail by Anna Haddow (1939). On the basis of the record she has set forth, several observations pertinent to present interests may be made.

Although the term "political science" was occasionally used from an early date (both in and out of academia), the usage was both broad and loose. Only gradually did the term acquire the implications that were to be given it through the growing prestige of science and the increasing connection between scientific enterprises and the university.

The object of teaching, perhaps first of all, was the formation of moral character (of the private person and of the citizen) and, second, training for participation in public life, as minister, magistrate, or whatever. The teaching of political science was not conducted in an academic "department" of political science. Rather, it was embedded in a "classical" curriculum modeled more or less on that of the English university of the time and having a prominent religious orientation. Three types of materials served as the main bases of instruction in political science: (1) selections from classical literature, including histories, which served to point a political moral as well as to instruct in language and history; (2) classics of political thought, such as works of Plato and Aristotle from antiquity and Locke and Harrington from the recent past; and—increasingly—(3) treatises and "textbooks." The works of the fathers of international law, Grotius, Pufendorf, Vattel, and Burlamaqui, were widely used. And especially favored were works of "philosophy." Frequently studied were Francis Hutchinson's *A Short Introduction to Moral*

*Philosophy* (several chapters of which were devoted to "Politics"); and above all, after its publication in 1785, William Paley's *The Principles of Moral and Political Philosophy*.

In a view of the entire period from the establishment of the first colleges to 1880, several evolutionary trends are evident. One is simply an increase in the stock of materials on which to draw for instruction, as well as increasing diversity in those materials. The works of Montesquieu, Guizot, Adam Smith, and de Tocqueville, for example, were drawn on to some extent when they became available. Another trend was toward differentiation and secularization. "Philosophy" was becoming differentiated and divided into separate pursuits. Not only was "natural" philosophy separating from "moral" philosophy, but "political philosophy" was becoming distinct from "ethics." History and economics were beginning to develop self-awareness; and the study of law was moving rapidly toward professionalization.

Another clear trend was toward "Americanization," especially, of course, after independence and union. American texts and treatises, such as the works of Francis Wayland, Laurens Hickok, Francis Bowen, James Kent, and Joseph Story, increasingly competed with foreign works for instruction in moral and political philosophy, political economy, and jurisprudence. Of much greater import, however, was a large and increasing attention to the documents of American nationhood, the citizen literature. The Declaration of Independence and the Constitution became central items in some courses of study. To these were added, according to time and political-sectional taste, *The Federalist,* the letters, papers, and speeches of statesmen (Washington's Farewell Address was of course a favorite), landmark judicial opinions, legislative resolutions, and patriotic addresses.

The "Americanization" of the study of political science was natural and under the circumstances unavoidable; it was also perhaps desirable. In any event, since education in citizenship and training for public service were central objectives of pedagogy, the ground was prepared for the ambiguities and tensions that were to become troublesome when political science aspired to become "truly" scientific.

### *Francis Lieber: Symbol and Portent*

At the same time that political science was rapidly becoming "Americanized," there appeared a portent of the Continental, especially Germanic, influence that was soon to become important: the career and writings of Francis Lieber.

As indicated, the Continental influence was exerted indirectly through the importation of institutional arrangements and academic values—the modern university—and through American study of political and social science abroad. But a significant amount of that influence has been exerted through the migration of German (and Austrian) trained scholars, especially after the rise of Nazism. Within the period from 1880 to the present, American political science was in many respects most "parochial" in the second and third decades of this century, after the replacement of the first generation of European-trained leaders by the products of the new American graduate schools and before the arrival of the able and influential scholars who fled Nazi persecution.

Berlin-born, university-trained, and of liberal persuasion, Lieber came to the United States (after a brief period in England) in 1827 to escape the conservative reaction following the Napoleonic wars. (As a patriotic Prussian he fought at Waterloo, but that fact did not prevent later imprisonment for his liberal ideas.) In 1835 he was elected Professor of History and Political Economy at South Carolina College, where he remained until elected to the chair of history and political economy at Columbia College in 1857. At his request, because he wished to emphasize *"Government,* Political Philosophy, or, as our great master [Aristotle] called it, Politics," his designation was changed to Professor of History and Political Science (though in 1865 the trustees transferred him to the Law School with the title of Professor of Constitutional History and Public Law).

While at South Carolina College, Lieber published the several works that established his reputation. His masterwork, *Civil Liberty and Self-Government,* was often used as a textbook after its publication in 1853. "Influence" is of course difficult to demonstrate, but in any event Lieber struck a new note in midcentury political science, and his innovative effort was widely recognized—as the call to Columbia signifies. Whatever his influence on the events of the 1880s (he died in 1872), he is interesting as a harbinger of the coming mingling of Continental and Anglo-American motifs and styles.

The essence of the matter is that Lieber's temperamental and doctrinal liberalism enabled him to bring a Germanic philosophic-juristic perspective to bear on Anglo-American political institutions. Of these political institutions he had great knowledge; indeed, for them he entertained great respect and affection. But his background saved him from a mere parochial adulation. He paired obligations with rights, duty with liberty, and he put all in context of philosophy and history. If his deep concern with civic duties was to seem quaint and stuffy to later generations of political scientists, his equal concern for civil liberties (perhaps inconsistently?) has not gone out of fashion.

### The Rise of University-Based Political Science

Stimulated by the social, institutional, and intellectual developments noted above, political science programs of a new type were created in the universities in the 1880s. Political science thereby was to reach a self-consciousness of a higher level—or at least of a different type—than had ever been reached before. In the 1970s these first attempts to achieve a "genuine" political science are likely to seem primitive and naive. But not only are there continuous lines of development down to the present; to a remarkable degree, problems and controversies that were to trouble the profession perennially were clearly foreshadowed in the first decades of the new political science.

The year 1880 marks, at least symbolically, the birth of the new political science. In June of that year the trustees of Columbia (even then still called Columbia College) authorized the creation of a School of Political Science. The moving spirit in this act of creation was John W. Burgess, who became head of the School and a potent influence in early political science, both through his shaping of this archetypical enterprise and through his writings. Burgess moved immediately and energetically, upon receiving the authorization of the trustees: "Although the period of gestation may have been long and painful, the School sprang almost fully formed at birth from the minds of Burgess and his young associates" (Somit and Tanenhaus, 1967, p. 21).[1] Training for a European-style Ph.D. began at once; research-based dissertation not only was required, but had to be published. In 1886 the School inaugurated the *Political Science Quarterly*, which for decades was the main channel for scholarly writings in political science and became the prototype for later political science journals.

A second major beginning, at The Johns Hopkins University, evolved more gradually. Johns Hopkins was founded in 1876 with the purpose of emulating European universities by offering instruction at the graduate level, and historian Herbert Baxter Adams became a member of its founding faculty. Adams took the lead in developing at Hopkins a program of advanced training and research in history and political science, which from his point of view were closely joined if not indeed the same enterprise considered in two aspects. In 1877 Adams founded the Johns Hopkins Historical and Political Science Association and in 1883 established *The Johns Hopkins Studies in Historical and Political Science*. Both were precedents for later associations and publication series.

Other universities, most notably perhaps the University of Michigan under the leadership of Charles Kendall Adams, made "starts" in establishing graduate training in this early period but, for various reasons, were unable to achieve lasting momentum. Until the twentieth century was well begun, it was to Columbia and Johns Hopkins that other universities chiefly turned for teachers with the doctorate when they wished to introduce the new political science. As the supply of American-trained political scientists built up, foreign training tapered off; it became less fashionable, as well as less necessary. By the time of World War I, political science was widely taught in colleges and universities. As a graduate-level enterprise it was well rooted in a score of leading academic centers, and some of the newer ones were now prepared to compete for leadership positions.

Of the two pioneer programs, it was that of Columbia, with a greater openness to interaction with disciplines other than history, which was to prove more relevant and influential for the political science of the mid- and late-twentieth century. But the characteristics the two programs shared were of greater import than their differences. In emulation of Continental models, both emphasized the graduate level rather than the undergraduate, and both sought to abandon the homiletic, memorization-and-recitation emphasis of the past. Both emphasized research, the production of new knowledge from the examination of data, as against philosophical speculation and deduction from "first principles." Largely in imitation of Continental scholarship but also somewhat influenced by Darwinism, both focused on the historical-comparative method as the basic scientific mode of discovering the laws of political life. Both emphasized the seminar and the lecture as methods of instruction. Both accepted *Lehrfreiheit* and *Lernfreiheit* as ideals, however qualified those principles were under the constraint of circumstances.

Most important and fundamental, the leaders of the new movement, wherever located, tended to share a commitment to scientism.[2] That is, impressed with the achievements of the natural sciences, they believed the way toward the discovery of greater (or "true") knowledge in the political sphere lay in the application of modes of thought and methods of research which had demonstrated their potency so effectively in such areas as physics and biology. The commitment to scientism, plus the belief that the political is analytically and to some degree empirically distinguishable from the total social field, plus the continuing dedication of institutions and resources to the attainment of scientific knowledge of the political—together these formed the base of a new American political science.

Something new and different in the study of politics was being created, not just for America but in history. To some extent the uniqueness is quantitative. Never before had persons in such number and resources in such amount been devoted to a scientific study of politics as was to be true in the coming decades. However, the uniqueness is also qualitative. Although the idea that the political is a distinguishable part of the total social field is to some extent ancient, to be sure, the adoption of the singular form, political *science,* nevertheless signified a departure in perspective and usage. The style chosen, political *science,* signified both a commitment to a sharpened understanding of the mandates of scientific method and a departure from a European, especially Gallic, view of "the political sciences," conceived as the various disciplines (sometimes including foreign languages) pertinent to statecraft. Although the new usage did not find immediate and universal acceptance—and occasionally it still contests with "politics" or "government"—nevertheless it did establish a clear dominance in the decades after 1880.

To argue the distinctiveness, indeed the uniqueness, of American political science and its importance for contemporary political inquiry is not to assert that a genuine and generalizable political science has in fact been realized. Perhaps the scepticism and open-endedness that are presumed to characterize science would itself pose the achievement of this goal as a continuing question. In any event, whether a "genuine" political science is yet in being is a question often readdressed, sometimes in cool appraisal, sometimes in heated contention. In such discussions and debates the significance of the Western-American context is obvious and undeniable. In addition to its self-imposed scientific mission, American political science has important tasks in greater or lesser degree imposed by (and often willingly accepted from) its political context, the most important of which are the transmission of a civic culture (or "teaching citizenship"), preparation of students for public careers, and participation in public affairs, if only indirectly, through studies that have impact on public policy. These activities, together with readily available domestic data and cultural immersion, tend to give an American coloration to American political science.

Ultimately, the problems presented by such considerations reach to the problematic if not opaque center of the enterprise of social science: What kind of social knowledge with what relationship to time, space, and culture is possible?

### *Pre-World War I Political Science: Developments and Characteristics*

No attempt can be made to treat the development of political science in rounded, narrative form. The names and themes are too many, the interrelations too complex. But for certain analytical and comparative purposes it will be useful to draw attention to some of the prominent aspects of political science in the pre-World War I period.

***Decline of the historical-comparative method.***   As noted, at both Columbia and Johns Hopkins (though with differing emphases) the historical-comparative method highly prominent in nineteenth-century Continental scholarship was accepted as integral to the enterprise of political science. E. A. Freeman's dictum "History is past Politics and Politics present History" was something of an official motto at Johns Hopkins, and at Columbia, despite greater openness to economics and other concerns, the primary emphasis was also on history. At center, the historical-comparative method was concerned with the discovery and elucidation of "laws" of development, in this case, of course, political development.

Almost from the beginning there was some resistance. Woodrow Wilson, at Johns Hopkins in the 1880s for graduate study, protested "rummaging" through documents as against observation of political "life." Immediate practical concerns soon began to draw attention of the comparatively few political scientists away from serious historical research. Other disciplines increasingly presented themselves as attractive sources of ideas and methods; the "grand" period of the historical-comparative method was passing, even on the Continent, with changing intellectual fashions. For whatever reasons, the vogue of the historical-comparative method, taken seriously, was comparatively brief. In general, the close joining of political science and history characteristic of early political science (academic departments of History and Political Science were common in the early period) declined decade by decade as other interests multiplied and newer conceptions of scientific method moved to the fore. By mid-twentieth century, history tended to be viewed, not as a primary source of political "laws" or even of political "understanding," but as one among other "sources"—a sometimes useful hunting ground for hypotheses, a convenient collection of illustrations, and a possible checkpoint for inferences derived in studies of the contemporary.

Dissociated from serious historical study, the comparative method was employed in two main areas. One was the study of foreign governments. But the study of foreign governments was limited for the most part to European and European-derived governments; and the "comparison" tended to be descriptive and formalistic. The other was the study of local and state governments. Those governments, particularly of the states, were often spoken of as "laboratories" in which comparative experimentation could take place. Again, however, when comparisons were actually made, they were primarily descriptive and formalistic, and they were more concerned with political action than with political knowledge. Only after World War II did the comparative method again emerge as a central concern of the scientific enterprise.

*The "Americanization" of political science.* The rapid decline of the historical-comparative method may be viewed as but one aspect of a more general tendency: the Americanization of political science. In general, concepts and styles of thinking characteristic of Continental political science and widely adopted by the first generation of self-conscious American political scientists tended to fade as domestic programs leading to the doctorate expanded and multiplied and as indigenous interests asserted themselves. Continental political science was centrally concerned with the state, sovereignty, and law. Early American political science echoed those concerns. Political science was "the science of the State," and several seminal early works had *State* in their titles. There was much concern for the nature and locus of sovereignty. The origins of law and its relationship to the political were matters of serious concern. Such subjects were approached, typically, with a method that mingled history, "theory," and philosophy. A "tradition" of graduate study was formed about these matters and the style in which they were addressed—a tradition that, though continuously eroding, proved long-lasting.

With considerable plausibility it can be argued that changes in vocabulary and style of address suggest more "progress" than exists, that there is more of Woodrow Wilson, W. W. Willoughby, and Frank Goodnow in contemporary political science than is suspected. Nevertheless, it is clear that significant changes in tone, scope, and emphasis took place between the formal founding of political science and World War I. A somewhat exotic import was shaped more or less to native uses, and certainly additional interests were successfully asserted to be a part of political science.

It is notable that "British imports" tended to rise as the Continental declined, obviously due in part to a common language but probably more importantly to the closer congruity of governmental institutions and problems, as well as greater commonality in intellectual fashions and approaches to problem-solving. James Bryce's *American Commonwealth* was recognized as an important work, and it was an influential one; and Bryce, though British, was elected fourth President of the American Political Science Association (Ions, 1968). Walter Bagehot's *English Constitution* and *Physics and Politics* were important in shaping the outlook of many. A. V. Dicey was widely read, and Graham Wallas's *Human Nature in Politics* had some immediate, as well as a lasting, influence. In general the British influence was in the direction of the factual, the empirical—broadly, "realism."

Of course, there was a range of political experience and concerns important for Americans to which few foreign works spoke directly or importantly—or indeed acceptably. Foreigners might, for example, have something to say to the problems arising from immigration, industrialization, and urbanization; certainly they could provide guidance with respect to such a problem as establishing an honest and efficient civil service. But did they have anything significant to say to important matters peculiarly American: a written constitution, federalism, the tripartite separation of powers, state government, and so forth? Whatever the answer given to this question (usually negative), such American institutions demanded and received increasing attention from political scientists as their numbers grew and specialization advanced.

This is an appropriate place to note that American political science has had from its beginning (whether the "beginning" is taken as the late eighteenth or the late nineteenth century) a certain ambivalence. On the one hand, it has been remarkably open to foreign experience and influence, with the important qualification that the experience and influence fall (on the whole) within the liberal-constitutional-democratic band of the spectrum. This receptivity is endlessly demonstrated, from the Founding Fathers of the Republic through the Founding Fathers of the discipline and up to the present. From "Roman" Senate to Scandinavian Ombudsman, from Aristotle to the latest "important" foreign scholarly work, the imports are legion. On the other hand, from the beginning of the national period there has also been a frequent and sometimes ardent sentiment that American political science (again, whether broadly or narrowly construed) is unique and perhaps uniquely important for the world, a type and range of knowledge deserving of export or emulation. This is hardly the place to explicate the ironies and explore the nuances of this ambivalence; or to relate the ambivalence to its context of American history and thought; or—even less—to try to sift evidence and weigh claims. But some appreciation of the foreign-American-foreign dialectic is necessary to an understanding of political science.

**Reformism.** "Reform" motives in political science are perhaps important at any time—even, paradoxically, when the motive is to purge political science of reformism in the interests of science. Certainly they were important in the early decades. American history provided proscenium, setting, and to some extent lines for the political science actors: How to deal with the stresses arising from exuberant capitalism, "rounding out the nation," massive immigration, the growth of cities? How to adjust a political system framed by eighteenth-century republicans, but significantly altered by Jacksonian democracy, to a new national experience?

The various reform motives and movements were to prove, if not incompatible in some grand logical resolution, at least contrary and confusing in what they seemed to require in and from political science. Problems and conflicts soon developed, and some of them still trouble political science.

Among the relevant reforms, one already noted was the reform—or "creation"—of the university. The institutional framework, the professional workways and mores it provided have been decisive for much that has happened. In the long run, these "institutional" factors have proved more important than the "contents" of the Continental political science, with which, in the importing, they appeared of a piece. The emphasis on the university as a fount of new knowledge (expressed in terms of research and publication), the importance attached to graduate training and the Ph.D. as the symbol of research competence, the conception that, above all, the university should be devoted to ideals expressed by the word *science*—these elements have been important in political science from its beginnings up to the present.

Another area of reform concerned leadership. The period in which national leadership was provided by the "natural aristocracy" was now long gone, and obviously (it appeared) the prescriptions of Jacksonian democracy would not meet the new needs. Means must be created, it was thought, to produce new leaders equal to new times; if received institutions did not meet the need, then new institutional means must be devised. The rise of political science unquestionably owes something to the notion that it could inspire and instruct the politicians, journalists, lawyers and others (including businessmen) who had public leadership roles.

Another reform movement centered on the civil service. The Jacksonian "spoils system" was judged to be, for the new conditions, not simply inadequate but pernicious as well. It not only failed to provide the necessary competence in government service; it poisoned politics as well. Dorman B. Eaton's *Civil Service Reform in Great Britain* (1880) provided both a spur and plausible remedies, and the assassination of President Garfield in 1883 by a "disappointed office-seeker" dramatized the need for change. The new political science, it was widely hoped, could not only provide guidance on the principles to be followed in purifying and strengthening the public service; it could provide the necessary expertise for administrative functions and impart it to potential civil servants.

Here Woodrow Wilson's essay of 1887, "The Study of Administration," is extraordinarily revealing. His central concern is America: How to preserve and strengthen the American democracy now that "it is getting to be harder to *run* a constitution than to frame one." "Running" the government must now be taken seriously; it is no longer a matter that "clerks" can arrange after "doctors" have agreed on principles. Where can we learn the necessary "science?" From European countries, where it has long been taken seriously. No matter that we do not approve of their undemocratic ways; their knowledge of efficient means can be borrowed, cleansed of autocratic contagion, and adjusted to serve *our* ends. A political science that merely provides "intelligent critics" of government does not go far enough. "We must prepare better officials as the *apparatus* of government."

It is worth noting that the example set by the École Libre des Sciences Politiques, created in France in the 1870s to train candidates for government service, was not lost on the founders of political science. Although the German university, with its research emphasis, was preeminent in their thoughts, the activities at the École Libre, as well as the British reforms flowing from the Trevelyan-Northcote report, often served as inspiration (though not necessarily as models to be closely copied).

Another reform motif was education for citizenship. The multifold increase in population since 1790 had been paced by the spread of democratic ideas and expectations: the Republic had become a Democracy. No longer would it suffice to ensure the political education of clergymen, lawyers, merchants, and gentleman farmers; the fate of the polity now depended on a multitude of homesteaders, laborers, shopkeepers, and—even—immigrants ignorant of the language of their adopted country. To "thinking people" in general the situation presented itself as perilous. Fortunately, the remedy seemed obvious. As put in the House of Commons after the reform bill of 1867: "Now we must educate our masters."

How should this be done? Through many means, including the press, mass education, and special programs. But did not higher education have an important role, and especially, was this not an obligation of the burgeoning land-grant universities, which owed their very existence to the Republic?

Much evidence indicates that the problem of education for citizenship was deeply involved in the establishment of the new political science. To some leaders it was obviously a matter of subordinate interest, but to others it was a prime mission—even a missionary duty. Political science was viewed not as an encapsuled pursuit of esoteric knowledge but as a vehicle for inculcating in the citizen the principles of the Republic and for strengthening those principles by the discovery of new knowledge appropriate to changed conditions. To teach *American* government was the first task and central obligation. Nor was the matter one to be determined solely by political scientists. The citizens had an interest and the means to make it felt, most importantly through frequent legislative injunction that American government (sometimes "citizenship") must be taught in the public universities as well as in primary and secondary schools.

The three motifs, leadership education, education for government service, and citizenship education are logically separable and were often separated in fact, in terms of primary interest and manifestations. But they were also sometimes closely related and intertwined. Nor do these three motifs stand alone as "reform" interests. To understand political science in the pre-World War I period, one must perceive that it was deeply involved in—it was an aspect of—the currents of reformism which came to be designated Progressivism, as well as, to some extent, Populism. The themes and movements of Progressivism and Populism—civil service reform, the direct election of senators, electoral reform, the reconstruction of municipal government, the initiative and referendum, and still others—were a part of the political science of the time, as the record abundantly attests.

**"*Professional*" considerations and characteristics.** The American Political Science Association was created in 1903, more or less as a consequence of an initiative of the previous year to found an "American Society for Comparative Legislation." The founding meeting took place in New Orleans in connection with meetings of the American Historical Association and the American Economic Association. (The former had been founded in 1884, the latter in 1885. The American Statistical Association was founded in 1888, the American Academy of Political and Social Science in 1889. The American Sociological Association was also created in 1903.) The membership of the Association in 1904, its first full year, was just over two hundred. By the beginning of World War I the membership was approximately fifteen hundred, but it declined to thirteen hundred by 1920, presumably for war-related reasons.

In 1906 the American Political Science Association began publication of the *American Political Science Review*. It had been preceded by the *Proceedings of the American Political Science Association* (which contained learned articles, especially those presented as "papers" at the annual meetings); in 1914 the latter was discontinued, in effect merged with the *Review*. The previously noted *Political Science Quarterly* (1886) and *The Annals of the American Academy of Political and Social Science* (1890) had preceded both—and still continue. (Other university-sponsored journal or serial publications also preceded the organs of the Association but proved less durable.) The journals of other learned societies, law journals, and organs such as the *National Municipal Review* (1912) provided additional outlets for publication.

College and university recognition of the new political science, reflected in the establishment of separate departments of political science, proceeded slowly. Only a few existed by the turn of the century, and in 1920 the number was still short of fifty. More common until long after the establishment of the Association was the combination of political science with another discipline (or disciplines). In 1914, at "89 colleges, political science was joined with history; with history and economics at 48; with economics and sociology at 21" (Somit and Tanenhaus, 1967, pp. 56–57). The "output" of American doctorates in political science is difficult to ascertain because of record-keeping and classificatory problems. On an annual basis it is estimated as: "From 1885 to 1900, three or four; from 1900 to 1910, six to ten; from 1911 to 1915, ten to fifteen; and from then to 1921 about eighteen to twenty" (Somit and Tanenhaus, 1967, p. 58).

As to "fields" in the early period, some broad generalizations are possible. By a wide margin, American government was the main object of attention and of pedagogy. (Most teaching, of course, was of undergraduates.) But "American government" is not a single thing, and courses devoted to selected aspects, such as constitutional law or municipal government, were common. Comparative government was a recognized area. Although much of its literature had the limitations indicated above, there were able men and durable works. International law and relations received a fair amount of attention; but distinguished work by Americans was not notable. The history of political thought was a small field, dominated by William A. Dunning at

Columbia and by those trained under him. Public administration and public opinion were hardly yet recognized fields, but works later credited as laying their foundations were published (for example, Frank J. Goodnow's *Politics and Administration* and A. Lawrence Lowell's *Public Opinion and Popular Government*).

Some of the earliest political scientists essayed major treatises aimed at "laying out" political science more or less entire. Some were ably done and still speak in some measure to the contemporary political scientist: thus works by John W. Burgess, William W. Crane and Bernard Moses, Woodrow Wilson, W. W. Willoughby, and Frank J. Goodnow. (These works were largely aimed at professional peers. They were supplemented and succeeded by textbooks, largely undistinguished, directed toward students.) But on the whole the early treatises, however ably done, were derivative, owing a large debt to European political science and advancing little beyond it. There was a conspicuous absence of major original works of a theoretical nature, grounded either in philosophy or the logic and method of natural science. An exception, perhaps, is Arthur F. Bentley's *The Process of Government* (1908), which later came to fame and influence. But Bentley was not a "political scientist," and his work was little noted and less praised at the time by those who so designated themselves.

From data such as the foregoing and from even a cursory survey of the early literature, a number of further observations can be made and generalizations drawn.

Political science on the eve of World War I was hardly of a clear and single mind about the identity it asserted and only with charity might be designated either a discipline or a profession. Differentiation from other social sciences was far from complete; the struggle for separate departmental status was only well begun. The establishment of the American Political Science Association certainly represented a forward step and was decisive for much of what was to happen in later decades. But clearly the Association was not, in this period, composed of a highly differentiated membership. Although academically trained and located political scientists assumed a dominant position from the beginning, the majority of the members were journalists, reformers, lawyers, politicians, administrators, and so forth—persons of many backgrounds and occupations who were obviously "interested" and whose knowledge might be considerable but whose entitlement to the designation "political scientist" would rest on the loosest construction of the term.

But then, on the other hand, academically located political scientists were less clearly differentiated, specialized, and "professional" than they would later become. For many who instructed in political science this was only a course or two along with courses in history, economics, or whatever. Furthermore, there was a tradition and presumption of activism born of the forces noted above: Political science was not merely for the library and classroom, not a withdrawn scientific quest. It was for purposes of national survival, of civic improvement, of democratic health. The political scientist, it was thought, has special responsibilities as citizen. Engagement in some form of political life was common, not just on the part of the rank-and-file academician, but on the part of the leaders of the new political science. Woodrow Wilson's career, from professor through university presidency and gubernatorial office to President of the United States, was merely the most notable in a general pattern.

Probably it is fair to say that there was some decline in the average level of scholarly-scientific writing as the volume increased. The "peaks" remained high, as, for example, the works of Charles A. Beard, Henry Jones Ford, Frank J. Goodnow, Albert Bushnell Hart, and A. Lawrence Lowell attest. But the valleys became broader as the ranks of would-be political scientists swelled and outlets for publication increased.

A number of factors were involved—in addition to the fact that "publication" early became a factor in professional visibility and academic promotion. One was the decline of the historical-comparative method. With the fading of its claims and aspirations, and in the absence of another authoritative "scientific" model to replace it, there came a degradation of its methods: a trivialization of its attention to "source" documents, formalistic description and comparison without clear purpose. But the widespread acceptance of "nonscientific" objectives was more centrally relevant. To the extent that political science has as objectives the transmission of civic culture, public enlightenment, and improvement of the polity, do other criteria than scientific criteria become relevant in judging research and publication? Whatever one's answer, pedagogic-reformist motives help to account for a great deal of reportorial, descriptive, and hortatory writing in the Progressive era—writing almost wholly "dead" to the contemporary reader.

## The Emergence of Enduring Motifs and Problems

As just suggested, one may, when perusing the literature of the pre-World War I period, have a sense that the material in hand is quite as remote from contemporary issues as a Byzantine theological disputation. But the opposite is also possible: a recognition of material bearing on an issue that is highly contemporary and perhaps even in heated contention. In the interest of gaining perspective on the enterprise of political science, it will be useful to note (or to note again) the emergence of certain enduring themes.

We may appropriately begin by focusing on the matter of definition, or more precisely, self-image. In what kind of enterprise did the early political scientists conceive themselves to be engaged? What were regarded as its distinguishing features, its divisions, its boundaries?

The early political scientists for the most part accepted the designation "political science" without serious question as to its appropriateness (though "government" and "politics" were the favored terms of some). It was easy for them to do so, given the context of language and history. The history of the term (sometimes "science of politics" or the "political sciences") would be difficult to write. Certainly the usage was not new. The Founders of the Republic spoke easily of the "science" of politics. W. J. M. Mackenzie notes that the term political science "was used unselfconsciously in the middle of the nineteenth century" (Mackenzie, 1967, p. 16). There was no need to search for a new term, since "political science" was so flexible it could accommodate tradition as well as signify ambition for the future.

Science in a new sense, to be sure, was "in the air," transforming the old usage, sharpening concepts, and whetting ambitions. But one must beware of viewing the scene with the lenses of twentieth-century science and scientific philosophy. The "newer" meaning of science was really "old," given by diffusion and refraction of the ideas of Bacon, Descartes, Newton, Darwin, and Spencer. Not just in the popular mind but in the minds of able publicists (sometimes even of bona fide natural scientists), science was intimately joined with "nonscientific" ideas and sentiments, above all, the idea of *progress*. Karl Pearson's classic statement of Victorian scientific philosophy and methodology, *The Grammar of Science*, was not published until 1892, and there is no evidence of its influence until much later. Bernard Crick's thesis that it was not science but *technology* that became the "image" of American political science (Crick, 1959) is perhaps overargued, but it contains much truth. Certainly the enterprise of political science was decades old before it seemed appropriate to reflect seriously on the implications of a distinction between pure science and applied science.

Nevertheless, it should be noted and emphasized that a number of the creators and leaders of the new political science were highly self-conscious about the "science" to which they aspired. They conceived that the future of political science lay in following the lead of natural science, and (given prevailing ideas) they were knowledgeable about what this appeared to mandate. John W. Burgess, Munroe Smith, and Jesse Macy were among those who argued for following the natural science model (Somit and Tanenhaus, 1967, pp. 28-29). In general, the argument was against "deduction" and debate; it was for induction, comparativeness, experiments, and search for "laws." This emphasis has a contemporary ring. Even the distinction between fact and value, which was to become so important later, may be said to have been enunciated (though these terms were not used) in 1884 by William W. Crane and Bernard Moses in *Politics* (p. 3).

On the other hand, then as now there were doubters and dissenters about the possibility of making politics into a true or exact science. Some were equivocal: thus, on the whole record, Woodrow Wilson. In any event, distinctions were not so clearly drawn in the early period, and neither scientific philosophy nor scientific method was much argued. Political scientists on the whole were content to pursue their own interests, confident that their labors satisfied *some* scientific standard as well as practical need.

Attempts to divide and delineate the object of attention are worthy of note; twofold and threefold divisions early became popular. The Crane and Moses *Politics*, the Theodore Woolsey *Political Science* (1877), and the Frank J. Goodnow *Politics and Administration* (1900) favored a twofold division. In the first two (depending on how one interprets the language) the division was between science and art, or theory and practice. In the last it was of course between politics (as determining the will of the State) and administration (as executing the will of the State). Threefold division was favored by Burgess in *Political Science and Comparative Constitutional Law* (1890) and by W. W. Willoughby, in *The Nature of the State* (1896). Somit and Tanenhaus (1967, p. 24) translate the language in which Burgess expressed his tripartite division into the contemporary distinction among political community, type of regime, and administration in power. Willoughby divided political science among "determination of fundamental philosophical principles," "description of political institutions, or governmental institutions considered at rest," and "the determination of laws of political life and development, the motives that give rise to political action, the conditions that occasion particular political manifestations. . ." ( pp. 382–383).

Contemporary dichotomies and trichotomies presumably carry us some distance beyond these, but it is not irrelevant to the gaining of perspective to ask critically: How? Why? Beyond cavil, much that has recently appeared as a gain in understanding can be found, at least in other language and in germ, in the early literature. Some of the early writers—for example, Bagehot and Bryce, Ford and Lowell—had a fair understanding of "functionalism," even if they did not use the term (Landau, 1968a, 1972).

As already more than merely suggested, in the early period there emerged the perennial problems of the relationship of political science to other disciplines: How—and how much—distinct and separate? How can other disciplines serve political science? And how can political science avoid being "used," even captured? The dialectical processes of (1) a drive toward specialization and autonomy in the social sciences and (2) a search for fruitful relationships, perhaps the recognition of a total social science, the creation of a unified social theory, were already in operation.

The initial intimate involvement with history was gradually relaxed. The decline of political economy may be read in the creation of separate disciplinary organizations for economics and political science. The professionalization of legal training in separate schools was well advanced by the turn of the century. Close relationships with all three, history, economics, and law, were writ deeply into the Western political tradition, but they were now being attenuated, changed qualitatively as well as quantitatively with the pressure of specialization and under the spur of scientific aspirations.

On the other hand, new relationships were becoming important. The concurrently emerging discipline of sociology exerted an attraction. A number of pre-World War I political scientists saw sociology, rather than history, as being the most closely cognate field of inquiry, perhaps as providing a general theory of society in which all specialties could be somehow united. The rising discipline of psychology began to reveal in the works of Graham Wallas and A. Lawrence Lowell the attraction it would exert. The work of Lowell, particularly his "Oscillations in Politics," also foreshadowed the use of statistics for analytical purposes.

Finally, in this noting of themes and problems, it is appropriate to return to the subject of the multiple roles of political science. The relationships between its several roles, especially the strain between scientific aspirations and "extrascientific" activities, emerged as problems in the early period of self-conscious political science. The problems presented, at least in their range and intensity, are distinctive for political science as an academically based social discipline. (Similar problems exist, I believe, in economics and history but to a lesser degree, less still in sociology, and hardly at all in anthropology.)

The extrascientific functions of political science concern, broadly, transmission of the political tradition and culture, considered both as a complex of beliefs and as a set of institutions, and aid in making received political ideas and institutions "work," improving them and adapting them to changing conditions. They include education or training for leadership roles (especially but not limited to those clearly political), for government service more or less professional in nature, and for exercising the general responsibilities of citizenship. They include engaging in research aimed (at whatever level and however direct or indirect) at providing guidance in public policy. And they may involve an extra responsibility, namely, to participate in some fashion in public affairs as one with a special knowledge of things political.

As indicated above, these extrascientific functions derived from both foreign and domestic sources. Given the problems of the American polity, it seemed only natural to expect the new political science to assist in their resolution by providing a special learning and a special teaching. In Europe, it was observed, academic political science (more generally, higher education) provided special training for government service, and political scientists were characteristically active in political life in addition to fulfilling their scholarly-scientific roles. Nor were the extrascientific functions accepted unwillingly. To the new political scientists the several roles of researcher-scientist, teacher of citizenship, guide in preparation for leadership or government service, and reformer or activist fitted together, on the whole, without incongruity or conflict. "Science" had yet to assume its narrower and firmer mid-twentieth century connotations, and role-conflict was more latent than overt.

Still, as World War I approached—the evidence in the proceedings of the annual meetings of the Association and in the reports of its committees is clear—the special problems arising from the multiple roles of political science were beginning to emerge.

## THE MIDDLE PERIOD: POLITICAL SCIENCE FROM WORLD WAR I TO WORLD WAR II

The selection of the two world wars as chronological "markers" in the development of political science is in part only a matter of convenience, serving to divide experience into sections of fairly equal length and manageable size. But it is also more. Both wars, in various ways, affected political science and political scientists directly, and both resulted in significant sociointellectual changes in the environment of political science. Each of the three periods has its distinctive tones and colors, as much because of changing circumstances as because of changes in leading actors; and the changes in circumstances were often war-related.

### The Interwar Matrix

The abrupt ending of the Progressive Era brought not only a change in the emotional climate; it brought changes in the agenda of reforms and activities to which political scientists addressed themselves. In the war "democracy" had triumphed; but in its victory it had lost some of its innocence and élan. The force of the notion that "the cure for democracy is more democracy" was hardly exhausted (and still is not). But there was a growing sense that, at least in simplistic forms, it was an idea whose time had passed. The enormities of the war induced an uneasy sense that, despite the dissolution of the Hohenzollern and Hapsburg autocracies abroad (and their replacement by self-determination, constitutionalism, and democracy) and the "return to normalcy" at home, all was not well. How had the war happened? What were the implications for government? For the enterprise of social science? It was a natural, if not inevitable, conclusion that the cause of past catastrophes and the potential for more lay in unequal development: The "power-producing sciences" had outstripped the "power-controlling sciences." In the interests of democracy, even of survival, this relationship must be changed. Not less science but more—in the social sciences. ("The cure for science is more science"?)

Of course, the Romanoff autocracy had been replaced not by constitutional democracy but by Bolshevik dictatorship, a major new feature in the world's political landscape. A new experiment in international order, the League of Nations, came into existence, faltered, and then "failed." The triumphs of fascism in Italy and then of Nazism in Germany were followed by the alarms, incursions, and crises that heralded World War II. A rising tide of restlessness, sometimes leading to civil disorder or rebellion, characterized the extensive colonial areas around the world. The world-encircling

Great Depression had resulted in the New Deal in the United States, a nexus of governmental changes, political realignments, and intellectual developments of deep and lasting significance.

These were only major features of a national and international situation replete with implications for the enterprise of political science. In various ways historical events in the interwar years affected political science, and some of these will be indicated. Retrospectively, however, perhaps the wonder is not that they affected political science but that the response to them was not greater.

### Disciplinary-Professional Developments

The middle period of political science was genuinely "middle" with respect to much of an intellectual nature. In various quantitative and organizational aspects also, it bridges between the first and third periods.

***Quantitative and organizational factors.*** In 1920 the membership of the American Political Science Association, down somewhat through the war years, was 1300. But it reached 2800 by the eve of World War II and this time increased during the war years, reaching 3300 in 1945. (Membership figures for all periods are approximations, and they include institutional as well as personal memberships.) Registrations at the annual meetings rose more sharply, from fewer than 200 in the early twenties to more than 1000 by 1940. Independent academic departments of political science gradually increased in number and in size. The number of departments offering training leading to the Ph.D. increased significantly; "leadership" or "prestige" departments grew in number and became more widely distributed about the country. (Somit and Tanenhaus estimate that Ph.D. "output" went from "35 Ph.D.'s in 1925 to 45 by 1930, 60 in 1935, and 80 in 1940," declining then during the war years [1967, pp. 101–102].)

The *American Political Science Review*, solidly established as the central organ (and main public evidence of the existence) of the Association, evolved slowly under the guidance of Managing Editor Frederic A. Ogg, who held that position for nearly a quarter of a century. The pattern of extensive coverage of "developments," inclusion of material of a reportorial-interpretive nature on such matters as constitutional law and state and local government, was continued. The coverage of materials of that type, plus "news and notes" on such matters as personnel and programs, often left, in the opinion of critics, inadequate space for learned articles and reports on research.

In organizational structure the Association changed hardly at all in the middle period. Up to and through World War II the structure remained (one might say) that of a learned society rather than of a profession. An annually elected President, a Council with overlapping three-year terms, a Managing Editor for the *Review*, and a part-time Secretary-Treasurer (to handle the business-administrative side) constituted the essential mechanism. To one now reviewing the record it seems obvious that it would be only a matter of time until a national office with a continuing staff would be established. But "reform" in this direction was resisted; it was in fact still opposed by many members of the Association when it finally did occur after World War II.

Meanwhile important organizational developments of another sort had begun to manifest themselves: the creation of regional and specialized or "field" organizations. To be sure, these were not entirely new. The early graduate programs had sponsored "associations" of colleagues, students and alumni, and there had been a short-lived midwestern political science organization in the early period. Various organizations, such as the National Civil Service Reform League and National Municipal League, in which some political scientists participated actively, had some of the qualities of later "field" organizations. But the establishment of the Southern Political Science Association in the interwar period was unquestionably an important new development. It has endured and grown, providing a prototype for other regional associations in the post-World War II period. The journals of these associations, beginning with the (Southern) *Journal of Politics* in 1939, have become important media for publication and information. Although these journals have a regional emphasis, all are more or less *general* political science journals in terms of coverage and authorship.

The creation of the American Society for Public Administration in the late thirties appears to be different in nature and in its implications for the future. Specialized "cause," "interest," and even "activity" organizations had long existed, and political scientists had participated in them, but the American Society for Public Administration was the first "field" organization. In the 1920s and 1930s, public administration had become one of the "fields" of political science in the sense of gaining specialized textbooks and courses under this rubric. The creation of the Society and the establishment (in 1940) of its organ, the *Public Administration Review*, represented in part a conviction by those specializing in public administration that their interests warranted attention beyond that given through the American Political Science Association.

The formation of the American Society for Public Administration represents one of the centrifugal forces at work in political science, the tendency of special interests and "fields" to assert a more or less separate identity, to create mechanisms for expression in addition to—perhaps even separate from—the American Political Science Association. With continuing growth of the Association and increasing specialization of interests, the formation of organizations to give special attention to these interests has emerged as a phenomenon. Whether and to what extent it is a "problem" depends on the perspective with which it is viewed.

***Americanization and "re-Europeanization."*** Though hardly world-embracing in its interests, political science in its origins and first decades was open to many Western influences. Indeed, its rise clearly cannot be understood apart from these influences. The election of James Bryce as the fourth President of the American Political Science Association is symbolic, as well as being a testimony to the accomplishments and influence of that able British scholar.

But by the advent of World War I a substantial "Americanization" had occurred. It was most notable, of course, in the establishment of domestic programs of training for the Ph.D. After the turn of the century it became rare for a political scientist to include even a year of foreign study in his preparation. Disciplinary interests turned inward. The grand design of Burgess for a comparative political science was forgotten, and attention tended to be focused on practical problems of governance in the United States.

World War I did not immediately and obviously do much to broaden the scope of political science. Public administration, emerging as a "field" with its first textbooks in the twenties, was almost wholly focused on the domestic scene, despite universalistic claims for its "principles." Indeed, the resulting national mood of isolationism found some direct reflection in political science, as in the work of Charles Beard.

But in various ways, some indirect and long-range (even paradoxical—an argument for "national interest" must be put into a frame of history and theory), World War I did result in broadening the range of political science and moving it toward internationalization. Immediately, the importance of international relations and law was of course underscored. The newly established democratic states provided fresh foreign-comparative materials, however superficial the treatment thereof. The establishment of the League of Nations and its collapse; the creation and endurance of the U.S.S.R.; the rise of Fascism-Nazism; the ominous threats of a new world conflagration—all the important political events flowing from World War I inevitably were reflected in political science to some degree. Perhaps the most important "broadening" effect was indirect in the sense that the cataclysm and its aftermath helped to motivate Charles Merriam and others in a crusade to achieve a political science sufficiently well grounded to anticipate and avoid political disasters.

Tendencies toward parochialism and inbreeding in the interwar period were significantly and increasingly countered by foreign scholars. In the twenties and thirties a number of able and influential British-trained political scientists, including G. E. G. Catlin, Herman Finer, and Harold Laski, became a "presence," not only through writing but through lecturing and sometimes teaching in American universities. More important for post-World War II political science, as the World War I "settlement" collapsed in ruins, the resulting dislocations and persecutions brought about the migration of a considerable number of Continental political scientists, primarily from the German-speaking areas, to the United States. Indeed, the migrants were not only political scientists but social scientists in other disciplines, some of whose work has significantly "impacted" political science. And the migration included not only Continental-trained scholars but younger émigrés, who were to receive at least their advanced disciplinary training in the United States—and become disciplinary leaders.

For illustrative purposes, a few names (representing both of the categories above) will suffice: Hannah Arendt, Karl Deutsch, Alfred Diamant, William Ebenstein, Heinz Eulau, Carl Friedrich, Ernest Haas, Stanley Hoffman, Hans Kelsen, Henry Kissinger, Hans Morgenthau, Fritz Morstein Marx, Franz Neumann, Sigmund Neumann, Leo Strauss. The list of important contributors to the literature is long, the "story" much too complex even to outline. The important point is that the contribution and influence of the Continental-derived political scientists have been so great during the past generation that it is impossible to imagine what the present contours of political science might be if they had not participated in its creation. It is not that the influence has been of a piece. On the contrary (as even a slight acquaintance with the names above indicates) the émigrés have represented many interests and "fields," as well as divergent traditions, philosophies, and methodologies. All parts of political science have been enriched, and the resulting total is more complex.

***Other disciplinary-professional factors.*** During the interwar period political science became decisively "academicized." On the eve of World War I fewer than half the members of the American Political Science Association held academic appointments; but on the eve of World War II a large majority of the members were academics. Whether the shift toward an academic center of gravity represented a tacit decision to become a "discipline", rather than a "profession" is a complicated matter that will receive some attention below. For the present the following factors are worthy of note.

Academics, by the nature of their role and position, have an unusual opportunity for study, analysis, and reflection. On the record, there is no doubt that this opportunity was involved in the creation of "self-conscious" political science. Moreover, at least those in favorable university locations have the incentive, the time, and the skills to develop positions of leadership. The American Political Science Association was essentially created by academics. From its inception down to the present, academics have been preponderant in the officialdom and meetings of the Association.

But as has been indicated, in the early period the distinction between academic and nonacademic, professor and "practitioner," scientist-specialist and political participant was far less sharp than it was later to become. The record indicates that some form of political participation (elective or appointive, part-time or occasional full-time, partisan or formally governmental) was widespread among the early academics, including those in leadership roles. They thus blended fairly easily into what, until World War I, constituted the majority of the Association's membership: elected and appointed officials, civic leaders, lawyers, journalists, reformers—whoever might have a special interest in public affairs and hoped thus to forward it.

Political party membership (or sometimes inclination or preference) also shifted significantly in the interwar period, a matter not irrelevant to the understanding of political science. Only for the fairly recent period are reasonably full data on party identification of rank-and-file members of the Association available. But it is a reasonable surmise that until the thirties party identification was fairly evenly divided between the Republican and Democratic parties (with perhaps some leaning, particularly in the early years, in the Republican direction). Down to that time, certainly, *prominent* political scientists were identified with both parties in not too unequal numbers. The Great Depression and the New Deal, however, brought a tidal movement in the Democratic direction. Responsibility for the former tended to be assigned to the Republicans. The Democratic party was nominally (if not entirely in fact) responsible for the latter, and it evoked wide support among political scientists for a number of reasons. Since the late thirties a substantial majority (at present approximately three-fourths) of the membership of the Association have been Democratic in their party identification.

In the interwar period the importance of history and law were slowly and gradually—but only slowly and gradually—diminished.[3] But anthropology, sociology, and psychology, also "rising" disciplines in the academic firmament, received increasing attention. Although they tended to be more praised and enjoined (Barnes *et al.*, 1925; Ogburn and Goldenweiser, 1927) than actually used there were exceptions, notably Harold Lasswell's *Psychopathology and Politics* (1930). Economics, ahead in the game of status and recognition, tended to be more envied as a model (thus, notably, G. E. G. Catlin's *Science and Method of Politics*, 1927) than substantively used; there was no significant impulse to recreate political economy. The serious use of quantitative methods did begin to gain ground; for this Stuart A. Rice's *Quantitative Methods in Politics* (1928) is a landmark volume. The thirties saw a serious and significant use of quantitative methods in several fields, well beyond past efforts.

The emergence of public administration as a recognized "field" has been noted. In the thirties public opinion also began to gain recognition as a specialized area of scholarly-scientific inquiry—if not exactly *in* political science, at least of great importance for it. In political theory the two decades produced a number of respectable, even impressive, works, as the following signify: Francis W. Coker, *Recent Political Thought* (1934), Charles H. McIlwain, *The Growth of Political Thought in the West* (1932) and George H. Sabine, *A History of Political Theory* (1937). However, these were in the historical-philosophical-interpretive style, and beyond such works "theory" for the period must be sought either in the methodological disquisitions and disputes or in substantive works addressed to particular problems or areas. The study of comparative government, still overwhelmingly centered on constitutional government in the West, responded sometimes sluggishly, sometimes imaginatively, if erratically, to the challenges presented by communist and fascist regimes. As suggested, the study of international relations was stimulated by World War I and the events following in its train. Although much of what was done was descriptive, hortatory, or legalistic, some works, particularly products of the "Chicago school" in the thirties, made both substantive and methodological advances. All things considered, it was probably in the study of American government, and especially in its more "political" aspects, that the greatest advances were made. Among the works recognized as important in their own day and symbolic for the future were the following: Harold F. Gosnell, *Getting Out the Vote* (1927); E. Pendleton Herring, *Group Representation Before Congress* (1929); Arthur N. Holcombe, *The Political Parties of To-Day* (1924); Charles E. Merriam and Harold F. Gosnell, *Non-Voting; Causes and Methods of Control* (1924); Peter H. Odegard, *Pressure Politics; The Story of the Anti-Saloon League* (1928); Stuart A. Rice, *Farmers and Workers in American Politics* (1924); and Elmer E. Schattschneider, *Politics, Pressure, and the Tariff* (1935).

## *The Reassertion of Scientism and the Sharpening of Role Conflict*

Some of the most important events of the interwar period have appeared only by implication in the account to this point. They concern the reassertion of the scientific ambitions of political science and the counter-assertion of the extrascientific aspects of the enterprise. These events gave direction and tone to much of what took place in the interwar period. They also were a preparation for—one might say a rehearsal for—the controversies of post-World War II centering on behavioralism.

One can speak of the "reassertion" of scientific ambitions because the force of the early ambition to make political science a "genuine" science after the model of the natural science was gradually diminished. It was diminished by the inherent difficulties of the task, by the often unfavorable circumstances under which it was pursued, by conflicting interpretations of what the objective enjoined, and especially by the fact that those who called themselves political scientists accepted, willingly or by force of circumstances, extrascientific obligations that not only competed for resources but often seemed to be in conflict with the dictates of science.

The reassertion of the scientific ambition came early in the twenties, "peaked" in the middle or late twenties, significantly diminished in the early thirties as other currents in political science became ascendant and the turbulent sociopolitical environment engaged the attention of political scientists, but again gathered force as the thirties drew to a close. The reassertion of scientism is closely associated with the name and activities of Charles E. Merriam. In his essay of 1921, "The Present State of the Study of Politics," and in his book of 1925, *New Aspects of Politics,* Merriam indicted contemporary political science for its lack of scientific vigor, sounded a call for renewed scientific endeavor, and set forth his own ideas for scientific progress. Merriam's efforts led first to the establishment in the Association of a Committee on Political Research and then to a series of three National Conferences on the Science of Politics (1923–1925). Under Merriam's leadership the University of Chicago became noted for a serious and sustained effort to stress the "science" in political science. Unquestionably, a disproportionate amount of the important work of the thirties was done by the "Chicago school" (the term is often used, but there was no "school" in a strict sense); and a significant number of the leaders of the later behavioral movement were trained there in the thirties.

The leader of the counterreformation was Thomas H. Reed of Harvard University. Reed represented and spoke forcefully for the interests concerned with citizenship education and preparation for political-governmental careers—in general, civic education and activism. In 1927 Reed became chairman of the Association's recently created Committee on Policy. This vantage point was skillfully used. Reed was successful in obtaining for his committee at first modest and then substantial foundation financing. With this support he was able, for several years, to mount a campaign aimed at making the Association more broadly based (i.e., less disciplinary-professional) and political science more directly effective in political life, a campaign that included, among other activities, a national radio program, "You and Your Government."

As Somit and Tanenhaus (1967, p. 88) put it, "Though neither Merriam nor Reed captured the Holy Land, or came close to it, both crusades left their mark on the discipline." Both "crusades" seized territory and produced converts; both left a legacy of ideas and attitudes important for future events. Each emphasized different potential roles for political scientists as individuals and for political science as a self-conscious enterprise. The role conflict that was engendered was clearer, more intense, than it had been during the early period, though not so sharp as it was to become following World War II.

Not knowledge of the past for its own sake but understanding of the present is the central objective of this essay. This objective warrants some further observations on the "crusades" of the twenties and thirties, apart from the fact that to say no more would be to oversimplify and distort history.

Although differences of opinion were many and often sharp, to picture two monolithic parties in contest is incorrect. There was little argument that political science should abandon all but one of its roles. Few believed that political science should forsake its claim to "science"—though many would insist on a "soft" definition of the term. The partisans on each side often had, among themselves, significantly different positions on important issues of method and strategy.

Merriam himself was not only scholar and academic, he was a sometime political activist. His belief in science was ardent and his understanding of it, in context, sophisticated. But above all, he was interested in democracy, and what he sought was to put science into the service of democratic principles. He felt no inconsistency at all in trying simultaneously to forward science and democracy. The historical context made it very easy to perceive the two goals as congruent, if not indeed the same goal. Both American democratic political thought and pragmatic philosophy, then prominent, saw democracy as essential for scientific progress and science as a reinforcement of democracy: Both require experimentation, an honest search for reality, a public test of truth.

For Merriam the need was essentially for what came to be called "policy science," and he saw aid coming especially from psychology and quantitative methods. William B. Munro saw physics as the proper model for a genuine political science; and unlike many others who emphasized the need for more science, he argued that it was not a proper function of political scientists to teach democratic citizenship. G. E. G. Catlin, in his *The Science and Method of Politics* and other writings, perhaps advanced furthest toward the value-free, "pure science" position. His thesis that "power" is the essence of the political and that a science of politics thus should address itself to political power was, as the record testifies, a persuasive one to many inclined in the direction of more science.

Those on the "other side" in the debates of the time—notable among them, William Y. Elliott, Edward S. Corwin, and Charles A. Beard—on the whole opposed neither the idea of science nor the aspiration toward it: To the extent that scientific methods are useful, let us use them. Rather, they decried what they regarded as pretentiousness and unrealistic ambitions, and they argued—strongly—against the possibility and (or) desirability of a value-free political science. Elliott's *The Pragmatic Revolt in Politics* (1928) was and is the appropriate "counter" to *The Science and Method of Politics*. In perusing these two works, one advances his understanding not only of the middle years but of the controversies following World War II.

Finally, it should be noted that the rank and file of political scientists were at most interested partisans in the debates of their leaders on the future of science in political science. Most were teachers of political science in colleges and universities, and the objectives of the teaching were seen (particularly at the undergraduate level, where most of the teaching was done) primarily as preparing students for public careers or for effective democratic citizenship. (Some saw themselves as humanists seeking the traditional goals of a liberal education. They saw the study of politics as useful in this context. But they were sceptical not only of scientific aspirations but of the efficacy of training for public service and "teaching citizenship.") In the increasing emphasis on graduate training and particularly in the growing power of the Ph.D. in securing place and status, the Continental emphasis on research had seemingly triumphed. But perhaps more in form than in substance. In the American context, teaching, for most academic political scientists (and most political scientists were academics), had to be placed ahead of research; and the aims of that teaching had to be other than competence in research—scientific or otherwise.

## THE RECENT PERIOD: POLITICAL SCIENCE SINCE WORLD WAR II

As the "recent" period becomes the "contemporary" period, clarity and objectivity become more difficult. The size and complexity of political science increase with every year while the perspective is simultaneously foreshortened. Later, some observations on and analyses of contemporary political science will be ventured. But immediately, the objective is to view the period since World War II as a whole, in the manner attempted for the preceding periods.

### Historical Factors

The major events and trends of the past three decades are hardly obscure, and their impact on political science is obvious and often noted. It is well, nevertheless, to put the recent period into context. Even the "purest" physical science exists in a unique historical context and is affected by it.

We may begin by noting that although the New Deal was an event of the thirties, much of its impact on political science was delayed and long-lasting. It brought about both an increased involvement of political scientists with government and a change in the type of involvement: more full-time employment in administrative positions—especially in federal government—for a significant period, followed by a return to academia. This increased interaction blended into and was increased by the mobilization for and prosecution of World War II, which brought social scientists by the thousands into government service. To be sure, in many instances the social scientists were only apprentice or potential, and the service was military; but this circumstance may have heightened, not lowered, the impact.

The often-noted result of personal governmental service for political scientists was to demonstrate to them a gap between governmental reality as experienced and the exhortations, abstractions, and "facts" of their discipline. Furthermore, political scientists found that their discipline, in comparison with economics, was less well understood and certainly less well recognized for employment purposes. (Public administration had found some recognition in the civil service classification system; but since political science as such was not a recognized expertise, many political scientists found themselves entering government employment as "economists," or whatever.) The effects of personal governmental experience were manifested in various ways. In public administration, for example, an enlarged and deepened "case study" movement was an attempt to close the gap between theory and facts. But beyond question the main result was to create a mood favorable to the postwar behavioral movement. The inadequacies of then-contemporary political science were exposed, and the need for greater penetration, more "realism," was demonstrated.

The War itself and the consequent altered world and national situations created new problems and opportunities, to which there were more specific responses. Following the second world cataclysm, a world organization was again created; but this time there was no "return to normalcy." Instead, there was intense competition between superpowers and their satellites and allies, cold war threatening to become—and marginally becoming—hot war. Old nationalisms were reasserted and new ones developed. The centuries-old Western penetration and domination of the non-Western world, already in decline, was decisively reversed; many "new nations" of greatly differing nature and size came into the arena of international politics. The United States, by force of circumstances now a superpower and by national decision resolved to play a major role in world affairs, set upon various courses of action: the maintenance, for the first time in history, of a sizeable action-ready military force; the "containing" of communism by means that might (and occasionally did) include military action; aid in restoring the economy of noncommunist Europe; military aid to allies and potential allies. A so-called Revolution of Rising Expectations occurred; "development" became a worldwide preoccupation and expectation, closely related to national and ideological competition. America's Marshall Plan assistance to Europe was followed by and broadened into "Point Four" aid to developing nations.

The study of international politics and related subjects was tremendously stimulated by these momentous changes. Both in numbers attending to such matters and in the vitality and creativeness of the response, there is a sharp contrast to the interwar period. The study of comparative government, now coming to be called comparative politics, was also greatly stimulated. Not only was its scope broadened geographically in an attempt to encompass government wherever found; its conceptual apparatus was reconstructed with the aim of embracing political phenomena of all ideological coloration, cultural variation, and socioeconomic complexity. Political scientists by the hundreds, especially those identified with public administration, had periods of service in "technical assistance" projects in developing countries. The result was a related and similar attempt to broaden and strengthen public administration to enable it to cope with administration —more widely, "development"—in non-Western contexts.

In a number of ways technical and scientific changes ("advances") rooted in or following World War II have been highly consequential for political science. The creation of fission-fusion bombs has profoundly affected the study of international politics and national security. The invention of the electronic computer and the rapid development of computer technology ("hard" and "soft") are of course closely related to advances in the size and sophistication of voting studies. More generally, the great development in data gathering, storing, and manipulating capacities, in the machine's ability to replace, expand, and simulate human thought, is consequential for all of political science. The rapid rise of national and international air travel has permitted and stimulated a level of intellectual interchange and foreign study never before possible. In addition to their effects on American political science, the development of travel and communications technology patently has contributed to an "internationalizing" of political science. The upsurge in the support of scientific research and development, particularly after the launching of earth-orbiting satellites by the U.S.S.R., resulted in some increased support for the social sciences and has, in one way or another, affected the research and attitudes of political scientists.

Relevant to much that has happened to and in political science is the fact that the past quarter century has been a period of rapid national growth and, on the whole, economic prosperity. The most obvious relationships concern the size of the enterprise and the level and types of support. The increase in population and especially the phenomenal increase in higher education meant a growing base of support for political science, inasmuch as academia is the location for most disciplinary activity. On an unprecedented scale, funding for special programs and for research was obtainable. For a number of reasons foundation support was often generous (but by no means equally available to all "interests" in political science), and government support became increasingly a factor (but, again, selective in its objectives).

Though the most obvious correlations of growth and affluence are with quantitative aspects of political science, there may have been effects on the tone and directions of political science: on problems researched, on concepts, on results. In the most recent period, especially, some have charged that political science, in attending to its personal and professional interests, has been opportunistic, thus lending its support to an unjust "Establishment."

It is of course impossible to treat in a few lines "intellectual" developments of the postwar years in relation to political science, but two factors deserve mention even in this brief sketch. One is the continuing decline of idealist philosophy and the rather abrupt decline of pragmatic philosophy; and the concomitant rise of logical positivism, together with a more general interest in "philosophy of science." The other (which is also a "quantitative" matter) is that the postwar years were "growth" years, not only for political science but for the social sciences in general. Other social sciences (and other fields, including psychology, statistics, logic, and mathematics) were also advancing rapidly, and the social sciences in general were striving toward more and "purer" science, under conditions that favored the diffusion of concepts and techniques. Cause and effect are tangled and obscure (to say the least). But both material and intellectual forces seem often to have worked together to stimulate and support the behavioral movement in political science.

Finally, in this sketch of factors providing the matrix of political science since World War II, note must be taken of major events, shifts in trends, and changes in emotional climate since the middle and late sixties: for the qualifying phrase "up to fairly recently" must be added to much of what has been set forth. Perhaps it is too much to say that in recent years the United States has entered into a Toynbeean Time of Troubles. But much has happened in recent years that, by wide agreement, is "down" or "bad"; and the national mood, as the sixties drew to a close and the seventies began, can perhaps be characterized as one of anxiety, exasperation, and malaise.

A mere listing of some of the events and problems must here suffice: a war that, in the manner in which it was entered into and in the issues it raised, created division and embitterment; a "war against poverty" that created expectations that perhaps could not be, and in any case were not, realized; an economic recession of serious proportions; the assertion of racial-ethnic rights and identity; an increase in and increasing recognition of urban-centered problems; episodes of violence and civil disorder; the rise of the so-called Counter-Culture; the revival of older forms of radicalism together with the emergence of a self-styled New Left; the rapid rise to prominence of problems of pollution and of ecological problems in general.

For present purposes there should be added explicitly what is to some extent implied: Recent years have witnessed what is probably a falling off of support for formal education. Certainly (here economic recession and demographic factors enter in) the postwar expansion of higher education has significantly slowed. There has been something of a wide-spectrum decline in respect or regard for governmental institutions and a decline in belief in the efficacy of "governmental solutions" (paradoxically, while legislatures continue to respond to requests for "solutions" and governmental employment continues to increase). There is a noticeable rise in hostility toward modern technology and even something of a "revolt" against the institutions and culture of science.

At this point one cannot know the full import for political science of the events and movements of recent years. What is temporary aberration and what the beginning of a long-term trend? What are transient symptoms and what underlying causes? What is peculiar to America and what related to broader currents of world history?

One can confidently assert that the events and trends of recent times have had some effect, to date, on political science—as will be observed below. But one can only hazard guesses as to the future.

### Professional-Disciplinary Developments

In general, the post-World War II period has been a good period for political science. To be sure, the "upward curve" may to some extent only reflect the national growth and prosperity (particularly the growth of higher education); and many political scientists are critical of some "achievements." Nevertheless, the enterprise of political science expanded greatly in size, and in many ways it prospered. And the opinion of most political scientists is that, by meaningful and legitimate criteria, the enterprise has significantly advanced from its position a generation ago.

***Growth and organizational change.*** At the close of World War II, the American Political Science Association had a membership of 3300. In late 1972 the membership stood at 15,800. The number of political science departments in colleges and universities has risen to approximately 1340, though in many (mostly the smaller institutions) political science is still combined with one or more other disciplines. The number of departments awarding the Ph.D. degree has risen to more than one hundred, and the number of Ph.D.s awarded annually is approximately 700. Although "excellence," as commonly judged, is certainly not equally distributed on a geographical basis, much less among all institutions awarding the Ph.D., nevertheless the "nationalization" of high standards and high reputation already apparent in the interwar years has continued.

In the post-World War II years major organizational changes were made in the American Political Science Association, changes which moved it away from the "learned society" mode toward the "professional association" mode. On the eve of World War II the Association still functioned without a continuing national center. Clerical-business matters were largely divided between a Secretary-Treasurer and the Managing Editor of the *Review*. The Executive Council and the President had limited powers; Association committees tended to have a life of their own, often a source of embarrassment or a cause of anger to many members; with increasing size and complexity, the planning and conduct of meetings became increasingly a problem.

Immediately after the war Association affairs entered into a period of crisis—or at least of reformism and contention. The result was major changes, adopted in 1949 and rapidly put into effect. The Executive Council was abolished and replaced by a Council with an inner Executive Committee. The office of President Elect was instituted to ensure greater continuity of leadership. A national office with a small but continuing staff was established in Washington, headed (at first part-time, but soon full-time) by an Executive Director. In the early fifties actions were taken to make the Association master in its own house by reducing the autonomy of its committees.

In the general view of the membership of the Association, the reforms have resulted in a greatly improved situation (certainly dissatisfactions have not run in the direction of a return to previous arrangements). Political science has a continuing "presence" in the national capital. Stability, continuity, and regularity in Association affairs have been forwarded, services to members expanded. Association communication with government organs and personnel, as well as with other professional associations and with foundations, has been greatly facilitated. With a national office and a continuing staff, the Association has been enabled to develop and administer a considerable number of programs and activities: internships, awards, training programs, and so forth.

During the same period that the overarching organization for political science has been strengthened, a development of another sort has taken place, namely, the establishment of regional political science associations. The creation of the Southern Political Science Association in the thirties was noted above. That organization has been joined by a Midwest Political Science Association, a Western Political Science Association, a Pacific Northwest Political Science Association, a New England Political Science Association, a Northeast Political Science Association, and a Southwestern Political Science Association. (The exact date of establishment of regional associations is difficult to fix, since characteristically they have begun on an informal basis.)

Further, a number of state political science associations have been formed; there are even a considerable number of associations representing cities, metropolitan areas, and parts of large, populous states. A national political science honor society, Pi Sigma Alpha, was founded in 1920; it is a member of the Association of College Honor Societies and has approximately 150 chapters. These regional and other associations are not "divisions" of the American Political Science Association; they are independent, though not in any important sense competitive. "Supplementary" may be the best term to characterize the relationship. Many, probably a majority, of political scientists have membership in two or more political science associations.

***Political science publications.*** In the recent period the volume of political science publications has burgeoned because of a number of interacting factors. They include the increase in the number of political scientists and the resulting increase in research and writing, a growing market (especially for teaching materials), and above all, changes in intellectual orientations and the exploration of new areas. In fact, the volume of publication is now so large that it is no longer possible for a political scientist, faced with many demands on his time, to have more than a superficial knowledge of the total enterprise of political science.

The American Political Science Association now has two main organs. The *American Political Science Review*, though increased in size through the years, has been supplemented since 1968 by *PS*. (Representing both Political Science and "post script," as the first issues indicate, *PS* now stands alone.) Though the material in the two organs is not sharply differentiated, the former contains chiefly reports on research, general essays, and coverage (through reviews and notes) of political science publications; the latter contains chiefly a variety of material relating to disciplinary-professional affairs (meetings, committee reports, personnel changes, etc.).

The journals published by the regional associations, though giving some special attention to the region served, are wide-spectrum, in the sense that they not only cover political science in general but also publish material from political scientists outside the region. The Southern Political Science Association publishes the *Journal of Politics*. The organ of the Western Political Science Association is *Western Political Quarterly*; that of the Midwest Political Science Association is *Midwest Journal of Political Science*; that of the Northeast Political Science Associations is *Polity*. General or wide-spectrum journals include two with university associations: *Political Science Quarterly* (Columbia University) and *Review of Politics* (University of Notre Dame).

As one moves beyond the wide-spectrum journals, it is impossible in short compass either to catalog or to describe the periodical literature (much less the occasional or irregular "soft-cover" literature) of contemporary political science. Some journals focus on what has conventionally been considered a "field" or subdiscipline; thus *Public Opinion Quarterly, Public Administration Review*, and *World Politics*. But quickly boundaries become indistinct, "field" labels useless. The variety is suggested by the following titles: *American Behavioral Scientist, American Politics Quarterly, Comparative Political Studies, Journal of Comparative Administration, Journal of Conflict Resolution, Philosophy and Public Affairs, Policy Studies Journal, Public Management, Public Policy.* (A number of the newer journals are published commercially, not as organs of learned or professional societies.)

The essential point is that although the literature of political science has a fairly well agreed-upon core, it has no recognizable periphery, in terms of where political scientists publish or in terms of materials germane to political science but produced by those not nominally political scientists. The interests and activities of political scientists move outward toward and become mingled with those of the other social sciences, with those of the other learned professions (especially law), with those of traditional intellectual endeavors (literature, philosophy, mathematics), with those of newer intellectual foci (systems theory, computer technology, operations research), with those of politicians, publicists and journalists. Journals of considerable, perhaps even crucial, value to political scientists run to several score (even putting aside for the moment foreign publications).

The "book" literature of political science—in annual volume several times that of a generation ago—is even less sharply edged than the periodical literature, lacking publishing sources that are identified only with political science. To be sure a "core" literature can be distinguished, each item of which is identifiable by the prominence of the author as a political scientist or by the fact that the book treats a subject that convention or emerging consensus regards as political science. But no meaningful boundary can be discerned. Political scientists write for many purposes and for many publics; and many persons from other disciplines and professions write books that contribute to (or at least contain material germane to) political science.

*"Academization" and "professionalization."* The "academization" of political science noted for the interwar years has continued in the post-World War II period. In the years before World War I the majority of the membership of the Association was nonacademic (in the sense of location and employment). Immediately after World War I academics became a majority, and the size of their majority has increased through the years, reaching approximately seventy-five percent of the personal membership. The shift did not occur as the result of Association policy; that is, there was no conscious intent to discourage nonacademic membership or to favor academic membership. Its causes, rather, must be sought in the "situation," in certain characteristics of American political and educational institutions, and in certain events and developments.

Obviously much that has been recounted indicates a raising of standards, the development of criteria for judging achievement, and the establishment of firm organizational bases for political science research and other activities. Beyond doubt political science has successfully asserted its claim as an academic discipline. Has it also, by virtue of what has been achieved, moved in the direction of professionalization? That it has done so is the common opinion of political scientists writing about political science. Such an opinion is not unreasonable. The development of group self-consciousness, criteria of excellence, and separate organizational bases are usual aspects of professionalization. But in moving toward an academic base and a disciplinary model, political science may have moved away from, not toward, congruency with other professional criteria. This matter receives further attention below.

### The Behavioral Movement

By almost any measure the most important aspect of post-World War II political science has been the rise of "behavioralism": the controversies it engendered, its success in coming to dominate much of organized political science, the changes it brought in the matters to which political scientists attend, and the manner in which they are addressed. A lengthy essay would be necessary to treat the subject even in moderate detail, and what follows can only be designated a sketch. However, no more (if indeed as much) is needed by those who have at least a general acquaintance with the "story." And for others, a vast literature—substantive, polemical, interpretative—is readily available; in fact, it is unavoidable in any moderately extended attention to the written record of the period.

The behavioral movement may be interpreted as a renewed and reinforced effort to take the "science" in political science seriously, to make political science a true or genuine science. The model taken was natural science, i.e., the physical and biological sciences. To a lesser degree (or at a different level) the models were psychology and other social sciences deemed to have been more successful than political science in approximating the natural science model, at least in some of their aspects.

The term "behavioralism" to designate the reinvigorated scientism had several sources. Well before midcentury "behaviorism" was a well-developed point of view and method in psychology, stressing observable behavior over introspection and subjectivism. Some debt exists in this direction, but there was no simple borrowing. What happened was more complicated—and somewhat obscure. Certainly part of the story concerns the fact that "behavior" grew in favor in the post-World War II years; to scientistically inclined social scientists it put the focus of attention where it should be, on what could be observed and "objectively" studied. Part of the story concerns the phrase "the behavioral sciences," which came into vogue at midcentury. "The behavioral sciences" conveyed a scientific intent, i.e., an intent to focus on observable behavior. It also served to divide the intellectual-disciplinary universe in a more or less new manner. Disciplines or parts of disciplines with the appropriate focus (e.g., much of psychology) were, by definition, included; those with an inappropriate focus (e.g., much of history) were excluded. Strictly intellectual and "strategic" motives were mingled, it appears, in this new usage. For a number of reasons foundation and governmental support for "behavioral science" was easier to secure than support for "social science." Be that as it may, the adjective "behavioral" was converted in the course of events into the noun "behavioralism," and within political science the term came to designate the movement toward a harder, sharper science.

The reasons for the resurgence of scientism have been suggested above. They include the New Deal, World War II, and its aftermath of reconstruction and "development." They include the emergence of communism and fascism, rapid change in the world's political map, the new position of the United States as a superpower, the cold war. Many political scientists, either from observation and reflection or from personal experience, were impressed with what seemed a wide gap between the political science they professed and a political science that could adequately explain and control the "real" political world. Also relevant were other types of motivation, for example, the discovery that a putative expertise in political science had little value in securing government employment and the feeling that other social sciences were more advanced along the road toward science.

Advances in technology, both "soft" and "hard" (typically in combination) also enter in. The emergence of operations research from World War II, for example, suggested new interrelations and potentialities for social science. The advance of survey techniques, both for social-political and for commercial purposes, and especially the invention and rapid development of the electronic computer and related data processing equipment provided the foundation for studies of a scale and complexity that had previously been impossible. Intellectual advances and changes in philosophic styles enter in as well. Some pertain to the other social sciences, some concern mathematics and statistics, often both together, as with game theory. Of especial importance was the "reception" of logical positivism, which largely displaced pragmatism as "the" scientific philosophy. Logical positivism's sharp separation of fact and value categories and its assertion that, though values lend themselves in various ways to scientific scrutiny, their "validation" is outside the realm of science presented an intellectual "map" quite different from that readily available to earlier political scientists with scientistic inclinations—and to their opponents.

Behavioralism was not—and is not, if it can be said still to exist "as such"—a clear and firm creed, an agreed-upon set of postulates and rules. It has sometimes, with reason, been designated a "mood" or "persuasion." Ideological and religious comparisons are not inappropriate. Marxists have in common certain basic beliefs about history, social causation, and morality, and in a sense they are "united" in what they oppose. But they are nevertheless often divided radically on doctrine, strategy, tactics, and objectives. Protestant Christians have had in common an opposition to the Catholic church; but the roads to salvation chosen by different branches and sects have varied. Behavioralists, like Marxists and Protestant Christians, have sometimes presented a more or less unified front against the "enemy"; but—like Marxists and Protestant Christians—they have often disputed and contested among themselves—over doctrine, strategy, tactics, and objectives.

Despite the lack of clarity and consensus, an attempt must nevertheless be made to indicate some main tendencies and tenets of behavioralism. Negatively, behavioralism set itself against "mere" description, "raw" ("barefoot") empiricism, "simple" factualism; against metaphysics, abstract speculation, and deduction from "first principles"; against "grand" interpretations of history, the contemporary world, and future evolution; against legalistic modes of thought and "institutional" modes of analysis; against entangling political science with moral or ethical matters—at least if that led the political scientist *qua* political scientist to "prescribe." Positively, behavioralism favored studying successful sciences to learn and know how to apply proper scientific modes of thought and methods of research; focusing attention on actual, observable behavior, i.e., on what actors in fact *do* of political significance; seeking, carefully appraising, and testing empirical theory, i.e., theory about the behavioral world; fully and scrupulously gathering data, but doing so with theoretical guidance and for theoretical (testing) purposes; learning and applying as much mathematics and especially as much statistical-quantitative methodology as the phenomena or data permit; working toward the attainment of "higher-level" generalizations, i.e., those which explain more phenomena with greater clarity, simplicity, and economy; in general, striving toward the goals of explanation, prediction, and control.

To some these generalizations may seem too pat or too sweeping, and to others they may seem inaptly put, with incorrect emphasis and misleading effect. In any case, it should be made explicit that there are a number of important matters on which avowed behavioralists have spoken with more than one voice. One of them concerns the feasibility and desirability of a "paradigm" for political science as a whole, a theoretical construct which would serve to orient and guide theory and research for the entire discipline. Another (somewhat related) concerns the uniqueness and purity of the political, the extent to which political science should seek its own separate identity as against integration with the constructs and activities of other social sciences. Another concerns the role and status of "applied" research, its importance measured against and its contribution to "pure" research (or theory). Another (related but not identical) concerns the possibility, potential, and desirability of "policy research"—whether it can be done without compromising scientific integrity, its proper means and limits, its claim on scarce scientific resources, its morality (in the service of what ends, determined by whom?).

Behavioralism gathered force in the forties, and its status in the fifties may fairly be described as a "movement." Though it lacked both a unifying organization and a single creed, it had effective leaders and ardent, able partisans, especially among the younger political scientists. As suggested, a number of factors worked in its favor. Not the least was comparatively advantageous financing in support of training (or retraining) and research. Research (more broadly, "publication") is the acknowledged, favored route to strategic location and promotion in academia. Behavioralists in number met the pragmatic test. In the fifties and especially in the sixties, they succeeded in reaching high and strategic positions in academia and in the Association.

The behavioral movement evoked strong and occasionally fierce resistance in academia and in the Association. The sources of the resistance have—again—been suggested. Some political scientists were essentially humanists, regarding the study of political experience as a source of insight and wisdom, to be sure, but not as a field for the application of "hard" science. Some, deeply steeped in philosophy and law, judged behavioralism a barbarian repudiation of an invaluable, hard-won heritage. Many were primarily interested in "practical" politics or pressing issues of policy, and they saw behavioralism as, at best, an irrelevance. Many saw their mission as the promotion of democratic citizenship and found shocking the sentiment that "the political scientist has no more responsibility for democracy than the sociologist has for the family." Still others were interested primarily in preparation for government service and found in behavioralism little or nothing pertinent to that end.

Even less than the behavioralists did their opponents present a united front; the professor of political philosophy and the professor of budgeting often had little in common but opposition to what both regarded as dangerous or irrelevant. They could and often did present telling arguments against behavioralism: the difficulties, practical and theoretical, in achieving behavioral goals; the urgent political-moral issues shunted aside; the importance of the immeasurable and imponderable; the gaps between data and theory; the ponderous methodological "packing" for inconsequential research "trips." The opponents also had their situational advantages. After all, they began in possession of most of the positions of status and strength. Ancient and respectable traditions could be drawn upon for support. Powerful forces in society were interested in their goals. And if foundations were primarily interested in financing behavioral research, legislatures were primarily interested in financing citizenship education and practical training.

The period of strong, sometimes bitter encounter lasted, roughly, from 1950 to 1965. By the latter date the behavioralists, it might be said, had won a qualified victory. They had captured many strategic positions, and the intellectual map of political science had been greatly altered through their efforts. It may be closer to correct to say that by the mid-sixties the situation had been so changed that one could not speak in any meaningful sense of "sides" or "victories": political science had become too complex, arguments too subtle, opinions too tempered, emotions too exhausted. What were now to become important were influences originating in the turmoil and ferment of the late sixties and early seventies. These again posed behavioralism as an issue, but in another context and in altered ways.

### *Public-Oriented Activities and Responsibilities*

The intent now is to take some note of activities and responsibilities of political scientists other than those with a strict intellectual-disciplinary orientation. The problem is to find a designation that does not imply a judgment on the worth of the activities and responsibilities *or* of their right to be regarded as a part of political science. The designation "public-oriented activities and responsibilities" is perhaps an acceptable solution. In any event, the activities and responsibilities discussed can be characterized by such terms as: outward-looking, applied, activist, "service."

The terminological problem pertains to the mixed heritage of political science and to differences of opinion, often sharp, on the present obligations and future development of an enterprise that designates itself as political science. To some these public-oriented activities and responsibilities are not properly regarded as a part of political *science*. They may be judged to be salutary, desirable for performance by someone in or out of organized political science. But they are regarded as beyond, or at least only marginal to, the *scientific* endeavor, as nonscientific or extrascientific. They *may* be judged as futile, wasteful, annoying, and even embarrassing to a scientific enterprise. This is not to imply that the strict scientist is without a sense of responsibility. Indeed, in his view the duty of political science is to achieve *science*. It is in the scientific pursuit that duty is fulfilled and the public truly served.

To other political scientists public-oriented activities and responsibilities are the heart of the enterprise. These political scientists may or may not be sceptical of the scientific claims and aspirations of their colleagues. But they believe that we already have more and better "political science" than is now in practice, and that the first priority is to ensure wider knowledge and application. They may believe that the political scientist has civic responsibilities beyond or additional to scholarship and research in politics, responsibilities that are not adequately fulfilled by separating the roles of political scientist and private citizen. For such beliefs there is, as observed above, warrant in tradition and etymology. Moreover, what is concerned is not simply an "academic" argument. Sometimes public-oriented activities and responsibilities are mandated by the source of funds, and thus an ingrained sense of duty and a formal requirement may be mingled—and thus also the politics of the polity and those of the academy may be mingled.

Public-oriented activities and responsibilities do not lend themselves to sharp categorization, and, when categorizing is attempted, two or more are often blended. But at least four types are distinguishable.

1. *Citizenship, or civic education,* centers on conveying a knowledge of American political institutions and of the rights and duties of citizens to undergraduate collegians (in some public institutions a legal requirement). But it has many other possible aspects, including the preparation of (or advising on the preparation of) teaching materials for secondary and even elementary curricula, as well as extra-academic lecturing.

2. *Education for public service* has three main aspects. One, beginning with citizenship education but going beyond it, seeks to impart extra knowledge (and perhaps an extra feeling of responsibility) to those, such as lawyers and journalists, whose careers will have a special relation to and impact on the political realm. The second concerns those who enter political life as such, seeking and holding elective office or at least supplying expert counsel to such persons. Recognizing that it does not have a monopoly, to say the least, on the source of practical political knowledge, political science nevertheless seeks to convey political expertise to those who aspire to elective office. It aims at conveying a practical knowledge, leading to success in achieving office; but it aims also, and more importantly, to convey knowledge and inculcate values that will make performance in office more intelligent and publicly responsible. The third aspect concerns those who will enter public service as appointed employees or officials. Here again political science occupies far from a monopoly position. But here again political science is active: and for this aspect discrete courses, curricula, and programs—typically under the rubric "public administration"—are much more apparent than for the first two. Sometimes the special education or training is undergraduate. Much more frequently it is graduate, and occasionally it is "special" or "mid-career."

3. *Policy study and guidance* covers a wide range of activities, centering in academia but often ranging far afield, as in advising as consultant (to government agency, political party, etc.) or in public lecturing. At one end of the spectrum, activity under this heading may be regarded as properly "scientific": inquiry aimed at increasing knowledge of how policy in general or in a particular area is in fact made. At the other end of the spectrum, by common agreement, advice on preferred policy in a certain area would be regarded as "normative." Between the extremes are many activities in which "scientific" and "normative" aspects are joined together in different combinations, often leading to theoretical and programatic disputes. The concept of "policy science," a frequently used term and one often used to designate a research ambition or program, is especially troublesome. The intent, obviously, is somehow to join the normative and the scientific. But whether this

can be done, and how it is to be done, are complicated and contentious matters.

4. *Participation in public affairs* warrants recognition as a distinguishable type of public-oriented activity undertaken by political scientists, even though, patently, the preceding categories may involve some participation in public affairs. Some political scientists are "activists" in either partisan or "issue" politics. Some seek elected office; if successful, they may continue in a political career, or they may return after a period to a teaching or research position. Many more political scientists spend some period, from a few months to several years, in some sort of appointed governmental position. Altogether, the range and variety of participation in public affairs is great. Political scientists with strong scientific interests may look askance at such activities, may in fact regard them as irresponsible defections from the proper role of the political scientist. Political scientists of another mind argue that political science has special responsibilities in public affairs, and that personal experience in the "stuff" to which political science is addressed is a valuable, perhaps even necessary, part of professional education in political science.

It is difficult to generalize about the public-oriented activities and responsibilities of political science in the post-World War II period. They are sometimes intermingled with scholarly-scientific pursuits, reliable data are unavailable, and interpretations vary. Nevertheless, some "global" observations are possible. One is that public-oriented activities often have been attacked by behavioralists, and those engaging in them have been sometimes placed in a defensive position by the strength of the behavioralist movement. Another is that despite the strength of the drive toward a "purer" science of politics, public-oriented activities generally have not only survived but have increased—in absolute terms if not in terms of proportion of comparative resources (as allocated to teaching and research in academia). Another is that in at least one area, namely, public service education, there has been an increase both in absolute and in relative terms.

**Developments in four areas.** Some further observations about each of the four areas will be hazarded.

With regard to citizenship education, though the total volume of such activity has remained high, the idea and the practice have suffered "erosion" from several sources. It is not simply that the scientifically inclined have found it an extrascientific drain on resources. There has often been a related sentiment that "indoctrination" or "teaching of values" is an improper academic activity. Ironically, a similar sentiment sometimes issues from the other end of the spectrum. Humanists, those to whom "liberal arts" is a sacred term, find "teaching citizenship" a crude form of mind manipulation, unworthy of education rightly conceived. Others, in and out of political science, have leveled the criticism that such teaching, in effect if not in intent, is ideologically biased: What is conveyed is a simplistic, idealistic upper- or middle-class view of the American experience and potential. A final and perhaps most telling observation is that some studies have produced what appears to be good evidence that "teaching citizenship" in the manner customarily attempted neither produces lasting knowledge nor improves civic efficiency or morality.

The response to such criticisms has been chiefly in accordance with the behavioral currents of recent years. An attempt has been made to make citizenship education (both collegiate and precollegiate) less formalistic and "romantic," more realistic and analytical. As this implies, an attempt has also been made to join citizenship education more closely with a realistic introduction to contemporary political science in general, introducing theoretical, comparative, and methodological considerations into an area previously dominated by formal description and moral exhortation.

This is an appropriate place to take note of the Citizenship Clearing House-National Center for Education in Politics (CCH-NCEP), which came into existence as the result of some postwar activities aimed at stimulating greater participation in politics by political scientists and more effective educational preparation via political science for political careers. (Though the efforts were focused as indicated, the objectives of CCH-NCEP might be characterized as, more generally, "political education.") In many ways the CCH-NCEP was successor and descendant of the Association's interwar Committee on Policy, noted above. (Thomas H. Reed, who had dominated the Committee on Policy, was highly influential in the creation of CCH-NCEP.) But CCH-NCEP, though largely a "political science" operation, was not formally a part of the Association. Nourished by substantial foundation support, CCH-NCEP mounted a sizable program of internships, conferences, and so forth. In the mid-sixties, when foundation support was no longer forthcoming, CCH-NCEP ceased operation; at that time, the Association, gaining some foundation support, launched a somewhat similar—though also somewhat different—program.

Education for public service, as suggested, has been expanded during the past quarter century, so far as concerns education for appointive positions. But what has taken place poses the question: Has the expansion taken place "within political science"? The answer depends on what definition of political science is accepted. Several trends make the question relevant. Most of the education (or "training," the term that many would regard as more apt), so far as it is carried on in political science departments, is centered in the subdiscipline or field of public administration. But public administration has long had a separate professional association, and political scientists specializing in public administration are often restive and sometimes secessionist, feeling that their interests are slighted.

Developments of another kind are relevant. What is taught in the educational programs is less and less derived from political science, more and more derived from other sources (including but not limited to the other social sciences). Some separate graduate schools of public administration or public affairs now exist, and their number is slowly increasing. Also, during the recent period, schools of business administration have been developing programs for "public sector" administration; and recently created generic "schools of administration" also have developed programs for public sector employment. Additionally, an increasing amount of education or training for public employment is now "in-house," that is to say, carried on within governmental jurisdictions.

As to policy study and guidance, perhaps it is desirable first of all to underscore the ambiguity or ambivalence of such activities vis-à-vis behavioralism. In some contexts and in some ways, policy study, even guidance, is regarded as quite respectable, scientifically considered, as well as morally desirable as a means of forwarding liberal-democratic interests. Harold Lasswell, often thought of as "the" behavioralist of recent decades, has firmly supported the "policy science" concept. But much, perhaps most, of what is done by political scientists in the name of policy research would not meet acceptable scientific standards in the judgment of those who are strong in their behavioral convictions, however desirable it may seem to those who do it and however useful it may be to those who receive it. This would be true, for example, of the bulk of the research output of the several score of bureaus—variously titled: bureaus (or institutes) of public administration, bureaus of state and local government, bureaus of public affairs—associated at least loosely with departments of political science. (Characteristically, such units have training, consulting, or some other "service" functions.)

Second, it should be observed that the area of policy research and guidance has some similarities to that of education for public service. It too has tended to become more interdisciplinary: less dominated by concepts and methodology originating in political science, more characterized by a mixture of concepts and methodologies. And it too has tended increasingly to be carried on under institutional arrangements that are outside political science departments and do not have "political science" in the institutional designation: often "institutes" for policy research, in general or for specific areas.

Participation in public affairs continues at a high level in absolute terms. Political scientists in number participate part-time or, for some period, full-time in some aspect of public affairs. They consult, testify, aid in campaigns, take "tours of duty" at home or abroad, make public addresses, and so forth.

But this activity must be viewed in the context of what was noted above in the discussion of "Academization and Professionalization." The dividing line between political scientist and non-political scientist is sharper than it once was, and the "rules" governing political participation, as well as the judgments placed on it, have subtly changed in half a century.

## Significant Changes in the Disciplinary Map

The intent in what immediately follows is to indicate some of the more significant changes in the disciplinary "map" of political science since World War II. The nature of these changes has been suggested—sometimes more than merely suggested—above; and the implications of some changes will be indicated more fully in what follows this section. But the objective of achieving a reasonably clear view of the recent and contemporary scene will be served both by emphasis and by further information at this point.

***From structure to process.*** Somit and Tanenhaus (1967, p. 133) conclude their review of political science as a learned discipline in the interwar years with the generalization: "There was, in fine, a gradual shift in interest from structure and policy to process." In the recent period the shift from structure to process has continued and accentuated. The injunction to move from static to dynamic modes of analysis has been a prominent theme of behavioralism. Two related reasons for this emphasis appear. One is scientific-methodological: Political science must move beyond descriptive-prescriptive, institutional-legalistic approaches and develop theory and data appropriate for a truly scientific enterprise. The other is related to the historical milieu: A world of rapid change and turbulence must have a political science appropriate to the times, one that can act intelligently in such a world.

Whether political science in the recent period has moved also from "policy" to "process" is a complicated question; the answer given will depend on interpretation and definition—eventually perhaps on the definition of political science. Certainly what came to be regarded as mainstream political science has evidenced little interest in policy in the substantive sense (e.g., labor policy, agricultural policy, tax policy). But attention to some aspect of the "policy-making process," in line with the stress on process, has been substantial; and the idea of "policy science," using scientific methodology to achieve democratic policy objectives, has had eminent sponsorship (including prominently, as noted above, that of Harold Lasswell). Typically, policy research by political scientists, whether "old style" or "new style," has involved interdisciplinary cooperation (chiefly with economists); and typically, it has taken place in bureaus and institutes only loosely connected with (or detached from) academic departments of political science.

***Expansion of the comparative method.*** For a number of reasons the use of some type of comparative method became a prominent feature of post-World War II political science.

The rise of communism and fascism and the rapid post-War increase of non-Western states were a spur to the comparative method. These developments created a challenge to develop conceptual and methodological means to embrace in meaningful comparison political phenomena across the ideological spectrum, across varying historical-cultural matrices and, geographically, around the entire world. The costs of turbulence, the risks of violence, the need for "development" seemed obvious. An expanded and deepened use of the comparative method, it was hoped, would produce knowledge useful in gaining control of events and guiding proper development.

What appeared to many to be scientific-methodological imperatives reinforced practical and altruistic motives. The scientific method (it was asserted) is comparative: Where scientific advance has occurred, some form of comparison, guided by theory and scrupulous in use of data, has been of the essence. The problem for political science is clear, however difficult the solution. It is to discern those modes of comparison that meet the criteria of scientific methodology, hold promise of significance of findings, and can in fact be carried out, given constraints of time, data, and so forth.

Not surprisingly, the impulse to use the comparative method in an expanded and methodologically more sophisticated way centered in that part of the discipline which had been designated comparative government, but which now came to be designated comparative politics. The shift in terminology signified a wish to shift from a focus on Western democratic institutions to conceptualizations and techniques that would permit significant comparisons across and among *all* political systems, cultures, and ideologies. To this end a search both intensive and extensive was made for appropriate theories and research methods, a search not only through the heritage of political science but through the entire inventory of theories and research methods of the social sciences. (The Social Science Research Council's Committee on Comparative Politics, 1954 to 1967, played a major role in the reinvigoration and transformation of comparative studies. That Committee, headed first by Gabriel Almond and then by Lucien W. Pye, was extraordinarily vigorous, and its influence extended beyond "comparative politics" in any strict sense.)

The new emphasis on comparative method affected all parts of political science to some degree. A vigorous comparative administration movement, arising in the fifties and flourishing in the sixties, was a prominent aspect of public administration. In international relations, experimentation with comparative methodology has ranged from relatively simple "models" to attempts to embrace all countries of the world in analyses that will yield significant comparative data. In the study of judicial behavior, legislative activity, policy "outputs," executive style, voting preferences, metropolitan organization, national and regional political "cultures"—across the span of interests and activities of political science—attempts have been made to use comparative methods with greater sophistication and precision.

***Transformation of international relations.*** As with comparative politics and for similar reasons, the area of international relations was significantly transformed in its nature. The causes are now obvious: the sweeping changes in the political map of the world, the impulses and resources of behavioralism, the emergence of the United States as a superpower in a situation of ideological conflict and cold war, the ever-present threat of catastrophe. In the new historic context, past approaches and "solutions" seemed largely shallow or irrelevant. New ideas and attitudes, much greater depth and breadth in research seemed patently and urgently needed.

Such older interests as diplomatic affairs and international law were not entirely abandoned, but they were subjected to new "approaches" in the intensified scientific mode. Above all, new interests, specializations, and activities emerged; and important interrelations with other disciplines, both in the other social sciences and beyond, were established. Somewhat as public administration had done in the post-World War II period, international relations tended to become a substantial, varied "world" in itself, with very important relations outside political science and some impulses toward autonomy.

***Expansion of voting and opinion studies.*** In the recent period a combination of factors led to such growth and vigor of voting and opinion studies that those studies came to represent "behavioralism" to many political scientists. Such studies were signaled by earlier works and nourished by deep and enduring interests of political scientists; and as indicated above, the study of public opinion had assumed an importance by the thirties that warranted a separate journal. In the thirties and forties two developments, opinion polling centered on predicting elections and motivational research centered on commercial objectives, though having only tenuous connections with political science, helped to develop techniques and concepts which could be turned to the purposes of serious political research. After the war, the rapid development of the computer and allied technologies, the availability of foundation support, related developments in other disciplines, and the reinvigorated drive toward science combined with the other factors to create a "critical mass." It appeared to many that a genuine "breakthrough" toward a genuine science of politics either was imminent or had now in fact occurred. Whatever the judgment of history will be, the accomplishments have been substantial. New levels of predictability and precision have been reached; a deeper, more comprehensive knowledge of political motivation has been attained; and more understanding of the relation of political to socioeconomic variables has been gained.

At the center of this area of political inquiry is one of the most important institutional developments of the recent period, the Inter-University Consortium for Political Research. Organizationally and geographically, the Consortium revolves about the Center for Political Studies (until 1970–1971, the Political Behavior Program) and the Survey Research Center, two of the constituent units of the Institute for Social Research of the University of Michigan at Ann Arbor. Formed in 1962, the Consortium is an association or partnership of educational and research institutions, now numbering several score. The membership includes substantially all universities offering graduate instruction, as well as some offering only undergraduate instruction; and it includes foreign (especially Canadian) institutions. Member institutions help to support the activities of the two centers, which provide research facilities, training, and data for member institutions; and the activities of the centers and the Consortium, thus mutually reinforced, are aided further by foundation or other "outside" support.

The significance of the Consortium runs far beyond "survey research." Ann Arbor became a center for summer training programs in quantitative methods and related matters long before the Consortium was formed, and special training and research programs more or less "behavioral" have been continued and expanded. Although the political act of voting and survey techniques of research have been at the center of attention, there is no clear periphery of research interests, much less of influence; the centers and the Consortium have been important both as symbols and as active centers of influence in the behavioral movement.

**Revitalization of theory.** In *The Political System* of 1953 David Easton writes in his preface: "Today in the United States . . . it has become increasingly difficult to appreciate why political theory should continue to be included as a central part of political science. Theory has become increasingly remote from the mainstream of political research" (p ix). The situation, as it presented itself to Easton (and to many others), was that in political science the study of political theory tended to turn backward toward history and outward toward philosophy and *belles lettres,* to concern itself mainly with interpreting theorists of the past rather than with guiding current research. Meanwhile, much research suffered from lack of theoretical sophistication, often displaying a crude "fact-gathering" empiricism.

Whatever the situation in 1953, two decades later a judgment can fairly be made that the recent period has been one of significant theoretical vitality and creativeness. Again, history must judge the full impact and lasting significance of the accomplishment; but that the accomplishment overshadows that of the earlier periods seems clear. Easton's argument, set forth in *The Political System,* that research and theory be brought together in a focus on the political *system,* proved to be highly influential and is itself part of and evidence for the theoretical vitality.

But though patently influential, Easton's argument for a focus on the political system did not carry all before it. In fact, the chief characteristic of "theory" in the recent period may be diversity. Often there has been theoretical contradiction and conflict (indeed bitter battles) centering on behavioralism; but the variety of theories has been too great, the arguments too varied and subtle, to represent the situation simply as a two-sided argument on the possibilities and merits of a "science" of politics.

It is possible only to suggest the variety of theoretical endeavor. Various kinds of traditional theoretical work—exegesis, analysis, textual examination, reinterpretation—have achieved a high level, both on the part of émigré scholars and on the part of younger, domestically educated scholars. On the other end of the spectrum, so to speak, behaviorally inclined political scientists have written sharply and creatively in the area where political research confronts philosophy and methodology. Much of what has taken place may be interpreted as a continuation of the Great Dialogue; certainly there has been considerable discussion and controversy about the place of the writings of the "Greats" in a possible science of politics. Much of what has been written, particularly by younger theorists during the past decade, is difficult to place on any "spectrum." Some of it returns to old themes (e.g., citizenship, authority) but in new ways; some is idiosyncratic (but possibly significant) speculation or projection; some argues for new ways of defining or perceiving the political; some works the borders of and expands on recent philosophic trends. Opinions, naturally, vary on the "correctness" and worth of what is produced. But what is clear is that able, well-trained, and sharply honed minds are at work.

In the conventional classification of political scientists, there are those designated "theorists," and the present discussion focuses on these. However, an outstanding feature of the recent period is that the line between "theorists" and other political scientists has become indistinct, problematical. In a way not true of the middle period of political science (though there are interesting resemblances to the first two decades of self-conscious political science), "theory" of some kind informs most work, and often it is consciously and carefully treated. A growing theoretical sensitivity and sophistication of political scientists in general may, in retrospect, prove to be the most important development of the recent period.

**Rise of scientific philosophy and methodology.** The rise to prominence of scientific philosophy and methodology testifies eloquently to the impact of behavioralism. In the interwar period a course on "scope and method in political science" was a regular feature of doctoral training; and a course on "research methods in political science" might also be required. The first was likely to be basically "orientation": a survey of the traditional literature of the "fields," of "relations" with other social sciences, and of methods (e.g., historical, legal, comparative). The second would almost certainly center on library research and the mechanics of scholarship, though it might also venture to give some skill in elementary statistical techniques. In the post-World War II period, particularly in the sixties, a radical change occurred. Courses in "scope and methods" and "research methods" now centered on the ideas and methods associated with behavioralism; in many graduate curricula new courses were introduced to deal in a more concentrated way with some aspect of scientific philosophy and methodology. Students were likely to be advised (or required) to take courses in other departments, courses in scientific philosophy, modern logic, statistical techniques, algebra, calculus, and so forth. Much attention was paid, one way or another, to the more scientific aspects of other social sciences, and to areas or foci (such as "operations research") without clear disciplinary location but with putative scientific value.

Accordingly, much of the "language" of political science has changed. Somit and Tanenhaus (1967) portray the change graphically.

> An older generation spoke knowingly of checks and balances, *jus soli*, divesting legislation, brokerage function, quota system, bloc voting, resulting powers, proportional representation, pressure group, sovereignty, dual federalism, lobbying, recall and referendum, Posdcorb, quasi-judicial agencies, concurrent majority, legislative court, Taylorism, state of nature, item veto, unit rule, and natural law. From today's younger practitioners there flows trippingly from the tongue such exotic phrases as boundary maintenance, bargaining, cognitive dissonance, community power structure, conflict resolution, conceptual framework, cross-pressures, decision making, dysfunctional, factor analysis, feedback, Fortran, game theory, Guttman scaling, homeostasis, input-output, interaction, model, multiple regression, multivariate analysis, non-parametric, payoff, transaction flow model, role, simulation, political systems analysis, T test, unit record equipment, variance, and, of course, political socialization.[4]

The literature of political science of course reflects the change. In the interwar years, the journals and books showed a gradual increase in the use of some sort of "quantitative method." In the post-World War II period, especially in the sixties, the use of statistical methods became more complex and sophisticated, mathematical and quasi-mathematical formulations were frequently used, and vocabularies became increasingly technical and esoteric. Even introductory textbooks came to reflect the new political science.

The changes in the map of political science wrought by the drive toward science are obvious and indisputable, but as much of the foregoing indicates, the behavioral movement has not—by a long measure—completely transformed political science. To begin with, many who regard themselves as behavioralists would deny any objective beyond "reform," that is, the purification and improvement of a basically sound tradition of inquiry. Certainly the older "world" of political science still exists in many places and in many ways. To some extent a new vocabulary may be that and little more, new terms for older, enduring concerns. To some extent, even, learning the new political science has been but a tactic of survival, a strategy for evading—and ultimately defeating—the "invader."

The topics treated in this discussion of significant changes in the map of political science were not selected at random. Neither, however, is there a presumption that they include all the significant matters to which a comprehensive survey of recent political science would attend. Not included, for example, are the revived and sharpened focus on the "group," the use of the concept of culture in studies of "political culture," the use of social-psychological concepts in studies of "political socialization." It has seemed more appropriate to discuss some important matters elsewhere; and many can at best be only mentioned.

## CENTRIPETAL AND CENTRIFUGAL TENDENCIES

Political science as a self-conscious enterprise is engaged in a continuous process of definition and redefinition. This process is conscious in that there are always those seeking to define "the political" and to specify the methods appropriate for its examination. It is also unconscious in that many factors (as is now clear) other than formal definition determine the shape and direction of the enterprise: the vagaries of national experience, influences from other social sciences, technological changes, and so forth. Not all changes lend themselves to the interpretation that they are "centripetal" or "centrifugal" in their effect; nevertheless, to view political science as continuously experiencing such opposing forces offers a useful perspective.

### The Problem of Identity

It is appropriate to begin by remembering the unique nature of the enterprise. The idea of *a* political science, as against the looser idea of "the political sciences," has enjoyed a pragmatic success in the sense that the enterprise begun under this style nearly a century ago has not merely survived but grown enormously and, in many ways, prospered. Few would deny that it has produced knowledge that is (in some sense) true and skills that are useful. Political science is widely recognized as a legitimate social science. There is no important threat to its continued independent existence. Rather, there are many reasons why further growth and achievement can be anticipated with confidence.

The reasons why political science has been able to maintain its identity are of various kinds and operate at different levels. Some are environmental and situational: the fact that political science, once conceived and born, was seen as a vehicle for conveying the political culture and has often been supported with this end in view; the fact that an enterprise devoted to "science" has been undertaken in a society with a high regard for things scientific; the fact that the enterprise has been undertaken in a modern society characterized by relative wealth, large size, and great specialization of function. Some of the integrating forces are sociopsychological. Those who are (so to speak) socialized into the subculture known as political science and whose social position, livelihood, and personal sense of identity are associated with the fortunes of political science have a natural interest in ensuring its identity, integrity, and prosperity. Organizations, once formed, strive toward growth—or at least perpetuation—and engage in behavior appropriate thereto, such as goal definition and redefinition.

Some of the integrating forces operate at the conscious level, such as attempts at defining the "political" or the "scientific," alone or in relation to each other, in a manner that will command the acceptance of those willing to march under the political science ensign. In the early period of political science it was conventional to define political science as inquiry into the nature and functioning of "the state." In the middle period the idea that the proper object of inquiry is "power," more precisely "political power," gained prominence. In the recent period, in which systems theory has enjoyed much popularity and acceptance, the idea that political science should concern itself with "the political *system*" has been persuasively argued and has been widely accepted. Other "defining" ideas have also, of course, been advanced; and both "state" and "power" continue to have their adherents and uses.

Characteristically, most of the forces that have or are intended to have a unifying effect also have a divisive effect, with resulting paradox. Although the wealth, size, and specialization of the American environment have supported the emergence of an independent political science, the same factors lend encouragement to further specialization and independence. Arguments aimed at unifying political scientists by agreement on some particular conception of subject matter or some program of proper methodology evoke controversy and raise threats of schism. Again, ideological and religious analogies are appropriate: In the "politics of political science" both strict partisan and popular front movements are discernible; political science has both ecumenicists and sectarians; "doctrine" is important in contests within political science and in relations between political science and other disciplines and groups. In the recent period the behavioral movement has of course been the center of much controversy, in some ways unifying, in some ways divisive.

*Relations With Other Disciplines and Foci*

Relations with other disciplines naturally constitute an important element in the continuing process of self-identification, one replete with contradiction and irony. Political science, it has been said, is "like Poland, open to invasion from every side." Patently, "the political" does not exist in isolation. In the existential world it is intricately intermingled with history, culture, law, economic life, social phenomena in general. Other disciplines not only lay claim to such areas but sometimes assert that the political, in part or even in whole, is properly viewed as subservient to the areas to which they claim jurisdiction. Political scientists cannot deny the *importance* of nonpolitical phenomena for the political, nor do they generally wish to deny the relevance of what other disciplines may have to "contribute" to understanding the political. Indeed, the idea of a total understanding of the social realm, the concept of a "unified social science," has not simply intellectual respectability but much emotional appeal. How, then, to find the optimum balance, the proper, fruitful interrelations?

Much of the history of political science could be written in terms of the relationships with other disciplines and with intellectual enterprises or foci which do not necessarily have disciplinary status. Some generalizations and observations on this subject are appropriate.

Political science, as noted, began in close conjunction with history. The relationship has remained important in many ways, despite many forces tending toward separation. Recently there has been some argument for a closer liaison. In any event, inertia and institutional convenience serve to maintain significant connections; in nearly two hundred undergraduate colleges, history and political science still are taught in a unified department. Political science also began in close relationship with the study of law. There, too, the record is one of gradually attenuating connection. Law has continued its professionalization, centered in graduate professional schools of law. Meanwhile political science has gradually lessened its interest in law on the "substantive" side, shifting its attention, under behavioral influences, to judicial-legal behavior, to law as a political phenomenon.

Well before World War I some leading political scientists argued that the crucial relationship of political science is with sociology, conceived as the study of the social realm entire, and various essays in the middle period made a case for the necessity of grounding the study of the political in the study of society in general. In the recent period relationships with sociology became very important. The currents of behavioralism moved in concert with important currents in sociology. Political scientists often looked to sociology for useful concepts and perspectives; and perhaps more important, leading sociologists turned their attention to the study of the political. The interchange between the two disciplines became so prominent, in fact, that "political sociology" came into use as a term to designate the substantial area of mutual concern.

As the record makes clear, economics and political science were not created simply by a sundering of nineteenth-century political economy. But the sundering has always been considered by some an error, leaving both of the separate disciplines without an adequate base, either for explanatory theory or for public policy guidance, and resulting in a varied pattern of ad hoc cooperation, amateur improvising, and "border raids." One of the salient features of the recent period has been movement toward a closer, more "rational" joining of the interests of economists and political scientists. What is judged to be some of the more original and useful work in political science has been done by economists applying to politics concepts and modes of reasoning taken from the economist's disciplinary tool kit. Some political scientists, attracted by the seeming success of economics in developing quantitative methods and "powerful" theory, have sought either to borrow useful ideas and methods or to reconstruct political science along lines analogous to economics. (The idea that "power" in political science should be analogous to "wealth" in economics was in fact forcefully argued in the twenties, and that relationship has remained to some a desirable and feasible objective.) Most important is the fact that in recent years the case for a construction of a new political economy (i.e., for a closer, more systematic joining, whatever the name and the resulting disciplinary rearrangements) has been made with cogency and, it appears, considerable persuasiveness.

The idea that a theory (or science) of politics must be grounded in a theory (or science) of human nature is one of the oldest and most respectable in the tradition. It is hardly surprising, therefore, that an important part of the development of political science concerns this ambition. It will be recalled that Merriam judged psychology to be of prime importance in the drive to make political science genuinely scientific, and much of Lasswell's work centered on the joining of the psychological (particularly psychoanalytic theory) and the political. In the post-World War II period the argument for the necessity for a firm psychological base has been carried forward with intelligence and force, and much substantive work in this vein is a characteristic of recent decades. In fact, so many, so varied, so intricate are the interrelations between the many branches and facets of psychology and political science in the recent period that they defy generalization—except *this* generalization.

Interrelations with and borrowing from other "domains" are important, but noting this fact must suffice. Some domains have disciplinary status, as does anthropology. Some are interdisciplinary "clusterings" or "foci" without distinct disciplinary bases (though they may be represented by learned journals), such as systems theory, cybernetics, and communications theory. Some of the "harder" behavioralists have seen the route to a genuine political science as running not through cognate fields but directly through the physical sciences and mathematics.

Obviously, the above-noted analogy to Poland's problem of maintaining its integrity has some force. Political science is not able and perhaps should not be able to assert exclusive claim to the study of the political; its domain is entered frequently and penetrated deeply by other disciplines. But clearly, too, the "invaders" are frequently welcomed and are judged as making useful contributions to the study of politics. Nor is the invasion simply one-way. Political scientists in the quest for more knowledge and better instruments enter other realms frequently and in number. Few would deny that the advance of knowledge is served by the considerable crossing of borders, whatever the severity of the accompanying "boundary problems."

## Satellite Organizations and Secessionist Movements

All organizations, no matter how large and successful, are faced with problems of division within and loss of members at their boundaries. Indeed, success and bigness, by their nature, create such problems (as the history of religious, political, business, and other organizations demonstrates). In a society characterized by much freedom to organize and by a high propensity to create organizations, as is the United States, internal division and loss of members is likely to take place through the creation of new, more or less supplementary, more or less competitive or "counter" organizations. The American Political Science Association is not exempt from universal tendencies in organizational behavior or from the general characteristics of our organizational culture. It is appropriate to take note of some of the divisive and "centrifugal" aspects of political science as they manifest themselves through the affairs of the Association.

In the Association as in many other organizations, including the overall social science "family" of disciplinary-professional organizations to which the Association belongs, the ferment, turbulence, and discord of the late sixties and early seventies have been reflected. Not surprisingly, there have been "antiestablishment" and "proestablishment" forces, which have reflected themselves in the creation of, respectively, a Caucus for a New Political Science and an Ad Hoc Committee, both representing loosely structured organizations-within-the-organization. Neither "side" has won all the organizational battles for control of the official apparatus of the Association and for guidance of the evolution of political science in the near future. In general, "proestablishment" forces have been decisively predominate; but "accommodation" and compromise have taken place, with some full or partial victories (in terms of personnel and policies) going to the dissidents and with a general relaxation of the ardent partisanship characteristic of turn-of-the-decade Association affairs. As this essay is being written, it appears certain that American political science will not suffer a major organizational schism, that the main lines of development in the political science of the sixties will continue to be predominate in the Association. This conclusion leaves open, however, the question of the long-range influence of some of the opinions and tendencies represented by the "antiestablishment." These could, in the long run, gain more acceptance and—conceivably—become decisive in "official" political science.

Although the struggle between "two sides" was often of the essence, to represent the organizational ferment and strife of recent years in that way is nevertheless a misleading simplification. Both "sides," especially the dissidents, represented varying points of view, causes, and constituencies; and calculations of a strategic or tactical nature in terms of group objectives, rather than general "ideology," were characteristically decisive. Representatives of the women's liberation movement, of blacks and other racial-ethnic minorities might be willing to join forces in support of a politically "activist" role for the Association, and of course they were likely to support each other; but ultimately each group represented distinctive interests. (Those interested in the politics of the Association will find of interest the several analyses of Association voting, as well as other materials, published in *PS*.)

The organized groups and loosely organized "groupings" that have emerged within the mainstream of political science in recent years constitute an important addition to the factors that certainly represent complexity and probably can be construed to represent some quantum of divisiveness (and at least potential dispersion). But additionally, there are at any given time a number of "normal" interests and groups that find that the Association (or more broadly, mainstream political science) does not fully or fairly represent their interests. A common response to that feeling is the establishment of a separate organization to express and promote those interests. Characteristically, such sectoral or "special purpose" organizations remain relatively small, do not aim at major Association change, and are not inclined toward secession. These groups may have a formal structure, with officers and dues, but most of their members remain members of the Association. The Association, on its part, "recognizes" the existence of such groups. Since they are not a part of the official apparatus of the Association, they cannot be treated as such. But relations with the satellite organizations are polite and may even be cordial; and some Association recognition and services may be extended to them.

The programs of the annual meetings of the Association are instructive. In addition to the official Association program, there are "events" and meetings in wide variety and in great number. It is now customary for the officially printed program to contain notice of many of them under the heading "Courtesy Listing of Unaffiliated Groups." In the most recent (1972) program this feature runs eight pages and contains much variety. Many of the listing are university social events or meetings of state or regional associations; there are also irregular and ad hoc concerns of no great import for present purposes. But also listed are meetings of a wide variety of "committees," "caucuses," "organizations," and "associations." Some, again, may have no great or continuing significance. But some do represent important interests of long standing, interests that may later be brought within the official apparatus or, conversely be removed from under the Association's roof.

To list some of the entities serves to illustrate a number of points: American Society for Political and Legal Philosophy, Caucus for a New Political Science, Caucus of Foreign Born Political Scientists, Committee on Health Politics, Comparative Urban Research, Conference for the Study of Political Thought, Conference Group on Communist Studies, Conference on Inter-University Gaming and Simulation, International Studies Association, Inter-University Consortium for Political Research, Latin-American Development Administration Committee, Policy Studies Organization, Political Scientists Interested in Diplomacy, The Polycentric Circle, Women's Caucus for Political Science.

It is impossible to know the extent to which the Association has lost individual memberships to alternative centers of attraction or clusters of interests that have "hived off" to complete independence (or that were independently created and have not been incorporated). What is clear and important is that the idea of *a* political science, embodied in the Association, has survived and continues to thrive. The question whether other related organizations, foci of study, and professional activity are also "political science," even though they do not bear that title, is at one level a matter of simple definition and arbitrary classification, but at another level (as we have seen) a question that involves in its answer questions of history, philosophy, tradition, and national experience.

It was observed above that a major sector of political science, international relations, has shown some secessionist tendencies. They are evidenced by the creation of the International Studies Association, by the existence of independent journals, and in other ways. Other sectors of political science, as evidenced by satellite organizations and otherwise, occasionally become restive and more or less seriously discuss "disaffiliation." In only one, however, is separation both important (with respect to size, at least) and fairly well advanced. This sector is public administration.

Public administration, gaining its separate textbooks and other literature after World War I, became a recognized field of specialization within political science. That is, it gained recognition as such in curricula, in the *Review*, and in Association program organization. In the fifties and especially in the sixties, however, the status of public administration as a part of political science became clouded. Its literature received less attention in the journals, it appeared less frequently as a topic on the programs of meetings, and so forth. Meanwhile, the American Society for Public Administration, established in 1939, proved durable. Its membership rivals that of the Association in number, and many who teach and do research in the field of public administration are primarily oriented toward the Society—though they may remain members of the Association and even have a lively interest in its affairs.

What is involved in this gradual but incomplete movement toward separation is very complex, beyond thorough probing here. But several observations—and a conclusion—are warranted. Public administration is the most "professional" part of political science in the sense that, though only a minor fraction of governmental administrators are trained in public administration, such training does lead (normally without difficulty) to employment in public administration, i.e., to a career other than that of teaching and research. The majority of the members of the Society are "practitioners," not academics.

The "applied" interests of the public administrationist and his professional "reference group" drew heavily on his energy and attention in the years when the behavioral currents gathered strength and centered the attention of most political scientists on matters other than administration. Increasingly, the public administrationist found the concepts and research findings of other disciplines, especially those of economics, sociology, and social psychology, more pertinent to his interests and needs than those of political science. Further, other organizations of professionals in or related to public administration exerted an attraction: organizations of personnel specialists, budget officers, planners, city managers, and so forth.

In short, it appears that public administration is a "special case," and that what has happened and may happen in this area has limited relevance to other areas of political science (Kaufman, 1956; Waldo, 1972).

## FIELDS AND FOCI

Whether to present in this essay quantitative data bearing on the fields and foci of political science, data indicating relative emphasis and changing emphases through time, has constituted a difficult question. In principle it seemed highly desirable to do so. But practical problems severely limit the usefulness of quantitative data. For some possible indices (e.g., Ph.D. specialization, courses taught) data are incomplete, unavailable, or, if available, questionable. For all indices (including books published or reviewed and programs of the annual meetings) there are baffling problems of classification and interpretation. The conclusion was that journal articles provide the best basis for an analysis.

Presented below are data on articles published in general political science journals during five selected periods. Undoubtedly of some value, these data give clear evidence of certain emphases and trends and provide a basis for various hypotheses and speculations. Plainly, however, their value is limited, and they are properly preceded by some explanations and warnings.

*Problems of Categorization*

A standard language for the "parts" of political science does not exist. Political scientists speak of "concentrations," "fields," and "subdisciplines," but they do so loosely and often interchangeably. Differing principles of classification—geographic, functional, methodological—are used, sometimes in combination, to indicate titles of courses, parts of curricula, sections of programs, and divisions of journals. Moreover, emphases shift and fashions in terminology change (e.g., comparative government becomes comparative politics), making longitudinal comparisons difficult and questionable. No warrant can be given, obviously, that the categories and classes selected for use in analyzing and presenting the data are "correct." They mingle an attempt to recognize the most widespread usage with judgments on the most reasonable analytic concepts.

Fitting journal articles into categories, however the latter are stated, is difficult. Journal articles are not written to suit the convenience of indexers and cataloguers, much less that of analysts at some future time. To be sure, most articles can be categorized without serious difficulty, but for some a more or less arbitrary decision must be made.

*The "Perimeter" Problem*

The problem of what is or is not to be recognized as "political science" is faced at a number of points in this essay. It is involved in the decision to include in the analysis only *general* journals of political science in the United States. (The names of the journals are listed in the explanatory notes following Table I.)

The results would have been different if specialized and "field" journals were included, for example, *World Politics* and *Public Administration Review*. To argue that they should be included is not unreasonable. But taking this route, one encounters nagging questions without reasonable answers. If the *Public Administration Review*, then the journals of public personnel administration? The entire large and heterogeneous periodical literature of public administration? On into the literature of public affairs in search of "public administration" items?

The decision to include only general journals of political science was a practical one, without prejudice as to broader as against narrower definitions of political science. But focusing on the "center" does help to clarify what political science has been and is in the minds of those most deeply committed to it in terms of education, position, and self-image.

By definition, a measure of quantity is not a measure of quality. Nevertheless, a special caveat may be desirable. Unless the data are interpreted with some knowledge of qualitative changes, they risk concealing more than they reveal. The above-noted changes in the disciplinary "map" in the recent period, for example, are little signified in the following data.

*Data from Five Periods*

The tables present data from five periods. The first, 1909–1914 (excluding 1913; see notes following Table I), was selected to represent political science at the conclusion of its formative period, after disciplinary status had been asserted and before World War I had caused any "distortions." The second period, 1925–1929, represents "normalcy" in the interwar period. The third period, 1939–1941, presents political science following the New Deal but before World War II had exerted a significant effect. The fourth period, 1952–1954, presents political science as affected by World War II, its consequences, and the beginning of significant behavioral influence. The fifth period, 1969–1971, represents political science in the latest period for which data were available.

Patently, the data in the tables speak clearly to some matters, in a Delphic manner to others, and what they "say" is subject to varying interpretations. The comments on the tables call attention to some salient features, suggest some explanations, and pose some questions. They are in no sense intended as authoritative. Those familiar with the history of political science or those highly specialized in some part of it undoubtedly will wish to question some of the interpretations. (The comments, by category, refer both to Table I and to Tables II-1 through II-13.)

*Explanatory Notes for Tables I through II-13*

Tables I through II-13 are based on the same data and should be construed as one consecutive table. The following information supports and amplifies the necessarily concise table headings.

As noted, journals included in the analysis were limited to general journals of political science in the United States. They were as follows:

1. *American Political Science Review*

1a. *Proceedings of the American Political Science Association*

2. *Political Science Quarterly*

3. *Journal of Politics*

4. *Review of Politics*

5. *Western Political Quarterly*
6. *Midwest Journal of Political Science*
7. *Polity*

The journals included were not the same in all periods, however. Numbered as above, the journals in each period were as follows:

1909–1914: 1, 1a, 2 (See note below)

1925–1929: 1, 2

1939–1941: 1, 2, 3, 4

1952–1954: 1, 2, 3, 4, 5

1969–1971: 1, 2, 3, 4, 5, 6, 7

Note: Because publication of the *Proceedings* was suspended during 1913, no journal articles for that year were coded. Therefore the first period was actually 1909–1912 and 1914.

In some of the tables, distribution by class within the given category resulted in classes with too few observations for analysis. Dashes appear in the appropriate columns of those tables.

Because of rounding, some of the columns showing percentages may not total 100%.

*Technical Note*

In addition to the terminological and categorization problems noted in the text, additional problems were encountered in using data from a previous coding of articles. The distribution of articles for the 1925–1929, 1939–1941, and 1952–1954 periods were adapted from a prior publication (Waldo, 1955, pp. 38–41). The 1909–1914 and 1969–1971 periods were coded for the present essay to permit a more extensive comparative analysis. Since it was obviously impossible to define objective standards of categorization, both coders were permitted to assign journal articles to more than one category. Thus, one article may yield more than one "observation."

This multiple classification procedure resulted in an obvious disparity that had to be reconciled to permit comparative interpretation. The first coder, it seems, was far more liberal than the second in his use of multiple classification. The ratios of the sum of "observations" to the sum of actual articles for the first coder were as follows: 2.33 for the 1925–1929 period, 2.85 for the 1939–1941 period, and 2.81 for the 1952–1954 period. The ratios for the second coder were 1.04 for the 1909–1914 period and 1.13 for the 1969–1971 period.

In order that some degree of numerical consistency between the two coders could be achieved, the total number of observations was assumed to

TABLE I. Distribution of articles in general American political science journals by category for given time periods.

| Articles by category | 1909–1914 | | 1925–1929 | |
| --- | --- | --- | --- | --- |
| | Number | Percent | Number | Percent |
| Normative and descriptive theory | 29 | 10 | 69 | 14 |
| Comparative government and politics | 66 | 23 | 130 | 26 |
| International politics, organizations, and law | 26 | 9 | 22 | 4 |
| Legislative affairs | 23 | 8 | 62 | 12 |
| Politics, parties, and pressure groups | 3 | 1 | 24 | 5 |
| Public opinion, voting, and elections | 9 | 3 | 33 | 6 |
| Presidency | 6 | 2 | 9 | 2 |
| Organization and administration | 1 | 0 | 34 | 7 |
| American government (other than federal) | 38 | 13 | 51 | 10 |
| Public policy analysis (substantive) | 58 | 20 | 32 | 6 |
| Judicial affairs | 3 | 1 | 8 | 2 |
| Public law and jurisprudence | 14 | 5 | 26 | 5 |
| Study of political science | 8 | 3 | 8 | 2 |
| Total observations | 284 | 100 | 508 | 100 |
| Total articles | 273 | — | 218 | — |

be the relevant referent on which the percentage distributions were based. Thus the percentage distributions presented in Tables I and II-1 through II-13 have been computed by dividing the number of observations within a category (class) and time period by the total number of observations for that time period. Clearly, this procedure will achieve a degree of numerical consistency only and will not account for variations in the categorical perceptions of the two coders.

### *Normative and Descriptive Theory*

The relatively little attention given to theory in any sense at the end of the formative period is clear, as is a consistent strength for this category in the

| 1939–1941 | | 1952–1954 | | 1969–1971 | |
|---|---|---|---|---|---|
| Number | Percent | Number | Percent | Number | Percent |
| 159 | 21 | 255 | 22 | 172 | 22 |
| 145 | 19 | 260 | 22 | 139 | 18 |
| 30 | 4 | 122 | 10 | 60 | 8 |
| 31 | 4 | 64 | 6 | 55 | 7 |
| 52 | 7 | 56 | 5 | 82 | 10 |
| 32 | 4 | 59 | 5 | 122 | 15 |
| 62 | 8 | 28 | 2 | 10 | 1 |
| 55 | 7 | 41 | 4 | 7 | 1 |
| 44 | 6 | 51 | 4 | 70 | 9 |
| 76 | 10 | 155 | 13 | 36 | 5 |
| 17 | 2 | 15 | 1 | 22 | 3 |
| 34 | 5 | 40 | 3 | 10 | 1 |
| 9 | 1 | 17 | 2 | 8 | 1 |
| 746 | 100 | 1163 | 100 | 793 | 100 |
| 262 | — | 718 | — | 702 | — |

last three periods. (See Table I.) The relationship between "History of political ideas, theory and ideology" and "Normative political theory and political philosophy" is worthy of note. (See Table II-1.) The "untheoretical" bent of the first period is again evident, as is a consistent near-equality between the two in all subsequent periods.

"Descriptive political theory and political science methodology" is minuscule in the first period, but it is up sharply in the second period (reflecting the Merriam-led movement toward scientism) and has grown relatively strong. "Construction of general political theory," showing a fairly high level in the first period, very high levels in the middle periods, and a sharp drop-off in the most recent period, presents special problems of in-

TABLE II-1. Distribution of articles in "Normative and descriptive theory" category in general American political science journals by class for given time periods

| Articles by class | 1909–1914 | | 1925–1929 | |
|---|---|---|---|---|
| | Number | Percent | Number | Percent |
| Normative and descriptive theory | 29 | 100 | 69 | 100 |
| History of political ideas, theory, and ideology[1] | 19 | 66 | 21 | 30 |
| Normative political theory and political philosophy[2] | 3 | 10 | 21 | 30 |
| Descriptive political theory and political science methodology[3] | 1 | 3 | 7 | 10 |
| Construction of general political theory[4] | 6 | 21 | 20 | 30 |

1. Includes primarily discussions, descriptions, developmental analysis of idea of particular theorists, particular tradition, particular doctrine, schools, or times.
2. Includes more general and/or analytical discussions of ideas, theories, and/or political "thought."
3. Includes simulation, rational model building, philosophy of science, and formal model building.
4. Includes general theories of State Rights, Politics, Government, Organization, and broad-scale model building.

terpretation because of the heterogeneity of materials it includes. (See note 4.)

### Comparative Government and Politics

The relative strength of comparative studies in the first and following periods is impressive; the decline in the most recent period is puzzling (see Table I). Obviously "interpretation" is necessary. Many of the "Informal or formal case studies" in the earlier periods (see Table II-2) would now be regarded as shallow and unworthy of publication. Certainly much comparative study in the most recent period has been published in newer, more specialized journals (e.g., *Comparative Political Studies, Journal of Comparative Administration*). Still, the dominant position of the case study in the recent period raises the question whether the wave of "comparativeness" following World War II is receding.

|  1939–1941 |         |  1952–1954 |         |  1969–1971 |         |
| :----: | :-----: | :----: | :-----: | :----: | :-----: |
| Number | Percent | Number | Percent | Number | Percent |
|  159   |   100   |  255   |   100   |  172   |   100   |
|   45   |   28    |   75   |   29    |   74   |   42    |
|   46   |   29    |   74   |   29    |   61   |   35    |
|    7   |    4    |   19   |    8    |   30   |   17    |
|   61   |   38    |   87   |   34    |    7   |    4    |

### *International Politics, Organization, and Law*

The attention given to international affairs immediately preceding World War I is surprising; but one might have expected more attention to international affairs in the interwar years, especially for the years 1939–1941 (see Table I). The move upward after World War II (and after the beginning of the cold war) is as expected. But the decrease in the most recent period, as with comparative studies, invites comment. The decrease is especially puzzling with respect to "International behavior," given that students of international politics have inclined toward behavioralism. (See Table II-3.) Presumably publication in specialized journals (e.g., *World Politics*) accounts for much of the drop-off.

The cyclical pattern for international law catches one's attention, but perhaps it is of no great significance. On the other hand, the upward slope for "Construction of general theory in international politics" and its sharp increase in the most recent period probably speak to something significant.

### *The "Domestic" Categories*

The following eight categories deal primarily with American politics, though not exclusively so. On the average, a little over 50 percent of the articles have fitted into these categories, with very little variation between periods. The relatively large drop in the fourth period (down to 44%) is as might be

TABLE II-2. Distribution of articles in "Comparative government and politics" category in general American political science journals by class for given time periods

| Articles by class | 1909–1914 | | 1925–1929 | | 1939–1941 | | 1952–1954 | | 1969–1971 | |
|---|---|---|---|---|---|---|---|---|---|---|
| | Number | Percent | Number | Percent | Number | Percent | Number | Percent | Number | Percent |
| Comparative government and politics | 66 | 100 | 130 | 100 | 145 | 100 | 260 | 100 | 139 | 100 |
| Informal or formal case studies | 57 | 87 | 67 | 52 | 72 | 50 | 162 | 62 | 110 | 79 |
| Cross-cultural and/or cross-nation-state analysis[5] | 9 | 14 | 63 | 49 | 73 | 50 | 94 | 36 | 26 | 19 |
| Construction of general theory of comparative politics | 0 | 0 | 0 | 0 | 0 | 0 | 4 | 2 | 3 | 1 |

5. Includes all comparative studies except U.S. or American state political party studies.

TABLE II-3. Distribution of articles in "International politics, organizations, and law" category in general American political science journals by class for given time periods

| Articles by class | 1909–1914 | | 1925–1929 | | 1939–1941 | | 1952–1954 | | 1969–1971 | |
|---|---|---|---|---|---|---|---|---|---|---|
| | Number | Percent | Number | Percent | Number | Percent | Number | Percent | Number | Percent |
| International politics, organizations, and law | 26 | 100 | 22 | 100 | 30 | 100 | 122 | 100 | 60 | 100 |
| Informal or formal case studies | 15 | 58 | 13 | 59 | 15 | 50 | 49 | 40 | 33 | 55 |
| International behavior[6] | 9 | 34 | 5 | 23 | 10 | 33 | 51 | 42 | 9 | 15 |
| Substantive studies of international law | 1 | 4 | 3 | 14 | 1 | 3 | 11 | 9 | 2 | 3 |
| Construction of general theory in international politics[7] | 1 | 4 | 1 | 5 | 4 | 13 | 11 | 9 | 16 | 27 |

6. Includes both national and supranational behavior analysis, relations between two or more states, policy formulation involving more than one state, world and regional activities. Also includes reports of international events of professional interest.
7. Includes simulation and decision-making studies.

TABLE II-4. Distribution of articles in "Legislative affairs" category in general American political science journals by class for given time periods

| Articles by class | 1909–1914 | | 1925–1929 | |
|---|---|---|---|---|
| | Number | Percent | Number | Percent |
| Legislative affairs | 23 | 100 | 62 | 100 |
| Biographical | 0 | 0 | 3 | 5 |
| Particular legislators and legislative problems | 4 | 17 | 19 | 31 |
| Particular bills and laws[8] | 1 | 4 | 19 | 31 |
| Legislative reform[9] | 13 | 57 | 20 | 32 |
| Theory of legislative functions | 5 | 22 | 1 | 2 |

expected (given the salience of overseas affairs), and the return to a normal pattern in the last period may be significant.

***Legislative affairs.*** The sharp dip downward for this category for the period 1939–1941 (Table I) and the intermittent or cyclical nature of some of the classes (Table II-4) present problems in interpretation. Perhaps explanation is to be sought more in the temper and problems of American politics than in the internal dialectic of political science.

***Politics, parties, and pressure groups.*** The small showing for this category in the first period (Table I) reflects the climate and interests of Progressivism: Reform and purification were dominant motifs; parties and politicians were only marginally respectable. The advance of "realism" in the middle period is evident (Table II-5): Pressure groups were "discovered," lobbying became a phenomenon worthy of professional attention, and the study of leaders and elites became a serious and continuous interest.

***Public opinion, voting, and elections.*** As for the preceding category and for similar reasons, the showing for the first period is minuscule (Table I); *all* items concern "Election laws and administration"—a practical and "reform" interest that generally slopes off to the present (Table II-6). Again, realism asserts itself in the interwar period and continues strong, particularly in the class "Political behavior, political socialization, and mass behavior." The

| 1939–1941 | | 1952–1954 | | 1969–1971 | |
|---|---|---|---|---|---|
| Number | Percent | Number | Percent | Number | Percent |
| 31 | 100 | 64 | 100 | 55 | 100 |
| 0 | 0 | 4 | 6 | 0 | 0 |
| 10 | 32 | 22 | 35 | 6 | 11 |
| 10 | 32 | 16 | 25 | 1 | 2 |
| 10 | 32 | 18 | 28 | 6 | 11 |
| 1 | 3 | 4 | 6 | 42 | 77 |

drop-off in "Political opinion formation and movement" in the recent period presumably is accountable to specialized publication.

***The Presidency.*** It is no surprise that interest in the Presidency was high following the New Deal (Table II-7). But what accounts for the more recent decline? Surely not that this institution has grown less consequential. Various hypotheses suggest themselves; for example, in a period in which comparative studies are in vogue, the Presidency does not lend itself (except in limited fashion) to comparative study. Perhaps the answer is to be found primarily in the peculiar nature of the institution: There are special problems of accessibility and availability of data. The large literature on the Presidency tends to be the product not of political scientists but of journalists, "publicists," and former White House officials.

***Organization and administration.*** The data here, taken as a category, are easily interpreted. In the first period, interest in public administration existed only in germ (as in issues of municipal reform), though the ground for its development had been prepared earlier, particularly by Woodrow Wilson and Frank Goodnow. The first textbooks appeared in the twenties, and rapid growth in curricula and programs was forwarded by a number of factors, including the activities of the President's Committee on Administrative Management in the mid-thirties (Table II-8). The creation of the American Society for Public Administration in 1939, as well as the growth of specialized (e.g., personnel and finance) organizations, created competing centers for professional loyalties and provided alternative publication media, thus effectively "draining" most of public administration from political science.

TABLE II-5. Distribution of articles in "Politics, parties, and pressure groups" category in general American political science journals by class for given time periods

| Articles by class | 1909–1914 | | 1925–1929 | | 1939–1941 | | 1952–1954 | | 1969–1971 | |
|---|---|---|---|---|---|---|---|---|---|---|
| | Number | Percent | Number | Percent | Number | Percent | Number | Percent | Number | Percent |
| Politics, parties and pressure groups | 3 | – | 24 | 100 | 52 | 100 | 56 | 100 | 82 | 100 |
| Political parties[10] | 2 | – | 11 | 46 | 19 | 37 | 17 | 30 | 17 | 21 |
| Political leadership or elite behavior | 1 | 0 | 6 | 25 | 19 | 37 | 16 | 29 | 25 | 30 |
| Pressure groups and lobbying | 0 | 0 | 1 | 4 | 5 | 10 | 6 | 11 | 11 | 13 |
| Construction of general theory in organized group behavior | 0 | 0 | 6 | 25 | 9 | 17 | 17 | 30 | 29 | 35 |

10. Includes all studies of political party activity on the federal, state, and local level.

TABLE II-6. Distribution of articles in "Public opinion, voting, and elections" category in general American political science journals by class for given time periods

| Articles by class | 1909–1914 | | 1925–1929 | | 1939–1941 | | 1952–1954 | | 1969–1971 | |
|---|---|---|---|---|---|---|---|---|---|---|
| | Number | Percent | Number | Percent | Number | Percent | Number | Percent | Number | Percent |
| Public opinion, voting, and elections | 9 | 100 | 33 | 100 | 32 | 100 | 59 | 100 | 122 | 100 |
| Election laws and administration | 9 | 100 | 12 | 36 | 3 | 9 | 6 | 10 | 11 | 9 |
| Political behavior, political socialization, and mass behavior | 0 | 0 | 12 | 36 | 20 | 63 | 32 | 54 | 84 | 69 |
| Political opinion formation and measurement | 0 | 0 | 4 | 12 | 6 | 19 | 15 | 25 | 23 | 19 |
| Communications and construction of general theory | 0 | 0 | 5 | 15 | 3 | 9 | 6 | 10 | 4 | 3 |

TABLE II-7. Distribution of articles in "Presidency" category in general American political science journals by class for given time periods

| Articles by class | 1909–1914 | | 1925–1929 | |
|---|---|---|---|---|
| | Number | Percent | Number | Percent |
| Presidency | 6 | – | 9 | – |
| Presidential institutions | 1 | – | 2 | – |
| Presidency-federal bureaucracy relations | 1 | – | 1 | – |
| Presidency-congressional relations | 0 | 0 | 7 | – |
| Presidency-judiciary relations | 3 | – | 0 | 0 |
| Presidential policy formulation and execution process | 0 | 0 | 3 | – |
| Construction of general theories of the Presidency | 1 | – | 0 | 0 |

***American government (other than federal).*** One "surprise" here may be that a renewed interest in state affairs (often involving economic analysis and/or interstate comparisons), in local affairs (spurred by the "urban crisis"), and in problems of the federal system (evidenced by many special commissions and new arrangements) does not suffice to bring the level of comparative attention up to the level of the first three periods.

Although the analysis by class within category may often seem to be too refined, it is still not subtle enough to make some significant points. Thus *none* of the items for "Local politics, administration, and law" for the recent period concerns local administration or law; i.e., they all concern the political dimension of local government.

***Public policy analysis (substantive).*** However imperfectly the data mirror the substantive policy interests of political scientists, they present more than random clues, and, when read in the context of history, they speak to our professional posture. Some policy areas, especially "Health, education, and welfare," have a certain constancy. Others have a "hot flash" quality: thus "Civil liberties" in 1952–1954, an obvious response to McCarthyism (Table II-10). But patently there is selectivity in responding to "hot" issues. In the

| 1939–1941 | | 1952–1954 | | 1969–1971 | |
|---|---|---|---|---|---|
| Number | Percent | Number | Percent | Number | Percent |
| 62 | 100 | 28 | 100 | 10 | – |
| 14 | 23 | 8 | 29 | 4 | – |
| 18 | 29 | 4 | 14 | 3 | – |
| 15 | 24 | 5 | 18 | 1 | – |
| 7 | 11 | 2 | 7 | 1 | – |
| 8 | 13 | 8 | 29 | 0 | 0 |
| 0 | 0 | 1 | 4 | 1 | – |

recent period of intense ecological concern, there has not been a single item addressed to "Resources and conservation policy."

The most significant datum is presumably the decline, in the most recent period, to 5 percent of the total for the category as a whole. This change appears to be an obvious reflection of behavioralist interests and influence.

*Judicial affairs, and public law and jurisprudence.* The data reflect the decline of interest in the substantive and philosophic aspects of law and the recent growth of behavioral studies (Tables II-11 and II-12).

## The Study of Political Science

The sharp upward movement for "Research trends and bibliography" in the period 1952–1954 is a patent reflection of the then-growing controversy over behavioralism (Table II-13). But perhaps the most significant point these data make is that political science has given little attention in its journals to the activity to which, by a large measure, the most time is given: teaching.

TABLE II-8. Distribution of articles in "Organization and administration" category in general American political science journals by class for given time periods

| Articles by class | 1909–1914 | | 1925–1929 | |
|---|---|---|---|---|
| | Number | Percent | Number | Percent |
| Organization and administration | 1 | – | 34 | 100 |
| Public fiscal activity | 1 | – | 5 | 15 |
| Personnel administration and organization development | 0 | 0 | 9 | 27 |
| Organization and management | 0 | 0 | 13 | 38 |
| Comparative administration and technical assistance | 0 | 0 | 1 | 3 |
| International administration | 0 | 0 | 1 | 3 |
| Administration of particular programs | 0 | 0 | 3 | 9 |
| Private administration | 0 | 0 | 0 | 0 |
| Construction of general organization and administration theory | 0 | 0 | 2 | 6 |

## "Science Manpower" Data: Political Science

Data from another source are available for use in trying to "get a picture" of the interests and activities of political scientists. The source, a report on "American science manpower," resulting from a survey conducted by the National Science Foundation in 1970 (published 1971), is the second issue of a proposed biennial National Register of Scientific and Technical Personnel.

These data are unquestionably of some value. They bear on place and type of employment, as well as specialization, and thus are relevant to the discussion (see below) of professionalization. But these data are also subject to various limitations and must be interpreted with caution. They were gathered from a questionnaire distributed to members of the American Political Science Association. Thus some who consider themselves political scientists would not have received the questionnaire. (Though trained as political scientists, they might have allowed their membership to lapse, particularly if employed outside academia.) And of course, not all who received

| 1939–1941 | | 1952–1954 | | 1969–1971 | |
|---|---|---|---|---|---|
| Number | Percent | Number | Percent | Number | Percent |
| 55 | 100 | 41 | 100 | 7 | – |
| 9 | 16 | 5 | 12 | 0 | 0 |
| 11 | 20 | 6 | 15 | 2 | – |
| 16 | 30 | 6 | 15 | 1 | – |
| 0 | 0 | 3 | 7 | 1 | – |
| 0 | 0 | 2 | 5 | 0 | 0 |
| 4 | 7 | 7 | 17 | 1 | – |
| 3 | 6 | 3 | 7 | 0 | 0 |
| 12 | 22 | 9 | 22 | 2 | – |

the questionnaire responded. (Were those with a "science" orientation more disposed to respond, given the sponsorship and name of the survey?)

The following tables were constructed from data in the report. The categories ("fields") used in the tables are those used in the questionnaire and the report thereon. (In the questionnaire and the report, the categories are broken into subcategories, which are ignored for present purposes. The report also contains data on "levels"—Ph.D., M.A., and A.B.—which are lumped together in the tables.)

Controlling for years of experience (Table III), one can draw some conclusions regarding specialization.

Political theory has been a comparatively steady, though relatively small, field of interest. Methodology has been a field of increasing interest for younger political scientists. Interest in public policy is fairly steady, but it "peaks" among those who became political scientists in the late thirties and early forties. Public administration has been declining in its attraction for

TABLE II-9. Distribution of articles in "American government (other than federal)" category in general American political science journals by class for given time periods

| Articles by class | 1909–1914 | | 1925–1929 | | 1939–1941 | | 1952–1954 | | 1969–1971 | |
|---|---|---|---|---|---|---|---|---|---|---|
| | Number | Percent | Number | Percent | Number | Percent | Number | Percent | Number | Percent |
| American government (other than federal) | 38 | 100 | 51 | 100 | 44 | 100 | 51 | 100 | 70 | 100 |
| Federal-state relations and regionalism | 6 | 16 | 2 | 4 | 12 | 27 | 20 | 40 | 3 | 4 |
| State politics, administration, and law | 9 | 24 | 31 | 61 | 22 | 50 | 22 | 43 | 40 | 57 |
| Local politics, administration, and law | 23 | 61 | 18 | 36 | 10 | 23 | 9 | 18 | 27 | 39 |

TABLE II-10. Distribution of articles in "Public policy" category in general American political science journals by class for given time periods

| Articles by class | 1909–1914 | | 1925–1929 | | 1939–1941 | | 1952–1954 | | 1969–1971 | |
|---|---|---|---|---|---|---|---|---|---|---|
| | Number | Percent | Number | Percent | Number | Percent | Number | Percent | Number | Percent |
| Public policy analysis (substantive) | 58 | 100 | 32 | 100 | 76 | 100 | 155 | 100 | 36 | 100 |
| Foreign policy | 0 | 0 | 8 | 25 | 10 | 13 | 22 | 14 | 2 | 5 |
| Industrial and commercial policy | 17 | 30 | 0 | 0 | 2 | 3 | 9 | 6 | 3 | 8 |
| Agriculture policy | 3 | 5 | 0 | 0 | 6 | 8 | 3 | 2 | 1 | 3 |
| Labor and management policy | 10 | 17 | 2 | 6 | 6 | 8 | 17 | 11 | 1 | 3 |
| Resources and conservation policy | 2 | 3 | 3 | 9 | 5 | 7 | 5 | 3 | 0 | 0 |
| Health, education, and welfare policy | 4 | 7 | 2 | 6 | 6 | 8 | 10 | 6 | 12 | 34 |
| Fiscal and budgetary policy | 9 | 15 | 0 | 0 | 0 | 0 | 2 | 1 | 0 | 0 |
| Civil liberties[11] | 4 | 7 | 1 | 3 | 1 | 3 | 18 | 12 | 4 | 10 |
| Other[12] | 9 | 15 | 16 | 50 | 40 | 53 | 69 | 45 | 13 | 36 |

11. Includes both internal security and civil rights.
12. Includes transportation, communications, civil-military relations, and general policy studies.

TABLE II-11. Distribution of articles in "Judicial affairs" category in general American political science journals by class for given time periods

| Articles by class | 1909–1914 | | 1925–1929 | | 1939–1941 | | 1952–1954 | | 1969–1971 | |
|---|---|---|---|---|---|---|---|---|---|---|
| | Number | Percent | Number | Percent | Number | Percent | Number | Percent | Number | Percent |
| Judicial affairs | 3 | – | 8 | – | 17 | 100 | 15 | 100 | 22 | 100 |
| Case studies and biography | 0 | 0 | 0 | 0 | 3 | 18 | 4 | 27 | 1 | 5 |
| Judicial organs and administration | 1 | – | 4 | – | 7 | 41 | 3 | 20 | 3 | 14 |
| Judicial behavior and activities | 1 | – | 4 | – | 7 | 41 | 5 | 33 | 15 | 68 |
| Construction of general theory of judicial behavior | 1 | – | 0 | 0 | 0 | 0 | 3 | 20 | 3 | 14 |

TABLE II-12. Distribution of articles in "Public law and jurisprudence" category in general American political science journals by class for given time periods

| Articles by class | 1909–1914 | | 1925–1929 | | 1939–1941 | | 1952–1954 | | 1969–1971 | |
|---|---|---|---|---|---|---|---|---|---|---|
| | Number | Percent | Number | Percent | Number | Percent | Number | Percent | Number | Percent |
| Public law and jurisprudence | 14 | — | 26 | 100 | 34 | 100 | 40 | 100 | 10 | — |
| Public law | 11 | — | 20 | 77 | 22 | 65 | 24 | 60 | 3 | — |
| Jurisprudence | 3 | — | 6 | 23 | 12 | 35 | 16 | 40 | 7 | — |

TABLE II-13. Distribution of articles in "Study of political science" category in general American political science journals by class for given time periods

| Articles by class | 1909–1914 | | 1925–1929 | | 1939–1941 | | 1952–1954 | | 1969–1971 | |
|---|---|---|---|---|---|---|---|---|---|---|
| | Number | Percent | Number | Percent | Number | Percent | Number | Percent | Number | Percent |
| Study of political science | 8 | — | 8 | — | 9 | — | 17 | 100 | 8 | — |
| Teaching of political science and citizenship education | 6 | — | 4 | — | 3 | — | 2 | 12 | 3 | — |
| Research trends and bibliography | 2 | — | 4 | — | 6 | — | 15 | 88 | 5 | — |

TABLE III. Percentage distribution of political scientists by field for given years of professional experience, 1970

| Field | Years of Professional Experience | | | | | |
|---|---|---|---|---|---|---|
| | 1 year or less | 2–4 years | 5–9 years | 10–14 years | 15–19 years | 20–24 years |
| Total | 100% | 100% | 100% | 100% | 100% | 100% |
| Political theory | 7.4 | 7.7 | 7.9 | 6.3 | 7.1 | 9.4 |
| Methodology— political science | 5.2 | 4.2 | 2.5 | 1.7 | 1.8 | 0.1 |
| Public policy formation and impacts | 6.9 | 6.8 | 6.8 | 8.4 | 8.1 | 8.9 |
| Public administration | 7.4 | 8.2 | 10.0 | 15.3 | 16.0 | 22.0 |
| Political stability, instability, and change | 3.5 | 4.3 | 4.0 | 3.0 | 2.9 | 1.9 |
| Foreign and cross-national political institutions and behavior | 28.0 | 23.8 | 25.0 | 19.5 | 17.8 | 13.5 |
| U.S. political institutions, processes, and behavior | 22.3 | 26.0 | 26.0 | 23.7 | 26.0 | 26.0 |
| International law, organization, and politics | 13.2 | 12.4 | 12.3 | 15.0 | 12.7 | 11.6 |
| Political science, other | 5.9 | 6.6 | 5.6 | 7.2 | 7.5 | 6.0 |

*Source:* Table A-52, p. 212, National Science Foundation, 1971.
*Note:* Because of rounding, columns may not total 100%.

younger political scientists; but this change must be interpreted in light of the separatist tendency of public administration. The evidence that "Political stability, instability, and change" shows comparatively little interest for any age group is difficult to interpret, because the category (however important) is not a customary "field."

The two areas that attract the greatest number of political scientists are foreign and domestic government. The former has been steadily increasing its share of political scientists since World War II. Interest in domestic government is relatively steady between cohorts, following something of a cyclical pattern. Interest in international affairs shows some decline since World War II; but perhaps this, too, represents more a tendency to separatism than an absolute decline in interest.

Table IV indicates the strong pedagogical orientation of political science

| Years of Professional Experience | | | | No report of years of experience |
|---|---|---|---|---|
| 25–29 years | 30–34 years | 35–39 years | 40 or more years | |
| 100% | 100% | 100% | 100% | 100% |
| 5.6 | 4.8 | 5.7 | 5.5 | 7.4 |
| 1.4 | 1.7 | 0.1 | – | 1.2 |
| 11.3 | 13.1 | 7.3 | 6.4 | 7.4 |
| 20.7 | 24.5 | 22.0 | 26.6 | 12.3 |
| 1.4 | 0.1 | 1.6 | 4.6 | 3.6 |
| 12.7 | 10.9 | 11.4 | 7.3 | 19.8 |
| 21.1 | 18.3 | 22.1 | 26.6 | 24.6 |
| 18.8 | 18.8 | 25.2 | 11.9 | 13.9 |
| 7.0 | 7.0 | 4.9 | 11.0 | 9.8 |

and the difference between fields in this respect. In all fields except public administration, teaching is reported as the primary work activity.

Table V again indicates the pedagogic orientation of political science. For political scientists in all ten age groups, educational institutions are the chief employer—by a significant margin. Employment outside academia is highest for those with 20 to 35 years of professional experience.

*"Social Science Manpower": Comparative Perspectives*

The data in Tables VI through X permit some comparisons between political science and four other social-behavioral disciplines: anthropology, economics, psychology, and sociology. The data are derived from *American Science Manpower, 1970* (National Science Foundation, 1971), from the 1970 annual report on National Science Foundation funding for research projects, and from the central offices of the several national disciplinary associations. The limitations of the data are obvious. Those pertaining to *American Science Manpower, 1970*, were noted above. In two tables data from this

TABLE IV. Percentage distribution of political scientists by primary work activity for given fields, 1970

|  |  | Primary Work Activity | | |
| --- | --- | --- | --- | --- |
| Field | Total | Research and development | Management or administration | Teaching |
| Political theory | 100% | 8 | 7 | 74 |
| Methodology—political science | 100% | 24 | 20 | 39 |
| Public policy formation and impacts | 100% | 15 | 23 | 45 |
| Public administration | 100% | 8 | 45 | 32 |
| Political stability, instability, and change | 100% | 17 | 11 | 52 |
| Foreign and cross-national political institutions and behavior | 100% | 13 | 8 | 65 |
| U.S. political institutions, processes, and behavior | 100% | 9 | 13 | 65 |
| International law, organization, and politics | 100% | 9 | 10 | 67 |
| Political science, other | 100% | 7 | 17 | 49 |

*Source:* Table A-50, p. 206, National Science Foundation, 1971.
*Note:* Because of rounding, rows may not total 100%.

source are combined with data from the two other sources.[5] Still, interpreted with caution the data are instructive in various ways.

Table VI indicates that political science is a middle-sized social science discipline, roughly comparable to economics and sociology, much smaller than psychology, much larger than anthropology. Table VI also offers evidence on the question raised above as to the representativeness of the political science respondents to the National Science Foundation survey. Only 39.1% of political scientists participated in the 1970 survey, presumably the more "scientifically" inclined. (However, what would account for the spread between the economists—95.3%—and the anthropologists—28.8%?)

Table VII indicates comparatively the primary work activity of the five

| | Primary Work Activity | | | | |
|---|---|---|---|---|---|
| Consulting | Exploration, Forecasting, reporting | Other | Not employed | No report of work activity |
|---|---|---|---|---|
| – | – | 2 | 6 | 3 |
| 2 | 8 | 1 | 3 | 3 |
| 2 | 3 | 5 | 4 | 3 |
| 5 | 3 | 4 | 2 | 2 |
| 2 | 5 | 4 | 7 | 3 |
| – | 2 | 2 | 7 | 2 |
| – | 2 | 2 | 6 | 3 |
| – | 2 | 2 | 6 | 3 |
| 1 | 4 | 5 | 10 | 6 |

disciplines. Political scientists more than any of the other four consider their primary work to be teaching. The second most frequent primary work activity is management and administration; in this they are roughly comparable to the other disciplines. But political science is lowest in the proportion of its members reporting research and development as the primary work activity.

Table VIII bears on place of work and indicates that more than three-fourths of political scientists work in educational institutions. But in this there is no striking contrast with the other disciplines; more than half of those in each of the other disciplines work in academia. Of all political scientists, 6.8% work in the federal government, 3.4% in government on other levels, 3.3% in nonprofit corporations, and 1.8% in business and in-

TABLE V. Percentage distribution of political scientists by type of employer for given years of professional experience, 1970

| Years of professional experience | Total | Type of Employer | | |
| --- | --- | --- | --- | --- |
| | | Educational institutions | Federal government | Other government |
| 1 or less | 100% | 70.6 | 3.5 | 3.5 |
| 2 to 4 | 100% | 76.3 | 4.2 | 3.6 |
| 5 to 9 | 100% | 82.1 | 4.8 | 3.3 |
| 10 to 14 | 100% | 76.8 | 6.4 | 4.0 |
| 15 to 19 | 100% | 77.8 | 6.6 | 4.9 |
| 20 to 24 | 100% | 76.5 | 8.1 | 5.2 |
| 25 to 29 | 100% | 67.3 | 10.9 | 4.7 |
| 30 to 34 | 100% | 72.8 | 11.6 | 2.7 |
| 35 to 39 | 100% | 72.9 | 3.4 | 3.4 |
| 40 or more | 100% | 70.4 | 3.7 | 1.9 |
| No report | 100% | 78.6 | 3.9 | 1.7 |

*Source:* Table A-10, p. 75, National Science Foundation, 1971.
Note: Because of rounding, rows may not total 100%.

Table VI. Distribution of association members, NSF registrants in 1970, and employment status for selected social sciences

| Discipline | Number of members in the national association (1) | Number of registrants with NSF in 1970 (2) | Percent of national membership who registered with NSF in 1970 | Number of registrants employed full-time (3) |
| --- | --- | --- | --- | --- |
| Political science | 16,600 | 6,493 | 39.1 | 5,552 |
| Anthropology | 4,600 | 1,325 | 28.8 | 1,188 |
| Economics | 14,052 | 13,386 | 95.3 | 11,959 |
| Psychology | 34,000 | 26,271 | 77.3 | 23,309 |
| Sociology | 10,950 | 7,658 | 69.9 | 5,943 |

*Sources:* (1) The latest association records as of March, 1973; (2) p. 31, National Science Foundation, 1971; (3) p. 43, National Science Foundation, 1971.

|  | Type of Employer ||||||  |
|---|---|---|---|---|---|---|---|
| Non-profit organization | Industry and business | Self-employed | Military | Other | Not employed | No report of type of employer |
| 3.2 | 3.0 | –   | 1.7 | 0.1 | 11.5 | 2.1 |
| 3.1 | 1.2 | 0.1 | 1.9 | 0.9 | 7.8  | 0.7 |
| 2.1 | 1.2 | 0.3 | 1.2 | 0.9 | 3.2  | 0.6 |
| 3.3 | 3.3 | 0.9 | 2.3 | 0.3 | 2.3  | 0.3 |
| 3.9 | 2.8 | 0.7 | .7  | 0.9 | 1.1  | 0.6 |
| 4.6 | 1.5 | 0.4 | 1.5 | 1.0 | 1.0  | 0.2 |
| 4.7 | 3.8 | –   | 2.4 | 1.4 | 2.8  | 1.9 |
| 5.8 | 2.2 | 1.3 | 1.8 | 0.4 | 0.1  | 0.4 |
| 6.8 | 1.7 | 3.4 | –   | 0.8 | 5.9  | 1.7 |
| 3.7 | 0.9 | 0.9 | –   | 0.9 | 17.6 | –   |
| 3.2 | 1.0 | 0.3 | 0.8 | 0.6 | 7.6  | 2.2 |

TABLE VII. Percentage distribution of NSF registrants in 1970 by primary work activity for given social science disciplines

| Discipline | Teaching | Research and development | Management and administration | Other |
|---|---|---|---|---|
| Political science | 58.3 | 10.5 | 16.5 | 14.7 |
| Anthropology | 55.7 | 21.2 | 11.2 | 11.9 |
| Economics | 39.5 | 20.5 | 21.9 | 18.1 |
| Psychology | 25.9 | 23.2 | 18.7 | 32.2 |
| Sociology | 51.2 | 18.6 | 13.7 | 16.5 |

Source: Table A-12, pp. 80-81, National Science Foundation, 1971.

TABLE VIII. Percentage distribution of NSF registrants in 1970 by type of employer for given social science disciplines

| Discipline | Educational institution | Federal, civilian and military | Other government | Non-profit | Business and industry | Other |
|---|---|---|---|---|---|---|
| Political science | 76.9 | 6.8 | 3.4 | 3.3 | 1.8 | 7.8 |
| Anthropology | 80.7 | 2.3 | 1.0 | 2.7 | 0.8 | 12.5 |
| Economics | 58.6 | 12.2 | 5.1 | 3.9 | 13.6 | 6.6 |
| Psychology | 56.5 | 6.8 | 9.7 | 7.8 | 7.3 | 11.9 |
| Sociology | 74.0 | 3.5 | 3.9 | 4.5 | 1.6 | 12.5 |

*Source:* Table A-8, pp. 55-56, National Science Foundation, 1971.

dustry. This pattern is somewhat similar to those of anthropology and sociology but rather different from those of economics and psychology.

Table IX indicates the distribution of all federal "grants and awards" to the five disciplines in 1970. (Data for the *level* of funding are not given for recipient disciplines as such. Hence caution in interpretation is necessary; but Table X provides at least partial clarification.) Political science is fourth in the number of members receiving any type of federal financial support. The rank order of the social sciences is *not* changed by removing those who work directly for the federal government. (Significantly, economists far outnumber political scientists in employment by the federal government, both in absolute numbers and in relative ratios.)

Table X confirms that political science has fared relatively poorly in generating federal financial support for its research activities. Of course, all the disciplines receive research funding from a wide variety of sources other than the federal government, and for political science during the past two decades, funding from the Ford Foundation and the Social Science Research Council has been significant. But the table does indicate the relative levels of support from one highly important source. Perhaps the relatively poor showing for political science is related to its late acceptance by the National Science Foundation as a "science" (a story much too complicated to be recounted here) and is due for rapid improvement. But as recently as 1970, at least, political science received the smallest amount of money as a discipline, received the smallest amount per capita, and had the fewest projects funded.

In sum: As a social science, political science attracts its "share" of adherents; but there is reason to believe that cleavage along a "science/nonscience" line is particularly significant for the discipline. Political scientists for the most part work in academic environments and identify their primary work activity as teaching, a pattern more like anthropology

TABLE IX. Distribution of federal financial support for selected social sciences

| Discipline | Number of registrants receiving federal support in 1970 (1) | Percent of registrants employed full-time receiving federal support* | Number of registrants working for federal government (civilian and military) (2) | Number of registrants receiving federal funds through contracts or grants in 1970 (1) | Percent of registrants employed full-time receiving federal funds through contracts or grants in 1970† |
|---|---|---|---|---|---|
| Political science | 1,516 | 27.3 | 442 | 1,074 | 19.3 |
| Anthropology | 417 | 35.1 | 31 | 386 | 32.5 |
| Economics | 4,660 | 39.0 | 1,637 | 3,023 | 25.3 |
| Psychology | 10,060 | 43.2 | 1,795 | 8,265 | 35.5 |
| Sociology | 2,297 | 38.7 | 273 | 2,024 | 34.1 |

*Sources:* (1) p. 31, National Science Foundation, 1971; (2) pp. 45-46, National Science Foundation, 1971.
\* Percentage derived by dividing column 1 of Table IX by column 4 of Table VI.
† Percentage derived by dividing column 4 of Table IX by column 4 of Table VI.

TABLE X. Distribution of National Science Foundation grants and awards for research projects in selected social sciences

| Discipline | Total, 1970 NSF support for research (in dollars) (1) | 1970 NSF support for research per association member in 1973 (in dollars) (2) | 1970 NSF support for research per registrant in 1970 (in dollars) (2) | Number of projects funded in 1970 (1) | Mean funding per project in 1970 (in dollars) |
|---|---|---|---|---|---|
| Political science | 1,200,072 | 72.29 | 184.83 | 45 | 26,668.27 |
| Anthropology | 3,554,352 | 772.69 | 2,682.53 | 160 | 22,214.70 |
| Economics | 4,539,150 | 323.03 | 339.10 | 95 | 47,780.53 |
| Psychology | n/a | n/a | n/a | n/a | n/a |
| Sociology | 3,558,990* | 325.02 | 464.74 | 86 | 41,383.60 |

*Sources:* (1) National Science Foundation, *Grants and Awards for the Fiscal Year Ending June 30, 1970*, Washington, D.C., U.S. Government Printing Office, 1971, pp. 35-42 (totals via additions); (2) see Table VI for association members and registrants.
\* Includes support for social psychology projects.
n/a-data not available

and sociology (the smaller disciplines) than like economics and psychology (the larger disciplines). Political science has been less successful than the other disciplines in gaining financial support for research from the federal government; but this circumstance needs to be interpreted in the light of history and in the context of many factors, some of which are not even mentioned in this essay.

## POLITICAL SCIENCE VIEWED INTERNATIONALLY

To give a brief survey of political science outside the United States proved to be the most vexing task imposed by the preparation of this essay. There are many sources of data, but often they are incomplete and not current. Characteristically—for reasons that are understandable and forgivable—collections of data for the world as a whole or any substantial part of it are undiscriminating and likely to be misleading. Differences in language, tradition, national "style," and ideology present severe problems of accuracy of knowledge and comparability of data. Above all, there is the problem of definition and perspective: What shall be called "political science" and by what warrant? The aim of inclusiveness and dictates of prudence lead to heaping in one basket labeled "fruit" apples, oranges, bananas, tomatoes, corn, coconuts, rice, and potatoes.

In the introductory section the legitimacy of a broad interpretation of "political science" was recognized and, indeed, argued. Premodern polities had and contemporary non-Western polities have political science, i.e., political knowledge. Also it may be reemphasized that American political science, though "something in size, content and method unique in Western intellectual history" (to repeat the words of Bernard Crick), owes incalculable debts to Europe. In its origins and in every stage of its development it has been inspired and enriched by European thought, as the account above testifies. Indeed, the record of influence and contributions is broader, involving the sweep of history and intercultural borrowings. In short, to speak of the growth of political science internationally is not simply to speak to the export and installation of a product labeled "Made in the U.S.A."

So much prefaced, the question posed is: What is the extent and status of self-conscious political inquiry of the type developed in the West and particularly in the United States? Some general observations are an appropriate beginning.

Since World War II the notion of a self-conscious political science, conceived in the singular (as against the "political sciences"), independent in status (as against subordination to or inclusion in other social sciences or law), and aspiring toward the type of scientific base and achievement of the natural sciences, has been slowly gaining acceptance in a significant number of countries. Important in the process of diffusion and acceptance has been the strong influence exerted by the United States in much of the world in the post-World War II period. Specifically, this influence has often been exerted through the exchange of scholars and professionals in the Fulbright and other (often foundation) exchange programs, and through programs of aid and technical assistance. The creation, via UNESCO, of the International Political Science Association, both provided an important channel for American influence (given the preponderance of American political scientists and the ease and attractiveness of foreign travel) and became itself a major source of interaction and influence.

Generally, the spread of political science has been forwarded by the spread and influence of the same forces that favored the growth of political science in the United States. For these forces "modernization" may be the best shorthand notation: industrialization, specialization, secularization, and so forth. Such forces have abetted the spread not simply of political science but of behavioral and statistical modes, of contemporary social science in general, that is, of the complex of ideas, attitudes, and methodologies which envelop and support political science.

Claiming a superior political knowledge and improved techniques for studying political reality, political science encounters resistance (often open hostility) from established elites concerned with studying and teaching the political, especially in the universities; and as a result, political science characteristically finds its home either in institutes or foundations separate from (or only loosely affiliated with) the older universities or in newer (often regional or provincial) universities, in which tradition is weaker and new experiments can more readily be undertaken. On the other hand, elites (including communist elites) may offer a qualified entrance, seeking what instrumental utility new tools may offer, or perhaps calculating that there may be a competitive loss if the "game" is not entered.

*A Geographical View*

Not surprisingly, western and central Europe evidence fair strength and considerable promise. British political science remains heavily weighted toward historical-philosophical-humanistic interests, but there is also a significant amount of political science in the newer idiom. (The more traditional view is represented by *Political Studies* [1953 to the present]; newer currents are better represented in *British Journal of Political Science* [inaugurated in 1971]). The newer political science (as against "the political sciences" and public law) has made considerable headway in France, some progress in Italy, very little in Spain. Here and there in West Germany significant progress has been made against deeply entrenched traditional approaches; little headway has been made in Austria. Switzerland is enigmatic: deeply traditional but still the base of influential "modern" social science. The Netherlands is moving rapidly and impressively; Belgium has made a start. There are important "enclaves" in the Scandinavian countries; and Sweden, where political studies have long been recognized as such (a Chair in Rhetoric and Politics was established as early as 1622), is especially strong.

In Russia and eastern Europe, political science experiences not only the constraints of the public law tradition but those of Marxist ideology and communist regime. In Russia these constraints are effective, for the most part, in preventing the rise of political science in the Western ("bourgeois") sense. Poland and Yugoslavia, however (and Czechoslovakia briefly, until 1968), are "freer" and, in differing ways, support a significant quantum of modern social science, including political science.

In Asia it is Japan that leads; despite the strength of traditionalism and law, an impressive effort is being made. India, combining indigenous materials and mingled British and American influences, makes a significant effort. Several of the other countries, including the Philippines, Malaysia, Pakistan, and South Korea, have at least the beginning of modern political science. The People's Republic of China has political studies in its own style, of course, but no (known) political science in the present meaning.

For a number of reasons, including the proximity of the United States, Canada mounts an impressive effort. Of the historic "settled" British dominions, Australia follows Canada. New Zealand and South Africa, in very different ways, have some teaching and research in political science. In Latin America, political science is generally in thrall to law, though there are occasional spurts of significant achievement.

In the Near East, Turkey probably leads, though the small Israeli effort is impressive. There are "islands" of political science in the Arab countries but only that. The same or a similar generalization can be made for Africa.

After this horseback survey, both caveats and apologies are in order. The perspective, to repeat, is not only Western but that of contemporary political science in the United States. No attempt has been made to judge the significance or achievements of political science of other types and in context. Judgments made for countries or areas were rough, and they were qualitative only in the sense indicated; outstanding work occurs wherever it occurs, and it occurs in many places. An adequate treatment of political science worldwide would require a lengthy book.

The following data must serve to conclude this brief treatment. A recent census of National Political Science Associations (in *PS*, Spring, 1972) indicates that thirty-one countries have one or more political science associations of some sort. But "of some sort" must be emphasized, since there is great heterogeneity (if not outright incompatibility). Approximately half of the national associations have an association publication of some sort. But the publications do not necessarily represent all political science—of whatever type—for the countries concerned. The UNESCO *World List of Social Science Periodicals* lists nearly two hundred journals that, on a *broad* interpretation, might be classified as political science journals. Considerably less than half of them would be "political science" in a sense recognizable to most of the membership of the American Political Science Association. Only about one-third of the associations hold meetings.

The International Political Science Association was founded in 1949 under UNESCO sponsorship. Formally, the Association is composed of national political science associations, but individual memberships are also possible. The Association holds triennial congresses and publishes *International Political Science Abstracts* and the *International Bibliography of Political Science*. Individual membership now (1972) stands at about 450. Although it has individual members in many countries, the great majority of individual members are western European and American. In fact, nearly half are American.

## *TOWARD A POSTBEHAVIORAL POLITICAL SCIENCE?*

It is hardly open to dispute that the tendencies collectively known as behavioralism, in the ascendant in the fifties, reached a position approaching dominance in American political science in the sixties. To be sure, political science was not reconstructed entire. Great numbers of political scientists remained unconvinced, even antagonistic. Many "nonbehavioral" activities continued; many deep-flowing currents (some generated long before American political science) continued largely undisturbed. But those known as "behavioralists" became prominent, probably dominant, in the affairs of the political science associations and in most of the leading faculties of political science. Books, journals, convention programs, research grants—many other indices testify to the vigor and wide acceptance of behavioralism.

As the sixties drew toward a close, however, behavioralism received a new challenge. This new challenge had its sources in the intellectual ferment and social-political turbulence that marked American life in the middle and late sixties and continued, if diminished, into the seventies. In general, the new challenge sprang from the two phenomena known as the New Left and the Counterculture. To speak thus in categorical terms is to oversimplify and risk misunderstanding, but an explication of recent history, taking account of the complexities of events and the subtleties of ideas, is beyond the scope of this essay.

In the late sixties the new dissent centered in the creation within the American Political Science Association of a so-called Caucus for a New Political Science. The Caucus (predominantly but by no means exclusively younger political scientists) acted vigorously, sometimes stridently, in an attempt to nullify or reverse dominant patterns of political science. That no major victories, in terms of election of officers or control of Association affairs, went to the dissidents is not necessarily a measure of effect, especially long-term, or of the validity (or invalidity) of the ideas and actions advanced.

The term "postbehavioral" came into use to designate the mood and programmatic intent of the new dissenters. Those who would accept this designation vary greatly among themselves, but some of the main tenets and tendencies can be indicated.

### *"Postbehavioral" Tenets and Tendencies*

Political science has become too narrowly defined, too "professional," too much identified with the established order. Political scientists, personally and collectively, should be more concerned with "values," with issues of justice, freedom, and equality, with political activity. In a period of stress, turmoil, and gross inequities, it is irresponsible to carry on "as usual" in academic detachment. At minimum, political scientists need to be concerned with issues of public policy and political reform; perhaps they should become engaged with issues of radical sociopolitical reconstruction.

Driven by the ambition to become a genuine science, political science has constricted and crippled itself philosophically and methodologically. The fact-value distinction has encouraged an undesirable foreshortening of vision and a moral insensitivity. Emphasis on methodology borrowed from the natural sciences has resulted in much research that is trivial—"elegant," perhaps, but inconsequential, even for its ostensible purpose of helping to create a science of politics.

A concentration on scientific philosophy (knowledge of which is not necessary to "do" political science) and on scientific methodology (which pertains only to methods of proof, not to the more important matters of discovery or creation) has squeezed the vitality from political science. No longer the Master Science of the Greeks, it concerns itself with a narrow range of phenomena that lend themselves to treatment by approved methods. In fact, political science is becoming apolitical.

Political science needs to become imaginative, creative (even playful), open to the world. Modern natural science, after all, is but a "school of consciousness," one among many. It represents a monopolistic expropriation of the meaning of "science," i.e., knowledge in its original sense. The monopoly must be broken.

Such views were expressed not just orally but in articles, monographs, and books. (Graham and Carey, 1972; Kariel, 1972; Marini, 1971; Surkin and Wolfe, 1970; Easton, 1969; McCoy and Playford, 1967) A newly founded journal, *Politics and Society*, though covering more than "political science," reflects the new currents. It seeks to provide an alternative to "the leading professional social science journals" which "continue to be obsessed with technique at the expense of politics."

*Effects and Implications*

Immediately, the effect of the formation of the Caucus for a New Political Science was to complicate the politics of political science. The interests of political scientists have always been too diverse, the opinions too varied and subtle, to permit division into a small number of sharply defined "parties." But the controversies concerning behavioralism (like the controversies of the twenties and early thirties) did create a certain bipolarity between those holding more traditional interests and opinions and those seeking to advance the cause of science. Probably by the mid-sixties there was decreasing tension and controversy. After years of sometimes heated disputation, the situation could perhaps best be conceived as a spectrum, with the position of the majority of political scientists on the philosophic-methodological issues represented by the central bands.

The rise of the Caucus, the events in the historical context that caused and accompanied it, the opinions it represented, and the issues it forwarded served to complicate issues and confuse the politics of political science—and to provide material for those with a taste for irony. In a formal sense, the positions argued by Caucus members often were those of the traditionalists (e.g., the importance of values, a loose as against a strict interpretation of science). On the other hand, the political causes they ardently espoused were likely to be abhorrent to the traditionalists—but attractive to many behavioralists.

On the crucial question of the nature of the American Political Science Association—whether it should become a more active force in political life (e.g., by passing resolutions on prominent issues of the day, "educating," and lobbying) or remain essentially neutral, focusing on disciplinary-professional concerns—the decisions have turned in the latter direction. On this question traditionalists and behavioralists (now become "establishment" and in that sense traditional) have been able to muster a substantial majority.

The long-range significance of the "postbehavioral" forces is another matter, complicated and problematical, hidden from view. Perhaps from the vantage point of 1980 the rise of the Caucus and the proclamation of a "postbehavioral sensibility" will appear but a temporary aberration, another detour in a march toward a more scientific politics. Perhaps a new balance of forces will emerge, a rearrangement of professional ends and means, motives and techniques, in which science is cultivated less for its own sake and used more in a conscious attempt to realize preferred values. Relevant to either of these possibilities is the fact that many of the recent dissidents are younger political scientists well schooled in scientific philosophy and well trained in behavioral research methods.

Whatever develops, it will develop in relation to cues and commands from the environment within which political science exists. The events and movements in recent political science have had their counterparts in the other social sciences. Indeed, they are a part of currents of thought and patterns of activity that also affect the humanities and the well-established natural sciences. Beyond these are the complexities and imponderables of unfolding history. The prudent will avoid prediction.

## THE FACES OF POLITICAL SCIENCE

If anything is clear from the foregoing, it is that political science is not a single, simple thing. Rather, it is an aggregation of varied interests and activities in a complex relationship with its environment—or its several changing environments. No doubt it has significant aspects that are not explored in this essay: political science as technology or as ideology, for example; or political science as a symbolic system; or as itself a political system (or subsystem). Perhaps these aspects deserve more than the hints and asides they have received.

Be that as it may, this essay can appropriately end with a focusing on five aspects of political science of undoubted importance. To some extent this presentation will be recapitulation and summary. But some new data will be included; and with good fortune, the understanding of political science will be forwarded by a more careful delineation of categories and their interrelation.

### Political Science as Tradition

The early part of this essay presumably made it indisputably clear that political science has traditional aspects. Political science exists in the context of a specific history. In important ways this history is a living presence. A heritage that is both intellectual and institutional inevitably contributes shape and color to political science.

Probably the heritage of the past, in one way and another, is more important for political science than for the other social sciences. Certainly this is true of the literary-philosophical heritage. No other social science approaches political science in the antiquity and richness of its historical literature. Some hold this to be a disadvantage and are apt to cite Alfred North Whitehead's dictum that a science that hesitates to forget its founders is lost. Others respond that a science that forgets its founders may also be lost, or they cite Shakespeare's "What's past is prologue." Whoever wishes a demonstration of the tensions and ambiguities posed for political science by its heritage need look no further than the *International Encyclopedia of the Social Sciences*, wherein the most eminent political scientists take diverse and even contrary positions on the relationship of classical political thought to contemporary scientific ambitions.

We cannot put tradition aside simply by deciding to do so. It is the past that gives us our language of politics, the categories by which the political is perceived and understood; and to devise a new language poses heroic difficulties. To do so as a scholarly scientific exercise can serve certain limited purposes. (To some extent, for certain purposes, political science does so.) But our political tradition, now become current culture and institutions, would remain largely unaffected by such an academic effort. The "stuff" political science addresses has a stubborn, intractable quality imparted to it by its history.

From one point of view, political science is a "natural" science. People, as well as objects and artifacts within the purview of political science, are of course physical phenomena. But political science is also inevitably a "culture" science, which must deal, however it can, with the intangibles of culture. These intangibles also may be held to be a part of the natural order and thus amenable to the methods of science. But even if this is granted in principle, the solution to crucial methodological problems does not necessarily follow. What language of politics is there, what language of politics can there be, that is not culture-bound? What is true of the "political animal" *qua* political animal, apart from the circumstances of any particular time, place, and culture? At less global levels, the questions posed are faced in day-to-day political science, especially when it turns its attention beyond national boundaries.

## Political Science as Discipline

Discussions of political science by political scientists characteristically refer to it as both a "discipline" and a "profession"; a writer often shifts from one to the other term from page to page or even within the same paragraph. Political scientists apparently believe that political science is both a discipline and a profession (in addition to being a science), and (or) that there is little difference between the two. Is this point of view warranted?

Etymology is of limited value here, but it is a legitimate starting point in addressing this question. "Discipline" derives fairly directly from the Latin *disciplina*—instruction, tuition. Medieval and early modern history add layers of association to the core meaning of teaching-and-learning. Moral rectitude, proper conduct, and operating skills, as well as cognitive knowledge, are a part of discipline in church, university, guild, and military contexts. But secularization and the rise of modern science act in turn to strip away the medieval and early modern associations. In the university, *Lehrfreiheit* and *Lernfreiheit* serve to reduce the authority of received knowledge and proliferate "fields" of knowledge. In common usage today a discipline means, both simply and loosely, "a subject that is taught," "a field of study."

Plainly, then, in common usage political science is a discipline. It is a subject that is taught; it is recognized as a field of study. Pragmatically, it has successfully asserted itself, it exists, and there is no important threat to its continuance. In leading colleges and universities it has departmental status with its accompanying (substantial though not complete) autonomy. It is (usually) independent from other social sciences, and its departmental status is similar to "disciplines" in the humanities and the natural sciences. But then—one must quickly note—departmental status goes also to such enterprises as physical education, home economics, and journalism, which are not ordinarily regarded, even by their practitioners, as disciplines.

When political scientists refer to political science as a discipline, they do have in mind the fact that it exists as a recognized field of study, has departmental status, and is formally equal to cognate fields of study. Quite plainly however, this pragmatic success and commonsensical meaning is not *all* they have in mind. Much of the foregoing evidences that there would be considerable diversity and some disagreement in the responses political scientists would give to the question: What claim does political science have to disciplinary status? But there would be wide agreement on certain matters, centrally on the assertions that "the political" is *important* enough to deserve concentrated study, and that it is both empirically and analytically distinguishable enough from other phenomena to warrant *separate* study.

The arguments and evidence that would be adduced in support of these contentions would relate, for the most part, to emerging "professional" qualities and—especially—to a claim that political science has attained or is in the process of attaining the status of a genuine theoretical science. This is the argument, for example, of David Easton in his treatment of "Political Science" in the *International Encyclopedia of the Social Sciences* (1968, pp. 282–298, p. 289). He begins by positing an "identity crisis" for political science at midcentury but then continues, "Through the efforts to solve this identity crisis it has begun to show evidence of emerging as an autonomous and independent discipline with a systematic theoretical structure of its own. The factor that has contributed most to this end has been the reception and integration of the methods of science into the core of the discipline." This statement illustrates a widely shared belief. It also illustrates the soft and slippery nature of "discipline": While political science shows evidence of *becoming* a discipline (first sentence), it already *is* a discipline with a core (second sentence).

### Political Science as Profession

Can political science be designated as a profession? In what ways is it a profession, in what ways not? These are questions it is difficult to answer because it is difficult to know what we are talking about. Here (as against discipline) it is not for lack of an extensive serious literature. Rather, perusal of the literature brings as much bewilderment as clarification.

Some of the difficulties in achieving a clear focus pertain to differences in history and thus to the empirical phenomena designated as professional. Whereas "divinity, law, and physick" are by wide agreement the archetypical professions, in the modern period there is divergence in the evolution of the professions on the Continent and in Britain. On the Continent the professions grew up in close association with the universities and the state. In Britain they grew up outside the universities and beyond the state. The United States inherits parts of both traditions (including the writings that interpret the two traditions), mixes them, and of course adds distinctive new ingredients.

The rise of modern science presents a major complication. Some of the alleged characteristics of professionalism antedate modern science and (or) seem to have no necessary relationship with it. On the other hand, the ideas and institutions of science have become so intermingled (especially in the university) with professionalism that some interpreters effectively equate the two. All interpreters find "knowledge" to be essential to the definition (or understanding) of professionalism. Must this knowledge meet certain epistemological and methodological criteria? Or are sociological characteristics, e.g., group norms and service to clients, determinative?

Some of the difficulties relate to perennial methodological problems in the social sciences. Most of the treatments of professionalism utilize an ideal-typical or attribute-cluster methodology. That is, from the empirical phenomena presumptively or ostensibly "professional," they select for attention (and designate as defining) those characteristics that seem most general and important. But what is an essential characteristic for one may be marginal or irrelevant for another. A persistent difficulty—somewhat related, somewhat different—is that the "is" and the "ought" are both involved. It is widely believed (by professionals and nonprofessionals) that professionals ought to act in certain ways, e.g., place client-interest above self-interest. Does the "ought" become an "is"? How and for what purposes?

Some social scientists find ideal-typical and attribute-cluster study of the professions to be of little value or perhaps even a misleading search for "essence." They would reject whatever cannot be "operationalized"; or they find that such approaches miss important aspects of social reality, or that they divert attention (especially by including altruistic "oughts") from the important matter of the distribution and exercise of power in society.

Such doubts and objections are not without force—obviously. But putting them aside, what help does the considerable body of writing on professions and professionalism give in addressing the question: Is political science a profession?

The most general and important attributes of a profession appear to be the following (here I use the methodology of the writers I survey, and the result is subject to the reservations noted).

1. The profession possesses a body of knowledge. This knowledge is, e.g., "generalized and systematic," "esoteric or difficult." It may consist of "abstract principles arrived at by scientific research and logical analysis." The

body of knowledge may be a "monopoly." In any event those who hold it make claims of extraordinary knowledge.

2. Inculcation of the body of knowledge comes from prolonged study and (or) socialization in the profession.

3. The practitioners, i.e., those who are already professionals, exercise a general surveillance over the body of knowledge, assist in and supervise the training of new professionals, articulate and enforce norms of professional behavior. Customarily the practitioners are organized in an association (or associations), and many of their professional functions are exercised through the association (or associations).

4. The profession is in some sense public. This public quality both confers privileges and imposes obligations. The former primarily constitute a certain autonomy in control of matters pertaining to the profession. The primary obligation is to render certain services, objectively and impartially.

Other characteristics are often specified: thus, that the profession have a place of "esteem" in society; that it have a set of symbols and symbolic functions; that it have a relationship with the university; that there be professional-client relationships.

Patently no unequivocal answer is possible to the question: Is political science a profession? Before one addresses the question, however, it is appropriate to adduce additional data regarding its scientific-professional characteristics. These data, again, are derived from the National Science Foundation's 1970 study of *American Science Manpower* (NSF, 1971).

Political scientists constitute only 2% of all scientists and technical personnel (these two categories hereafter combined as "scientists").

Of all scientists, 40% have Ph.D.s, 30% have M.A.s, and 27% have B.A.s. Of all political scientists, 61% have Ph.D.s, 38% have M.A.s, and 1% have B.A.s. (Remember: These data are based on reports from "working" political scientists. The total number of those with B.A.s in political science is of course larger than the number with higher degrees.)

Of all scientists, 31% work in business or industry, 42% in educational institutions, and 10% in the federal government. Of all political scientists, 1.8% work in business or industry, 76.9% in educational institutions, 5.4% in the federal government, 3.5% in state and local government, and 1.4% in the military. Of those in the federal government, 65% are engaged in administration, 14% in research and development, 13% in exploration and forecasting. The proportion of managers is larger for state and local government (71%), and the proportion of teachers is higher for the military (28%).

Of all scientists, 31% reported their primary work as research and development, 22% management and administration, and 23% teaching. Of political scientists, 10.5% reported their primary work as research and development, 16.5% management and administration, 58.3% teaching. In proportion to the whole, a significantly larger number of political scientists teach than economists, a somewhat larger number than sociologists.

Of all political scientists, 3.4% are employed by nonprofit organizations. Of these, 66% are engaged primarily in administration, 32% primarily in research and development. Very few political scientists are self-employed; most of those who are self-employed engage in consulting.

Though subject to the limitations noted above, these data point to the following conclusions. Political science is centered in academia. This is true compared with the sciences in general. It is true compared with the closely related disciplines of economics and sociology. Whatever the size or significance of the research product of political science in academia, teaching is the main "work" of academically employed political scientists. This does not necessarily signify that political scientists—more precisely, those who teach primarily or exclusively—are not professionals. For teaching is an "occupation" for which the claim of "profession" is common.

These data, together with what has been said above about the history and "nonscientific" functions of political science, permit the following conclusions. The teaching of citizenship, the interpretation and inculcation of a civic culture, political socialization (however such matters may be designated) absorb a great deal of the time and energy of political science. Political science generally does little to train for roles other than teaching and research, though some parts of it do so to a significant degree (e.g., public administration for practicing public administration).

The following observations are also in order. Much of the time and energies of those who teach political science goes not only beyond science and beyond civic education in any narrow sense, but to realization of the purposes of "liberal education" in terms of conveying a sense of the political in history, in human destiny. Much of the "product" of political science is invisible, in the sense that no statistics display it; it is woven into lives and careers that become statistics in other categories. Political science becomes the undergraduate specialization ("major") of a large number of students. Many of them follow careers, such as in law and journalism, to which political science contributes knowledge and skills. To a number of professions, political science, as a "discipline," plays a role analogous (of course the analogy is not exact) to that which biology plays to medicine or physics to engineering: a shaping, contributing role.

Let us now return to the criteria of profession. To what extent, in what ways, does political science fit or not fit the criteria?

Without doubt political science possesses a "body of knowledge." The question whether this body of knowledge is based in science is not irrelevant, but neither is it necessarily determinative of the question of professionalism.

Recognized professions have been based on and many utilize knowledge that is other than that based on modern empirical theoretical science.

Without doubt the knowledge of political science is inculcated in a course of training that is prolonged, and socialization through teacher-student interaction (and peer group interaction) is a lengthy, complicated process.

Again, those who are already the acknowledged "professionals" (as evidenced by higher degrees, professional achievement—especially research and formal status) perform a surveillance function. They set standards, judge competence, admit through "gates," enforce norms. Some of this is done through professional associations (admission to the publication media, awarding of places on convention programs, and so forth), but centrally it is performed through academic organization, combining hierarchical and collegial-peer styles.

The question whether political science is in some sense public is rather more complicated. Unquestionably in some ways it *is;* in fact, its connection with the civic tradition gives it certain "sacral" aspects. Unquestionably it has a large amount of autonomy. Ordinarily the state does not, crudely and blatantly, reach into university and association to set standards, determine promotions, and so forth. But often government does, in one way and another, "intervene," as in the setting of "required" courses; and occasionally its intervention may be regarded (by many political scientists at least) as mischievous or despotic. The questions that are raised in the balance between public expectations and control, and professional performance and autonomy, go beyond the relation between state and profession. They reach to the nature of the university (and the principle of "academic freedom") and to general questions of civil rights.

Of other criteria for professional standing that have been advanced, the one that may be most relevant is a professional-client relation. (Some discussions place much weight on fee-for-service and on mutual obligations, such as obedience and confidentiality.) Here political science seems to have trouble, though to regard the student as client goes some distance in fitting political science to the criterion.

However, it is probably better not to press the case for professional standing beyond a certain point, but rather to argue the relevance of other "models," such as discipline and science. After all, few professions *are* professions, if the criteria are applied rigorously. And under the influence of science and of modern organizational styles, all professions, even the archetypical ones, may be becoming less rather than more professional in terms of historically derived criteria.

### Political Science as Science

Whether political science is a science, whether it can become a science, how it can become a science, what kind of science it is or can become—such matters have been discussed since the study of politics attained self-consciousness. They have been discussed frequently and at length in the literature of American political science, especially during the recent period. Much of this essay has been a commentary on the subject—on the points of view held, on the arguments advanced, on the "politics of political science" as shaped by changing opinion on the issues.

This, then, is hardly the place to review the many and complex issues, much less to explore them in depth. I shall simply set forth again a personal perspective: I reject both the view that the ancients "knew it all" and that we have only to return and drink of their wisdom; and the view that the only way political science can become a science is to cast off the "yoke of the past."

On a broad construction of the term "science," *political science is a science.* The information and theory that it musters and organizes is *knowledge.* This knowledge is both true and useful. This knowledge is also cumulative.

Each one of these four assertions would have to be explained and qualified in an extended discussion. But they would also have to be explained and qualified if made about biology or astronomy. For that matter, except for the first assertion, they would have to be explained and qualified if made about physics, which is the "defining case" for the strict as against broad use of the term "science."

Whether or to what extent political science can become a science in the strict sense, i.e., one that resembles physics and (or) fits the specifications of an "advanced" or "true" science as set forth in the literature known as philosophy of science, is an open question to be answered by the future. The aspiration is an understandable and legitimate one. The aspiration is also open to serious doubt and respectable contrary argument. In any case, growth in political knowledge will continue; political science will advance in understanding of the political.

*Political Science as Enterprise*

Whether (or to what extent or in what ways) political science is a discipline, a profession, or a science clearly depends on definition of terms and interpretation of facts.

From my point of view, it is or has aspects of all three. No single organizational style can (or should try to) contain or embody it. It has and should have a variety: professional associations, learned societies, academic departments or bureaus, "invisible colleges." No single "paradigm," however strictly or loosely that much used and abused term is interpreted, can (or should try to) contain or embody it. Political science is multifaceted, and it needs perspectives and theories appropriate to purpose and circumstance.

"Professions profess, sciences know." What is appropriate for one is not appropriate for the other. A distinction between theoretical (or "pure") and practical (or "applied") science has utility for certain purposes. But it does not, without straining the ordinary usage of terms, serve to classify and contain all that is relevant to what political science is and should be.

Only a broad-spectrum term, such as "enterprise" or "endeavor," serves to indicate all that is involved. The range of concerns and activities indicated by *the political* is of central importance in the human experience. The political has been an important dimension of the human experience since the beginning of civilization (and before, by some interpretations). It will remain as an important dimension if and when the state system is supplanted. The task of political science is to muster as much knowledge, skill, and wisdom as possible in attending to this dimension.

## NOTES

1. The author acknowledges his debt to Somit and Tanenhaus, 1967, for the discussion in this section.

2. In this discussion, "scientism" has the dictionary-authenticated meaning of "advocacy of the application of the principles derived from the natural sciences to other disciplines." That is, though sometimes used pejoratively, the term has in this essay (as in Somit and Tanenhaus) its simple descriptive sense.

3. If I may be permitted a personal note: Well over a third of my own graduate training in the late thirties consisted of constitutional history, English and American; international, constitutional, administrative, and municipal law; and jurisprudence. Perhaps no doctoral program during recent years would have permitted such an allotment of effort.

4. Reprinted by permission from *The Development of American Political Science: From Burgess to Behavioralism* by Albert Somit and Joseph Tanenhaus (Boston: Allyn and Bacon, 1967), pp. 190–191.

5. Membership figures for the disciplinary associations are especially troublesome. Not only do they vary by the month and move with academic and economic trends, but the membership categories among associations vary, e.g., "institutional," "student," "interested."

## REFERENCES

Alker, Hayward R. (1965). *Mathematics and Politics.* Toronto: Collier-Macmillan.

Almond, Gabriel (1966). "Political theory and political science." *American Political Science Review* 60:869–79.

American Political Science Association Committee on Pre-Collegiate Education (1971). "Political education in the public schools: the challenge for political science." *PS* 4:431–57.

Anderson, William (1964). *Man's Quest for Political Knowledge: The Study and Teaching of Politics in Ancient Times.* Minneapolis: University of Minneapolis Press.

Averini, Shlomo (1968). *The Social and Political Thought of Karl Marx.* London: Cambridge University Press.

Bailey, Stephen K., et al. (1955). *Research Frontiers in Politics and Government.* Washington: Brookings Institution.

Barents, Jan (1961). *Political Science in Western Europe: A Trend Report.* London: Stevens.

Barnes, Harry E., with K. W. Bigelow, Jean Brunhes, and others, eds. (1925). *The History and Prospects of the Social Sciences.* New York: Knopf.

Bluhm, William T. (1965). *Theories of the Political System: Classics of Political Thought and Modern Political Analysis.* Englewood Cliffs, N.J.: Prentice-Hall.

Brecht, Arnold (1959). *Political Theory: The Foundations of Twentieth Century Political Thought.* Princeton: Princeton University Press.

Brecht, Arnold, and Sheldon Wolin (1968). "Political theory" (I Approaches, Brecht; II Trends and goals, Wolin). In David L. Sills (ed.), *International Encyclopedia of the Social Sciences*, Vol. 12. New York: Crowell Collier and Macmillan.

Butler, David E. (1959). *The Study of Political Behavior.* London: Hutchinson.

Catlin, George E. G. (1927). *Science and Method of Politics.* New York: Knopf.

——— (1939). *The Story of the Political Philosophers.* New York: McGraw-Hill.

——— (1962). *Systematic Politics.* Toronto: University of Toronto Press.

Charlesworth, James C., ed. (October 1962). *The Limits of Behavioralism in Political Science* (special issue). Philadelphia: American Academy of Political and Social Science.

——— (December 1966). *A Design for Political Science: Scope, Objectives, and Methods* (Monograph 6 in a series). Philadelphia: American Academy of Political and Social Science.

——— (October 1968). *Theory and Practice of Public Administration: Scope, Objectives, and Methods* (Monograph 8 in a series). Philadelphia: American Academy of Political and Social Science.

Childe, V. Gordon (1946). *What Happened in History.* New York: Penguin.

Committee for the Advancement of Teaching, A.P.S.A. (1951). *Goals for Political Science.* New York: Sloane.

Connery, Robert H., ed. (1965). *Teaching Political Science: A Challenge to Higher Education.* Durham: Duke University Press.

Cowling, Maurice (1963). *The Nature and Limits of Political Science.* Cambridge: Cambridge University Press.

Crane, William W., and Bernard Moses (1884). *Politics: An Introduction to the Study of Comparative Constitutional Law.* New York: Putnam.

Crick, Bernard (1959). *The American Science of Politics: Its Origins and Conditions.* Berkeley: University of California Press.

Dahl, Robert A. (1961). "The behavioral approach in political science: epitaph for a monument to a successful protest." *American Political Science Review* 55:763–72.

———— (1963). *Modern Political Analysis*. Englewood Cliffs, N.J.: Prentice-Hall.

de Jouvenel, Bertrand (1961). "On the nature of political science." *American Political Science Review* 55:773–9.

de Sola Pool, Ithiel, ed. (1967). *Contemporary Political Science: Toward Empirical Theory*. New York: McGraw-Hill.

Deutsch, Karl W. (1963). *The Nerves of Government: Models of Political Communication and Control.* New York: Free Press of Glencoe.

Easton, David (1953). *The Political System: An Inquiry into the State of Political Science*. New York: Knopf.

———— (1965a). *A Framework for Political Analysis*. Englewood Cliffs, N.J.: Prentice-Hall.

———— (1965b). *A Systems Analysis of Political Life*. New York: Wiley.

———— (1968). "Political science." In David L. Sills (ed.), *International Encyclopedia of the Social Sciences,* Vol. 12. New York: Crowell Collier and Macmillan.

———— (1969). "The new revolution in political science." *American Political Science Review* 68:1051–61.

Eaton, Dorman B. (1880). *Civil Service Reform in Great Britain*. New York: Harper.

Eisenstadt, Shmuel N. (1963). *The Political Systems of Empires*. Glencoe, Ill.: Free Press.

Elliott, William Y. (1928). *The Pragmatic Revolt in Politics: Syndicalism, Fascism and the Constitutional State*. New York: Macmillan.

Eulau, Heinz (1963). *The Behavioral Persuasion in Politics*. New York: Random House.

———— (1968). "The behavioral movement in political science." *Social Research* 35:1–29.

Eulau, Heinz, and James G. March, eds. (1969). *Political Science*. Englewood Cliffs, N.J.: Prentice-Hall.

Franklin, Julian H. (1963). *Jean Bodin and the Sixteenth Century Revolution in the Methodology of Law and History*. New York: Columbia University Press.

Friedrich, Carl J. (1963). *Man and His Government: An Empirical Theory of Politics*. New York: McGraw-Hill.

Germino, Dante (1967). *Beyond Ideology: The Revival of Political Theory*. New York: Harper.

———— (1972). "Some observations on recent political philosophy and theory." *The Annals* 400:140–8.

Gosnell, Harold F. (1927). *Getting Out the Vote: An Experiment in the Stimulation of Voting*. Chicago: University of Chicago Press.

Graham, George J., and George W. Carey, eds. (1972). *The Post-Behavioral Era: Perspectives in Political Science*. New York: McKay.

Haas, Michael, and Henry S. Kariel, eds. (1970). *Approaches to the Study of Political Science*. Scranton, Pa.: Chandler (Intext).

Hacker, Andrew (1963). *The Study of Politics: The Western Tradition and American Origins*. New York: McGraw-Hill.

Haddow, Anna (1939). *Political Science in American Colleges and Universities, 1636–1900*. New York: Appleton-Century.

Herring, E. Pendleton (1929). *Group Representation Before Congress*. Baltimore: Johns Hopkins Press.

Holcombe, Arthur N. (1924). *The Political Parties of To-Day; A Study in Republican and Democratic Politics*. New York: Harper.

Holler, Frederick L. (1971). *The Information Sources of Political Science*. Santa Barbara, Cal.: A.B.C.-Clio Press.

Hyneman, Charles S. (1959). *The Study of Politics: The Present State of American Political Science*. Urbana: University of Illinois Press.

International Political Science Association (1969). *Synthesis Report on the I.P.S.A.: 20 Years Activities, 1949–1969*. Brussels: International Political Science Association.

Ions, Edmund S. (1968). *James Bryce and American Democracy, 1870–1922*. London: Macmillan.

Irish, Marian D., ed. (1968). *Political Science: Advance of the Discipline*. Englewood Cliffs, N.J.: Prentice-Hall.

Isaak, Alan C. (1969). *Scope and Methods of Political Science: An Introduction to the Methodology of Political Inquiry*. Homewood, Ill.: Dorsey.

Kaplan, Morton A. (1968). "Systems theory and political science." *Social Research* 35:30–47.

Kariel, Henry S. (1972). *Saving Appearances: The Reestablishment of Political Science*. North Scituate, Mass.: Duxbury Press.

Kaufman, Herbert (1956). "Emerging conflicts in the doctrines of public administration." *American Political Science Review* 50:1057–73.

Kirkpatrick, Evron M. (1971). "Toward a more responsible two-party system: political science, policy science, or pseudo-science?" *American Political Science Review* 65:965–90.

Landau, Martin (1968a). "On the use of functional analysis in American political science." *Social Research* 35:48–75.

———— (1968b). "The myth of hyperfactualism in the study of American politics." *Political Science Quarterly* 83:378–99.

———— (1972). *Political Theory and Political Science: Studies in the Methodology of Political Inquiry*. New York: Macmillan.

Lasswell, Harold D. (1963). *The Future of Political Science*. New York: Atherton.

Lasswell, Harold D., and Abraham Kaplan (1950). *Power and Society: A Framework for Political Inquiry*. New Haven: Yale University Press.

Lepawsky, Albert (1964). "The politics of epistemology." *Western Political Quarterly* 17:Supp. 21–52.

Lerner, Daniel, and Harold D. Lasswell, eds. (1951). *The Policy Sciences*. Stanford, Cal.: Stanford University Press.

Lichtheim, George (1964). *Marxism: An Historical and Critical Study,* 2nd edition. London: Routledge.

———— (1971). *From Marx to Hegel.* New York: Herder and Herder.

Lipset, Seymour M., ed. (1969). *Politics and the Social Sciences.* New York: Oxford.

Luttbeg, Norman R., and Melvin A. Kahn (1968). "Ph.D. training in political science." *Midwest Journal of Political Science* 12:303–29.

Mackenzie, William J. M. (1967). *Politics and Social Science.* Baltimore: Penguin.

———— (1971). "The political science of political science." *Government and Opposition* 6:277–302.

———— (1971). *The Study of Political Science Today.* New York: Macmillan.

Marini, Frank, ed. (1971). *Toward a New Public Administration: The Minnowbrook Perspective.* Scranton, Pa.: Chandler.

Massimo, Salvadori, ed. (1950). *Contemporary Political Science.* Liege, Belgium: Thone.

Mayer, Jacob P. (1960). *Alexis de Tocqueville: A Biographical Study in Political Science.* New York: Harper.

McCoy, Charles A., and John Playford, eds. (1967). *Apolitical Politics: A Critique of Behavioralism.* New York: Thomas Y. Crowell.

McNeill, William H. (1971). *A World History,* 2nd edition. New York: Oxford University Press.

Meehan, Eugene J. (1965). *The Theory and Method of Political Analysis.* Homewood, Ill.: Dorsey.

Merriam, Charles E. (1921). "The present state of the study of politics." *American Political Science Review* 15:173–85.

———— (1925). *New Aspects of Politics.* Chicago: University of Chicago Press.

Merriam, Charles E., and Harold F. Gosnell (1924). *Non-Voting; Causes and Method of Control.* Chicago: University of Chicago Press.

Merritt, Richard L., and Gloria J. Pyszka (1969). *The Student Political Scientist's Handbook.* Cambridge, Mass.: Schenkman.

Merry, Henry J. (1970). *Montesquieu's System of Natural Government.* West LaFayette, Ind.: Purdue University Studies.

Mitchell, William C. (1968). "The new political economy." *Social Research* 35:76–110.

Morgenthau, Hans J. (1946). *Scientific Man Versus Power Politics.* Chicago: University of Chicago Press.

National Science Foundation (1971). *American Science Manpower, 1970: A Report of the National Register of Scientific and Technical Personnel.* Washington: Government Printing Office.

Odegard, Peter H. (1928). *Pressure Politics: The Story of the Anti-Saloon League.* New York: Columbia University Press.

Ogburn, William F., and Alexander Goldenweiser, eds. (1927). *The Social Sciences and Their Interrelations.* Boston: Houghton Mifflin.

Orlans, Harold (1971). "Social science research policies in the United States." *Minerva* 9:7–31.

Pennock, J. Roland, and David J. Smith (1964). *Political Science: An Introduction.* New York: Macmillan.

Pollock, Frederick (1960; first published 1890; revised edition, 1911). *An Introduction to the History of the Science of Politics.* Boston: Beacon Press.

Ranney, Austin (1958). *The Governing of Men: An Introduction to Political Science.* New York: Holt, Rinehart, and Winston.

——————, ed. (1962). *Essays on the Behavioral Study of Politics.* Urbana, Ill.: University of Illinois Press.

——————, ed. (1968). *Political Science and Public Policy.* Chicago: Markham.

Rice, Stuart (1924). *Farmers and Workers in American Politics.* New York: Columbia University Press.

—————— (1928). *Quantitative Methods in Politics.* New York: Knopf.

Sabine, George H. (1964). *A History of Political Theory,* 3rd edition. New York: Holt, Rinehart, and Winston.

Schattschneider, Elmer E. (1935). *Politics, Pressures, and the Tariff.* New York: Prentice-Hall.

Shackleton, Robert (1961). *Montesquieu: A Critical Biography.* New York: Oxford University Press.

Somit, Albert, and Joseph Tanenhaus (1964). *American Political Science: A Profile of a Discipline.* New York: Atherton.

—————— (1967). *The Development of American Political Science: From Burgess to Behavioralism.* Boston: Allyn and Bacon.

Sorauf, Francis J. (1965). *Political Science: An Informal Overview.* Columbus, O.: Merrill.

Spiro, Herbert J. (1970). *Politics as the Master Science: From Plato to Mao.* New York: Harper and Row.

Storing, Herbert, ed. (1962). *Essays on the Scientific Study of Politics.* New York: Holt, Rinehart, and Winston.

Stretton, Hugh (1969). *The Political Sciences: General Principles of Selection in Social Science and History.* New York: Basic Books.

Surkin, Marvin, and Alan Wolfe, eds. (1970). *An End to Political Science: The Caucus Papers.* New York: Basic Books.

Truman, David B. (1951). *The Governmental Process.* New York: Knopf.

—————— (1965). "Disillusion and regeneration: the quest for a discipline." *American Political Science Review* 59:865–73.

Van Dyke, Vernon (1960). *Political Science: A Philosophical Analysis.* Stanford, Cal.: Stanford University Press.

Veysey, Laurence (1965). *The Emergence of the American University.* Chicago: University of Chicago Press.

Voegelin, Eric (1952). *The New Science of Politics: An Introductory Essay.* Chicago: University of Chicago Press.

Waldo, Dwight (1956). *Political Science in the United States of America: A Trend Report.* Paris: UNESCO.

―――――― (1972). "Developments in public administration." *The Annals* 404:217–45.

Wasby, Stephen L. (1970). *Political Science—The Discipline and Its Dimensions: An Introduction.* New York: Scribner's.

Willoughby, Westel W. (1896). *An Examination of the Nature of the State: A Study in Political Philosophy.* New York: Macmillan.

Wilson, Woodrow (1887). "The study of administration." *Political Science Quarterly* 2:197–222.

Wolin, Sheldon S. (1960). *Politics and Vision: Continuity and Innovation in Western Political Thought.* Boston: Little, Brown.

Young, Oran R. (1968). *Systems of Political Science.* Englewood Cliffs, N.J.: Prentice-Hall.

Young, Roland, ed. (1958). *Approaches to the Study of Politics.* Evanston, Ill.: Northwestern University Press.

# 2

# THE LOGIC OF POLITICAL INQUIRY:
## A SYNTHESIS OF OPPOSED PERSPECTIVES

*J. DONALD MOON*

## 1 INTRODUCTION: ALTERNATIVE MODELS OF POLITICAL INQUIRY

In any almanac or book of records one can find a vast number of indisputably "political" facts: the number of seats in different legislatures, the number who voted in various elections, the type of political system enjoyed by particular countries at particular times, etc. Although it cannot be doubted that these are facts about politics, no one would argue that their presence qualifies such compilations as works of political science. Even if such repositories of miscellaneous information were limited to specifically political facts, they still would not qualify. Political science differs from the activities of professional fact compilers by its systematic character and by its concern for the *explanation* of political phenomena. We do not simply assemble information; we seek coherent accounts of political life.

So much is obvious—a part of the familiar litany we hear on the occasion of a presidential address or read in our textbooks. The interesting and controversial issues concern how this coherence is achieved. What constitutes a satisfactory explanation? On what principles can the data of political inquiry be organized? On what grounds ought we to accept a particular finding? What support does a finding give to a generalization, or what inferences can we draw from it? What kinds of concepts are admissible in political inquiry? Questions such as these pose the fundamental methodological is-

---

I would like to thank Brian Barry, Brian Fay, Dante Germino, Arthur Goldberg, Fred Greenstein, Felix Oppenheim, Nelson Polsby, and Stuart Thorson for reading and commenting on this essay. Special thanks to Fred Greenstein for support and encouragement, and to Brian Fay for his guidance through much philosophical literature and for our many long discussions, which were essential in clarifying the issues and arguments I present here.

sues of political science and of the other social sciences as well. They have been widely and often hotly debated, since they strike at the very heart of what we are doing—or ought to be doing—as political scientists. The answers one gives to these questions define a particular model of political and social inquiry specifying what can count as political or social knowledge, rules governing the formation of admissible concepts, etc.

Perhaps the most popular methodological position in political science is one that might broadly be called the "naturalist"[1] or "scientific" model, for it seeks to structure political science in terms of the methodological principles of the natural sciences. Indeed, this view of political science might also be called the "positivist" model, since it is inspired at least in part by an essentially positivist account of the methodology of the natural sciences. Adherents of this model deny the existence of any fundamental methodological differences between the natural and social sciences. For both natural and social science, the goals of the "scientific enterprise" are the explanation and prediction of natural or social phenomena. In both areas of inquiry, moreover, scientific explanation consists in showing that the particular event or state of affairs to be explained could be expected, given certain initial conditions and the general laws or regularities in the field. For example, we might explain the freezing of a pan of water on a winter night by reference to the general law that water freezes when it is cooled below 32°F and the fact (or initial condition) that the temperature that night was lower than 32°F. (This is a variant of the example Hempel, 1942, uses to illustrate scientific explanation.) Laws or regularities, in turn, can be explained by deducing them from more general laws, or sets of laws, which are organized into comprehensive theories that have implications for a wide range of phenomena. These theories, by giving an account of a multitude of diverse kinds of events and situations, represent the crowning achievement of science, for they provide coherence to, and the systematic character of, a particular area of inquiry.

Although it is sometimes said—or more often suggested—that the scientific model is the only model of political inquiry capable of providing either unity to a field or genuine explanations of some phenomenon, this claim is clearly false. If "social science is . . . simply a way of being careful about studying human affairs" (Polsby *et al.*, 1963, p. 10), it is certainly not unique in that respect. In particular, there is an alternative methodological position which underlies what might be called the model of an interpretative social or political science. In opposition to the naturalist ideal, adherents of this model, whom I will, with some trepidation, call "humanists," insist on the methodological distinctiveness of the human sciences. The phenomena of the social sciences consist of human actions, and these are fundamentally different from the phenomena of the natural sciences, for they are constituted by the ideas and self-understandings of the social actors themselves. In the natural sciences we are free to create categories, define concepts, or group events in any way we please, so long as it helps us to advance our explanatory aims. In the social sciences we do not enjoy such freedom, for the human actions we would explain are intentional, which is to say that their very existence depends on the ideas that the actors themselves have. To describe someone as "saluting," to take a simple example, is possible only if the actor himself has certain conceptions of hierarchy and respect in terms of which this practice is defined; and to understand what he did when he "saluted," we must first grasp these notions. Hence the investigator must understand the meanings of the actions and social forms he is studying, and to do so he must interpret their significance in terms of the actor's intentions and in terms of the conventions and the fundamental conceptualizations of the actor's society. Thus the social scientist is necessarily committed to the hermeneutical or interpretative techniques and perspectives which are characteristic of the humanities, and this fact marks a fundamental break between the philosophy of the social sciences and the philosophy of the natural sciences.

In the next two sections of this chapter, I will present the central elements of these two models of political inquiry. In Section 2 I will outline the "scientific ideal," focusing on the nature of scientific explanation as it involves the use of laws and theories. In Section 3 I present a number of criticisms of the naturalist model and then outline the essential elements of the interpretative conception.

My main purpose in this chapter, however, is to attack the opposition between these two positions by showing that the claims of both are unfounded. If we must concede that the social sciences are methodologically distinct from the natural sciences, the differences are not so great as adherents of the hermeneutical model insist, for some of the things that happen in social life are things no one *does*, and so we cannot think of them simply in terms of the categories of intentional action. Of course, we must understand the conventions of a society to recognize such events as a stock market crash or a war, but since these events do not (necessarily) express anyone's intentions, an analysis of their meanings will not explain why they occurred. For such an explanation a methodology modeled on the natural sciences will be more appropriate. In particular, we will have to make use of generalizations and theories analogous to those of the natural sciences, in order to explain how the events in question result from the kinds of situations that precede them.

In the fourth section of this chapter, I develop these criticisms of the interpretative ideal and offer the outlines of a methodological position which represents a genuine synthesis of these two equally one-sided accounts. Following recent works in the philosophy of science which emphasize the conceptual presuppositions of scientific theories, I show that theories in the social sciences make certain implicit assumptions regarding human motivation, sociality, and rationality, and that these assumptions underlie both the interpretative understanding that the humanist seeks and the explanatory generalizations and theories to which the naturalist aspires. Since the principal criterion of adequacy of an essay of this type must be its ability to illuminate political inquiry, especially its capacity to account for the variety of forms political inquiry can take, I have illustrated the argument of this section with a number of examples drawn from the literature of political science. Although the conception of political inquiry I develop is rather schematic, I hope that it can contribute to a more adequate methodology of political science, providing a better account and understanding of the processes and results of political inquiry.

## 2   THE "SCIENTIFIC" IDEAL

### 2.1   Explanation, Theories, and Theory-Testing: An Overview

At least since the time of Hobbes an important school of political research has endeavored to place the study of politics on a "scientific" footing. The attractiveness of such an undertaking is obvious. Indeed, the success of the natural sciences in providing explanations and descriptions of the world is so great that some have even taken science to be the paradigm of rationality: "science . . . is the only method available for responsibly assigning maximally reliable truth status [to statements]" (Gregor, 1971, p. 27). From such a perspective, the desirability of the scientific ideal requires little argument: to be concerned with what actually goes on in the political world, that is, to be interested in the empirical study of politics, requires that we follow the procedures of science.

Apart from its intellectual attractions, the scientific ideal answers to our practical interests as well. Hume, along with many classical thinkers, hoped to reduce politics to a science in order to moderate political conflicts. Once we understood the "general truths" of politics, Hume reasoned, many political disputes could be settled, and the factitious struggles which threaten to "change a good administration into a bad one" could be controlled or ended (Hume, 1952, p. 23). More ambitiously, Gabriel Almond sees the need for "an explanatory, predictive, and manipulative political theory" that can be used to solve "the problem of violence and coercion in human affairs" (Almond, 1967, pp. 7, 18). Science, by providing us with the causal laws or mechanisms which operate in a particular field, tells us which variables or conditions we must manipulate in order to achieve results that we desire: "Prediction implies the possibility of control. . ." (Falco, 1973, p. 55). Scientific theories are validated in the context of successful instrumental action, whether in experiments or in technological applications (Habermas, 1966; 1971, Part II). As our manipulations of the "independent" variables produce desired changes in the "dependent" variables, we justify our account of the underlying causal structure while advancing our control over the world. We might say that technological control is imminent in experimental procedure, and that science therefore holds the key to our acquiring greater control over our environment and over the processes of our own society.

Although the appeals of a scientific study of politics are clear, just what such a study requires is not so obvious. As our understanding of the methods and procedures of science has changed, our conception of a science of politics has also varied. Hobbes's vision, for example, featured an axiomatic deductive method modeled on geometry, whereas John Stuart Mill is celebrated for his emphasis on the primacy of observation and induction. At the present time there are a number of partially competing, partially overlapping accounts of scientific procedure that have gained acceptance among political scientists who have written on these issues. A central feature of most accounts, however, is the concept of scientific explanation, for the goals of understanding and control which the scientific enterprise advances are realized in the explanations science provides. The concept of explanation is also crucial, for it is this idea which separates the two models of political inquiry, the "scientific" and the "interpretative," which I am contrasting in this chapter.

The standard account of scientific explanation is known as the "covering-law" model. According to this model, scientific explanation requires generalizations or laws, and so most of Section 2.2 is devoted to an explication of the nature of these laws. The analysis of the role of laws in explanations however, leads directly to a discussion of scientific theories, for the conditions which must be imposed on laws in order to account for their explanatory force can be justified only by going beyond the laws themselves to a consideration of the theories in which they are "embedded," so to speak. In Section 2.3, therefore, I discuss the structure of scientific theories. I first outline the different uses of the term "theory" and then offer a very abbreviated account of the "orthodox" view of theories—the model of scientific theories which was developed by the logical empiricists and which has dominated much of the discussion of theories since. This model is briefly criticized in Section 2.3.2. The criticisms, which emphasize what might be called the "conceptual foundations" of scientific inquiry, lead at once to a consideration of the problems of testing and evaluating scientific theories, and these questions are taken up in Section 2.4. Finally, the argument is summarized in Section 2.5.

## 2.2 Scientific Explanation

To explain why something occurred is to show why, given the circumstances, it *had* to occur—to show that nothing else could have occurred under these conditions. If I want to know why an event, $p$, occurred and am told that, under these circumstances, $p$ or $q$ or $z$ might have happened, my curiosity will be somewhat abated, but it will certainly not be satisfied—especially if the differences between the alternatives were significant. For example, one would be dissatisfied with an explanation of the fall of the French Fourth Republic in terms of its high level of governmental instability if the author of the account was quite prepared to admit that the Fourth Republic, like the Third, could have continued in spite of this disability, though at a declining level of performance. Surely we would be entitled to object that what we were promised was an account of why it *fell*, but all we were in fact told was that it was unstable.

Of course, to the extent that the range of possible events or outcomes has been limited, this account could be considered helpful. Moreover, it suggests a line of further inquiry: given the set of possible outcomes, what further factor(s) present in the situation led to the actual collapse of the system, rather than to its continued erosion? Carrying the example further, we might point to the threatened military revolt: it was this, given the background of ministerial instability, that precipitated the collapse. We could say that ministerial instability and the threatened coup jointly account for the fall of the Fourth Republic.

Quite apart from any question of its truth, this account is still not satisfactory since it does not show that the Fourth Republic fell *because* of the military coup in conjunction with ministerial instability. Obviously the collapse *followed* these earlier events or conditions, but if they are also to *explain* it, something more is required. And this "more" is a generalization or scientific law to the effect that if a political system has a high level of instability and is threatened by a military coup, it will collapse.[2] This generalization, together with the singular statements already provided, logically implies the statement that describes the event to be explained and thus shows that it was necessary. It is the generalization or law that provides the *force* of the "because" in our putative explanatory account and transforms it from a description of a mere sequence of events into a genuinely causal account.

It must be stressed that some generalization (or set of generalizations) is necessary if an account is to be explanatory—if we are to show that the event to be explained was necessary, given the initial conditions.[3] This is evident from a simple logical consideration: no set of singular statements denoting the initial conditions could logically imply the singular statements denoting the event to be explained, without the addition of some universal premise. From such statements as "This $x$ is a $y$" we could never deduce "This $x$ is a $z$" unless we could add the universal premise "All $y$'s are $z$'s." And it is essential that we deduce the (description of the) event to be explained (the "explanandum") from the description of the initial conditions if we are to say that the explanandum was necessary, given these conditions.[4]

Because of the critical importance of laws or generalizations in this analysis of scientific explanation, it is often called the "covering-law model" of scientific explanation or, simply, "nomological" explanation (from the

Greek "nomos," meaning "law"). Similarly, the generalizations which figure in such explanations may be called "nomological statements." One of the major issues regarding this pattern of explanation concerns the nature of these nomological statements. Although generalizations of some sort are required, it is obvious that not just any kind of general statement will do. Consider, for example, the following putative explanation of Canada's relatively painless progress to autonomy and independence.

| | |
|---|---|
| Initial conditions: | Canada was a white (or white-ruled) British colony during the nineteenth century. |
| General law: | All countries that were white (or white-ruled) British colonies during the nineteenth century achieved independence without a prolonged struggle. |
| Explanandum: | Canada achieved independence without a prolonged struggle. |

Although this explanation looks superficially like an example of the covering-law model, the appearance is deceiving. The subject of the generalization in the example—the set of white-ruled British colonies between 1800 and 1900—contains only a finite number of examples, namely, Canada, Australia, New Zealand, and South Africa. Hence our "general law" is equivalent to the following series of statements (I have abbreviated the longer phrases):

Canada is a WBC and Canada achieved independence painlessly,
and
Australia is a WBC and Australia achieved independence painlessly,
and
New Zealand is a . . . ,
and
South Africa is a . . . .

When we put our "general law" in this form, it is obvious that the "explanation" in question is no explanation at all, because the conclusion of the argument simply repeats one of the premises. Far from being given an account of *why* Canada achieved independence painlessly, we are simply told *that* she did—once as a premise and once again as a conclusion!

The problem here is not that a proper name (British) appears in the putative "law," for there are other recognized laws which include proper names. Galileo's law mentions the earth (the acceleration of bodies in free fall in the vicinity of the earth is constant), and Kepler's laws specifically refer to the sun. But both laws can be interpreted as applying to an unrestricted class of objects which might satisfy the conditions of the law. Thus Galileo's law holds for any object which might become unsupported near the earth, and Kepler's laws enable us to predict that all planets which have been, are, or might come into the "vicinity" of the sun will revolve about it in elliptical orbits. What is essential is that a generalization be an unrestricted universal statement, that its subject term designate an open class of objects or instances. Only then can it be said to explain or predict its instances, rather than merely summarizing our observations. (See Nagel, 1961, p. 63; Hempel, 1965, pp. 342–343.)

Although universality in this sense may be a necessary condition of a law, it is hardly sufficient since some unrestricted generalizations may be merely "accidental." Consider two time-honored examples, "All swans are white" and "All crows are black." Apart from questions of truth or falsity, neither statement provides a satisfactory explanation of its instances because, one might say, there is no "necessity" to either of them. It is often held that, in order to provide a ground for extension to new cases, as a law must do if it is to provide an explanation of *any* case, a law should support subjunctive conditional statements, including statements contrary to known or presumed facts. For example, if it is a law that water, under normal pressure, vaporizes when heated, then we should be able to form the subjunctive conditional statement "If there were anything that is a sample of water and if it were heated, then it would vaporize." Now suppose that we had ascertained that some given sample of liquid was indeed water, and suppose that we then destroyed it by electrolysis; then this physical law should justify the counterfactual statement "If that sample of water had been heated under normal pressure, then it would have vaporized." Generalizations which do not support such conditionals may be called "accidental" generalizations, as opposed to laws. Because the generalizations about swans and crows do not support such conditionals as "If there were swans in Australia, they would be white," or "If there were crows in Anarctica, they would be black," we would not call them laws.

This test can be used to determine whether some of the generalizations which are or have been advanced in political science are actually laws. Consider, for example, the generalization[5] "If a democratic country has a single-member, plurality electoral system, then it will have only two electoral political parties." (See Duverger, 1950, for the classic discussion of this "sociological law" and Grumm, 1958, and Rae, 1971, for empirical tests of it.) If this is a sociological law, then it should permit us to say that if countries not now democratic were to become so, and if they were to have single-member electoral systems, then they would all have two-party systems. For example, writing in 1950, we might have said, "If India should adopt this electoral system, it will have only two electoral parties," or perhaps, "If (only!) France would adopt this electoral system, it would then experience (the blessings of) a two-party system." If we were unwilling to affirm such statements, we would betray our belief that this famous law was no law at all but merely an accidental generalization of some sort. It may be a "spurious correlation" or a result of the contingent fact that the logically and empirically possible combination of factors producing multipartyism had not occurred in countries which happen to have such electoral systems (such as, perhaps, a federal system marked by intense, regionally based cultural, linguistic, or religious cleavages).

The laws which figure in explanations, then, must be unrestricted universals, and they must "support" counterfactual and subjunctive conditionals. These requirements arise from the need to make sense of our intuitive idea that laws must apply to all possible cases and not simply reflect an "accidental" concomitance of events. If an explanation shows that the event in question *had* to occur, that it could not have been otherwise, then the generalization on which the explanation is based must not simply be a summation of some set of particular instances or express the coincidence that the empirically and logically possible combination of factors which would falsify the generalization does not happen to occur.

Because of these requirements, it is often held that laws must express some kind of "necessity," but the idea involved here is difficult to explicate. One unambiguous interpretation would be to hold that laws are *logically* necessary, i.e., that laws are necessarily true in view of the meanings of the terms they contain. In this case, laws would be analytic statements, and their truth would be guaranteed by the conventions of the language in which they are stated. Thus, if "All swans are white" is a scientific law, then finding a black bird which in all other respects resembles a swan would be grounds not for denying the "law" but for recognizing a new category of bird. Indeed, if laws were logically necessary, their denials would be self-contradictory, and no amount of empirical evidence could possibly bear upon their truth. This, however, is a major difficulty with this position, because it makes the empirical character of science problematic. If laws express "necessary truths," then, as Nagel (1961, pp. 53–54) points out, scientists should proceed like logicians and mathematicians. They should develop demonstrative proofs for their scientific laws, rather than setting up experiments or engaging in other forms of controlled observation.

Diametrically opposed to the logical-necessity or "conventionalist" view of laws is the Humean or "empiricist" position, according to which a law simply states the existence of some uniformity that happens to exist in the world but which is in no way "necessary." For example, in the Humean view, the law that water under normal pressure vaporizes when heated simply expresses the fact that all past, present, and future cases in which water under normal pressure is heated also happen to be cases in which the water vaporizes. But there are deep problems with this view as well, for it does not seem to meet the intuitive requirement that laws apply to all possible cases. In this view, it is difficult to see how laws can be said to "support" counterfactual or subjunctive conditionals. If laws simply express the fact that a particular relationship holds, how could they support our belief that, in possible instances which did not actually occur, the relationship *would have held*? For example, how could such laws support our belief that if we had heated a certain sample of water yesterday, it would have vaporized?

Empiricists are quick to recognize this difficulty, but they insist that it can be met by viewing laws and the explanations in which laws figure, in terms of their functions and places in scientific theories. Nagel (1961, pp. 68–73) argues that subjunctive and contrary-to-fact conditionals are asserted not simply on the basis of some particular law but on the basis of other laws and theories one accepts. One cannot propound a particular universal statement—all ravens are black—and then ask whether it supports a subjunctive conditional statement—if ravens were found in polar regions, they would be black—for even if we accept the statement as a law of nature, the conditionals it supports depend on the set of other laws, assumptions, and theories we accept. In this case, the conditional appears to conflict with some of our beliefs regarding the color of plumage, and so we would not assert it. But this does not mean that the putative law is not a law *because* it fails to support such conditionals, since it fails only to support *this* conditional, and the reason is that the "law" in question is only part of the evidence that bears upon our accepting or rejecting particular statements. Of course, we may still decide for other reasons that "All ravens are black" is not a law of nature, but such a decision will, once again, depend on the role this statement plays in the "system of explanation" constituting a particular science. Thus, to understand the structure of scientific explanation, we are led from a consideration of laws to a discussion of theories and the relationships between laws and theories.

## 2.3 Scientific Theories

That adequate explanations ultimately rely on theories is a cardinal tenet of modern political science. Van Dyke expresses a widely shared belief when he argues that

> Explanation by reference to a . . . law is ordinarily incomplete. Among other things, it is incomplete in the sense that we are likely to want to know . . . why the law holds. For this purpose we seek a theory. Having explained the event by reference to . . . a law, we seek to explain the . . . law by reference to a theory. (Van Dyke, 1960, p. 41)

One of the reasons why so much attention has recently been paid to the development of theories (or "conceptual frameworks" which can provide the basis for the development of theories) is the general belief that only a systematic theory of politics, or some aspect of politics, will provide adequate explanations of an accumulating body of empirical material. For example, Deutsch (1963, pp. 3ff) describes the history of science as a dialectic of "philosophic stages," in which the development of theories is emphasized, and "empirical stages," in which theories are tested and refined. In this subsection I will present a brief characterization of the structure of scientific theories, and in the next subsection (2.4) I will discuss some of the issues involved in the testing and acceptance of a theory.

The subject of scientific theories has probably given rise to greater contention and dispute than has any other topic in the philosophy of science. To outline the contrasting positions regarding the structure and meaning of theories would require another essay of this length and would contribute little to an explication of the actual work of political scientists. It is possible, however, to discern three different uses of the term "theory" which are relatively unproblematic. The first use is clearly informal, as when the term "theory" designates a set of basic ideas about a subject—a fundamental conceptualization of a field or of a set of phenomena. In this sense, the term "theory" could be replaced by such words as "paradigm" (Kuhn, 1970b; Masterman, 1970), "research program" (Lakatos, 1970, 1971), or simply "conceptual framework." Conceptualizations of politics in terms of cybernetics (e.g., Deutsch, 1963), systems (e.g., Easton, 1965a, 1965b), functions (e.g., Almond, 1960; Almond and Powell, 1965), and the "rational choice" behavior of individual actors (e.g., Downs, 1957) are examples of "theories" in this sense. These fundamental conceptualizations play an important role in the testing and construction of theories, a role that will be discussed in Section 2.4 and Section 4 below.

A second informal use of "theory" is so vague that it might be replaced by "conjecture" or even "hypothesis." Any set of loosely articulated reasons for expecting a particular outcome may be called a "theory" in this sense. For example, one might have a theory that education is related to democratic stability, since "democracy" requires voting, which requires the ability to choose alternatives, and that ability is probably strengthened with education. This usage may be the most common, and I will occasionally use the term in this way, especially when constructing illustrations. No doubt, scientific theories may actually grow out of such vaguely formulated conjectures, but in this form they do not represent the systematic qualities which are required in a genuinely explanatory theory.

### 2.3.1 Hypothetico-Deductive Theories: The "Orthodox" View

The third use of "theory" is more formal, referring to such well-developed, systematically related sets of propositions as the kinetic theory of gases or the special theory of relativity. Although there is little agreement regarding the analysis of these theories or regarding their relationship to informal theories, one very influential position is developed in the positivist or logical empiricist tradition within the philosophy of science. This conception can be called "the 'orthodox' view of theories," to use the title of the excellent article by Feigl (1970), which provides a remarkably succinct summary and exposition of this model and of the debate it has triggered. This view, which is offered as a "rational reconstruction" of theories and *not* as an account of how theories are actually discovered and developed, sees theories as consisting of an uninterpreted postulate system or "pure calculus," together with a set of semantical rules which provide an empirical interpretation for some of the symbols of the postulate system. An uninterpreted postulate system consists of a purely formal set of symbols or elements, a set of axioms, and a number of "transformation rules," or rules of inference. The set of symbols consists of two kinds of terms. Some of the symbols of this system are explicitly "defined" in terms of other symbols in the sense that they could be replaced by the other symbols in any formula in which they occur. Obviously, however, not all the elements of the system could be explicitly defined in terms of others, without at least some of the definitions being circular. Hence there must be a set of symbols which are undefined within the system, and these elements are called "primitives." Some of the symbols of the system, including all the primitives, will be used in formulating the axioms or postulates of the system. Then, with the use of the rules of inference which the system allows (such as the standard rules of elementary logic), "theorems" can be derived from these axioms. "Theorems," then, are the formulas which can be logically derived from the axioms of a system.

So far this construction is a purely logical affair—it consists of a completely formal set of symbols and the rules for manipulating them. But this sytem can be "interpreted" by semantical rules which assign empirical meaning to some of the symbols of the system. The semantical rules say that certain elements of the calculus are to designate certain objects in the world, such as empirical entitites, relations, etc. These rules are formulated in what is called a "metalanguage," which is generally some natural language, such as ordinary English. For example, suppose that we have a system composed of the following elements: $a$, $b$, $c$, and $R$. Let the system have an axiom which reads: $(aRb) \& (bRc) \rightarrow (aRc)$. This system can be interpreted by using the following semantical rules: $R$ designates the relation "is preferred to," and $a$, $b$, and $c$ designate positions a political party could take on an ideological spectrum. The axiom, then, would say that if one position is preferred to a second (e.g., "conservative" to "liberal") and the second to a third (e.g., "liberal" to "radical"), then the first is also preferred to the third (i.e., "conservative" to "radical").

Once semantical rules have been specified, the "pure calculus" becomes a system of *statements* and no longer simply a system of formulas. Now that the symbols have been given an interpretation, the "formulas" in which they figure are not simply abstract "formalisms" but are assertions about the world. An empirically interpreted calculus, then, is a theory.

It is important to note that, in this account, not all the elements of the uninterpreted system are provided with empirical interpretations or semantical rules specifying the observable properties, relations, or entities which the term is to designate. Some of the terms of a theory will not be assigned an empirical interpretation and are called "theoretical terms." Similarly, some of the sentences of the theory will be made up only of empirically interpreted terms, and so they will be equivalent to sentences in the observation language, or the language with which we describe the empirical world. Other sentences will include only theoretical terms, and so we can say that they will be sentences in the language specific to the theory, or the theoretical language. Finally, there will be sentences which include both kinds of terms. These sentences are called "correspondence rules," and they serve to provide a partial interpretation of the theoretical language by linking it to the observational language.

Because this "orthodox" view of theories draws a sharp distinction between the "theoretical" and the "observational" languages of a theory, it has been called the "dual language" conception of theories. In this view there are two crucial components of a theory: a set of theoretical principles and a set of correspondence rules which link the theoretical principles to observations, thereby providing an indirect or partial empirical interpretation to the theoretical principles. A theory of this type is what is often called a hypothetico-deductive system.[6]

Theories constructed on this model are said to "explain" laws by permitting us to deduce them from the basic principles of the theory.

> . . . empirical science raises the question "Why?" also in regard to the uniformities expressed by . . . laws and often answers it, again, by means of a deductive-nomological explanation, in which the uniformity in question is subsumed under more inclusive laws or under theoretical principles. (Hempel, 1965, p. 343)

A theory provides a higher "level of explanation" than laws provide, because it "construes . . . phenomena as manifestations of entities that lie behind or beneath them, as it were." These entities "are assumed to be governed by characteristic theoretical laws, or theoretical principles, by means of which the theory then explains . . . empirical uniformities" (Hempel, 1966, p. 70). In general, however, a theory will not enable us to deduce the precise form of the laws which had been discovered before the theory was developed. Rather, the theory will frequently show that the laws in question hold only within certain limits, and/or it will provide a more accurate version of these laws. Moreover, theories provide an account of how a number of diverse laws and types of phenomena are systematically related, and so we can say that they do much more than simply enable us to explain laws.

If the explanatory work of the theory is done by the theoretical entities and the theoretical principles a theory posits, the correspondence rules are equally vital. Without the correspondence rules, the theoretical principles would have no meaning, since they do not refer to observable things. Hence the correspondence rules are necessary if the theory is to have empirical import, because they link the theory to statements which can be tested by experiment and observation. Indeed, without correspondence rules the theory would have no explanatory power either, for the phenomena or laws we wish to explain are described or stated in the observation language, and so the theory could explain them only if there were some means to link the language of the theory to the language of our observations.

From this brief and unfortunately abstract discussion of the structure of scientific theories, it must be obvious that we do not have such theories in political science. There are no theories which have actually been put into axiomatic form, and with the possible exception of some "rational choice" theories borrowed from economics, none of our theories is even a candidate for such axiomatization. Nonetheless, the development of such theories represents the highest aspiration of the "scientific" ideal—what many hope will grow out of the loose formulations of basic ideas which presently constitute the "theories" of our discipline. Without theories such as these, the explanatory power and systematic coherence promised by the scientific ideal will not be realized.

### 2.3.2 Some Criticisms of the Orthodox View of Theories

Before we go on to a consideration of the process of theory-testing and acceptance, it is necessary to consider some of the criticisms that have been leveled against the orthodox view of theories. Some of these criticisms are important in that they bear upon the process of theory-testing, and because they have implications for the way in which "informal" theories are related to well-developed ones.

Although a great variety of objections have been urged against the received view of scientific theories, those I will consider here all emphasize what might be called the "conceptual presuppositions" of scientific theories, or scientific inquiry in general, and they all bear upon the distinction between the "theoretical" and "observational" terms of a theory. Spector has shown that this distinction does not withstand analysis, for these categories are not mutually exclusive. He shows that there are a number of distinct uses of the terms "observable" and "unobservable" which "make different points about a term or entity. No one of these [is] such that all and only those terms which [adherents to the orthodox view] have called observable will turn out to be observable, nor will they be such that direct meanings can be given only for those terms which turn out to be observational" (Spector, 1966, p.

3). Moreover, the same is true of the notion of "theoretical terms" (Spector, 1966, p. 89).

In a similar vein, Hempel has argued that the orthodox view of theories should be reformulated. Theoretical principles should not be viewed as an uninterpreted calculus but as the "internal principles" of a theory, and correspondence rules should be reformulated as "bridge principles" linking the internal principles to an antecedently understood vocabulary, which may include previously understood theories.

> . . . the phenomena to which bridge principles link the basic entities and processes assumed by a theory need not be "directly" observable or measurable: they may well be characterized in terms of previously established theories, and their observation or measurement may presuppose the principles of those theories. (Hempel, 1966, p. 74)

Moreover, theoretical terms will often be understood before they are used in a new theory, since they will have been used in other theories, and therefore it cannot be said that they derive their meanings simply from the correspondence rules of the new theory. Hence "it is misleading to view the internal principles of a theory as an uninterpreted calculus and the theoretical terms accordingly as variables, as markers of empty shells into which the juice of empirical content is pumped through the pipelines called correspondence rules" (Hempel, 1969, p. 31).

If theories are not composed of two distinct kinds of terms, then the testing of a theory is rendered problematic. In particular, if the bridge principles do not link theoretical concepts to observables, and if theoretical terms can be given meaning directly, then it would be possible to use a theory to criticize and reject the observational statements themselves. But the observational statements are supposed to be independent of a theory so that they can be used to test it. If they are not independent but are subject to theoretical criticism, then how can we ever test a theory? And since the explantory power of a theory is dependent on its being testable, the very status of theories in the scientific enterprise seems to be called into question. This issue is taken up in the next subsection.

## 2.4 The Choice and Testing of Theories

### 2.4.1 The Difficulty of Falsifying a Theory

Political scientists have often been critical of the "theories" in our discipline because they have been "informal," consisting of sets of basic ideas about, or conceptualizations of, politics. Such informal theories may be vital to the discovery of genuine theories, but they are no substitute for the latter, because they are not testable, and therefore they cannot be explanatory.

> The complex theoretical structures of Plato, Aristotle, Aquinas, Harrington, Hobbes, Hegel, and Marx attest to no lack of imaginative abilities. What have been lacking have been the casting of theory into universal, empirically falsifiable form, and the provision of criteria of falsification. (Goldberg, 1963, pp. 34–35)

Theories are genuinely explanatory only if we can use them deductively to infer statements cast in observational terms, which can then be seen to be true or false. If such observable consequences cannot be deduced from a theory, it is not explanatory. In the absence of such consequences, the theory could not be used to show that some phenomenon could be expected (given the initial conditions), and so it could hardly be said to "explain" the event in question.

The particular conception of theory-testing involved here stresses the "falsification" of theories. According to this view, theories can be *rejected* by empirical tests, since theories entail observational statements which can be found to be false, and this finding implies that the theory itself is false. But a theory cannot be completely confirmed in this way, even if all its observational consequences are found to be correct—roughly because a false statement (or a set of statements, some of which are false) may validly imply a statement that happens to be true, as in the example, "If the Sears Tower in Chicago is over two miles tall, then it is the tallest building in the world." Once a theory has been proposed and has been shown to have observational consequences that are false, the theory must be rejected or at least reformulated. Furthermore, according to this view, it is necessary to put theories to increasingly severe tests, for it is only in this way that we can discover a theory's limitations and see where it must be changed in order to strengthen it.[7]

Unfortunately, this whole conception of how theories are tested is thrown into doubt by the considerations presented in Section 2.3.2 above. If theories do not consist of sharply distinguished observational and theoretical vocabularies, then any test of the "internal principles" of a theory is also a test of the various theoretical assumptions and principles which are part of the observational or experimental component of the theory. Hence it is always possible to save a theory by arguing that "observational" statements describing the alleged counterexample are themselves defective, and so they cannot be used to refute the internal principles of the theory.

Such moves can take two basic forms. One is to argue that there are factors extraneous to the theory operative in the situation in which the theory is tested, and so this situation does not satisfy the assumptions of the theory. For example, one might have a theory of political coalitions which predicts that only groupings of a certain sort will form. If, in a given instance, one finds that the prediction fails, the theory could be saved by discovering a further factor, such as imperfections in the structure of communication in the test situation, which shows that the theory is not applicable to this case. Hence what appeared to be a refutation turns out to be an irrelevancy.

A second move is to deny the truth of the observational statement which contradicts the theory. This can be done in several ways. One is to deny some of the theoretical principles which are part of the observational language in question. For example, if one has a "theory" that an increase in political participation by people with authoritarian personalities will undermine the stability of a democratic system by increasing the strength of extremist parties, and if this theory is not borne out by studies correlating such participation and stability, then one might save the political theory by rejecting the psychological theory used to measure or classify people as authoritarians.

A radical variant of this move would be to deny what are apparently purely "factual" statements—those which seem only to report our "rock-bottom" observations and not to "interpret" them at all. Even these elementary statements, however, do not constitute a "fancyless medium of unvarnished news" (Quine, 1960, p. 2), for they must make use of the conceptual structure of our language. What we "see"—in the sense of what statements we are prepared to affirm or deny in response to a particular stimulus—is already structured by the conceptual system we hold. Even these "rock-bottom" statements reflect "natural interpretations" (Feyerabend, 1970a, pp. 48ff), a structuring of perception (or, rather, perception-reports) so immediate that we are not aware of any structuring at all. But we can come to be aware of these natural interpretations by criticizing them from the vantage point of an alternative set of concepts, which may be the framework of a scientific theory. Hence, instead of rejecting a theory in response to certain factual statements we make, we might decide to revise our "factual" statements in light of our new theories. For example, we might come to say that the sun only *appears to rise,* rather than that it *rises*.[8] (See, e.g., Hanson, 1958, p. 5 and Chapters 1 and 2.)

It must be emphasized that it is not open to us to get around these problems by declaring such methods of saving a theory to be *ultra vires,* for the theories which underlie our observations may be wrong, and the theories which we have proposed may be correct. The desire to ensure the empirical character and testability of our theories may prompt us to forbid these stratagems, but such a move would be self-defeating. Not only would this suggestion have foreclosed a number of the most important scientific developments, but it would also effectively preclude the criticism of those elements of our observational language which may genuinely be in need of criticism. It would remove from empirical investigation and control the auxiliary sciences and theories needed to generate observational statements bearing on a theory under test, and it would therefore reduce the empirical content of science by investing our observational language with an unquestionable, "metaphysical" status. (See Feyerabend, 1963, 1965; Lakatos, 1970, pp. 93–116.)

Enough has been said to indicate that the problem of falsifying a theory or finding evidence that supports it is extremely difficult. Indeed, that problem raises fundamental questions regarding the cognitive status of science and whether or not rational grounds can ever be given for the choice of one particular theory over another. Instead of pursuing those issues,[9] however, I will present the solution to this problem which has been developed by Lakatos. In addition to showing that there are rational grounds on which theories can be evaluated, it has the merit of bearing upon the kinds of theories we actually have in the social sciences.

## 2.4.2 The Criticism and Choice of Theories

At first glance, the discussion above seems to have left us in a real dilemma. On the one hand, it seems to be possible to save a theory from refutation by using any one of a number of possible strategems, and the use of these strategems cannot be ruled out without reducing the empirical content of our knowledge. But on the other hand, if there is no way to refute a theory, then it must have lost its empirical character since its immunity from refutation can be purchased only at the cost of depriving it of any determinate implications regarding specific, observable events, processes, entities, or whatever.

In order to escape this dilemma, one must recognize that a theory is not abandoned simply because it is inconsistent with some well-confirmed observations or data. To give it up is rational only when there is a better theory to replace it. Tests of theories "are—at least—three-cornered fights between rival theories and experiment," not confrontations of isolated theories with particular facts. Indeed, inconvenient facts are never allowed to "shoot down" elegant theories, for all theories are "born refuted" (Lakatos, 1970, p. 121n). All theories face an "ocean of anomalies" (Lakatos, 1970, p. 135) or data which, at least superficially, contradict the theory, but such evidence bears on our decision to reject a theory only when we have a better theory at hand.

This observation enables us to shift our attention from the problem of evaluating or testing an individual theory to that of evaluating or testing a series of theories. Placed in this context, criteria for evaluating such a series can be stated which preserve the testability and empirical character of theories, but which do not ignore or dismiss the various strategems that can be used for "saving" them. These new criteria will "impose certain standards on the theoretical adjustments by which one is allowed to save a theory," thereby providing room for using such strategems when that use can be justified.

The basic standard governing our evaluation of a series of theories is that each subsequent theory in the series should enable us to predict "some novel, hitherto unexpected fact," and that at least some of these predictions should be corroborated. A series of theories which satisfies this criterion can be called "progressive," and a series which fails to do so can be called "degenerating." This idea can be illustrated by returning to the examples presented earlier. In one case I suggested that a theory of coalition formation might be saved from refutation by introducing a new variable, "communication imperfections," into the description of the test situation, thereby showing that it failed to meet the assumptions of the theory. According to the criterion developed here, this strategem would be permissible only if adding this variable to the theory would enable us to predict new facts. Otherwise, it would be prohibited as a "content-decreasing" move which must be rejected as pseudo-scientific. Similarly, in the case of the theory relating increased participation by "authoritarians" to political instability, any attempt to save the theory by rejecting the psychological theory on which the measures of "authoritarianism" are based would be progressive only if it led to a new theory which not only removed the anomaly in question but also predicted additional findings, such as other features of the behavior of "authoritarians" or, possibly, other consequences of their political participation. In both of these cases we are concerned with evaluating possible theoretical adjustments. Until one of the adjustments we try "works," there is no need to reject the theory—at least, there is no need to reject it simply on the grounds that it contradicts known facts.

The latter example is of additional interest since it bears directly on the idea of a theory being "confronted" with and tested by the "facts." In this case and in all such cases, this is a misleading formulation—at least, once we have given up the orthodox conception of theories which sharply distinguishes between "observational" and "theoretical" statements. What is to be counted as the "facts" depends on the perspective we decide to adopt. If we focus on the theory of instability, the factual statements are those describing the effects of increased participation by authoritarians. But those statements amount to two different sets of claims. One is that certain individuals behaved in certain ways, and the other is that they had certain characteristics, $c_1$, $c_2$, etc., which imply that they are authoritarians. Hence, accepting those statements as "factual" amounts to accepting the psychological theory according to which characteristics $c_1$, $c_2$, etc., are indicators of authoritarianism. If instead we should decide to accept the political theory as "factual," or "correct," then the statements describing the behavior of those particular individuals would serve to refute the psychological theory. Hence, what we have here is an inconsistency between two theories, in light of certain observations.

> . . . experiments do not simply overthrow theories, [and] no theory forbids a state of affairs specifiable in advance. It is not that we propose a theory and Nature may shout NO; rather, we propose a maze of theories, and Nature may shout INCONSISTENT. (Lakatos, 1970, p. 130)

This conflict or inconsistency is resolved by determining which adjustment in either or both theories leads to the greatest increase in empirical content.

By setting up the standard of increasing empirical content to govern theoretical adjustments, and by conceptualizing the problem of theory-testing in terms of evaluating a series of theories, we preserve the empirical—and therefore explanatory—character of scientific theories. By developing standards which we can use to evaluate successive or proposed theories, we avoid the dilemma which the criticism of the orthodox view of theories posed. We no longer need to choose between, on the one hand, blocking off some areas of empirical inquiry in order to preserve some statements as "factual" so that they can be used in testing theories and, on the other hand, permitting our theories to become trivial by opening up the flood gates to a multitude of strategems for saving a theory. Since we are not trying to test a single, isolated theory but are evaluating a series of theories, we can permit the floodgates to open and allow all theory-saving strategems to be used. But we insist that these moves count as creating a new theory, and we insist that this new theory have a greater empirical content than the original one.

The demand that we continuously increase the empirical content of our theories may, at first glance, seem to get us out of one thicket only to land us in another. Although it bars both those ploys (usually verbal reformulations) which simply remove an anomaly without predicting new facts, and those theoretical adjustments which predict new "facts" that turn out to be wrong, it fails to stop those theoretical adjustments which simply amount to adding another hypothesis to a theory when that hypothesis has no real relationship to the rest of the theory. For example, this standard does not rule out a "research strategy" which consists in selecting one's "independent variables" from a correlation matrix simply with a view to maximizing the "variance explained" in the dependent variables.

In cases such as these, the theoretical adjustment is merely "empirical" or "formal"; it provides us with a better "fit" between theory and data but at the cost of increasing the "complexity" of the theory to the same degree that the fit is improved. Thus the resulting theory fails to provide unity and coherence to a field by representing diverse phenomena as the result of a few basic, underlying theoretical principles. Since this is one important purpose of scientific theories, our standards for evaluating theories must be strengthened to prevent such (non)theoretical growth by agglomeration. Lakatos has formulated such standards in terms of what he calls "research programs."

## 2.4.3 Scientific Research Programs

The basic way to prevent theories from growing as a result of the piling up of a number of unrelated hypotheses is to require that there be some continuity between them. This rather vague requirement can be clarified in terms of the idea of a "research program." A new theory which has more empirical content than the preceding one will be acceptable only if it meets one of two conditions: (1) it is developed in accordance with the same underlying program of research as the preceding theory, or (2) it launches an altogether new program. From this point of view, a research program "consists of methodological rules: some tell us what paths of research to avoid (*negative heuristic*), and others what paths to pursue (*positive heuristic*)" (Lakatos, 1970, p. 132; emphasis in original). These rules reflect or provide an "implicit definition of the conceptual framework" or the "language" of the scientific theory. That is, the research program may be said to define the fundamental conceptualization of the phenomena within an area of study and the system of concepts and basic principles which are to be used in ordering and explaining those phenomena. Lakatos provides several examples of research programs in the natural sciences, including Newton's gravitational theory. In the political and social sciences there are several such research programs, or "proto-research programs," since some have yet to be very well defined. Perhaps the most successful is the conception of politics in terms of the "rational choice" model, a program I will analyze in some detail in Section 4. Similarly, "functionalism," "group theory," Marxism, and "systems theory" could all be considered research programs, or nascent research programs, for they have provided the conceptual frameworks for some research within political science.

Lakatos argues that research programs may be characterized by a "hard core," which he calls the "negative heuristic," and a "protective belt" of auxiliary hypotheses and theories, which he calls the "positive heuristic." The negative heuristic consists of those basic assumptions which the theorist refuses to change, irrespective of the evidence. For example, the hard core of Newtonian mechanics, according to Lakatos, consisted of the "three laws of dynamics and the law of gravitation" (Lakatos, 1970, p. 133). In the rational choice research program, the hard core consists of the conceptualization of social phenomena in terms of the rational choices of individual actors responding to the structure of incentives they face (see Section 4). The negative heuristic comprises the theorist's basic ideas about a field, and if a test goes against a theory, or if mathematical or logical difficulties arise in the course of articulating a theory, the theorist will refuse to make adjustments in these basic principles, but will alter some feature(s) of the protective belt in order to "save" the hard core. One of the factors that make a series of theories continuous, then, is that each theory in the series has the same "hard core" as the others.

The "positive heuristic" or "protective belt" is the second component of a research program. Whereas the negative heuristic tells us what assumptions or principles are *not* to be altered, the positive heuristic provides, as it were, the "plan" for future research on the program. Any theory or research program is always subject to a host of apparent counter-examples or anomalies, and it is impossible to deal with all of them at once. Rather, they must be attacked in an orderly fashion, and it is the function of the positive heuristic to create that order by providing directives to guide research. From this perspective, the positive heuristic "consists of a partially articulated set of suggestions or hints on how to change, develop the 'refutable variants' of the research-program, how to modify, sophisticate, the 'refutable' protective belt" (Lakatos, 1970, p. 135). By working on a research program in accordance with the positive heuristic, the theorist will generate "a chain of ever more complicated models simulating reality," in which each successive model is developed from the preceding one by altering some of the restrictive or simplifying assumptions of the earlier model in accordance with the directives of the positive heuristic. In the case of the Newtonian research program, for example, Newton began with a highly simplified model of the solar system consisting of only one pointlike planet orbiting the fixed pointlike sun, and as he developed a satisfactory analysis of this case, he relaxed these assumptions and developed a series of ever more complex models. In a similar fashion, Downs's theory of political action in a democracy began with a highly simplified model of perfectly informed parties, and those restrictive assumptions were gradually relaxed until a reasonably complex, explanatory theory emerged.

A research program can be called "progressive" so long as work in accordance with the positive heuristic continually yields theories which are progressive. But eventually a point will be reached where the program begins to "run out of steam." Theoretical innovations will be proposed which are degenerating, and it will become increasingly difficult to save the hard core of the program without resort to various ad hoc strategems. When this occurs researchers will—and ought to—gradually abandon the program in favor of one which is, at the time at least, progressive.

The hard core and the protective belt of a research program, then, constitute the continuities between successive theories which serve to rule out the use of auxiliary hypotheses which reflect a different way of conceptualizing the subject matter in question. This conception of a research program gives substance to the second principal criterion for evaluating, testing, and choosing theories. We require that successive theories, in the first place, have increased empirical content in the sense that later theories predict facts which are not predicted by earlier ones, and that some of these predictions be confirmed. Second, we require either that successive theories be continuous in the sense that they develop within the same research program, or that a new theory launch a new research program altogether. Finally, when we evaluate competing research programs, we judge one program to be better than another if it is generating a series of theories which are progressive, whereas the other is plagued with degenerating theories. These criteria provide us with standards which can be used in rationally evaluating theories, but which recognize that no theory can be conclusively falsified. Although there are certain difficulties with Lakatos's program,[10] and no doubt it will be amplified in the future, it is sufficient to demonstrate the testable, and therefore explanatory, character of scientific theories.

## 2.5 The Scientific Ideal: Summary and Conclusions

In this section I have presented an outline of some important features of the methodology of the natural sciences. I have focused on the interrelated problems of scientific explanation and the empirical import or testability of scientific theories. These are certainly among the features which make scientific methodology so attractive to students of society and politics. Moreover, those who reject the naturalist model of social and political inquiry generally focus on the covering law pattern of explanation. They argue, as I shall show in the next section, that social and political inquiry requires a *different* model of explanation—one that is equally empirical but does not require laws or generalizations and does not lead to the development of theories. In order to appreciate this position, then, it is essential to outline as fully as possible the main features of the covering law model of explanation, and to show that it is related to other aspects of the scientific ideal.

The nomological pattern of explanation, as its name implies, requires the presence of general laws in any explanatory account. When we say that one thing—for example, military aggressiveness—occurs because of something else—for example, rapid economic growth—we require a general law linking these factors in order to "provide force" to the "because." But not just any kind of general statement can perform this explanatory function. Not only must laws be unrestricted universals (i.e., they must be in universal form and must apply to an unrestricted class of objects), but they must also support "counter-to-fact" and subjunctive conditional statements. For example, if it really is a law that rapid economic growth leads to military aggression, then we should be willing to say that if England's rate of economic growth had been a few points higher, she would have started World War I. But to make such an assertion requires a great deal more information than that conveyed by a particular law, and so in order to understand the explanatory force of laws, we had to examine them in relation to scientific theories.

The term "theory" is used in a number of different ways, and even when it refers to the fairly well articulated theories of the natural sciences, there is considerable controversy regarding their logical structure. The received or orthodox view of theories has the merit of being reasonably well specified, but it makes what appears to be an untenable distinction between "theoretical" and "observational" concepts. And when this distinction is dropped, the process of theory-testing becomes problematic. Once we admit that even our "rock-bottom" observation statements are conceptually structured and can therefore be criticized, we realize that "facts" cannot serve as an independent basis on which to judge "theories." This does not mean that our choice of scientific theories can be made in a purely subjective manner, however, and I outlined Lakatos's argument showing that there are rational standards for testing and evaluating theories. These standards presuppose the concept of a "research program," or a fundamental conceptualization of some phenomena, together with the basic concepts and principles which are used in ordering and explaining them. They require that theories be developed within such research programs in order to avoid an essentially ad hoc agglomeration of hypotheses passing as thoretical progress. Then, theoretical development within a research program is to be governed by the demand that new theories have more empirical content than the theories they replace. Finally, a research program can be evaluated by the extent to which it gives rise to a progressive series of theories.

Not only does this concept of a research program show that theories can be tested and therefore that they can have explanatory import, but it also helps us to see the manner in which science provides unity and coherence to a field of inquiry. Scientific theories represent a range of diverse phenomena and regularities as the manifestations of a small number of theoretical entities and their interrelationships, and they do so in terms of a conceptual structure with "heuristic power," which provides a basis for the further articulation and development of theories of even greater scope. This systematically progressive nature of science is one of its greatest attractions. But some have argued that the methods of science are unable to account for the kinds of phenomena which the social and political scientist seeks to understand. Their arguments and their ideal of political inquiry are examined in the next section.

## 3  THE INTERPRETATION AND EXPLANATION OF POLITICAL ACTION

### 3.1  The Distinctive Character of Social Phenomena

In this section I will outline the "interpretative" model of political inquiry, a methodological position opposed to the naturalist conception. The fundamental opposition between these two models concerns the account of "explanation" which each espouses. We have already seen that the naturalist model insists on the crucial role of laws and generalizations in scientific accounts. As Hempel argues, "all scientific explanation involves, explicitly or by implication, a subsumption of its subject matter under general regularities; . . . it seeks to provide a systematic understanding of empirical phenomena by showing that they fit into a nomic nexus" (1965, p. 488).

The interpretative model of political inquiry insists that laws and generalizations are not necessary to an understanding of human actions and institutions. Although generalizations may have heuristic value in alerting us to the kinds of factors we should look for in a situation, they are *not* part of the logical structure of an explanation itself. The reason is that social phenomena are fundamentally different from natural phenomena in that they are "intentional": they express the purposes and ideas of social actors. Therefore actions, like language, have an essentially meaningful or symbolic character. Hence they must be understood in terms of the intentions of the actor and in terms of the conventions of his society, which specify the meaning or significance of particular acts. Such understanding does not require generalizations, and it certainly does not require "causal" laws. Rather, it requires a process of *interpretation* in which the meanings of an action are uncovered by analyzing the action in light of the agent's particular situation and in light of the conventions, practices, and rules of his society. It is analogous to the way we understand what a person says by explicating the meanings of his utterance in terms of the conventions of the language and in terms of its relationship to the other things he is saying and doing.

Not only does the interpretative model of social inquiry develop a different pattern of explanation, but it also organizes and provides coherence to social phenomena in a way different from that of the naturalist model. Where the scientist articulates theories and research programs and tries to reduce a welter of events to the operation of a few basic principles, the humanist identifies and analyzes traditions of discourse and action and articulates the fundamental ideas and "constitutive meanings" that provide unity or coherence to a particular society or form of life. And where the naturalist unearths the causal mechanisms which underlie phenomena and so provides us with the knowledge that is requisite to control, the humanist clarifies meanings and intentions and so increases our capacity to communicate with and understand one another.[11]

My presentation of the interpretative model begins with its criticisms of the nomological pattern of explanation as an account of how we understand actions. Then, in Section 3.3, I present the basic explanatory scheme of the interpretative model, the practical inference. Although the practical inference links actions to the intentions of the actor, it is incomplete as an explanatory account. Just as scientific laws require theories, so the explanation of an individual action requires an analysis of the conventions and "constitutive meanings" of a society. These concepts are developed in Section 3.4, and some implications of this model for the testing and acceptance of explanatory and descriptive accounts are discussed in Section 3.5. Finally, in Section 3.6, I present and answer several objections to this model of political inquiry.

Extravagant claims are made for both the interpretative and the naturalist accounts of social and political science. Both are offered as complete descriptions of the methodology of political science, and neither recognizes the other position. The central thesis of this chapter, however, is that both models are necessary, for neither is alone able to recognize the full complexities of political and social life. Indeed, I will argue in Section 4 that these ostensibly conflicting accounts can be viewed as presupposing and complementing each other, and that only a synthesis of the two approaches can provide an adequate methodology for political research. Before I can develop that synthesis, however, it is necessary to present the interpretative model in its own terms.

## 3.2 The Naturalist Explanation of Action

The scientific ideal outlined in Section 2 purports to account for the structure of explanations in political science. This does not mean that all of our explanations are actually cast in the form of the covering law model; it means only that they can be *reconstructed* to fit it. In particular, it means that we should be able to ferret out lawlike generalizations in the explanatory accounts offered by political scientists for such generalizations are essential to any explanation. But if we find that such generalizations do not figure in our explanations, then the applicability of the naturalist model to social phenomena will be called into question. In this section I shall argue that at least one kind of explanatory account does not appear to fit the covering law model.

One common type of explanation in political science is what might be called "rationale explanations," in which the political scientist explains the actions of some political actor by presenting the "rationale," or reasons, for his actions. For example, Dahl in *Who Governs?* (1961) analyzes Mayor Lee's decisions in two cases involving support for his appointees on the New Haven School Board. In one case, Lee decided to support them by working for the appointment of their nominee to a post within the school administration; in the other situation, Lee decided not to support them and did not put his influence behind their proposal to change the promotion policies of the school system. Dahl's explanation presents the rationale for Lee's first decision.

> Had he failed to support Miss White the Mayor might have permanently alienated important support: the candidate of Golden and Barbieri would have been appointed; their influence within the schools and

within [Lee's Democratic Party] would have increased relative to his own; and his highly favorable public image would probably have been damaged. (1961, p. 213)

Lee's second decision, however, was a "different story"

> The Mayor was a busy man; he could not be expected to intervene every time his appointees on the Board ran into a snag; if he did so too often he might easily step over the ill-defined boundaries beyond which his intervention would appear to many persons as illegitimate political interference in the school system. (1961, pp. 213–214)

It goes without saying that this summary is an "explanation-sketch," not a complete account of the mayor's decisions. Dahl had earlier supplied a great deal of information about these decisions, which he did not recount in his summary, and even in the more complete analysis he did not feel it necessary to present some possibilities, since the reader could be presumed to understand them already—for example, that Lee would not arrest the rival candidate, thereby preempting the field, although this alternative was theoretically open to him. But in order to show that Dahl's explanation of Mayor Lee's decisions conforms to the covering law model, it is not necessary to supply such additional details but it *is* necessary to discover the implicit generalizations or laws which it contains. If we cannot find such laws or generalizations, then we shall have to conclude that this kind of explanation does not conform to the covering law model of scientific explanations. And this would mean that there is a fundamental methodological distinction between natural and social science.

Hempel, of course, argues that this kind of explanation does depend on laws, and he offers the following reconstruction of rationale explanations to show that they can and must be understood as instances of the nomological pattern.

| | |
|---|---|
| Initial conditions: | A was in a situation of type C. |
| | A was a rational agent. |
| Law: | In a situation of type C, any rational agent will do X. |
| Explanandum: | A did X. |

Applying this schema to one of Dahl's examples, we might have the following.

| | |
|---|---|
| Initial conditions: | Mayor Lee could back his appointees and would incur a net gain of political support. |
| | Mayor Lee was a rational agent. |
| Law: | In situations in which one will incur a net gain of political support by backing his appointees, any rational agent will back them. |

Explanandum:        Mayor Lee did back his appointees.

Although this reconstruction has effected a drastic simplification of Dahl's analysis, it does at least superficially correspond to the covering law model. The problem with it is the status of the "law" it contains. It appears that this putative law actually expresses (at least part of) what we mean when we call an action rational: What is it to be rational except to act so that the "gains" from one's actions exceed the "costs?" Hence the explanatory force of the argument rests on the singular statements which describe the kind of position Lee found himself in and which attribute "rationality" to the mayor. The generalization not being an empirical law, the explanation does not conform to the covering law model of explanation.

A defender of the naturalistic ideal might rebut this interpretation, as Hempel does, by arguing that "rationality" is "a broadly dispositional concept" (1965, p. 472). A dispositional concept attributes a disposition to an object to react in a certain way under certain conditions. When we say that glass is brittle, for example, we are saying that it will shatter if struck with a certain amount of force. Similarly, when we say that opium has a "dormitive power," we are saying that it tends to put one to sleep when one smokes it. Frequently explanations using dispositional concepts are question-begging, the classic example being the explanation of one's falling asleep after smoking opium by invoking opium's dormitive powers. But dispositional concepts can legitimately be used in explaining some item of the behavior of some object, provided that our grounds for attributing the disposition to the object are different from the behavior the disposition brings about. For example, if we know that a person who is tired is always irritable, then we can explain his becoming angry with little provocation in terms of his being irritable, without simply repeating our original observation that the person got angry for nothing, since we can attribute irritability to him on the basis of his being tired.

If we were to treat "rationality" as a dispositional concept, we would have to define the behavior which is sufficient to attribute rationality to a person and the behavior which a rational individual necessarily displays. We would then have statements of the form

"If an individual does Z in situations of type A, then he is rational."

and

"In situations of type C, any rational agent will do X."

Together these statements entail

"Individuals who do Z in situations of type A will do X in situations of type C."

For example, we might say that Mayor Lee's rationality was shown by his advocacy of urban redevelopment, and we could come up with a statement like

"Politicians who advocate redevelopment when redevelopment appears to be popular will back their appointees when backing them will result in a net gain of political support."

We could then provide a new analysis of Dahl's explanation of Mayor Lee's actions.

Initial conditions: Mayor Lee was in a situation in which he could attain a net gain of political support by backing his appointees.

Mayor Lee advocated redevelopment when it was popular.

Law: Individuals who advocate redevelopment when it is popular will back their appointees when doing so results in a net gain of political support.

Explanandum: Mayor Lee backed his appointees.

In this case there can be no doubt that the "law" in question is an empirical statement, since one could deny it without fear of contradicting himself. This reformulated syllogism, then, is a proper example of a nomological explanation.

If we have finally succeeded in developing a nomological explanation for Mayor Lee's actions, it is far from obvious that we have shown that social science explanations are at least implicitly of the same form as natural science explanations. To do so we must demonstrate that this syllogism is a *reconstruction* of Dahl's argument—that what it supplies is already implicit in, or logically required by, the original explanation. But in Dahl's exposition there is nothing even analogous to the "law" which figures so prominently in this account. We do not find Dahl marshaling a great number of examples of political figures who supported or failed to support their appointees in similar circumstances, nor does he try to show that any particular combinations of Lee's characteristics or behavior can be taken as sufficient conditions for attributing "rationality" to Lee or to any political actor. Indeed, we must conclude that this putative reconstruction of Dahl's explanation is, in actuality, a *substitution* for it. And in the absence of a demonstration that the original analysis is seriously deficient, it is not at all obvious why we should accept this substitute.

On the other hand, there are two fundamental reasons why we might *not* accept it. The first is that it is little more than a promissory note. We do not have laws of the form this explanation requires, and until we do have such laws, the demand that we cast our explanation in these terms can only express a pious faith in the future of a naturalistic social science. Hempel, of course, is quick to grant that the required laws are not available and even notes that the concepts in terms of which such laws would be stated—"belief," "purpose," "moral standard," etc.—have yet to be satisfactorily explicated. That is why he insists on calling "rationality" only a "broadly dispositional" concept (1965, pp. 472–474). But however the argument may be qualified, until we have the laws we do not have a substitute for traditional explanations—much less a reconstruction of them.

Second, and more important, it is not at all clear that what is lacking in Dahl's analysis is a generalization of any sort. Consider, for example, someone who doubted Dahl's account and argued that the reasons offered for Lee's behavior in these two cases do not explain what he did. Even if we could present example after example of politicians who behaved in that way for those reasons, we would not be likely to convince an objector of the adequacy of this account in this particular case. Rather, such doubts would normally be stilled only by a more detailed description of the actual case, enabling us to dismiss other possible motives for Lee's actions. But this shows that the explanatory power of this account rests on the particulars which are adduced to support it, rather than in any generalization which might be added to it.

We do make use of generalizations in developing explanations of why an agent takes some particular action. But when we use generalizations, they do not play the role attributed to them by the covering law model. For example, if someone were to doubt whether politicians ever acted to maintain or increase their political support, we should point to a number of cases in which that was the motive for their actions. But in each case cited we would have to show that maintaining political support was the motive, and we would have to do so *without* invoking general laws linking this motive to their actions. Indeed, if we were willing to risk a generalization to the effect that politicians usually (or always) act to maintain political support, it would be because we had found this reason to explain their behavior in each particular case—and we would have to find it so *before* we could offer the generalization. Obviously, then, the explanation of the actions could not require that we already have the generalization in question.

In the explanation of action we use generalizations in a fundamentally different way from the way they are used in the explanation of natural events. In the natural sciences we must have a generalization before we can explain a particular event in terms of earlier events or conditions. Until we are ready to formulate such a law, all we have is the coincidental occurrence of two events in succession, and we cannot explain one in terms of the other. But in explaining human actions, we can know the connection between an action and the reasons for an action without reference to any general laws or lawlike statements. (See Hart and Honoré, 1959, Chapter 2, for an excellent statement of this argument.)

The idea that generalizations are necessary in the explanation of actions, just as in the explanation of the behavior of things, is based on a misunderstanding about the nature of action and therefore about the type of explanation that is appropriate to it. In the next part of this section I further explicate the concept of human action and present a schema that is appropriate to the explanation or, as I would rather say, to the *understanding* of action.

### 3.3 Action, Intention, and Practical Inference

We have seen that one common form of explanation in social science, "rationale explanations," does not appear to rest on generalizations. Significant doubts about such accounts seem to be ultimately reducible to doubts about particulars and can be expressed by such questions as whether a politician had other purposes than those suggested or whether there was additional background information which would lead us to wonder whether his conduct could properly be described, for example, as supporting or failing to support his appointees. The reason rationale explanations do not require generalizations is that they serve to explicate the *meanings* of the actions in question; the attempt to cast such explanations in the deductive-nomological form neglects this essential aspect of human action.

In saying that actions have "meanings," I am, at least initially, merely invoking the familiar distinction between "action" on the one hand and "movement" on the other—between what a person *does* and what *happens* to him. To use a well-worn example, one can raise one's arm, but the action of raising one's arm cannot be identified with the fact that one's arm rises. One might be "hooked up" to some kind of machine that stimulates one's nervous system in such a way that one's arm goes up. An action is something that we *do*, and it is distinguished from mere movements of our body, from things that might happen to us, by its irreducibly intentional or purposive character. In acting, we not only have "control" over our movements, but we *intend* to do what we are doing, and the movement of our body is carried out more or less in accordance with our intentions. Because of this intentional character of action, it is always appropriate to ask of any action, "What is its point?" This question is clearly not in order regarding mere movements or events in nature.

The question "What is the point of that action?" expresses part of what we mean when we ask, "What does that action mean?" This idea is familiar to social scientists who are acquainted with Weber's notion of "action" as "subjectively intended" or "subjectively meaningful" behavior—behavior that has a "sense" or "significance" for the agent. One of the ways of explicating the sense or "meaning" of behavior is to subsume it under some intention or purpose it realized or was intended to realize. Thus we observe someone raising his arm, and we say, "He's signaling." In doing so, we are describing his action (raising his arm) in terms of one of its conventional "consequences": raising an arm in such circumstances constitutes "signaling."

Similarly, we might describe someone's "lighting the stove" as "preparing supper," since it is part of a complex performance intended to realize that goal. Again, we might say that a person who is opening a window is cooling the room, thereby describing what he does in terms of one of its causal consequences. Or yet another example, we might describe someone as enjoying his walk, indicating that he has no ulterior or further purpose in taking a walk. In each example we redescribe an action in terms of some purpose or intention which it advances or of which it is a part, and the variety of these four cases indicates something of the complexity of the relationship between intention and action.[12]

It should be emphasized that in each case it is an action that is explained or redescribed in terms of some intention, not a set of "movements," such as "arm-risings" or "feet-going-up-and-down," that are explained. What we want to have explained are someone's actions and what we directly observe are his actions. We do not observe various physical movements and then infer that the person is acting. For example, we do not see an arm going up and then infer that someone is raising his arm unless we find ourselves in very unusual circumstances (such as viewing what we believe to be a corpse and suddenly seeing its arm begin to go up). We no more "see" movements and "infer" actions than we "see" blotches of color with varying intensities of light and shadow and "infer" the existence of material objects. Of course, we are sometimes mistaken; what we think is an action may turn out to be merely a reflex movement, just as we may be mistaken in seeing a material object when there is only light and shadow. Actions are an essential and basic constituent of our perceptual world, just as they make up our social world.

Explaining the meaning of an action is also explaining the action, for in describing the end or the intention which the action realizes, we explain why the action was performed. This form of explanation can be set out as a "practical syllogism."[13] Such an argument consists of a (set of) premise(s) stating the end to be achieved, another (set of) premise(s) stating the means believed to be necessary or expedient in realizing the end, and the conclusion: that the agent attempts to do what is required and therefore does it unless he is prevented or fails. Although the practical syllogism is a very old idea, it has not received much attention until recently, when a number of philosophers have used it to develop a more adequate analysis of human action. As formulated by Aristotle, the major premise is a characterization of something as desirable—"dry food"—and a description of something as falling under the major premise—"Here is some dry food." These premises issue in an action—eating the dry food. Whereas a theoretical syllogism issues in a proposition whose truth is guaranteed by its premises, a practical syllogism issues in an action whose appropriateness or justification is guaranteed by the premises.

There is obviously something odd about holding that there are logical relations among such disparate items as value judgments, empirical statements, and actions. Indeed, it may be thought that logical relations can hold only among propositions, so that the very idea of a practical syllogism is incoherent. However, von Wright (1971, 1972) has recently formulated an account of the practical syllogism which promises to be adequate for the purposes of explaining actions. He argues that the premises must be construed as statements describing the end the actor has in view and the actions he considers necessary to realize that end. The conclusion, then, is a statement to the effect that the agent intends to perform the action or that he sets himself to do what is required at the appropriate time. Making allowance for all possible qualifications, his schema is as follows:

From now on A intends to bring about $p$ at time $t$.

From now on A considers that, unless he does $a$ no later than at time $t'$, he cannot bring about $p$ at time $t$.

Therefore, no later than when he thinks time $t'$ has arrived, A sets himself to do $a$, unless he forgets about the time or is prevented. (von Wright, 1971, p. 107)

If the practical inference schema in this form is acceptable, then there is a type of explanation in social science which does not rely on general laws, and this conclusion means that there is a fundamental methodological distinction between natural and social science. The major issue concerning practical inferences, then, is whether the link between the premises of the argument—or the agent's *reasons* for his action—and the conclusion—the agent's setting himself to act—is logical or contingent. If it is contingent, the reasons can be considered "causes" of the agent's behavior, and we will have to amend this practical inference schema by adding a general law to it. The general law is necessary to make the schema into a satisfactory explanation, for only then will the premises actually entail the conclusion. Such a law might take the form (using the language of the schema above: "If a person intends to bring about $p$ at time $t$, and if he considers that, unless he does $a$ no later than at time $t'$, he cannot bring about $p$ at time $t$, then he will do (or set himself to do) $a$ at $t'$, unless he forgets about the time or is prevented." If this putative law should be analytically true, then the link between the premises and the conclusion would be logical, not contingent. We would not need to have a general law in order to have a complete explanation of why the agent did what he did, and we could conclude that the naturalistic model of social science is not adequate as a complete account of social science methodology.

If the relationship between reason and actions is merely contingent, it should be possible to demonstrate the existence of the two things —intentions and actions—independently of each other. If we cannot determine the existence of the action apart from ascertaining the intentions, and if we cannot ascertan an agent's intentions without thereby verifying that he acted in a certain way, we have to conclude that his intentions and his actions are logically linked—two aspects of the same thing, like "being a material object" and "being extended."[14] Thus, supposing that the conditions of a practical inference are satisfied, we must determine whether it is possible to show that some agent, A, performed some action, *a*, without thereby assuming that the premises of an associated practical inference are true.

To show that a certain action—say, voting—has taken place, we can point to certain physical occurrences: his fingers wrapped around the lever, his arm moved down depressing it, and so forth. But the conclusion of the practical inference is that an *action* was performed—that the behavior or the "movements" were *intentional* under some description. What is at stake is not the *movements* of a person's fingers, arms, etc., but that he *voted*. In this case, the movements in question were relevant but not conclusive. The sequence could have been produced by some machine that stimulates the nerves to produce just those movements, or the person could have been acting in a movie or learning how to vote. Alternatively, an entirely different set of movements could have counted as voting—raising his arm, marking a ballot, saying "aye," etc. And the situation would have been even more complicated if the "action" in question had been a forbearance—refusing or failing to vote, not because he forgot or tried unsuccessfully but because he deliberately did not vote. Thus, verifying that an action or a forbearance has occurred requires us to verify the premises of an associated practical inference, for only then can the intentional character of the action be confirmed and the movements (or lack of movement) be characterized as an action of a particular type.

Just as we cannot verify the conclusions of a practical inference without verifying the premises, neither can we establish the premises without establishing the conclusion, because we cannot show that a person had certain intentions without showing that he acted in a certain way. Of course, there is normally no question of verifying either the action or the intentions. When an American enters a voting booth on election day and marks a ballot, we *see* that he is voting, and the fanciful possibilities canvassed above do not even occur to us. As a member of American society, the person can be presumed to have the requisite knowledge, abilities, and interests which qualify his behavior as "voting." That he is voting is evident from the way his behavior fits into a "story about the agent" (von Wright, 1971, p. 115), his education, his party identification, his having planned to arrive home late, his having registered to vote, his expressed concern for public issues, the "fact" that it is election day, the similar actions of others, etc.

If we are dissatisfied with such indirect evidence that his behavior was intentional, we might resort to the rather obvious expedient of asking the actor what he intends in doing what he is doing. (See von Wright, 1971, pp. 112ff.) In response, he is no doubt likely to say that he is voting. But have we advanced our project significantly? When he answers us, he is performing another action in many respects similar to the action we were originally trying to explain. How are we to establish that he *says* he is voting, as opposed to uttering the noise "I am voting?" Perhaps he does not *mean* "I am voting" when he makes these sounds. Perhaps he did not understand our question. And of course, there is always the possibility that he is dissimulating regarding his intention. Perhaps he has even "deceived" himself—saying, for example, that he intends to vote when in fact he does not *really* intend to vote at all.

Then are we to say that only the agent himself can really know whether the premises of a practical inference are true—that only he can know what the reasons for his actions *really* are? Is it that the premises are descriptive of the inner states of the agent's mind, and only the agent can "see" what state his mind is in, and so only he can say whether any statement correctly reports it or not? This move may have great appeal, at least superficially, for am I not the best judge of my own intentions? But this leads directly to the question of how we ascertain the intention of an act. In the first place, contrary to the widely held position stemming from Dilthey and Weber, recognizing one's own intentions is not analogous to perception; it is not like seeing something—in this case a something that just happens to be "inside" and visible only through a special faculty called "introspection." On the contrary, we justify our saying that we have certain intentions and beliefs in the same way that others come to judge them—by reflecting on our actions, on what we do, how we choose, how we react, and so on. And our immediate knowledge of our intentions—the knowledge we have while we are actually engaged in some activity—is not based on perceptions of any inner states. (At the end of a day's work we do not "look inward" and proclaim, "Ah, yes! I now see that I want to go home.") Rather this knowledge

> *is* the intentionality of my behavior, its association with an intention to achieve something. It is therefore of no use for verifying the premises of a practical inference which say what my intentions and cognitive attitudes are, since it *is* itself the very thing which has to be established. . . . (von Wright, 1971, p. 114)

The mistake in this move to inner states is to suppose that the intention is some sort of mental event which lurks behind the manifest behavior. It is encouraged, no doubt, by our common experience of resolving to do something. Sometimes a person says to himself, "I will now do *x*," and since we all have this experience, we may come to think of intentions as if they were such "internal resolutions." But even in this case, how does the person know that he really intends to do it? How does he know that this "internal resolution" is his real intention unless he knows that he really means what he (internally) says? And how could he know this—except in terms of how he actually acts? Even in this case, then, intentions are not private mental events.

The intention is not something different from the behavior: ". . . to intend to be doing something is to be performing or trying to perform some action in order to realize some state of affairs (Locke, 1969, p. 145). An action is not an item of behavior which is (somehow) associated with something else called an "intention." On the contrary,

> Behavior gets its intentional character from being *seen* by the agent himself or by an outside observer in a wider perspective, from being set in a context of aims and cognitions. (von Wright, 1971, p. 115)

An action, in short, is a behavioral "sequence *meant* by me or *understood* by others as an act" of a particular kind (von Wright, 1971, p. 115). Thus one cannot identify an intention independently of the act it explains.

Since actions cannot be identified independently of intentions and intentions cannot be determined apart from actions, it follows that they are logically rather than contingently related. Therefore the explanation of action in terms of practical inferences does not rest on any nomic connections between the intention and the act. The nomological-deductive model, then, does not provide an adequate reconstruction of "rationale" explanations of behavior, since the "rationale" of an action is (part of) what establishes something as an action in the first place! A practical inference, on the other hand, by providing the intention of an action, explains why the agent performed it and enables us to understand at least part of the meaning of the action—what the actor intended in doing what he did. Moreover, on the basis of an account of the agent's intentions, a practical inference justifies our redescribing an action in accordance with its intention. Thus raising one's arm can be redescribed as "voting" when it is meant or understood as an act of voting. Similarly, under rather special circumstances, pumping water can be redescribed as "killing Nazis," provided that the water is poisoned, that it is being pumped into a cistern from which Nazis are drinking, and that the person responsible knows that the water is poisoned, etc. (For this example, see Anscombe, 1957, pp. 37ff). The practical inference, then, is an indispensable tool of the social sciences.

## 3.4 Action, Convention, and Meaning

### 3.4.1 Conventions and Practices

The emphasis on discovering the purposes of an individual actor has sometimes led people to neglect the intrinsically conventional character of all human action and to overemphasize its instrumental nature. In the first place, there is a whole class of actions, particularly important in politics, which are meaningful not because they express intentions but because they involve an application of a rule or convention. For example, even if we are dealing with a person who cannot provide a reason for the way he voted in some election—or even for his voting at all—his action clearly has "sense" so long as elections are an operative institution in his society and he has some understanding of the conventions governing political life and the place or "function" of elections therein. As Winch has argued, so long as "it makes sense to distinguish between a right and wrong way of doing things in connection with what [a person] does," we can say that his actions involve the application of a rule to a particular situation and that they are therefore meaningful (Winch, 1958, p. 58).

Looked at in this way, however, all action descriptions, including those of instrumental actions, clearly presuppose a set of conventions or rules, for even instrumental actions can be well executed or poorly executed, done properly or improperly. In particular, any instrumental action presupposes a particular interpretation or understanding of the situation in which it is performed, and any such action can be evaluated according to the correctness of the interpretation. (See Wellmer, 1971b, pp. 72ff.) More significantly, most action (even of an instrumental character) is defined in terms of some set of "constitutive norms," which prescribe what shall count as an action of a certain type. Thus "marrying," "voting," "greeting," "running for office," and "conducting interviews" are all examples of activities which are constituted by a set of social conventions. Even "natural" activities like eating are not exempt from this "normative background," as the briefest reflection of such concepts as "munching," "dining," and "feeding" suggests. "Man is a rule-following animal" (Peters, 1958, p. 5), and to understand his behavior we must set it in the context of the rules and conventions, of the social practices of his society.

One aspect of a social practice, then, is a set of norms which define particular actions, when performed under specified circumstances, as actions of a particular type. John Searle has given an elaborate analysis of the practice of "promising," which we can use as an example of a social practice constituted by a particular, well-defined set of rules. To make a promise, one utters certain words, under a particular set of circumstances, by which one expresses an intention to do a certain act in the future (irrespective of whether the speaker is sincere in expressing this intention). And in going through these motions, one undertakes an obligation to perform the action at the required time—that is to say, going through these motions *counts* as making a promise (Searle, 1969, pp. 63–64). Similarly, a set of constitutive rules defines any number of other things we may be said to do: playing a game or making a move within a game, issuing an order, making a request, giving a warning, taking a job, assassinating a political leader, lobbying, making a representation, engaging in "horseplay" (as opposed to fighting), "waiting" (as opposed to loitering), legislating, judging, and so forth. But such a set of rules is not all there is to a practice. Rarely are our social practices well articulated in the sense that we could draw up a list of necessary and (jointly) sufficient conditions enabling us to discriminate actions which accord with the practice and those which do not. Moreover, practices are themselves defined in terms of other practices; they are stated in terms of certain concepts and can be said to have a point, or meaning. Thus we may define "promise" in terms of "obligation," "assassination" in terms of the "public" character of the act and/or the person killed, "order" in terms of "command" or "authority," etc. It thus becomes necessary to introduce a higher level of interpretation in order to account for these characteristics of practices.

### 3.4.2 Constitutive Meanings and the Interpretation of Practices

If actions are made intelligible in terms of practices, practices can be interpreted in terms of the "constitutive meanings" of a society (Taylor, 1971) or, as Wittgenstein and Winch would say, in terms of a "form of life." The notion of a "constitutive meaning" can be explicated by considering further what is involved in following even a simple rule, such as completing a series of numbers.

> Learning the series of natural numbers is not just learning to copy down a finite series of figures in the order which one has been shown. It involves *being able to go on* writing down figures that have not been shown one. In one sense, that is, it involves doing something *different* from what one was originally shown; but *in relation to the rule* that is being followed, this counts as "going on in the *same* way" as one was shown. (Winch, 1958, p. 59; emphasis in original)

Even in such simple and well-defined cases, following a rule involves knowing its point, and this means that acting in accordance with a rule presupposes a context of meaning within which the rule must be set. To know how to write down the natural numbers means understanding something about ordering things, about size or quantity, and about counting. In social settings, this context of meaning is supplied by the "constitutive meanings" of a society.

In learning the series of natural numbers, it is evident that what can count as "going on in the same way" cannot be exhaustively specified without ending up in an infinite regression of definitions and rules. If we have a rule which specifies what we are to do in a particular situation, then to apply it we must be able to recognize situations of that type. But this requires a further rule, which enables us to discriminate those features of a situation which would make it "count" as the kind of situation covered by the rule. But recognizing those features requires a rule of interpretation by which we can discriminate them from their environment in terms of their properties and/or relations. But in order to recognize those properties and/or relations, we would need . . ., and so on and on we would go. Even in mathematical and logical inference, we must at some point simply be able "to see that the conclusion does in fact follow," since "the actual process of drawing an inference . . . is something which cannot be represented as a logical formula" (Winch, 1958, p. 57; see also Polanyi, 1964, Sections 6.10, 8.8, and *passim*).

If we cannot exhaustively specify a practice, we can nonetheless attain a high level of agreement about the descriptions and evaluations carried out in terms of it, since the practice presupposes a set of constitutive meanings which partially specify the "point" of the activity and which relate various practices to one another. Although the "paradigm case" of a promise may involve a speaker uttering the words, "I promise you, Y, to do action *a* at time *t*," it is doubtful that most "promises" are made according to such a formula. It is even possible that the word "promise" appears more often in contexts in which promises are not made than it does in contexts, in which they are, as in "He is a very promising student." But our understanding of the *point* of the activity of promising enables us to recognize cases of "promising" which are quite different from the idealized paradigm that a philosopher might construct. Thus we can discriminate between those situations in which a person simply expresses an intention—"I'll be there tomorrow"—and those in which he makes a commitment—for example, when the context is such that his utterance will be relied on by another person in making his own plans. And we can make such discriminations because we understand that part of the point of promising is to enable people to coordinate their activities with each other by entering into obligations regarding their future behavior, and we can use this understanding to recognize utterances or actions which do so, as opposed to those which do not.

Apart from defining practices, constitutive meanings are presuppositions of the possibility of certain practices. The concept of "voting," for example, presupposes the necessity for human decision regarding collective affairs (as opposed, for example, to social decision procedures involving consultation of oracles), and it presupposes that the participants in the social decision process are, in some way, autonomous. These ideas are constitutive of social reality inasmuch as they enter into and define the type of social relationship that must exist in a society in which the practice of voting occurs. The constitutive role of human ideas marks a crucial distinction between the social and natural worlds; in the latter, we presume, the patterns displayed by phenomena are independent of human ideas regarding them: the rotation of the earth did not depend on our conceiving of a heliocentric universe, and the relationship between thunder and lightning existed long before men conceived of it. But in the case of social reality, the matter is different: we could not have the phenomenon of giving and receiving orders, for example, unless the idea of obedience was among the constitutive meanings of the society (Winch, 1958, p. 125).

This conception of constitutive meanings must be distinguished from the related notion of a distribution of attitudes or cognitive orientations—even from a "distribution" which approaches consensus. As Taylor has pointed out (1971, pp. 27ff), when social scientists deal with social meanings using survey research, they usually approach this subject through the expressed beliefs or attitudes of social actors (for example, see Almond and Verba, 1963). Now it is true that within the framework of the ideas and practices of a society, its members may formulate beliefs and values on which they may agree or disagree: they may even formulate beliefs about their society itself—such as the belief that the country's leaders do not listen to or care about what the average person says or thinks. Attitudes or beliefs such as these are what the survey research interviewer elicits when asking questions of various members of a social group. However, the "convergence of belief or attitudes or its absence presupposes a common language in which these beliefs can be formulated and in which these formulations can be opposed," and much of this common language comprises these constitutive meanings (Taylor, 1971, p. 28). As social actors, we may agree or disagree about whether citizen groups can influence the behavior of government officials and legislators, for example, but in order for our agreement or disagreement to be significant, we must share conceptions of representation and authority, and perhaps also a notion of the overriding purpose or function of government. It is against the background of such orientations, defining the relationship between "citizen" and "government" within which "influence" is to take place, that we can form attitudes or have opinions, for unless something of the scope and purpose of such influence is given, we do not know what people are agreeing or disagreeing about when they tell an interviewer that the government is impervious or open to influence. Responsive behavior in a system in which representation consists in presenting petitions on behalf of some corporate or territorially defined party would be quite different from such behavior in a system in which representation includes the authority to make law. And under neither of these conceptions of representation would the failure of a criminal organization to affect public policy be taken as indicating a lack of citizen influence.

### 3.5 The Testing and Acceptance of Interpretative Accounts

Surveys are an inadequate device to determine the constitutive meanings of a social order since such "meanings" are implicit in a community's forms of action or practices. We must therefore discover them through a process of interpretation, just as we discover the meaning of a literary work through interpretation. Banfield's *The Moral Basis of a Backward Society* (1958) provides us with an illustration of the process of interpretation through which constitutive meanings are articulated, as well as with an example of the use of such interpretation in social explanation.

The most obvious feature of this aspect of Banfield's study is that it *is* an interpretation of what members of Montegranesi society say and do. We cannot simply *ask* members of a society to explain the basic assumptions and orientations underlying their actions, since it is in terms of these constitutive meanings that people understand themselves and their own actions. Even if our informant understood the question, his answer would not be privileged, since we are concerned, for example, not with what would be the proper thing to do in some context but with understanding the concepts and the presuppositions in terms of which something can be said to be what is "done" or "appropriate." Understanding actions, in this respect, is analogous to understanding a language; a native speaker's intuitions may be decisive when it comes to determining whether a given statement is properly formed, but he may be totally ignorant of the rules according to which proper utterances can be formed or of the logical and other presuppositions of a given utterance.

For the same reason that even an ideal informant cannot tell us what the constitutive meanings of a society are, interpreting actions and practices in terms of constitutive meanings does not involve "rethinking" anyone's thoughts or discovering anything inside anyone's head through some process of empathy. Like intentions, constitutive meanings are not private, mental events that live a ghostly existence "behind" people's manifest behavior—including verbal behavior. On the contrary, since constitutive meanings are the conditions of the intelligibility of our practices, it is obvious that they must be intersubjective, i.e., common to the members of a society. And so the activity of interpretation must be public in the sense that it is governed by public rules and standards. An interpretative account must be justified by the evidence, and the testing and acceptance of such accounts is no more "subjective" than is the testing and accepting of theories or research programs in science.

The essential feature of interpretation is the so-called *hermeneutical* or *interpretative circle*. (For these terms, see Radnitzky, 1970, Vol. 2, pp. 23ff, and Kaplan, 1964, p. 362. The term "hermeneutical," of course, means "belonging to or concerned with interpretation" [Oxford English Dictionary], and "hermeneutics" refers to the "art or science of interpretation."). The hermeneutical circle consists of a movement back and forth between the particular and the general, as the meaning and significance of specific actions, practices, texts, etc., are judged in relation to a conception of the whole, and our ideas about the whole are corrected and amplified by testing them against the "parts." When we are puzzled about the meaning of a particular phrase, for example, we attempt to infer what meaning it must have in order to provide coherence to the speech or text of which it is a part. Hence, to understand the part, we must already have an understanding of the whole. But this understanding of the whole is "built up from" and corrected by our understanding of the parts. Therefore, having interpreted the parts of a text in terms of a notion of the meaning of the whole, we are in a position to correct this understanding in terms of our interpretations of the parts. This process of "tacking" between the particular and the general continues until a coherent account of the text has been developed. And what holds true for texts can be applied to the interpretation of actions as well.

This mutual dependence of the meaning of the parts on the meaning of the whole and vice versa can be seen in Banfield's study. The structure of Banfield's argument begins with a number of basic notions which govern his understanding of Montegranesi society. Banfield begins with the generalization that the Montegranesi are overwhelmingly oriented toward private affairs and show little interest or inclination to take on public roles or responsibilities. He conjectures that this tendency may be rooted in any number of alternative ways that they may have of understanding themselves and their situation. Perhaps they have a "fatalistic worldview," or a "pathological distrust of the state and all authority"[15] (p. 36). Banfield uses these conceptions to interpret specific practices of the society and finds them wanting. For example, if the Montegranesi were fatalists, some of their actions would be unintelligible—such as the attempt many were making to limit the size of their families—and any supposed distrust of government is belied by their relatively positive beliefs about members of the government. After examining some other aspects of Montegranesi society, Banfield suggests that it is organized almost exclusively by the individual's relationship to his family. "In fact, an adult hardly may be said to have an individuality apart from the family: he exists not as 'ego' but as 'parent'" (p. 103). Moreover, the family exists in an extremely uncertain world in which calamity may overtake it at any time and in which little depends on one's own efforts.

> In such a fearful world a parent cannot count on achieving anything by means of his own effort and enterprise. The conditions and means of success are all beyond his control. He may struggle to get ahead, but in

the end he will probably be crushed by the insane fury of events. (p. 107)

In such a hostile world, the only recourse the individual has is to attempt to maximize the short-run, material interest of his immediate family and to assume that others will do likewise (p. 83). This maxim Banfield calls "amoral familism," and with it he is able to provide interpretations of a vast array of Montegranesi practices, attitudes, beliefs, etc. The interpretation of these practices, in turn, elaborates and extends the conception of amoral familism itself.

Explicitly hermeneutical or interpretative analysis has been a central feature of many of the humanities, as well as such fields as intellectual history and political theory; in the social sciences it has been less formalized, though certainly very common. Moreover, many of the standards that govern interpretation in literature or philosophy carry over to interpretative explanation of social action and social practices.[16] The most obvious standards are coherence and scope: an interpretative account should provide maximal coherence or intelligibility to a set of social practices, and an interpretative account of a particular set of practices should be consistent with other practices or traditions of the society. Banfield uses both of these standards in developing his account of Montegranesi society; for example, he rejects the view that the Montegranesi are fatalists on the grounds that such a view of the world would render some of their practices unintelligible.

In spite of the possibility of using these standards to evaluate and criticize an interpretative account, interpretation in social science has been criticized because it necessarily involves an interpretative or hermeneutical circle—using an account of the constitutive meanings of a society to interpret the meanings of a particular practice, while at the same time explicating the constitutive meanings of the society in terms of the meanings of its practices. "How," one might object, "can we explain something, $x$, in terms of something else, $y$, and then turn around and explain $y$ in terms of $x$? Isn't this an obviously circular procedure?"

The "hermeneutical circle," however, is not a "vicious circle," for it merely signifies the fact that our understanding of meaningful behavior (including texts and verbal behavior) develops by making our presuppositions more explicit and testing them to determine whether they enable us to make intelligible those actions or statements which previously were puzzling or obscure. An example of such hermeneutical analysis and of a resulting "hermeneutical circle" is Hempel's explication of the concept of "explanation" in empirical science. Hempel defends his explication by arguing that it "does justice to such accounts as are generally agreed to be instances of scientific explanation" while at the same time providing a "systematically fruitful and illuminating" construal of the concept (1965, p. 489). We must have some notion of what an "explanation" is before we begin, but this notion is made explicit and can then be used to show just how particular scientific explanations are "explanatory," and to provide rational reconstructions of others. In coming to understand our own language and our own social practices, there can be no alternative to such "circular" reasoning.

> We are like sailors who must rebuild their ship on the open sea, never able to dismantle it in dry-dock and to reconstruct it there out of the best materials. (Neurath, 1932/33, p. 201)

Hempel's explication of the concept of explanation brings out another important feature of the activity of interpretation: its tendency to refine or alter the meaning of an idea, expression, or practice. Having developed a satisfactory concept of explanation, we can now criticize certain practices within science and provide guidelines for future work. Similarly, the process of interpretation in social and political inquiry not only discovers the constitutive meanings of a society but may also affect these meanings. This, of course, is a version of the familiar problem of the self-fulfilling prophecy. Banfield mentions an example, the influence of Carlo Levi's *Christ Stopped at Eboli* on at least upper-class interpretations of their village society.

> It should be remembered that Levi's observations were made during an exile which began in 1935 and that his book, which was widely read by the upper class in Montegrano and other southern towns, no doubt produced an effect. At any rate, it was curious in 1955 to find upper class people quoting him with approval. . . . (Banfield, 1958, p. 36)

So far I have spoken as if a society were a uniform, integrated, and static "whole," in which there is a well-defined stock of "action descriptions," each couched in terms of a different set of "practices," which in turn presuppose a set of "constitutive meanings" that link the various practices to each other, provide a "point" to the different practices, and constitute the "framework" in terms of which the practices can be understood. Social science, then, might consist in providing explanations of individual actions by subsuming them under general action descriptions, the action descriptions under practices, and the practices under constitutive meanings—a "layer cake" theory of social explanation. But this schema differs from that presented in Section 2, the scientific model, since each level here corresponds to successively higher levels of interpretation; this schema serves to explicate the meanings of what people do rather than to provide an account of the nomological structure underlying the observed correlations among different events.

Different societies, from this point of view, could be defined or identified in terms of the differences among their overarching sets of constitutive meanings; a corollary, of course, is that "actions" which appear to be the same but are performed in two different social settings may actually be quite different, since the practices and frameworks from which they derive their meaning may be very different. In particular, it may be quite impossible to perform certain kinds of actions in certain kinds of society—such as principled public action in Montegrano. The "meanings" of different societies must be learned contextually, and only after they are given will it be possible to understand what people are doing in that society. But this means that it will be difficult and sometimes impossible to establish equivalences among action descriptions in different cultures, since superficially similar behavior may have very different meanings because of differences in their cultural and institutional backgrounds. And this implies that the naturalist model of political inquiry, to the extent that it requires actions in different societies to be comparable, will be unable to provide us with a comparative science of politics. (See MacIntyre, 1971, for a clear and provocative statement of this argument.)

Significantly, adherents to the naturalist model conceptualize this problem of cross-cultural comparability in remarkably different terms. When measurements of what we take to be the "same" social phenomena in different social systems yield different results, according to Przeworski and Teune (1970), "we need to explain those differences. The first step is to test the 'equivalence' of measurement statements. If this attempt to account for the differences fails, what we need to do is control for theoretically significant system-level differences that can be expressed as variables." (p. 134) According to the interpretative model, however, the problem is not that we have neglected certain "variables," but that the meanings of the concepts in terms of which people in different cultures act may be fundamentally different. That is why (or at least one reason why) measures of social phenomena in different cultures can be expected to lead to incompatible findings—the phenomena measured in one culture will be different from the phenomena measured in another. Attempts to make them comparable run up against the fact that social phenomena are constituted by the self-definitions or constitutive meanings of a society. Hence even those types of actions which appear to be similar will have different meanings and so will yield different "readings" when attempts are made to measure them.

Now it is certainly true that the emphasis on the uniqueness of each set of constitutive principles is incompatible with the naturalist model of a generalizing science of politics. But an interpretative political science could certainly be comparative, and indeed, it would have to be if it were to deal with the existence of change within a single society. If social systems really were the monadic unities the sketch above assumes they are, it is hard to see how change could ever come about. More important, a social science which could not make comparisons among different societies at one point in time could not explain changes within a single society since, from this perspective, the "same" society at a later point in time would simply be a "different" society, in that it would have a different set of practices, defined by a different set of constitutive meanings. But the assumption that the practices and constitutive meanings of a society are fully integrated and coherent is introduced only for expository convenience. Indeed, it is precisely because of the shifting, overlapping, and conflicting meanings that coexist within a social system that a hermeneutical problem arises. It is, for example, when the received or traditional ideas of a society become subtly transformed in the course of acting in terms of them in different situations that communication and understanding are likely to break down. And it is at this point that a need for interpretation arises.

In the normal course of events, we are able to operate perfectly well, there is no problem in understanding what people say or do, and we do not experience a need to inquire behind the "taken-for-granted" world. It is primarily when we come to deal with strange cultures or time periods, or when there are dramatic shifts within our own society, that the need for interpretation arises. From the perspective of clashing traditions or practices, it is possible to see the presuppositions underlying alternative sets of practices and to construct ideal-types which enable us to understand them. Hermeneutical understanding, then, is frequently historical and comparative, perhaps necessarily so, and it involves the construction and comparison of ideal-types as interpretative constructs enabling us to understand the practices of one society during different periods of time or of many societies at one point in time. In political science there is no better illustration of this method than Beer's study of modern British politics.

Beer begins his analysis of British politics by focusing on British political culture, specifically the notions of representation, authority, and the purposes of government which characterize British political life. These notions are among the essential "images and sentiments that function as operative ideals in a community, or section of a community" (Beer, 1969, p. xiii) and are vital "in explaining the political behavior of individuals, groups, and parties" (p. xii). What men do depends on what they think, and to understand what they think we must grasp not only the values and beliefs they express but also the fundamental orientations they have toward politics and the concepts in terms of which they understand political life. But these basic orientations cannot be approached directly; they must be seen from a comparative and historical perspective, for only then can we become aware of the "common and familiar" and have a background from which the features of the present period can be determined. Thus the first section of Beer's book is devoted to an analysis of the "five types of politics" that have characterized British politics in the past four hundred years. By looking at modern, "collectivist" politics in light of earlier forms of political life, we are able to see its constitutive meanings more clearly and to assess the significance of such features as party government, functional representation, and organizational concentration in the determination of political behavior.

It should not be thought that the political culture of a particular period is one integrated whole; just as conceptions of representation and of the legitimate purposes of political power have changed over time, each period is characterized to some degree by conflict over some of the fundamentals of political life. The notion of "class," for example, is basic to both Labour and Conservative understandings of modern politics, but it has a very different meaning for each of the two parties. Although both Labourites and Conservatives might refer to the same groups when they use the term,[17] the "sense" it has for them differs. The Labourite conceives of "class" as a solidarity grouping of people sharing a common economic status, as opposed to those who occupy a different economic status. On the other hand, the Conservative sees "class" as a functional grouping of individuals sharing a common background or training that fits them for political rule or fails to do so. Because of these differences in their conceptions of "class," the two parties see the role of classes in modern society in quite different terms. For the Conservatives, "class" and "hierarchy" are part of the "natural order" of things and contribute to the integration and stability of a society. The Labour party views class as dividing society and as marking the lines of political conflict. In a similar vein, the two parties differ over their conceptions of "democracy," "leadership," "security," etc. (See Beer, 1969, Chapter 3 and *passim.*)

It is precisely because the structure of British politics is partially constituted by these conflicting ideas that the political scientist must understand them if he is to explain or even describe political behavior in Britain. Beer's work, then, illustrates the need for a hermeneutical understanding of the constitutive meanings of a set of political practices, and it demonstrates that such understanding, far from being vitiated by the existence of serious cleavages within a society or by fundamental changes taking place over time, is essential to the explanation of these conditions.[18]

### 3.6 *The Interpretative Ideal of Social Inquiry*

In this section I have presented an "interpretative model" of social science, differing in certain fundamental respects from the naturalist ideal presented in Section 2. Before closing this section, I would like to summarize its argument by responding to two criticisms which have been made against this theory of social and political inquiry. Although I will be defending certain aspects of this methodological position here, I do not mean to endorse its extreme claims. In the following section I will criticize this position and offer an alternative model of political inquiry.

The interpretative view of social science begins with the basic assumption that human behavior is essentially different from the phenomena studied in the natural sciences in that it is intentional and meaningful. This difference means that fundamentally different methods must be employed in the human sciences. In particular, the social scientist faces the task of *understanding* the actions, practices, and forms of life of his subjects. He must grasp the conventions and the constitutive meanings which make up the field of social action, and he must do so by attending to the actions, concepts, and ideas of social actors. Only by interpreting the meanings of what these actors do will the social scientist be able to make their behavior intelligible.

The natural scientist does not face this hermeneutical problem. When he inquires into the "meaning" of a phenomenon, he is interested in its nomological relations to other phenomena. "What does its turning red mean?" can be stated roughly as "What caused it to turn red and/or what will its turning red lead to?" But when we ask, "What does his refusal mean?" we could be asking a very different question indeed, one that might be rephrased as "What does his behavior amount to, or just what was it that he did?" And the answer to this question may be an explication of his action in light of the conventions and practices of the society: "His refusal meant that he was breaking off negotiations," or "His refusal meant that he was playing for time." And of course, "refusal" is already a concept which is highly "interpreted." For what he *did* was to say something, "I will not accept your proposal," or perhaps to do something, like walk out of a conference. These issues cannot arise for the natural scientist, because he is not concerned with intentional behavior and therefore with behavior which can have "meaning" in this sense. There are no "self-understandings" or "self-interpretations" of atoms or elements that the scientist must come to terms with before he proceeds to develop his own concepts and ideas to describe and explain the behavior he observes. In this sense, Winch's comparison between the engineer (or natural scientist) and the social scientist is apt.

> If we are going to compare the social student to the engineer, we shall do better to compare him to an apprentice engineer who is studying what engineering—that is, the activity of engineering—is all about. His understanding of social phenomena is more like the engineer's understanding of his colleague's activities than it is like the engineer's understanding of the mechanical systems which he studies. (Winch, 1958, p. 88)

An obvious objection to this line of argument would be to ask whether we could not simply replace the concepts of social actors with concepts that we, as scientists, find convenient to work with for our purposes. Granted that action is meaningful, why must we understand it in terms which the actors themselves use? There is an analogy to natural science here, in that the natural scientist comes to his studies with a "pre-formed" vocabulary and conceptual system which includes notions like "The sun rises in the east." But he is not bound by these concepts, and he is quite free to ignore them and to introduce others when doing so will advance the purposes of exact description and adequate explanation. Indeed, as this example shows, that has been the constant tendency of scientific progress, and so, following the lead of the natural sciences, we should be entirely free to ignore the "meaningful" or intentional aspects of behavior if it serves our purposes to do so. The natural sciences have been freed from the constraints of anthropomorphism; it is time for the social sciences to be free to conceptualize their phenomena in any scientifically fruitful way. (See Gellner, 1968, for a forceful statement of this argument.)

The second objection to an interpretative social science is much more serious. Whereas the first objection insists that we should be free to dispense with intentional concepts, the second claims that this model of political inquiry is itself fallacious. According to Rudner (1966), the form of understanding of actions and rules which the interpretative model seeks to provide is really a psychological experience, for it involves "having the experiences of behaving in conformance with those rules" (p. 70). The idea that science should provide us with such "direct experiences" of phenomena is a form of what Rudner picturesquely calls the "reproductive fallacy," for it rests on the belief that science should reproduce "the conditions or states of affairs being studied." But, Rudner argues, "It is the function of science to describe the world, not to reproduce it." And this is true whether we are studying people or such natural phenomena as tornadoes.

> Of course a description of a tornado is *not* the same thing as a tornado! And incidentally, the description does not "fail" to be a tornado on account of being incomplete, truncated, generalized, or abstract. Even if it were a "complete" description of a tornado—whatever that might be—it would still be a *description* of a tornado and not a tornado. Moreover, a description of a tornado no more *fails* to be a tornado than does a tornado fail to be a description. (Rudner, 1966, p. 83)

So even though we can understand human actions from the "inside," so to speak, such understanding is not what science seeks, and we should study them in the same way that we study natural things.

Since this objection strikes at the heart of the interpretative model, I will deal with it first. I will show that it rests on two errors, the first being the claim that "knowing the phenomena from the inside" amounts to "having the experiences of behaving in conformance with [certain] rules." As I have argued throughout this section, to know the meaning of an action is to make an interpretation of that action in terms of the intentions of the actor and the practices and constitutive meanings of his society. I have gone to some length to show that grasping the intention of an act or interpreting the practices of a society does *not* involve thinking anyone's thoughts or having anyone's feelings: it is not a psychological process at all.

Unfortunately, the first advocates of this model of social inquiry often spoke as if the "understanding" it provided was psychological. For example, Collingwood (1946) argued that the task of the historian (and the social scientist generally) is to "re-live" the thoughts of historical actors, and Weber frequently spoke of *verstehen* in similarly "psychological" terms, as when he emphasizes the *subjective* character of intentional action.[19] The view that understanding the "meaning" of one's actions depends on the ability to "get inside" the other person's "mind" rests on a primitive mind-body dualism which is certainly indefensible.

Of course, it is because action is subjectively intended that it can have meaning at all. It is because people are agents who form purposes in accordance with their own conceptions of themselves, and in accordance with norms and standards of their society, that action has a symbolic, meaningful character in the first place. But the meaning of an action is not simply what a person intends by it, just as the meaning of what a person says is not what he meant by saying it. Rather, the meaning of the utterance is at least partly a matter of the conventions of the language (or the society, in the case of actions). Searle (1969, pp. 44ff) illustrates this with the imaginary example of an American soldier, captured by Italian soldiers during the Second World War, who tries to convince his captors that he is a German soldier, thereby inducing them to release him. To do so, naturally, he must tell them that he is a German soldier, but he does not know enough German or Italian to do so, and he obviously would fail to advance his goals by saying, "I am a German soldier." In fact, the only German he knows is a line from one of Goethe's poems that he once had to memorize, "Kennst du das Land wo die Zitronen blühn?" So he utters these words with the intention that the Italians will take him to be saying that he is a German soldier, or at least that they will understand that he is a German soldier. But whatever his intention, the meaning of what he says is not "I am a German soldier" or even "Ich bin ein deutscher Soldat." In short, meaning is public:

> To say that culture consists of socially established structures of meaning in terms of which people do . . . things . . . is no more to say that it is a psychological phenomenon, a characteristic of someone's mind, personality, cognitive structure, or whatever, than to say that Tantrism, genetics, . . . [or] the Common Law . . . is. (Geertz, 1973, p. 13)

That meaning is something psychological, a matter of directly experiencing something which some actor in some situation intends in saying or doing something, is a particularly egregious error in the context of Winch's analysis, for Winch has gone to some length to deny precisely this aspect of the Weber/Collingwood analysis of *verstehen*. Indeed, he has argued (following Wittgenstein) that even

> the concepts in terms of which we understand our own mental processes and behavior have to be learned, and must, therefore, be *socially*

established, just as much as the concepts in terms of which we come to understand the behavior of other people. (Winch, 1958, p. 119)

If an interpretative social science is unacceptable, it cannot be due to its attempting to convey the psychological experience of participating in a form of life to its practitioners and students.

The second error in Rudner's argument is his (at least implicit) suggestion that the "understanding" that we seek of a tornado is analogous to the "understanding that we seek of meaningful or symbolic behavior." On the face of it this is a most implausible position. Surely we should be dissatisfied with an explanation of a poem which consisted of an elaborate description of what the printer did in setting up his type, inking it, and producing the sheets with these particular configurations of shapes on them. Likewise, any explanation of the course of a tornado in terms of what the tornado "wanted" to do would be immediately dismissed as absurd, for the tornado's behavior is not intentional. As long as we admit, then, that action does have a meaningful character, we admit the legitimacy of systematic, disciplined procedures for explicating and analyzing its meaning.

If the second objection to an interpretative social science—that it commits the "reproductive fallacy"—is untenable, what of the first objection—that we may replace the concepts of ordinary language, of action, purpose, intention, meaning, etc., by scientifically acceptable terms, thereby obviating the need for an interpretative understanding of social life? Is interpretation a necessary condition of social inquiry, or is it just one *possible* form such inquiry can take? There is no obvious reply to this question. But we can note that what most political scientists are interested in explaining is what people *do* in *political* contexts. And both their "doings" and the concept of "political" are part of the field of meanings which it is the task of a hermeneutical science to explicate. The natural scientist may be free to shape his concepts in any way he sees fit, but the social scientist's subject matter is the social relations and the ideas constituting those relations, which are part of our experience as social actors. If he ignores those ideas, he is, so to speak, no longer studying the same subject. If we are interested in legislative behavior, for example, we must take the criteria of what is to count as legislative behavior from the self-understandings of the actors involved. It is the conventions of the political system that determine what a "legislature" is, who is a member of it, and which of a member's actions are done in his "official" capacity and which are not. And as we saw by examining Beer's and Banfield's works, interpretation of these practices and orientations in terms of the fundamental, constitutive meanings of the society are valuable contributions to our understanding of the political life of the society in question.

Having said this, I find it safe to conclude that we cannot conduct political science, as we understand it today, while totally ignoring the meaningful aspects of human behavior. But this argument, at best, shows that we *ought not* to abandon "anthropomorphic" concepts in the study of man, not that we cannot do so. It is conceivable that a social or, perhaps more accurately, a "behavioral" science modeled on the strict scientific ideal, eschewing the use of intentional concepts, is logically possible. It is at least possible that some kind of neurophysiological theories of "behavior" could be developed and extended to the "interactions" of large numbers of individuals without making reference to any of the concepts which they use in ordering and understanding their "actions." Discussion of such an ideal seems to be quite pointless, however, since it is completely programmatic at this time, and totally foreign to the methodologies and interests of virtually all contemporary political scientists.[20]

## 4 INTERPRETATION, THEORY, AND MODELS OF MAN.

### 4.1 *The Limitations of Interpretative Explanations*

If we must concede the claim that interpretation is integral to social science, we should not make the mistake of supposing that it exhausts the legitimate activities of social scientists. From the perspective of political science, the major limitation of interpretative explanations is that they are tied to the explication of particular contexts. The point of hermeneutical understanding is to explicate the meanings of particular actions, texts, practices, institutions, and other cultural objects, by setting out the internal relations which link each particular to other particulars and to the social wholes of which they are parts. Although interpretation serves to lay bare the meanings of things which would otherwise be obscure, to express the particular in terms of the general categories of language and action which the political scientist shares (or comes to share through the process of hermeneutical understanding) with the actors involved, its task is limited to the analysis of historically unique configurations.

But political science, like economics, sociology, and anthropology, is not only concerned to understand particular events and traditions; it also aspires to compare and to generalize about social phenomena. And though such generalization must presuppose interpretative explanations of particulars, such explanation does not provide a sufficient basis for the construction of more general comparisons and theories. Quite apart from the theoretical pretensions of the social sciences, there are features even of particular situations which escape hermeneutical understanding. The outbreak of World War I, the scale of violence following the partition of India, and the pattern of American involvement in Indochina are a few examples of events which were, to some degree, the unintended (and undesired) consequences of the actions of large numbers of individuals, each responding to his own particular situation and concerns.

In addition to the analysis of such particular cases, then, social scientists must deal with the general regularities resulting from particular kinds of actions. For example, from economics we have the "paradox of savings," in which the attempts of many individuals within a society to increase their rates of savings results in a general fall in the level of national income and a fall in the aggregate level of savings: because of their attempts to increase their savings, many will find that their savings decrease. Political science also provides such examples, including the convergence of party platforms to the median position on the political spectrum, given two-party competition and a unimodal (or uniform) distribution of attitudes over the electorate. A more controversial example is the growth of political instability as a result of increasing participation in politics. Tracing the unintended consequences of actions in particular cases and discovering regularities associated with particular kinds of behavior are important parts of the work of political science and of social science in general.

Closely related to the problem of unanticipated consequences is that of explaining the structure of a social or political system, particularly changes in the institutional framework of a society over time. Rarely do the "gross" characteristics of social and political systems correspond to the intentions or conscious designs of anyone, even (or especially?) revolutionaries and "nation-builders" who try to shape them. It is a commonplace that practices change gradually as people confront new situations and adjust their behavior and expectations accordingly. Likewise, a given set of conventions can result in dramatically different effects, and its meanings can be subtly transformed, as changes in its context occur. Population movements, to take an obvious example, may have a seriously disruptive effect on patterns of representation. Similarly, an electoral system reform designed to provide for the representation of new groups, such as proportional respresentation, may have the effect of impeding the consolidation of older parties. And a revolution to destroy clerical power and consolidate secularism may have the effect of creating a permanent religious cleavage within a society, ultimately culminating in deep splits within the working class—a class not even in existence when the revolution occurs! (See Rokkan, 1970.)

Some of the things that *happen* in social life are things that no one *intends,* and for such events the categories of intentional action and the associated schema of explanation cannot provide a satisfactory account. Of course, such "happenings" take place against a "background" of intentional action; they may even designate the *actions* of a very large number of people. For example, "outbreak of a war" is a summary phrase denoting the different actions of a very large number of differently placed individuals: government officials who make various declarations, generals who give various orders, soldiers who march and shoot, merchants who abandon plans or find their goods requisitioned, etc. Moreover, such a phrase is intelligible only in terms of certain conventions which constitute "war" as a particular relationship among people (or organized groups—two individuals may *fight*, and a crowd may *riot*, but in neither case is it a "war"), and there are a number of regulative norms applicable to the conduct of individuals at war. (See Winch, 1958, pp. 130ff.) "War" must be *understood* before we can significantly speak of the "outbreak of war," but its outbreak cannot always be *explained* using the hermeneutical or interpretive techniques of *verstehen*, as when a war "results" from an escalating series of skirmishes, diplomatic moves, propaganda barrages, etc. In this case there is no actor for whom we can construct a practical inference linking his intentions to the action "starting a war," and so the explanation will have to proceed along other lines.

One way of explaining such events is to develop practical inferences, or *verstehen* explanations, for the actions of the various individuals involved, and to arrange the explanations in such a way that the consequences of one person's actions on the situation which another person faces are evident. A simple and totally artificial example of such a pattern of explanation is the Richardson (1960) theory of the course of an arms race. In that theory each nation is assumed to want to maintain its sense of security, which depends on the relative level of its armaments and those of its neighbors, but each nation's response to the other's armaments depends partly on the costs of raising the necessary military forces. Starting with a situation in which nation A has a certain level of arms, nation B finds its security threatened, and so it increases its own level of spending on defense. This action, of course, creates a new situation, in which the relative level of arms has changed, and so nation A reacts by further increasing its own arms expenditures. But this alters B's situation, and so the process continues until they converge on a level at which neither side finds the security provided by additional forces "worth" the costs of those forces, or the "system" breaks down into war. Depending on the relative rates at which they respond to each other, the system may or may not have a stable equilibrium, and depending on their starting point, they may or may not reach an equilibrium level of expenditure.

Richardson's work is an analysis of the structure of a recurring situation, but social scientists are more commonly concerned with tracing the unanticipated consequences of particular events, or analyzing the structure of concrete political processes or institutional configurations by linking together particular interpretative explanations to form a chain, the end point of which is unintended by any of the participants during the process of interaction and response. Von Wright offers a typical example of the analysis of such a concrete situation in his discussion of the beginning of World War I (1971, pp. 135ff). We commonly say that the war resulted from (or was "triggered by") the assassination of the Austrian Archduke Franz Ferdinand, but that is a summary statement of a very complex set of linkages between those events. The linkages can be understood in terms of the chain of practical inferences which the actors involved made as they assessed the impact of the assassination and the impact of subsequent decisions made by other parties to the conflict on the situation they faced. Thus the assassination provided Austria with a justification, given contemporary standards, for taking action against Serbia, and swift action provided the opportunity to so weaken Serbia (and its ally, Russia) that Austria's position in the Balkans could be maintained. On the other hand, failure to act against the nationalists might well have encouraged them in their projects, thereby presenting a threat not only to Austrian interests in the Balkans but to the survival of the Hapsburg empire itself. So Austria issued an ultimatum to which Serbia could hardly conform without jeopardizing its own vital interests, as well as Russia's. The ultimatum, then, "forced" Russia to back Serbia, but the subsequent Russian mobilization presented a danger to Germany. And so it went, each nation reacting to the changed situation in which it found itself as a result of the actions and decisions of others.

Von Wright calls explanations such as these "quasi-causal," since they resemble causal patterns of explanation, at least in that the antecedent conditions, or "causes," are logically distinct from the consequences of effects. We can say that the cause of the outbreak of World War I, for example, was the assassination of Franz Ferdinand, because an assassination and the outbreak of a war are not conceptually linked. Unlike the relationship between rationale or intention and action, nothing about the assassination logically implies anything about the initiation of hostilities, not to mention world war. Similarly, the Richardson model can be represented by a set of differential equations such that, from the state of the system at one point in time, we can deduce its states at subsequent periods. But there is nothing in the description of the relative armaments of two countries at a particular point in time that logically implies specific values for those figures later. To determine those values we must know the regular pattern which characterizes the way each country reacts to the actions of the other.

Although these explanations link events which are logically separate, they are nonetheless not nomological explanations for the linkages and do not depend on genuine laws. As the initial description of the explanations made clear, the linkages in question are the effects of one agent's actions upon the situation of the other, and this means that the change in the situation becomes part of the *premises* of a new practical inference of the other actor. Nation B sees the increasing armaments of nation A as threatening and therefore finds an increase of its own to be necessary. Russia sees Serbia's complying with the Austrian ultimatum as involving a decrease in Russian influence in the Balkans, and so Russia must help Serbia resist it.

Each of these necessities is a "practical necessity": it points to a logical or conceptual link between the actor's situation, goals, and actions. The actions are not "necessitated by" causal laws which link the actor's beliefs and values, on the one hand, and its actions, on the other, because these links, as we have seen, are conceptual, not contingent. Amending Richardson marginally, we can say that our equations do not describe what people have to do; rather, they "are merely a description of what people would do if they did not stop to think [ahead]" (1960, p. 12).

However, one should not think that all the linkages between antecedent conditions and the results to be explained are practical inferences; a number of important links may be of a significantly different type, although their "nomic status," as it were, is still problematic. In studying the outbreak of World War I, for example, Holsti, North, and Brody (1968) have argued that it is necessary to consider the situation which the actors perceived to exist, rather than their "actual" situation, since their perceptions were frequently, even systematically, distorted. For example, both the Triple Entente and the Dual Alliance perceived the level of violence in their own actions to be lower than it actually was and saw their own actions as less hostile than the actions of the opposing alliance. Holsti (1965) also found that, as the crisis deepened, each side tended to see itself as having progressively fewer alternatives, while at the same time thinking that the other side's range of options had increased. Obviously, such perceptual distortion is not something one consciously creates (although it may be something one can consciously prevent), and if it varies with the intensity of the crisis, for example, we may have a relationship between "intensity of crisis" and "perceptual distortion" that has many of the qualities of a genuinely nomological relationship. As important as such a relationship may be, however, it does not destroy the quasi-causal character of the explanation of the outbreak of the war. Even if the linkage between a situation and the perception of the situation is causal, the relationship between an actor's perception of the situation and his action is a practical inference. Hence the overall relationship between the situation and its outcome is quasi-causal, since at least some of the essential linkages involved are practical inferences.

### 4.2 Quasi-Causal Explanations and the Nature of Political Theory

Just as some explanations are quasi-causal in character, so our *theories* are quasi-causal. As I pointed out in Section 2, the term "theory" is frequently used rather loosely. One "informal" use of theory is to refer to a relationship between two or more variables or factors which can be generalized beyond a specific, concrete setting, but in which the linkages between the related events include chains of practical inferences rather than causal or functional laws. For very good reasons analysts are seldom content with enunciating a general relationship between two political variables, however impressive the observed correlation between them, without offering some "theory" of why they should be related, a "theory" couched in terms of the motivations and perceptions of the actors involved. These "theories," of course, are interpretative explanations, reconstructions of the practical inferences of the relevant individuals.

An example of the interaction between developing such explanations and finding statistical correlations might be the recent and growing interest in the relationship between inequality and political instability. At first the systematic attempts to correlate such variables may not present an explicit theory—even of this informal variety—to justify the relationship. Russett, for example, in his study of the relationship between land tenure and politics, introduces a hypothesis in the following terms.

> Extreme inequality of land distribution leads to political instability only in those poor, predominantly agricultural societies where limitation to a small plot of land almost unavoidably condemns one to poverty. In a rich country, the modest income a farmer can produce from even a small holding may satisfy him. (Russett, 1964, p. 133)

We can take it for granted, apparently, that people who are poor or relatively poor are apt to engage in acts of violence. Before long, however, explicit attention must be paid to explaining why there may be a relationship between inequality and violence or instability, especially when examples are found in which the posited correlation is reversed—such as Mitchell's (1968) finding that government control in South Vietnam was directly, not inversely, related to inequality.

Such findings are important for two reasons. First, they suggest the need for some kind of reassessment of accepted theories: What aspects of the previously accepted theory do they call into question? How can the theory be modified to encompass these findings? Second, such negative results call into question the data and the interpretations of the data of both the earlier work and the disconfirming study itself. In particular, they pose the question whether the "indicators" of the variables in the theory are themselves adequate. Both factors require us to make the implicit linkages between our variables explicit, and in the example at hand, Mitchell's essay stimulated work on both issues. The "effects" of inequality of land holding on the motivational situation of the peasantry were conceptualized more precisely, and this refined theory was used to question Mitchell's data and his techniques of data analysis, specifically on the grounds that they were ill-designed to test the theory in question, e.g., that of Paranzino (1972). On the other hand, some of his adverse findings could be incorporated into considerably refined variants of the original "theory." (For example, see Zagoria, 1971, p. 152.)

A good example of such a refined theory (though drawing its immediate inspiration from a different set of problems) is Zagoria's study, "The Ecology of Peasant Communism in India" (1971). Zagoria finds a high correlation between voting for communist parties and two explanatory variables, "high rural population density" and "landlessness," the latter being "a composite of three variables: agricultural laborers as a percentage of all cultivators, tenants as a percentage of all cultivators, and holdings of less than one acre" (p. 147). His explanation of these findings is quite complex. He observes that regions of high population density tend to be irrigated, rice-growing areas, which are very productive and yield fairly large agricultural surpluses. Because the land in these regions tends to be distributed very unequally, there are large numbers of peasants without land or with only "dwarf" holdings, insufficient to support themselves and their families. Because of the competition for land and its high productivity, landlords are able to extract large surpluses from the peasants. Moreover, in the absence of large farms organized on capitalist principles, in which the owner provides such important factors as seeds, expertise, marketing connections, etc., the landlord extracts the peasant's surplus without providing anything in return, thereby undermining any "natural basis of respect for the landowners and renters" (p. 159). If the landowners are not capitalists, they rarely constitute a small, quasi-feudal class; rather, they tend to be a large, faction-ridden class of petty landlords, most of whom own small to medium-sized plots. Thus they are not in a position to enforce a traditional pattern of deference and respect for their social "betters" from the poorer strata of the peasantry. On the other hand, since many of the peasants own small amounts of land, they are not entirely dependent on the landlord. Hence it should be easy for the peasants to envisage a situation in which they own enough land to satisfy their needs and can be entirely free from the demands of landlords who not only provide them with little or nothing but are also of roughly the same social status as the peasants themselves. Thus the peasant-landlord relationship becomes ridden with conflict, and the peasant expresses his discontent politically by voting communist, since there is no other party which advocates significant land reform.

It is clear that Zagoria's "theory" represents an interpretation of the situation of the peasantry which renders their actions intelligible to us. The explanatory factors he presents specify the "beliefs" the peasants hold about their situation, a set of conditions disposing the peasantry to form these particular beliefs about their situation and not others, and an (implicit) set of values, norms, and objectives which peasants and landlords have. Given these factors, the behavior of the peasantry is understandable, and it is in terms of this background of understanding that the correlation between density and landlessness, on the one hand, and peasant voting, on the other, is explained. Moreover, his theory has further empirical consequences, which can be checked and whose truth would tend to corroborate it. For example, communist voting should be high among sharecroppers and laborers who own minuscule amounts of land and possibly among those who own no land at all. It should not be high in areas in which landlords provide significant inputs, such as large plantations worked by landless laborers; areas in which substantial land reform takes place should experience a drop or at least a leveling off of communist support. Finally, the relationship between these aggregate variables can be used to explain other events and conditions —such as why certain provinces or districts in other countries should have relatively high levels of communist organization and activity. And it should provide support for subjunctive and counterfactual conditionals—"had Diem carried out a vigorous land reform program, Viet Cong control in the Mekong Delta would be attenuated."[21]

In spite of these similarities to genuine nomic statements, the correlation of communist strength and patterns of land tenure and population density remains quasi-causal, since the relationship is mediated by the practical inference describing the actions of the peasants. In a very schematic fashion, this situation can be represented as shown in Fig. 1. The linkage

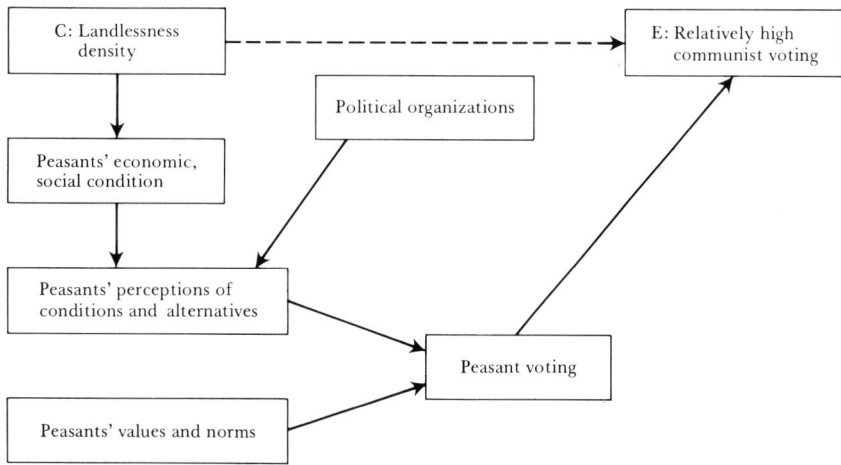

*Fig. 1   The Structure of Quasi-causal Relationships.*

between C and E is the result of the underlying pattern of linkages between C and the other "intervening variables," including the peasants' awareness of their condition in terms of certain alternatives, and their actions. Now *some* of these linkages may be genuinely nomological (though, no doubt, of a probabilistic type). In order for a political organization to exist, it is logically necessary that there be communication among its members, between the organization and its supporters, and among its supporters. High population density facilitates such communication, and in the absence of highly developed technologies of communication and the economic resources to utilize them, it may well be a necessary condition of such communication and therefore of political organization. Whether or not this necessity is nomic, however, the linkage between the peasants' beliefs and values, on the one hand, and their actions, on the other, is conceptual, as we saw in Section 2. Hence the overall relationship between C and E cannot be causal, since the relationship rests on certain intermediate links, and one essential intermediate link is not contingent but conceptual.

Zagoria offers his theory of peasant communism somewhat tentatively, since it represents the beginning of a larger study of peasant radicalism that will include a greater variety of explanatory factors. The importance of his work for my purposes is not that it is completed or finished but that it is representative of a particular type of empirical "theory" in political science. Such theories explain observed correlations between two or more variables by showing what patterns of behavior would produce those correlations, and showing that such behavior is intelligible, given the circumstances described by the "independent" variable. Other examples of this type of theory include the various "relative deprivation" theories of rebellion, violence, and instability, such as Feierabend and Feierabend (1966), Gurr (1970), and Eckstein (1966).

The central purpose of Gurr's elaborate theory, involving scores of variables and their interrelationships, is to explain how a diffuse (naturalistically conceived) feeling of anger comes to be transformed into political violence. Discontent becomes politicized when people come to think of political institutions or leaders as responsible for their discontent or as capable of alleviating it, and when violence is seen as efficacious and legitimate. Whether violence will be seen in this way depends on such factors as the success of the regime in the past in alleviating discontent, the success of violence in the past in securing desired ends, people's expectations of the use of violence, the pervasiveness of violence in the political system, and the availability of alternative means of influence over government policy. Similarly, the type and magnitude of violence is explicable in terms of the relative resources which are available to government and dissidents. Even the generalized feelings of discontent which "begin" the process are not simply reactions to stimulus conditions, understood only in terms of the external regularities they reveal; rather, these conditions are mediated by the knowledge, beliefs, and values of the participants. For example, we experience relative deprivation if we believe the "stock" of some good is fixed and we observe another group increasing its share when that group has no greater claim to it than we do. "Frustrations" such as these are possible only against a background of shared norms, values, and beliefs in terms of which such changes can count as deprivations. Far from producing a kind of diffuse anger on some kind of "stimulus-response" pattern, such changes can be understood only in terms of the intentionalist concepts of the actors themselves. In this respect, such "potential for collective violence" differs profoundly from the diffuse anger, discontent, and irritability that might be the (nomic) effect of a higher level of noise, or pollution, or sounds of a certain frequency in one's environment. Laws describing these relationships would be essentially physiological, and they would not explain particular actions.[22]

The importance of interpretative explanations in those theories which explicitly stress psychological factors may come as no surprise, but the argument can be generalized to include theories emphasizing functional and structural aspects of political situations as well. For example, Dahrendorf's theory of social change (1959) places the structural features of social situations at the center of analysis. Although it is based on a theory of conflict, it does not view conflict as a result of the malintegration of the individual and society, or as the effect of some adverse change in the life situations of a significant number of persons; rather, conflict and its attendant social change are rooted in the very structure of "imperatively coordinated associations," in which some rule and others are ruled. Dahrendorf's theory, then, is an account of the conditions under which groups sharing an interest (what he calls "quasi-groups") in change will become mobilized, will articulate their demands, confront ruling groups, and precipitate changes in the political or social order. But even in this structuralist theory, the transformation of quasi-groups into conflict groups depends on the group members' coming to recognize that they have common interests due to their sharing a common position of power—or powerlessness—in the hierarchy of the association in question, and on their coming to see action in accordance with these interests as both possible and legitimate. Although a number of external conditions must be satisfied before such a transformation occurs, it is clear that Dahrendorf's theory, far from dispensing with interpretative explanations, provides the framework for an extended interpretation of the meanings of certain actions and social situations; it provides a basis for the systematic reconstruction of the practical inferences of social actors as they come to recognize and respond to the opportunities afforded by their situations. Here, as in the Zagoria example, the pattern is to seek regularities which are based on a prior understanding and interpretation of social action in intentional, meaningful terms, and to provide for the reconstruction of the practical inferences linking an actor's situation to his actions. As Eckstein has argued, "to ask *why* certain relations exist in social life is always to ask what there is about one state of society that induces behavior leading to another" (1966, p. 253).

## 4.3 Theory and Models of Man

So far I have been arguing that social science theories presuppose an interpretative understanding of action, and that the regularities they discover and explain are "quasi-causal" in nature. A further, essential characteristic of these theories is that they make certain implicit assumptions regarding human motivation, sociality, and rationality. Such assumptions are essential, for they structure our interpretations of action and provide part of the premises of the "practical inferences" that underlie the quasi-causal relationships which social science theories discover and explain. These theories, we might say, presuppose a particular "model of man," a set of fundamental assumptions regarding human behavior, in terms of which the actions the theory requires are intelligible.

This can be seen in Dahrendorf's work, for example. Dahrendorf assumes that there is a necessary conflict of interest between controlling and controlled classes in all associations, and this assumption is essential to his theory, for it distinguishes his theory from the functionalist theories, with their presuppositions of integration and normative consensus within a society. But why should there be such a conflict? Why do we require only propitious circumstances of communication, organization, leadership, etc., for it to become manifest? Why should the interests of those occupying subordinate positions necessarily clash with the interests of those occupying ruling positions? Dahrendorf attempts to justify his assumption of contradictory interests by construing these interests in analogy to the concept of role expectations in Parsonian theory. Just as the functionalist assumes "certain 'objective' expectations of behavior" for analytic purposes, so Dahrendorf proposes to use the notion of "role interests, i.e., expected orientations of behavior associated with authority roles in imperatively coordinated associations" (1959, p. 178). But the "expectations" defining Dahrendorf's role interests are the "expectations" the *investigator* has regarding social behavior, not the expectations which the social actors themselves entertain. Because actors have certain expectations, we are justified in speaking of "roles," since particular expectations *constitute* particular roles. In Dahrendorf's argument, this concept of "expectation" is used to define the notion of authority roles: "Where there are authority relations, the superordinate element is socially expected to control . . . the behavior of the subordinate unit" ( p. 166). It may well be that those in positions of authority are generally conservative and those in positions of subjection are generally opposed to the status quo, but these generalizations are not part of the ideas which constitute the social relations of domination and subjection. Thus conflicting "role interests" are not analogous to "role expectations," and this device will not justify the central tenet of Dahrendorf's theory. Only if we make certain further assumptions about the motivations or needs of social actors will we have adequate grounds for positing an irreducible conflict of interests within imperatively coordinated associations.

That social conflict is a necessary feature of a class society is a plausible claim only if one adopts a model of man which posits that men have a propensity to dominate (or at least a propensity to resist domination) or a desire for the "goods" or "'values" which authority brings—prestige, wealth, approval, or whatever. For only such a model excludes the possibility that certain inequalities in power will become fully legitimized by a consensus among the actors as to the norms or values in terms of which position in society is assigned. That this is so can be seen by contrasting Dahrendorf's theory of social change with an alternative theory based, at least in part, on fundamentally different assumptions regarding human behavior. Chalmers Johnson (1966), for example, begins his analysis by positing "a basic human need for an explanation of the social and material environment in which a human organism finds itself." However we came by this need, and whatever its importance relative to other needs, "people . . . provide themselves with (or accept) some intellectual construct that lends significance to their being together and working together. Values thus provide meanings for social action; they are symbolic interpretations of reality." (pp 24–25) Thus a description and analysis of a society's value system is central to an adequate social theory, since the value system provides people with ways of orienting themselves to their situations. By specifying the criteria governing the allocation of roles within the society, and by legitimizing the sets of norms to which people are subject and which give concrete form to the value system in actual practice, the value system enables individuals to satisfy their basic need to have and understand some purpose and significance in their lives. In particular, the value system "defines the roles and statuses of [political] authority, and at the same time is the source of this authority's legitimacy" (p. 30). Now it is the role of one's value system in a person's psychic economy that allows Johnson to claim that a class system need not be one of conflict among those in power and those not in power. For political authorities can use their monopoly of legitimate force to maintain the system of rights and obligations, power and responsibilities—in short, the normative structure of the society in terms of which their power is legitimized. Thus, given effective means of socialization and a reasonably high degree of coherence in the society's value system and in the norms expressing it, conflicts of interest over material rewards and positions of power can be meliorated, and they can be subjected to routinized procedures to resolve them. A social system can be—and we can normally expect that it will be—in "equilibrium," able to adapt to environmental changes and to internal sources of strain through marginal adjustments.

In both of these particular cases, then, certain fundamental conceptions about human needs and purposes provide an essential element in the explanations the theories provide, for the presuppositions specify the decisional premises of the actors which, together with descriptions of their situations, provide the rationale for the actions which bring about the overall pattern of social behavior—conflict, violence, social change—that the theorists desire to explain.

Unfortunately, it cannot be said that most theories in political science are based on clear, well-articulated images of man. On the contrary, the fundamental conceptions of human rationality, purposes, sociality, etc., tend to be left vague and inarticulate, and all too often they are shifted as one moves from one context to another. No doubt, this reflects an abiding distrust of "a priorism" or "rationalism" in American political science. But such vagueness is inimical to the development of systematic empirical theory, for not specifying one's basic assumptions encourages reliance on the correlation of available data, interpreted with ad hoc reasonings which supply a plausible basis for the observed relationships. The validity of these correlations may be buttressed by statistical tests of significance, but the relevance or value of such tests is rarely discussed—even when they are applied to statistics based on a population rather than a sample. Or the data may be subjected to one or another currently popular technique of "causal analysis," often without more than a cursory justification of the applicability of such a technique to the problem and data at hand. Even when the techniques are not abused,[23] there is a tendency in such cases to generate a series of studies which, to use Lakatos's terminology (see Section 2.4), are "progressive" in the sense that later studies contain more corroborated empirical content than earlier ones. But these studies do not develop out of a well-articulated research program, and so they do not provide greater coherence or lend a more systematic character to our knowledge of a subject. If these efforts do increase our knowledge of politics—and in some cases their value cannot be doubted—this result reflects the fact that they unwittingly contribute to or provide confirmation for essentially interpretative accounts of the particular political context in which they are set.

As I argued in Section 2.4, a systematic empirical theory requires a research program, that is, the specification of a fundamental conceptualization of a field of investigation or, as I have been calling it in the context of the human sciences, a model of man. A model of man can provide the basis for the development of systematic theories similar to those of the natural sciences, while at the same time providing the interpretative explanations required by the subject matter of the social sciences. In defining a research program, a model of man specifies the negative heuristic: the regulative principles which must not be violated in developing empirical theories. Like the principle "no action at a distance," the negative heuristic of political theory may specify that "social systems are made up not of individuals, but of roles" (Almond and Powell, 1965, p. 19). Such statements, intended to express the "ultimate nature" of political or social things, are the principles *around which* theories are to be constructed. They are not descriptive of anything; rather, they direct our attention to certain factors and forbid explanations in terms of others. Similarly, the *positive* heuristic consists of a set of regulative principles or directives for the articulation of a theory. By specifying salient features of the subject matter, it suggests the concepts, analogies, and hypotheses guiding the articulation of a rigorous, formalizable theory. The problems encountered in articulating such a paradigm and the outstanding empirical anomalies it generates represent the "puzzles" which structure and engage scientific attention. Finally, *scientific progress* will be possible once a particular research program is accepted, for it is the research program which presents a standard in terms of which theoretical innovation can be assessed and the empirical content of alternative theories can be compared.[24] Given a common conceptual framework, it should be relatively unproblematic to determine whether a newly proposed theory is consistent with the preceding theory, in the sense of being able to account for all the phenomena which the earlier theory explained, and whether it predicts additional facts—facts incompatible with or, at best, not predictable by the original theory. Finally, given a research program, we should also be able to distinguish between what we might call "humdrum science" and "normal science" (see Kuhn, 1970b), between mere variations and refinements—a succession of small papers—and genuine theoretical innovation, advancing the solution to puzzles the research program, or paradigm, poses. The paradigm, as I stressed in Section 1, provides the necessary continuity to the scientific enterprise, such that it can become cumulative. Without such frameworks, the results of research would be a motley assemblage of miscellaneous observations, at best merely a storehouse of "facts," but facts of doubtful significance.

### 4.4 The Rational Choice Paradigm

In political science we have few well-articulated research programs rooted in clearly worked-out models of man. Indeed, it might be argued that there is really only one: the rational choice model of human behavior. On the basis of this model, a number of particular theories have been developed, including Downs's *Economic Theory of Democracy* (1957), Riker's *Theory of Political Coalitions* (1962), and Olson's *Logic of Collective Action* (1965). This paradigm has long been fundamental in economics, and it is attracting increasing interest in the other social sciences; in sociology it goes under the name "exchange theory" and has been developed in the writings of Homans (1961) and Thibaut and Kelley (1959). Downs's study is one of the first works of this school in political science. It was originally motivated by an anomaly in economics, specifically within the subfields of public finance and welfare economics. In those areas government action is a central variable, and economists had been remarkably successful in using theories based on the rational choice model to analyze the impact of alternative government policies. Based on such analyses, they could recommend policies to government decision makers, but, Downs complained, economists had been notably lax in developing theories which would predict or explain what policies a government would actually follow. They were generally content to indicate what actions should be taken and to assume that the government would take them. However, given the rational choice model, there is no reason to suppose that the government will act on their advice. Like other people, the members of the government must be assumed to be rational utility maximizers, and they must be presumed to make government policy as a means of maximizing their *own* utility—just as the baker bakes bread not to do good for his fellow man but as a way of earning his living. Hence they will follow the economists' recommendations only if those recommendations happen to be in their own interests—obviously a contingent matter. Hence, in order that an adequate theory of public finance may be developed, some account of government behavior is necessary.

It must not be supposed that this difficulty can be avoided simply by assuming that the government is "special," and so it will act to maximize the public interest. Such a "solution" is not adequate because it would contradict the assumption underlying the economic theories on which the recommendations themselves are based, for if government decision makers can act in a nonmaximizing manner, the same assumption can be made for the other actors whose behavior is to be explained, and the predictions of the entire corpus of economic theory would then be called into question. Such a situation, then, violates the "negative heuristic" of the research program underlying economics. It is for this reason that Downs set out to develop an adequate theory of government decision-making.

### 4.4.1 Rational Choice and the Nature of Action

The fundamental assumption of Downs's work is that the behavior of an individual must be explained in terms of his maximizing his own "utility," and that all social phenomena must be explainable on the basis of this conceptualization of individual behavior. This is the core of the negative heuristic of this reasearch program, since it specifies a fixed point around which theories must be developed. It involves a certain image of man and a corresponding image of the relationship of individuals to each other and to society. As a conceptualization of human action, it reduces all behavior to the making of choices among alternatives which confront the actor or subject. The rational agent is to analyze the various courses of action open to him in terms of the consequences each will have. These consequences will be different "states of the world," so to speak, or different probability distributions over the set of all possible states of the world. (The complications of uncertainty will be ignored here, since they do not affect the argument.) The actor is also supposed to have a preference ordering of all possible states of the world which satisfies certain axioms. The most important of them are an axiom of choice (between any two alternatives he can say that one is preferred to the other or that he is indifferent between them) and an axiom of transitivity (if an alternative, $x$, is preferred to an alternative, $y$, and if $y$ is preferred to an alternative, $z$, then $x$ is also preferred to $z$). Then, from the set of alternatives or "states of the world" the agent actually confronts, he chooses that set which has the highest ranking in his preference orderings.

In the modern version of the rational choice approach, no assumption is made about the way in which people come to prefer one thing to another. In particular, a relation of preference between two items is *not* interpreted to mean that the agent derives greater pleasure from the one he prefers than from the other. The wants, values, satisfactions, or whatever it is that underlies the valuations represented by a preference ordering is quite immaterial. All that is required is that a person be consistent in his choices, and to be consistent is to order possible states of the world in terms of the axioms of choice and transitivity, for only if these axioms are satisfied will it always be possible for the individual to make a determinate choice in any situation he may happen to confront.

It is obviously very important how these alternative states of the world are described. For example, if all the concepts we use in discriminating different states are such that the rational agent attaches no importance to them, he will necessarily be indifferent among them. Although he may recognize that the worlds so described are indeed different, they will all be the same from an evaluative point of view. It is hard even to imagine describing the world in such terms—so closely are our concepts tied to our interests. But most of us would find little to choose between alternatives differentiated solely by the amount of sun spot activity on Alpha Centauri, or by the number of donkey hairs present in each, or even states of affairs described jointly by these characteristics. Obviously, then, the description of these different situations will have to be couched in dimensions that are evaluatively significant for the decision maker concerned. Moreover, if this schema is to do its job, *all* of the evaluatively significant variables will have to be included; otherwise we would find our agent expressing a preference between things which, in terms of our descriptions, are the same.

In the theory of consumer behavior these evaluatively significant dimensions can be called "goods," since the consumer's choice problem is to select that bundle of goods or mix of commodities and services which he prefers to all other bundles, given the choices he faces. Now if (and only if) the consumer's preference ordering satisfies certain conditions, his choice behavior can be represented as maximizing some index of his overall value position. Such an index is called a "utility function," and it assigns a single number to each consumption bundle in such a way that if one bundle is preferred to another, the number assigned to the former will be greater than the number assigned to the latter. If the consumer's preference ordering can be represented by a utility function, it is possible to deduce determinate statements about how he will respond to certain conditions. For example, assuming that the utility of most consumers increases at a decreasing rate as the amount they each consume of a particular commodity grows while the amounts they have of other commodities are held constant, one can deduce the Law of Demand: the quantity of a good which consumers are willing to buy is inversely related to its price.

### 4.4.2 Theory Construction and the Positive Heuristic

The point of developing this analysis of preference ordering is to use it to generate such laws. But the analysis presented here is compatible with virtually any pattern of choices. Whatever an individual chose, we could always "explain" his choice by saying that the alternative chosen was the "best" among those he confronted. In order to use this model to develop generalizations, we must constrain it in some way. The most common constraints follow.

1. The individual prefers "more" to "less." If two states of the world, A and B, are equal on all evaluatively significant dimensions except one, and if A has "more" of some good or value than B, then A is preferred to B. This implies that there is no satiation point; no matter what the individual's situation, there will always be some other position he will prefer.
2. Preference orderings can be represented by a utility function.
3. Diminishing marginal utility: as a person gets more of one particular good, the "value" of successive increments (in terms of what he would be willing to give up to obtain them) decreases.
4. The individual is indifferent to the value of other individuals' preference orderings. His evaluation of a situation does not depend on the satisfactions (or lack of satisfactions) which others derive from it.

These constraints limit the indefiniteness of the general model, and the concept of individual "rationality" amounts to the assumption that the individual's actual choices reflect a preference ordering that satisfies these constraints.

In addition to these very general assumptions, further restrictions may be placed on preference orderings in order to construct theories of specific social or political processes. Thus Downs, for example, assumes that parties are interested only in securing the rewards of office—including power, prestige, money, etc. Such assumptions form part of the context within which the theory is to work; the context includes the identification of the actors and their (relevant) relationships, the specification of the "boundaries" within which they must work, etc. Downs begins with a model of a set of voters facing two parties, one forming the government, the other the opposition, in which the government must take a stand on "issues" prior to the opposition's doing so, in which the government does not alter the electoral system itself, and in which all actors have perfect information. Assumptions such as these are part of the "protective belt," or the positive heuristic of a theory. They are the hypotheses and concepts which can be manipulated, arranged, and altered in order to develop theories of increasing verisimilitude, but which conform to the negative heuristic of the governing research program or paradigm. In developing his theory, Downs relaxes the assumptions of perfect information, two parties, and the requirement that the government move first.

The positive heuristic structures the course of theoretical development by providing the theorist with the concepts, definitions, hypotheses, etc., which he can use in solving the puzzles that the paradigm poses and overcoming the major anomalies the theory faces or those which develop as the paradigm is articulated. One such puzzle for Downs's theory—and I will show how it arises in a moment—is that it predicts that no one should vote, because voting cannot yield net benefits to the individual voter. The seriousness of this problem does not result from the fact that people vote, even though the theory implies that they should not. If it were merely that an empirical finding contradicted the theory, we could ignore it while continuing to articulate the paradigm in the expectation that this apparently disconfirming evidence would be explicable on the basis of a more refined theory. The difficulty this problem poses, however, is not merely "empirical," for it questions the central tenets of the paradigm itself. In the first place, part of the *point* of the theory is to explain voting patterns, and yet the theory predicts that people will not vote! And this is just the beginning. For it seems that the prediction that people will not vote should be included as part of the beliefs of the rational voters whose behavior the theory predicts, since, being rational, they should see that everyone will reach the decision that voting is not worthwhile. But allowing for this belief causes the theory to break down completely in the following way. The reason no one should vote is that the value of one's vote depends on the probability of its affecting the outcome of the election, and that probability is negligible. Hence, no matter how much one stands to gain as a result of his preferred party's being elected, it will not pay him to vote so long as there are any measurable costs to voting at all. Therefore he should not go to the polls. Moreover, since everyone is in the same position, no one should vote. But there is no reason to stop with this conclusion; the rational individual can see that no one will vote, so he can only conclude that if he should change his mind and decide to vote after all, he will be the only voter, and his vote will therefore decide the election! Hence it will pay him to vote if he sees any difference between the parties at all. But once again, there is no reason to stop here; each person can reason in this way, leading to the conclusion that everyone will vote! But, our rational man must conclude, it no longer pays him to vote, so he will stay home; but then everyone should reach the same conclusion at this round, and so it continues. Clearly, the problem here is a theoretical one, concerning the very enterprise of deducing patterns of social phenomena from individual behavior when that behavior is based on certain beliefs and values. It therefore goes to the heart of the rational choice paradigm itself, given its commitment to explain all social and political phenomena in terms of the incentives facing representative or typical individuals. What began simply as a problem for Downs's theory of democracy turns out to be a "puzzle" for the paradigm on which Downs's theory is based. And indeed, the same problem arises in different forms in different theories based on this paradigm. The indeterminancy of game theory in the face of the "prisoner's dilemma" (for example, see Rapaport, 1966, pp. 140ff) and accounting for the development of organizations catering to the needs of large groups (see Olson, 1965) are other examples of this problem.

### 4.4.3 Scientific Progress

Having seen that the positive heuristic of the rational choice research program defines a set of puzzles structuring scientific investigation, we might find it valuable to examine, however briefly, a sequence of attempts to solve these puzzles, thereby illustrating how the paradigm enables us to recognize scientific progress. The problem of whether to vote can be taken as an example once again. I will outline three attempts to solve it, the first two representing theoretically degenerating problem shifts[25] and the third a progressive innovation.

Having formulated the problem of voting turnout, Downs was also the first to propose a solution. He argued that a rational individual would vote, even if his vote would make little difference to the outcome of an election, because he derives "long-run participation value" from voting. The rational man, Downs argued, recognizes that the survival of democracy depends on a sufficiently high level of participation in elections, since universal failure to participate would bring about the collapse of the system—and of the benefits which democracy generates. Thus, to the short-run value of his vote he must add the reward he receives in the way of system maintenance. "Of course," Downs continued,

> . . . he will actually get this reward even if he himself does not vote as long as a sufficient number of other citizens do. But . . . he is willing to

bear certain short-run costs he could avoid in order to do his share in providing long-run benefits. (Downs, 1957, p. 270)

But it is irrational to do one's share, to incur some cost, when one can acquire the benefits in question without doing one's share, without incurring costs. There is no reason to expect such socially desirable behavior on the part of the actors in Downs's model, and the entire theory on which it is based is inconsistent with such behavior. Not only are these actors supposed to be self-regarding and therefore insensitive to the effects of their actions on the well-being of others, but they are also supposed to calculate the benefits of their actions only in terms of the consequences; they are assumed *not* to govern their behavior in accordance with general rules. Indeed, the point of the theory is to explain behavior without reference to such notions.

What is involved here, let me emphasize, is the conception of instrumental rationality itself, not simply the assumption of self-regarding behavior. Even if one were a perfect utilitarian and acted to maximize the total utility resulting from much of his actions, regardless of the person to whom it accrued, he would face a similar problem so long as he acted "rationally" in the sense that Downs uses the term. With regard to an indivisible good, such as the maintenance of the democratic system, the contribution of any one individual's vote is insignificant in bringing about the result.

True, my action could make a contribution if I were joined by a sufficiently large number of other individuals; if enough of us voted, we could look back and see that the total benefit resulting from our actions exceeded the total costs, and so in a sense we could say that the average utility produced by each of us was greater than the average cost each of us bore. But prospectively, when we are deciding whether to vote, each of us can only calculate the expected value of his own individual action. And since an individual's voting or not voting has no impact on whether anyone else does, the benefits directly attributable to a single person's actions are virtually nonexistent.

As a group, we can secure these benefits for ourselves only if each of us—or some significant proportion of us—acts in accordance with some sort of general rules. These rules may be designed in such a way that, if a large number of people observe them, the best consequences for all will result. But a commitment to act in accordance with such norms is a commitment which may well lead one to do things which do not, on occasion, produce any desirable results for himself or anyone else. It may be *socially rational* to act on such principles, but it is not *individually rational* to do so, in the sense that one "moves towards his goals in a way which, to the best of his knowledge, uses the least possible input of scarce resources per unit of valued output" (Downs, 1957, p. 5). It is not, then, simply that most of the time our goals may not include the well-being of others, for even if they did, we would still not have an adequate incentive to realize the common good.

Downs's solution to this puzzle is unsatisfactory because it contradicts the negative heuristic of the rational choice research program itself. A second solution, proposed by Riker and Ordeshook (1968), is unsatisfactory in that it represents a "degenerate problem shift." They propose that the determinants of the "expected utility of voting" be expanded to include those which do not depend on the individual's contribution to the outcome of the election. Notoriously, the costs of voting are independent of one's vote having any effect, but are there any benefits in this category? Riker and Ordeshook suggest that there are indeed satisfactions to be gained in the act of voting, irrespective of whether one's vote makes a difference, and they provide a long list of such rewards: the citizen derives "satisfaction from compliance with the ethic of voting, . . . from affirming allegiance to the political system, [and] . . . from affirming a partisan preference" (p. 28). These "satisfactions," clearly, are in the same camp as Downs's "long-run participation value": they presuppose the efficacy of normative orientations to behavior, thereby contradicting the assumptions of the rational choice paradigm, which requires that behavior be explained in terms of incentives and consequences.

Riker and Ordeshook also suggest other sources of gratification, particularly the pleasure of acquiring political information, going to the polls, choosing which party to support, etc. (p. 28). That is, they suggest that some citizens may find voting and political activity enjoyable, in and of itself. And when the enjoyment one derives from the act of voting is counted, it becomes rational for many people to vote.

The problem with this hypothesis, of course, is its ad hoc character in the context of this research program. Merely on empirical grounds it cannot be faulted; some people do derive pleasure from participation, and those who score higher in terms of "citizen duty" (which, for the sake of argument, may be taken as a surrogate for the intrinsic satisfactions from political activity) are more likely to vote than others. But this innovation is not progressive, because it is not developed in accordance with the positive heuristic of the research program, since it amounts to making an assumption about a *specific preference,* rather than attempting to explain behavior in terms of general assumptions regarding preference orderings. Indeed, by adding such ad hoc constraints to voters' preferences, we would be able to make this theory "predict" any behavior we might require! And this has the consequence of saving the theory only by duplicating, in the assumptions of the theory, all the vagaries of the empirical situation we are trying to explain.

The third solution to the paradox of voting *is* theoretically progressive. Ferejohn and Fiorina (1973) propose an innovation in the positive heuristic of the rational choice paradigm, specifically, a shift from a maximizing conception of rationality to an alternative formulation. They assume that voters do not act to maximize their total level of utility, since such a course of action is not well defined when the outcome of one's action depends on the actions of others, and when there is no way of determining how others will behave. Previous theorists had treated the voting decision as a case of decision-making under risk, and they required the voter to estimate the probabilities of various events taking place—in particular, that the election would be very close—but there is no basis for estimating such probabilities. Hence, according to Ferejohn and Fiorina, we must treat the voting decision as a problem of decision-making under uncertainty, as a situation in which the probability of the various outcomes is unknown. Thus the voter cannot try to maximize his expected utility from voting, since he does not have the necessary information to do so; he must therefore adopt an alternative strategy, such as minimizing his maximum loss (minimax), or minimizing his maximum "regret," where the "regret" associated with an action, $a_1$, is "the difference between what the decision maker could have attained had he known the true state of nature before he chooses his action, and what he actually gets by choosing $a_1$" (p. 8). The minimax regret voter, then, will go to the polls with only a slight incentive.

> If asked why he voted, a minimax regretter might reply "My God, what if I didn't vote and my preferred candidate lost by one vote? I'd feel like killing myself." Notice that for the expected utility maximizer the probability of such an event is very important, whereas for the minimax regretter, the mere logical possibility of such an event is enough. (Ferejohn and Fiorina, 1973, p. 26)

Assuming that voters adopt a minimax regret decision rule, we can predict much higher levels of voting turnout. Moreover, this innovation permits the deduction of further empirical consequences as well—e.g., that in a three-cornered race, the minimax regret voter will not vote for the candidate who is his second choice, even when his first choice is likely to lose and his third choice to win!

Ferejohn and Fiorina's innovation, then, is progressive inasmuch as it involves a reconceptualization of the voting decision, making use of the "positive heuristic" of the rational choice research program, but without positing an essentially ad hoc constraint on preference orderings which is designed simply to account for the troubling anomaly. It dissolves the paradox of voting at the theoretical level by showing that the indeterminacy which resulted from the earlier formulations can be avoided. Moreover, it predicts a number of new facts in addition to providing an explanation for the anomaly of the original theory. Finally, this innovation generates new "puzzles" which can be used to structure further research. By introducing the possibility of a number of different decision rules which are consistent with the rational choice paradigm, it poses the problem of which criterion is used under which circumstances and why. And this, of course, suggests the ultimately promissory character of their theory as well, for there is no guarantee that research along these lines will prove progressive, and in the future we may have to begin again with the question of why a rational actor should vote.

## 4.5 Interpretative Explanations and Generalizing Theories

If rational choice theories of politics illustrate the importance of a well-articulated model of man for theory construction, they also illustrate the close relationship between interpretative explanations of particular political events and generalizing theories of politics. In fact, there are three separate ways in which they are related, and I will close by examining each of the ways. In the first place, political theories are akin to interpretations of action in that they are quasi-causal in nature. The quasi-causal character of the laws based on the rational choice paradigm is so obvious that it requires little comment. The convergence of electoral parties in two-party systems with unimodal distributions of attitudes over the electorate, or the necessity for "selective incentives" to organize large "latent groups"—these and other implications of rational choice theories follow from the reconstructions of the practical inferences of large numbers of individuals; in fact, it is precisely the purpose of this paradigm to provide such reconstructions.

The explanatory power of these theories rests on their systematizing these practical syllogisms by showing how a given situation, together with certain values, justifies a particular course of action on the part of those affected and how their actions, in turn, affect the situation, creating a new motivational context for subsequent behavior. Thus, in the party convergence example, the reason the parties converge is that their leaders respond to increases and/or decreases in popular support. Their actions are based on the following considerations: changes in popular support are related to the relative distance between the parties and the voter since each voter casts his ballot for the party which is "closest" to him; because there are more voters in the "center" of the spectrum, movements away from the center by one party results in its losing voters as some now find the other party relatively closer to their own positions; thus movements toward the center result in net increases in voter support. Whether or not party leaders actually recognize what is happening, so long as they realize that they gain votes by moving in one direction and lose votes by moving in the other, they will tend to move toward the center; and they will gain votes or lose votes if the voters reason as the model suggests. These background processes of reasoning underlie and explain the tendency of political parties to converge.

The relationship between attitude distribution and party position, then, is mediated by the practical inferences of voters and parties, and it is therefore a quasi-causal relationship rather than an instance of a genuine law. Because rational choice theories are intended to provide general accounts of the structural and dynamic features of particular kinds of situations, they are not a species of interpretative explanation; but, like other social science theories, they presuppose a set of interpretative explanations as links between general social or political variables.

In the second place, rational choice theories depend on interpretative explanations to provide the context within which these theories function. Any theory of politics, for example, must at least implicitly include a conception of "politics" as a kind of behavior differentiated from other kinds of behavior. In rational choice theories, naturally, such a conception may not be a central part of the theory itself—the point of these theories being to exhibit political behavior as continuous with "economic" behavior. Nonetheless, shifting the focus of the analytical apparatus from economics to politics requires that the theorist come to terms with the phenomenon of collective choice and group behavior, and that he redefine what will count as an incentive or "good." These changes reflect a conceptualization of the political sphere which may or may not be articulated, but which involves an interpretation of the meanings of certain actions or practices.

This situation may be most evident in the majoritarian conception of democracy implicit in most rational choice theories. Quite in keeping with their emphasis on explaining all social phenomena in terms of the incentives facing typical individuals, a major puzzle of the rational choice paradigm lies in the way individual preferences are mapped into collective decisions; such a paradigm must seek to explain collective decisions in terms of individual preferences, together with the resources and procedures available to individuals to advance these preferences. Politics, in this view, is the activity of men advancing their interests through collective action. From this perspective, the commonsense notion of democracy—the rule of the people—is adopted and defined as that set of decision rules which consistently provides for the realization of the preferences of more people rather than less.[26] On this basis, Rae (1969) develops an index of democracy that reflects the extent to which majority rule is actually realized within each institution of the polity, and his index systematically qualifies most of the traditional devices of "constitutionalism," including bicameralism, qualified majorities, etc., as (relatively) undemocratic.

Of course, majoritarianism is a well-established, even venerable tradition in democratic theory. But there are other traditions, and the differences among them depend in part on their underlying conceptions of politics. The constitutional democrat, who sees politics primarily in terms of the protection of rights, in terms of checking and resolving conflicts among men, takes a very different view of "democracy," or "rule of the people." For example, Buchanan and Tullock (1962), who insist that the problem of politics arises only *after* a set of human property rights has been specified, and who implicitly see politics in terms of the settlement of disputes arising against the background of such a normative order, develop a theory of democracy centered on the concept of unanimity rather than majoritarianism.[27]

Interpretative explanations provide the context for rational choice theories of politics in a second, more specific way as well. Quite apart from their dependence on a general understanding of political life, rational choice theories presuppose the constitutive norms defining actions and practices within the society or societies whose politics are to be explained. Although this point is obvious, it cannot be stated too forcefully that we must have a participant's understanding of voting, legislating, judging, electing, in order to claim that we are explaining his political activities. The meanings of these concepts can be understood only in terms of the practices and/or actions they denote, and these practices and actions can be understood and related only in terms of the concepts they express. They are learned and defined contextually in the process of political action, and a theory which would explain political activity presupposes them, for in their absence there is no political activity to be explained.

Generalizing theories of politics are closely related to interpretative explanations of political action in yet a third way. The rational choice paradigm conceptualizes politics as a sphere of instrumental action; political actors are interpreted as pursuing certain objectives and regulating their behavior in accordance with those objectives. This paradigm therefore excludes interpretations of political action in expressive, symbolic, and communicative terms, as action engaged in for its own sake, or to affirm one's personal identity or one's solidarity with a larger community, or to exercise and display one's powers and capabilities. Thus the rational choice paradigm constitutes a particular interpretation of the constitutive meanings of politics and political activity—or at least it radically restricts the range of possible interpretations. The conceptions of political activity espoused by a long tradition of political thinking, from Aristotle to Arendt, fall outside the pale of acceptable interpretations, given this paradigm. And by so restricting interpretations at this level, the rational choice paradigm limits the kinds of *interpretative* explanations of political actions and practices which can properly be given as well.

To the extent that an explanatory theory requires such a fundamental conceptualization of politics, then, the activities of explanation and interpretation presuppose and complement each other. Far from being antithetical to each other, the naturalist and interpretive models of social science must be synthesized within a common framework. To develop such a framework and to apply it to actual theories in political science have been the objectives of this section.

## 5 EXPLANATION, INTERPRETATION, AND POLITICAL INQUIRY: AN OVERVIEW

My intention in this essay has been to present and defend a methodological position which transcends the differences between the naturalist and the interpretative views of social and political science. The central questions I have addressed concern the structure and testing of explanatory accounts. As I argued in Section 2, the scientific model requires laws, or lawlike generalizations, in all explanations, for laws serve to link the event we wish to explain to the "antecedent conditions" which led to it. Without laws, there is no way to show that we have correctly identified the factors which brought about the event in question. But how are we to identify a statement as a "law?" To answer this question requires a consideration of scientific theories, for the theory explains and, one might say, gives "force" to laws. Theories represent a range of phenomena in terms of the operation of a few basic principles and thus show *why* observed regularities hold. Theories provide systematic unity to our knowledge and so represent the crowning achievement of the scientific enterprise.

Unfortunately, there is no commonly accepted explication of the structure of scientific theories, and even more significantly, it is not clear how theories can be tested and rejected. And since the explanatory power of theories depends on their testability, even the generally accepted account of scientific explanation becomes problematic. In Section 2.4, however, I presented a possible solution to this problem, which was developed by Imre Lakatos. His solution has the merit of showing that the testing and choice of theories is a rational affair, while at the same time recognizing the "conceptual presuppositions" of scientific inquiry. It involves viewing the process of theory-testing as a contest between or among theories, developed in terms of a research program. And as I argued in Section 4, his "methodology of scientific research programs" is directly applicable to political science and can help us clarify some of the issues of theory construction in our own field.

The second methodological position, the interpretative model of political inquiry, offers a fundamentally different account of the nature of political science, and I presented this model in Section 3. In opposition to the naturalist model, this position holds that explanations of social phenomena do not require laws or generalizations. Social phenomena are different from natural phenomena in that they are in part ideational and linguistic, and therefore they must be *interpreted* or *understood* in terms of their meanings, rather than simply *explained* in terms of *generalizations*. The explanatory schema appropriate for the human sciences, according to this account, is the practical inference, which links a person's intentions or reasons for action to his action. The practical inference enables us to interpret an action in terms of the agent's intention, but it must be emphasized that this intention is not some shadowy thing in the agent's "mind." Rather, the intentional character of our behavior is due to our viewing it in the context of the conventions of our society and the purposes, values, and beliefs of social actors. Hence, to construct a practical syllogism requires us to view the action in question in terms of the practices and conventions of a society. These practices, in turn, are expressed in the language of the society, and they can be interpreted in terms of what I called "constitutive meanings," which are the fundamental ideas which define a particular way of life. By understanding these ideas, we are able to grasp the point or significance of a practice and to see how or the extent to which a social order constitutes a unified, coherent whole.

At the end of Section 3 I stressed that the interpretative understanding provided by this model of inquiry is no more "subjective" or "psychological" than the understanding provided by scientific explanations. Of course, the testing of interpretative accounts involves problems which are different from those involved in the testing of scientific theories. In particular, interpretative understanding involves what is called the "interpretative" of "hermeneutic" circle, in which the meaning of a particular action or utterance is explicated in terms of the "global meaning" of the whole sequence of actions or speech, and then the "global meaning," in turn, is tested and corrected against the meanings of the parts. But this does not mean that interpretative understanding is not objective, or that it is identical with any kind of private, psychological experience.

Neither the interpretative nor the naturalist model of political inquiry is adequate, however. The former is correct in insisting on the symbolic or meaningful nature of human actions, but it is mistaken in arguing that the categories of intention or rules exhaust social and political phenomena. On the contrary, many of our actions have unintended consequences, and the structure of our society and the processes of social change are seldom deliberately planned. So what is required is a methodological position which represents a genuine synthesis of these two accounts.

In section 4 I presented, in a highly schematic form, the basic elements of such a synthesis. My conception makes use of the idea of a "model of man," a fundamental conceptualization of man and society, of human rationality, needs, sociality, etc. Such a conceptualization, I argued, could function as a research program in formulating rigorous theories describing and explaining the "quasi-causal" relationships which characterize political and social life. But many elements of the interpretative model are also preserved in this conception of political research. In the first place, the relationships which these theories describe are only quasi-causal, for they presuppose or systematize the practical inferences of large numbers of individuals. Second, these theories depend on interpretative explanations which identify the "actions" and other social phenomena the theories are to explain. Third and most important, the model of man which defines a research program for political inquiry also serves to guide the articulation of these interpretative explanations. Hence it serves as a bridge between the generalizing theories, on the one hand, and the interpretation of particular actions, practices, and forms of life, on the other. This shows that *the naturalist and interpretative accounts of political inquiry, when properly understood, complement and, in fact, presuppose each other.* Only on the basis of this recognition can we have an adequate understanding of the logic of political and social inquiry.

## A POSTSCRIPT ON THE RELATIONSHIPS AMONG POLITICAL THEORY, POLITICAL PHILOSOPHY, AND POLITICAL EVALUTION.

One of the most vexing issues in the methodology of political science is the relationship between empirical inquiry and theory, on the one hand, and political philosophy and political evaluation, on the other. One of the advantages of the conception of political inquiry developed in this chapter is that it enables us to see how closely these activities are related to each other. The purpose of this "postscript," then, is to bring out some of the more important continuities between political theory, political philosophy, and normative inquiry. Since political philosophy and normative inquiry are treated elsewhere in this volume, I shall be concerned only with the connection between them and political theory, and I will not deal with them in their own terms.

The most obvious connection between political theory and political philosophy is to be found at the level of theoretical paradigms: political philosophy, in addition to its other features, is a source of paradigms, or "models of man." Hobbes, for example, entitles the first two books of his *Leviathan,* "Of Man," and "Of Common-wealth," respectively, and basic conceptions of human nature and action are scarcely less explicit in the writings of other political philosophers as well. The articulation of these paradigms involves separable (though seldom explicitly separated) kinds of activities, one corresponding to the interpretive concerns of political inquiry and the other to the generalizing activities of political theory. The first task of the political philosopher is to reflect on the basic assumptions and conceptualizations which underlie and constitute the political relationships of his own society, to lay bare the political practices of his political order by interpreting their meanings. Professor Germino, in his contribution to this volume, stresses the "radical" character of political philosophy, its insistence on explicating the root assumptions, the "hegemonic idea," or, to use the term employed above, the "constitutive meanings" of a society or a political order. In this respect, political philosophy is continuous with the interpretative dimension of political inquiry.

An interpretative account of political life is possible, of course, only at a certain "distance" from one's society, for only at a distance is it possible to see the "taken-for-granted world" in any perspective, and to reflect critically on what is normally only tacitly understood. This is why political philosophy flourishes in times of political crises, when the nature of a particular social and political order is undergoing profound change or is under severe attack, for such periods of clashing self-understandings and self-definitions expose the basic assumptions and conceptualizations underlying social practices, as disagreement and conflict lead men to articulate their orientations more explicitly and thoroughly than they did before the period of crisis. And because political philosophy flourishes during periods of crisis, the interpretations political philosophers provide tend to have a "practical" or "diagnostic" character; because they offer an interpretation of the political and social practices of one's society at a period in which these practices are in question, they will inevitably have implications for the positions of some or all of the parties to the conflict, and they may help new groups to understand and articulate their own standpoints.

The "diagnostic" character of political philosophy involves the second type of activity in which political philosophers must engage: the development of analytical, general theories which transcend the experience of any particular polity. It is often thought that political philosophy is concerned essentially or only with the basic normative features of political life, but this view is seriously deficient precisely because political philosophy also serves as the basis for developing generalizing theories of politics; as Germino argues, political philosophy has empirical relevance. Of course, the extent to which and the direction in which a philosopher develops systematic theories based on the model of man he presents depends on his specific purposes and the particular puzzles posed by his fundamental conceptualization. A central puzzle for Hobbes's paradigm, for example, is the possibility of political stability, given his basic assumptions about human motivation and rationality. This, combined with the radical problems of revolution and civil war which provide at least a part of the occasion for his work, accounts for his developing an elaborate theory of political stability. Similarly, Locke's attention to the evolution of forms of political authority is dictated by the apparent anomaly that traditional forms of rule represent for a theory which rests on a "voluntarist" conception of political order. Plato's attention to a theory of social change may be traced to a need to articulate the interdependence of "personality and politics," so prominent a feature of his basic conceptualization, as well as to his practical concern with the possibilities and strategies of political action.

The aspects of a model of man and society that are developed as systematic theories may vary with the distinctive features of the model, as well as with the practical interests and problems which led to its articulation, but unless some parts are developed in this way, the claim of a philosopher to have provided an adequate justification for a particular set of political principles or a particular form of political order will not be fully credible. The reason a justification of a political order requires the development of theories of political behavior is that a justification involves the evaluation of alternative political orders or institutions, and to make such an evaluation requires that we understand the consequences of alternative institutional arrangements. But this means that we must have at least an implicit theory of politics in terms of which the consequences of alternative institutional arrangements can be predicted. Hence, the political philosopher is forced to elaborate his philosophical model of man by developing systematic theories of at least some aspects of political life.

Even if a philosopher is not interested in articulating and justifying a particular set of political principles, the model of man he offers still has empirical implications. Indeed, unless it is developed in the form of an explicit theory of some aspect of politics or used to interpret some concrete form of political life, it is unlikely to be very meaningful, simply because it will appear to be so abstract and pointless. A few of the issues around which such political philosophers as Plato, Hobbes, Burke, Montesquieu, Marx, and Mosca have developed explicit theories include the breakdown of traditional forms of authority, the conditions of political instability, the possibility of consciously planned social and political change, the conditions necessary for constitutional government, the succession of distinct social, political and economic systems, and the conditions of revolution. Naturally, one might say (if one so wished) that a political philosopher, when he goes beyond articulating a general conceptualization of man and society to develop explicit theories or to interpret political practices, thereby becomes a political scientist. Although such a distinction might be possible in principle, there would be little point in making it in practice, because the statement of a model of man and the articulation of a set of theories based on it are closely linked and interwoven in the work of most political philosophers.

It should not be thought that the provision of paradigms or models of man exhausts the activities of political philosophy which are continuous with the construction of political theories. Quite apart from its *substantive* continuity with political theory, political philosophy has an important contribution to make to the *methodology* of political inquiry. Indeed, among philosophers it is often argued that the *only* relationship philosophy can have to empirical discipline is methodological, for philosophy is thought to be a "second-order" activity, in that it asks questions about how we are to *understand* the world, and it answers them in terms of *meta* theories, or theories about theories of politics.[28] And this is surely an important activity; in the course of empirical work in a particular discipline, problems may arise which a philosopher is equipped to handle, since they concern conceptual issues of one sort or another and are not decidable simply by ascertaining the relevant "facts." In political science, for example, we might be concerned with the status of a concept, such as the notion of a "political system": In what sense can a "system" of any sort be said to exist? Can there be properties of the "system" that are not simply concatenations of properties of identifiable individuals? Can a political theory that includes "system" as one of its basic concepts be reduced to a political (or psychological) theory that does not? A similar set of questions can be asked regarding more specifically political concepts; in this volume Oppenheim offers analyses of such terms as "control," "influence," "power," "freedom," and "legitimacy." A myriad of other political concepts essential to the vocabulary of political science are explicated in the literature of political philosophy, including "law," (e.g., Hart, 1961), "representation," (e.g., Pitkin, 1967), "sovereignty," (e.g., Rees, 1956), "state," (e.g., De Jouvenel, 1962), "revolution," (e.g., Arendt, 1965), "coercion," (e.g., Nozick, 1972), etc.

Quite apart from the analysis of specific concepts, philosophical questions are raised by certain types of political inquiry and by the kinds of knowledge claims a political scientist might advance. The widely cherished belief that the findings of political science should be relevant to policy decisions and the ideal of a policy science raises numerous philosophical issues, including the contrast between "facts" and "values," the related distinction between "means" and "ends," the possibility of a value-free political science, and the nature of political decision. (For contrasting discussions of these points, see Fay, 1974, and the chapter by Oppenheim in this volume.) Similarly, the conceptions of theory and inquiry reviewed in the first three sections of this chapter and the considerations relevant to choosing among them are essentially philosophical issues.

In answering "second-order" questions regarding the logic of certain concepts or the possibility of different kinds of political knowledge, the political philosopher may root his analysis in more general areas of philosophical analysis, such as epistemology, metaphysics, ontology, philosophical logic, theology, etc. Traditionally, many of the foremost philosophers of politics have attempted to base their political views on or even deduce them from more general philosophical positions, particularly epistemology. Hegel is often held up as an archetype of such an approach, since he consciously presented his political philosophy in terms of the concepts developed in his philosophical logic and epistemology. Although this concern may appear to mark a decisive break between political theory and political philosophy, the sharpness of the contrast must not be exaggerated, since the fundamental conceptualization or paradigm of a political theory cannot be adopted independently of one's other philosophical commitments. There is, in particular, a close relationship between epistemology and metaphysics, on the one hand, and the philosophies of mind, action, and language, on the other. That there should be such connections seems intuitively obvious: there must be some relationship between theories concerning what we *can* know, or what we must think about the world or what there is, and the logical structure of concepts we use to refer to our actual thinking, believing, perceiving, feeling, sensing, intending, etc. To hold, for example, that all knowledge is based on reports of sense experience or on logical combinations and implications of such reports is vacuous without some analysis of perception and an account of the intersubjectivity of knowledge that is consistent with this claim—i.e., how or in what sense the sense experience of one individual could be the "same" as that of another. In developing an analysis of such mental concepts, one provides an account of human consciousness and rationality, of the relationship between a person and the external world, and of a significant part of the relationship between one person and another. In short, one is developing an image of what it is to be a person, to be a conscious, human agent. But this is to say that our fundamental conceptualizations of human behavior are bound up with more general philosophical commitments, which the political philosopher must make explicit, and whose implications for the study of politics and society he must spell out and clarify. (These points are elaborated in the context of two important traditions of modern thought in Wood, 1972.)

These fundamental continuities between political theory and political philosophy suggest that the pursuit of either subject in isolation from the other is impossible. Even one who eschews all interest in one of these subjects will implicitly be drawing upon it and making assumptions about it. Similarly, both political theory and political philosophy are intimately related to political evaluation. That political philosophy is concerned with normative issues will come as no surprise; to reflect upon and to take a critical stance toward the basic principles, concepts, and assumptions of a polity *is* to engage in normative analysis and criticism. The relevance of political theory to normative concerns is no less striking, even if it may be (or appear to be) less direct.

I do not mean to deny that the intention of political theory is analytical and descriptive, or to suggest that the activities of description and prescription are really the same or that in doing one, the theorist necessarily does the other as well. Nonetheless, political theory has normative implications, or is "valuationally relevant," in at least three ways. In the first place, it is commonly recognized that, by clarifying our concepts and increasing our understanding of political phenomena, an empirical theory of politics becomes relevant to our normative commitments. By showing that certain goals cannot be attained, or by accurately projecting the range of effects a particular policy might have, in addition to its impact on our immediate objectives, we may be led to alter our choices. Similarly, by clarifying the meanings of some of our principles in order to facilitate their empirical application, we may be led to see ambiguities or contradictions within our value system. These and similar uses of political science have long been recognized.

A more direct continuity between political theory and political evaluation follows from the fact that an essential feature of political theory is the interpretation of specific forms of political life, the clarification and explication of the meanings of political actions and practices. Like any process of explication, this activity necessarily has implications for our appraisal of actions, practices, or beliefs in that any interpretation is to some degree reconstructive of the text or activity that is its object. By making explicit the sense something has, and by making the meanings and implications of what we say or do conscious, an interpretation affects the way we can regard our practices and perhaps even what those practices are. By interpreting voting solely in terms of the categories of instrumental action, for example, we implicitly exclude a whole range of possible ways of relating to this activity, and we restrict the standards which are appropriate for evaluating it. As this interpretation comes to be widely accepted, the practice itself may change, or become better defined, since people may consciously orient their behavior in terms of the new interpretation. Whatever stigma may now be attached to nonvoting, for example, should come to be recognized as baseless, and the force of some arguments from participation to political obligation ("because you voted, you are bound to accept the outcome of the electoral process") will be muted.

The third and most important continuity between political theory and political evaluation is the direct relationship between the former and what Barry and Rae call the "general ground of evaluation," human well-being. Complicating the task of political evaluation is the fact that people differ over their conceptions of human well-being, and these differences are related to differences in their conceptions of a "person." Most of the major normative disputes in the history of political philosophy have not been between those who advocated political arrangements based on considerations of human well-being and those who justified their recommendations on some other grounds—racial, religious, or whatever. The differences between Plato and Thrasymachus, for example, concern not whether the good of man should be advanced but what the good of man is! And their differences on this score are rooted, at least in part, in fundamental differences of philosophical psychology and philosophical anthropology. Thrasymachus argues that a person's well-being consists in his being able to satisfy whatever desires he happens to have, a situation which implies that the good of one person conflicts with the welfare of another; Plato contends, however, on the basis of a different conception of human faculties and needs, that following Thrasymachus's ideal would lead to frustration, unhappiness, and (eventually) regret. Similarly, Hobbes differs fundamentally from Aristotle, and Marx from Bentham, and Rousseau from Burke on the meaning of the phrase "human well-being" and on the conditions of achieving it, rather than on whether human welfare is a value.[29] Even when the well-being of particular groups is discounted, the form of argument is usually to deny them the status of "human" (or "fully human"), rather than to argue against human well-being as a basis for evaluation. Thus Aristotle notoriously held that slaves were incapable of enjoying certain values (autonomy, self-direction, participation in political life), from which stand he concluded that such goods could (and should) be withheld from them.

As Barry and Rae's essay clearly shows, considerable progress in political evaluation can be made without complete agreement on a particular formulation of the "foundation of political evaluation." Nonetheless, political philosophers have generally been concerned to articulate the conceptions of human well-being implicit in their theories of man and society, to explicate the political principles which flow from these theories, and to analyze the institutional arrangements which their theories justified. The attention paid to this aspect of their work varies considerably, of course, with Marx and Machiavelli spending relatively little time explicitly discussing normative issues, whereas Kant's political writings are heavily weighted in this direction.

In developing the normative implications of their political theories, political philosophers have been sensitive to what we now call the "fact-value" dichotomy. Rousseau's formulation of this thesis is characteristically penetrating and politically acute.

> Grotius denies that all human power is established in favour of the governed, and quotes slavery as an example. His usual method of reasoning is constantly to establish right by fact. It would be possible to employ a more logical method, but none could be more favourable to tyrants. (Social Contract, I, ii)

Although we cannot "establish right by fact," we cannot suppose that our well-being is independent of what we are or the conditions in which we find ourselves. And although a particular political theorist may not be interested in articulating the normative implications of his views of politics, doing so is a legitimate and necessary task and one that is continuous with the activity of political theory.

Political theory, political philosophy, and political evaluation are related, then, in that each presupposes and makes use of a fundamental conceptualization of man and society, or what I have been calling a model of man. This is not to say that these activities are the same; they differ in emphasis and in some of their concerns. Political theory looks to the elaboration and formalization of a model of man in explanatory theories of political processes, whereas political philosophy analyzes the fundamental presuppositions of political theories, and political evaluation is concerned with the analysis of principles and the elaboration of standards. But these differences should not be permitted to obscure their interdependence, justifying rigid divisions within a subject whose parts cannot be adequately treated in isolation from each other. Only by recognizing the fundamental continuities among these three kinds of activities can we appreciate the basic unity of the field of political theory.

**BIBLIOGRAPHICAL NOTE**

In an essay of this length it is impossible to deal with all the relevant issues in a satisfactory manner. Inevitably, a number of important positions will not be discussed. The purpose of this note is to call attention to some of the literature and arguments which bear on the questions discussed in this chapter, but which could not be explicated in the text.

The account of scientific explanation which I gave in Section 2 is essentially based on the work of Hempel and Nagel, but this position has a number of critics. In addition to those mentioned in the text, the work of Rom Harré should also be cited. Harré has developed an account of science and the analysis of causal relationships which do not depend on covering laws. See Harré (1972, 1973) and Harré and Madden (1973, 1973a). Von Wright (1971) offers an experimentalist account of causal relationships that does not require covering laws and that provides an interesting view of the nature of subjunctive and counterfactual conditionals. It also bears a close resemblance to the causal analysis techniques of Simon (1952) and Blalock (1964). For further criticism of the covering law model, see Achinstein (1971).

On the distinction between observational and theoretical terms and the role of models and conceptual frameworks in science, see Maxwell (1962), Achinstein (1965), Campbell (1920, Chapter 6), Hesse (1966), Spector (1965), Körner (1966, 1970), Masterman (1970), Hanson (1970), and Toulmin (1972). This is a small part of a vast and rapidly growing literature which emphasizes the dependence of our theories and "observational" statements on a basic categorical framework, paradigm, or model or which is critical of the empiricist treatment of these issues.

General accounts of the methodology of the social sciences which adopt a naturalist stance, in addition to those cited in the text, are Nagel (1961, Chapters 13–15), Brodbeck (1968), Gibson (1960), and—an oversimplified but provocative account—Homans (1967).

In my presentation of the interpretative model of political inquiry I drew almost exclusively on the tradition of analytic philosophy stemming from Wittgenstein (1958). Of equal importance is the continental tradition of phenomenology, represented in America primarily by Schutz (1967), Natanson (1970), Garfinkel (1967), and Berger and Luckman (1966). Natanson (1963) includes many of the earlier articles in this tradition, together with several essays critical of it. An anthology edited by Douglas (1973) includes a wide range of material drawn from anthropology, sociology, and philosophy; it includes an extensive bibliography as well. Another source of the interpretative model is the hermeneutical and dialectical traditions in German social science and philosophy, in which this model is developed and severely criticized. Of particular importance here is the work of the Frankfurt school (see Jay, 1973) and the work of Apel (especially 1967, 1972), Wellmer (1971b), and the writings of Habermas, cited previously. Radnitzky (1970) presents a comprehensive survey and explication of continental, especially German, philosophical work which is relevant to an understanding of both natural and social science inquiry.

For critical discussions of various aspects of the interpretative ideal in addition to the advocates of the naturalist model and the writings cited immediately above, see MacIntyre (1964, 1967). The latter is a critique of Winch (1958), and Winch criticizes the former in his (1964), which is reprinted as Chapter 2 of his (1972). MacIntyre's essays are reprinted in Wilson (1970), together with a number of other articles which develop the issues in this debate. A more general anthology is Emmet and MacIntyre (1970). A standard critique of the interpretative model is Abel (1948), whose argument is demolished by Apel (1972). Martin (1969) is a more recent criticism of the interpretative ideal. For works in the philosophy of action which argue for a causalist or nomological approach to action and against the kind of schema presented in Section 3, see Davidson (1963), Brodbeck (1963), Brandt and Kim (1963), and Goldman (1970).

## *NOTES*

1. This use of the term "naturalist" should be distinguished from the "naturalist" position in metaethics, according to which "certain moral principles can be shown to be true by reducing them somehow to true descriptive generalizations" (Oppenheim, 1968). Although this metaethical position may have been inspired by a desire to make ethics "scientific," it is not part of the "naturalist" position regarding the methodology of the social sciences. Indeed, it is specifically repudiated by this model, which insists on a sharp distinction between "facts" or "descriptive" statements, which are subject to scientific investigation, and "values" or "prescriptions," which are expressions of preference or personal values and do not represent any kind of knowledge at all, let alone any kind of scientific knowledge. For a discussion of these issues, see the chapter by Oppenheim, "The Language of Political Inquiry," in this volume.

2. The concepts employed in this example, needless to say, would have to be considerably refined. In particular, "high level of instability" would have to be defined independently of the regime's collapsing. For a discussion of this issue, see the chapter by Oppenheim, especially Section IVB.

3. I am obviously assuming that a complete explanation of a particular event would show how it was that this event had to occur. I thus neglect the problems associated with "inductive-statistical" explanations, those in which an event is "explained" by showing

that it was very *likely,* given the initial conditions. I doubt that "inductive-statistical" explanations are adequate if our interest is the explanation of a particular event. As Scriven puts it, "statistical statements are too weak—they abandon the hold on the individual case" (1959, p. 467). See also von Wright, 1971, pp. 13-15. In spite of my reservations, my main reason for neglecting statistical explanations is convenience of exposition. I do not believe that including them would materially alter my argument.

4. This account glosses over a number of difficulties which cannot be treated fully here for want of space. The need for generalizations, it might be argued, could be dispensed with if an explanatory account consisted of a material, rather than a formal, inference. Given the inference license "An $x$ being a $y$ is a ground for saying that it is a $z$," we can explain its being a $z$ without invoking any generalizations. Whether or not we construe explanations in this way, replacing generalizations with material rules of inference is not likely to avoid the difficulties associated with the former. For a contrary view, see Toulmin, 1958, especially Chapter 3. The classic statement of this "nomological" account of explanation can be found in Hempel, 1942, and Hempel and Oppenheim, 1948. Both are reprinted in his (1965), which includes an essay (1965a) considerably amplifying his views and giving his response to various objections which have been advanced against the nomological model. For a critique of Hempel's views, see Scriven, 1959, 1962, 1966.

5. Of course, this generalization is false. The discussion in the text is intended simply to suggest some considerations which would lead one to doubt its status as a law, even if one did not know of any exceptions to it.

6. This account of the orthodox view of theories is highly schematic, since a complete exposition would represent too great a digression from the main issues of this essay. For accounts of this view, see Carnap, 1939, Nagel, 1961, Chapters 5 and 6, Hempel, 1962, and Rudner, 1966, Chapter 2, as well as Feigl, 1970. The notion of observational and theoretical concepts is discussed in the chapter by Oppenheim in this volume, especially Section II.

7. The view that testing involves falsification is vigorously defended by Popper (1959, 1963). Popper opposes falsification to the view that theory testing may lead to the progressive confirmation of a theory by inductively marshaling evidence for it. The differences between these positions need not concern us, since evidence can count *for* a theory only if it is possible for evidence to count *against* a theory. For a clear, concise account of the differences between "inductivists" and "falsificationists" and the problem of confirmation, see Smart, 1968, Chapter 6.

8. At least when we are speaking literally. The point is that before we adopted the heliocentric theory, we *were* speaking literally in saying that the sun "rises." The term "natural interpretations," together with an extended discussion illustrated with examples from the history of science, can be found in Feyerabend, 1970a, pp. 48ff, or 1970c, pp. 304ff.

9. For arguments and explications of these issues, see the writings of Feyerabend mentioned above, as well as his (1962, 1970b). Kuhn (1970a; 1970b, especially the "Postscript") raises similar issues. Achinstein (1964), Shapere (1966), Scheffler (1967) are critical of some of Feyerabend's and/or Kuhn's arguments. Rorty (1972) offers a succinct statement of these issues and a plausible resolution of many of them.

10. For example, see Feyerabend's criticisms in 1970b and the comments by Kuhn, Feigl, and Koertge in Cohen and Wartofsky, 1971.

11. These models of social science differ profoundly in terms of their bearing on political practice; the relationship between these models of social inquiry and conceptions of political action are analyzed in Fay, 1974. Habermas (1966, 1971, 1973) presents a very general account of the relationship between "theory" and "practice," which focuses, in part, on fundamental epistemological issues.

12. Naturally, an action may not be intentional under a particular description: "I never intended to do that!" or "I didn't mean to do that!" and a myriad of other locutions are available to draw a line at some of the "consequences" of our actions.

13. The argument of the next several pages draws heavily on von Wright, 1971.

14. For a discussion and elaboration of this argument, see von Wright, 1971, pp. 91ff.

15. Banfield offers other suggestions which could not count as interpretations of the Montegranesi's self-understandings and therefore could not function as constitutive meanings for Montegranesi society. These other explanations for the absence of associations and a vigorous public life in Montegrano are basically "causal" in nature (e.g., the widespread poverty in the area), and this kind of explanation in social science will be treated in Section 4 below.

16. Explanations of actions and practices in terms of their "meanings" may be called "verstehen explanations" after the example of Weber (1949), since they "explain" by rendering the action or practice "intelligible" or "understandable."

17. It is not obvious that they do use this term to refer to the same groups. For the Labourite, there are essentially two social classes, whereas the Conservative has a more differentiated picture. Moreover, the Labourite would divide people into classes on the basis of their economic position, whereas the Conservative includes a distinctly political element here. Thus the groups into which they divide society may also be quite different.

18. Such understanding may be essential, but it is not sufficient to explain these conditions. In discovering the "basic orientations" underlying political behavior by interpreting the actions, practices, and statements of political actors, one is in a position to describe the major features of political life, and to "bring out the motivation on which behavior depends" (Beer, 1969, p. 404). But there are other aspects of political life that require a different kind of analysis, as will be brought out in the next section. This kind of analysis is not simply interpretative but uses the results of interpretative studies to construct what I will call (following von Wright) "quasi-causal" relationships. Much of Beer's work consists in such analysis, and the brief discussion I have devoted to his book is intended to illustrate my argument, not to summarize even the major arguments of that outstanding work.

19. This may not be a correct interpretation of Weber's views. He argues, for example, "For the verifiable accuracy of interpretation of the meaning of a phenomenon, it is a great help to be able to put one's self imaginatively in the place of the actor and sympathetically to participate in his experiences, but this is not an essential condition of meaningful interpretation." The ability to imagine performing a similar action

oneself is not a prerequisite to understanding the action of another: "one need not have been Caesar in order to understand Caesar" (Weber, 1949, p. 90).

20. For discussion of these issues, see Taylor, 1964, 1970, and Bernstein, 1971. For an argument espousing the possibility of eliminating intentional and other "mentalistic" concepts, see Feyerabend, 1965, and Sellars 1963, Chapters 1 and 5.

21. These further consequences, especially those involving generalizations to other cultural settings, can be derived from a theory such as this only with the implicit aid of a *ceteris paribus* clause. The explanation of high communist voting may be true in India, but land reform might not have done Diem any good, since the peasants in South Vietnam may have religious or, more broadly, cultural values, norms, and orientations which lead them to act differently under similar circumstances. Or the meaning of the communist appeal in Vietnam may be quite different from its meaning in India; for example, it may express nationalist aspirations in Vietnam while the government is seen as alien, whereas the Indian Communists failed to take the leadership of the nationalist movement—or even to cooperate with it—at critical points during the struggle for independence.

22. Social-psychological theories of conflict such as Gurr's have not been without their critics. For a particularly incisive criticism, see Charles Tilly's chapter, "Revolutions and Collective Violence," in Volume 3 of this *Handbook*. It is significant that Tilly rejects Gurr because Gurr neglects the structural dimension of conflict, and because of the very abstract nature of Gurr's categorial scheme. Far from pressing for the elimination of interpretative explanations from our theories, Tilly would have us work within a framework that is closer to the actual historical record and which pays more attention to the self-understandings of the individuals and groups involved in conflict, especially their interests and aspirations, their control over resources, their organizational structures, etc.

23. As Meehl (1967) points out, because social science theories are so general, they tend to resist "falsification," and improvements in experimental design and the correct use of such statistical techniques may actually increase the chances that a theory will be corroborated by the data. What significance, then, can we impute to studies which misuse even these research techniques?

24. For a discussion of the research-guiding functions of paradigms, which examines a number of contemporary approaches, see Holt and Richardson, 1970.

25. This puzzle and two attempts to solve it are masterfully presented in Barry, 1970, Chapter 2. That book also provides an excellent comparison of two research programs, the rational choice and the sociological approaches.

26. This formulation, of course, presupposes the impossibility of "interpersonal comparisons of utility." Significantly, even Bentham espoused pure majoritarianism, although he seemed to treat utility as additive.

27. As several critics have pointed out, Buchanan and Tullock's arguments for unanimity are unsatisfactory. I suggest that the contradictions in their account derive from their trying to utilize the rational choice model of individual behavior, according to which each person attempts to maximize his own well-being, in the context of a basic normative framework and its associated view of politics, which requires each individual to moderate his demands by reference to the rights of others. So long as

one confines himself to the rational choice maximizing framework, the only decision rule the rational man will accept is majority rule. For example, see Rae, 1969, and Barry, 1965, Chapters 14 and 15.

28. This view of political philosophy is presented and defended by Oppenheim in his chapter in this volume.

29. Note, however, that a person could accept the value of human well-being but deny that it is the sole value. God's purposes for man or aesthetic values may, possibly, compete with human well-being.

## REFERENCES

Abel, Theodore (1948). "The operation called verstehen." *American Journal of Sociology* 54. Reprinted in Feigl and Brodbeck (1953).

Achinstein, Peter (1964). "On the meaning of scientific terms." *Journal of Philosophy* 61: 497–509.

─────── (1965). "The problem of theoretical terms." *American Philosophical Quarterly* 2. Reprinted in Brody (1970).

─────── (1971). *Law and Explanation*. Oxford: Clarendon Press.

Almond, Gabriel A. (1960). "Introduction: a functional approach to comparative politics." In Almond and Coleman (1960).

─────── (1967). "Political theory and political science." In pool (1967).

Almond, Gabriel A., and James S. Coleman eds. (1960). *Politics of the Developing Areas*. Princeton: Princeton University Press.

Almond, Gabriel A., and Sidney Verba (1963). *The Civic Culture*. Princeton: Princeton University Press.

Almond, Gabriel A., and G. Bingham Powell, Jr. (1965). *Comparative Politics*. Boston: Little, Brown.

Anscombe, G.E.M. (1957). *Intention*. Oxford: Basil Blackwell.

Apel, Karl-Otto (1967). *Analytic Philosophy of Language and the Geisteswissenschaften*. New York: Humanities Press.

───────(1972). "The a priori of communication and the foundation of the humanities." *Man and World* 5: 3–37.

Arendt, Hannah (1965). *On Revolution*. New York: Viking.

Ayer, A. J. ed. (1959). *Logical Positivism*. New York: Free Press.

Banfield, Edward C. (1958). *The Moral Basis of a Backward Society*. New York: Free Press.

Barry, Brian. (1965). *Political Argument*. London: Routledge and Kegan Paul.

─────── (1970). *Sociologists, Economists and Democracy*. London: Collier-Macmillan.

Beer, Samuel H. (1969). *British Politics in the Collectivist Age*. New York: Random House.

Berger, Peter L., and Thomas Luckman (1966). *The Social Construction of Reality.* Garden City, N.Y.: Doubleday.

Bernstein, Richard J. (1971). *Praxis and Action.* Philadelphia: University of Pennsylvania Press.

Blalock, Hubert M., Jr. (1964). *Causal Inferences in Nonexperimental Research.* Chapel Hill: University of North Carolina Press.

Brandt, Richard, and Jaegwon Kim (1963). "Wants as explanations of actions." *Journal of Philosophy* 60: 425–35.

Brodbeck, May (1963). "Meaning and action." *Philosophy of Science* 30. Reprinted in Brodbeck (1968).

_____, ed. (1968). *Readings in the Philosophy of the Social Sciences.* New York: Macmillan.

Brody, Baruch A., ed. (1970). *Readings in the Philosophy of Science.* Englewood Cliffs, N.J.: Prentice-Hall.

Buchanan, James M., and Gordon Tullock (1962). *The Calculus of Consent.* Ann Arbor: University of Michigan Press.

Campbell, Norman (1920). *Physics: The Elements.* Cambridge: Cambridge University Press.

Carnap, Rudolf (1939). "Theories as partially interpreted formal systems." In Brody (1970).

Cohen, Robert S., and Marx W. Wartofsky, eds. (1971). *Boston Studies in the Philosophy of Science,* vol. VIII. New York: Humanities Press.

Collingwood, R.G. (1946). *The Idea of History.* New York: Oxford University Press.

Dahl, Robert A. (1961). *Who Governs?* New Haven: Yale University Press.

Dahrendorf, Ralf (1959). *Class and Class Conflict in Industrial Society.* Stanford: Stanford University Press.

Davidson, Donald (1963). "Actions, reasons, and causes." *Journal of Philosophy* 60. Reprinted in Brodbeck (1968).

DeJouvenel, Bertrand (1962). *On Power.* Boston: Beacon.

Deutsch, Karl W. (1963). *The Nerves of Government.* New York: Free Press of Glencoe.

Douglas, Mary, ed. (1973). *Rules and Meanings.* Baltimore: Penguin.

Downs, Anthony (1957). *An Economic Theory of Democracy.* New York: Harper & Row.

Duverger, Maurice (1950), *Political Parties.* Translated by B. and R. North. New York: Wiley.

Easton, David (1965a). *A Framework for Political Analysis.* Englewood Cliffs, N.J.: Prentice-Hall.

_____ (1965b). *A Systems Analysis of Political Life.* New York: Wiley.

Eckstein, Harry (1966). *Division and Cohesion in Democracy.* Princeton: Princeton University Press.

Emmet, Dorothy, and Alasdair MacIntyre, eds. (1970). *Sociological Theory and Philosophical Analysis.* London: Macmillan.

Falco, Maria J. (1973). *Truth and Meaning in Political Science.* Columbus, Ohio: Merrill.

Fay, Brian C. (1974). *Social Theory and Political Practice.* New York: Humanities Press. London: Allen and Unwin.

Feierabend, Ivo, and R. Feierabend (1966). "Aggressive behaviors within polities, 1948–1962." *Journal of Conflict Resolution* 10: 249–71.

Feigl, Herbert (1970). "The 'orthodox' view of theories: remarks in defense as well as critique." In Radner and Winokur (1970).

Feigl, Herbert, and May Brodbeck, eds. (1953). *Readings in the Philosophy of Science.* New York: Appleton-Century-Crofts.

Feigl, Herbert, and Grover Maxwell, eds. (1962). *Minnesota Studies in the Philosophy of Science,* Vol. 3. Minneapolis: University of Minnesota Press.

Feigl, Herbert, Michael Scriven, and Grover Maxwell, eds. (1958). *Minnesota Studies in the Philosophy of Science,* Vol. 2. Minneapolis: University of Minnesota Press.

Ferejohn, John, and Morris Fiorina (1973). "The paradox of not voting." California Institute of Technology: Social Science Working Paper Number 19.

Feyerabend, Paul K. (1962). "Explanation, reduction, and empiricism." In Feigl and Maxwell (1962).

——— (1963). "How to be a good empiricist—a plea for tolerance in matters epistemological." In Bernard Baumrin (ed.), *Philosophy of Science: The Delaware Seminar,* Vol. 2. New York: Wiley.

——— (1965). "Problems of empiricism." In Robert G. Colodny (ed.), *Beyond the Edge of Certainty.* University of Pittsburgh Series in the Philosophy of Science, Vol. 2. Englewood Cliffs, N.J.: Prentice-Hall.

——— (1970a). "Against method." In Radner and Winokur (1970).

——— (1970b). "Consolations for the specialist." In Lakatos and Musgrave (1970).

——— (1970c). "Problems of Empiricism II." In Robert G. Colodny (ed.), *The Nature and Function of Scientific Theories.* University of Pittsburgh Series in the Philosophy of Science, Vol 4. Pittsburgh: University of Pittsburgh Press.

Garfinkel, H. (1967). *Studies in Ethnomethodology.* Englewood Cliffs, N.J.: Prentice-Hall. Inc.

Geertz, Clifford (1973). *The Interpretation of Cultures.* New York: Basic Books.

Gellner, Ernest (1968). "The New Idealism." In Lakatos and Musgrave (1968). Reprinted in Gellner (1973).

——— (1973). *Cause and Meaning in the Social Sciences.* London and Boston: Routledge and Kegan Paul.

Gibson, Quinton (1960). *The Logic of Social Inquiry.* London: Routledge and Kegan Paul.

Goldberg, Arthur (1963). "Political science as science." In Polsby, Dentler, and Smith (1963).

Goldman, Alvin I. (1970). *A Theory of Human Action.* Englewood Cliffs, N.J.: Prentice-Hall.

Gregor, A. James (1971). *An Introduction to Metapolitics.* New York: Free Press.

Grumm, John G. (1958). "Theories of electoral systems." *Midwest Journal of Political Science* 2: 357–76.

Gurr, Ted Robert (1970). *Why Men Rebel.* Princeton: Princeton University Press.

Habermas, Jürgen (1966). "Knowledge and interest." *Inquiry* 9. Reprinted in Emmet and MacIntyre (1970) and Habermas (1971).

———(1971). *Knowledge and Human Interests.* Boston: Beacon Press.

——— (1973). *Theory and Practice.* Boston: Beacon Press.

Hanson, Norwood Russell (1958). *Patterns of Discovery.* Cambridge: Cambridge University Press.

——— (1970). "A picture theory of theory meaning." In Robert G. Colodny (ed.), *The Nature and Function of Scientific Theories.* University of Pittsburgh Series in the Philosophy of Science, Vol. 4. Pittsburgh: Pittsburgh University Press.

Harré, Rom (1972). *The Principles of Scientific Thinking,* 2nd edition. London: Macmillan.

——— (1973). "Surrogates for necessity." *Mind* 82:358–80.

Harré, Rom, and E.H. Madden (1973). "In defence of natural agents." *The Philosophical Quarterly* 23:117–32.

——— (1973a). "Natural powers and powerful natures." *Philosophy* 48:209–30.

Hart, H.L.A. (1961). *The Concept of Law.* Oxford: Clarendon Press.

Hart, H.L.A., and A. M. Honoré (1959). *Causation in the Law.* Oxford: Clarendon Press.

Hempel, Carl G. (1942). "The function of general laws in history." *Journal of Philosophy* 39. Reprinted in Hempel (1965).

——— (1958). "The theoretician's dilemma." In Feigl, Scriven, and Maxwell (1958). Reprinted in Hempel (1965).

——— (1965). *Aspects of Scientific Explanation.* New York: Free Press.

——— (1965a). "Aspects of Scientific Explanation." In Hempel (1965).

——— (1966). *Philosophy of Natural Science.* Englewood Cliffs, N.J.: Prentice-Hall.

——— (1969). "On the structure of scientific theories." *The Isenberg Memorial Lecture Series.* n.p.: The Michigan State University Press.

Hempel, Carl G., and P. Oppenheim (1948). "Studies in the logic of explanation." *Philosophy of Science* 15. Reprinted in Hempel (1965).

Hesse, Mary B. (1966). *Models and Analogies in Science.* Notre Dame, Ind.: University of Notre Dame Press.

Holsti, Ole R. (1965). "The 1914 case." *American Political Science Review* 59:365–78.

Holsti, Ole R., Robert C. North, and Richard A. Brody (1968). "Perception and action in the 1914 crisis." In J. David Singer (ed.), *Quantitative International Politics.* New York: Free Press.

Holt, Robert T., and John M. Richardson, Jr. (1970). "Competing paradigms in comparative politics." In Robert T. Holt and John E. Turner (eds.), *The Methodology of Comparative Research*. New York: Free Press.

Homans, George Caspar (1961). *Social Behavior: Its Elementary Forms*. New York: Harcourt, Brace & World.

──────── (1967). *The Nature of Social Science*. New York: Harcourt, Brace & World.

Hume, David (1952). "That politics may be reduced to a science." In *Political Essays*, edited by Charles W. Handel. Indianapolis: Bobbs-Merrill (This essay was originally published in 1741.)

Jay, Martin (1973). *The Dialectical Imagination*. Boston: Little, Brown.

Johnson, Chalmers (1966). *Revolutionary Change*. Boston: Little, Brown.

Kaplan, Abraham (1964). *The Conduct of Inquiry*. San Francisco: Chandler.

Körner, Stephan (1966). *Experience and Theory*. London: Routledge and Kegan Paul.

──────── (1970). *Categorical Frameworks*. Oxford: Basil Blackwell.

Kuhn, Thomas S. (1970a). "Reflections on my critics." In Lakatos and Musgrave (1970).

──────── (1970b). *The Structure of Scientific Revolutions*, 2nd edition. Chicago: University of Chicago Press.

Lakatos, Imre (1970). "Falsification and the methodology of scientific research programmes." In Lakatos and Musgrave (1970).

──────── (1971). "History of science and its rational reconstruction." In Cohen and Wartofsky (1971).

Lakatos, Imre, and Alan Musgrave, eds. (1968). *Problems in the Philosophy of Science*. Amsterdam: North-Holland.

──────── eds. (1970). *Criticism and the Growth of Knowledge*. Cambridge: Cambridge University Press.

Landau, Martin (1972). *Political Theory and Political Science*. New York: Macmillan.

Laslett, Peter (1956). *Philosophy, Politics, and Society*, 2nd series. Oxford: Basil Blackwell.

Laslett, Peter, W.G. Runciman, and Quentin Skinner (1972). *Philosophy, Politics, and Society*, 4th series. Oxford: Basil Blackwell.

Locke, Don (1969). "Intention and intentional action." In J.J. Mackintosh and S. Coval (eds.), *The Business of Reason*. London: Routledge and Kegan Paul.

MacIntyre, Alasdair (1964). "Is understanding religion compatible with believing?" In John Hick (ed.), *Faith and Philosophers*. London: Macmillan. Reprinted in Wilson (1970).

──────── (1967). "The idea of a social science." *Proceedings of the Aristotelian Society*, Supplementary Volume 41. Reprinted in Wilson (1970).

──────── (1971). "Is a comparative science of politics possible?" In MacIntyre, *Against the Self-Images of the Age*. Reprinted in Laslett, Runciman, and Skinner (1972).

Martin, Jane R. (1969). "Another look at the doctrine of verstehen." *British Journal for the Philosophy of Science* 20: 53–67.

Masterman, Margaret (1970). "The nature of a paradigm." In Lakatos and Musgrave (1970).

Maxwell, Grover (1962). "The ontological status of theoretical entities." In Feigl and Maxwell (1962).

Meehl, Paul E. (1967). "Theory-testing in psychology and physics: a methodological paradox." *Philosophy of Science* 34:103–15. Reprinted in Denton E. Morrison and Ramon E. Henkel (eds.), *The Significance Test Controversy*. Chicago: Aldine, 1970.

Mitchell, Edward J. (1968). "Inequality and insurgency." *World Politics* 20:421–38.

Nagel, Ernest (1961). *The Structure of Science*. New York: Harcourt, Brace and World.

Natanson, Maurice (1970). *The Journeying Self: A Study in Philosophy and Social Role*. Reading, Mass.: Addison-Wesley.

_____, ed. (1963). *Philosophy of the Social Sciences: A Reader*. New York: Random House.

Neurath, Otto (1932/33). "Protocol Sentences." In Ayer (1959).

Nozick, Robert (1972). "Coercion." In Laslett, Runciman, and Skinner (1972).

Olson, Mancur, Jr. (1965). *The Logic of Collective Action*. Cambridge, Mass.: Harvard University Press.

Oppenheim, Felix E. (1968). *Moral Principles in Political Philosophy*. New York: Random House.

Paranzino, Dennis (1972). "Inequality and insurgency in Vietnam." *World Politics* 24:565–78.

Peters, R.S. (1958). *The Concept of Motivation*. London: Routledge and Kegan Paul.

Pitkin, Hannah F. (1967). *The Concept of Representation*. Berkeley: University of California Press.

Polanyi, Michael (1964). *Personal Knowledge*. New York: Harper & Row.

Polsby, Nelson W., Robert A. Dentler, and Paul A. Smith, eds. (1963). *Politics and Social Life*. Boston: Houghton Mifflin.

Pool, Ithiel de Sola (1967). *Contemporary Political Science*. New York: McGraw-Hill.

Popper, Karl R. (1959). *The Logic of Scientific Discovery*. New York: Basic Books.

_____ (1963). *Conjectures and Refutations*. New York: Basic Books.

Przeworski, Adam, and Henry Teune (1970). *The Logic of Comparative Social Inquiry*. New York: Wiley.

Quine, Willard van Orman (1960). *Word and Object*. Cambridge, Mass.: MIT Press.

Radner, Michael, and Stephen Winokur, eds. (1970). *Minnesota Studies in the Philosophy of Science*, Vol. 4. Minneapolis: University of Minnesota Press.

Radnitzky, Gerard (1970). *Contemporary Schools of Metascience*. New York: Humanities Press.

Rae, Douglas W. (1969). "Decision-making rules and individual values in constitutional choice." *American Political Science Review* 63:40–56.

_____ (1971). *The Political Consequences of Electoral Laws*, 2nd edition. New Haven: Yale University Press.

Rapoport, Anatol (1966). *Two-Person Game Theory*. Ann Arbor: Univeristy of Michigan Press.

Rees, W.J. (1956). "The theory of sovereignty restated." In Laslett (1956).

Richardson, Lewis F. (1960). *Arms and Insecurity*. Pittsburgh: Boxwood Press.

Riker, William H. (1962). *The Theory of Political Coalitions*. New Haven: Yale University Press.

Riker, William H., and Peter C. Ordeshook (1968). "A theory of the calculus of voting." *American Political Science Review* 62: 25–42.

Rokkan, Stein (1970). *Citizens, Elections and Parties*. New York: McKay.

Rorty, Richard (1972). "The world well lost." *Journal of Philosophy* 69:649–65.

Rudner, Richard S. (1966). *Philosophy of Social Science*. Englewood Cliffs, N.J.: Prentice-Hall. Reprinted by permission.

Russett, Bruce M. (1964). "Inequality and instability." *World Politics* 16. Reprinted in Ivo K. Feierabend, Rosalind L. Feierabend, and Ted Robert Gurr (eds.), *Anger, Violence, and Politics*. Englewood Cliffs, N.J.: Prentice-Hall.

Scheffler, Israel (1967). *Science and Subjectivity*. Indianapolis: Bobbs-Merrill.

Schutz, Alfred (1967). *The Phenomenology of the Social World*. n.p.: Northwestern University Press.

Scriven, Michael (1959). "Truisms as the grounds for historical explanation." In Patrick Gardiner (ed.), *Theories of History*. New York: Free Press.

_____ (1962). "Explanations, predictions, and laws." In Feigl and Maxwell (1962).

_____ (1966). "Causes, connections, and conditions in history." In William H. Dray (ed.), *Philosophical Analysis and History*. New York: Harper & Row.

Searle, John R. (1969). *Speech Acts*. Cambridge: Cambridge University Press.

Sellars, W.F. (1963). *Science, Perception and Reality*. London: Routledge and Kegan Paul.

Shapere, Dudley (1966). "Meaning and scientific change." In Robert G. Colodny (ed.), *Mind and Cosmos*. University of Pittsburgh Series in the Philosophy of Science, Vol. 3. Pittsburgh: University of Pittsburgh Press.

Simon, Herbert A. (1952). "On the definition of a causal relation." *Journal of Philosophy:* 49. Reprinted in Simon, *Models of Man*. New York: Wiley, 1957, pp. 50–62.

Smart, J.J.C. (1968). *Between Science and Philosophy*. New York: Random House.

Spector, Marshall (1965). "Models and theories." *British Journal for the Philosophy of Science* 16: 121–42. Reprinted in Brody (1970).

_____ (1966). "Theory and observation." *British Journal for the Philosophy of Science* 17: 1–20; 89–104.

Taylor, Charles (1964). *The Explanation of Behavior.* London: Routledge and Kegan Paul.

———— (1970). "The explanation of purposive behaviour." In Robert Borger and Frank Cioffi (eds.), *Explanation in the Behavioural Sciences.* Cambridge; Cambridge University Press.

———— (1971). "Interpretation and the sciences of man." *Review of Metaphysics* 25: 3–51.

Thibaut, John W., and Harold H. Kelley (1959). *The Social Psychology of Groups.* New York: Wiley.

Toulmin, Stephen (1958). *The Uses of Argument.* Cambridge: Cambridge University Press.

———— (1972). *Human Understanding,* Vol. 1. Oxford: Oxford University Press.

Van Dyke, Vernon (1960). *Political Science: A Philosophical Analysis.* Stanford: Stanford University Press.

Von Wright, Georg Henrik (1971). *Explanation and Understanding.* Ithaca, N.Y.: Cornell University Press.

———— (1972). "On so-called practical inferences." *Acta Sociologica* 15: 39–53.

Weber, Max (1949). *The Methodology of the Social Sciences.* Translated and edited by Edward Shils and Henry Finch. New York: Free Press.

Wellmer, Albrecht (1971a). *Critical Theory of Society.* New York: Herder and Herder.

———— (1971b). "Some remarks on the logic of explanation in the social sciences." In G.N.A. Vessy (ed.), *The Proper Study.* Royal Institute of Philosophy Lectures, Vol. 4. London: Macmillan.

Wilson, Bryan, ed. (1970). *Rationality.* New York: Harper & Row.

Winch, Peter (1958). *The Idea of a Social Science.* London: Routledge and Kegan Paul.

———— (1964). "Understanding a primitive society." *American Philosophical Quarterly* 1. Reprinted in Wilson (1970) and Winch (1972).

———— (1972). *Ethics and Action.* London: Routledge and Kegan Paul.

Wittgenstein, Ludwig (1958). *Philosophical Investigations,* 3rd edition. New York: Macmillan.

Wood, Ellen Meiksins (1972). *Mind and Politics.* Berkeley: University of California Press.

Zagoria, Donald S. (1971). "The ecology of peasant communism in India." *American Political Science Review* 65: 144–60.

*3*

# THE CONTEMPORARY RELEVANCE OF THE CLASSICS OF POLITICAL PHILOSOPHY

*DANTE GERMINO*

Philosophy is something lonely; it does not belong on the streets and in the market-place, yet it is not alient to man's actions. . . . As a matter of fact, there is no better proof than contemporary events that education is triumphing over philistinism [*Roheit*] and spirit over spiritless understanding and mere cleverness.

Daily do I get more convinced that theoretical work achieves more in the world than practical work does. Once the realm of ideas is revolutionized, actuality does not hold out. (G. W. F. Hegel, Letters of January 23, 1807, and October 28, 1808, in Shlomo Avineri, 1972, pp. 64 and 68)

## PREFACE

"What has Athens to do with Jerusalem?" demanded Tertullian, one of the early Church fathers. "What have the classics of political philosophy to do with contemporary political science?" ask some skeptics in the profession today. I hope that the case for political philosophy—and more particularly

I am grateful for the comments of Fred I. Greenstein, J. Donald Moon, Felix Oppenheim, Nelson Polsby, and Melvin Richter on an earlier draft of this chapter. Any errors of judgment, interpretation, and conceptualization which may remain are of course exclusively my responsibility. I also wish to acknowledge the able assistance of Daniel Stroup, graduate student at the University of Virginia, and to express my thanks to Marvin E. Wolfgang, President of The American Academy of Political and Social Science, for permission to incorporate portions of my article, "Some Observations on Recent Political Philosophy and Theory," published in the *Annals* of the Academy, Vol. 400 (March 1972), pp. 140-148. As with my other recent writings, Frances Lackey has served as both editor and decipherer of my baroque style and handwriting, and I continue to be most grateful for her assistance.

for the classics of political philosophy—made in this chapter will at least be sufficiently compelling to persuade some skeptics to rethink their position on such an important matter.

It is difficult to imagine a single key concept of political science which does not have its roots in one of the classics of political philosophy. The very word "politics" comes to us from the Greeks; the symbol "state" was articulated as a result of the attempt in early modern times to free the governmental power structure from feudal and ecclesiastical control; and such terms as power, sovereignty, consent, representation, tyranny, democracy, and the public interest have a precise prehistory in the Western intellectual tradition.

Thus the classics of Western political thought have "uses" for every political scientist, regardless of his field of specialization. For example, the specialist in public administration can ill afford to ignore Rousseau's "general will" in grappling with the concept of the public interest; the student of comparative government who wishes to construct a new typology of governments will want to refer explicitly to the earlier formulations of Aristotle and Montesquieu; scholars of international politics will wish to be familiar with the teachings on war and peace of Augustine, Machiavelli, Hobbes, Grotius, Kant, and Hegel; and those who teach and write about American politics can scarcely be unaware of the influence of Locke and the Calvinist tradition on early American political thought. Nor would it do for students of political behavior to ignore hypotheses about patterns of political and social change and the conditions of political rule found in Aristotle, Machiavelli, Harrington, Rousseau, Marx, and other authors of the past.

But the proposition I wish to advance is a more fundamental one than the mere indication of the extent to which contemporary political inquiry is indebted to past thought for this or that concept or insight. Rather, I wish to make a more difficult (because it goes against the grain of today's "conventional wisdom") and more controversial point, i.e., that we "need" the classics (and note that I use the plural, implying a conversation of many voices) because the study of them helps to convince us that politics *per se* is an activity or process far more extensive than our ordinary way of conceiving it suggests. Certainly some of the preoccupations of the authors of the classics of political philosophy discussed in the following pages will at first seem labored, strange, and "foreign" to our conventional understanding of competitive, electoral politics. And yet I contend that the idea of politics suggested in the "great conversation" that is the history of political philosophy is an *expansion from* rather than an *opposition to* the conventional view of politics accepted today. For what, after all, initially turned the minds of most of the great political philosophers of the past to philosophy, if not the awareness that one cannot begin properly to understand the problems attendant on the breakdown of the established political order (politics in the lower-case sense) without viewing that breakdown against the background of the larger order of things (Politics in the upper-case sense)? Thus, for example, Plato turned to philosophical reflection about politics in an attempt to understand better the breakdown of constitutional order in fifth-century Athens; Augustine did so to make sense out of the "fall" of Rome to Alaric the Goth, Machiavelli in response to the political decadence in the midst of economic and artistic greatness in the fifteenth- and sixteenth-century Italy, Hobbes because of the English civil wars of the 1640s, and Hegel after the turmoil of the French Revolution and in the wake of the Napoleonic conquests.

Metaphorically speaking, let us view political reality as an immense canvas before which we stand and which, with the help of political scientists, we wish to understand more fully. Depicted in the foreground of the canvas is the political struggle—domestic and international—in all its bewildering detail. Certain kinds of scholars—let us designate them foreground theorists or scientists—assist us in discerning certain patterns and relations between different scenes and figures in the painting. Other theorists and scholars—let us refer to them as background theorists or political philosophers—insist on our "seeing" the foreground in relation to the whole canvas—or to as much of the whole as we can discern. The background theorists point out that if we concentrate our gaze exclusively on the foreground, we shall inevitably have a distorted vision of the whole, neglecting the larger context in which it is situated.

Now let us take as a specific example the subject of "representation." It is, of course, of major importance to study the role of the representative in the American political system and in other parliamentary governments, as Wahlke and Eulau (1962), Stokes and Miller (1966), and Lewis Dexter (1963) have done in recent years, and to generalize about the role of representatives and their relationships with their constituents, with interest groups, with the bureaucracy, etc. But such analyses need to be related to other aspects and dimensions of the question, such as those suggested by Eric Voegelin in *The New Science of Politics* under the heading "Truth and Representation." Briefly, Voegelin distinguishes three "levels" or types of representation: elemental, existential, and transcendental. Elemental representation deals with the fact that societies everywhere organize themselves for action in history by designating certain officials to "stand in the place" of the whole citizenry in making public decisions. These officials are authorized to act on behalf of the community. In addition to that aspect of representation, however, there is also the question whether, in the existential sense, the elemental representatives, juridically empowered to legislate on behalf of the whole community, are perceived to be acting on its behalf by the greater part of the active and influential citizenry. As John Locke took pains to point out in the *Second Treatise of Civil Government,* a legitimately established government might make itself illegitimate by acting in a capricious and arbitrary fashion over a sustained period of time against the interests of the majority. In that event, he argued, it might be forcibly restrained or removed, if necessary. The inability of legally established governments to recognize that adverse circumstances were conspiring to bring about their *de facto* delegitimization helps to explain why in Europe between the wars even the best-constructed constitutions went to pieces when they failed to prevent the alienation of the newly emerging social forces from the established order. As Gaetano Mosca showed decades ago in *The Ruling Class (Elementi di una scienza politica)*, formal legal guarantees and arrangements (what he called the "juridical defense") were ineffectual unless they were backed up by sufficient support mobilized by "social forces" among the citizenry.

There is yet another level of analysis of representation, however, which may be penetrated solely by recourse to the kind of philosophical reflection found in the greatest, most comprehensive "classics" of Western political philosophy. This level Voegelin calls "representation in truth." Elemental and existential representation are concerned chiefly with who represents *whom;* representation in truth is concerned with who represents *what.*

What Eric Voegelin discovered (or rediscovered) as he went about his work as an "empirical" political scientist studying political institutions in his native Austria during the 1930s was that, undergirding every viable legal-constitutional order, there is a self-interpretation of society (in our secular age we might call it the society's "invisible religion") which attempts to provide some sense of the meaning of existence as a whole and to relate human affairs to an enduring moral order. If this self-interpretation breaks down and no longer carries conviction for the greater part of the active citizenry, even the most expertly devised constitution can go to pieces overnight.

Thus Voegelin was led in his analysis of representation from the "foreground" to the "background," from a study of the institutional workings of his own country to a concern with the "symbolic forms" which provide the larger moral frame of reference for all societies. He concluded that Arnold Toynbee was correct in arguing that only *civilizations* (rather than nation-states) were "intelligible units of study," and he found that, within Western civilization, of which both his native and his adopted countries[1] were fragments, Greek philosophy, Judaism, and Christianity were the symbolic forms that in their interpenetration constituted the basis of civilizational order. The unprecedented problems of the modern period resulted from a gradual atrophy of the experience of transcendental truth that Socrates, Amos, and Jesus had attempted to communicate to men. The erosion of the key interpretive symbols of a civilization without their replacement by alternative ones capable of illumining the character of political reality in all its complexity threw certain portions of the Western world into a full representational crisis at the deepest level. That event ineluctably made its shock waves felt throughout the other (elemental and existential) dimensions of society as well. Voegelin argued that a critical science of politics can fully deal with the subject of representation only by taking into account the time dimension within the unfolding of the Western civilizational order itself. We thus dispense with the study of the history of political philosophy only at our peril.

"Political society" in this extended sense is that dimension of total reality which concerns man's continuing attempt to order his life with his fellows in the light of his imperfect but noetically differentiated understanding of the structure of existence. Therefore political activity, in this larger sense, must be seen as the process of participation by mankind in the drama of humanity. Man exists not only in his local community, his nation, or his region, but also in the open society (Bergson, 1935) embracing all mankind. This open society, to be experienced in the depths of the psyche, is less tangible, immediate, and visible than the narrower forms of community, but it is no less real. The fact that in Charlottesville, Virginia, where I live, we cannot see the surrounding mountains on a foggy day does not mean that those mountains are thereby less real. Although philosophy is frequently called obscure, its true role is to help dissipate the mental fogs which so frequently obscure our understanding of ourselves and the reality in which we participate.

To summarize, then: In the more extended but nonetheless concrete and "empirical" conception implicit in the work of the great political philosophers, politics is the participation by man with his fellows in a greater order of things, and the history of philosophy is the continuing story of man's imperfect yet impressive attempts to articulate and symbolize this experience.[2]

The analysis of the "uses of political philosophy" that follows is nothing more than an attempt by the present author to set forth his own interpretation of this controversial subject. That interpretation, of course, proceeds from a particular intellectual and historical perspective. There is, to be sure, a truth that escapes all our imperfect attempts at symbolic articulation and that judges and measures us all, regardless of our "approaches" and "perspectives." Before such a truth, the appropriate attitude is doubtless one of humility and renunciation of all desire to see our own partial and imperfect insights foisted on the discipline. For diversity can be the stimulus to philosophy, and its occurrence in a context of openness should gladden the heart and delight the mind.

## INTRODUCTION: ON THE "USES" OF POLITICAL PHILOSOPHY

In a sense, to speak of the "uses" of philosophy is paradoxical, because all philosophy originates in "wonder" (Aristotle, *Metaphysics*) and, as a free activity of man beyond all necessity, is literally "useless." Nor would it have made sense to Plato and Aristotle to inquire of the utility of political *philosophy* for political *science,* because to them political science (*epistēmē politikē*) and political philosophy (*philosophia peri ta anthropina*) are essentially one and the same, in that it is fallacious to speak of a nonphilosophical political science. Political science was conceived in Greek philosophy to be a *noetic, self-critical interpretation of man and society,* which was made possible by the emergence of philosophy itself in tension with the compactness of the *polis* myth. "Noetic" is derived from *noesis* (thinking) and from *nous* (mind or intellect). To Aristotle, a noetic interpretation of reality was contrasted with a "mythical" interpretation. Noetic discourse is self-consciously critical about its basic assumptions and does not accept the legends and traditions of a society as expressions of truths beyond debate although it by no means rejects all myth and tradition. Indeed, much of mythical thought, reinterpreted and clarified, is accepted into philosophic discourse by Plato and Aristotle, especially when it confronts experiences at the boundary of the consciousness, such as immortality, creation, openness, the measure of right judgment, liberation, redemption, etc. Aristotle in old age described himself as a "lover of myth." But the myths used by the philosopher have lost the rigidity they possessed for the man of traditional piety; there is a new freedom of symbolic recreation and reconstruction enjoyed by the philosopher, as Plato showed so well in the occasional use he made of myths in the *Phaedo, Republic, Timaeus,* and other dialogues.

Nevertheless, it will not suffice here simply to recall the Platonic and Aristotelian conceptions of political science and philosophy, however important such recollection is. Much has happened both in philosophy and in society since the pristine days of the creation of political science to make the topic of this essay relevant to our concerns. We live in a culture (Max Weber would have said in an "iron cage"; Weber, 1950, Conclusion) dedicated to activities and priorities which Plato and Aristotle would have found to go ill together with the philosophic or "theoretic" life *(bios theōretikos).* The thrust of much of the modern experiment has been to downgrade pursuits considered "unproductive" or "disfunctional" in favor of those rated "useful" and "instrumental."[3] Beginning with Machiavelli, for whom the most praiseworthy figures were men of action rather than of thought, continuing with Luther, Melanchthon, and Calvin in their attack on the "idleness" of the monastic life, and culminating in Marx's dictum that philosophy's purpose is to "change the world,"[4] we encounter a sustained revolt against the premodern understanding of the subordination of the active to the contemplative or philosophic life. Perhaps an even more emphatic proclamation that philosophy has a practical function in the modern world is found in the work of the Polish "left" Hegelian, August von Cieszkowski, who declared in his *Prolegomena zur Historiosophie* of 1838, that philosophy after Hegel "must . . . now be content *primarily* with being *applied,* and just as the poetry of art has been transformed into the prose of thought, so philosophy must descend from the heights of theory into the *battlefield of practice.* Practical philosophy or, to put it more accurately, the *philosophy of practice*—the most concrete action of life and social conditions, the development of truth in concrete activity —is the future lot of philosophy as such." (Quoted in Fetscher, 1971, p. 48) And yet if Marx and Cieszkowski were bent on making philosophy more practical, they were also committed to making practice more philosophical. They surely did not intend for philosophy to be absorbed into the practice of contemporary industrial society, which they had judged to be the ruination rather than the realization of a humanistic philosophy.

There is considerable truth in Antonio Gramsci's observation that "philosophy in general does not exist; instead, diverse philosophies or conceptions of the world exist and it is always a choice between them" (Gramsci, 1966, p. 5). However, there is also a sense in which we may speak of philosophy and political philosophy as such, despite the divergencies among their practitioners regarding their conception of philosophy in general and the substantive content of their philosophies in particular.

The meaning of philosophy is not contained in the works of any one philosopher but in the dialogue or conversation that is the *history* of philosophy. Philosophy as such has no essence; it is an activity which has taken place over a specific segment of time and which originated in a specific civilization. Its meaning is bound by its history as a tradition of inquiry. What philosophers have in common from Plato onwards is their *radicalism*, or their attempt to reexamine the root assumptions (*radices*) and categories of their own and their society's thinking without according the deference normally accorded to received opinion. The philosopher descends like a diver into the depths of his experience in an effort to discover new symbols which illumine the character of the reality in which he participates.[5]

All philosophers view reality from a limited perspective, and no thinker occupies an Archimedean point outside history. As Hegel put it, "every man is a son of his time." Thus any given philosophy, no matter how profound, is one-sided. Philosophy, considered as the conversation that has taken place with a variety of participants from Plato to Marx and beyond, however, is many-sided, and our study of the philosophical classics of the past enables us to multiply the perspectives with which we view the world. Philosophy is concerned with the expansion of the consciousness to the point at which we are able inwardly to see other dimensions of reality than those visible to unreflective thought and received opinion. Expansion of the consciousness and the multiplication of perspectives do not add up to omniscience, however. There are limits to what philosophy can show us, so that after all its work is done, at the core of his being man remains a mystery to himself. One of the uses of philosophy should be to teach us humility about what man may accomplish.

Kenneth W. Thompson ably expressed the multiperspectival character of political and social philosophy when he wrote with reference to theories of international relations:

No single perspective holds any monopoly on wisdom; the quality of insight of the observer and his intellectual power outweighs the merits of a particular social theory or methodology. If this is heresy for modern social science, it is orthodoxy in the long history of social thought. For any other conclusion would obscure the timeless importance of Thucydides, Machiavelli, Marx, or Burke. . . . The world of international studies has many mansions and our debt to their inhabitants is continuing and far-reaching. (Thompson, 1967, p. 147)[6]

## POLITICAL PHILOSOPHY AS A CONVERSATION OF MANY VOICES

As the position taken in my previous remarks indicates, there is no single substantive answer to the question "What is philosophy?" Just as philosophy may be most fruitfully seen as a conversation or dialogue between different perspectives and interpretations of reality as a whole, political philosophy may be most profitably viewed as a conversation between different orientations toward political reality, or that part of reality as a whole which concerns man and his relationships in society with his fellows. Although there is no unity to the answers given, there is a commonness in the *quest* and a basic restlessness in all the participants, who refuse to accept ready-made interpretations of political reality supplied by the conventional wisdom of the time. In this sense, all philosophers are moved by a sense of their ignorance about the human condition to inquire into its character and structure. The interpretations they supply are varied, but out of such variety there do emerge certain leitmotifs or types of answers which can afford us considerable help in making sense out of the conversation. A conversation is not a babble of voices but rather a reflection of certain predominant lines of argument, which can be identified by those who will listen.

In opening our consciousness to the "conversation of mankind" (Thomas Hobbes's phrase), we must exercise considerable care in avoiding biases respecting past thought which may be very pronounced in our present culture. One such bias—perhaps the overriding one—is that which favors "modern" or even very recent thought over that of the premodern or ancient and medieval world. Openness to the different voices in the conversation requires an assumption on our part that the time location of the philosopher we are interrogating be regarded as irrelevant to the contribution he can make to our self-understanding. In other words, we who today survey the history of political philosophy are asked to proceed *as if* the conversation were taking place in the present. As Michael Oakeshott once observed, "history is 'made' by nobody save the historian . . . and the course of events is not a mere series of successive events, but a world of co-existent events—events which co-exist in the mind of the historian" (Oakeshott, 1933, 1966, pp. 99–100).

I do not go so far as Oakeshott in maintaining that in the reconstruction of historical events the historian cannot possibly hope to understand the way events were viewed at the time they actually occurred but must rather impose an alien pattern on them.[7] However, it is extremely helpful to be mindful of the inescapable role played by our own interpretative categories in our examination of past thought. By being aware and self-consciously critical of the truth that past events are not just "there" waiting to be "objectively" *described* but that, on the contrary, we perceive them through "lenses" and selective categories, we can be as careful as humanly possible to employ criteria that are not ideological in inspiration but that assist us in elucidating the ongoing significance of the political philosophies of the past.

Thus, if for analytical purposes we regard the history of philosophy as an ongoing conversation, we will not be prejudiced for or against any of the voices because they appear chronologically in the distant or the recent past. We will not reject the political philosophy of Plato out of hand because it is ancient and therefore "obsolete," nor will we praise more recent developments because they are presumed to be "modern" and therefore "relevant."[8] To reverse the assumptions above, however, we will also avoid any automatic aversion to more recent or modern thought because of a sweeping rejection of "modernity" as inherently pathological, diseased, or anomic.[9]

For the most philosophical approach to the history—and the reality—of political philosophy, we will wish to extend as much as possible the range and depth of the conversation so that no important and distinctive voice will be omitted arbitrarily. This question brings us to a consideration of the "classics" of political philosophy as touchstones for what is significant in the conversation.

## THE CLASSICS AS TOUCHSTONES OF POLITICAL PHILOSOPHY

A classic is a work in a "class" by itself, a work "of the first rank and of acknowledged excellence" (*Oxford English Dictionary*). Over the nearly two and one-half millennia since the initial emergence of philosophy on the soil of ancient Hellas, certain treatises of political philosophy stand forth as so notable for their depth and penetration of insight, conceptual luminosity, freshness of vision, and quality of thought as to be commonly accorded the designation "classic." Plato's *Republic* and *Laws*, Aristotle's *Ethics* and *Politics*, Augustine's *City of God*, Aquinas's *Treatise on Law* in the *Summa Theologica*, Machiavelli's *Prince* and *Discourses*, Hobbes's *Leviathan*, Locke's *Second Treatise*, Rousseau's *Social Contract*, Hegel's *Philosophy of Right*, and Marx's *Philosophic-Economic Manuscripts* and *German Ideology* are among the works generally accorded this designation.[10]

As is obvious from even a cursory inspection of this list, there is no unity of substantive philosophy among these disparate authors. What unites them is not the conclusions reached but the questions to which they address themselves. Those questions—the topics discussed with varying degrees of explicitness in the great treatises of political theory—are:

1. What is man?
2. What is society?
3. What is history?

There appear to have been three principal positions, from which we derive answers to the three principal questions, that have emerged in the course of Western political philosophy. We may conveniently designate them as (1) theocentric humanism, (2) anthropocentric humanism, and (3) metastatic humanism,[11] respectively, recognizing that these terms are abridgments of complex realities and that within each subtradition of the philosophy of Western humanism there are numerous important disagreements among the various representatives. Of the authors of the principal classics, Plato, Aristotle, Augustine, and Aquinas are representatives of theocentric humanism; Machiavelli, Hobbes, and Locke of anthropocentric humanism; and Rousseau and Marx of metastatic humanism. Hegel remains difficult to place, as befits a great synthesizer.

Now, what has been the answer of each of the three subtraditions to the three questions for discussion: What is man? What is society? What is history? Before proceeding, we had best comment on the significance of the tiny but nonetheless momentous word "is" in the questions themselves. When the Greek philosophers for the first time in recorded history asked the question "What is?" they were not asking for a detailed description of a particular thing (this kind of activity, of course, had long been performed by prephilosophical thought). Rather, they were seeking an account of what was *distinctive* and *fundamental* to that thing which unites it with all other phenomena of a similar class. They were asking the question of *essence*. (The essence of something is what is always present in a class of phenomena, regardless of the presence or absence of other characteristics—i.e., what is essential to it.)

The "is" in the above questions, then, is of decisive importance. The philosophers do not ask what this particular man is like or how most men behave under certain conditions. Rather, they ask what it is that is *distinctively human in man,* that "defines" his humanity, that enables us to call ourselves "men" and not some other name. Nor does the question about society have to do with a description of the majority of communities in history. Rather, it has to do with what a (hypothetical) society would look like if it reflected and ministered to the best in men. Finally, the (philosophical) question about history refers not to a flat, descriptive chronology of events but to those occurrences which have illumined the existence of men in time and the world with meaning.

Even though some of the authors of the classics were explicitly antiessentialist in their epistemologies (Hobbes, for example, was a nominalist, and Hegel and Marx denied that man had a fixed "nature"), they nonetheless may be seen to have in effect continued and contributed to the dialogue on the nature of man, society, and history begun by the Greek philosophers. As Plato taught, man exists in the In-Between *(metaxy),* aware of the pull of the realm of essences but anchored in existence, which is the realm of flux, indeterminacy, and contingency. A given thinker may choose to emphasize either the "essentialist" or "existentialist" poles of the tension. But whenever he speaks of the "optimal" or "good" or "rational" or "fully developed" society—and all political philosophers do—he is postulating a theory of what man essentially is or under the proper conditions can become.

## WHAT IS MAN?

### The Answers of Theocentric, Anthropocentric, and Metastatic Humanism

Now let us return to the three subtraditions and their answers to the three questions. *Theocentric humanism* conceives of man as "theomorph," the creature endowed with the capacity self-consciously to participate in the world-transcendent Ground of Being. The philosopher (or in the language of Revelation, the prophet) is the representative human type because he seeks to attune himself with divine Being. For theocentric humanism, the philosopher is the man who takes God for his measure (Plato, *Laws*, 716) and who aspires, within the limitations of his finite humanity, to be "like God."[12] In the splendid language of Plato's *Republic*, the philosopher

> contemplates a world of unchanging and harmonious order, where reason governs and nothing can do or suffer wrong; and, like one who imitates an admired companion, he cannot fail to fashion himself in its likeness. So the philosopher, in constant companionship with the divine order of the world, will reproduce that order in his soul and, so far as man may, will become godlike.... (Plato, *Republic*, 500)

In his famous allegory of the cave, Plato portrays philosophy as a conversion of the person from an inverted mode of being-in-the-world or as liberation from the prison of closed existence. When the philosopher accomplishes the *periagogē* (turning around) and has ascended to the mouth of the cave, he beholds the vision of the *agathon* ("The Good"). He inwardly "sees" the highest good, or ultimate reality. The *agathon* is "beyond being" and is the source of all goods of the spirit. It lights the inner world of the consciousness as the sun lights the visible world. The Good is not sensual pleasure or wealth or honor or power. (All these ends are good only if properly related to the absolute Good; if taken by themselves, as if they were the highest good, they fail to assuage man's thirst for contact with reality and become deformed into false goods.) The Good in Plato's teaching is that which comes closest to God, and the chief end of man is to know and do The Good, insofar as it lies within his capacity. For theocentric humanism, man's humanity is defined with reference to his capacity to participate, through his partial and finite reason, in the divine reason.

Aristotle had serious diagreements with Plato over the nature of the paradigm or of the good society, but in his anthropology, or theory of man, he continues the work of his mentor. In both the *Nichomachean Ethics* and the *Politics* he speaks of the "mature" man as one who is capable of leading the *bios theōretikos*, or contemplative life:

> But such a life [the *bios theōretikos*] would be too high for man; for it is not in so far as he is man that he will live so, but in so far as something divine is present in him; and by so much as this is superior to our composite nature is its activity superior to that which is the exercise of the other kind of virtue. If reason is divine, then, in comparison with man, the life according to it is divine in comparison with human life. But we must not follow those who advise us, being men, to think of human things, and, being mortal, of mortal things, but must, so far as we can, make ourselves immortal, and strain every nerve to live in accordance with the best thing in us; for even if it be small in bulk, much more does it in power and worth surpass everything. This would seem, too, to be each man himself, since it is the authoritative and better part of him. It would be strange, then, if he were to choose not the life of his self but that of something else. And what we said before will apply now; that which is proper to each thing is by nature best and most pleasant for each thing; for man, therefore, the life according to reason is best and pleasantest, since reason more than anything else *is* man. This life therefore is also the happiest. (Aristotle, *Nichomachean Ethics*, 1177b25–1178a10)

The Western tradition of theocentric humanism has three principal sources: Classical philosophy, Judaism, and Christianity. In Judaism and Christianity revelation takes its place with reason as the medium through which man apprehends and is apprehended by the world-transcendent God. Revelation is the manifestation of the Hidden, in which the God who is "wholly other" than man is experienced as gratuitously revealing his presence to man through an encounter in the soul of the prophet or, as with Christianity, in the assumption by the divine of a human form. (The Word "became flesh and dwelt among us" *John* 1, 1–14.)

The differentiation of the revelatory component from the structure of existence, which was the achievement, within the West, of Judaism and Christianity, created the possibility of a rivalry between the truths of revelation and those of philosophy; in particular, the question of the relationship between reason and the truth of revelation was raised. Several different answers were given, but the predominant one for theocentric humanism was that of Thomas Aquinas: *gratia non tollit naturam sed perficit* ("Grace does not annul nature but perfects it"). Through Clement of Alexandria, who called Greek philosophy the "second *Old Testament*" of Christianity, and other theologians, theocentric humanist philosophy was accepted by Christianity as containing a truth that was in need of being supplemented and "perfected" by grace. Augustine, Aquinas, and Richard Hooker, for example, accepted the analysis of Greek philosophy that the fulfillment of life was to be found in contemplation rather than in such illusory "highest goods" as pleasure, honor, power, or wealth. However, the contemplative life, extolled by Aristotle as the true highest good for man within the *polis*, was itself interpreted as but a preparation for fulfillment beyond this mortal life in the eternal *visio Dei*.

For these great Christian thinkers, not the contemplative life within time but eternal life beyond time is the true *summum bonum* (highest good) for man. Reason and nature are in themselves unable to account for all that is present in experience; they need to be supplemented by the truth of revelation and grace. Thus a further differentiation of the concepts of Greek philosophy, which itself had emerged against the background of the compactness of the cosmological myth, was achieved by Christianity and resulted in a further development of the anthropology of theocentric humanism. Man is conceived as a creature with an amplitude of possibilities for development; he is to be defined in relation to his maximal possibilities for development in existence under the world-transcendent God. Thus the highest character types are the saint and the philosopher, and when they come together, as in the lives of men such as Augustine or Aquinas, we become aware of the range of possibilities for man's development in humility within the Christian theocentric humanism of the premodern period.

Christian theocentric humanism remained for over a millennium the principal unifying cultural force of the West. It is the background of the emergence of modernity, and however "secular" our public life has become in modern times, Christianity—some would say "Christendom"—remains the silent partner of our history. Indeed, the predominant "voice" of the modern period, anthropocentric humanism, emerged as the result of claimed incompatibilities experienced between the theocentric humanist understanding of the world and the needs for man's survival.

For Machiavelli, Hobbes, Locke, and the other masters of modern anthropocentric humanism, man's lonely, formidable struggle to overcome obstacles to the enjoyment of life in *this* world, rather than his anguished efforts at orientation toward attunement with a Being beyond time and the world, constituted the proper point of departure for political philosophy. In the understanding of these humanists, what was the good life for man, who is the measure of all things, called for a vital, expanding civilization. In particular, they judged the "other-worldly" orientation of medieval Christianity to be a grievous hindrance in dealing with most men as they actually live and in meeting their needs for security and economic well-being. Christian "idealism" was to them not wrong so much as it was irrelevant; as Machiavelli observed in Chapter 15 of the *Prince,* many have imagined republics that never were, but the point was to "follow the effectual truth of the matter rather than its imagination."

Accordingly, the emphasis shifts in anthropocentric humanism from man in existence under God (wherein his obligation is to follow his "higher" faculties and impulses to live in attunement—however imperfect—with the divine) to man in uneasy but manageable relationship with his fellowman. *Political* man, as distinct from the man of the saints and theologians, is seen to have certain concrete objectives in this world. Reason is to be the servant of the passions rather than the ruler over them, and in particular the master passion, which is to avoid untimely death, is to be obeyed. The importance of man's being at liberty to attain the objects of his desire and will—to the extent compatible with a like liberty for others—is recognized, as is his responsibility to work actively to secure a more commodious existence for himself and his posterity.

Anthropocentric humanism achieved notable success in reorienting the Western political consciousness, so much so that the West established itself as an "active society" to an extent unknown in world history. Striking gains were made in the civil liberties enjoyed by men, in their freedom of movement, both physically and socially, in the "standard of living" of greater and greater numbers of people, in the cure and prevention of disease, and in technological discovery and innovation. At the same time, there emerged contradictions in the world of the anthropocentric humanist, which with time became increasingly severe and which created the conditions for the emergence of a third type of humanism, a humanism that called for a "new man" who would for the first time create history instead of serving forces beyond his control.

Jean-Jacques Rousseau was perhaps the earliest major modern political philosopher to sense the need for a new humanism radically different from that which had accompanied the growth of modernity. In his *Discourse on the Arts and Sciences* of 1749 (a work which made him famous), Rousseau in effect rejected the argument that modern "progressive" civilization had benefited man. On the contrary, he argued, it had only alienated him. Modern man had become a stranger to himself, a prey to false needs and a false consciousness. He was consumed with vanity and had lost all capacity for enduring natural relationships. Inasmuch as a retreat to a presocial "state of nature" was impossible, there remained only the alternative of creating a new society in which man could develop a "second nature" that would allow him to expand his distinctive capabilities. This new society was held to be extremely difficult to achieve, however, and Rousseau's *Social Contract* leaves us with the impression that, though possible of creation, it would remain unrealized.

It was left for Marx to work out consistently the view of the radical humanism that I have labeled metastatic. The Greek term *metastasis* refers to a fundamental change in the structure of existence. Whereas theocentric humanism had emphasized man's need for and dependence on God, the "author of our being," and whereas anthropocentric humanism stressed the human condition as one of competition for scarce resources, metastatic humanism saw man as potentially the creator of his own reality and called for transcending *within history* the alienation of modern man. Man has no essence fixed in advance, Marx proclaimed. Rather, "man is the essence for man." Or as Antonio Gramsci, Italy's foremost Marxist theoretician, was later to put it, "Man is what he is capable of becoming."

Unlike both theocentric and anthropocentric humanism (though more like the former than the latter), metastatic humanism envisages the emergence of a man qualitatively distinct from the contradictory creature we have come to know in recorded history. Furthermore, this *novus homo* is to materialize in *this* world and in *this* life, which for the metastatic humanist is the only life (all notions of "another" world or "afterlife" being condemned as "mystifications"). Marx held these new possibilities for *qualitative* change to be empirically based, since they were, paradoxically, the result of the unprecedented advances in technology and the control of the environment produced by the "alienated" consciousness of anthropocentric humanism. Man, conscious for the first time of the significance of his capacity to modify the environment in ways conducive to the enhancement and multiplication of his senses rather than to their restriction and confinement, is capable of a radically new beginning. For the first time, he will be able to rule the world by thought rather than be ruled by external "forces of production."

Paradoxically, Marx's "materialism" ends by being negated by the author himself, but this outcome is not surprising inasmuch as he was a close student of Hegel. Hegel's insistence on the primacy of spirit, on the possibility that man might create a world "suitable for the spirit to inhabit," and on the ultimate rationality of the historical process made its imprint on Marx's philosophy, leaving it more supple and humanistic and leavening its reductionist tendencies.

## WHAT IS THE PARADIGMATIC SOCIETY?

Just as the three types of humanism adumbrated in the previous section differ in their philosophical anthropologies, so do they diverge in their teaching regarding the best polity or paradigmatic society. Although in one sense the paradigm (from the Greek *paradeigma*, as used in Plato's *Republic*,

591) is a hypothetical construction or "city in speech" rather than a description of an existing society, it is not put forth as the product of mere speculative fancy. In that respect, Plato's paradigm was quite different from Sir Thomas More's "utopia," although the two are frequently confused. Far from being an example of "utopian" speculation hopelessly divorced from "reality," the paradigm was elaborated precisely to indicate those real potentialities of men which were often distorted or repressed in existing polities. The *polis*, Plato tells us, is the "soul writ large," and the paradigmatic *polis* is the soul of the "best man," the representative exemplar of the human species, the philosopher, writ large. The point behind Plato's metaphor of society as the soul writ large is that the paradigm, if it is to be an instrument of political science (or the noetic interpretation of man and society), must be an extrapolation from real potentialities in human nature. In effect, the political philosopher-theorist asks the question "What would society resemble if it brought out the best of which men are capable and if it were organized around the norms and priorities of the most fully developed human types?"

The contours of the Platonic paradigm are well known. The "city in speech [*logos*]"—which might also be translated as the "city of reason"—was to possess a three-class system paralleling the tripartite division of the human soul (psyche). The philosophers, with the aid of auxiliaries in whom the "spirited" element of the soul is predominant, were to rule over the majority of the people in whom, if they are not restrained by good laws and examples, there reigns the appetitive and acquisitive part of the soul. The philosophers and auxiliaries were to live under an austere regimen, perhaps somewhat misleadingly called communism. They were to possess neither family nor property; they were to think only of the good of the community.

In the *Statesman* and the *Laws,* Plato undertakes the task of "diluting" the paradigm so that it might have greater prospect of realization under existing conditions. The Platonic Socrates had already proclaimed (in *The Republic,* 591) that it is "no matter" whether the city in speech ever became an actual city; it remains for all time a "pattern [*paradeigma*] laid up in the heavens," which good and wise men may use as a standard for governing their own souls. In the *Statesman* we encounter a dilution of the principle that philosophers must rule and an acceptance of the rule-of-law principle under ordinary conditions. This surprising *bouleversement* is partially mitigated in the *Laws,* wherein Plato offers his "second best" paradigm; communism of women and property are gone, but the author makes clear that a truly good society, as distinct from a tolerably defective one, would acquire somewhat the form of philosophy through its system of education and through its scrupulous attempts to follow a law code set down by the philosopher himself.

Although in Book II of his *Politics* Aristotle strenuously criticized the "communistic" features of the paradigm elucidated by Socrates in Plato's *Republic,* Books VII and VIII, he nonetheless offered an abbreviated paradigm of his own, which he doubtlessly regarded as "purified" of the *Republic's* institutional excrescences. The best regime was held to be an aristocracy of mature men. Rewards and offices in the good society would be apportioned in accordance with virtue, rather than with wealth (as in oligarchies) or numbers (as in democracies). The avoidance or rectification of social injustice resulting from the inequality of possessions was left primarily to the beneficent influence of education on character, and the Socratic (Platonic?) emphasis on specialization according to functions was discarded in favor of the principle of ruling and being ruled in turn. Thus the virtuous citizen in his youth served as a solider, in his middle age as a political leader, and in his old age as a priest. The aim of the Aristotelian paradigm, just as much as the Platonic, was to give widest possible scope and social efficacy to the contemplative or philosophic life, designated by Aristotle as the *bios theōretikos*. For Aristotle as for Plato, in the best *polis* war was waged for the sake of peace, and activity was carried on for the sake of that leisure which is the mother of philosophy.

For all their impressiveness, the paradigmatic societies of Plato and Aristotle were burdened with what Eric Voegelin has called the "mortgage of the *polis*." It remained to Stoicism and Christianity to draw out the universalism latent in the paradigm concept itself. The walls of the *polis* were flung down, and the symbol of the universal *cosmopolis* of the spirit, coeval with all men of good will, was articulated by the Stoic philosophers. In these later stages of the development of theocentric humanism, all men were perceived to be brothers, offspring of a common father, God. Every man was perceived to have not one country but two: his native land and the universal community, the city of reason, open to all, regardless of race, place of birth, or social status.

In Augustine's masterful formulation of the paradigmatic society as the *civitas dei,* or "city of God," all resemblances between the paradigm and the condition of the division of the human species into closed societies were overcome. The invisible city of God, to which all belonged who had abandoned their allegiances to the fallen self of pride *(amor sui)* in order to be governed by the love of God *(amor Dei),* was incompatible with the politics of parochial division and war. (It will be recalled that both Plato and Aristotle assumed the continuation of war, even for the paradigmatic society, for they both made provision for soldiers in their best regimes.) Nonetheless, the spiritual purification and universalization of the paradigm by Augustine was accomplished at the price of widening the gulf between the paradigm and its historical realization to the point where it became unbridgeable. To the paradigmatic city of God, the destination of all men who adhere to God in faithfulness and love, Augustine juxtaposed the *civitas terrena,* or earthly city, in which was conducted the politics of this fallen world. True and complete justice, a true and authentic peace, a full and abiding unity could not be attained within time and the world. Human fulfillment could not be achieved *within,* but only *beyond* time and the world through God's grace.

Augustine's true city or paradigm clarified, within the context of Christian universalism, the nature of the ultimate perfection of man as lying beyond history. To the chiliastic revolutionaries who would achieve the Kingdom of God on earth, Augustine had only one answer: Don't attempt it! The effort to immanentize the *eschaton,* or to bring heaven down to earth, through revolutionary action could lead only to disaster. Human existence is ineluctably the realm of division and conflict. The members of the city of God, while keeping their eyes fastened on the true city, contours of which they could see dimly in the distance, had no alternative in their pilgrimage on earth but to endure as best they might the imperfections and injustices of the fallen world.

The Augustinian paradigmatic construction was immensely influential in shaping the medieval world view. Its ascendancy began to be challenged by the apocalyptic movements of the twelfth to the fourteenth centuries (as in the tripartite historical schema of Joachim of Fiore, for example) but it was only in the modern period with the development of the anthropocentric humanist version of the paradigm that it was successfully overthrown.

Regardless of Augustine's intentions, the practical effect of his teaching about man and society was to discourage men from actively seeking to improve their lot in this life and from striving for such relative justice in temporal affairs as they might by reason and artifice contrive. Accordingly, the modern masters of anthropocentric humanism, such as Machiavelli, Hobbes, and Locke, offered up paradigm constructions that were closer to the ways in which they perceived men actually to behave than were any devised by either the classical or the Christian theocentric humanists. With the modern masters we witness a certain increase in "realism" with regard to their paradigms, accompanied by a new activism and a new emphasis on transforming current political mores and institutions.

Anthropocentric humanist political philosophy proved prodigiously successful in assisting the rise of a secular, activist-oriented, expansionist civilization that, as has been mentioned, was unprecedently effective in fostering material wealth for many of its inhabitants. The political doctrine of liberalism, which received its earliest coherent formulation at the hands of John Locke, stressed the liberation of the individual from the weight of restrictions, both intellectual and institutional, inherited from the medieval past. The paradigmatic society was conceived of as one in which individuals had the greatest scope possible to exercise their initiative and enterprise and to seek their private ends. Government, which assumed a monopoly of the means of force and violence, though potentially extremely powerful (the medieval intermediary institutions having been either swept away or enfeebled), was to have carefully limited domestic functions, and these were to be supervised by a legislature responsible to the majority of the property owners if not initially of the whole adult citizenry. With the age of "Enlightenment" in the eighteenth century, the triumph of secular liberal ideas seemed assured, and an increasing confidence in man's ability to ensure indefinite "progress" in attaining peace and prosperity reigned supreme, even though few would have gone so far in the direction of heady optimism as had Condorcet in his *Sketch of the Progress of the Human Mind*.

Even in the midst of the eighteenth-century celebration of the new era, in which the representative figure was the French *philosophe* (who was hardly a philosopher in the Platonic sense), certain voices were to be heard in opposition. From very different perspectives, Jean-Jacques Rousseau and Edmund Burke challenged the progressivist ethos on the grounds that it failed to fulfill man's need for community. Burke advocated a moderate conservatism as the cure for this neglect. Rousseau proclaimed the need to fashion a modern version of the ancient Greek city-state; man's alienation from himself in modern society could be overcome at the public level, if at all, only by constituting an egalitarian society in which the individual found his realization in selfless service to the "general will" or public interest of the community.

It remained for Karl Marx, however, to develop a "philosophy of *praxis*" in which he attempted to demonstrate the possibility of the merger of philosophy and practice through a final "radical" revolution which would result in the overcoming of man's alienation and the "negation" of man's enslavement to irrational forces beyond his control. In the *Philosophic-Economic Manuscripts* of 1844, in the *German Ideology* of 1846, and, with reduced explicitness, in his later detailed analyses of capitalism, Marx proclaimed the view that the historical conditions were maturing in which man for the first time could consciously grasp the truth that he is the author of social reality; if "[material] circumstances make man, man can make the circumstances human." Both sides of this dialectical proposition had to be grasped by a philosophy that was truly "radical"—i.e., that penetrated to the roots of man's condition.

Marx's metastatic humanism proclaimed not only the *possibility* but even the *necessity* for achieving a *qualitative* change in man's existence. Capitalist civilization, through one-sided development of industry and technology, had created the means of production which could now be appropriated, following the Communist revolution, and used for the benefit of all. Marx never claimed to be a prophet and did not pretend to be able to predict the details of the future course of history. He was not a "determinist" in the sense that he envisaged the revolution as occurring *automatically*, without the conscious intervention of men. What he argued, rather, was that the objective material (economic-technological) conditions existed for the overcoming *(Aufhebung)* of class society and for the eventual creation, after several intermediate stages, of a world civilization which would be self-regulating and in which the free development of each would be the condition for the free development of all. In such a society man would no longer have to spend his most valuable waking moments in irksome, mindless toil; rather, he could "create according to the laws of beauty" and choose to perform one task at one time, taking up a variety of activities in turn, as suited his multifaceted nature. For Marx, philosophy, like the state, would be "overcome" by being "realized" in the final, fully developed communist society.

## WHAT IS HISTORY?

The third of the major topics, or themes, of political philosophy can be succinctly discussed on the basis of what we know of the responses of each philosophic grouping to the other two. Indeed, much of what we retrospectively learn about the philosophers' understanding of history is implicitly rather than explicitly stated in their works. Among the previously cited authors of the classics, only Augustine, Hegel, and Marx may be said to have full-fledged philosophies of history. That this is so does not mean, of course, that an interpretation of history as a pattern of events unfolding in time is absent from the works of the other philosophers; it means only that such an interpretation has been prevented from surfacing to maximal clarity by their preoccupation with other problems or by the limited perspective afforded by their intellectual milieu. Thus Plato and Aristotle failed to develop an explicit philosophy of history, because their consciousness of living in a new epoch (that of philosophy as distinct from that of the myth) was obscured by the persistence of the myth of cyclical recurrence of events within time. Machiavelli was similarly bound to the classic myth of cyclical repetitiveness, even while possessing a consciousness of embarking on a completely new (or "modern") era, and Hobbes and Locke were too eager to get on with the negative task of making a "clean slate" *(tabula rasa)* of inherited ideas to notice the extent to which they were contributing to the positive task of laying the groundwork for a "progressive" theory of history. Granted that the theories of history of many of the classical political philosophers remain embedded in their anthropologies and theories of the paradigmatic society, it is nevertheless both possible and necessary for the present-day interpreter to draw out the implications of their views on history. Indeed, we live in an era in which the philosophy of history has again become a flourishing enterprise.

*Theocentric* humanism emphasizes the gulf which separates the human from the divine and conceives of history as a series of attempts (even though imperfect ones) by man to attune his existence with divine reality, interrupted by periods of revolt and *hubris*. Thus neither Plato nor Augustine, for example, promises the realization of the paradigm within time. Although history is seen to possess a meaning, primarily in man's increased understanding of his humanity through the experiences of philosophy and revelation (experiences which are seen to be representative for all men), that meaning in its entirety cannot be grasped by the finite human mind. The "mystery of history" (Voegelin) is impenetrable, and philosophy cannot tell us why the historical process possesses the character of a field of forces in tension. We cannot know why history is transacted in the "In-Between," between openness and closure, attunement and revolt, life and death, or why there is no promise of deliverance from its ambiguities save through faith and trust in a transcendent divine reality, the experience of which is on principle incommunicable in terms of the categories of immanent existence.

The theocentric humanist conception of history as the record of man's imperfect attempts at attunement with the world-transcendent God—and, in the Christian formulation, of the descent of that God in the unrepeatable event of the Incarnation to take on human form—left the way open for other interpretations of history with emphasis on man's action here and now, within time and world immanent existence. Although theocentric humanism scarcely ignored the dimension of man's immanent existence, it subordinated events at the pragmatic level of history to what Jacques Maritain once called the "primacy of the spiritual." Anthropocentric humanist philosophy sought to stress the need for deliberate action to change the political order so as to provide greater amplitude of maneuver for man within time and the world. Man was conceived as a creature of autonomous reason, capable of fabricating the "little world" of his understanding and of rescuing himself from decadence (Machiavelli), from the constant threat of violent death (Hobbes), and from the vagaries of an arbitrary and paternalistic government (Locke). Instead of being the story of critical events which had already taken place (i.e., the birth of philosophy and the irruption of revelation), history was conceived of as a process which was only about to begin. Man, who had been looked on as a plaything of the gods or a "pilgrim" whose ultimate destination was in another world, was seen as the being who, within the limitation of his finiteness, would remake his entire culture through will and artifice. For the first time, he could become an "individual" and as an individual participate in a new era for mankind, wherein the bonds of tradition, irrationality, and inherited privilege would be broken. History was conceived of as the story of liberty, "progress," and "enlightenment."

The "new secular order" of anthropocentric humanism, though impressive insofar as it unleashed the unprecedented expansion of man's material productivity, was itself subject to the objection that, while claiming to free man, it had only subjugated him to external forces of production, and while pretending to liberate him for self-determining individuality, it only locked him into an ever more oppressive and coordinated conformity. Hence the historical construction of metastatic humanism promised to "build a heaven in hell's despite" (Blake) and to "make of Augustine's two cities, one city" (Brown, 1966, p. 179).

Metastatic humanism, the humanism of Karl Marx, Herbert Marcuse, and other "radical" writers of the past century, envisions a qualitative transformation of both man's consciousness and his institutions. Such a *metastasis*, or *qualitative change* of existence, will establish a new man and a new world civilization, founded on the realization of man's highest noetic and aesthetic capabilities and on a human symbiotic relationship free of exploitation and fear. To premodern theocentric humanism's conclusion that the paradigm was transhistorical, metastatic humanism replies that philosophy must be realized and the promises of the city of God must be fulfilled in the city of man.

It now remains to us, who continue the "great conversation" in the present day, to decide (provisionally, at least) to what extent the differences between the three humanisms are incompatible and to what extent their insights are complementary to each other. If there is to be a (presumably irreducible) plurality of humanisms—meaning that for each of us one of the languages is our controlling language—then how can we nourish the capacity of empathy (which is more than tolerance) between men for perspectives other than our own? The last sentence presupposes that an important lesson we learn from the philosopher's search for meaning is openness to voices in the conversation other than the one we accept most fully, with which we feel most comfortable. To be open means *both* to have ground on which to stand *and* to have a respect for (and insofar as possible even a delight in) the perspectives of those who similarly engage in the quest, regardless of whether they stand among us or somewhere else.

## PHILOSOPHY, THEORY, AND NONNOETIC THOUGHT

The interpretation of philosophy suggested here, while taking into account the importance of later developments, is related to the Platonic conception of *philosophia:* Philosophy is conceived of as a conversation or dialogue about the reality in which man participates; it is best portrayed as the *love (philiá)* of rather than the *possession* of wisdom *(sophia);* it involves the whole person, including the passionate side of man (his erotic constitution), rather than being solely an affair of the intellect; and the effect of its consistent pursuit is to open the psyche to new dimensions of reality and new priorities for life and action. Thus conceived, philosophy is seen to have its origins in the preintellectual disposition of the individual philosopher; or as Enzo Paci has expressed the matter in a felicitous phrase, philosophy has a "precategorial genesis."[13]

However, if philosophy is true to itself, it cannot remain inarticulate but must achieve expression in symbols; what is precategorial must be expressed in categories if it is to be intelligibly communicated to others, or to put it another way, what is subjective must become intersubjective. It is precisely because of the difficulty inherent in the act of philosophizing itself that the symbols used by the philosopher seem always inadequate to describe his experience; for he must try to perform the literally impossible but humanly necessary task of expressing his "subjective" experience in "objective" language. The poetry of philosophy must be translated into the prose of "theory."

Thus we find, for example, Plato's philosophic experience of reality expressed in a theory of forms or "ideas," and his experience of the forces of order and disorder encountered in the consciousness is reported as a theory of the three "parts" of the "soul." Indeed, political philosophy itself, as we have seen, is broadly divisible in its concerns between a "theory" of man, a "theory" of society, and a "theory" of history.

Although theory needs to be *distinguished* from philosophy, it should not be *separated*. Philosophy gives rise to and nourishes theory. I attempted to formulate the relationship between the two activities in a recent volume:

> One thing seems clear (to me, at least) as a result of my labors on this volume: theory (or the disinterested observation and explanation of a given segment of reality) derives its nourishment from philosophy (or the attempt to see reality, insofar as a man can, as a meaningful whole). While theory can be analytically *distinguished* from philosophy, it is disastrous to separate these two activities. Thus one can have theories of social change, types of regime, the circulation of elites, voting behavior, and political development, for example, but if they are separated from the concerns that have perennially preoccupied political philosophy, their meaning will appear distorted or prove barren and irrelevant. For the intellectuality of theory must be leavened with the poetic vision of philosophy. (Germino, 1972a, p. 389)[14]

Thus, if theories in the social sciences are put forward, as they too often are, without any explicit philosophical underpinning, they may lose their noetic character and uncritically support particular interests, whether of a nation, regime, religion, party, or socioeconomic class. Strictly speaking, the alternative to a philosophical political science is one that is parochial. One of the principal criticisms of recent "behavioral" social science has been that under the label of science it has so often implicitly and uncritically endorsed the policies and practices of the established order instead of performing the

Socratic function of "speaking truth to power," as Hans J. Morgenthau has so felicitiously expressed it (Morgenthau, 1970). Bernard Crick, one of the more astute foreign observers of American society, even went so far as to term postwar behavioral political science the *"American* science of politics" (Crick, 1959), so parochial did he find its predilection for uncritically absorbing the leading assumptions of the uniquely American civil theology or hegemonic idea.

Following the argument of Louis Hartz (1955), Crick found American political thought dominated by a Lockean liberal consensus which uncritically accepted individualism, the contractual basis of society, rationalism, "enlightenment," and "progress" as self-evident ideals, not only for America but for the human race at large. From an examination of the work of Charles Merriam, T. V. Smith, Harold Lasswell, and other prominent recent figures in the development of American political science, Crick reached the controversial conclusion that the study of politics in this country has been more a doctrine than a science. Without wishing entirely to subscribe to his views or the unusual acerbity with which they are sometimes expressed, I must admit that this perceptive and by no means unfriendly critic has given us much food for thought.

In arguing for the crucial importance of the distinction between noetic and nonnoetic thought, one should of course not overlook the fact that even the greatest and most philosophically open thinkers show parochial preoccupations that in retrospect seem incompatible with their basic commitment as philosophers. Thus, for example, Plato may be severely criticized for his theocratic impulse, Aristotle for his preoccupation with the vanishing world of the *polis* and his moral obtuseness on slavery, Augustine for his overreaction to the moral perfectionism of the sects and his acceptance (as inevitable in this fallen world) of specific injustices that we now know to be remediable, Machiavelli for not having written more clearly about his intentions and for thus having left himself open to vilification without parallel, Hobbes and Locke for leaving too much out of the psychologies of their "rational" men, Rousseau for the unresolved tensions in his thought between universalism and parochialism, Hegel for his failure to draw out the implications of his teaching for a world state, Marx for the reductionist and mechanistic aspects of his teaching that have constantly threatened its humanistic core, and all of them for having failed sufficiently to recognize what the history of their dialogue demonstrates: that the consciousness of any one participant in the human drama is severely limited in its perspective. The authors of the classics were men and therefore flawed, but looking back over the history of political philosophy, one can see that the whole is greater than the sum of its parts.

Recall that Aristotle used the term "philosophy of man" *(philosophia peri ta anthropina)* to designate what has come to be called political philosophy

(*Nicomachaean Ethics*, 1181b15). Aristotle is also important for having developed the distinction of three kinds of knowledge or "science": theoretical practical, and productive. Theoretical knowledge is knowledge for its own sake rather than for the sake of action or production. It is concerned with things which cannot be other than they are, whereas the other two kinds of knowledge deal with the area of contingency. A question raised by Aristotle, though nowhere definitively resolved by him, is this: Does political science or philosophy belong in the realm of theoretical or practical knowledge?

Perhaps there is no "definitive" resolution to this problem, and it may be that the study of the history of political philosophy shows us that we need to keep before our minds two different conceptions of the relationship between philosophy and practice, one put forward by the premodern authors of the classics, which stressed contemplation before action, and the other, most fully developed in Marx's thought, which emphasized the unity of theory and practice. Whereas the former runs the risk of needlessly enfeebling philosophy and suppressing the leavening effect it may have on practice, the latter courts the contrary danger of pressing philosophy into the service of a particular interest in the mask of a universal interest. Nonetheless, irrespective of the difficulties attendant on dealing with this problem, I offer the following attempt, on the basis of my own understanding of the matter, as a provisional resolution, recognizing that if it errs it does so on the side of the contemplative pole of the existential situation.

It seems that political philosophy, or a philosophical political science, is of a hybrid character and belongs to the realm of both theoretical and practical knowledge. Or better, it exists between the two poles of (philosophically nourished) theory and practice. Its aim is understanding, irrespective of its effect on the immediate self-interest of a particular individual, group, or nation; the passion that informs it is a passion for truth, not for power. The aims of political philosophy and the theories it produces are to further our understanding of political reality and to raise perennial questions valid for man *qua* man.

Insofar as political philosophy concerns itself with the "nature" or realized essence of man, it is in the area of Aristotle's theoretic knowledge. Insofar as it has consequences for the world of practice, however, it is a form of practical knowledge. Such knowledge has greater claim to epistemic validity to the degree that it is removed from the advocacy of specific policies. For example, it is legitimate for the political philosopher to enunciate general principles with regard to property arrangements (that concentration of property in a few hands is detrimental to social justice, for example)[15] and to attempt to defend them; however, when and if he enters the list for a specific, immediate reform (whether of governmental institutions, taxes and welfare, or foreign policy), he ceases to act as a philosopher and cannot claim the "disinterested" status of the same. He has entered the arena instead of remaining in the stadium as a spectator or "theorist,"[16] and he must expect to be treated as a competitor by those with opposing policies and recommendations. This is not to suggest that the philosopher should never enter directly into the arena of practical politics—he may conclude that inaction is wholly inadmissible in a given set of circumstances or that he has an unusual opportunity to tame and civilize the exercise of power—but only to note that when he does, he is adopting another role.

What I have just maintained about the relationship between philosophy and practice is no doubt controversial; specifically, it militates agnst the tendency of the modern ethos to exalt action over contemplation. Nonetheless, I hold that this relationship is basically the one that prevails within the works of the great political philosophers themselves. Wherever they enunciate general principles of right action and of the good society, they continue to be read with interest for their contribution to the philosophical conversation. Wherever they descend to advocating specific reforms or to defending specific practices, they are thought to have become enmeshed in the timebound disputes of their day. My point here, once again, is *not* that philosophers should refrain from direct advocacy of policies; it is simply that, if that were all they did, we should have no philosophy but only political advocacy. Thus we value Rousseau's *Social Contract,* Hegel's *Philosophy of Right,* and even Marx's *Philosophic-Economic Manuscripts* for the extent to which they manage to transcend their immediate practical problems to contemplate the perennial problems of man *qua* man. I furthermore maintain (on grounds similar to the Thomistic distinction between a thesis—statement of a general principle—and a hypothesis—application of the principle to a concrete situation) that, given the contingency of human affairs and their contextual character, it is often extremely difficult to translate general principles into practice, for they frequently seem capable of being applied in a number of alternative ways. Such application is the preoccupation of the practical or prudential reason, and it is rightly considered a mark of wisdom in practical politics to know *when* to "hang up" philosophy. There is no clearer indication that someone has misunderstood the character of political philosophy than his or her wish to reduce its teaching to a few rigid, apodictic propositions, which all who hold office in government and society are in lockstep to obey. Political philosophers—and by extension, political scientists—are not the superlegislators of mankind. Sheldon Wolin has nicely captured the flavor of the kind of wisdom to be gathered from the study of the classics of political philosophy in the following passage.

> Taken as a whole, this composite type of knowledge . . . is mindful of logic, but more so of the incoherence and contradictoriness of experience. And for the same reason, it is distrustful of rigor. Political life does not yield its significance to terse hypotheses, but is elusive, and

hence meaningful statements about it have to be allusive and intimative. Context beomes supremely important. . . . (Wolin, 1972)

If there is a way of deducing detailed, concrete proposals for political action directly from one's philosophical understanding of man, society, and history, I have been unable to find it. Thus I would argue that when political philosophers *claim the prestige of philosophy* for their personal choices on immediate policies, issues, movements, and candidates of the day—whether they are on the "right," in the "center," or on the "left" in terms of the contemporary political debate—they run the grave risk of endangering the disinterested status of the philosophical enterprise itself. They should make every effort to distinguish between their philosophical analyses—made for the "common benefit of everyone," in Machiavelli's memorable phrase *(Discourses,* Book I, Preface)—and their immediate practical decisions, whether on domestic or international issues.

The philosophical political scientist is on safer ground *qua* philosopher if he speaks *against* what he concludes to be abuses of power that threaten the *unity of mankind* (as in condemning an unjust war or the persecution of political dissenters or the injustices of racial discrimination) than he is in *advocating* specific reforms or policies which lie in the area of decision by the practical reason and where no obvious and fundamental violation of the right by nature or "right philosophically understood" (Hegel, *Philosophy of Right,* Preface) has occurred. In arguing in this vein, I am in part at least following Julien Benda's contention (1959) that the philosopher should insofar as possible stay detached from the advocacy of "lay passions" which serve only to enhance group or national hatreds. In sum, the philosopher's first duty is to serve truth and the open society embracing all mankind as persons sharing an equal dignity and right to respect. However, even in this latter category of abuses of power deserving moral censure, the philosopher should never forget his own frailty and fallibility, and he should constantly recall Richard Hooker's injunction: "Think ye are men; deem it not impossible for you to err" *(Laws of Ecclesiastical Polity,* Preface).

Inevitably, this discussion brings to mind Plato's famous dictum that man's only hope was for philosophers to become kings or kings philosophers. If baldly and literally stated, of course, realization of such a proposition is an impossibility, because rulers notoriously do not have the leisure to philosophize, and they cannot "speak truth to power" while they have power themselves. However, I am far from suggesting that political philosophy is irrelevant to the practice of politics or that students of political philosophy should refrain from seeking office.

Indeed, in a society becoming more open, one wishes to see in power more persons with an education in political philosophy. Although the ascendency to power of philosophically inclined persons would scarcely induce a perfect, problem-free world (for philosophy cannot instruct the world in the solution of immediate practical issues of war and peace, domestic turmoil, etc.), it would mean that problems would be *approached* with a different quality of mind. The study of philosophy can teach us the existential virtues of (1) openness—or the ability to transcend one's immediate preoccupation to view matters from a more universal perspective; (2) disinterested love of truth for its own sake; (3) respect for the human in man *behind* the ideological, ethnic, or national label; (4) distrust of simplistic, apodictical thinking with respect to complex, multifaceted realities; (5) recognition of one's fallibility and limitation of his perspective; (6) recognition of the multidimensional character of reality and of the difficulty of achieving among men a uniform level of awareness in the world of practice; (7) tolerance of intellectual diversity without ceasing to search for that truth of existence which lies beyond all imperfect attempts to formulate its character; and (8) an empathy, which goes beyond tolerance, for perspectives that are different from our own and that are the result of an equally disinterested search for symbols that illumine the universal character of the human condition. We are enriched by a multiplicity of perspectives.

Throughout this discussion an assumption has been made, following Eric Voegelin, about the different character of noetic and nonnoetic thought. Political philosophy and theory are attempts at a noetic (or self-critical) interpretation of reality, and they presuppose a radical questioning of basic assumptions. Nonnoetic thought, however, takes for granted its basic assumptions and is concerned, above all, with creating or defending certain institutions or regimes. No society has ever existed whose self-interpretation is entirely noetic. Therefore political philosophy always exists in tension with various other intellectual and spiritual forces in society, and most especially with the prevailing "hegemonic idea" (Gramsci) or "political formula" (Mosca) of the time. It now remains to be seen whether a new hegemonic idea of the open society, to which philosophy would be related both as friend and critic and which could serve as the basis for a world civilization, can be developed in time to avoid either ecological catastrophe or nuclear annihilation. Although at the present time the prospect seems elusive, philosophy by its nature is an enterprise based on hope and trust, and those who engage in it will continue to speak of the "things that are absent" in the hope that they may become more present.

## CONCLUSION: THE RELEVANCE OF POLITICAL PHILOSOPHY[17]

We are now in a position to gather up the threads of our argument and to make some concluding observations on the "relevance" or "uses" of political philosophy for political science and, indeed, for our culture in more general terms as part of the core of liberal learning, the transmission of which is a principal mission of the university.

If we study the classics of political philosophy with appropriate seriousness, we shall draw the following conclusions.

1. Political science is the attempt to achieve a noetic, as distinct from a nonnoetic, interpretation of political reality.

2. Political science is in the realm of "sciences of the person" rather than that of "sciences of phenomena" (to employ Max Scheler's fruitful distinction), and its methods must be appropriate to the investigation of the multidimensional participation in political reality experienced from within by the philosopher-theorist-scientist himself.

3. The philosopher exists not in a vacuum but within a specific political culture and civilization, whose collective cultural memory he shares. Thus he gives a time dimension to political reality that must be explored in depth through the process of self-conscious historical recollection.

4. The political philosopher (or noetic participant in political reality) is one who "descends" to the depths of the consciousness and on his "return" articulates symbols designed better to illumine the character of political reality within the structure of existence.

5. Political science is a science of the whole man, and reductionist theories which pretend to explain all of man's behavior on the basis of only a part of his experience must be rigorously examined and placed in a broader context before they may be regarded as contributions to political science.

6. A major function of a critical science of politics is to "speak truth to power," however unpalatable that truth may be to the powers that be at the time.

7. There are certain intellectual and existential virtues to be gained from the study and practice of philosophy, such as increased critical awareness, a distrust of single-vision apodictical argumentation, a love of philosophical reflection as a means of experiencing dimensions of reality absent from contemporary historical existence, intellectual integrity, openness to perspectives beyond those of one's immediate practical concerns and predilections, and respect for the inquiring human person behind the labels (or masks) conventionally attached to them in political life.

8. Technique is only a tool of thought, despite the seeming assumption of advanced industrial society to the contrary, and "decision-makers" who remain ignorant of philosophy cut themselves off from a vital source of the intellectual and existential virtues so necessary to making tolerable, let alone wise, decisions.

Political philosophy emerges, then, as a species of "speculatively practical" knowledge. Its representatives are human beings who, however much they may have been originally attracted to the study of politics by some immediate practical interest, become captivated by the pull of the contemplative life and are led to another level of reflection. And in turn, we are able, retrospectively as it were, to perceive the ultimate "relevance" of these representatives' philosophical reflections to practical politics as well. As Benedetto Croce once commented, "Contemplation, which has its origins and end in itself, by educating the mind, prepares one for *eupraxia*," or "good practice" (1925, p. 58).[18]

As we enter what has been called the "post-behavioral era" in political science,[19] we appear to be witnessing, particularly in the United States, a renewed interest in and appreciation of the classics of political philosophy. The search of numerous scholars, young and old, in response to the multiple crises of the 1960s, for a "value-related" political science has inevitably led many to reexamine the classics of political philosophy for suggestions for alternative models of political and social science. Given the humanistic orientation exemplified by all the authors of the philosophical classics, we may, as a result of the increasing philosophical sophistication of political scientists, eventually even be spared the naive and arrogant exhortations of occasional simplistic "behavioralists" that political science devote itself to "social engineering."[20]

There is abroad in the world today a tendency to downgrade the creative works of man and to view man as a creature "beyond freedom and dignity."[21] But the authors of the classics testify to the capacity of the human spirit to articulate symbols and concepts which endow the "little world of our understanding" with meaning and coherence. They show us that the world is not determined *a priori* and that particular human beings can make a difference by enriching the cultural content of our shared interpretation of the world. The human response is varied and variable, and the way in which facts are interpreted can shape social reality.

It makes a huge difference for mankind that Plato lived and wrote, and that later philosophers took the trouble to become "footnotes" (in Whitehead's memorable phrase in *Process and Reality*) to his work. It is difficult to envisage how, without political philosophy, the open society (in the Bergsonian sense) would be even a remote possibility for mankind. A world leavened by the self-criticism of philosophy is open to the unexpected and to the free activity of the human spirit as it struggles to articulate a paradigm of the good society for the future building on the insights of the past.

It would doubtless be more comfortable to dwell in a closed society, a city without gadflies and without the influence of philosophy. In such a society the ends of life would be accepted as given, and attention would be focused exclusively on the techniques of achieving or maintaining those ends. Indeed, the technocratic ethos abroad in the contemporary world tends to reject the study of the classics as useless and irrelevant. But the more this ethos establishes itself and the more successful it becomes in permeating society, the more discontented and fretful do the subjects of our world appear to become. Without the free activity of thought, which Aristotle once identified as the *bios theōretikos,* contemporary man in his newfound leisure turns restlessly and compulsively to distractions of various kinds which become ever more sensational and bizarre, eventually leading to the phenomenon of what Herbert Marcuse has designated "repressive desublimation."

The study of the classics in our educational institutions and in our leisure time can assist us in some measure, at least, to remove the blockage (resulting from the pressures and "imperatives" of industrialized societies) in the way of the *bios theōretikos,* which so often distorts the psychology of contemporary man.

The authors of the classics, experiencing their world as in crisis, cast themselves on the open seas of thought to discover new symbols or to reexpress previous ones that illumine the character of the *ensemble* of relationships in which human beings find themselves. The primary purpose of a political philosopher is to explore the individual's relationship to society, and he inevitably concludes that man cannot be exhausted in his social relationships, that experience is multidimensional, that the open personality participates in reality through relating to others, to himself, to the external world of nature, and to the principle of reality itself, which gives coherence to all things. The psyche of man fulfills itself maximally and escapes the distortion that results from the atrophy of the noetic faculties only when it is capable of defining its own world through an inner experience uncontrolled by the taskmasters of the immanent productive order.

Some years ago in *Beyond Ideology* I argued that we were then in the midst of a revival of political philosophy. Today I hold this view even more strongly. Whether we take as our criterion published work of quality or college and university enrollments in political philosophy courses, the record of the past decade has been encouraging.

Still, the pressures against a renaissance of political philosophy are immense. The contemporary university agonizingly attempts to juggle a host of activities, some of them only marginally relevant to the free life of the mind. The case for a humanistic approach to the study of man and society has to be made again and again, not only without but even within the universities. Always, however, the thirst in our psyche for contact with modes of experience other than the productive and the manipulative brings us back to the recognition of the higher utility and ultimate relevance of "that most useless thing," philosophy.

What, after all, does one learn from immersing himself in, studying, living with the classics? Certainly it ought not to be some slavish fascination with the literal meaning of a text. Note that we are concerned here with the relevance of the classics (in the plural). To study the classics is immediately to be struck by the immense divergency in the interpretation of experience and in the understanding of psyche, society, and history between, for example, Plato and Hobbes, Aristotle and Marx, Aquinas and Machiavelli, Augustine and Rousseau, Locke and Hegel. In fact, a major lesson we can derive today from the study of the classics is that we should beware of reifying the symbolic formulations of our philosophical opponents and of rejecting out of hand political teachings at variance with our own. The fact that so many sensitive, gifted, and learned men could come up with such different readings of experience should give us considerable pause about exclusive reliance on the categories and symbols for defining reality shared by one particular culture or group, even if it happens to be our own.

Another lesson to be gleaned from the study of the classics is respect for the quality of thought of someone with whom one may profoundly disagree. For example, I personally find Hobbes's psychology and theory of the rational society highly unconvincing. Yet I readily acknowledge that if one keeps coming back to him, one detects a far greater complexity of thought than one had initially expected to find expressed in a philosophy seemingly mechanistic and reductionist. Even if we continue ultimately to reject a given philosopher's counsel and interpretation of reality, however, we benefit greatly from following him through the rigors of his thought, and we learn at what level of discourse we ourselves must think and write if we are to offer an alternative interpretation which deserves the name of political philosophy.

When the leading theoretician of Italian Marxism, Antonio Gramsci, was imprisoned by the Fascists, he spent much of this time writing his famous *Prison Notebooks*. Of all the writers with whom Gramsci conducted his inner dialogue during his long ordeal, none was taken more seriously than Benedetto Croce. In terms of conventional labels, of course, Croce and Gramsci were in opposing philosophical schools, and their political conceptions did indeed substantially diverge. But Gramsci never caricatured Croce's views and, in the process of refuting what seemed to be his errors, learned much from him, so that Gramsci's own Marxism, tempered as it is with some of Croce's philosophical "idealism," became much more vital and alive than it would have been under the inspiration of the reductionist and mechanistic interpretation of historical materialism given such wide currency in "Marxist" circles after the death of the master.

Gramsci displayed a rich zest for dialogue that is all too rare among us. We today, instead of viewing philosophical disagreement as normal—given what B. J. Lonergan (1957) has called the "polymorphous" shape of the consciousness—tend to become apprehensive or impatient about the diversity of conceptions and ideas we encounter in the history of political theory. We wonder whether the history of philosophy has anything to teach us today, for it seems but a babble of voices recalling the words of Macbeth that life is a "tale told by an idiot, full of sound and fury, signifying nothing."

Actually, if we look over the history of Western political thought, of which political philosophy is only a part, we can identify certain epochs or periods, each characterized, in Gramsci's phrase, by a given "hegemonic idea." The hegemonic idea may be the *polis* myth or the Roman civil theology (the *respublica christiana*) or liberalism or Marxism. Such hegemonic ideas have been highly effective practical forces in integrating societies or in founding new ones, but it needs to be emphasized that philosophy by its very nature exists in tension with such ideas, born as they are of practical need. Imitating its founder, Socrates, political philosophy takes nothing for granted and includes within its purview for critical inspection even the most basic assumptions of the hegemonic idea prevailing at the particular time and in the particular culture in which the philosopher finds himself.

A given political philosopher may endorse, tolerate, or oppose a given hegemonic idea, and in practical politics he may be "conservative," "liberal," or "radical," but one thing he can never do without forfeiting his right to be called a philosopher is to argue that we do not need the voice of political philosophy and that a particular hegemonic idea is sufficient unto itself for defining political reality.

The study of the classics of political philosophy has a vital place in a curriculum devoted to liberal learning. Such learning (and experiencing) is concerned above all with multiplying the perspectives from which we may view our world. We expand our inward sight by following the authors of the classics on their quests, for we are enabled thereby to behold vicariously the world of human relationships from a multiplicity of perspectives. None of them will be identical with our own, for ultimately a man thinks, as he dies, uniquely and alone. But how much more impoverished we should be if we did not take advantage of the opportunity to see political reality through the lenses of a Plato, a Machiavelli, and a Marx!

Plato, Machiavelli, and Marx: Here we have archetypically represented three types of humanism—theocentric, anthropocentric, and metastatic. Each variety has something to contribute. From Plato we learn the crucial significance of inner conversion, by which we orient ourselves in terms of new priorities attempting, however imperfectly, to attune ourselves to the presence of Being. The Platonic philosopher becomes the theomorphic man. There is in Plato an opening of the psyche to the contemplation of the transcendent ground of Being, as captured so superbly in Bergson's *Two Sources of Morality and Religion*. From Machiavelli we learn the dangers of neglecting the world of appearance, where "the many" call the tune, and where significant human achievements must be fashioned against a background of temporal uncertainty and moral ambiguity. From Marx we learn that it is not idle speculation or utopian fancy to suppose that men may in time create a new world that is truly brave, a world in which they may see reflected the image of their best selves instead of some distorted caricature, a world, in the words of Marx's politically more moderate mentor, Hegel, "worthy of the spirit of man to inhabit."

The classics of political philosophy, then, invite us to share in a great adventure of the mind and spirit by continuing their authors' quest for a broadening of perspective and a deepening of awareness. We are asked neither to "imitate" these authors in some mechanical fashion nor to "compete" with them in a bootless search for glory, but meditatively to reenact the inner experiences on which the classics were based and to strike out on fresh attempts to elaborate symbols for the guidance of contemporary man on his troubled journey.

We have until now spoken repeatedly of "Western" political philosophy, and this characterization of our subject matter makes us sharply aware, in an era marked by what F. C. S. Northrop (1966) once called the "meeting of East and West," that philosophy as we have known it is the product of only one of the world's civilizations. We need today to recognize that from the "classics" of Buddhism, Confucianism, and Islam we in the West doubtless have much yet to learn. Such a concern to learn from the insights of other civilizations is in keeping with the spirit and essential relevance of political philosophy, which is to shatter any complacency that we might have in living in a closed society and to send us on our way in a search for that "true city" without walls, embracing all humanity, the tower of which, with Dante, we may see dimly in the distance.

> Convenne rege aver, chi discernesse
> Della vera cittade almen la torre.
>
> Needful to have a ruler who might discern
> At least the tower of the true city.[22]

Dante Aligheri, *The Divine Comedy: Purgatory*, XVI, 95–96.

## BIBLIOGRAPHICAL ESSAY

### A. Editions and Translations of the Classics of Political Philosophy Discussed in this Chapter

*Introductory Note*

Few students of the history of political philosophy can attain sufficient mastery to read all the classics in their original languages. Therefore it is most important to make use of accurate and, if possible, felicitous translations. In the list that follows, translations which are generally regarded to be reliable are given, along with critical editions of the texts in their original languages.

In general, for Plato, Jowett frequently sounds a bit Victorian and old-fashioned to contemporary ears, and Cornford's translation of the *Republic*, in my judgment, reads better than any other currently available. However, Cornford omits a few passages (they are so indicated in the text), and Allan Bloom's translation has the virtue of both completeness and greater literalness. Many translators of both Plato and Aristotle render *polis* and *politeia* as "state," and thus the two authors are made to seem to be advancing theories of the "ideal state," when actually they are discussing the "best regime" (*aristē politeia*).

The *Republic, Statesman,* and *Laws* are generally recognized as Plato's principal political dialogues, but many others are also important, including the four early dialogues dealing with Socrates's trial and death (the *Euthyphro, Apology, Crito,* and *Phaedo*), as well as the *Gorgias* and the *Timaeus.* The *Laws* can scarcely be read all at once; it is far longer than any of the others and was not finished even at Plato's death. Probably Books III, X, and XII are of greatest interest to the student of political philosophy.

That Aristotle's *Politics* is frequently read without his *Ethics* in political thought courses is a grave mistake, for the author regarded the two works as halves of a single whole; i.e., his political science (*epistēmē politikē*) is expounded in the two works together. The *Rhetoric* has some interesting passages on the "right by nature," and parts of the *De Anima (On the Soul)* and the *Metaphysics* are also highly relevant to his political philosophy. See also Aristotle's *Constitution of Athens.*

As for St. Augustine, who wrote 117 books, St. Isidore of Seville later observed that anyone who claimed to have read all of them had to be a liar. Even the *City of God* is too vast and rambling to take in at once; it is perhaps best to begin with the Preface, then go on to Book V, Chapters 11–24, and then to the entirety of Book XIX, as well as Book XX, Chapter 7. The *Confessions,* a literary masterpiece, had best be read in entirety rather than excerpted.

Thomas Aquinas's *Summa Theologica,* though intended as a textbook for the beginning university student of theology, requires twenty-two volumes for the English translation. Even so, it was never completed, because three years before his death Thomas had a vision that led him to regard all he had written as of "so much straw" compared to the beauty that had been revealed to him. Although a great synthesizer and practitioner of the scholastic method, he did not aspire to construct a complete airtight philosophical system. Like Aristotle, whom he so much admired, Aquinas investigated *problems* and left his thought open-ended and capable of further development. His undeserved reputation as a rigid, dogmatic, and wholly deductive thinker derives from the work of too many unimaginative later interpreters, who used his teaching in an authoritarian and mechanical fashion foreign to its spirit.

The major portion of the *Summa* that is of particular interest to students of political philosophy is the famous *Treatise on Law.* It is contained in the First Part of the Second Part of the *Summa,* Questions 90 to 108. In addition,

Aquinas wrote part of the *De Regimine Principum (On the Governance of Princes)* and brief commentaries on Aristotle's *Politics* and *Ethics*, which, with other selections of interest to the student of his political thought, have been included in two handy volumes, one edited by Alexander Passerin d'Entrèves (with the Latin text on alternate pages) and the other by Dino Bigongiari. Substantial portions of the *Summa Theologica* and the shorter *Summa Contra Gentiles* are available in Anton C. Pegis's carefully edited *Basic Writings of Saint Thomas Aquinas* (two volumes; Volume II is more valuable for political theorists).

Machiavelli's principal writings have been ably translated in a three-volume edition by Allan Gilbert. His notorious *The Prince* should be supplemented by the *Discourses on Livy*, the play *Mandragola*, and the sermon *Exhortation to Repentance*, by everyone wishing a more accurate impression of Machiavelli's thought. In addition, one could usefully read in the *Florentine Histories* and the *Art of War*.

Hobbes's *De Cive* may profitably be read in addition to the *Leviathan*, although the latter clearly serves as the fullest expression of the Malmesbury sage's political philosophy. Locke's *First Treatise*, a lengthy and often tedious refutation of Sir Robert Filmer's *Patriarcha*, is probably not worth reading except for a passage here or there. However, *An Essay Concerning Human Understanding* is very important as a means of seeing the epistemological underpinnings of the *Second Treatise*. His *Letters on Toleration* and *Thoughts on Education* also need to be read by anyone wanting a deeper knowledge of Locke's teaching.

Of Rousseau one should read (preferably in the following order) the *Discourse on the Arts and Sciences, Discourse on the Origins of Inequality*, and *Social Contract*. Minor works of particular interest to the political theorist are the *Government of Poland* and the *Constitution of Corsica*. Rousseau's *Confessions* and other attempts at autobiography, if used with care, can also help in illuminating his political teaching.

Hegel's political philosophy is expounded in parts of his *Phenomenology of the Spirit* (1807) and in his political masterpiece, *The Philosophy of Right* (1821). The great philosopher also wrote a number of political essays with regard to contemporary issues that are helpful in illuminating the concrete quality of his allegedly "abstract" political philosophy. The available English translations of Hegel's *Lectures on the Philosophy of History* should be used with caution, because the author's own notes are there interspersed with the lecture notes of students who attended his course. An excellent edition in German of Hegel's own notes for the philosophy of history is available: *Die Vernunft in der Geschichte*, edited by Johannes Hoffmeister (Hamburg: Felix Meiner, 1956). Valuable collections of Hegel's political essays and selections from various writings may be found in *The Philosophy of Hegel*, edited by C. J. Friedrich, and for the political essays, *Hegel's Political Writings*, edited by

Knox and Pelczynski. Both volumes have excellent introductions; Friedrich stresses the philosophical and Pelczynski the practical dimension of the thought of the great German master.

Several able English translations of Marx's political writings have appeared in recent years. Perhaps the most useful for the important early writings (i.e., from 1843 to 1848) is *Writings of the Young Marx on Philosophy and Society*, edited by Loyd D. Easton and Kurt H. Guddat. Tucker's recent *Marx-Engels Reader* gives a picture of Marx's thought throughout his life. Although it is sometimes difficult to separate the two men, the reader, bearing in mind that Marx was far more philosophical and creative than Engels, should take care not to confuse the formulations of one man with those of the other.

## *Plato*

*Works.* 10 vols. With an English translation. Loeb Classical Library. London: Heinemann; New York: Putnam, 1917–1929.

*The Works of Plato.* Translated into English with analyses and introductions by B. Jowett. New York: Dial Press, 1936.

*Plato.* Collected dialogues of Plato, including the letters. Edited, with introduction and prefatory notes, by Edith Hamilton and Huntington Cairns. Translated by Lane Cooper and others. New York: Pantheon Books, 1961.

*The Republic.* Translated, with introduction and notes, by Francis Macdonald Cornford. Oxford: Clarendon Press, 1941. Paperback.

——————————— Translated, with notes and an interpretive essay, by Allan Bloom. New York: Basic Books, 1968. Paperback.

*The Statesman.* Translated, with introductory essays and footnotes, by J. B. Skemp. London: Routledge and Kegan Paul, 1952. Skemp translation also available in paperback, Bobbs-Merrill, 1957.

*The Laws.* Translated by A. E. Taylor. London: J. M. Dent, 1934. Translation by T. J. Saunders available in paperback, Penguin, 1970.

*Gorgias.* Translated by W. Hamilton. Baltimore: Penguin, 1971.

*The Last Days of Socrates: Euthyphro, Apology, Crito, Phaedo.* Translated by Hugh Tredennick. Baltimore: Penguin, 1971.

*Timaeus.* Translated by Benjamin Jowett. Indianapolis: Bobbs-Merrill, 1959.

## *Aristotle*

*Works.* 12 vols. Translated into English under the editorship of W. D. Ross. Oxford: Clarendon Press, 1908–1952.

*Works.* Loeb Classical Library, Greek authors. 17 vols. Cambridge, Mass.: Harvard University Press, 1926–1965.

*Aristotle's Constitution of Athens.* Translated by Kurt von Fritz and Ernst Kapp. New York: Hafner, 1950.

*The Ethics of Aristotle* (Nichomachean). Translated by J. A. K. Thompson. London: Allen and Unwin, 1953. Thompson translation also in paperback, Penguin, 1955.

*The Politics of Aristotle.* Translated, with an introduction, notes, and appendixes, by Ernest Barker. Oxford: Clarendon Press, 1946. Paperback, 1958.

*Rhetoric.* Translated by W. Rhys Roberts. *Poetics.* Translated by Ingram Bywater. New York: Modern Library, 1954.

*Metaphysics.* Edited by Werner Jaeger. London: Oxford University Press, 1957.

*De Anima.* Translated by W. Davis Ross. London: Oxford University Press, 1961.

*Augustine*

*De Civitate Dei.* Edited by Dombart-Kalb. Leipzig: B. G. Tuebner, 1928.

*The City of God.* Translated by Marcus Dods with an introduction by Thomas Merton. New York: Modern Library, 1950. Paperback abridgement, edited by Vernon J. Bourke, introduction by E. Gilson, Anchor-Doubleday, 1958.

*Introduction to St. Augustine, The City of God.* Selections from *De Civitate Dei*, with translation and commentary by R. H. Barrow. London: Faber and Faber, 1951.

*Confessionum Libri Tredecim.* Edited by P. Knoll. Leipzig: B. G. Tuebner, 1898.

*The Confessions.* Translated by E. B. Pusey. London: J. M. Dent; New York: E. P. Dutton, 1946. Translation by R. S. Pine-Coffin available in paperback, Penguin, 1961.

*Thomas Aquinas*

*Summa Theologica.* 22 vols. Translated by the Fathers of the English Dominican Province. London: Oates and Washburne, 1912–1925.

*Basic Writings.* 2 vols. Edited and annoted, with an introduction, by Anton C. Pegis. New York: Random House, 1945.

*The Political Ideas of Thomas Aquinas: Representative Selections.* Edited, with an introduction, by Dino Bigongiari. New York: Hafner, 1953. Paperback.

*Selected Political Writings.* Edited, with an introduction, by Alexander Passerin d'Entrevès. New York: Macmillan, 1959.

*Machiavelli*

*Tutte le opere di Niccolo Machiavelli.* A cura di G. Mazzoni e Mario Casella, Firenze, 1929.

*Machiavelli: The Chief Works and Others.* 3 vols. Translated by Allan H. Gilbert. Durham, N.C.: Duke University Press, 1965.

*Literary Works: Mandragols; Clizia; A Decalogue on Language; Belfagor; with Selections from the Private Correspondence.* Edited and translated by J. R. Hale. London: Oxford University Press, 1961.

*The Art of War.* Edited with an introduction by Neal Wood. Translated by Ellis Farneworth. Indianapolis: Bobbs-Merrill, 1965. First published as *Dell'Arte della Guerra.*

*The Prince.* Translated by George Bull. Baltimore: Penguin, 1961. Paperback.

*The Discourses.* Translated by Leslie Walker. Edited, with an introduction, by Bernard Crick. Baltimore: Penguin, 1970. Paperback.

*History of Florence and of the Affairs of Italy, From the Earliest Times to the Death of Lorenzo the Magnificent.* With an introduction by Felix Gilbert. New York: Harper, 1960. First published as *Le Istorie Fiorentine.*

## Hobbes

*De Cive;* or *The Citizen.* Edited, with an introduction by Sterling P. Lamprecht. New York: Appleton-Century-Crofts, 1949. Paperback.

*Leviathan.* Edited, with an introduction by Michael Oakeshott. Oxford: Blackwell, 1951. Paperback, Dutton, 1950.

## Locke

*The Works of John Locke.* 10 vols. Aalen, Germany: Scientia Verlag, 1963. Reprint of 1823 edition.

*Letter Concerning Toleration.* Indianapolis: Bobbs-Merril, 1955. Paperback.

*Two Treatises of Government.* Edited, with notes and introduction by Peter Laslett. Cambridge University Press, 1960. Available in paperback, Mentor, 1965.

*An Essay Concerning Human Understanding.* 2 vols. New York: Dutton, 1961.

*Some Thoughts Concerning Education.* Edited by F. W. Gargorth. Woodbury, N.Y.: Barron, 1965. Paperback.

## Rousseau

*The Social Contract and Discourses.* Translated, with an introduction by G. D. H. Cole. New York: Dutton, 1950. First published as *du Contrat Social.* Paperback translation by Maurice Cranston, Penguin, 1968. A new critical edition is being prepared by Victor Gourevitch.

*The Confessions of Jean Jacques Rousseau.* 2 vols. New York: Dutton; London: Dent, 1960.

*Jean Jacques Rousseau: The Political Writings.* 2 vols. Edited by C. E. Vaughan. New York: Wiley, 1962.

## Hegel

*The Philosophy of Hegel.* Edited with an introduction by Carl J. Friedrich. New York: Modern Library, 1953. Paperback.

*Hegel's Political Writings.* Translated by T. M. Knox, with an introduction by Z. A. Pelczynski. Oxford: Clarendon Press, 1964.

*The Phenomenology of Mind.* Translated, with an introduction and notes, by J. B. Baillie. New York: Harper and Row, 1967. Paperback. First published as *Phañomenologie des Geistes.*

*The Philosophy of Right.* Translated, with notes and introduction by T. M. Knox. Oxford: Clarendon Press, 1942. Paperback. First published as *Grundlinien der Philosophie des Rechts.*

*The Philosophy of History.* Translated by J. Sibree. New York: Dover, 1956. Paperback. First published as *Vorlesungen über die Philosophie der Weltgeschichte.*

The late Johannes Hoffmeister began a new critical edition of Hegel's works. Several volumes appeared before his death, including the *Philosophie des Rechts,* published in 1953. Felix Meiner Verlag, of Hamburg, is the publisher of this series, which is being continued. Other critical editions of Hegel are also underway in Germany.

## Marx

*Historischkritische Gesamtausgabe, Werke, Schriften, Briefe.* 12 vols. Edited by D. Rjazanov under the commission of the Marx-Engels Institute, Moscow. Glashutten in Taunus: D. Anvermann, 1970.

*The Marx-Engels Reader.* Edited by Robert C. Tucker. New York: Norton, 1972. Paperback.

*Writings of the Young Marx on Philosophy and Society.* Edited and translated by Loyd D. Easton and Kurt H. Guddat. New York, Anchor-Doubleday, 1967. Paperback.

*Capital,* Vol. 1. Translated by Samuel Moore and Edward Aveling. New York: Modern Library, 1936. A complete English translation was published in Moscow.

## Some Recent Works on Approaches to Political Philosophy and Theory

A good indication of the contemporary diversity of viewpoints respecting the nature and character of political philosophy and theory may be gleaned from some of the following works.

Benn, S. I., and R. S. Peters, eds. (1959, 1965). *The Principles of Political Thought*. New York: Free Press.

Bluhm, William T. (1965). *Theories of the Political System*. Englewood Cliffs, N.J.: Prentice-Hall.

Brecht, Arnold (1959). *Political Theory: The Foundations of Twentieth-Century Political Thought*. Princeton: Princeton University Press.

Connolly, William (1967). *Political Science and Ideology*. New York: Atherton.

Cox, Richard, ed. (1967). *Politics, Political Theory, Ideology*. Belmont, Cal.: Wadsworth Press.

d'Entrèves, Alexander Passerin (1967). *The Notion of the State*. London: Oxford University Press.

Flathman, Richard (1972). *Political Obligation*. New York: Atheneum.

Germino, Dante (1967). *Beyond Ideology: The Revival of Political Theory*. New York: Harper.

Kaplan, Abraham (1964). *The Conduct of Inquiry: Methodology for Behavioral Science*. San Francisco: Chandler.

Kateb, George (1968). *Political Theory: Its Nature and Uses*. New York: St. Martin's Press.

Murphy, Joseph S. (1968). *Political Theory: A Conceptual Analysis*. Homewood, Ill.: Dorsey Press.

Oppenheim, Felix (1961). *Dimensions of Freedom: An Analysis*. New York: St. Martin's Press.

Pocock, John Greville Agard (1971). *Politics, Language and Time: Essays on Political Thought and History*. New York: Atheneum.

Young, Roland, ed. (1958). *Approaches to the Study of Politics*. Evanston, Ill.: Northwestern University Press.

### B. Recent Leading Secondary Works on the Classics of Political Philosophy

Many able studies on individual thinkers in the history of political philosophy and theory have appeared in recent years. Indeed, a kind of renaissance in interpretive scholarship has occurred in political philosophy, and never before has the student had available such an impressive array of critical scholarship to aid him in interpreting past thought. Without any pretense of being definitive, I have singled out the following secondary works as particularly useful in orienting the beginning student to the texts themselves. In addition, I have listed at the end some general histories of political thought as of possible assistance. However, there is no substitute for reading the authors of the classics themselves extensively.

## Plato and Aristotle

Morrow, Glenn (1960). *Plato's Cretan City: A Historical Interpretation of the Laws.* Princeton: Princeton University Press.

Strauss, Leo (1964). *The City and Man.* Chicago: Rand McNally.

Vlastos, Gregory, ed. (1971). *Plato: A Collection of Critical Essays*, Vol. 2. Garden City, N.Y.: Anchor-Doubleday.

Voegelin, Eric (1957). *Order and History.* Vol. 3: *Plato and Aristotle.* Baton Rouge: Louisiana State University Press.

## Augustine and Aquinas

Deane, Herbert A. (1966). *The Political and Social Ideas of St. Augustine.* New York: Columbia University Press.

Gilby, Thomas (1958). *The Political Thought of Aquinas.* Chicago: University of Chicago Press.

Pieper, Josef (1962). *Guide to St. Thomas Aquinas.* Translated by Richard and Clara Winston. New York: New American Library.

## Machiavelli

Gilbert, Felix (1965). *Machiavelli and Guicciardini.* Princeton: Princeton University Press.

Parel, Anthony, ed. (1972). *The Political Calculus: Essays on Machiavelli's Philosophy.* Toronto: University of Toronto Press.

Ridolfi, Roberto (1963). *The Life of Niccolo Machiavelli.* Chicago: University of Chicago Press.

## Hobbes

Brown, Keith C., ed. (1965). *Hobbes Studies.* Cambridge, Mass.: Harvard University Press.

Oakeshott, Michael (1951). Introduction to Hobbes's *Leviathan.* Oxford: Blackwell.

Watkins, J. W. N. (1968). *Hobbes's System of Ideas.* New York: Barnes and Noble.

## Locke

Dunn, John (1969). *The Political Thought of John Locke.* New York: Cambridge University Press.

Seliger, Martin (1969). *The Liberal Politics of John Locke.* London: Allen and Unwin.

Yolton, John W., ed. (1969). *John Locke: Problems and Perspectives.* New York: Cambridge University Press.

## Rousseau

Chapman, John W. (1956). *Rousseau—Totalitarian or Liberal?* New York: Columbia University Press.

Dodge, Guy H., ed. (1971). *Jean Jacques Rousseau: Authoritarian Libertarian?* Lexington, Mass.: D. C. Heath.

Masters, Roger (1968). *The Political Philosophy of Rousseau.* Princeton: Princeton University Press.

Shklar, Judith (1969). *Men and Citizens: A Study in Rousseau's Social Theory.* London: Cambridge University Press.

## Hegel

Avineri, Shlomo (1972). *Hegel's Theory of the Modern State.* Cambridge: Cambridge University Press.

Pelczynski, Z. A. (1964). Introduction to *Hegel's Political Writings.* Edited by T. M. Knox and Z. A. Pelczynski. New York: Oxford University Press.

## Marx

Avineri, Shlomo (1969). *The Social and Political Thought of Karl Marx.* London: Cambridge University Press.

Hypolite, Jean (1969). *Studies on Marx and Hegel.* Edited and translated by John O'Neill. New York: Basic Books.

## Recent General Works on the History of Political Philosophy

Cropsey, Joseph, and Leo Strauss, eds. (1964). *A History of Political Philosophy.* Glencoe, Ill.: Free Press.

Cumming, Robert F. (1969). *Human Nature and History: A Study in the Development of Liberal Political Thought.* 2 vols. Chicago: University of Chicago Press.

Friedrich, Carl J. (1958). *The Philosophy of Law in Historical Perspective.* Chicago: The University of Chicago Press.

Germino, Dante (1972). *Modern Western Political Thought: Machiavelli to Marx.* Chicago: Rand McNally.

Hallowell, John H. (1950). *Main Currents of Modern Political Theory.* New York: Holt.

McDonald, Lee C. (1968). *Western Political Theory from its Origins to the Present.* 3 vols. New York: Harcourt, Brace and World. Paperback.

Plamenatz, John Petrov (1963). *Man and Society: A Critical Examination of Some Important Social and Political Theories from Machiavelli to Marx.* 2 vols. London: Longmans.

Sabine, George H. (1961). *A History of Political Theory*, 3rd edition. New York: Holt.

Sibley, Mulford Q. (1971). *Political Ideas and Ideologies.* New York: Harper and Row.

Sigmund, Paul (1971). *Natural Law in Political Thought.* Cambridge, Mass.: Winthrop.

Wolin, Sheldon (1960). *Politics and Vision.* Boston: Little, Brown.

### C. Observations on Works of Recent Political Philosophy

*Continuation of the "Revival of Political Theory"*

In my study of contemporary political theory published in 1967, I identified a number of writers who in my judgment had made particularly significant contributions to what I had first referred to in 1963 as the contemporary "revival" of political theory and philosophy, after an eclipse of some decades. (Germino, 1967). For a time there was a genuine danger that critical theories of politics would be overwhelmed by a combination of sterile conformism parading as "value-free" analysis, on the one hand, and by the proliferation of unreflective, imitative ideology (whether of left, right, or center) on the other. Although that danger has hardly disappeared as this essay is being written, the intellectual situation in many parts of the world seems relatively much more open and promising for independent, critical inquiry into the basic elements and assumptions of politics than it was even twenty years ago.

The writers and teachers whom I emphasized in *Beyond Ideology* as typifying the resurgence of interest in political theory have continued to play their creative, catalytic, and/or synthetic roles. Most of them have been, or were until recently retiring, great teachers as well as significant authors, and their influence on numerous younger scholars and teachers has been felt.

*Some Leading Figures*

Hannah Arendt has continued to apply her extraordinary knowledge of the history of political thought and her gift for fruitful conceptual distinctions to problems of exceptional relevance to our contemporary condition. Her *On Violence* (1970) distinguishes between violence, force, and power, and it examines political violence from the perspective of a rich and multidimensional analysis.

Carl J. Friedrich, whose *magnum opus* Karl Deutsch hailed as "the most important work of its kind to appear during the last several decades,"[23] has since produced several additional books, including *Introduction to Political Theory* (Friedrich, 1967), and numerous articles that attest to the splendid catholicity of his interests and of his approach to the study of politics. A *Festschrift* in his honor, edited by Klaus von Beyme, was published in 1971 by

Martinus Nijhoff in The Hague. Having recently retired from his professorships at Harvard and Heidelberg, Friedrich has recently completed works entitled *The Pathology of Politics* and *Limited Government*.

Bertrand de Jouvenel has in recent years been particularly active in studies oriented toward future political trends and possibilities, and he has edited an extensive series of publications entitled *Futuribles*, published in Paris. In 1967 he published *The Art of Conjecture* in English.

Michael Oakeshott's great but relatively unknown work, *Experience and Its Modes*, originally published in 1933, was reissued by Cambridge University Press in 1966. Since his recent retirement from his chair at the London School of Economics and Political Science, Oakeshott has been at work on a major study of the nature of politics. An anthology of essays dedicated to him and edited by Preston King and B. C. Parekh was published in 1968.

Leo Strauss, whose death in October 1973 was a great loss to political philosophy, wrote an important article on "Natural Law" for the *International Encyclopedia of the Social Sciences*. Of late, he had also published *Socrates and Aristophanes* (1966) and *Liberalism: Ancient and Modern* (1968), both issued by Basic Books. In 1971 he published *Xenophon's Socratic Discourse: An Interpretation of the Oeconomicus*, which was issued by the Cornell University Press. Strauss had recently completed a book entitled *Xenophon's Socrates* (1972), also from Cornell University Press, and was working on an interpretation of Plato's *Laws* at the time of his death. He had also completed other essays and articles on different Platonic dialogues.

Eric Voegelin brought out a major work in German, *Anamnesis: Zur Theorie der Geschichte und Politik* (1966), which deals with his efforts over a number of years to achieve a reorientation of contemporary political science through a renewed philosophy of the consciousness. Voegelin has also written a number of major articles, and he brought to completion the fourth and final volume of his *Order and History*, scheduled for publication by the Louisiana State University Press in 1973. This volume contains an essay, "Equivalences of Experience and Symbolization in History," which marks a further development in his complex and evolving political philosophy. In the spring of 1971 a symposium, the proceedings of which are expected to be published, was held in his honor at the University of Notre Dame. Voegelin gave the concluding address.

With the publication of his mammoth *A Theory of Justice* in 1971, the Harvard philosophy professor John Rawls appears to have emerged as a political philosopher of the first rank among contemporary scholars. His book attempts to restate, through arguments which will carry weight in present-day philosophical circles, the contract theory of the basis for political obligation as against utilitarianism. Rawls is impressively learned, both in the history of political philosophy and in the more recent techniques of linguistic philosophy. Along with such political theorists as Felix Oppenheim (1961) and Richard Flathman (1972), Rawls has attempted to refine concepts used in political philosophy so that they may be brought to bear on current problems of political analysis.

## Theoretical Works Relevant to Current Problems

Despite the accusation one often hears of political theory's "irrelevance" to problems of practical life, one can report in recent years an increase in the number of theoretically informed works which satisfy even the most demanding criteria of "relevance." Some of these studies have not always been adequately appreciated for their intellectual content and creativity in theory construction by scholarly reviewers—if they have been reviewed in scholarly journals at all—but nonetheless they deserve inclusion in any discussion concerned with the revival of political theory. Particularly worthy of note in this respect are the following titles: Charles A. Reich, *The Greening of America* (1970); Jacques Ellul, *The Technological Society* (1967); Victor Ferkiss, *Technological Man* (1969); Amitai Etzioni, *The Active Society* (1968); Sebastian de Grazia, *Of Time, Work, and Leisure* (1964); and the late Yves Simon, *Work, Society, and Culture*, edited posthumously by Vukan Kuic (1971).

## The Radical Criticism of Society

Political philosophy or theory has always been "radical" in one sense, in that it attempts to penetrate to the roots of its own fundamental assumptions with respect to man's existence in the world and his knowledge of it. As critical, self-aware, self-conscious thought, it often finds itself in tension with the conventional wisdom of the day. What is particularly significant about the most recent period in the United States is the outpouring of political theory which is also radical in other senses: its outright opposition to and rejection of the prevailing political consciousness (or "hegemonic idea," to borrow a phrase from Antonio Gramsci), and its insistence on the need for a revolution of consciousness which would also bring about profound institutional and structural transformations.

The names of Norman O. Brown, Noam Chomsky, Paul Goodman, Christopher Lasch, Herbert Marcuse, Barrington Moore, Jr., Charles A. Reich (previously cited), and Robert Paul Wolff would be included under the rubric of philosophical-political radicalism.

Herbert Marcuse has become well known (he is almost a household word in some quarters, except that his name is often mispronounced) as the so-called father (or grandfather) of the New Left, a title to which he has taken exception. He continues to write prolifically in his retirement, and his *Essay on Liberation* (1969) is perhaps his most important recent book. Marcuse's political ideas are discussed in Paul Breines (ed.), *Critical Interruptions* (1970). Norman O. Brown's *Love's Body* (1966) is a path-breaking work with far-reaching implications for political philosophy by an author who combines insights from Freud, the Freudian tradition, early Christianity, and the world of the myth. Brown is Professor of Philosophy at Cowell College, University of California, Santa Cruz.

Currents that had been thought to have run dry and never to have left much of an impression on political theory in the United States and that now indicate a resurgence of creative activity are socialism and anarchism. *The Revival of American Socialism* (1971), edited by George Fischer, contains essays by various younger scholars who call themselves socialist and are attempting to bring about a creative rebirth of that tradition. Robert Paul Wolff in his provocative short essay, *Anarchism* (1970), attempts to demonstrate the weakness of all accepted theories of political obligation.

## *NOTES*

1.  Voegelin emigrated to the United States after the Nazi occupation of Austria and became an American citizen.
2.  I am deeply grateful to my friend, Professor Gregor Sebba of Emory University, for clarifying to me in personal correspondence some of these points about politics.
3.  On the modern opposition to the priority assigned to the *vita contemplativa* in premodern as opposed to modern thought, see Germino, 1972a, Ch. 1.
4.  Karl Marx, eleventh "Thesis on Feuerbach," in *The German Ideology* (1846): "Philosophers hitherto only *interpreted* the world in various ways; the point now is to change it."
5.  The metaphor of the diver descending into the depths is suggested by Eric Voegelin in his important essay "Equivalences of Experience and Symbolization in History," to appear in *Order and History IV* (forthcoming, L.S.U. Press).
6.  Quoted by permission of *The Review of Politics*.
7.  The late Leo Strauss, in contrast to Oakeshott, went to great lengths to argue in all his works that it is of crucial importance to come as close as possible to understanding the teaching of a political philosopher in the way that he understood it himself. I do not quarrel with this objective, but say only that it is far more difficult to achieve than Strauss appeared to acknowledge. I also dissent from Strauss's notion that we should approach the great philosophers of the past with piety and awe. After all, they too were men with limited vision. But these are minor objections; the study of political theory in recent decades would have been much the poorer without the presence of Leo Strauss.
8.  See Richard Cox's (1962, p. 266) perceptive discussion of the widespread conviction among social scientists from World War II until quite recently with respect to the presumed "obsolescence of political philosophy in its traditional form." Thus classical and Christian political *philosophers* are supposedly "normative," "utopian," "deductive," "idealistic," "moralistic," "unscientific," etc., whereas modern political *theorists*, beginning with Machiavelli and Hobbes but really getting going in the last three or four decades with positivism, behavioralism, etc., are supposedly "empirical," "realistic," "scientific," etc.

9. On the twin perils of negative and positive hypostatization of modernity, see the critique of monistic interpretations of modernity in Germino (1972a, pp. 10–15). Although following Eric Voegelin on many points, I disagree with his assessment of much of modern political thought.

10. This list is not meant to be exhaustive. Many careful students of the history of political philosophy would include the relevant works of Jean Bodin, David Hume, Montesquieu, and John Stuart Mill as worthy of citation among the major classics, and some would add the *Federalist Papers,* James Harrington's *Oceana,* Richard Hooker's *Laws of Ecclesiastical Polity,* and Vico's *New Science,* as well as others. Space limitations and the economy of this chapter require discussion of only relatively few authors, however, and I have attempted to single out those authors generally acknowledged by persons learned in the history of political thought to be preeminent as political *philosophers.* I have included no writer later than Marx among the authors of the classics for the simple reason that it is extremely difficult to know what recent or contemporary works will withstand the test of time. The passage of time and the judgment of successive generations are required for the designation of a work as of "classic" stature.

11. "Theocentric" means God-centered, "anthropocentric" man-centered; "metastatic" implies belief in the possibility of a radical, qualitative change within human existence (from the Greek *metastasis,* change of condition).

12. In this account of theocentric humanism, I am relying in part on my *Beyond Ideology: The Revival of Political Theory* (Germino, 1967, pp. 18 ff). My interpretation of the third type of humanism, here called metastatic, has obviously undergone evolution, especially with reference to Marx. Some readers might therefore wish to consult my chapter on Marx as well as my remarks on the three humanisms in Chapter 1 of my *Modern Western Political Thought.*

13. Quoted in Fred R. Dallmayr, "Phenomenology and Marxism: A Salute to Enzo Paci," to appear in George Psathas (ed.), *Phenomenology and Sociology* (Wiley, forthcoming).

14. Quoted by permission from *Modern Western Political Thought* (Chicago: Rand McNally).

15. As John Rawls has done in *A Theory of Justice,* 1971, in which he argues that differentials in wealth are justifiable *only* if they are conducive to the benefit of the least advantaged.

16. For the original meaning of *theōros,* or theorist, as an observer at the Olympic games, see Germino, 1967, p. 8.

17. This section is adapted in part from my paper, "The Relevance of the Classics," delivered to the American Political Science Association Annual Meeting, Washington, D. C., September 1972.

18. *Eupraxiá* means "right action or practice."

19. See Graham and Carey (1972) and many of the essays contained therein. The phrase "the post-behavioral era" began to be disseminated widely following David Easton's employment of it in his presidential address to the American Political Science Association in September 1969 (reprinted in the *American Political Science Review,* December 1969).

20. Eugene J. Meehan (1972, pp. 54–70) asserts that the "questions posed by traditional philosophy bear little relation to the kinds of questions for which social scien-

tists must [?] have answers" (p. 61). However, had he taken time to reflect on Aristotle's cardinal distinction between theoretical, practical, and productive knowledge, he would never have conceived "social engineering" to be a major task of a critical science of politics in the first place. Meehan's readers would have also been spared his incredibly arrogant remarks on the need for "convinc[ing] black workers . . . that they should adopt the Protestant ethic and the behavior that goes with it—punctuality, thrift, hard work, tidiness, and so on" (p. 65). Let me add at once that Meehan's essay is in no way typical of the quality of the other contributions to the volume edited by Graham and Carey, which, taken overall, superbly illustrate the increased openness of contemporary American political science to the philosophical dimension.

21. This phrase, of course, is from the title of B. F. Skinner's latest proclamation on behalf of a reductionist scientism, *Beyond Freedom and Dignity* (1971).

22. I am grateful to Alexander Passerin d'Entrevès for pointing out the relevance of these lines to the idea of the "open society" in a paper at the Villa Serbelloni, Bellagio, Italy, July 1972.

23. Karl W. Deutsch and Leroy N. Rieselbach, "Recent trends in political theory and political philosophy," *The Annals of the American Academy of Political and Social Science* 360:145. Reference is to Friedrich's *Man and Government: An Empirical Theory of Politics* (New York: McGraw-Hill, 1963).

## *REFERENCES*

Arendt, Hannah (1963). *The Human Condition*. Garden City, N.Y.: Doubleday.

────── (1970). *On Violence*. New York: Harcourt, Brace and World.

Avineri, Shlomo (1969). *The Social and Political Thought of Karl Marx*. London: Cambridge University Press.

────── (1972). *Hegel's Theory of the Modern State*. Cambridge: Cambridge University Press.

Benda, Julien (1959). *The Treason of the Intellectuals*. Translated by Richard Aldington. Boston: Beacon Press.

Benn, S. I. and R. S. Peters, eds. (1959, 1965). *The Principles of Political Thought*. New York: Free Press.

Bergson, Henri (1935). *The Two Sources of Morality and Religon*. Translated by R. Ashley Audra and Cloudesley Brereton, with the assistance of W. Horsfall Carter. New York: Holt.

Bluhm, William T. (1965). *Theories of the Political System*. Englewood Cliffs, N.J.: Prentice-Hall.

Brecht, Arnold (1959). *Poltical Theory: The Foundations of Twentieth-Century Political Thought*. Princeton: Princeton University Press.

Breines, Paul, ed. (1970). *Critical Interruptions*. New York: Herder and Herder.

Brown, Keith C., ed. (1965). *Hobbes Studies*. Cambridge, Mass.: Harvard University Press.

Brown, Norman O. (1966). *Love's Body*. New York: Random House.

Campbell, Angus, *et al.*, eds. (1966). *Elections and the Political Order.* Survey Research Center, Institute for Social Research, University of Michigan. New York: Wiley.

Chapman, John W. (1956). *Rousseau: Totalitarian or Liberal?* New York: Columbia University Press.

Connolly, William (1967). *Political Science and Ideology.* New York: Atherton.

Cox, Richard (1962). "The role of political philosophy in the theory of international relations." *Social Research* 29: 261–92.

_____, ed. (1967). *Politics, Political Theory, Ideology.* Belmont, Cal.: Wadsworth.

Crick, Bernard (1959). *The American Science of Politics.* Berkeley: University of California Press.

Croce, Benedetto (1925). *Elementi di Politica.* Bari: Laterza.

Cumming, Robert F. (1969). *Human Nature and History: A Study in the Development of Liberal Political Thought*, 2 vols. Chicago: University of Chicago Press.

Dahl, Robert (1968). "Truth and consequences." In Robert Dahl and D. Neubauer (eds.), *Readings in Modern Political Analysis.* Englewood Cliffs, N.J.: Prentice-Hall.

Dallmayr, Fred R. (1973). "Phenomenology and Marxism: a salute to Enzo Paci." In George Psathas (ed.), *Phenomenology and Sociology.* New York: Wiley.

Deane, Herbert A. (1966). *The Political and Social Ideas of St. Augustine.* New York: Columbia University Press.

d'Entrèves, Alexander Passerin (1967). *The Notion of the State.* London: Oxford University Press.

de Grazia, Sebastian (1964). *Of Time, Work, and Leisure.* Garden City, N.Y.: Doubleday.

de Jouvenel, Bertrand (1948, 1949). *On Power: Its Nature and the History of its Growth.* Translated by J. F. Huntington. New York: Viking.

_____ (1957, 1959). *On Sovereignty: An Inquiry into the Political Good.* Translated by J. F. Huntington. Chicago: University of Chicago Press.

Deutsch, Karl W., and Leroy N. Rieselbach (1965). "Recent trends in political theory and political philosophy." *The Annals of the American Academy of Political and Social Science* 360: 139–62.

Dexter, Lewis (1963). "The representative and his district." In Nelson W. Polsby and Robert L. Peabody (eds.), *New Perspectives on the House of Representatives.* Chicago: Rand McNally.

Dodge, Guy H., ed. (1971). *Jean-Jacques Rousseau: Authoritarian Libertarian?* Lexington, Mass.: D. C. Heath.

Dunn, John (1969). *The Political Thought of John Locke.* New York: Cambridge University Press.

Easton, David (1953). *The Political System.* New York: Knopf.

_____, ed. (1966). *Varieties of Political Theory.* Englewood Cliffs, N.J.: Prentice-Hall.

_____ (1969). "The new revolution in political science." *American Political Science Review* 63: 1051–61.

Ellul, Jacques (1967). *The Technological Society.* New York: Random House.

Etzioni, Amitai (1968). *The Active Society.* New York: Free Press.

Eulau, Heinz (1964). *The Behavioral Persuasion in Politics.* New York: Random House.

Ferkiss, Victor (1969). *Technological Man.* New York: Braziller.

Fetscher, Iring (1971). *Marx and Marxism.* New York: Herder and Herder.

Fischer, George, ed. (1971). *The Revival of American Socialism.* New York: Oxford.

Flathman, Richard E. (1972). *Political Obligation.* New York: Atheneum.

Fleischer, M., ed. (1972). *Machiavelli and the Nature of Political Theory.* New York: Atheneum.

Friedrich, Carl J. (1963). *Man and His Government: An Empirical Theory of Politics.* New York: McGraw-Hill.

──────── (1967). *An Introduction to Political Theory: Twelve Lectures at Harvard.* New York: Harper and Row.

Germino, Dante (1967). *Beyond Ideology: The Revival of Political Theory.* New York: Harper.

──────── (1972a). *Modern Western Political Thought: Machiavelli to Marx.* Chicago: Rand McNally.

──────── (1972b). "Some observations on recent political philosophy and theory." *The Annals of the American Academy of Political and Social Science* 400: 140–8.

Gilbert, Felix (1965). *Machiavelli and Guicciardini.* Princeton: Princeton University Press.

Gilby, Thomas (1958). *The Political Thought of Thomas Aquinas.* Chicago: University of Chicago Press.

Graham, George J., Jr., and George W. Carey, eds. (1972). *The Post-Behavioral Era.* New York: McKay.

Gramsci, Antonio (1966). *Il materialismo storico e la filosofia di Benedetto Croce*, 8th edition. Turin: Eianadi.

Hallowell, John H. (1950). *Main Currents of Modern Political Thought.* New York: Holt.

Hartz, Louis (1955). *The Liberal Tradition in America.* New York: Harcourt, Brace.

Hypolite, Jean. (1969). *Studies on Marx and Hegel.* Edited and translated by John O'Neill. New York: Basic Books.

Kaplan, Abraham (1964). *The Conduct of Inquiry: Methodology for Behavioral Science.* San Francisco: Chandler.

Kateb, George (1968). *Political Theory: Its Nature and Uses.* New York: St. Martin's Press.

Kuhn, Thomas S. (1962). *The Structure of Scientific Revolutions.* Chicago: University of Chicago Press.

Lichtheim, George (1967). *The Concept of Ideology.* New York: Random House.

Lonergan, Bernard J. (1957). *Insight: A Study of Human Understanding.* London: Longmans; New York: Green.

McDonald, Lee C. (1968). *Western Political Theory from its Origins to the Present.* New York: Harcourt, Brace and World.

Marcuse, Herbert (1969). *An Essay on Liberation.* Boston: Beacon Press.

Masters, Roger (1968). *The Political Philosophy of Rousseau.* Princeton: Princeton University Press.

Meehan, Eugene J. (1972). "What should political scientists be doing?" In George J. Graham and George W. Carey (eds.), *The Post-Behavioral Era.* New York: McKay.

Morgenthau, Hans (1970). *Truth and Power: Essays of a Decade, 1960–1970.* New York: Praeger.

Morrow, Glenn (1960). *Plato's Cretan City: A Historical Interpretation of the Laws.* Princeton: Princeton University Press.

Murphy, Joseph S. (1968). *Political Theory: A Conceptual Analysis.* Homewood, Ill.: Dorsey Press.

Northrop, F. S. C. (1966). *The Meeting of East and West.* New York: Collier.

Oakeshott, Michael (1933, 1966). *Experience and Its Modes.* Cambridge: Cambridge University Press.

_____ (1951). *Introduction to Hobbes' Leviathan.* Oxford: Blackwell.

Oppenheim, Felix (1961). *Dimensions of Freedom: An Analysis.* New York: St. Martin's Press.

Pieper, Josef (1962). *Guide to St. Thomas Aquinas.* Translated by Richard and Clara Winston. New York: New American Library.

Pocock, John Greville Agard (1971). *Politics, Language and Time: Essays on Political Thought and History.* New York: Atheneum.

Polanyi, Michael (1960). *Personal Knowledge: Towards a Post-Critical Philosophy.* Chicago: University of Chicago Press.

Rawls, John (1971). *A Theory of Justice.* London: Oxford University Press.

Reich, Charles A. (1970). *The Greening of America.* New York: Random House.

Ridolfi, Roberto (1963). *The Life of Niccolo Machiavelli.* Chicago: University of Chicago Press.

Sabine, George H. (1961). *A History of Political Theory*, 3rd edition. New York: Holt.

Seliger, Martin (1969). *The Liberal Politics of John Locke.* London: Allen and Unwin.

Shklar, Judith (1969). *Men and Citizens: A Study of Rousseau's Social Theory.* London: Cambridge University Press.

Sibley, Mulford Q. (1971). *Political Ideas and Ideologies.* New York: Harper and Row.

Sigmund, Paul (1971). *Natural Law in Political Thought.* Cambridge, Mass.: Winthrop.

Simon, Yves (1971). *Work, Society, and Culture.* Edited by Vukan Kuic. New York: Fordham University Press.

Skinner, B. F. (1971). *Beyond Freedom and Dignity.* New York: Knopf.

Stokes, Donald E., and Warren E. Miller (1966). "Party government and the saliency of Congress." In Angus Campbell *et al.* (eds.), *Elections and the Political Order.* Survey

Research Center, Institute for Social Research, University of Michigan. New York: Wiley.

Strauss, Leo (1953). *Natural Right and History.* Chicago: University of Chicago Press.

———— (1964). *The City and Man.* Chicago: Rand McNally.

———— (1966). *Socrates and Aristophanes.* New York: Basic Books.

———— (1968). *Liberalism: Ancient and Modern.* New York: Basic Books.

———— (1971). *Xenophon's Socratic Discourse: An Interpretation of the Oeconomicus.* Ithaca, N.Y.: Cornell University Press.

Strauss, Leo, and Joseph Cropsey, eds. (1964). *History of Political Philosophy.* Glencoe, Ill.: Free Press.

Thompson, Kenneth W. (1967). "The empirical, normative, and theoretical foundations of international relations." *The Review of Politics* 29: 147–59.

Vlastos, Gregory, ed. (1971). *Plato: A Collection of Critical Essays*, Vol. 2. Modern Studies in Philosophy Series. Garden City, N.Y.: Anchor-Doubleday.

Voegelin, Eric (1952). *The New Science of Politics.* Chicago: University of Chicago Press.

———— (1956), 1957). *Order and History*, 3 vols. Baton Rouge: Louisiana State University Press.

———— (1966). *Anamnesis: Zur Theorie der Geschichte und Politik.* Munich: Piper Verlag.

Wahlke, John C., and Heinz Eulau, eds. (1962). *The Legislative System: Explorations in Legislative Behavior.* New York: Wiley.

Watkins, J. W. N. (1968). *Hobbes's System of Ideas.* New York: Barnes and Noble.

Weber, Max (1950). *The Protestant Ethic and the Spirit of Capitalism.* Translated by T. Parsons. New York: Scribner.

Wolff, Robert Paul (1970). *Anarchism.* New York: Harper.

Wolin, Sheldon (1960). *Politics and Vision.* Boston: Little, Brown.

———— (1972). "Politics as a Vocation." In M. Fleischer (ed.), *Machiavelli and the Nature of Political Theory.* New York: Atheneum.

Yolton, John W., ed. (1969). *John Locke: Problems and Perspectives.* New York: Cambridge University Press.

Young, Roland, ed. (1958). *Approaches to the Study of Politics.* Evanston, Ill.: Northwestern University Press.

# 4
# THE LANGUAGE OF POLITICAL INQUIRY:
## PROBLEMS OF CLARIFICATION

FELIX E. OPPENHEIM

The language of political inquiry has long been the language of everyday life, as used by politicians and citizens. Utterances in everyday language, especially about politics, tend to be imprecise and emotive and as such detrimental to the scientific study of politics. It is true that political scientists have lately adopted more and more technical terms such as 'political culture', 'role', 'socialization', 'equilibrium', and 'function'.[1] Why, then, have they not abandoned everyday language altogether and taken up an entirely technical vocabulary, like their colleagues in the natural sciences and even in economics? Because political thought and action have been traditionally tied to such nontechnical concepts as authority, legitimacy, democracy, liberty, equality, justice, each with its own history—a heritage that cannot simply be brushed aside. Furthermore, concepts in ordinary language often correspond to distinctions essential for comprehending the richness and nuances of political life, which an entirely technical language could hardly hope to capture. We do distinguish in ordinary discourse between competition and conflict, persuasion and bargaining, preference and interest. Awareness of the implicit rules governing such usages is a necessary prelude to an understanding of political phenomena.

Yet political science cannot effectively use the language of everyday life as it stands. To adapt ordinary discourse for scientific purposes, one must make explicit the rules governing the use of its concepts, sharpen the criteria of their application, reduce their vagueness and eliminate their ambiguity, and hence sometimes modify their meaning.

---

The whole chapter benefited from William E. Connolly's constructive criticism, the more so as it stemmed from a different point of view. I am grateful to him for all his help, and also to Hugo A. Bedau, A. James Gregor, and J. Donald Moon for their critical comments on an earlier drafts.

Clarifying the language of political inquiry consists, then, in constructing an adequate scientific language out of elements of ordinary discourse. This task involves explicating the basic concepts, analyzing the logical structure of the statements, and investigating the logical relationships between those statements. I shall deal principally with the explication of basic concepts but I shall engage in the actual elaboration of definitions only to illustrate the more general problems of conceptual analysis. I shall not pay close attention to the more technical concepts, even though they, too, are often in need of elucidation. I believe that the analysis of concepts such as power, freedom, and authority will reveal more effectively the problems of clarification. I hope to show that the elucidation of the language of political science is by no means an idle exercise in semantics, but in many instances a most effective way to solve substantive problems of political research.

There are few works dealing with the analysis of the language of political science as a whole. Lasswell and Kaplan's seminal work (1950), now more than twenty years old, supplies definitions of many important political concepts but does not deal with other aspects of the logic of political discourse. More recent works by Weldon (1953), Simon (1957), Benn and Peters (1959), Hart (1961), Oppenheim (1961), Barry (1965), and Flathman (1966 and 1972) represent efforts to provide a more complete analysis of a smaller number of the many concepts central to political theory. (The *Nomos* volumes should also be mentioned in this connection.) Nagel (1961) and Kaplan (1964) are concerned with problems of linguistic analysis other than (and as well as) definitional, but in the context of the social sciences generally rather than of political science specifically. Gregor (1971) is perhaps the only recent work dealing with our topic. Fortunately, however, if we look to the writings of analytic philosophers over the past generation, we will find a great deal of linguistic analysis relevant to the subject that is missing from the writings of political scientists themselves. For this reason, this essay will include more references to the work of philosophers than of political scientists, and one of its purposes is to acquaint the latter with the relevant trends in analytic philosophy. We can expect that during the next decade political scientists will avail themselves more and more of the tools of analytic philosophy to clarify their own language and thus to increase the effectiveness of their research.

## *I. DESCRIPTIVE POLITICAL CONCEPTS IN GENERAL*

For the moment, I shall presuppose a fundamental distinction between the language of factual and of normative political inquiry and shall consider later (Section V) arguments which qualify that distinction.

## A. Choice of Concepts

Which are the concepts that are to be taken over from ordinary language into the language of political science? Although logically speaking the choice of a concept is arbitrary, there are nevertheless certain objective criteria by which to assess its fruitfulness for scientific purposes. This situation may be illustrated by the concept of power, which fulfills all the following conditions of fruitfulness for political science. (1) It refers to phenomena which are of central interest to political inquiry. According to Lasswell and Kaplan, "Political science, as an empirical discipline, is the study of the shaping and sharing of power" (1950, p. xiv; see also Simon, 1957, p. 5). If so, power should be taken as *the* pivotal concept in political science. Although some writers have recently questioned the centrality of the concept of power (e.g., Easton, 1968, p. 283; Eulau, 1968, p. 208; March, 1966; Riker, 1964), few would deny that the language of political science must include it as *one* of the basic notions. (2) The concept of power draws attention to the behavioral aspects of politics. We shall see that it can be defined in terms of certain relationships of interaction. (3) It has a wide range of applicability. It covers a great variety of interpersonal and intergroup relations, political and nonpolitical, governmental and other. It thus brings out the similarity among various kinds of power phenomena. (4) As we shall see, the concept of power can be linked by a network of definitions to other basic political notions which help to define it or which it helps to define. (5) The concept of power has great explanatory force, because it is highly abstract and theoretical, and because statements about power implicitly refer to causal relations between actors and their respective actions. (6) The notion of power has great "systematic import"; i.e., it

> lend[s] itself to the formulation of general laws or theoretical principles which reflect uniformities in the subject matter under study, and which thus provide a basis for explanation, prediction, and generally scientific understanding. (Hempel, 1965, p. 146)

Indeed, a relatively great number and variety of empirical generalizations are concerned with political power. For example: "Power will determine the distribution of nearly all the surplus possessed by a society" (Lenski, 1966, p. 44). "Privilege is largely a function of power" (*ibid.*, p. 45). "The greater one's resources, the greater one's power" (Dahl, 1968, p. 409). "A major objective of all actors in the political process is the use and development of power . . ." (Gross, 1968, p. 268).

Yet these conditions are not decisive. In general, investigators first decide on a topic which they consider worth investigating, and that selection in turn determines their choice of concepts.

> A concept is introduced into language when certain kinds of phenomena are selected for attention. . . . We cannot give any recipes for selecting the concepts and finding the hypotheses to which the method of science is then applied. (Brodbeck, 1968, pp. 8–9)

In political science, the choice of topic itself is often influenced by normative considerations. For example, an investigator who is concerned with the question of responsibility for political decisions is likely, for this reason, to adopt power as a key note (Connolly, 1970). In general, controversies in political science focus less on whether or not a concept should be adopted than on the way it should be defined.

### B. Logical Structure of Concepts

After deciding to take a concept from everyday language into the vocabulary of political science, we want to determine its meaning. Now one might think that the meaning of a *concept* (e.g., of freedom) is the meaning of the *word* ('freedom') by which it is expressed. First of all, the fact that a given concept (e.g., of freedom) can often be expressed by several synonymous words ('freedom', 'liberty', 'liberté', etc.) is one reason that we are concerned with the analysis of concepts rather than of words or terms. Second, meaning can usually not be attached to words in isolation; it adheres only to sentences in which the words typically occur. Words like 'length' and 'freedom' do not have meaning; expressions like 'the length of $x$ is $y$ units' and 'with respect to $P, Q$ is free to do $x$' do.

Before we can determine the meaning of a concept, we must uncover its logical structure; and to do so we must specify the type of sentence by which the concept is generally expressed. Before we can *define* a concept, we must exhibit the *expression to be defined*. Let us consider some illustrations of this procedure.

*1. Property concepts.* In logic, a property is anything which can be asserted or predicated of something else. Thus, in the expressions '$x$ is green', '$x$ is a law', '$x$ is President of the United States', the words after '$x$ is . . .' express in each case properties, regardless of whether, grammatically, they are adjectives or nouns. Democracy, too, is a property concept; i.e., the word 'democracy' stands for a property, namely, one which can be attributed to human organizations like trade unions, universities, or large-scale political organizations. To define the concept of democracy is to say what property it is that we attribute to an organization when we say that it is democratic. Not 'democracy' but '$x$ is democratic' (or '$x$ is a democracy') is the expression to be introduced into the language of political science (and later to be defined).[2] Egalitarianism is another example of a property concept. In the expression 'x is egalitarian', the variable x typically refers to certain kinds of rules of distribution (legal or moral or customary).

**2. Relational concepts.** The concept of equality refers neither to a "thing" nor to a property (unlike the concept of egalitarianism), but to a relation, like the concepts of heavier than or between. Again, the corresponding terms cannot be taken in isolation but must be considered contextually: '$x$ is heavier than $y$'; '$x$ is between $y$ and $z$'. In the case of equality, the expression typically to be examined is: '$P$ and $Q$ are equal with respect to characteristic $x$', where the variables $P$ and $Q$ refer to objects (often to persons) and $x$ refers to characteristics such as age, sex, citizenship, income, need. To say that $P$ and $Q$ are equal with respect to age or need means simply that they have the same age or need (Bedau, 1967). But "all men are equal" is an incomplete statement, if taken literally. (It is usually meant to express the *normative* principle that governments should grant all citizens the same rights.)

Power, another relational concept, refers to a relationship of interaction, which can be construed as: '$P$ has power over $Q$ with respect to $x$', where $P$ and $Q$ stand for actors (persons or groups) and $x$ for an action of $Q$ (actual or potential). Failure to take all three variables into account, e.g., to specify the range of $Q$'s activities over which $P$ is said to have power, "often leads political observers astray" (Dahl, 1970, p. 24).

Perhaps less obviously, the concepts of social and political freedom and unfreedom, too, designate relationships of interaction. Thus the latter (which is the simpler one) must be construed as follows: 'With respect to $P$, $Q$ is unfree to do $x$'. This means, as we shall see later, that $P$ makes it either impossible or punishable for $Q$ to do $x$. Although we tend to think of citizens being unfree primarily with respect to government (e.g., to choose their religion or occupation), we must keep in mind that, as with power, the variables $P$ and $Q$ can range over actors of any kind, and that $P$ may use other than legal devices to make $Q$ unfree to act in a certain way. Similar considerations apply to the concept of political freedom: With respect to $P$, $Q$ is free to do or not to do $x$ (Oppenheim, 1961, p. 113). Authority and legitimacy, if taken in the legal sense, are also relational concepts. Here the expressions to be defined are: 'according to legal system $S$, $P$ (or any person $P$ occupying a certain office) has authority over $Q$ with respect to $Q$'s doing $x$'; 'according to legal system $S$, $P$ is the legitimate government over territory $Q$'.

**3. One term for several concepts.** I have mentioned that several terms in current language (e.g., 'freedom' and 'liberty') may refer to the same political concept; conversely, one and the same word may cover different concepts in the language of political science. We have seen that the ordinary word 'equality' is used in the sense of both equality of personal characteristics and an egalitarian rule of distribution. Benn questions the view that power is a relational concept, since "we talk about . . . the power of speech, about seeking power as a means to future enjoyment (Hobbes), or about power as 'the production of intended effects' (Russell)" (1967b, p. 424). The reply is that 'power' in ordinary language can refer either to an actor's power over another actor's activity (a relationship of interaction) or—as in Benn's examples—to an actor's ability to do something (which is, incidentally, also a relational concept, namely, between an actor and his own potential action: '$P$ has the power to do $x$'). Even though both expressions contain the word 'power', they stand for two different concepts, with different logical structures and meanings.

The word 'freedom' is used in ordinary language to refer to at least four different concepts.

a. *Social or political freedom*, the relationship of interaction mentioned above.

b. *Freedom of choice*, "the power of acting or not acting, according to the determinations of the will" (Hume, *Human Understanding*, Sec. 8, Pt. 1). The distinction between (a) and (b) parallels that between the two senses of 'power' just discussed. '$Q$ has freedom of choice with respect to $x$' means that $Q$ can do $x$; otherwise he lacks freedom of choice in this respect. It is ambiguous to say that "when someone . . . has the power to do or not to do something . . . he is said to be free to do so" (Friedrich, 1963, p. 351). He has *freedom of choice* in this respect (i.e., he can do it), but he may be *unfree to do so* with respect to someone who would punish him if he did. Most people have freedom of choice to commit most crimes, but they are unfree to commit them with respect to government. Vice versa, I may be free (with respect to everyone) to become a physician, but I lack freedom of choice in this respect, because I cannot stand the sight of blood—let alone go through medical training. Inability to do something is an instance of unfreedom to do so with respect to another actor only if the latter caused the former's incapacity.[3] Consider the "four freedoms." To advocate freedom of speech is to oppose governmental sanctions against citizens' utterances of any kind. To demand freedom from want is not to champion political freedom of any kind, but to demand that those now unable to secure the necessities of life (i.e., lacking freedom of choice in this respect) be enabled to do so. (As a matter of fact, "freedom from want" usually requires governmental limitations of certain individual freedoms, such as to dispose of income.) Civil liberties and social welfare are different concepts, standing for different goals.

c. *Feeling free*. To say that freedom is "the absence of obstacles to the realization of desires" (Russell, 1940, p. 251) is ambiguous, because the reference here is to still another concept of freedom. Political liberty consists in not being prevented from, or punished for, doing something which one may or may not desire. In this sense, it is not paradoxical to say that we are (with respect to most others) free to cut off our ears (contrary to Benn and Weinstein, 1971, p. 195). Furthermore, some *feel* free to the extent to which they *are left* free to do many things, *including* those they want to do. Others feel free provided that the only things they are made unfree to do are those they would not want to do anyhow. Effectively indoctrinated citizens in a totalitarian system may feel very free, even though they are socially unfree to deviate from the official party line.

d. *Free actions.* That $Q$ is, with respect to $P$, free to do $x$ (or that he is unfree to do so) does not imply that he can, that he wants to, or that he does do $x$. If $P$ makes it punishable for $Q$ to do $x$, $Q$ is unfree to do $x$, whether he does $x$ and suffers the penalty or whether he abstains from doing $x$, and if the latter, whether he refrains on his own accord (e.g., because he deems doing $x$ immoral) or out of fear of punishment. Cassinelli (1966, p. 34) considers it "logically most cumbersome" to say that "a man is unfree to perform an activity that he in fact performs." He evidently confuses social unfreedom and lack of freedom of choice. However, 'free' and 'unfree' may also designate characteristics of actions. An action may be said to be unfree if it is motivated by fear of punishment; otherwise it is free. In this sense, committing a crime in spite of some threatened penalty is a free action. Not committing a crime may be a free or an unfree action, depending on the motive; it is free unless motivated by fear of sanctions.

Since the word 'freedom' stands for such a variety of concepts, it is highly ambiguous to say that "America is a free society" or "men possess freedom" or "$P$ is free" without specifying whether one means to refer to social freedom (and one must then specify with respect to whom he is free to do what) or to any of the other three concepts to which this everyday language term may refer.

## II. THE ROLE OF EXPLICATION

After having chosen certain concepts to be taken over from ordinary speech into the language of political science—or rather of some particular area of political research—and after having expressed them in a way which clearly reveals their logical structure, we must next determine their meaning. Now "the meaning of a word is its use in a language" (Wittgenstein, 1953, par. 43; cf. Parkinson, 1968, p. 12). Hence to specify the meaning of a *word* is to construct a definition for an *expression* in which it typically occurs. We have seen that the vocabulary of politics is made up largely of relational terms, and that such words must be defined, not in isolation, but contextually. For example, to ascertain the meaning of the concept of power is to define not the word 'power' but the expression '$P$ has power over $Q$ with respect to $x$' (cf. Gregor, 1971, pp. 136–137).

## A. Kinds of Definition

According to a venerable philosophical tradition going back to Plato, meaning is a characteristic of things rather than of words, and to define a concept is to discover the true meaning or essence of its referent. A definition which is valid constitutes a truth which is certain. Political reality is revealed, not through empirical investigation, but by answering such questions as: What *is* the state? What is the "true nature" of sovereignty? What is the "essence" of freedom?—as if somewhere in the universe, but outside empirical reality, there existed such abstract entities as the state, sovereignty, freedom, to be captured through definitional scrutiny. This approach has been rightly criticized as involving the fallacy of reification, i.e., of treating property concepts like justice or relational concepts like freedom "as though they were proper names and denoted abstract entities . . . in much the same way as proper names denote individuals" (Pap, 1949, p. 507; see also Oppenheim, 1961, p. 13).

In opposition to classical essentialism, modern formalism holds that meanings are attached to linguistic expressions, not to things, and that definitions specify the meanings of the expressions to be defined. Accordingly, definitions do not convey "new" information about "reality" but embody rules governing the use of linguistic symbols. Here we must distinguish several kinds of definitions.

***1. Stipulative definitions.*** A stipulative or nominal definition "may be characterized as a stipulation to the effect that a specified expression, the *definiendum*, is to be synonymous with a certain other expression, the *definiens*, whose meaning is already determined" (Hempel, 1952, p. 2). Stipulative definitions are typically provided for technical terms. For example, Dahl (1963, p. 73) stipulates that "we shall use as interchangeable the terms 'popular government' and 'polyarchy'." He proposes to define the technical term 'polyarchy' by the expression 'popular government', presuming that the meaning of the latter (the *definiens*), couched in ordinary language, is already clear. A stipulative definition cannot be true or false, since it constitutes a speaker's or writer's arbitrary decision to use synonymously two linguistic symbols, a newly introduced term and a familiar expression.

***2. Explicative definitions.*** We are concerned mainly with expressions taken into the language of political science from ordinary language, rather than with newly introduced technical terms. Such concepts as authority, liberty, and democracy (unlike polyarchy) are generally "understood." Why do they have to be defined nevertheless? Because their meaning in everyday discourse tends to be vague and ambiguous. To be suitable for the purpose of political science, they must be provided with explicative definitions.

Taking its departure from the customary meanings of the terms, explication aims at reducing the limitations, ambiguities, and inconsistencies of their ordinary usage by propounding a reinterpretation intended to enhance the clarity and precision of their meanings as well as their ability to function in hypotheses and theories with explanatory and predictive force. (Hempel, 1952, p. 12)

Thus, after having defined the technical term 'polyarchy' by the ordinary-language expression 'popular government', Dahl (1963, p. 73) in turn defines 'popular government' as a political system "in which power over state officials is widely, though by no means equally, shared." Although both the *definiendum* and the *definiens* are expressed in everyday language, the latter narrows down, clarifies, *explicates* the meaning of the former. Explications of the concepts chosen may be judged more or less adequate by certain standards to be discussed shortly.

*3. Reportative definitions.* The purpose of definitions such as those which make up a dictionary is to report the meaning actually attached by a certain group to the words listed. Other examples of reportative definitions are: 'Freedom' in Rousseau means obedience to the general will. 'Democracy', as used in the United States, refers to a competitive party system as an essential, defining characteristic, whereas in Yugoslavia the same term refers primarily to workers' participation in the management of economic enterprises. Reportative definitions are always based on empirical statements about linguistic habits. Thus their basis is empirically either true or false. As will be shown, explicative definitions of political concepts must sometimes deviate from the commonly accepted usage reported by the lexicon.

### B. Methods of Explication

Contemporary political science has been influenced by several philosophical movements, all of which have some bearing on the question: What conditions must an explicative definition meet to fulfill its function? Here we shall ask to what extent these various approaches have contributed to a satisfactory answer to this problem.

*1. Empiricism.* In its broadest sense, empiricism is the view that objective factual knowledge is based on data which are intersubjectively ascertainable through sense experience. Radical empiricism of the early twentieth century held that a sentence has empirical (as opposed to purely logical) meaning if and only if it can be tested by experiential evidence. In the classical formulation of Schlick (1936): "The meaning of a proposition is the method of its verification." It soon became apparent that such a stringent criterion would make it necessary to ban from the language of science as factually meaningless all universal laws, since "no sentence of the form 'all *s* is *p*' . . . where *s* denotes an infinite set . . . can be verified by any finite number of observations" (Berlin, 1938, p. 21). Assertions like 'My toothache is more violent than yours' would also have to be excluded, since "each observer . . . can vouch for the occurrence or non-occurrence only of events in his own experience" *(ibid.,* p. 32).

In the light of such criticisms, modern empiricists assign factual meaning also to assertions which are only indirectly testable by observation, i.e., which can somehow be linked to statements "that could, at least in principle, be shown to be true or false, or to some degree probable, by reference to empirical observations" (Ashby, 1967, p. 240).

**2. Behaviorism.** Proponents of radical behaviorism applied the principles of radical empiricism to the study of human behavior. This movement arose as a reaction against the "subjectivism of introspectionist psychology" (Kaufman, 1967, p. 268). Since overt movements are the only human events which are publicly observable, psychology was to be concerned solely with the observation of overt responses to external stimuli. This approach would have to proscribe as unscientific the study of verbal behavior (an especially important component of politics) and of such mental phenomena as beliefs, preferences, wants, feelings of deprivation (also of particular significance in the context of politics, as we shall see). Surely, speaking and writing (e.g., legislating), believing and choosing cannot be viewed simply as bodily movements. In line with the shift from radical to modern empiricism, behaviorism was soon willing to consider such phenomena as "intervening variables" between observable stimulus and response, and to readmit corresponding concepts referring to mental states into the language of science, provided that they could be *defined* in terms of expressions containing only nonmentalistic terms. Later on, even those who denied this possibility were no longer willing to proscribe concepts such as intentions, preferences, and wants from the vocabulary of the sciences of individual or collective behavior. Modern behaviorism, like present-day logical empiricism, puts the main emphasis on the unity of *method* of all the empirical sciences.

> What unites behavioral science to physical and biological science is not that the "behavior" it studies is physical and biological, but that the study itself is, like the other sciences, an empirical one. (Kaplan, 1964, p. 79)

Behaviorism in political science arose as reaction "against what was felt to be an unduly historical-descriptive, legal-formal, or normative orientation in the study of government and politics" (Eulau, 1968, p. 204). Contemporary political scientists of the "behavioral persuasion" (Eulau, 1963) have shifted from radical to modern behaviorism, and for this reason some prefer to call themselves behavior*al*ists.

> As far as I know, there is probably no one in political science who would consider himself a behavorist. . . . I know of no one associated with political research who has advocated a position that even begins to approximate so rigid an exclusion of subjective data. Ideas, motives, feelings, attitudes, all appear as important variables. (Easton, 1967, p. 12. The distinction between behaviorism and behavioralism is also emphasized by Sibley, 1967, p. 52, and Berelson, 1968, p. 44.)

In other words, political science is not primarily interested in political *behavior* in the strict sense, describable and explainable as response movements to external stimuli. Political science is concerned with political *action*, characterized in terms of such mental concepts as beliefs, motives, intentions, preferences, choices—and these cannot in turn be explicated in terms of publicly observable events (cf. White, 1968, especially the introduction; Care and Landesman, 1968; Flathman, 1962, p. xvi). There is hardly a political scientist who would question behavioralism in this broad sense, which admits concepts referring to mental states. The emphasis of political behavioralism, too, has been on unity of science: Political behavior is one species of behavior; political science is one of the behavioral sciences; all behavioral sciences use the method of all empirical sciences (see the list of "the intellectual foundation stones" of political behavioralism in Easton, 1965a, p. 7).

*3. Operationalism.* As another outgrowth of empiricism, operationalism is concerned more particularly with the requirements of explicative definitions of scientific terms. In its original form, operationalism

> maintained that every scientifically meaningful concept must be capable of full definition in terms of performable physical operations and that a scientific concept is nothing more than the set of operations entering into its definition. (Schlesinger, 1967, p. 544)

For example, '$x$ is harder than $y$' means that $x$ scratches $y$ and not vice versa. Operationalism in this strict sense would ban from scientific language dispositional and theoretical concepts which are of special importance in science.

Dispositional predicates, like 'soluble', refer to a disposition of something to exhibit certain characteristics under specified conditions, which may or may not actually be realized in a given instance. We do not hesitate to say that a lump of sugar is soluble in water, even without performing the appropriate "operation."

Hence, an operational definition of a concept will have to be understood as ascribing the concept to all cases that *would* exhibit the characteristic response if the test conditions *should* be realized. (Hempel, 1965, p. 126)

As I shall point out later, many basic political concepts are dispositional.

As with empiricism and behaviorism, the original thesis of operationalism has been relaxed under the pressure of philosophical analysis. It is not possible to state the exact relationship which must exist between a theoretical concept and observable phenomena in order to consider it operational. The emphasis is on negative criteria. "That which is conceptualized need not be completely defined in terms of operations, although it must make contact with the world of public experience" (Schlesinger, 1967, p. 545).

There is a tendency among some researchers to hold others (but not themselves) to operational requirements that no research project could approximate. It might be thought that this analysis, combined with this tendency, constitutes a good argument for dropping altogether references to an "operational requirement." I think not. One can resist such tendencies without losing the advantages that operationalism, even in its relaxed form, provides. For the revised thesis still does eliminate some definitions from empirical political science, namely, those which cannot be linked even indirectly to observational evidence. In this context, the operational requirement may even be considered especially relevant, since political concepts have so often been defined with the help of value words; e.g., freedom by 'what one *ought* to do'; rights by '*just* claims'; the public interest by 'the common *good*'. (Further examples will be given in V, D, 2.) Unless one holds that the underlined value words can in turn be definitionally linked to descriptive terms, one must conclude that such definitions fail to meet the operational requirement even in the broadest sense. The operational approach exhorts political scientists to try to replace such valuational definitions as far as possible by explications which specify precisely the observations necessary for their applications, and thereby to salvage the concepts in question for empirical political inquiry.

**4. Verstehen.** The most recent influential opponents of the behavior approach are proponents of *Verstehen* (the German word for intuitive understanding, as opposed to knowledge based on inductive and deductive reasoning, or *Wissen*). Early *Verstehen* advocates often supported introspection as the best method for formulating and testing hypotheses about human conduct. Today most proponents of this approach hold that the appropriate method of inquiry into human affairs is to comprehend the agent's conduct, not by introspecting one's own motives, but by ascertaining the rules of conduct *he* is following. The investigator's central task is to learn the purposes the agent seeks to promote and to understand the reasons he invokes or could invoke within his particular social setting to justify his action as an appropriate response. Indeed,

> The same overt behavior (say, a tribal pageant as it can be captured by the movie camera) may have an entirely different meaning to the performers. What interests the scientist is merely whether it is a war dance, a barter trade, the reception of a friendly ambassador, or something else of this sort. (Schutz, 1963, p. 237)

In this view, gaining knowledge about a social practice is closer to the way we gain understanding of a foreign language or to the process by which a trial judge weighs evidence and pronounces a verdict than it is to the models of inquiry adapted from the natural sciences.

The controversy between behavioralism and the advocates of *Verstehen* concerns us only insofar as it is bound up with different interpretations of concepts pertaining to mental states or events such as wanting, intending, choosing. We shall see that such mental concepts in turn help to define such key political notions as power, interest, and politics.

Behavioralists, as we have seen, have sometimes assumed that terms such as 'want', 'desire', and 'intention' can be construed as dispositionals. But the dispositional analysis of mental terms has been subjected to serious criticism. For example, Alston has shown that, especially in situations where an agent has conflicting wants, one *could* want something without ever manifesting the want behavior (1967, pp. 403–405). Similarly, Winch (1958), an advocate of *Verstehen*, has claimed that there

> is no contradiction in saying that someone who never before manifested any signs of a jealous disposition has, on a given occasion, acted from jealousy; indeed, it is precisely when someone acts unexpectedly that the need for a motive explanation is particularly apparent. (p. 80)

Concluding that a dispositional analysis can provide only a partial interpretation of mental terms, many advocates of *Verstehen* (such as Winch, 1958, and Louch, 1966) adopt a contextualist approach. In this view, describing an action, as opposed to a mere movement, is analogous to describing a move in, say, a game of chess. A statement like 'the player moved his knight' can be understood only by those who know the rules of chess, which tell us what a player is, what the purpose of the game is, and what it takes to win the game. In social and political life, too, actions are taken for reasons, and the reasons can be comprehended only by understanding the conventional rules, institutional arrangements, and moral standards of the given society. For example, voting or engaging in nonviolent protest can be explicated only within the system of rules and social practices accepted by participants. On this account, when I interpret an actor's intention as a reason for his action, I am merely displaying its point or purpose as seen within the system of rules accepted by the agent.

Two conclusions, closely related to questions about concept clarification in political inquiry, are thought to follow from this analysis. First, since intentions, reasons, motives, etc., are part of what we mean by an action (as distinguished from a mere movement), they cannot be causes of that action. If $C$ is a cause of $E$, then $C$ cannot, on this account, have a logical connection with $E$, such as a definitional one. Second, actions can be understood only when they are placed within the context of rules, practices, and reasons followed in the culture to be studied. We understand the rationale of given patterns of conduct by understanding the conceptual world within which the participants move. In this reading, it can never be legitimate for the investigator to introduce concepts in his explanation which are not part of or "rooted in" the conceptual system of the participants themselves, because doing so would wrench the described conduct out of the very context which makes it conduct rather than mere movements without purpose (Louch, 1966). As Winch suggests, we cannot describe a relationship as one of command and obedience unless the participants themselves understand the requisite concepts, since "an act of obedience itself contains, as an essential element, a recognition of what went before as an order" (1958, p. 125). Winch concludes that, in general, concepts in the social sciences must be explicated in ways that remain faithful to the tacit rules of application adopted by the population to be studied.

This approach seems first, to be based on too restrictive a view of the conditions necessary for causal explanation. There is a partial definitional connection between reasons and action, but the two are surely not equivalent in meaning. Items which have such a partial noncontingent connection may also be related causally. Thus we speak of the lack of confidence in a parliamentary government as the cause of its collapse; yet there is *some* conceptual connection between the existence of a particular government and lack of confidence in it. Having the notion of a government is a necessary but not sufficient condition for lacking confidence in government.

> It is not enough merely to point out *some* logical connection between the concept of desire, belief, and feeling and that of action; the connection must be one which is clearly absent in undisputed cases of causal connections. (Donnellan, 1967, p. 87)

Once the view that reasons cannot logically be causes of actions has been undermined, a strong presumption can be provided in favor of the ordinary view that such a causal connection actually exists. My reasons for acting in a certain way cannot, it seems, be *my reasons* unless *they* lead me also to act that way, that is, unless I act *because* of those reasons. The difference between a reason and a rationalization is precisely that the former is causally related to action but the latter is not (Shaffer, 1968, Ch. 5; Davidson, 1963; Goldman, 1970).

Furthermore, the advocates of *Verstehen* inflate the importance of adopting the conceptual system of the participants. True, we must start with the concepts adopted by the participants themselves if we really want to understand their practices. But this does not require that we always stop there. A tribe may understand a crop failure as punishment for sins, whereas we might usefully employ concepts alien to that tribe in explaining that failure and its possible connection with political problems. A society may lack a clear notion of class, but we, as investigators, might find that the notion of class helps us to explain why certain patterns of distribution persist. Or the very fact that the members of a given society treat 'old' and 'wise' as synonyms may help the outside investigator to understand the persistence of gerontocracy (Gellner, 1970).

Empiricism, behaviorism, operationalism, and *Verstehen*, then, in their earlier and more vigorous formulations, each purport to offer clear and overriding requirements which concepts of political inquiry must meet if they are to perform their tasks effectively. In their later, more relaxed form each provides some insight into appropriate standards and approaches to conceptual clarification.

## III. EXPLICATING POLITICAL CONCEPTS

Like the choice of concepts to be introduced into the language of political science, the choice of explicative definitions for these concepts must fulfill certain criteria of adequacy.

### A. Meeting the Operational Requirement

That explications, to be adequate, must be operational applies also within the field of political inquiry. But operational in what sense? Deutsch claims in his textbook (1970) that "each concept is defined in terms of some operation that can be repeated and tested by different people regardless of their preferences" (p. ix). One may wonder, however, what "operations" are referred to by his definitions: *politics,* "the making of decision by public means" (p. 3); *interest,* "anyone's 'interest' in a situation consists in the rewards which he can extract from it" (p. 10); *liberty,* "the ability to act in accordance with one's own personality, without having to make a great effort at self-denial . . ." (p. 13); *legitimacy,* "the terms 'legitimate' and 'just' will be used interchangeably" (p. 14). And are the definitions of the last two terms operational in any sense? These examples show that the task of constructing operational definitions for political concepts presents a number of special difficulties, even if we apply the broader criteria of modern operationalism, for which most contemporary political scientists (unlike Deutsch) are no doubt willing to settle. In the following I shall illustrate some of the problems political scientists must face in their efforts to provide definitions for their basic concepts which meet the operational requirement in the broadest sense.

*1. Few observables.* Lord Bryce, who wrote in the heyday of extreme empiricism, advised political scientists to "keep close to the facts." But where do we find political facts? "It seems unlikely that Lord Bryce meant for us to deal simply with data of the senses—to examine such characteristic political phenomena as revolutions in terms of quantities . . . of reddish liquid" (Goldberg, 1968, p. 18). A revolution is not a "fact," because 'revolution' is neither an observation term nor definable exclusively by observation terms such as 'reddish liquid'. 'Revolution' is a theoretical term, and so is 'voting'—to take a previous example. We could not observe that $P$ voted in the last election (let alone that he voted Republican); we could observe only that $P$ dropped a paper in a box. And we cannot infer from this observation alone that a voting act took place; we must also "understand" the complex institution of casting a vote. Political behavior, at least in its nonviolent manifestations, consists in large part of "speech acts." The typical data of political science are interviews, attitude and opinion scales, statistics of elections and party affiliation, or legal documents. Among the concepts of political science there are few observation terms and consequently few statements which can be tested by direct experience. Most political concepts, even those "closest" to observable reality, are theoretical, and most assertions of political science are made up of such theoretical concepts. In the words of Easton: "Despite some post-behavioral objections to scientific abstractness and remoteness from the world of common sense, by its nature science must deal with abstractions" (1969, p. 1054). We have seen that modern operationalism no longer questions the legitimacy of abstract, theoretical concepts.

*2. Collectivities and their characteristics*

> Although concrete political action is invariably the behavior of individual human actors, the politically significant units of action are groups, associations, organizations, communities, states, and other collectivities. (Eulau, 1968, p. 209)

And the politically significant characteristics are attributes of those collectivities, such as a union's cohesion, a party's morale, a nation's aggressiveness. Collectivities and their properties are designated by collective terms (theoretical terms of a special kind), in contradistinction to individual terms, which are names of individuals (e.g., 'Napoleon') or designate attributes of individuals (e.g., 'ambitious'). How to explicate concepts referring to groups and their attributes remains a matter of controversy among social scientists and philosophers of science. The theory of methodological individualism holds that collective terms can be explicated with the help of individual terms exclusively. For example, according to Brodbeck (1958, p. 16), "Group concepts refer . . . to complex patterns of descriptive, empirical relations among individuals." While of course not denying that groups exist and that groups have properties different from their members, this theory claims that the former can be defined in terms of the latter. Methodological holism maintains, on the contrary, that social "wholes" cannot be explicated by referring to individuals exclusively. Thus, according to Mandelbaum (1955, p. 307), "those concepts which are used to refer to the forms of organization of a society cannot be reduced without remainder to concepts which only refer to the thoughts and actions of specific individuals."

Although strict behaviorism and operationalism must lead to methodological individualism, the contemporary broadened version of these theories is compatible with methodological holism as well (see Kaplan, 1964, p. 81). The language of political science may include statements about political "wholes" provided that they can be verified by statements about individual political actors and actions. Concepts such as group cohesion or political culture might well fulfill this requirement; but notions like group mind must be proscribed even by methodological holists if they want to remain empiricists. Collective concepts which refer to legal institutions, such as government or authority, present special problems in this connection which will be examined later.[4]

**3. Mental states.** We have seen (II, B, 2) that even a concept as "close" to empirical "reality" as that of human *action* cannot be explicated without referring to mental states such as feeling, believing, intending, choosing. Let us now show, for the sake of illustration, how the latter concepts are used to define certain basic notions of political *interaction,* namely influence, coercion (or restraint), and punishment—concepts which in turn will help to explicate those of control, power, and freedom.

a.  $P$ influences $Q$ not to do $x = df.$ $P$ causes $Q$ to choose not to do $x$.
b.  $P$ restrains $Q$ from doing $x = df.$ $P$ causes $Q$'s attempt to do $x$ to fail.
c.  $P$ punishes $Q$ for having done $x = df.$ $P$'s belief that $Q$ did $x$ causes $P$ to deprive $Q$ (i.e., to perform some action, $y$, that causes $Q$ to feel deprived).

Indeed, to influence someone to do (or not to do) something is to change his original *intention,* so that he now *decides* on a different course of action. To restrain or coerce is to frustrate an attempt; and to interpret an instance of behavior as an attempt to do something, is to refer to the agent's *goal.* Similarly, the definition of 'punishment' refers to $P$'s *beliefs* and $Q$'s *feelings*.

With the help of the concepts of influence and restraint, it is possible to define that of exercising control.

d. *P controls Q's not doing x* = *df*. *P* influences *Q* not to do *x* or restrains him from doing so.

Thus, if *Q*'s attempt at *x* was frustrated by *P*, it follows by definition that *P* exercised control over *Q* with respect to his not doing *x*. Statements about the exercise of control in the future are empirical hypotheses which, as such, can be asserted with a certain degree of probability, depending on the answers to questions such as: If *Q* attempts *x*, will *P* restrain him? Such hypotheses can, at least in principle, be tested by reference to similar actual occurrences in the past.

**4. Causation.** We have seen (II, B, 4) that it is debatable whether accounting for an action (e.g., *Q*'s doing *x*) in temrs of the actor's own motives constitutes a causal explanation. But there can be little doubt that an explanation of one action (*Q*'s doing *x*) by reference to an action of another actor (*P*'s doing *y*) is causal, and hence that the notion of cause enters the definitions of concepts of interaction such as influence. Indeed, the expression '*P* causes *Q*' figures in the first three definitions just mentioned. Causation is not an observational concept even in the broadest sense, but a highly abstract notion. It is also an obscure one, and it may for this reason be doubted whether it is at all practical to use it in the defining expressions of political concepts which are reasonably clear in ordinary language. This is indeed a difficulty, but an unavoidable one. One actor causing another to act in a certain way is precisely what is involved in all the above-mentioned relationships of interaction, and this causal relationship just cannot be "defined away."

There is a relatively simple way of clarifying the notion of causality, which will serve our purposes. That a certain kind of event, *C*, causes another, *E*, means either that *C* is a necessary or a sufficient condition for the occurrence of *E*, or that it is both. In which of these three senses the concept of social and political causation is to be taken remains controversial. For reasons pointed out elsewhere (Oppenheim, 1958; Shaffer, 1968, p. 63; von Wright, 1971, p. 38), causation in the context of political interaction relations had best be interpreted in terms of sufficient condition. Accordingly, '*P* influences *Q* not to do *x*' means that some influence action, *y*, of *P* is a sufficient condition for *Q*'s decision not to do *x*. This means, under the given circumstances, that if *P* does *y*, then *Q* decides not do *x*. In other words, if *Q* persisted in his original intention to do *x*, then *P* did not perform the influence action *y*. (In the case of punishment, causality flows in the opposite direction. It is *Q*'s action *x* which is a sufficient condition for *P*'s deprivatory action.) If concepts such as influence, control, power have great explanatory power, it is partly because they are defined with reference to causation. Indeed, to affirm, e.g., an influence relation is not merely to state some empirical facts about $P$'s action $y$ and $Q$'s choice of non-$x$, but to provide what Hempel (1965, p. 453) has called an "explanation-by-concept" of the latter event. For example, by affirming that Russia influenced Egypt to provoke Israel in 1967, one does not simply describe historical events, but explains (at least partially) *why* Egypt acted as it did.

**5. Dispositions.** Political scientists are often interested not merely in actual but in potential control relationships (as to this distinction, cf. Dahl, 1970, pp. 28–30). They want to affirm that the United States *has* control over Mexico's not joining the Soviet bloc, even though they cannot point to any actual American influence or restraint actions with respect to Mexico's foreign policy, let alone to causal connections between such events. Having control is a dispositional concept, like that of solubility (see II, B, 3). Such concepts, we have seen, are operational in the broad sense that statements in which they occur refer to hypothetical or contrary-to-fact conditionals which can, in principle, be verified by reference to actual occurrences. Accordingly, the following constitute operational definitions of the concepts of having influence, preventing, and having control.

e. $P$ has influence over $Q$'s not doing $x = df.$ Were $Q$ to intend $x$, $P$ would influence $Q$ not to do $x$.

f. $P$ prevents $Q$ from doing $x = df.$ Were $Q$ to attempt $x$, $P$ would restrain $Q$ from doing $x$.

g. $P$ has control over $Q$'s not doing $x = df.$ $P$ has influence over $Q$'s not doing $x$ or prevents him from doing $x$.

In the same way, the concept of political unfreedom may be defined in a dispositional way.

h. With respect to $P$, $Q$ is unfree to do $x = df.$ $P$ either prevents $Q$ from doing $x$ or makes it punishable for him to do so.

Statements about influence, prevention, having control, and unfreedom (in this particular sense) are again empirical hypotheses. They can in principle be tested empirically by reference to statements of the type: Were $Q$ to attempt $x$, $P$ would restrain him; had $Q$ done $x$, $P$ would have punished him for having done so.

**6. Legal institutions.** In contradistinction to such notions as political power or freedom, concepts like, e.g., property, voting, representative (or any other public office), democracy (or any other form of government), government, or state refer to "institutional facts" (Searle, in Foot, 1967, p.

111), i.e., to rules of positive law of a given legal system. To understand their meaning, we must clarify the concept of law itself and inquire whether legal rules can be explicated in behavioral terms. Consider the utterance: "Speed limit 60 mph." As a formal enactment, this is a normative sentence: Drivers are permitted to drive up to sixty miles an hour, but they may not go faster. But if *I* say to a speeding driver "Speed limit 60 mph," I may be informing or reminding him of the *fact* that it is illegal to drive more than sixty miles an hour on this highway. "The existence of a norm is a fact" (von Wright, 1963, p. 106). We are concerned not with the first but with the second kind of utterance, not with normative enactments by public officials (e.g., legislators) in their official capacity but with factual assertions by lawyers or political scientists. So the question is: Can statements like "'abortion is punishable by imprisonment' is a rule of the legal system S" be inferred from assertions about the behavior of members of S?

An affirmative answer is given by those political behavioralists who conceive of political institutions as "patterns of individual behavior that are more or less uniform and regular" (Eulau, 1968, p. 203). Now, from observing some regular pattern of behavior in S (e.g., few abortions), we can of course infer that there is a *habit* of that kind in S, habit being indeed "a fact about the observable behavior of most of the group" (Hart, 1961, p. 55). A prevailing habit of acting in a certain way is no doubt one of the indicators of a legal rule requiring that behavior. "Laws" which exist exclusively "in books" are in general not considered part of the positive law of a given society. But just from observing that there are few abortions or that most drivers don't drive faster than sixty miles an hour, we cannot infer that there is a law making abortion or speeding punishable. And if we find out that a particular speeder was actually fined, we may conclude that he was officially unfree to speed, but not that all are under a legal obligation not to drive more than sixty miles an hour. Or—to return to a previous example—from the mere observation that a certain number of persons in S dropped certain papers in certain boxes on a certain day, it does not follow that an *election* took place, that others who did not perform this visible act also have the *suffrage*, that certain persons were *elected* to the office of *representative* (which in turn is circumscribed by a bundle of legal powers, rights, and duties). Antibehaviorists therefore conclude that "the legal system itself cannot be defined in terms of individual behavior" (Mandelbaum, 1955, p. 312), and that political concepts which refer to legal institutions are not behavioral, either.

Most modern legal philosophers agree that we cannot infer the existence of legal rules within a given society from patterns of overt behavior of its members, but that we must also examine those persons' beliefs, normative as well as factual. We have seen, however, that statements to the effect that a person or group believes that something is the case or that something ought to be done are at present considered behavioral in the larger sense. Hart's

*Concept of Law* is the most influential example of this view, and I shall adopt his interpretation.

Legal rules belong to the larger class of social rules. That a certain social rule prevails in S means that: (a) there is a social habit to that effect in S; (b) deviations from the habit are usually criticized, either verbally or physically, and "threatened deviations meet with pressure for conformity" (Hart, 1961, p. 54); (c) "criticism for deviation is regarded as legitimate" (p. 54) and compliance is regarded "as a general standard to be followed by the group as a whole" (p. 55), but not necessarily on moral grounds. Indicators (a) and (b) are strictly behavioral, and criterion (c) is behavioral in the broader sense, since it refers to the normative convictions of members in S. A legal system has the additional characteristic that it comprises not only primary rules which prescribe or prohibit or authorize certain types of conduct or "confer powers on private individuals to make wills, contracts, or marriages" (p. 26), but also secondary rules which "specify the ways in which the primary rules may be conclusively ascertained" (p. 92). Secondary legal rules, too, must meet conditions (c) of any social rule. More particularly, they "must be effectively accepted as common public standards of official behavior by its officials" (p. 113). In principle, an anthropologist could reconstruct the legal system of a society by studying its habits and the prevailing normative beliefs about them, including those concerning the secondary rules of authoritative determination.

> The existence of every law depends on the existence of the legal system to which it belongs, and the existence of legal systems depends on persistent and pervasive patterns of behaviour on the part of a large proportion of the population to which they apply. (Raz, 1970a, p. 150)

This is quite true, provided that 'behavior' is taken in the widest sense. We may therefore conclude that political concepts referring to legal institutions are operational—again in the broadest sense.

Legal concepts must nevertheless be distinguished from those which do not refer to legal institutions. For example, all drivers have the *legal duty* not to speed; drivers are *unfree* to speed only to the extent that speeders are actually fined. If a given legal system confers on those who occupy a certain office the legal right to issue orders, they have *authority* in this respect, but they may be *powerless* to enforce compliance (e.g., policemen unable to quell a riot); conversely, someone may have power without legal authority (e.g., the gunman).

### B. Other Criteria of Adequacy

*1. Establishing definitional connections.* In general, the smaller the number of undefined terms within a language system and the greater the number of terms definable with their help, the "better." Thus all terms within the system of Euclidean geometry can be defined, directly or indirectly, by a small number of primitive terms. In the social sciences, such an ideal can of course be only approximated at best. With the help of the "undefined" terms 'choosing', 'attempting', 'doing', 'depriving', and 'causing', we have been able to construct explicative definitions for three basic theoretical concepts of political science, namely, influencing, coercing (or restraining), and punishing. These in turn help to define the still more abstract concepts of control and unfreedom. Further links in this chain of definitions lead to the concepts of power and freedom.

i. $P$ has power over $Q$ with respect to $x = df.$ $P$ has control over $Q$'s not doing $x$ or makes him unfree to do $x$ (that is, $P$ has influence in this respect or makes it impossible or punishable for $Q$ to do $x$).

j. With respect to $P$, $Q$ is free to do $x$ or $y$ (for example, not to do $x$) = $df.$ With respect to $P$, $Q$ is not unfree to do $x$, and not unfree to do $y$ (that is, $P$ makes it neither impossible nor punishable for $Q$ to do $x$, and neither . . . to do $y$).

Power in turn helps to define authority in Dahl's sense of accepted power (1970, p. 33), and the concept of authority enters Easton's definition of politics or political interaction as "authoritative allocation of values for a society" (1965a, p. 50).

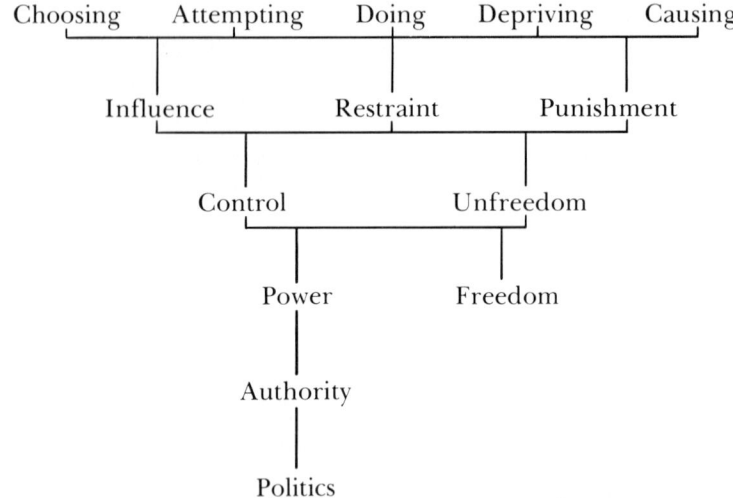

The construction of such a system of concepts linked together by suitable definitions may well be considered a theory, at least in the weaker sense.

In the stronger sense, a theory must contain logically deduced propositions, which, if referring to portions of the real world, must be in principle verifiable. In its weaker sense, a theory can simply be a preparation of a conceptual scheme in which a theory in the stronger sense will one day be developed (Rapoport, 1966, p. 132).

**2. *Establishing factual connections.*** Another test of the adequacy of explicative definitions of a series of related concepts is that they draw attention, explicitly or by implication, to certain features of the subject matter which are of theoretical importance but often not readily apparent. Thus, on the basis of the previous definitions, we can point to connections between various relationships of political interaction like the following.

If $P$ prevents $Q$ from doing $x$, $P$ has control over $Q$'s not doing $x$ and also makes him unfree to do so. But there may be control without unfreedom and unfreedom without control. If $P$ influences $Q$ not to do $x$, $P$ controls $Q$'s not doing $x$ but does not make him unfree to do so. (By influencing you to vote Democratic, I do not make you unfree to vote Republican.) If $P$ punishes $Q$ for having done $x$, $Q$ was, with respect to $P$, unfree to do $x$, but $P$ did not control $Q$'s behavior. Punishment indicates failure to control—but not absence of power; $P$ had (and exercised) power over $Q$ with respect to the action $x$ for which $Q$ was punished. This shows that it is not fruitful to equate power with control, disregarding punishment, as is often done.

If political freedom is interpreted as referring to alternative actions open to $Q$, then freedom is not the contradictory of unfreedom: I am not unfree to pay taxes; nor am I free to pay them or not; rather, I am unfree to withhold payment. "Freedom to propagate the truth" is a euphemism for 'unfreedom to spread "error"'. Both freedom and power relationships may hold between the same pair of actors. With respect to $P$, $Q$ remains free to do $x$, if $P$ influences $Q$ not to do $x$, or if $P$ refrains from preventing $Q$ from doing $x$ even though he has the power to do so.

Contrary to the widespread view that social power and social causation are synonymous (Simon, 1957, p. 5; Deutsch, 1970, p. 24), these are overlapping categories. There may be causation without control, e.g., if $Q$'s action cannot be causally linked to a determinate person or group but was caused, say, by prevailing general economic or social conditions. And if $P$ does not exercise the power he has over some action, $x$, of $Q$, $x$ is not the causal effect of $P$'s activity.

**3. *Not precluding empirical investigations.*** A further criterion of the adequacy of an explication is that it should not make true "by definition" what had better be left open to empirical investigation. Indeed, we do not want the very problems which are generally considered substantive in the field to be solved by definitional fiat. Let us illustrate this problem by an example taken from Dahl. He asserts that a regime which imprisons members of the opposition

> is by definition not a polyarchy. Yet it would be wrong to conclude that the relation between polyarchy and peaceful adjustment is wholly a logical circularity stemming from the way we define our terms. For there is good evidence for the belief that in polyarchies conflicts really are more likely to be settled peacefully . . . than in nonpolyarchies. (1970, p. 62)

Dahl does not bring out clearly in this passage that the logical status of "belief" depends on how we decide to *define* 'polyarchy'. If we were to take 'high probability of peaceful adjustment' as one of the criteria, it would indeed follow logically that polyarchy promotes peaceful adjustment. Such a definition, Dahl correctly implies, would be unpractical. Political science is interested in the empirical question whether and to what extent peaceful conflict resolution is a function of institutional arrangements. It would therefore be pointless to settle this question by definitional fiat. Dahl's allegation that a regime which stifles opposition "is by definition not a polyarchy" presumes that we have already made the protection of freedom of opinion one of the defining characteristics of polyarchy.

'Polyarchy', as we have seen (II, A, 2), is usually characterized by a wide distribution of power over political decision-makers (and only incidentally by freedom of opinion). 'Polyarchy' is also sometimes taken as *definiens* of 'democracy'. Thus, according to Verba (1969, p. 3), "democracy refers in some rough way to the degree to which power and influence over significant decisions for a society is diffused throughout that society." But then it becomes true by definition that the more widely political power is diffused, the more democratic the society. Therefore this definition, too, could be criticized from the point of view of adequacy now under consideration. It seems more fruitful to explicate the concept of democracy as a set of formal institutions, such as free elections by universal suffrage and majority vote in parliament, and to leave to political science the task of determining the empirical connections between democratic institutions and the diffusion of power over political decisions. Incidentally, it might turn out that democracy in the institutional sense is compatible with various distributions of political power, ranging from a single power elite through a multiplicity of countervailing power groups to genuine polyarchy.

For the same reasons it would be unpractical to define democracy in terms of "majority rule," even in Braybrooke's weaker sense that a system is democratic only if its policy makers implement the citizens' "collective preference" (1968, Part 3), e.g., that of the majority of the voters. This condition, of course, is not necessarily fulfilled by a democracy in the sense of a representative system, since elected representatives are not the voters' delegates. Only if we explicate the concept of democracy in institutional terms can we raise the empirical question whether the citizen's desires are more likely to be implemented in a democratic system than under different institutions. Incidentally, political writers often fail to make it clear whether they mean to deal with definitional or empirical questions. For example, Hook's statement that "governments are more or less democratic depending on whether political power or influence on political power is shared equally" (1959, p. 27) could be understood either as a definition or as a statement of fact.

***4. Remaining reasonably close to ordinary language.*** Explictations of political concepts should draw on ordinary discourse as far as possible. By ordinary discourse I do not mean the way most people would define a given term; rather, I mean the set of rules they implicitly follow when applying it to a given situation. Thus people commonly distinguish between shame and guilt or between public and private acts without being readily able to formulate all the rules marking those distinctions.

Why should political analysts stay close to ordinary language? As the philosopher John Austin has pointed out, the vocabulary of every day discourse is already rich in distinctions and connections.

> These surely are likely to be more numerous, more sound, since they have stood up to the long test of the survival of the fittest, and more subtle, at least in all ordinary and reasonably practical matters, than any that you or I are likely to think up in our arm-chairs of an afternoon —the most favoured alternative method. (Austin, 1970, p. 182)

By keeping explications relatively close to ordinary discourse, we can draw on its rich resources when we confront new situations with unforeseen features, as happens especially often in the area of politics. Consider the concept of politics itself. For a long time, political scientists applied it exclusively to formal governmental policy-making processes. Thus Hynemann interpreted the study of politics as the study of "that part of the state which centers on government and that part of government which speaks through law" (1959, pp. 26–27). More recently, some political scientists, such as Reagan (1963), Hacker (1964), and Bachrach (1967), have called attention to the extent to which corporate behavior manifests many of the characteristics which ordinarily are considered political: Corporations choose policies from among alternative possibilities; their choices carry consequences of importance for wide segments of society; some of their policies are contested by other groups; society at large tends to invest corporate decisions with legitimacy. Not that people in ordinary life have habitually applied the concept of politics to corporate activity. Rather, the rules which they implicitly follow when using it have encouraged political scientists to extend its application to corporate activities. Drawing on ordinary usage in this way, they have begun to study the "political" aspects of extragovernmental organizations.

However, "reasonable" closeness to ordinary language may require reasonable deviation. Ordinary usage tends to be vague or ambiguous and to vary among and within societies. "Conceptual analysis aims at the clarification and systematization of concepts and is not bound to reflect usage where that usage is confused and liable to mislead" (Raz, 1970b, pp. 303–304). Everyday language often uses the same term in different senses without distinguishing between them (as in the case of 'freedom') or makes distinctions where the scientist is more interested in similarities. The concept of power again provides an illustration. According to the explication proposed in III, B, 2, $P$ may have power over $Q$'s doing $x$ without intending that $Q$ does $x$. However, Benn has correctly pointed out that this explication "has some odd results" when viewed from the perspective of ordinary language. "Instead of suffering a *loss* of power, the crashing financier who brings down thousands with him in his fall would be exercising power that is perhaps greater than ever before" (1967b, p. 426). Benn therefore proposed to include among the criteria of power the powerholder's intention to modify the respondent's behavior in accordance with the former's purposes. This explication is closer to the ordinary usage of at least some segments of the population. But others, often those who identify with the bottom of society, seem to apply different rules here. In this usage, those "in power" are agents whose decisions carry consequences, whether intended or not, of importance for wide segments of society and who *could* alter future decisions producing those consequences. In this interpretation, the crashing financier does have power over those he brings down with him, even though he does not intend to cause their fall. In such instances, where ordinary discourse varies, it cannot provide a sufficient guide to scientific concept formation.

Yet some analysts proceed as if it were sufficient to explicate political concepts by reporting their use in ordinary language. Braybrooke, for example, tries to arrive at a definition of democracy by "surveying" how the concept if used by *advocates* of democracy, by "real people, alive today, ordinary men and women with some experience of politics in the English-speaking countries, who consciously favor their governments because they believe the governments have democratic features" (1968, p. 7). Surely, the way the concept is used—often quite differently—by non-English-speaking pro-democrats, and by avowed opponents of democracy as well, would be no less relevant. However, reportative definitions can be only the starting point. The construction of an adequate explicative definition must be guided by all the various criteria of adequacy we have mentioned, and reasonable closeness to ordinary language is only one of them. Both those analysts who tend to ignore ordinary discourse in favor of the construction of an artificial language of political science and those who seek to reflect fully the complexity of common usage in their explications of political concepts would do well to heed J.L. Austin's advice: "Ordinary language is *not* the last word; in principle it can everywhere be supplemented and improved upon and superseded. Only remember, it *is* the *first* word" (1970, p. 185).

**5. Openness of meaning.** We have seen (II, B, 3) that it is not always possible to provide definitions in terms of fixed criteria once and for all, and that old and established political concepts must often be used to capture new and unforeseen situations (II, B, 4). "We are tempted to think that new applications only add to our knowledge of truth but leave meaning unchanged" (Kaplan, 1964, p. 65). Instead, we should deliberately leave the meaning of such concepts "open," i.e., allow for "their permanent possibility of change in meaning" (*ibid.*, p. 69; cf. Waismann, 1951, p. 125). However,

> that meanings are open does not imply that they are altogether unspecified: as with minds, "open" is not the same as "empty." Initial contexts of application must provide enough closure to contain a usable empirical meaning. . . . Openness of meaning is fundamentally a consequence of the fact that there are no terminal contexts of inquiry. (Kaplan, 1964, p. 70)

Nor is "open" the same as "vague," i.e., using words in a fluctuating way (Waismann, 1951, p. 126). Fruitful explications of political concepts require us to steer a middle ground between vagueness and rigidity (cf. Gregor, 1971, p. 134).

## IV. CATEGORICAL AND COMPARATIVE CONCEPTS

Theoretical political science may be said to start with classification and to proceed from there to the more sophisticated methods, first of nonmetric ordering and ultimately of quantification and measurement.

### A. Categorical Concepts

**1. Classification.** A classification consists in subdividing all objects having a certain property in common into subclasses, according to whether they also share a certain other property. According to this simple, Aristotelian mode of analysis, all minerals (i.e., all objects having the property of being mineral) could be classified into hard and soft minerals; all political systems could be subdivided according to whether they are democratic or not. Aristotle himself classified all possible forms of government into the six categories of monarchy, aristocracy, constitutional government, and their respective "perversions": tyranny, oligarchy, democracy. A modern example is Almond's classification of political systems into four types: Anglo-American, Continental European, preindustrial (or partly industrialized), and totalitarian (1956, p. 392). Most of the concepts we have analyzed so far can be taken in a classificatory sense. *P* either has or lacks power over *Q*'s doing *x;* with respect to *P, Q* is or is not unfree to do *x;* a given rule of distribution is either egalitarian or inegalitarian.

Classificatory concepts are thus categorical. Their application is a matter of yes or no: a given mineral falls either into the category of hard or outside it; political systems are either democratic or nondemocratic.

**2. Criteria of adequacy.** How to classify political phenomena is a matter of fruitfulness, not of truth or falsity. In political research, as in any science,

> the taxonomic categories used for descriptive purposes recommend themselves not because they make any claim upon "reality" (whatever that might be), but because they prove capable of employment in the process of formulating genuine generalizations. (Gregor, 1971, p. 170)

Categorical concepts used for classificatory purposes must of course fulfill the conditions of adequacy of any concept. Thus they must be defined in such a way that it becomes possible to ascertain empirically whether any given member of the overall class has or lacks the characteristics which define the subclass. Concepts that meet this requirement are operational, even if they are not quantifiable. Contrary to a widespread view, operationalization does not require quantification. How best to categorize political phenomena depends of course on the topic under investigation. For most purposes, it will be more interesting to classify political systems by their form of government than by geographic location—or by miles of seashore.

There is a further, logical requirement for classificatory concepts: A set of concepts used to subdivide a given class must be mutually exclusive and jointly exhaustive (Hempel, 1952, p. 51). As pointed out by Kalleberg (1966, p. 74), Almond's categories are not mutually exclusive, since a given political system could be European, partly industrialized, and totalitarian. Or consider Aristotle's influential classification of rules of distribution into egalitarian and inegalitarian. An egalitarian rule allots "equal shares to equals" *(Ethics,* 1131a). If this defining expression means equal shares of something to all who are equal in some respect, then every conceivable rule turns out to be egalitarian. Universal suffrage means that every adult citizen shall have one vote, but minors and aliens shall have none; suffrage to whites assigns voting rights to all adult white citizens and none to nonwhites. Conversely, an inegalitarian rule—"when either equals are awarded unequal shares or unequals equal shares"—is a *logical* impossibility. A rule cannot allot unequal shares to those who are equal as to the characteristic the rule itself specifies, nor can it allot equal shares to those who differ in that respect. Racial discrimination treats those of the same race the same way and those of different races differently. For the same reason, every rule of distribution meets the requirement of "proportional equality" if this means that the more someone has of the characteristic specified by the rule, the greater (or smaller) his share; to each according to his need or ability or height. However, if a rule of distribution is considered egalitarian when it equalizes, or at least reduces, the difference between the holdings of those to whom the rule applies (Oppenheim, 1970, p. 149), then, given some initial distribution, certain rules can be shown to be egalitarian (e.g., extending the suffrage or establishing a graduated income tax), and others inegalitarian (e.g., limiting suffrage or levying a sales tax).

### B. Comparative Concepts

***1. As opposed to categorical concepts.*** The "real world" is not made up of neat pigeonholes. Substances we encounter in nature exhibit varying *degrees* of hardness. There are degrees of political development and stability, of party cohesion and competition. Some rules of distribution are more egalitarian than others. Some political systems are democratic to a relatively high degree, others less so. The United States and the Soviet Union are perhaps equally powerful, and there is a greater extent of freedom of speech in the former than in the latter. To capture phenomena exhibiting such gradations, it would be necessary to introduce expressions such as 'harder than', 'more democratic than', 'as powerful as', which enable us to establish a nonmetrical rank order among members of a given class. Yet political science has been slow to outgrow the classificatory stage. For example, the terminology political scientists use to characterize different political regimes "is almost hopelessly inadequate, for it is a terminology invariably based upon classifying rather than ranking" (Dahl, 1971, p. 6).

There is now an increasing tendency to use the comparative approach and to view political phenomena "as possessing in varying degrees continuous characteristics" (Scarrow, 1969, p. 17). Replacing categorical by comparative concepts enables us to ignore such merely verbal disputes as those about whether the Soviet Union is totalitarian, or Spain fascist, or Turkey democratic, or Chile underdeveloped. But the main reason for the greater fruitfulness of comparative concepts is that they lead to more sophisticated generalizations of the type: the higher the rank order of an object is in one respect, the higher (or lower) it is in some other. For example, the more developed a society is, the more democratic it is likely to be (certain specified conditions remaining the same).

***2. Problems of operationalization.*** Comparative concepts must be defined in a way that enables us to determine for any two members of the class under consideration whether they stand to each other in a relation of having the characteristic to the same degree or whether one ranks higher than the other. The concept of 'harder than' can be defined very simply by reference to the "scratch test," which is strictly operational: '$x$ is harder than $y$' means that $x$ scratches $y$ but not vice versa. Then we can assert, e.g., that steel is harder than copper but less hard than diamond. Similarly, given some initial distribution, a rule of redistribution can be said to be the more egalitarian, the smaller the difference between the holdings after the rule has been applied. However, many comparative political concepts are more complicated in several respects.

a. They can seldom be defined by reference to a single operation. The relative degree to which political phenomena exhibit certain characteristics must usually be construed as a function of several indicators. Thus the degree of $P$'s power over $Q$'s not doing $x$ may depend on such factors as the probability that $P$ will influence $Q$ not to do $x$ or punish him if he does, and the severity of the threatened penalty. Dahl views "democratization as made up of at least two dimensions: public contestation and the right to participate" (Dahl, 1971, p. 5). Each of these various dimensions in turn is comparative.

b. These criteria are often nonmetrical and therefore a matter of appraisal. For example, 'sectionalism' has been defined as

> the phenomenon in which a *significant* percentage of the population of a nation lives in a *sizeable* geographic area and identifies self-consciously and *distinctively* with that area to a degree that the cohesion of the polity as a whole is *appreciably* challenged or impaired. (Banks and Textor, 1963, p. 88, italics added; quoted by Scarrow, 1969, p. 13)

The italicized words are appraisal concepts which are comparative but, as we shall see, not normative. The investigator must appraise each of these factors in terms of some presupposed standard, in order to determine the relative degree to which a nation manifests sectionalism or to arrive at comparative estimates such as: Nation A manifests a higher degree of sectionalism than Nation B.

c. The various criteria vary independently. Thus, if one judges by the probability of punishment, drivers are perhaps officially more unfree to speed in Connecticut than in Massachusetts; but if one judges by the severity of the penalty, it may be the other way around. A democratic system may be democratic to a relatively high degree from the point of view of equal right of participation, but it may rank rather low on the scale of equal opportunity to act politically. The question then arises whether it is possible to draw these several dimensions together, as it were, and to arrive at an overall comparative concept of degree of democracy, power, development, sectionalism, etc. Haas (1966) points out some major difficulties involved in such efforts, which have nevertheless led to "the formulation since the early 1960s of several broad conceptual schemes for the comparative analysis of culturally dissimilar political systems" (p. 106).

**3. Extreme-type concepts.** Comparative locutions like 'more democratic than' naturally lead to extreme-type expressions like 'most democratic'. Thus 'a political system is most (or fully or purely) democratic' could be defined in Dahl's sense by the expression: *'All* its members are entitled to participate *to the fullest* in public contestation'. Extreme-type concepts are a special kind of comparative concept, since they designate

> simply the end points of a series that is ordered by certain criteria; that is, any property or set of properties that admits of degree, such as reverence for tradition or social status, will have extremes that may or may not have instances. (Brown, 1963, p. 179)

Political extreme-type characteristics more often do not. There has never been a fully democratic or a purely egalitarian society, and it is unlikely that there ever will be. Contrary to Cnudde and Neubauer (1969, p. 11), however, it does not follow that, e.g., full political equality is "operationally . . . a quite literally 'meaningless' concept because it has no empirical referent." It is a descriptive concept, and it is operational in the broader sense, since it is in principle possible to ascertain which of any two concrete political systems is closer to being fully egalitarian. Thus extreme types "may serve as conceptual points of reference or 'poles', between which all actual occurrences can be ordered in a serial array" (Hempel, 1965, p. 157).

Since "no large system in the real world is fully democratized," one may consider a concept like full democracy as an *ideal type,* and "maintain the distinction between democracy as an ideal system and the institutional arrangements that have come to be regarded as a kind of imperfect approximation of an ideal" (Dahl, 1971, pp. 8–9). Accordingly, Dahl uses the concept of polyarchy for actual political systems that are *substantially* democratic (*ibid.*), as distinguished from the extreme-type concept of democracy, i.e., *full* democracy.

**4. Quantitative concepts.** These concepts may be considered a refinement of comparative concepts.

> Once we have replaced a categorical statement of the type: 'x has property P' by a comparative statement to the effect that x has property P to a higher degree than y, it may under certain conditions be possible to introduce units and to define a quantitative measure of the degree to which a given object x exhibits property P. Thus we may be able to define numerical expressions such as length, temperature, price. Quantitative concepts in turn permit the formulation of empirical laws in

> which the value of one variable is represented as a mathematical function of one or more other variables. For example: The length of a metal bar is an increasing function of its temperature. The quantity demanded varies inversely with the price of the commodity in a linear relationship. (Oppenheim, 1961, p. 180)

Some of the comparative concepts mentioned before can be quantified, e.g., the degree to which a given rule of distribution is egalitarian. The same is true of some of their defining criteria. Thus the degree of $Q$'s unfreedom to do $x$ with respect to $P$ depends on, among other factors, the *probability* of $P$'s punishing $Q$ if $Q$ does $x$, and on the *severity* of the penalty (measurable by the amount of fine or the number of months in prison). Similarly, it has been suggested that an overall index of disequilibrium in a social system might be constructed on the basis of several measurable indicators, such as increased suicide and crime rates, "heightened ideological activity" (measurable by "circulation figures for ideological newspapers"), "growing numbers of police in relation to the size of population" (Johnson, 1966, Ch. 6). Again, the problem remains how to combine such a variety of independently varying magnitudes into a single measure, e.g., of social disequilibrium. Furthermore, even where quantification is possible, precision of measurement sometimes draws attention away from the vagueness of the concepts used to describe what has been measured.

> Thus we may get very precise looking results correlating degrees of prejudice toward Jews with degrees of acceptance of oneself. But . . . in taking our final numerical results to give us degrees of acceptance of oneself, we are subject to all the indeterminacy that attaches to the question of the form, "Does Jones accept himself?" (Alston, 1964, p. 93)

This example illustrates that the sense of pride and achievement political scientists often derive from their quantification may sometimes be misplaced.

## V. THE LANGUAGE OF NORMATIVE POLITICAL INQUIRY

Political inquiry does not aim only at describing and explaining (or predicting) political events; it is also concerned with what should be done or avoided in the area of politics. We are thus led to an examination of the other main variety of the language of our discipline, which may be broadly characterized as normative.

The language of norms serves two main purposes, prescribing and evaluating.

*Prescriptions* include: (a) commands (or prohibitions or permissions); (b) rules (e.g., rules of games, of grammar, of logic, customary or legal rules); (c) moral principles,[5] i.e., stipulations to the effect that certain kinds of actions are morally right or wrong, e.g., John Stuart Mill's advocacy of the moral principle that "actions are right in the proportion as they tend to promote happiness" (*Utilitarianism*. Ch.2). 'Right', 'just', 'ought', 'legitimate', 'obligatory' are typical moral terms. Moral norms are of special concern to normative political inquiry.

*Evaluations* are stipulations to the effect that certain kinds of objects or states of affairs are good or bad, or better or worse than others, e.g., Mill's valuational principle that "pleasure, and freedom from pain, are the only things desirable as ends" *(ibid.)*. 'Good', 'better', 'desirable', 'preferable', 'beautiful' are value words. Normative political discourse serves to propound standards of political evaluation as well as principles of political morality.[6]

### A. Descriptive and Normative Discourse

It might be thought that whether a statement is descriptive or normative depends only on whether it consists exclusively of descriptive terms or also includes normative terms. However, as we shall see later, normative principles in general and moral norms in particular are sometimes expressed without the use of normative words. Conversely, expressions containing moral or value terms may be descriptive, as the following examples show.

*1. Appraisals.* To appraise something is to assert that it does or does not meet a *given* valuational standard or does so to a certain degree. "The statement that something fulfills or fails to fulfill a clearly defined standard is an empirical statement" (Paul Taylor, 1961, p. 77). For example, the affirmation that "most state constitutions today are old, lengthy, poorly written, and often inadequate for modern state governments" (Buediner, 1967, p. 54; quoted by Scarrow, 1969, p. 26) constitutes an appraisal in terms of certain presupposed norms of a good state constitution. So does the statement that a certain nation manifests a relatively high or low degree of sectionalism, if one accepts the definition of 'sectionalism' given previously (IV, B, 2). Appraisals, which are sometimes labeled "characterizing value judgments" (e.g., Nagel, 1961, p. 492), are descriptive, even though they may include normative terms. Appraisals must therefore be distinguished from normative statements. Thus Mill first propounds the norm that "some *kinds* of pleasure are more desirable and more valuable than others" (namely, those preferred "by those competently acquainted with both"). He then makes an appraisal in terms of this standard, namely, that it is "better to be Socrates dissatisfied than a fool satisfied" *(Utilitarianism,* Ch. 2). Hence, this is a descriptive affirmation. The same is true of statements to the effect that "an act is in accordance with or violates a clearly defined rule (as distinct from the statement of the rule itself)." (Paul W. Taylor, 1961, p. 77) Thus, Mill's assertion that policies forbidding marriage among indigents "are not objectionable as violations of liberty" *(On Liberty,* Ch. 1) is descriptive, since it is an appraisal in terms of the moral principle (previously propounded) that governments ought to restrict a person's liberty "to prevent harm to others" *(ibid.),* but for no other purposes.

Certain utterances, however, are not unambiguously either descriptive or normative, since they serve both to make an appraisal in terms of a norm and to express one's commitment to that norm. Someone who says that *A* was a good President may mean to appraise *A* favorably in terms of farsightedness or concern for the underprivileged and at the same time to express the moral judgment that Presidents ought to have those qualities.

**2. Instrumental value judgments.** Like so-called characterizing value judgments, so-called instrumental value judgments, which assert that something is good or that it should be done as a means to a given end, are descriptive, since means-end statements can be translated without loss of meaning into cause-effect (if-then) assertions. An example is Machiavelli's advice that "in capturing a state, the conqueror should consider all the injuries he must inflict, and inflict them all at once" *(The Prince,* Ch. 8).

**3. Descriptive statements about normative statements** are also descriptive. For example, consider Machiavelli's assertion: "Let a prince, then, conquer and maintain a state; his methods will always be judged honorable and praised by all, for the vulgar is always taken by appearances" *(ibid.,* Ch. 18). This statement expresses not the "Machiavellian" morality that "the end justifies the means" but the factual generalization that the "vulgar" (i.e., most people) do hold this moral view.

**4. Metaethical statements.** There is still another group of statements which contain normative terms but are not normative. Unlike the three types discussed so far, however, they are not descriptive, either. Rather, they are metaethical, and they therefore belong to the language of analytic philosophy. Metaethics "consists, not in making moral statements, but in making statements *about* moral statements; not in moral reasoning, but in reasoning *about* moral reasoning" (Paul Taylor, 1963, pp. xi–xii). To cite a classical example:

> [The] law of nature . . . obliges everyone; and reason which is that law, teaches all mankind who will but consult it, that . . . no one ought to harm another in his life, health, liberty, and possessions. (Locke, *Second Treatise of Government,* Ch. 2)

Here Locke does not merely propound the moral principle that nobody *ought* to harm anybody else; he also affirms that this moral principle is a rule of natural law, and that as such it is determinable by "reason." The natural law thesis is a metaethical theory, since it tries to establish that there are moral principles of politics which are demonstrably valid, independently of subjective moral commitments (Oppenheim, 1968, pp. 35–52).

## B. Descriptive and Normative Political Discourse

*1. Significance of the distinction.* It is, then, the function of a statement in its context, not its vocabulary, which determines whether it is normative. "What makes a statement the expression of a value judgment is not *which words* are used but the ways in which, and the purpose for which, they are used" (Paul Taylor, 1961, p. 54). These considerations apply also, of course, to any statement about politics. Whether it is descriptive or normative depends on the kind of speech act the writer or speaker is performing in making the statement in question. If its function is to inform, it is descriptive, even if it contains normative terms, as in the following examples. 'In terms of promoting racial equality, *A* was a good President'. 'Promoting racial equality is desirable for the sake of strengthening democratic institutions'. 'Promoting racial equality is considered desirable by many Americans'. We have seen, indeed, that appraisals in terms of a given standard, affirmations about the desirability of certain means to a given goal, and assertions about normative beliefs are descriptive. (That is why the language of the history and sociology of political thought is of descriptive character.) On the other hand, language used to prescribe or to guide conduct is normative, regardless of whether it includes normative terms. Thus 'racial equality is desirable for its own sake' is an instance of normative discourse; and so (at least in many contexts) is 'all men are equal'.

Political theorists sometimes engage in discourse that is neither descriptive nor normative but that might be characterized as philosophical. They do so when they deal not with political phenomena directly but with linguistic expressions about politics. We have seen that metaethical statements belong to this category. Now, analytic political philosophy is concerned with all problems of the logic of political inquiry, descriptive as well as normative. These include not only the possibility or impossibility of validating normative principles of politics but also the method of verification of descriptive statements about politics and the explication of political concepts. In the language of political philosophy, expressions about political matters can (but often do not) occur, so to speak, in (single) quotation marks—as they do in the present study, which does indeed belong to analytic political philosophy.

It is precisely because we cannot go by linguistic appearances that it becomes an important task of the clarification of the language of political inquiry to determine whether a given statement about politics is descriptive or normative or philosophical (in the sense of dealing with descriptive or normative *expressions* about politics). This distinction should not be confused with the traditional division of political inquiry into political science (in the narrow sense of empirical political research), political ethics, and political philosophy. This classification according to *disciplines* is of no interest when one is dealing with the analysis of *language*. Using these categories at all might lend support to the view that political scientists are—or should be—concerned only with "facts," leaving questions of "values" and logical analysis to the philosophers. I prefer to interpret 'political science' in the largest sense of inquiring into the descriptive, normative, and linguistic (including the methodological) aspects of political inquiry, using different types of discourse in each case. I agree with the following statement (which deals, however, only with the first two kinds of discourse).

> Ethical evaluation and empirical explanation involve two different kinds of propositions that, for the sake of clarity, should be kept analytically distinct. However, a student of political behavior is not prohibited from asserting propositions of either kind separately or in combination as long as he does not mistake one for the other. (Easton, 1965a p. 7)

**2. Objectives to the separation of "facts" and "values."** However, to say that two kinds of statements are "analytically distinct" need not imply that there are *no* logical connections between them. The question still remains, then: Is there any such relationship at all between descriptive and normative statements about politics?

One affirmative answer has been given by Searle (1964), who claims that an 'ought' statement can be derived from an 'is' statement if the latter is about an institutional fact. Thus "to recognize something as a promise is to grant that, other things being equal, it ought to be kept" (in Foot, 1967, p. 108). Accordingly, the institutional fact that $A$ promised $B$ to do $x$ entails that $A$ ought to do $x$. Searle's view has been criticized by Hare (1964): "But this conclusion can be drawn only by one who accepts, in addition, the non-tautologous principle that one ought to keep one's promises" (in Foot, 1967, p. 126).

Others—e.g., Baier (1958), Foot (1958–59), Charles Taylor (1967), and Connolly (1972)—though not claiming that statements of empirical science entail normative conclusions, maintain nevertheless that "a given framework of explanation in political science tends to support an associated value position, secretes its own norms for the assessment of polities and policies" (Charles Taylor, 1967, p. 48). This is due to the "grammar" of words such as 'good', i.e., the rules that we implicitly follow when we use them and that distinguish them from expressions of feeling, e.g., of approval or dislike. Taylor agrees that

> we can never say that 'good' *means* 'conducive to human happiness'. . . .

But that something is conducive to human happiness, or in general to the fulfillment of human needs, wants, and purposes, is a *prima facie* reason for calling it good, which stands unless countered. 1967, (p. 55)

That there is a logical link, however tenuous, between a descriptive statement and a normative principle has been denied by, e.g., Stevenson (1944), Hare (1952), Frankena (1963), and Oppenheim (1968). In this view, acceptance of, say, the theory of the power elite might be psychologically connected with certain normative commitments but is not logically related to any view about the morality or immorality of the elite's power. The argument is similar to Hare's (mentioned above): To move from '$P$ dominates $Q$ in ways which suppress $Q$'s interests' to 'the power relationship between $P$ and $Q$ is undesirable' (even as a prima facie conclusion) requires the implicit adoption of another, normative premise, namely, 'relations of domination are undesirable'. The latter premise, it is claimed, does not flow from the grammar of 'undesirable'.

Arguments such as those of Searle and Charles Taylor are instances of the metaethical theory of naturalism. *Naturalism* in its broadest sense contends that moral rules can be somehow verified, or at least supported, by empirical evidence (e.g., Taylor), or derived from empirical statements (e.g., Searle), or deduced from descriptive definitions of ethical terms. *Intuitionism*, on the other hand, claims that certain moral principles can be demonstrated on the basis of moral or rational or religious insight. Naturalism and intuitionism are the two main varieties of the metaethical theory of *value cognitivism*, which holds that normative, including moral, principles are statements for which there are tests that count for or against them. *Value noncognitivism* maintains, on the contrary, that intrinsic normative utterances have no cognitive status; that they cannot be said, much less shown, to be either true or false; that they express the speaker's value commitments or moral attitudes. (Both cognitivists and noncognitivists agree (1) that appraisals and instrumental value judgments are descriptive, hence true or false; (2) that moral choices can be said to be or not to be rational in terms of some given standard.) This is not the place for a critical appraisal of these metaethical positions. I wanted merely to show that value cognitivists tend to affirm and value noncognitivists to deny that there are logical connections between descriptive and normative statements.

Sometimes the argument of a connection between descriptive and normative statements is used to deny the thesis of any "separation between facts and values." Thus Searle concludes that "the alleged distinction between descriptive and evaluative statements" is of limited use at best (1964, p. 114). However, even those who emphasize the connection between descriptive and normative statements typically presuppose at least implicitly some functional difference between them. For instance, to claim, as Taylor does, that certain descriptions "support an associated value position" is to imply that the former is not equivalent to the latter. Of course, to value noncognitivists the distinction between moral discourse and factual statements is of particular importance, since they consider the *logic* of the former to be different from that of the latter. But even value cognitivists need not deny that there is a functional difference between saying that something is the case and saying that it should be brought about. (For further discussion of this issue, see Urmson, 1968.)

### C. Some Moral Concepts of Political Discourse

The criteria of adequate explication of *descriptive* political concepts do not apply to such basic *normative* terms as 'good' and 'ought'. Invoking the operational requirement in this connection would be a commitment to the view that value words are definable in descriptive terms (e.g., '$x$ is good' *means* '$x$ is conducive to the happiness of the majority'). I shall point out later (D, 2) why I do not subscribe to this particular version of metaethical naturalism. Many philosophers hold that such value words cannot be defined at all but must be taken as primitive terms. Anyhow, the analysis of valuational and moral concepts is a matter of philosophical controversy beyond the scope of the present study.

I shall, however, deal briefly with some other normative concepts which relate more specifically to political matters, namely, those of rights, legitimacy, and justice.

**1. Rights.** '$X$ has a right to $x$' may refer to either a legal or a moral right. If the former, the statement asserts that some given legal system contains a legal rule under which "some other person $Y$ is, in the events which have happened, obliged to do or to abstain from some action . . . if $X$ (or some authorized person) so chooses . . ." (Hart, 1953, p. 16). That $X$ has some legal right implies that others have the legal duty to leave $X$ free "to exercise his right." Taken in the legal sense, the statement 'Americans have the right to refuse combat service under certain conditions' means that American draft laws contain a provision conferring on draft registrants the right to claim C.O. status, and hence imposing on draft boards the legal obligation to exempt any who meet these conditions and who avail themselves of this right. In the mouth of a lawyer or a political scientist, the statement describes a feature of a legal system. When uttered by the legislator in his official capacity, the same words constitute a legal enactment.

When such statements refer to moral rights, they are normative. '$X$ has a moral right to $x$' means that someone else (to be specified) has the moral duty to do (or to abstain from doing) something if $X$ wishes it. A political moralist may say, 'Americans have a right to refuse participation in a war they consider ethically or politically wrong'. This statement means that persons holding such beliefs are morally entitled to refuse induction, and that draft boards (or the armed forces in general) have the moral obligation to exempt them, even when they cannot legally claim C.O. status. Implicitly, this statement may also express the moral judgment that existing legislation should be modified accordingly. "One of the most important uses of statements of moral rights is in advocating that people be given legal rights they do not have" (Brandt, 1959, p. 436). In accordance with this position, let us consider the Declaration of Independence. It must not be interpreted as an assertion that "all men" have the *legal* rights of "life, liberty, and the pursuit of happiness" (an affirmation which would have been false in 1776—as it is today). Neither is it an act of legislation conferring such legal rights on all men (the framers had no legal authority to do so). Rather, it is an ascription of certain *moral* rights to all men, i.e., the proclamation of the moral principle that all governments have the moral duty "to secure" the corresponding legal rights to their respective citizens. Ascriptions of moral rights are often expressed by statements which appear to be descriptive. 'All men "possess" the right to life' looks like 'all Americans possess the right to life', or 'all men possess a nose', or 'some possess television sets'. Only the first is normative; the other three are descriptive.

Statements about *natural* rights, like the natural law thesis itself, belong to analytic political philosophy. An example: "The aim of every political association is the preservation of the *natural* and imprescriptible rights of man." Here the French Declaration of 1789 affirms that the statement 'men have certain moral rights' is demonstrably true (and proclaims that every political association ought to legislate accordingly). The Declaration of Independence expresses a similar idea; the moral principle that all men have certain unalienable rights is self-evident.

Another important distinction is that between a moral right and what is morally right. Unlike 'X has a moral right to do x', 'it is morally right for X to do x' carries no implication as to corollary moral obligations of others to X.

**2. Legitimacy.** Governments, policies, legal enactments are said to be legitimate or illegitimate. Like the notion of a right, the concept of legitimacy is used both in a descriptive-legal and in a normative-moral way. In the legal sense, 'legitimate', 'legal', and 'lawful' may be taken as synonyms. "Legal and legitimate are used indifferently to describe the way in which State activity conforms to the particular rules of the legal system or the general directives which the Constitution lays down" (d'Entreves, 1967, p. 141). Accordingly, "statements of the form 'X is the lawful government of Y' refer implicitly to a given legal system" (Raz, 1970b, p. 301). 'X is the legitimate or lawful government of Y' simply means that X is a government according to the legal system in Y, i.e., that "according to that system it is recognized as possessing certain powers and rights and is subject to certain duties" *(ibid.)*. Keeping in mind our explication of the concept of a legal system (III, A, 6), we note that this statement implies the following *empirical* assertions: (a) Those who claim governmental authority have acceded to office in conformity with the secondary rules of the given system (e.g., the constitution), and their enactments and policies do on the whole conform to these rules. (b) Inhabitants of Y tend to comply with X's enactments. (c) They tend to accept these enactments as general standards to be followed (but acceptance does not imply that they consider them morally obligatory). Thus one could argue that the regime of the Greek colonels was illegitimate, because it came into power by overthrowing the legitimate, constitutionally established government. One could also claim that the government of the colonels was legitimate in terms of their own "constitution" (and point out that most Greeks complied with their enactments and believed that they must do so, however reluctantly). Similarly, those who considered United States war policies in Indochina illegitimate sometimes meant that they violated American constitutional or international law. 'X is the lawful government of Y' may also constitute an act of recognition of government X by some other government. (To this point, see Hare, 1967.)

"Legitimate authority is precisely that which *ought* to be obeyed" (Pitkin, 1966, p. 39). Here the concept of legitimacy functions normatively. Taken in this sense, the expression 'X is the legitimate government of Y' means—or rather, implies—that X is morally entitled to the allegiance of the people of Y, and that the latter have at least a prima facie moral duty to comply with X's enactments. That a certain government is illegitimate in the moral sense expresses the judgment that it is morally permissible or even obligatory to disobey its commands or resist its power. Thus the government of the Greek colonels may be judged illegitimate from the moral point of view, even if it is considered legitimate from the point of view of the legal system of 1968, and even if a large segment of the Greek population *judged* it morally legitimate as well. That the United States was waging an illegitimate war in Indochina may refer to the immorality of that war (rather than its unconstitutionality). It is perfectly consistent to speak of illegitimate acts of legitimate governments, provided that one makes it clear that the same word functions first as a moral term and then as a descriptive term. Too often, however, the concept of legitimacy is used ambiguously.

**3. *Justice*.** "We are looking for justice, a thing much more precious than gold" (Plato, *Republic*, I, 336). No, justice is not a "thing," and it is certainly not visible (even in Plato's sense). Again, to avoid the fallacy of reification, let us avoid the noun and use the adjective. 'Just', too, can function in both a legal and a moral sense. A judge's decision is just if it is impartial, i.e., if it is determined exclusively by the legal rules which govern the case and not, e.g., by his like or dislike of the claimant or defendant. Any rule can be applied justly or unjustly. In terms of a provision limiting suffrage to whites, denying this right to a black person is legal, and hence it is just in the legal sense. Such assertions constitute appraisals and are therefore descriptive.

Whether a rule itself is just or unjust is a moral question. 'Racial discrimination is unjust' belongs to normative discourse, as does 'racial discrimination is wrong'. Justice is "part of virtue" (Aristotle, *Ethics*, 1130a), a subcategory of moral rightness. "Justice is not to be confused with an all-inclusive vision of a good society; it is only one part of any such conception" (Rawls, 1958, p. 165). 'Just' and 'unjust' can be predicated only of rules of distribution (including institutions based on such rules), and more specifically of the way in which such rules allocate benefits or burdens. One can ask whether it is right or wrong to legalize abortion or divorce, not whether such provisions are just. Examples of rules which can be judged just or unjust are provisions stipulating how offices, voting rights, tax burdens, educational opportunities are to be distributed—e.g., according to (or regardless of) ability or need or wealth or color.

Justice may conflict with utility (see Rawls, 1971, especially pp. 22–33). One may condemn slavery as unjust, even when the advantages to the slaveholders outweigh the disadvantages to the slaves. One may advocate wage differentiation according to ability for utilitarian reasons while conceding its injustice. This raises the ethical problem of which of these two competing values, justice or utility, ought to prevail. However, our topic does not require us to deal with normative issues of justice. We need only to emphasize that 'just', when applied to rules of distribution, is a moral notion and, e.g., 'racial discrimination is just (or unjust)' a moral principle of politics.

## D. Persuasive Definitions

Descriptive statements sometimes look like normative ones (e.g., so-called characterizing and instrumental value judgments). Conversely, normative principles, especially of politics, are often couched in factual language —usually for the sake of rhetorical effectiveness. Locke's statement that "all men are by nature equal" was an especially forceful way to express his moral conviction that all men *should* be given the same basic legal rights by their respective governments. Similarly,

> when some social institution is said to have a certain function, this may mean either the function which it actually fulfills or the function which it should fulfill—its proper and true function. (Gibson, 1960, p. 68)

More often still, political rhetoric disguises normative principles as definitions.

***1. In descriptive terms.*** Because words like 'freedom', 'equality', 'democracy' have acquired, in our culture (though not, e.g., in Plato's view), positive valuational connotations, they are sometimes said to stand for "political values," and they are therefore considered value words. We have seen, however, that these concepts are descriptive, that they can be explicated in descriptive terms, and that such definitions can often be accepted by persons with different normative attitudes. Meaningful disagreement about the desirable extent or limit of freedom, etc., presupposes agreement about the meaning of 'freedom' in descriptive terms. But 'freedom' is often "defined" to cover only those relationships of *both* freedom and unfreedom (in the sense defined above, III, B, 1) one wishes to commend. Thus classical liberals held that government ought to restrict a citizen's freedom to do whatever he wants only to prevent him from violating another's basic rights. They often expressed this normative view in definitional language: A free society *means* one in which freedom is restricted for such purposes but not for others. Modern liberals advocate governmental restrictions of individual liberty for the purpose of securing a minimum standard of living to all. But again, instead of using the language of 'ought', they like to say that freedom, or "true" freedom, *is* "freedom from want"—which, as we saw (I, B, 3) does not refer to social freedom at all but to welfare. And so 'freedom' acquires the meaning of desirable unfreedom. Rousseau, for example, by stating that "obedience to a law which we prescribe to ourselves is liberty" *(Social Contract,* Book I, Ch. 8) did not intend to *explicate* the meaning of 'freedom' but to *exhort* citizens to comply with restrictions of freedom prescribed in accordance with the "general will." And his statement that compelling someone to obey such injunctions "means nothing less than that he will be forced to be free" *(ibid.,* Ch. 7) expresses the moral judgment that it is right to make him *unfree* (in the usual sense) to disobey them.

In all such instances, words with laudatory connotations are assigned meanings which cover just those situations the speaker values positively. Stevenson (1944) has called such statements "persuasive definitions." Indeed, 'freedom is absence of want' or 'freedom is obedience' is a very persuasive way of *advocating* the welfare state or *exhorting* citizens to comply with governmental policies. We have seen that political scientists often disagree as to the most appropriate explication of a given political concept, and that such disagreements often reflect divergent political ideologies. Applying the criteria of adequacy discussed earlier can help to clarify and to reduce such differences. To adopt persuasive definitions, on the contrary, is to disregard these criteria and to capture political concepts for the purpose of advancing particular normative views.

**2. In normative terms.** The definitions above, even though persuasive, are couched in descriptive language. Sometimes, however, the defining expression in turn includes normative terms, as in the following examples: Freedom is "the power of doing what we ought to will and not being constrained to do what we ought not to will" (Montesquieu, *Spirit of the Laws*, Book XI, Ch. 3). "The true opposite of equality is arbitrary, i.e., unjustifiable or inequitable treatment" (Von Leyden, 1963, p. 67). Such statements must be criticized, not only for being persuasive definitions, but also for violating the basic operational requirement of connecting with empirical data. The presence of freedom or equality in a given situation is here made dependent, not on descriptive, but on normative criteria, namely, on whether someone is being compelled to do what he *ought* to will, or whether some inegalitarian distribution is *justified*. Furthermore, on the basis of the latter definition, it would be logically contradictory to say that a differential wage scale is justified *and* inegalitarian, or that paying equal salaries to all is inequitable yet egalitarian. If we adopt instead the descriptive definition of egalitarianism mentioned previously (IV, A, 1), there can be no doubt that the former rule is inegalitarian and the latter egalitarian, and it becomes then possible to disagree in a meaningful way as to whether one or the other rule is just or equitable.

Like 'egalitarian', 'political' can be used as a descriptive predicate and can be defined in descriptive terms, so that assertions that a given activity is political or is nonpolitical depend exclusively on empirical data. Not so when 'politics' is made to refer to "some conception of human welfare or the public good," in contradistinction to "pseudopolitical" activities concerned with "promoting private or private interest-group advantage, deterred by no articulate or disinterested conception of what would be just or fair to other groups." Here Bay (1965, p. 40) defines 'politics' persuasively to apply only to those political activities (in the descriptive sense) which are motivated by considerations of altruism, whereas those based exclusively on self-interest are labeled 'pseudopolitical'. Therefore the quoted passage must, first of all, be interpreted as an exhortation to policy makers to act "politically" and not "pseudopolitically." (The usual pejorative connotation of the former word has been transferred to the latter.) Furthermore, the "defining" expressions include not only 'human welfare' and 'private interests' but also 'the public good' and 'just'. Although the first two concepts may perhaps be defined descriptively, the last two are clearly normative. Consequently, to enjoin policy makers to act politically is to advocate whatever policies are deemed to fulfill these normative conditions.

Or take the concept of violence.

> Strictly speaking, *violence is the illegitimate or unauthorized use of force to effect decisions against the will or desire of others.* Thus, murder is an act of violence, but capital punishment *by a legitimate state* is not. (Wolff, 1969, p. 606)

If 'illegitimate' in the defining expression is taken in the descriptive-legal sense (see V, C, 2), then the two assertions are factual—and true, since murder is an illegal but capital punishment a legally valid use of force. On the other hand, if 'illegitimate' is interpreted normatively, then, whether the use of force constitutes an act of violence will depend on one's normative judgment as to whether those who performed or ordered the action had a moral right to do so or acted immorally. "Descriptively speaking, the attack on Hitler's life during the second World War was an act of violence, but one might perfectly well deny that it was violent in the strict sense, on the grounds that Hitler's regime was illegitimate" (Wolff, 1969, p. 606). Morally speaking, one might deny it. 'The attack on Hitler's life was not an act of violence' now means that the attempt was not morally wrong (but right).

Another common fallacy consists in adopting the reverse procedure, namely to express the *advocated* goal in valuational terms and to use descriptive terms to define the latter. Instead of advocating egalitarianism and equating egalitarianism with justice, one propounds justice as a goal and defines justice in terms of egalitarianism, as does Aristotle ("the unjust is unequal, the just equal" *Ethics,* 1131a). "If such definitions are acceptable, then by virtue of them, one can go logically from Is to Ought or from Fact to Value" (Frankena, 1963, p. 80). Thus, if 'just' is synonymous with 'equal', then, if a rule is egalitarian, it follows that it is just. Similarly, if a right action is defined as one "that is conformable to the principle of utility" (Bentham, *Principles of Morals and Legislation,* Ch. 1), then an action which is conducive to the general happiness is right and ought to be done. Or after having defined 'good' as what is approved by the majority or what fulfills human needs, one argues that $x$ is approved by the majority, hence good, that it is conducive to the fulfillment of human needs, hence desirable. But are such definitions "acceptable" in the sense of fruitful? It would then be logically contradictory to consider some egalitarian rule of distribution unjust or a policy approved by the majority undesirable. In all these instances, normative conclusions are logically derived from unacceptable definitional premises. To define either descriptive terms normatively or normative terms descriptively violates the rules of clear language.

***3. In appraisal terms.*** An even more widespread practice consists in defining political concepts persuasively with the help not of normative but of appraisal terms. We have seen that the latter are descriptive only if reference is made, at least implicitly, to a standard or rule. Thus the definition of 'sectionalism' given previously (IV, B, 2, b) is descriptive, since the standards in terms of which to appraise "significant percentage," "sizeable area," etc., are clearly implied. This condition is not fulfilled by Hayek's definition of freedom as "that condition of men in which coercion of some by others is reduced *as much as possible* in society," or as "independence of the *arbitrary* will of another" (1960, pp. 11, 12; italics added). Accordingly, if $Q$ has been coerced by *P* in a nonarbitrary way, *Q* is in a condition of freedom, even though *P* has made him unfree (in the ordinary sense of the word) to do *x*. In the absence of a specified standard of arbitrariness, investigators are bound to disagree as to whether *P* acted arbitrarily, and a Hitler or Stalin can "prove" that their subjects were "free." Everyone is left to make his appraisal in terms of his own normative commitments, and the concept thus "defined" refers not to some determinate state of affairs but to anything held desirable by anyone. Definitions in terms of appraisal words without reference to standards of evaluation therefore fail to meet the requirement of operationalism even in the broadest sense.

The concept of egalitarianism may again serve as a further illustration. According to another of Aristotle's definitions, a rule of distribution is egalitarian, provided that "the relative values of things given correspond to those of the persons receiving" (*Politics*, 1280a). Now, the relative values of things are often appraised in monetary terms, and this may be the implied standard. But by what standard shall we appraise the values of persons (relative to one another)? Clearly, '*A* is more valuable than *B*' is a value judgment, not an appraisal. Or consider the following, at present widely accepted definition: A rule of distribution is egalitarian if differences in allotments correspond to *relevant* differences in personal characteristics (e.g., Ginsberg, 1965, p. 79). It is then argued that it is egalitarian to limit the franchise to adult citizens but inegalitarian to restrict it to white men, because age and citizenship are "relevant" to voting rights, but race and sex are not. However, the standard of relevance is left open, and so the last statement means the same as: It is *just* to require a minimum voting age, unjust to base franchise on color or sex. Here again, whether a given rule is egalitarian or inegalitarian depends not on empirical criteria but on moral judgments.

One last example will illustrate the use of terms of appraisal left floating, so to speak, in midair, without connections to specified standards of value. Marcuse advocates restricting tolerance for

> movements of a demonstrably *aggressive* and *destructive* character . . . "where the other side" is demonstrably *"regressive"* and impedes possible *improvement* of the human condition. . . . If *vital* ideas, values, and ends of human *progress* no longer [or rather, not yet] enter, as competing equals, the formation of public opinion, . . . is there any alternative other than the dictatorship of an *"elite"* . . .? (Marcuse, 1969, p. 129; italics added)

To avoid ambiguities, normative concepts had best be used only to express the *advocacy* of some political action or goal, and the *advocated* policy or state of affairs must be characterized exclusively in descriptive terms; if appraisal terms are used, some standard must be indicated. Following this practice will make for clarification of both the normative and the descriptive dimensions of the language of political inquiry.

## VI. CONCLUSION: UNRESOLVED ISSUES

A study like the present one is bound to raise more issues than it can resolve. One reason is that at least some of them are linked to rather fundamental philosophical controversies. Instead of ending with a set of affirmative conclusions, it seems therefore more appropriate to restate these unresolved problems and to indicate, for the sake of illustration, two contrasting positions one might take concerning each of them.

### A. The Function of Linguistic Analysis in the Area of Politics

1. According to the view expressed at the start, one of the principal purposes of the clarification of the language of political inquiry consists in constructing for political concepts of ordinary language explicative definitions which make them more suitable for a scientific study of the political process. To that effect, such explications must depart from current usage whenever it is ambiguous or vague, as is so often true in the area of politics. This approach stresses the difference between the language of political rhetoric and of political science.

2. However, in the course of outlining this procedure, we have met repeatedly the objection that an efficient technical language of political science can be constructed only at the price of ignoring the complexities and shadings of political life. According to this view, analysts should stick more closely to the ways political concepts are actually used in ordinary discourse. They should keep in mind that many of them are "open-ended." Making these differences explicit and exploring the implications of alternative uses constitute an essential part of linguistic clarification.

### B. The "Fact-Value" Distinction

1. I began this study with the presupposition that there is a fundamental distinction between the language of factual and the language of normative political inquiry. The argument is that informing what is the case and advocating what ought to be done constitute different types of speech acts, serving different kinds of purpose (regardless of the grammatical appearance of the corresponding statements). Furthermore, many analysts hold that different kinds of reasons must be adduced to back up one or the other of these two types of discourse.

2. Nevertheless, we have encountered doubts as to whether—or at least to what extent—the distinction between "facts" and "values" can be maintained. Those sympathetic to position A,2 tend to consider appraisals in terms of a

valuational standard to have normative as well as descriptive features. They also point to the great number of political concepts which, in ordinary language, have both factual and evaluative dimensions. And they tend to be sceptical as to whether political concepts can be defined at all in a value-neutral, nonpersuasive way.

### C. Operationalism

1. According to empiricism (of which operationalism is an outgrowth), concepts, to be useful tools for empirical science, must be defined in such a way that statements in which they occur can in principle be tested by observational, publicly available evidence. There is common agreement that the original requirements of operationalism must be greatly relaxed to provide criteria for fruitful explications, especially of political concepts, which refer so often to mental states and to institutional rules. Proponents of positions A,1 and B,1 will nevertheless continue to attach importance to the operational requirement, if only to eliminate value words from explicative definitions of political terms, since otherwise the truth of factual statements would depend on the investigator's value position.

2. Many opponents argue that operationalism, if broadened to such an extent, no longer establishes a clear line between explications acceptable in political inquiry and those to be excluded. They consider some of the other criteria of fruitfulness to be more important.

### D. Lawlike and Verstehen Explanations

1. Concepts of political inquiry can and should be constructed in a way that makes possible an empirical science which provides lawlike explanations of political behavior.

2. Political concepts should rather reflect the rules of discourse adopted by participants in political life and thereby contribute to a mode of inquiry which understands conduct within the terms of reference adopted by the participants. These advocates of *Verstehen* tend to be sceptical as to whether causal explanations in general, and those of the covering law type in particular, are applicable to the study of social and political interaction.

Political philosophers and political scientists are likely to be more sympathetic toward the same position (either 1 or 2) on each of these issues. It remains to be seen whether one or the other will prevail in the long run, or to what extent compromises will receive rational support.

## NOTES

1. Following standard procedures adopted by logicians, single quotation marks are placed around an expression (word or sentence) whenever something is said about

that expression (e.g., about its meaning, its logical status) as distinguished from what the expression refers to. Thus, as the title of this essay indicates, I will deal, not with politics, but with 'politics' (i.e., with the concept of politics; note that no quotation marks occur in the latter expression).

2. Once '$x$ is democratic' has been defined, we can say that the noun 'democracy' refers to the property $x$ has just in case $x$ is democratic.

3. Hence it is not true that "a man who has inadvertently fallen into a natural pit with unscalable walls is unfree in the same sense as the prisoner at night in his cell" (Cassinelli, 1966, p. 28). Both lack freedom of choice to get out (i.e., they cannot leave); but only the latter is unfree to leave—with respect to the prison warden, etc.

4. Methodological individualism and holism also refer to two opposing views as to whether generalizations about group phenomena can be derived from laws of individual psychology (Brodbeck, 1958). This controversy does not concern us here, since it is independent of the issue about the meaning of group concepts.

5. It is a matter of controversy among moral philosophers whether moral norms are prescriptive (e.g., Hare) or evaluative (e.g., Paul Taylor) or neither (e.g., von Wright).

6. Ethics in general includes not only moral judgments in the strict sense but also value judgments. But not all evaluations are of a moral kind (e.g., esthetic judgments are not). (Cf. Frankena, 1963, pp. 9–10.)


## REFERENCES

Two frequently cited sources in the references that follow are given in abbreviated form: *EPH* stands for *Encyclopedia of Philosophy*, New York, Macmillan, 1967; *ESS* stands for *International Encyclopedia of the Social Sciences*, New York, Macmillan, 1968.

Almond, Gabriel A. (1956). "Comparative political systems." *The Journal of Politics* 18:391–409.

Alston, William P. (1964). *Philosophy of Language*. Englewood Cliffs, N.J.: Prentice-Hall.

Ashby, R.W. (1967). "Verifiability principle." *EPH* 8:240–7.

Austin, J.L. (1970). *Philosophical Papers*, 2nd edition. London: Oxford University Press.

Banks, Arthur, and Robert Textor (1963). *A Cross-Polity Survey*. Cambridge, Mass.: M.I.T. Press.

Bachrach, Peter (1967). *The Theory of Democratic Elitism, a Critique*. Boston: Little, Brown.

Baier, Kurt (1958). *The Moral Point of View*. Ithaca: Cornell University Press.

Barry, Brian (1965). *Political Argument*. New York: Humanities Press.

_____ (1962). "The use and abuse of 'the public interest'." In Carl J. Friedrich (ed.), *Nomos V: The Public Interest*. New York: Atherton Press. Pp. 191–204.

Bay, Christian (1965). "Politics and pseudopolitics: a critical evaluation of some behavioral literature." *The American Political Science Review* 59:39–51.

Bedau, Hugo A. (1967). "Egalitarianism and the idea of equality." In J. Roland Pennock and John W. Chapman (eds.), *Nomos IX: Equality*. New York: Atherton Press.

Benn, Stanley I. (1967a). "Political philosophy, nature of." *EPH* 6:387–92.

_____ (1967b). "Power." *EPH* 6:424–7.

Benn, S.I., and R.S. Peters (1959). *Social Principles and the Democratic State*. London: George Allen and Unwin.

Benn, S.I., and W. L. Weinstein (1971). "Being free to act, and being a free man." *Mind* 80:194–211.

Berelson, Bernard (1968). "Behavioral sciences." *ESS* 2:41–5.

Berlin, Isaiah (1938). "Verification." *Proceedings of the Aristotelian Society* 39:225–48. Reprinted in Parkinson (ed., 1968, pp. 15–34).

Brandt, Richard B. (1959). *Ethical Theory*. Englewood Cliffs, N.J.: Prentice-Hall.

Braybrooke, David (1968). *Three Tests for Democracy: Personal Rights, Human Welfare, Collective Preference*. New York: Random House.

Brodbeck, May (1958). "Methodological individualism: definition and reduction." *Philosophy of Science* 25: 1–22.

_____ (1968). "General introduction." In May Brodbeck (ed.), *Readings in the Philosophy of the Social Sciences*. New York: Macmillan. Pp. 1–12.

Brown, Robert (1963). *Explanation in Social Science*. Chicago: Aldine.

Buechner, John C. (1967). *State Government in the Twentieth Century*. Boston: Houghton Mifflin.

Care, Norman S., and Charles Landesman, eds., (1968). *Readings in the Theory of Action*. Bloomington and London: Indiana University Press.

Cassinelli, C.W. (1966). *Free Activities and Interpersonal Relations*. The Hague: Martinus Nijhoff.

Cnudde, Charles F., and Deane E. Neubauer, eds. (1969). *Empirical Democratic Theory*. Chicago: Markham.

Connolly, William E. (1967). *Political Science and Ideology*. New York: Atherton Press.

_____ (1970). "Liberalism under pressure." *Polity* 2:55–66

_____ (1972). "On interests in politics." *Politics and Society* 2:459–77.

Dahl, Robert A. (1963). *Modern Political Analysis*. Englewood Cliffs, N.J.: Prentice-Hall.

_____ (1968). "Power." *ESS* 12:405–415.

_____ (1970). *Modern Political Analysis*, 2nd revised edition. Englewood Cliffs, N.J.: Prentice-Hall.

_____ (1971). *Polyarchy: Participation and Opposition*. New Haven: Yale University Press.

Davidson, Donald (1963). "Actions, reasons, and causes." *The Journal of Philosophy* LX 23:685–700. Reprinted in May Brodbeck (ed.), 1968. *Readings in the Philosophy of the Social Sciences*. New York: Macmillan, pp. 44–588.

Deutsch, Karl W. (1970). *Politics and Government: How People Decide Their Fate.* Boston: Houghton Mifflin.

Donnellan, Keith S. (1967). "Reasons and causes." *EPH* 7:85–8.

Easton, David (1965a). *A Framework for Political Analysis.* Englewood Cliffs, N.J.: Prentice-Hall.

──────── (1965b). *A Systems Analysis of Political Life.* New York: Wiley.

──────── (1967). "The current meaning of 'behavioralism'." In James C. Charlesworth (ed.), *Contemporary Political Analysis.* New York: Free Press. Pp. 11–31.

──────── (1968). "Political science." *ESS* 12:282–98.

──────── (1969). "The new revolution in political science." *The American Political Science Review* 63:1051–61.

d'Entreves, Alexander Passerin (1967). *The Notion of the State.* Oxford: Clarendon Press.

Eulau, Heinz (1963). *The Behavioral Persuasion in Politics.* New York: Random House.

──────── (1968). "Political behavior." *ESS* 12:203–14.

Flathman, Richard E. (1966). *The Public Interest.* New York: Wiley.

──────── (1972). *Political Obligation.* New York: Atheneum.

Foot, Philippa (1958–59). "Moral beliefs." *Proceedings of the Aristotelian Society* 59: 83–104. Reprinted in Philippa Foot 1967, pp. 83–100.

──────── (1967). *Theories of Ethics.* London: Oxford University Press.

Frankena, William K. (1963). *Ethics.* Englewood Cliffs, N.J.: Prentice-Hall.

Friedrich, Carl Joachim (1963). *Man and His Government: an Empirical Theory of Politics.* New York: McGraw-Hill.

Gellner, Ernest (1970). "Concepts and society." In Dorothy Emmet and Alasdair MacIntyre (eds.), *Sociological Theory and Philosophical Analysis.* London and Basingstoke: Macmillan. Pp. 115–49.

Gibson, Quentin (1960). *The Logic of Social Enquiry.* London: Routledge and Kegan Paul.

Ginsberg, Morris (1965). *On Justice in Society.* Baltimore: Penguin Books.

Goldberg, Arthur S. (1968). "Political science as science." In Robert A. Dahl and Deane E. Neubauer (eds.), *Readings in Modern Political Analysis.* Englewood Cliffs, N.J.: Prentice-Hall. Pp. 15–30.

Goldman, Alvin (1970). *A Theory of Human Action.* Englewood Cliffs, N.J.: Prentice-Hall.

Gregor, A. James (1971). *An Introduction to Metapolitics; A Brief Inquiry into the Conceptual Language of Political Science.* New York: Free Press.

Gross, Bertram M. (1968). "Political process." *ESS* 12:265–72.

Haas, Michael (1966). "Aggregate analysis." *World Politics* 19:106–21.

Hacker, Andrew (1964). "Power to do what?" In I. L. Horowitz (ed.), *The New Sociology.* New York: Oxford University Press. Pp. 134–46.

Hare, R.M. (1952). *The Language of Morals.* Oxford: Clarendon Press.

_____ (1964). "The promising game." *Revue Internationale de Philosophie* 70: 398–412. Reprinted in Philippa Foot, 1967, pp. 115–127.

_____ (1967). "The lawful government." In Peter Laslett and W. G. Runciman (eds.), *Philosophy, Politics and Society,* 3rd series. New York: Barnes and Noble. Pp. 157–72.

Hart, H.L.A. (1953). *Definition and Theory in Jurisprudence.* Oxford: Clarendon Press.

_____ (1961). *The Concept of Law.* Oxford: Clarendon Press.

Hayek, F. A. (1960). *The Constitution of Liberty.* Chicago: University of Chicago Press.

Hempel, Carl G. (1952). *Fundamentals of Concept Formation in Empirical Science.* Chicago: University of Chicago Press.

_____ (1965). *Aspects of Scientific Explanation.* New York: Free Press.

Hook, Sidney (1959). *Political Power and Personal Freedom.* New York: Criterion.

Hyneman, Charles S. (1959). *The Study of Politics.* Urbana: University of Illinois Press.

Johnson, Chalmers (1966). *Revolutionary Change.* Boston and Toronto: Little, Brown.

Kalleberg, Arthur L. (1966). "The logic of comparison: a methodological note on the comparative study of political systems." *World Politics* 19:69–82.

Kaplan, Abraham (1964). *The Conduct of Inquiry: Methodology for Behavioral Science.* San Francisco: Chandler.

Kaufman, Arnold S. (1967). "Behaviorism." *EPH* 1:268–73.

Kovesi, Julius (1967). *Moral Notions.* London: Routledge and Kegan Paul.

Lasswell, Harold D., and Abraham Kaplan (1950). *Power and Society: a Framework for Political Inquiry.* New Haven: Yale University Press.

Lenski, Gerhard (1966). *Power and Privilege.* New York: McGraw-Hill.

Louch, A.R. (1966). *Explanation and Human Action.* Los Angeles: University of California Press.

Mandelbaum, Maurice (1955). "Societal facts." *The British Journal of Sociology* 6: 305–17.

March, James G. (1966). "The power of power." In David Easton (ed.), *Varieties of Political Theory.* Englewood Cliffs, N.J.: Prentice-Hall. Pp. 39–70.

Marcuse, Herbert (1965). "Repressive tolerance." In Robert Paul Wolff et al., *A Critique of Pure Tolerance.* Boston: Beacon Press. Pp. 81–123.

Nagel, Ernest (1961). *The Structure of Science: Problems in the Logic of Scientific Explanation.* New York: Harcourt, Brace and World.

Oppenheim, Felix E. (1958). "An analysis of political control: actual and potential." *The Journal of Politics* 20:515–34.

_____ (1961). *Dimensions of Freedom: an Analysis.* New York: St. Martin's Press.

_____ (1968). *Moral Principles in Political Philosophy.* New York: Random House.

_____ (1970). "Egalitarianism as a descriptive concept." *American Philosophical Quarterly* 7:143–52.

Pap, Arthur (1949). *Elements of Analytic Philosophy.* New York: Macmillan.

Parkinson, G.H.R., ed. (1968). *The Theory of Meaning.* London: Oxford University Press.

Pitkin, Hanna (1966). "Obligation and consent—II." *The American Political Science Review* 60:39–52.

Rapoport, Anatol (1966). "Some system approaches to political theory." In David Easton (ed.), *Varieties of Political Theories.* Englewood Cliffs, N.J.: Prentice-Hall.

Rawls, John (1958). "Justice as fairness." *The Philosophical Review* 67:164–94.

——— (1971). *A Theory of Justice.* Cambridge, Mass.: Belknap, Harvard University Press.

Raz, Joseph (1970a). *The Concept of a Legal System.* Oxford: Clarendon Press.

——— (1970b). "On lawful governments." *Ethics* 80:296–305.

Reagan, Michael D. (1963). *The Managed Economy.* New York: Oxford University Press.

Riker, William H. (1964). "Some ambiguities in the notion of power." *American Political Science Review* 58:341–9.

Russell, Bertrand (1940). "Freedom and government." In Ruth Nanda Anshen (ed.), *Freedom, its Meanings.* New York: Harcourt, Brace, pp. 249–64.

Scarrow, Howard A. (1969). *Comparative Political Analysis: an Introduction.* New York: Harper and Row.

Schlesinger, G. (1967). "Operationalism." *EPH* 5:543–7.

Schlick, Moritz (1936). "Meaning and verification." *The Philosophical Review* 45.

Schutz, Alfred (1963). "Concepts, constructs and theory formation." In Maurice Natanson (ed.), *Philosophy of Social Science.* New York: Random House. Pp. 231–49.

Searle, John R. (1964). "How to derive 'ought' from 'is'." *Philosophical Review* 73: 43–58. Reprinted in Philippa Foot, 1967, pp. 101–114.

Shaffer, Jerome A. (1968). *Philosophy of Mind.* Englewood Cliffs, N.J.: Prentice-Hall.

Sibley, Mulford Q. (1967). "The limitations of behavioralism." In James C. Charlesworth (ed.), *Contemporary Political Analysis.* New York: Free Press. Pp. 51–71.

Simon, Herbert A. (1957). *Models of Man: Social and Rational.* New York: Wiley.

Stevenson, Charles L. (1944). *Ethics and Language.* New Haven: Yale University Press.

Taylor, Charles (1967). "Neutrality in political science." In Peter Laslett and W.G. Runciman (eds.), *Philosophy, Politics and Society,* 3rd series. New York: Barnes and Noble. Pp. 25–57.

Taylor, Paul W. (1961). *Normative Discourse.* Englewood Cliffs, N.J.: Prentice-Hall.

———, ed. (1963). *The Moral Judgement: Readings in Contemporary Meta-Ethics.* Englewood Cliffs, N.J.: Prentice-Hall.

Urmson, J.O. (1968). *The Emotive Theory of Ethics.* New York: Oxford University Press.

Verba, Sidney (1969). "Political participation and strategies of influence: a comparative study." In James D. Barber (ed.), *Readings in Citizen Politics.* Chicago: Markham.

Von Leyden, W. (1963). "On justifying inequality." *Political Studies* 11:56–70.

von Wright, Georg Henrik (1963). *Norm and Action: A Logical Enquiry.* London: Routledge and Kegan Paul; New York: Humanities Press.

——— (1971). *Explanation and Understanding.* Ithaca: Cornell University Press.

Waismann, Friedrich (1951). "Verifiability." In Anthony Flew (ed.), *Logic and Language,* 1st series. Oxford: Blackwell. Pp. 115–45.

Weldon, Thomas D. (1953). *The Vocabulary of Politics.* Baltimore: Penguin Books.

White, Alan R., ed. (1968). *The Philosophy of Action.* London: Oxford University Press.

Winch, Peter (1958). *The Idea of a Social Science.* London: Routledge and Kegan Paul.

Wittgenstein, Ludwig (1958). *The Blue Book.* Oxford: Oxford University Press.

——— (1953). *Philosophical Investigations.* Oxford: Blackwell.

Wolff, Robert P. (1969). "On violence." *The Journal of Philosophy* 66:601–16.

# 5
# POLITICAL EVALUATION

*BRIAN BARRY AND DOUGLAS W. RAE*

## SECTION I: INTRODUCTION

For some decades political scientists have focused attention on writing accounts of how political decisions are made and have said relatively little about which decisions ought to be made. This emphasis has been useful in drawing attention to the complexities of political behavior, increasing our knowledge of concrete structures, and avoiding the confusion of earlier work, in which naive and inexplicit leaps between the realms of fact and value abounded. In the long run, however, such a withdrawal from engagement with the problems of evaluation is untenable. The "behavioral revolution" has in no way obviated the relevance of evaluation to the study of politics. The evaluations made by political actors are part of the phenomenon to be studied. How can we talk sensibly about values (a key concept in much contemporary political science) without a sound understanding of the way evaluative concepts work? The appalling crudity of much of the literature of political science when it ventures into the discussion of "values" and the evaluative aspects of "political culture" illustrates only too clearly the dire results of venturing into this field without adequate preparation. To take just one example, Lipset in *The First New Nation* (1963) compares countries in terms of "equalitarianism" without ever discussing what he means by "equality." Some of the evidence he produces would be relevant to some conceptions of that word, other evidence to others; but when a crucial explanatory variable is simply not defined, the results of using it must be of limited value.

Moreover, even if "value neutrality" is accepted as an ideal, having a

---

Sections II and III were drafted by Rae and IV, V, VI, and VII by Barry; responsibility for the final version lies with Barry. Kenneth Macdonald, Michael Taylor, Donald Moon, and Fred Greenstein gave very helpful comments on earlier drafts of this chapter.

clear understanding of evaluation helps one to achieve it. Value neutrality is a state in intellectual life as rare as virginity in sexual life, and it is as likely to result from letting nature take its course. Value neutrality is a highly unnatural condition, and it will be achieved, if at all, only on the basis of a sophisticated understanding of the way in which evaluation is a central human activity. The problem of values cannot be evaded merely by suppressing the words "good" and "bad." When this fact is not recognized, one gets comedies such as those in political science during recent years, in which scholars identify the evaluative mote in others' eyes without being aware of the evaluative beam in their own.

We also think it would be useful if scholars would recognize explicitly the point argued long ago by Weber (1949) and Myrdal (1958); that, however objective a scholar may be in his work, his reason for taking it up can hardly fail to be connected at some remove with his own evaluations. In the selection of subjects for scientific study, normative considerations are entirely in place. Of all aspects of all social interactions, the social scientist must somehow decide to study some and not others. The only criterion for choice we can imagine being plausibly defended is that it should make a difference that one thing happens rather than another. What does "make a difference" mean here? It is a tautology that if one thing happens rather than another, the state of the world is in some sense different from what it would otherwise have been, so that cannot be the relevant sense. We think it would be hard to come up with a sense for "make a difference" not involving the idea that one state of the world is preferable to the other. This notion, we shall suggest, is closely connected with political evaluation.

We do not mean, however, that we believe social scientists should feel it necessary to relate every piece of research directly to one of the "great issues of our time." The most direct route is usually not the best.

> . . . On a huge hill,
> Cragged, and steep, Truth stands, and hee that will
> Reach her, about must, and about must goe;
>
> Donne, "Satyre III"

We are far from joining those who disparage work on concepts or techniques of analysis or studies of occurrences that are not intrinsically important but increase our knowledge of social behavior. We simply insist that the whole enterprise makes sense only insofar as it helps us to obtain answers to questions to which it is important to have answers, and that "importance" cannot be understood without reference to evaluation.

Finally, we believe that political scientists have some positive responsibility to confront evaluative questions. Why should students and members of the public care to know (and pay for knowing) what we have to say about politics? Surely one reason, among others, is that they find the moral, ethical, *evaluative* problems raised by political choice puzzling and would like to think more clearly about the difference between good policies and bad ones. This, in part, is what our most thoughtful students are asking for when they demand "relevance" in political analysis. Relevance to what? Relevance to the urgently puzzling problems of political evaluation. We think this is a legitimate demand. Indeed, we go further and suggest that it would be an actual breach of duty not to engage with the evaluative efforts of students. Otherwise we might turn out efficient technocrats whose sense of political direction would be as unreflective—consisting perhaps of a handful of slogans—as it was when they arrived at university. "'That's not my department,' says Werner von Braun" (according to Tom Lehrer) when asked about the destination of his rockets. As Adam Smith observed, division of labor makes for efficiency, but it may be bad for people.

Political evaluation, then, is of interest for at least four reasons. First, we must understand the difficulties of evaluation if we are to understand politics itself; an understanding of evaluation is important to even the most dispassionate analysis of political action. Second, a "value-neutral" stance itself requires some sophistication about evaluation. Third, if we are to invest our energies fruitfully, we must make evaluative decisions about the questions we choose to study. And finally, we ourselves have some responsibility to confront difficult evaluative questions. In this chapter, we therefore explore some of the problems which arise in any attempt at political evaluation and some of the ways in which people try to evaluate in spite of those problems.

Our strategy is as follows. First, we set out the requirements that any system of evaluation should satisfy, and we introduce briefly some of the difficulties (Section II). In Section III we focus on one difficulty: that posed by the existence of potentially conflicting criteria of evaluation to which the evaluator wishes to adhere. We consider the possible ways of coping with this problem and try to show that no simple solution is likely to be acceptable. In the light of this we turn in Section IV to examining the heroic way out: the attempt to stick to one criterion of evaluation only. Having shown the weaknesses of each proposed single criterion, we discuss in Section V some ways in which the task of evaluation may be simplified. One way is to combine aspects of the general basis of evaluation with various recurrent features of the world to create new evaluative criteria that are more easily applicable—but at the cost of having built into them assumptions about causal relationships that run the risk of being wrong. In Section VI we analyze five of the most important of these political *principles* and show how they can be derived from aspects of the general basis of evaluation plus certain factual assumptions. A concluding section (VII) summarizes the argument and relates it to alternative views of the status of political principles.

## SECTION II: REQUIREMENTS OF EVALUATION

Evaluating is assigning value to things—roughly speaking, determining whether they are good or bad. We shall take political evaluation to consist in the first instance in assigning value to alternative policies, laws, or general decisions (either one-off or standing decisions) binding on a collectivity. We say "in the first instance" because political evaluation can move outward from this central point of collectively binding decisions in several directions. A move in one direction, to which we shall be devoting much attention, is to the consequences of political decisions. If we wish to evaluate a decision, one obvious question to ask about it is what its likely consequences are (and what consequences are possible, though unlikely). The evaluation of the possible consequences of alternative decisions may be described as political evaluation by a natural extension from the meaning of "political evaluation" already mentioned, namely, the evaluation of the policies themselves. A second move from policies is to the institutional settings in which they are made. It has always been assumed that normative political theory is heavily concerned with the evaluation of alternative political arrangements, both in terms of constitutional provisions and other written or unwritten constraints and in terms of the actual practices of, for example, political parties. The assessment of such arrangements is undoubtedly to be included in the scope of political evaluation, but in regarding it as secondary, we are taking the position that in the last analysis political arrangements stand or fall evaluatively by the decisions they are expected to bring about. In this chapter we concentrate on what we see as the fundamentals of political evaluation and have little to say directly about the evaluation of institutions. The problem of developing evaluative political theory in relation to contemporary political institutions is a challenging one, since such a theory requires as a part—but only a part!—the development of theories about the connection between institutions and outputs, and these theories are still quite primitive. A third move from political evaluation as the evaluation of collectively binding decisions is to political evaluation as the evaluation of acts intended to modify the content of those decisions, either by changing the personnel or by influencing the existing personnel. It is possible to evaluate kinds of act as well as individual acts. Thus there are discussions of the ethics of various kinds of pressure-group activity, the ethics of assassination, etc. We accept these as examples of political evaluation but do not discuss them in this chapter.

In this section we shall present seven requirements that we suggest must be met by any proposed method of making political evaluations. We shall relate the discussion to political evaluation in the sense we have posited as primary, but it can be applied without substantive changes to the other senses we have suggested. Of the seven requirements, three seem to hold for nearly any sort of evaluation. They are (1) internal consistency, (2) the interpretability of criteria, and (3) the ability to produce an answer where more than one criterion is invoked. The remaining four, which are more specifically related to political evaluations, are (4) the recognition of forced choice, (5) the recognition of risk and uncertainty, (6) the relevance of time, and (7) the relevance of criteria of evaluation to the condition of individual human beings. We shall examine these requirements in order.

## 1. Internal Consistency

An evaluation may take the form of saying simply that one thing is good or bad, but often evaluations say that one thing is better than another. When recommending a policy, we want if possible to say that the policy we recommend is not only a good one but the best available. Once we introduce comparisons, we may also introduce internal inconsistency. Suppose that we have a set of mutually exclusive policies, labeled $A_1, A_2, A_3, \ldots, A_n$.[1] We cannot consistently say both that $A_1$ is better than $A_2$ and that $A_2$ is better than $A_1$. This kind of inconsistency is not hard to avoid, of course. But when more than two alternatives are being evaluated, a more subtle form of inconsistency can arise. For example, we might find ourselves saying that $A_1$ is better than $A_2$, that $A_2$ is better than $A_3$, and that $A_3$ is better than $A_1$.

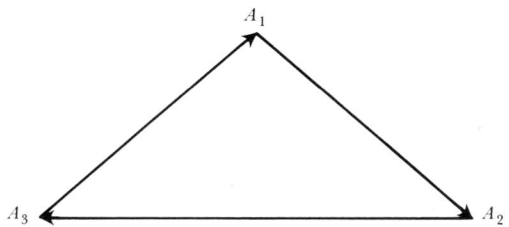

Cycles of this kind are well known in the results of collective decision-making (Condorcet, 1785; Black, 1958; Arrow, 1951; Sen, 1970). A *group* may contradict itself in this fashion even if each individual's "recommendation" is internally consistent. But even an *individual's* evaluation of three alternatives may take this form if he bases it on the rankings of the alternatives on the basis of a number of partly conflicting criteria, if he uses the rule that when conflict occurs, no one criterion is consistently put aside. It can be proved that there is no possible procedure for personal decision-making which ensures a transitive ordering of alternatives in this way unless all the criteria used to rank them can be reduced to a single consideration. In other words, if we rank three or more alternatives according to their ranks on more than one effective criterion, we cannot be sure of avoiding an intransitive recommendation (May, 1952). This will be recognized as a variant of the "paradox of voting" which underlies Arrow's General Possibility Theorem.

## 2. Interpretability of Criteria

If a criterion of evaluation is to do what is wanted of it, the least we can ask is that it have a sufficiently clear content to permit a different value to be assigned to alternative policies. A common symptom of vacuity in criteria is the notion that "everyone agrees on ends; we disagree about means only." Thus presidential candidates as different in their actual criteria for policy choices as Richard Nixon, Eugene McCarthy, and George Wallace no doubt would have been glad to agree in 1968 that all were in favor of internal and international "peace." But such criteria are so vacuous that they can be made to justify almost any policy—dropping more bombs on Vietnam or dropping none, meeting the demands of blacks or repressing them more vigorously, for example. If we are to sort out reasonable evaluations from unreasonable ones, we must insist on some test for the meaningfulness of the criteria invoked. Ideally, it might be hoped that any single criterion would be well enough defined to make it likely that any two independent observers would produce identical rankings of the members of a set of alternatives if told to take only that criterion into account. But this is too much to expect with broad-gauge criteria. There are differences about causal relationships (see requirement 5), differences of time-horizon (6), and differences in the interpretation of the criterion itself (see Section VI). All we can say, then, is that the more a criterion leaves open to individual interpretation, the less useful it is in evaluation.

## 3. Aggregation of Criteria

As we have already noted, many evaluative judgments turn on more than one relevant criterion, and that fact may produce certain special problems. Of course, we may be lucky enough to find that the same policy is best on all the relevant criteria, but we cannot count on this to happen. When there is a conflict, we have to have some higher-order criterion for dealing with it. We often find, though, that some particular alternative is worse on all counts than some other. We can then discard the first alternative from consideration. For, however we weight the criteria, it cannot possibly come out ahead of the second. We say that the first alternative is *dominated* by the second in such a case. Suppose, in a deliberately simplified example, that a town is deciding the location of its only fire station, that the town contains three well-defined neighborhoods on a straight road *(X, Y,* and *Z)*, and that the fire station has to be on the road. There are only three possible locations: $A_1$, $A_2$, and $A_3$.

| $A_1$ | | $A_2$ | | $A_3$ |
|---|---|---|---|---|
| X | Y | | Z | |

Two well-interpreted criteria emerge in the evaluation of these locations:

1. *Efficiency:* Choose a location which minimizes the average distance between the station and the neighborhoods it serves.
2. *Equality:* Choose a location which, as nearly as possible, equalizes the distances between the station and the neighborhoods it serves.

The efficiency criterion leads to the ranking $A_1$, $A_2$, $A_3$ —the last being extremely inefficient. But the equality argument leads to the diametrically opposite ranking: $A_3$, $A_2$, $A_1$. However inefficient it is to locate the station at some distant point ($A_3$), that location undeniably minimizes relative inequalities among the three neighborhoods: everyone suffers, but suffers in relative equality. We arrive, then, at a two-dimensional ranking, as shown in Fig. 1.

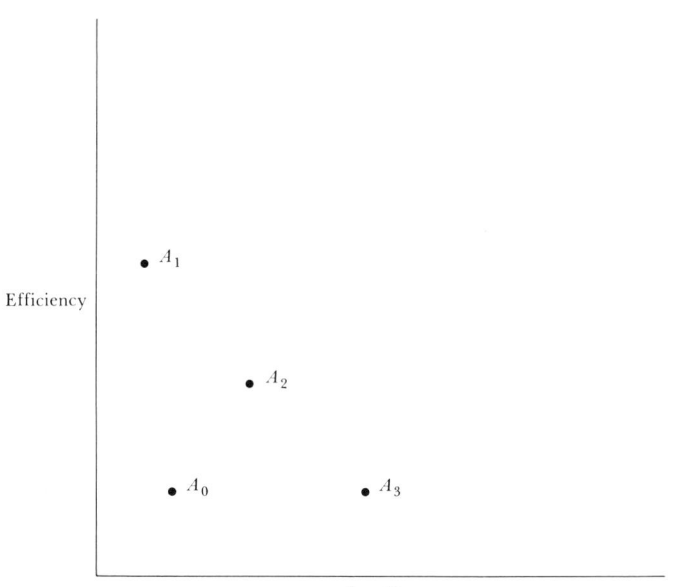

*Figure 1*

The status quo, $A_0$, we will suppose to be both inefficient and inequitable (since, let us say, there is no fire engine but only a fixed pump which works off a single standpipe). However, none of the other alternatives is dominated, thus posing the problem of aggregation. The most obvious solution is to disregard one criterion (say, equality), locating the station at the most efficient point ($A_1$). This *choice of a dominant principle* obviates the question of aggregation, returning us to a simple one-criterion problem. If there is a tie for first place on the dominant criterion, the next important criterion may be brought in simply as a tie-breaker, and if that still leaves a tie, the third most important criterion can be brought in, and so on. This ordering is called "lexicographic" because of its similarity to the way dictionaries are arranged. It may be an attractive option in our simple example, but it is not usually very plausible. As we have already noted (requirement 1), merely ranking policies on each criterion and using the ranks as the basis of aggregation presents difficulties. If we are to go beyond using rankings, we must make explicit judgments of the form "$A_1$ is a lot better on criterion $x$ than $A_2$, whereas $A_2$ is a bit better on criterion $y$ than $A_1$," and we must have some standards for choosing between a big advantage on criterion $x$ and a small advantage on criterion $y$. We devote the whole of Section III to a discussion of the problems thus raised.

### 4. Forced Choice

Evaluation in general we defined at the start of this section as assigning value to things, as determining whether they are good or bad. But we also posited a primary definition of *political* evaluations, according to which they are concerned with alternative collective decisions. This practical aspect makes the demands on political evaluation (in the sense we have identified as primary) more stringent than those on evaluation in general. The reader may have noticed that we have already on occasion slipped into speaking of rankings of policy alternatives. This reflects the fact that, in order to recommend or judge a choice, we wish to know not merely which alternatives are good and which bad but which alternative is best. It must of course be agreed that, because of the potentially infinite number of alternatives, this prescription to choose the best policy available can in practice mean only that of the alternatives that have been explored, the best should be chosen, and (rather vaguely) that the exploration of alternatives should be pushed up to the point where the marginal cost of inventing fresh alternatives and estimating their value exceeds the difference between the value of the outcome that can reasonably be expected from further exploration and the value of the best of the currently known alternatives.

Simon's concept of "satisficing" (Simon, 1955; March and Simon, 1958) no doubt describes some behavior, for example, the behavior of the managements of some firms. That is, so long as some adequate level of profit can be obtained without looking for new markets or methods of production, they may do little to look for possible new developments. However, in the light of our analysis, we suggest that such a rule of behavior is not inherently rational (the behavior it gives rise to may or may not be so in any given case), because big opportunities to increase profits are perhaps being missed. The behavior may of course be seen as rational if we drop the assumption that profit is the only criterion for evaluation recognized by the management. If we suppose instead that the management is trying to maximize the chances of living a genteel and unstressful life, the behavior depicted is perfectly rational, but it is no longer merely "satisficing." Thus David Landes (1969) says of the unenterprising, uninvesting British manufacturer of the late nineteenth century and after,

> Either his tacit assumption was that tomorrow would be the same as today or . . . he was unconsciously trying to minimize the need to make decisions—as always, the most demanding and disagreeable duty of the entrepreneur (p. 353).

An obvious but sometimes neglected point, to which this quotation leads us, is that doing nothing is in fact opting for a decision in favor of the status quo. The status quo is logically on a par with all the possibilities of change, and a collectively binding decision to do nothing is still a decision.[2] To say that we will do nothing unless an alternative to the status quo reaching some given standard of goodness can be identified is precisely to give a privileged position to the status quo. It is this feature of the context of political evaluation to which we refer in saying that it must be able to deal with forced choice. In any situation our machinery of evaluation should let us decide what is the best choice to make out of the alternatives we perceive. We are not free to say that no available alternative is acceptable; even under the most adverse circumstances, we must opt for least bad (or relatively best) options. A schoolmaster can responsibly conclude that no student's essay merits a prize, because he enjoys the luxury of unforced choice and may wait for a "better crop." Those involved in political evaluation do not enjoy this luxury. We are not denying that it may make sense in a given situation to say that all the alternatives involve wrongdoing (e.g., one breaks a promise, one will cause avoidable suffering, and so on). But unless we are to be paralyzed, it must be possible to say that one action would in the circumstances be less wrong than the alternatives. Barrington Moore, Jr. (1972) has recently reiterated this point. "If [a person who abhors violence on principle] refuses to use violence against a cruel oppressor, to make political sense such a refusal has to be based on an empirical judgement that the result will be less cruelty for humanity as a whole or some segment of it" (p. 27).

## 5. Risk and Uncertainty

Political evaluations, as we have said, are concerned in the first instance with policy alternatives. But the criteria invoked in evaluating policy alternatives are normally concerned not with the intrinsic characteristics of the policies but with the consequences of adopting one policy rather than another. The rub is this: Very seldom, in complex and dynamic situations, can we establish the consequences of a policy choice with certainty. Instead, most policy choices involve either (1) *risk,* by which we mean a known probabilistic relation between policies and their consequences; or (2) *uncertainty*, by which we mean that not even a known probability relation can be established between policies and their consequences (Luce and Raiffa, 1957, p. 13).

In the face of risk, one may proceed in three stages. First, one evaluates the various possible consequences of alternative policies on their merits. Second, one specifies the probability relationships between given policies and these evaluated outcomes. And finally, one tries to rank policies by the probabilistically weighted values of the consequences to which they may lead. A general formulation of this procedure is the "expected value" hypothesis developed by the economists. Say that we consider $n$ relevant conditions that may result from a policy choice, $C_1, C_2, \ldots, C_n$, some of which may be valued negatively and some positively. And consider that each alternative, $A_1, A_2, \ldots, A_m$, has a given probability of leading to each of these conditions. The chance that the $i$th policy will produce the $j$ condition may be labeled $P_{ij}$, and the "expected values" of the alternatives $(V_1, V_2, \ldots, V_m)$ are expressed by a set of equations.

$$V_1 = P_{11} \cdot C_1 + P_{12} \cdot C_2 + \cdots + P_{1n} \cdot C_n$$
$$V_2 = P_{21} \cdot C_1 + P_{22} \cdot C_2 + \cdots + P_{2n} \cdot C_n$$
$$\ldots$$
$$V_m = P_{m1} \cdot C_1 + P_{m2} \cdot C_2 + \cdots + P_{mn} \cdot C_n$$

One then chooses the policy whose value sum is most positive (or least negative).

But such strategies are rather strenuous in their requirements. They need cardinal values and definite numerical probabilities to be assigned to the various possible outcomes. Thus we might have to say whether a twenty percent decrease in the murder rate was 2.7 times as valuable as, say, a forty percent decline in the suicide rate, and that a given policy would have a 0.3 chance of achieving the former as against another policy's having a 0.2 chance of achieving the latter. Uncertainty means that we are unable to assign probabilities to outcomes.

One expedient for dealing with these complexities is a strategy of "incrementalism," by which one considers only marginal alternations of status quo policies. Aside from its tendency to constrain political conflict, Lindblom (1968) attributes three pertinent functions to this restriction on the range of choice, namely, that it

1. concentrates the policy-maker's analysis on familiar, better-known experience;

2. sharply reduces the number of different alternatives to be explored; and

3. sharply reduces the number and complexity of the factors he has to analyze.

These claims (Lindblom, 1968, pp. 26–7) are correct and no doubt account for a good deal of actual behavior. But by giving the status quo a special position in restricting the range of alternative policies to be considered, this strategy obviously risks the incurring of "opportunity costs" by missing other alternatives which might have proved more attractive. It is in fact very much a stable companion to "satisficing," which we discussed above (requirement 4).

## 6. Time

Even if all these difficulties are overcome, one faces the problem of *time*. One cannot usually consider outcomes as instantaneous events but must think of them as sequences of events through time. Thus the value terms of the analysis must be projected temporally on the basis of one's attitude toward the importance of distant as opposed to immediate values. This adds a further complication and source of potential disagreement among people who may even have basically similar values.

## 7. Individual Relevance

Finally, we must remember that people, not abstractions, experience the consequences of choice in politics. This is not to say that abstract criteria must be avoided; indeed, we recognize the necessity of reliance on abstractions if only because they allow us to think effectively about complicated problems. But there is always the danger that we will forget that such abstractions are important only insofar as they pertain to the experiences of individuals. Thus "the public interest" must be understood as "the public's interest." It is, we think, quite misleading to claim that the public interest "is whatever strengthens governmental institutions. The public interest is the interest of public institutions" (Huntington, 1968, p. 25)—especially if one recognizes a distinction between these institutions and the individuals bound together by them.

We do not mean that one cannot legitimately invoke criteria which pertain to some abstraction—the state, for example—so long as the argument goes on to recognize that they are instruments for the cultivation of individual goods. If we praise, say, Franklin Roosevelt for having "strengthened the presidency," we are obliged to argue that, in some direct or indirect way, a strengthened presidency is of use to some class of individuals, presumably the general public of the United States or perhaps the inhabitants of the world as a whole.

The limiting case, of course, occurs when individuals quite voluntarily equate their personal goods with the aggrandizement of an abstraction—a church, a messianic movement, a state. In this event, the good of the abstraction and those of individuals may be distinguished only by the imposition of an external definition for individual goods, and one then faces a genuine dilemma: In order to insist on an individual's irreducible standing as a unit of value, one must deny that individual's competence as a judge of his own good.

---

With this statement of requirements we have set up the paradox lying at the heart of political evaluation: that it is on the one hand inescapable and that it seems on the other hand to be far beyond human capacity to carry out succesfully. It is not altogether our wish to suggest that the paradox can be resolved. We live, after all, in a world which is becoming overpopulated at an accelerating rate, whose natural resources are becoming depleted and polluted in an apparently uncontrollable way, and much of whose population at any time is within minutes of either annihilation or agonizing death. Why should we suppose that we have to explain man's capacity for rational behavior in spite of the odds stacked against him? "With one bound Dan Dare escaped"—the classic solution of all our childhood cliffhangers—is not what we offer. Nevertheless, we do think the stark picture we have painted can be somewhat softened.

Can the requirements themselves be weakened? We do not see a great deal of room for maneuver here. It is surely inherent in the whole idea of evaluation that the procedures used should be capable of ordering the alternatives in a noncircular way and that they should be capable of coping with uncertainty and the fact that outcomes extend over time. Of requirements 1 through 6, the only relaxation we think might be accepted is to settle for a procedure that will always produce a single preferred alternative (or more than one in equal first place) even if it cannot give a consistent ordering of the other possibilities. However, a little thought will show that this is a worthless concession, because any procedure capable of always providing a first choice from any list of alternatives must be capable of providing a complete ranking (ties being permitted, of course). We need only to imagine that the procedure is applied first to the full range of alternatives, then to the set of alternatives minus the first choice, then to the set minus the first and second choices, and so on until the complete set is ordered. In any case, in collective decision-making, actors may have to make choices between alternatives which are all some way down on their order of preference.

The seventh requirement, we admit, is in a different category from the others. It reflects, if you like, secular liberal assumptions. We do not, however, regard it as in any sense arbitrary. On the contrary, we see it as a direct implication of what we shall suggest later is the ground of evaluation, namely, the advancement of general human well-being. Even if someone does not himself accept this universal secular goal as the only basis for grounding any evaluation, we do not see how anyone can hope to achieve *common* ground with the rest of the human race unless he is prepared to argue in terms of general human well-being. It is apparent that religious truths (if there are any) are not demonstrable and that divisions based on religious beliefs are bound to persist; while it can hardly be expected that the deification of particular collectivities will gain support from those outside the particular nation, Volk, class, or whatever is in question. If anyone remains entirely unconvinced by this contention and insists that the only point of evaluation is to express the will of God or advance the interests of some specific group, he will find certain parts of the rest of this chapter unacceptable. We shall merely note that those who reject our assumption that political evaluation must be referable to valuable states of human beings are likely to disagree substantively with one another more than with those who accept our assumption.[3]

If no worthwhile reduction can be made in the requirements of evaluation, we have left only the other side to operate on: Can procedures of evaluation meet the requirements by means of devices that somehow simplify the task or break it down into elements, each of which is within the compass of human capacity? The attempt to answer this question is the thread running through the rest of this chapter.

## SECTION III: CONFLICTS AMONG CRITERIA

The evaluative criteria used in policy recommendation, as we have pointed out, may offer conflicting advice in a given case. What is more egalitarian may be less just; what is more efficient may be less egalitarian; what maximizes total welfare may be less just; what maximizes the aggregate welfare of one group may be very bad for another. Whenever we evaluate on the basis of more than one criterion, we are liable to find an internal tension between the rankings offered by the different criteria. In this section, we outline some of the ways people try to resolve these tensions to produce an integrated evaluation from conflicting criteria. There are three broad responses to the difficulty: (1) to violate the implications of forced choice (Section II, requirement 4) by taking a brittle, "absolute" position; (2) to undo the conflict between criteria by arranging them in a hierarchy or (in the extreme) by allowing one to dominate the other(s); and (3) to accept both sources of difficulty and make "trade-offs" between criteria. We will survey the possible responses in the order given.

### 1. Absolutist Response to Conflict

Suppose that we are interested in two criteria, equality and efficiency, and that they offer conflicting advice. By "conflicting advice" we mean that for at least one pair of alternatives the criteria lead to opposed judgments. Thus, if $A_i$ is the more egalitarian, the conflict may arise from the view that $A_j$ is the more efficient. A common analog might be the choice between sales-tax and income-tax revenue. A sales tax is easy to collect, and since it is levied on all purchases in the state, including those made by nonresidents, it raises money at less cost to the state's public than does an income tax. On the other hand, an income tax offers the possibility of raising relatively more from the rich than from the poor. Often during recent years, this choice has been painfully encountered by state governors and legislative party leaders.

One response to difficulties of this kind is very simply a refusal to accept them. It is possible to say, in effect, "We will have an outcome which is *both* egalitarian and efficient!" In Fig. 2 this imperious decision is represented by the area of "acceptable" policies. The difficulty, of course, is that this area may be empty, that there may be no outcome that meets the requirement of simultaneous efficiency and equality. If we insist, when there is no policy at least as good as $A_i$ on each dimension, that we will stay at $A_0$, we are clearly acting irrationally (and giving a privileged position to the status quo) since we could have policies on the line connecting $A_j$ and $A_k$.

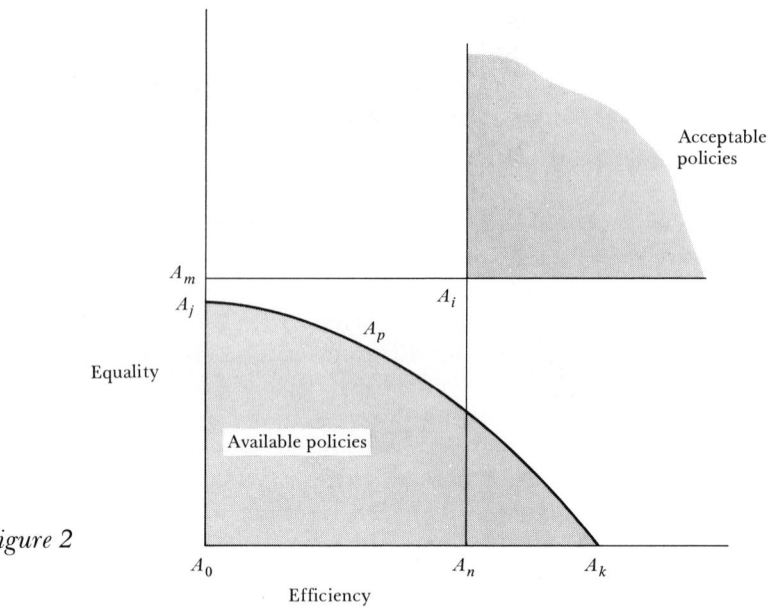

Figure 2

The kind of "relativism" implied here must not be mistaken for the variety which suggests a sheeplike acceptance of dreadful choices. It does not imply that one should not do whatever is possible to expand the set of available choices from which an acceptable one may emerge. For example, this antiabsolutism would not rule out recourse to drastic action, including violence under circumstances like those of Nazi Germany, carried out in the hope of producing new and acceptable prospects. Nor, less dramatically, would it rule out a search for new and better candidates for public office. But we are suggesting that, *after* all such efforts have been exhausted and a set of available policies is defined, pure and simple absolutism is not a rational approach to the resolution of conflict among criteria.

An apparent exception here is what may be termed "strategic absolutism," in which one rejects "least bad" alternatives on the ground that their adoption will in fact retard the search for radically preferable alternatives not now available. This is only an apparent exception, however. All it does is to reinforce the rejection of "satisficing," which we have already argued is irrational. The point remains that if, after all possible efforts have been made to find new alternatives, the best available choice of action is still bad but better in its consequences than inaction, it is irrational not to make that choice. (Bennett, 1968, argues that no principle of the form "It would always be wrong to . . . whatever the consequences of not doing so" can be accepted by anyone who has not handed over his moral judgments to some unquestioned authority, unless he is morally confused.)

The problem posed by adopting absolutist criteria may be solved after a fashion by a sequential application of less and less rigorous definitions for "acceptability." If a given level of stringency produces no acceptable outcome, one relaxes the requirements to see whether such a policy emerges, and if none does, one accepts a further relaxation and then another until finally some "acceptable" course of action is discovered. This procedure is quite straightforward in one dimension, but it requires additional specification if two or more partly conflicting criteria come into play. In Fig. 2, for example, does one drop efficiency to get $A_m$ or equality to obtain $A_n$, or does one relax both to finish up at, say, $A_p$? Both methods in fact involve the backdoor introduction of the techniques for coping with conflict of criteria that we discuss below.

## 2. *Hierarchical Response to Conflict*

A most attractive solution to conflict among criteria is to settle on a single dominant criterion and let it govern one's judgments. Thus, to continue our example, one might opt for efficient solutions, whatever their implications for equality, or vice versa. Or one might try to apply a third, more powerful criterion as a substitute for those which produce the conflict. We shall discuss proposed single criteria in Section IV, but we may anticipate the conclusion of that discussion here and say that no single criterion seems to be acceptable.

Lexicographic hierarchy, which we introduced briefly in Section II (requirement 3), is a refinement of the single-criterion approach (Taylor, 1970). With this method, one begins by ranking the criteria themselves from most important to least important. Then one applies the lexicographic principle within this hierarchy. This principle consists in nothing more complicated than the method by which names are placed in alphabetical order. We consider the first letter first (Ingles before Jacobs) and rank alternatives accordingly. If two names are "tied" on first letters, we rank them by second letters (Jacobs before Jones), and so forth until a complete ordering is the result. In evaluation, the most important criterion is like the first letter, the next most important criterion is like the second letter, and so on. In Fig. 3 we have specified equality as a first principle and efficiency as a second principle. Thus alternatives $A_1$ and $A_2$ are ranked above $A_0$ and $A_3$ because they are more egalitarian, and the distinction between $A_1$ and $A_2$ is based on the former's greater efficiency, producing $A_1$ as the outcome (and the ordering $A_1, A_2, A_3, A_0$ overall).

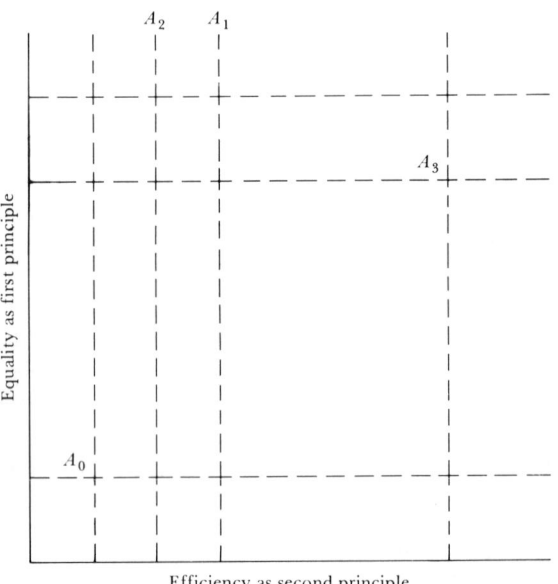

Figure 3

The example points up an obvious implication of the principle: $A_3$ is much more efficient than $A_1$, and only slightly less egalitarian; yet $A_1$ must be our choice. To commit oneself in general terms to a lexicographic hierarchy means, in fact, that the higher-ranking of any two criteria must be *infinitely* more important than the lower-ranking one: we must be prepared to make any sacrifice on the latter, however great it may be, to attain even an infinitesimal gain on the former.[4] In the example, the slight gain in equality is preferable to an enormous potential gain in efficiency. In other words, lexicography is tantamount to simply picking a dominant principle—other principles play their parts only when all higher-ranking principles produce exact indifference. And if one is prepared to accept all this, it may fairly be suggested that for all practical purposes he is operating on a single-criterion system of values, all other considerations being trivial by comparison.

In practice, the unacceptable implications of lexicography are probably evaded to a large extent by fudging. By adjusting the amount of difference there must be between two policies on a given criterion before they are judged unequal, an evaluator can reflect any desired weighting between that criterion and another one which is supposed to be lexicographically inferior. For example, an appointing committee might agree to rank its criteria and to take the best candidate on the first criterion, moving to the second criterion only if two or more candidates are considered equally good on the first. But if the second criterion is one to which members of the committee attach more than infinitesimal importance, there will be strongly felt pressure to count as equal on the first criterion two candidates who are in fact only fairly close on that criterion. This is a device for allowing the second criterion to come into play, and it is of course likely to be attractive if the candidate who is a little ahead on the first criterion is considered significantly inferior on the second.

If this account of lexicography in practice is anything like correct, what it amounts to is that one brings about an implicit weighting of the criteria by altering the maximum difference between alternatives that makes them count as equal. But when the supposed method of evaluation does not correspond to the real method, the chance of being irrational is increased. The selection committee is likely only to confuse its discussions by inextricably mixing up the question of the differences between the candidates with the question of the relative importance of the criteria of evaluation. If one is in fact "trading off" values against each another, it is advisable to be clear that one is doing so.

## 3. Trading, off Response to Conflict

If we admit that more than one criterion is important—and not just in the trivial sense that one will be used to break ties if alternatives are equal on another—we are inevitably in the trading-off business. Therefore we must think about marginal rates of substitution: How much fulfillment of criterion $x$ would we sacrifice for a given increase in fulfillment of criterion $y$ in order to conclude that the two positions were equally valuable?

In the simplest case the marginal rates of substitution are the same for all combinations of fulfillment of $x$ and fulfillment of $y$. Let us go back to the problem of locating the fire station and the choice between equality and efficiency that it occasioned (Section II, requirement 3). One way of conceptualizing the relation between the two criteria would be to suppose that we regard a degree of equality $a$ as equivalent to an amount of efficiency $b$. Stated another way, there is a marginal substitution rate of $a$ equality for $b$ efficiency, because it follows from what has been said that, if one policy leads

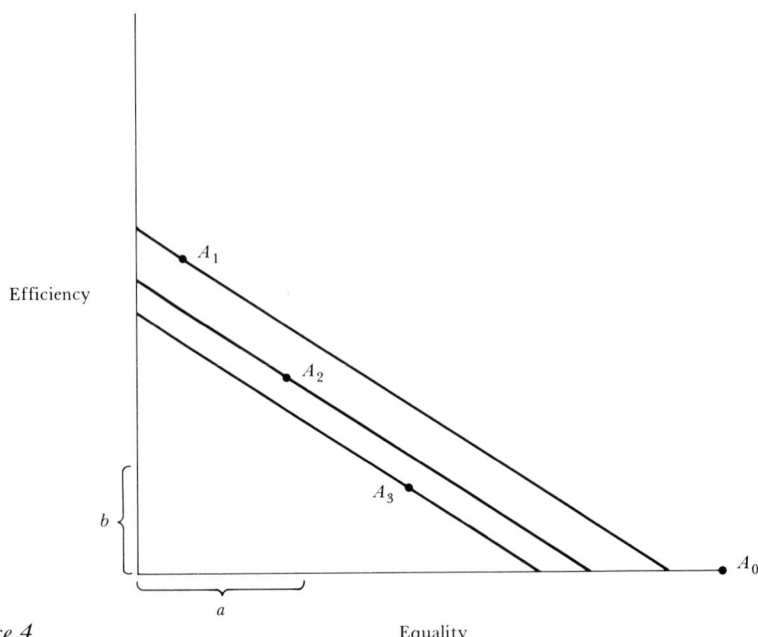

Figure 4

to *a* more equality and *b* less efficiency (or *a* less equality and *b* more efficiency) than does another policy, each policy is as good as the other.

If we redraw Fig. 1, we can add lines to represent hypothetical trade-off rates between equality and efficiency. In Fig. 4 we show for one such rate the points that equal in value each of the three available alternatives. (These sets of points are called *indifference curves* by economists.) Since there is a uniform marginal rate of substitution, each set of points lies on a straight line. The equivalent amounts of equality and efficiency (*a* and *b*) are shown on the axes. Figure 5 shows the lines corresponding to a different trade-off rate between equality and efficiency. Note that at the first rate $A_1$ is best and $A_3$ worst, whereas at the second rate the positions are reversed. In common-sense terms, we can say that in Fig. 4 we are positing that a little efficiency is as good as a close approach to equality, so the relatively efficient solution looks attractive, whereas in Fig. 5, we are positing that a big increase in efficiency is required to make up for a small drop away from equality, so the solution closer to equal comes out ahead.

In both Figs. 4 and 5 we were assuming uniform marginal rates of substitution, under which a given amount of equality is always equivalent to a certain fixed amount of efficiency. For most trade-offs, however, this as-

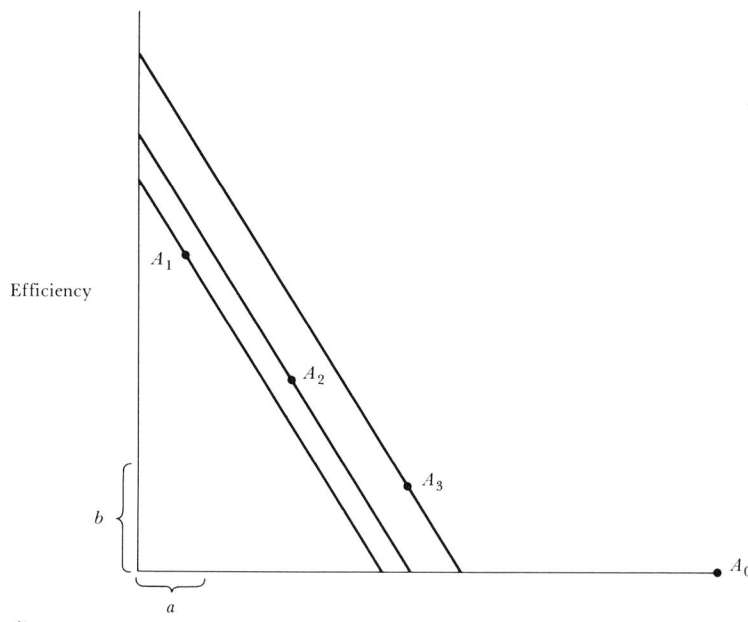

Figure 5

sumption is not very plausible. It seems much more likely that in a very egalitarian but very inefficient position, efficiency would be more valuable relative to equality than in a very efficient but very unequal position. This relationship is most clearly apparent if we make a new assumption about $A_0$, which is the situation where there is no fire engine at all. Let us now suppose that there is not even a single pump working from a standpipe, that the only way to obtain water is to fill up buckets from the nearest available domestic tap, that all the houses are equally spaced, and that all have running water. This arrangement is perfectly equal but much more inefficient even than having an engine but siting the fire station far away. If we locate this position, $A_0$, at the point shown in Figs. 4 and 5, it "beats" all the other alternatives by a big margin.

To allow for variable trade-off rates, the indifference curves which connect equally valuable points should be conceived of not as straight lines but as curves concave to the origin. Figure 6 illustrates a possible set of indifference curves which exhibit this property. Note that $A_2$ is now the most attractive position. In common-sense terms, we are now supposing that the more each criterion is fulfilled, the less important it is in relation to the other. The effect is to make a position that provides a balanced fulfillment of both

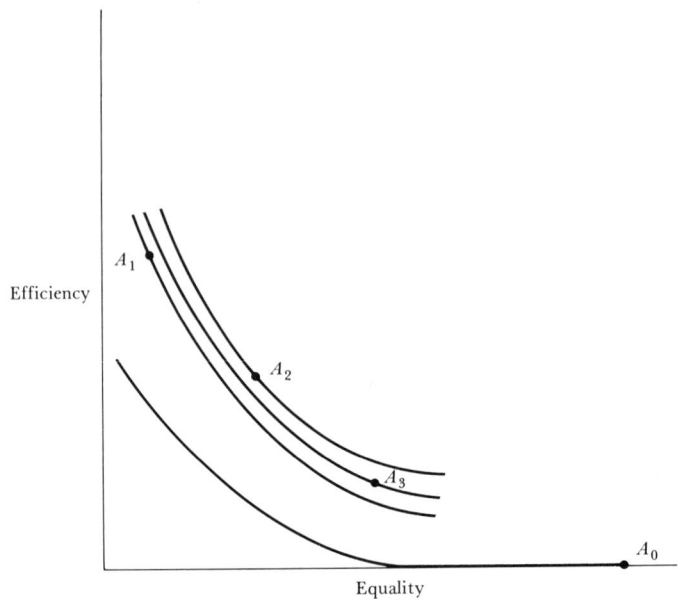

Figure 6

criteria look good. (There is in fact no uniform trade-off rate which would make $A_2$ best, since a straight line drawn between $A_1$ and $A_3$ leaves $A_2$ below and to the left of it.) At the same time, $A_0$ becomes highly unattractive.

We have simplified the discussion by considering only a few alternatives and two criteria. We can easily extend it to any number of alternatives. At the limit, we have an infinite number of alternatives, and by connecting all that are not dominated by others, we can draw a continuous line defining the frontier of available alternatives. (Recall that one alternative dominates another when it is better than the other on all the relevant criteria.) Thus the frontier of feasibility in Fig. 7 is $pp$, and the shaded area includes all available alternatives. The best alternative of those available is simply the one that lies on the highest indifference curve (the one that is highest and farthest right). In Fig. 7 the best alternative is $A_i$, which lies on the indifference curve $qq$.[5] When we go beyond two criteria, simple graphical representation becomes impossible, but nothing else changes. We assign a dimension to each criterion and give each alternative a position on each dimension. This defines its overall position in three dimensions or more. As before, we can then take sets of positions of equal value and arrange them in order of value, thus producing an $n$-dimensional equivalent of indifference curves. We can also concentrate attention on those available alternatives which are not dominated, thus producing an analog of the frontier of feasibility. The best

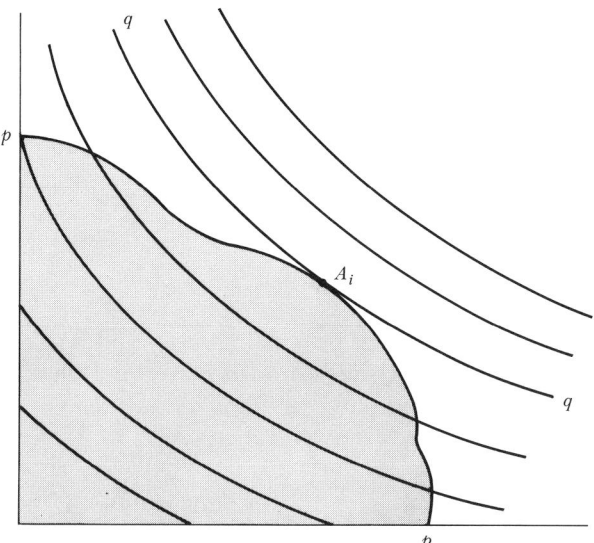

Figure 7

policy, again, is simply that feasible policy which is in a more valuable set of alternatives than any other.

It may be objected that the whole discussion of trading off has rested on the possibility of measuring the degree of fulfillment of different criteria, and that this cannot in fact be done. We admit that people cannot be expected to say that $n$ units of equality and $m$ units of efficiency are as good as $n + 1$ and $m - 3$ units. Our analysis is not a description or a blueprint, but it is defensible as a way of making clear what must underlie much actual evaluation. We do believe that trading off takes place, even when the process is not made explicit and all that emerge into the light of day are the criteria and the resulting evaluations of alternatives. Similarly, although we were idealizing in our statement that identifying the best policy is simply a matter of finding the point on the feasibility curve that touches the highest indifference curve, we still maintain that this statement sets out the logic of evaluating available alternatives as a basis for choice and helps to elucidate the respective roles of on one side judgments about causal sequences and practical possibilities and on the other criteria of evaluation and ways of aggregating them.

## SECTION IV: SIX PURE CRITERIA

In this section we shall backtrack and try to support the conclusion already anticipated in the previous section that no single criterion of evaluation is satisfactory. We shall do this by looking at six criteria which have been more or less influential and have some claim to plausibility. They are not of course the only single criteria that can be imagined, but we feel it is up to anyone who rejects our conclusion to produce a criterion that is not subject to objections of the kind we shall be raising to the six we do discuss.

The six criteria are utilitarianism, equality, Pareto optimality, majority, minimaximization (which we consider in two forms), and dominance. After examining them separately as single criteria of evaluation, we shall ask whether any lexicographic ordering of these criteria would prove acceptable and conclude that, although some could solve some of the problems, no lexicographic ordering would be likely to be completely acceptable.

In this section we shall pay no further attention to the problems of getting from the evaluation of states of affairs to the evaluation of policies. We shall confine ourselves to asking whether the criteria we are to consider can produce a satisfactory ordering of states of affairs. If they cannot, then the question of mapping from states of affairs to policies does not arise. However, if the reader disagrees with our conclusion and believes that one of these criteria (or more than one arranged lexicographically) is satisfactory, the remainder of the chapter is not thereby irrelevant, since the practical difficulties of getting a policy ordering from an ordering of states of affairs remain. These difficulties are inherent in the problems of uncertainty and so on, already discussed.

It is worth noting also that even if these practical difficulties were removed, there would still be no logical connection between an ordering of states of affairs and an ordering of policies. To say that the best policy is the one that leads with certainty to the best state of affairs is an evaluative assertion, not a tautology. And as an evaluative statement, it is in fact one that has often been denied. Those taking this line would maintain that certain kinds of policy would be wrong whatever their consequences; that is to say, they would invoke principles which characterize policies as such. In the later part of this chapter we shall be discussing some of these principles, and, although we shall treat them as shortcuts to evaluation in terms of consequences, there is nothing to prevent their being interpreted as having an independent basis. Principles characterizing policies will be related to what we called at the end of Section II the general ground of evaluation, so long as it is claimed that human well-being will be advanced if such principles are followed.

The minimum requirement we can ask of a criterion for ordering states of affairs described in appropriate terms is that, given any two states of affairs, it should in principle be able to say whether or not each state is at least as good as the other. If the two states of affairs are $x$ and $y$, we can write the relationship "$x$ is at least as good as $y$" in the form "$x \, R \, y$." From this we can define the two relationships we have already met in connection with policies, P (preference) and I (indifference). We say that $x \, P \, y$ if and only if $x \, R \, y$ and not $y \, R \, x$; that $x \, I \, y$ if and only if $x \, R \, y$ and $y \, R \, x$.

This, however, is too weak a condition for making evaluations of alternative states of affairs. As we noted before in connection with policies, a set of alternatives with all possible pairs ordered still may not produce a single ordering for the set as a whole. We may (to take the simplest case) get $x$ P $y$ and $y$ P $z$ but $z$ P $x$, and we then have no way of ranking $x$, $y$, and $z$. For an ordering we therefore require that if $x$ R $y$ and $y$ R $z$, then $x$ R $z$ (Sen, 1970, p. 9). What this means in terms of P and I is as follows: If $x$ P $y$ and $y$ P $z$, then $x$ P $z$; if $x$ P $y$ and $y$ I $z$, then $x$ P $z$; if $x$ I $y$ and $y$ P $z$, then $x$ P $z$; and if $x$ I $y$ and $y$ I $z$, then $x$ I $z$.

Obviously, to say that a criterion for evaluating states of affairs produces an ordering of any number of alternatives is not to say that it is a good criterion; and the number of criteria capable of producing orderings is indefinitely large. But if a criterion fails to produce an ordering, it fails to get to first base. We shall not introduce any other formal condition for judging criteria. We shall simply ask in addition whether each criterion is plausible. In the end this is something each person must decide for himself, since the answer is not derivable from the ground of evaluation but will constitute one interpretation of it. But we can show what the implications of accepting a given criterion of evaluation could be in particular cases.

We said that a criterion must be able to order states of affairs described in appropriate terms. By this we meant that those features of the states of affairs to be compared that are relevant to the criterion must be described before the criterion can be expected to order them. What features will be relevant depends on the criterion, of course. All the six criteria we are to consider now have in common the very important point that they require no information about any feature of a situation except how well-off people are in it. To put it another way, if two situations are alike in the well-being of the people in them, then as far as these criteria are concerned, they are to all intents and purposes the same situation—even if the two situations are widely separated by space or time.

Now, this is a great abstraction from the unlimited range of features of a situation that might be regarded as relevant. A particularly significant piece of information which these criteria ignore is the relation between any feature in the past behavior or present qualities of the people involved and their prosperity or adversity in the situation to be evaluated. This rules out, as we shall see more fully in Section VI, any reference to considerations of justice, since such considerations are inherently concerned with the connection between past behavior or present qualities and the good or bad outcomes (rewards and punishments) that people experience. It is, as we have observed, a vast abstraction to represent an entire situation in terms of the amount and distribution of well-being. It is also very difficult to do, and indeed it can be done only in rough terms. But even rough terms may sometimes be enough to make it possible to say that one situation is better than another according to one of these criteria; and as we shall see, the amount of information about well-being required by the different criteria varies a great deal. We shall not discuss further the practical problems of operationalizing our six criteria, since we think our negative conclusions about all of them will apply, irrespective of the precise sense given to "well-being"—whether, for example, one emphasizes individual preference, material prosperity, or the more intangible notion of happiness.

With these preliminary remarks we now proceed to an examination of each of the six criteria in turn.

## 1. Utilitarianism

We begin with the criterion of utilitarianism—Bentham's "greatest happiness principle" (Bentham, 1948, p. 1n). The usual way of defining it is to say that of two situations, the one to be preferred is that in which the sum of the utilities of the people involved is higher. "Utility" means welfare, happiness, want-satisfaction, or in general, the range of things we have been covering with the concept of well-being. Given the sums of utility for $x$ and $y$, we can immediately decide from this criterion whether $x$ P $y$, $y$ P $x$, or $x$ I $y$; and we can see that transitivity will hold for any criterion which is defined in terms of amounts of any homogeneous entity, since if $x$ has at least as much of something as $y$ and $y$ has at least as much of it as $z$, it follows that $x$ has at least as much of it as $z$. Thus the conditions for an ordering are satisfied.

What is more dubious is plausibility. One question that has been raised arises where situations with different numbers of people in them are to be compared. If we take the sum of utilities as the criterion, we presumably have to say that a state of affairs in which a large number of people are fairly miserable can be preferable to a state of affairs in which a smaller number of people are rather happier. This difficulty can be met by reformulating the criterion so that $x$ is better than $y$ if the *average* utility (the total divided by the number of people) is higher in $x$ than in $y$. Pushed to extremes, this too seems unacceptable: Would a hundred inhabitants of Britain be better than 60 million if the hundred were on the average a tiny bit happier?

For practical purposes, however, this difficulty is not too serious except in the (admittedly important) area of population control. Most comparisons of states of affairs which are relevant to policy choice involve one of two kinds of comparison. One is a comparison between some status quo position and that expected to come about if some policy is adopted, where the population in the second situation, though not identical in composition with that in the first, is unlikely to be grossly different in size. The other frequently made comparison is between two possible states of affairs at the same (future) time, which are the expected consequences of alternative policy choices now. Here, unless the alternatives themselves seriously affect population size, it will be the same in both hypothetical situations.

A much greater drawback of the utilitarian criterion is that it is compatible with preferring grossly unequal distributions to more equal ones. For example, gladiatorial combats would be justifiable if the pleasure of the spectators outweighed the pain of the gladiators. Admittedly, it can be argued that this is unlikely to happen, but is it satisfactory to accept unconditionally a criterion which would produce such an answer if it did? We think that the introduction of some explicitly distributive criterion in addition to utilitarianism is unavoidable.

## 2. Equality

Swinging to the opposite extreme, we might adopt a single criterion which involves a reference only to distribution. Since it will be recalled that we are dealing with criteria which are defined in terms only of the distribution and amount of utilities, without introducing any information about the histories or characteristics of the people involved, the only distributive criterion possible seems to be that utility should be distributed as equally as possible.

Like utilitarianism, this criterion can in principle produce an ordering. However, we must first establish the conditions for one of two sets of numbers to be more or less equal than the other. For example, we might say that the situation is more equal which has the lower average deviation from the mean. Once we can say that $x$ is at least as equal as $y$, there are no difficulties with transitivity, so an ordering will result from pairwise comparisons.

Again, the problem is plausibility. To illustrate, we shall introduce a notation which will prove particularly useful later. Let us consider sets of three situations which have the same three people in them—this degree of complication will suffice to make all the points we shall need. We shall say that people can be either well-off or badly-off, and that we can distinguish up to three slightly different degrees of well-offness and badly-offness. Well-off conditons will be denoted by numbers around 100 and badly-off conditions by numbers around 10, but—to illustrate the point that rough estimates are often enough—the same answers would be given by our criteria if well-offness were 20 or 1000 to the 10 for badly-offness. What is essential for our examples is that the differences between 9 and 10, etc., are much smaller than the differences between 10 and 100, etc. The extent to which interpersonal comparisons are required (a) for the working of a criterion and (b) for the criticism of its implications varies from case to case.

In Table 1, the three situations are 1, 2, and 3, the three individuals are A, B, and C, and their well-offness of badly-offness is shown by the numbers in the cells. On the equality criterion, 3 is clearly preferred to 2, but strictly speaking, it is preferred even to 1. Although the comparison of 1 and 3 seems to turn on an implausibly fine comparison of the degree of equality between two very different situations, there is no such difficulty with the comparison between 3 and 2—and any number of similar comparisons could of course be manufactured. The equality criterion thus requires in some circumstances the gratuitous destruction of well-being (for none is actually transferred between 2 and 3) and this, although it might be felt right in certain conditions (the specification of which would almost certainly require one to go beyond anonymous arrays of utilities) does not seem to be the formula for a universally applicable sole criterion of evaluation.

TABLE 1

|   | A | B | C |
|---|---|---|---|
| 1 | 100 | 100 | 99 |
| 2 | 100 | 100 | 10 |
| 3 | 10 | 10 | 10 |

## 3. Pareto Optimality

Both utilitarianism and equality, though based on nothing but arrays of utilities, made heavy demands for information. Utilitarianism requires that it should be possible to add A's utility to B's utility and produce a sum of utilities, and then perhaps to divide by two to get an average. Equality similarly requires the interpersonal comparison of amounts of utility (or whatever precisely the ground of evaluation is taken to be), since it requires the calculation not just of an average of utility but also, even in the simplest form, of average deviations from that average. We shall now consider a criterion which avoids the demand for so much information. Instead of demanding amounts of utility that can be added, whomever they belong to, this criterion requires only that as between two situations we can say for each person whether he is better-off (by any unspecified amount) in one or the other or equally well-off in both. This is the criterion of Pareto optimality, which says that one situation is at least as good as another if everyone is at least as well-off in the first as in the second.

Unfortunately, this criterion falls down on both internal consistency and plausibility. To show that it cannot produce an ordering, we offer Table 2. For the present purpose, the only relevant feature of the numbers is the order of size within each column. We shall use other features when we come to plausibility.

In fact, Pareto optimality does not satisfy even the condition that between two states of affairs, $x$ and $y$, either $x$ R $y$ or $y$ R $x$ (or both). If we compare 1 and 3 in Table 2, we see that on Pareto optimality it is not the case that 1 R 3 (since B and C are better off in 3 than in 1), but it is also not the case that 3 R 1 (since A is better off in 1 than in 3). Therefore we cannot say 1 P 2, 2 P 1, or 1 I 2.

TABLE 2

|   | A   | B   | C   |
|---|-----|-----|-----|
| 1 | 100 | 10  | 10  |
| 2 | 101 | 10  | 10  |
| 3 | 99  | 100 | 100 |

There are two ways of dealing with this. One is to say that wherever this happens, if one of the states of affairs is the status quo or the anticipated future consequence of not adopting any new policy, it is to be preferred to the alternative. This procedure does not of course produce an answer for all pairs, but it does produce an answer whenever one member of a pair is the status quo. Under this modified version of Pareto optimality, then, the status quo is better than any state of affairs which is not Pareto optimal (in the originally defined sense) in relation to it. However, this solution violates our condition that the status quo should have no logically special position but should be treated on a par with other alternatives. It is also implausible since if 1 were the status quo, it would be preferred to 3.

The alternative route is to say that if not $x$ R $y$ and not $y$ R $x$, then $x$ I $y$. In other words, if we can't choose between two situations on the basis of Pareto optimality as originally defined, we simply say that they are equally good. Unfortunately, although this solves the formal problem for each pair taken one at a time, it fails to produce an ordering. For in Table 2, 2 P 1 and 1 I 3. In order to produce an ordering, it must then be true that 2 P 3 (see the definition of transitivity above). But in fact, 2 I 3. Moreover, even if the pairs are taken separately, this version of Pareto optimality is not very plausible, since it requires us to say that 1 and 3 are equally good, whereas most people would surely say that, in the absence of any other information, 3 is a better state of affairs than 1.

## 4. Majority

Another criterion which avoids interpersonal comparisons or, even for one person, talking in any terms other than more and less, is the majority criterion. This is the principle that, where the interests of people come into conflict over policy alternatives, that policy should be preferred which advances the interests of more people rather than fewer. (See Dahl and Lindblom, 1953, pp. 44ff.) As a criterion of social choice, this suffers from the same two main defects as Pareto optimality: It does not allow a consistent ordering of states of affairs to be constructed, and it may in any case lead to implausible recommendations. Both of these assertions can be illustrated by another example, using the same conventions as before (Table 3). Starting at 1, we note that two people (A and B) would benefit from a change to 2, though C would lose heavily. If the change is then made to 2, we note that 3 would be preferred by B and C, though A would lose heavily. Finally, however, we can see that from 3 a majority (A and C) would benefit substantially by a move to 1, while B would lose slightly. Thus we get back to the beginning, and the whole cycle can begin again. This is the argument showing that no consistent ordering can be produced. The implausibility of the criterion may be tested by looking at the three states of affairs and observing that, although each is capable of getting a majority over one other, they are very different in their implications for the welfare of the people concerned. According to the conventions we set up for interpreting the numbers, in the first state of affairs all three participants are well-off, and in the second state two are well-off and one badly-off. Thus we cannot accept at all that circularity merely shows that it doesn't matter which is chosen.

TABLE 3

|   | A | B | C |
|---|---|---|---|
| 1 | 99 | 99 | 99 |
| 2 | 100 | 100 | 10 |
| 3 | 10 | 101 | 11 |

What is said here refers to the treatment of individuals as passive receptacles of utility. Note that it does not invalidate majority voting as a method of political decision-making that can have a value derived from the way in which it may be believed to be connected empirically with the furtherance of human well-being. In our discussion of democracy (Section VI) we shall consider the majority principle in this quite different perspective.

## 5. Minimax

The minimax criterion was introduced into social evaluation by Rawls (1958; see also Rawls, 1971). It says that of two states of affairs, $x$ and $y$, $x$ R $y$ if the worst-off person in $x$ is no worse-off than the worst-off person in $y$. Hence, if the worst-off person in $x$ is better-off than the worst-off person in $y$, $x$ P $y$; and if they are equally well-off, $x$ I $y$. A variant, which we can call the strong minimax condition, says that if $x$ I $y$ on the minimax condition as stated, we compare the next-to-worst-off in $x$ and $y$, and $x$ P $y$ if the second-worst-off person is better-off in $x$ than in $y$; and if that produces $x$ I $y$, we go on to the third-worst-off, and so on until either $x$ P $y$ or $y$ P $x$, or until it has been found that, starting from the bottom, each of the utilities in one situation can be matched by an equal utility in the other. (If the numbers of people are unequal in the two situations, the situation with more people would have some at the top left over. We shall ignore this complication in the present summary treatment.) The minimax criterion requires interpersonal comparisons of utility, but it does not require addition of utilities and, in its weak form, requires only that the utilities of two people should be compared, namely, the worst-off person in each situation. Even in its strong form it is not likely to be very demanding in the amount of interpersonal comparison of utility required.

Minimax produces coherent evaluations of pairs of situations, and it can also put them together to form an ordering, since if A is at least as well-off as B and B is at least as well-off as C, we can assert that A is at least as well-off as C. (Strong minimax also produces an ordering.) Where minimax falls down, at least in our view, is on plausibility. Thus, referring again to Table 1, we note that on the minimax criterion, 1 P 2 and 1 P 3, which seems reasonable enough; but 2 I 3, which does not. If we invoke strong minimax, this problems is solved and 2 P 3, but we can still produce a questionable result by modifying Table 1 to read as in Table 4. Now we get the answer

TABLE 4

|   | A | B | C |
|---|---|---|---|
| 1 | 100 | 100 | 99 |
| 2 | 100 | 100 | 10 |
| 3 | 11 | 11 | 11 |

that 3 P 2 on the basis of the ordinary minimax criterion; hence the tie-breaking feature of the strong minimax criterion has no opportunity to come into play.

## 6. Dominance

Minimax could claim to be an ingenious attempt to give some weight to equality and utilitarianism in a single criterion, though the satisfaction of the minimax condition is of course no guarantee that either the most egalitarian or the most utilitarian state of affairs has been selected. The criterion of dominance has the following property: If $x$ R $y$ on dominance, then $x$ R $y$ on minimax (in both ordinary and strong versions); and if $x$ R $y$ on dominance, then $x$ R $y$ on utilitarianism, provided the numbers in the two situations are the same. In fact, since Pareto optimality entails dominance, it has the same property in relation to minimax and utilitarianism, but the conditions for $x$ P $y$ under Pareto optimality are extremely restrictive. The same people have to be in both situations and each of them has to be at least as well-off in $x$ as in $y$. Dominance is a kind of anonymous version of Pareto optimality; alternatively, it can be looked at as an extension of strict minimax. What it says is that, when $x$ and $y$ have the same number of people in them, $x$ R $y$ if each person in $x$ can be paired off with one person in $y$ in such a way that the person in $x$ is at least as well-off as his opposite number in $y$.[6] The simplest way of thinking about this (though it requires more information than is necessary for the criterion to work) is to imagine that in situation $x$ the people are ranged in order of well-offness from best to worst, and then the same is done for situation $y$. The worst-off in $x$ is compared with the worst-off in $y$, and so on up the list until each person in $x$ has been compared for well-offness with the person in $y$ who has the same ranking (Table 5). Thus,

TABLE 5

| Rank | Utility | |
|---|---|---|
| | $x$ | $y$ |
| 1 | 9 | 8 |
| 2 | 6 | 5 |
| 3 | 5 | 5 |
| 4 | 5 | 4 |
| 5 | 2 | 2 |

if we suppose that the numbers in Table 5 represent interpersonally comparable utility values, we can see at once that $x$ R $y$ and not $y$ R $x$, hence $x$ P $y$.[7]

Although dominance is most easily visualized in the way we have just described, one of its strengths is that it does not actually require the people in the situation to be ranked; thus we can say that $x$ R $y$ on the minimax criterion if $x$ R $y$ on dominance, even if we cannot identify the worst-off person in each situation. All we need to know is that each person in $y$ can be paired with someone in $x$ who is at least as well-off. A further strength is that, although the operation of the dominance criterion does require interpersonal comparisons, it requires only a limited number of them, and they have to be only in terms of better- and worse-off. No estimate of the amount better- or worse-off is needed, nor is the even stronger condition of the addibility of utilities. This is significant in view of the fact that whenever dominance is satisfied, utilitarianism is satisfied.[8]

The cost of this apparent creation of something for nothing is that dominance shares two weaknesses of Pareto optimality. First, although dominance is less demanding than Pareto optimality, it still involves the considerable requirement that, roughly speaking, to each person in one situation there should correspond a person in the other who is at least as well-off. Second, dominance, like Pareto optimality, can easily produce a result where neither $x \, R \, y$ nor $y \, R \, x$ holds; and, if this result is interpreted as meaning that $x \, I \, y$, inconsistency can arise when more than two situations are compared. Thus, in Table 6, 1 P 2 and 2 I 3. For an ordering this combination requires that 1 P 3, but we in fact find that 1 I 3.

TABLE 6

|   | A   | B   | C  |
|---|-----|-----|----|
| 1 | 100 | 11  | 11 |
| 2 | 100 | 10  | 10 |
| 3 | 100 | 100 | 9  |

The conclusion we can draw about Pareto optimality and dominance is that, when they give rise to nothing but relations between pairs of people which satisfy either $x \, R \, y$ or $y \, R \, x$, the situation in the resultant ordering of all possible situations which comes out ahead of the rest has strong claims since it also leads on minimax and utilitarianism. (The converse does not hold, incidentally: one situation can be preferred to another on the criterion of both minimax and utilitarianism without being better on either Pareto optimality or dominance.) Unfortunately, however, the condition that all the situations to be compared should be related in this way is a very restrictive one.

It might be thought that the answer is to introduce lexicography to break the ties that arise when neither $x \, R \, y$ nor $y \, R \, x$. This is a wild goose chase, however. If we have Pareto optimality or dominance followed by minimax or utilitarianism, we may as well simply have minimax or utilitarianism, since the outcome will always be the same. If we have Pareto optimality or dominance followed by equality, we can still get inconsistency. Table 7 illustrates such a situation for the case of dominance. Here 2 P 3 by the dominance criterion. The dominance criterion does not produce any other preference ordering, so 1 I 2 and 1 I 3. However, by the equality

TABLE 7

|   | A   | B   | C  |
|---|-----|-----|----|
| 1 | 11  | 11  | 9  |
| 2 | 100 | 100 | 11 |
| 3 | 10  | 10  | 10 |

criterion, 3 P 1 and 1 P 2, which entails that 3 P 2. We thus get a *more* severe form of inconsistency than we had with dominance alone. Finally, majority as a second criterion will obviously do no good since it cannot itself produce an ordering.

Lexicography makes more sense in relation to equality, the ordinary form of minimax and utilitarianism. Thus, if two situations are just as good on the equality criterion, it seems minimally daring to say that if one is better than another on the dominance criterion, it is to be preferred, but we might well put in utility or minimax as tie-breakers instead. Similarly, minimax in its ordinary form cries out to be followed by something else, since two situations in which the worst-off persons are equally well-off might well be very different in other respects. Utility or equality could function as tie-breakers unless one follows the logic of minimax and adopts the strong form of the criterion. The criterion of utilitarianism could be followed sensibly by either minimax or equality.

The introduction of lexicographic orderings of criteria serves to cut out certain flagrantly absurd results of using a single criterion. Thus it rules out any implication that if two situations are equally good on the egalitarian criterion, there is nothing to choose between them, even if one satisfies the conditions of dominance—or even Pareto optimality—in relation to the other. But even so, it does not really help very much. All we have to do is to alter the example just given. We say that situation $x$ satisfies the criterion of dominance (or Pareto optimality) in relation to $y$, but $y$ is an infinitesimal amount more equal than $x$, and we get the result that $y$ is to be preferred to $x$, lexicography or no.

It might be argued that this is an artificial example and that two situations should be regarded as equally good on a criterion if they are within some range of similarity. But what range? Implicitly the criterion must be the range that produces sensible results. This may be a fair description of the way we sometimes operate. That is to say, we have some idea of the amount of difference on the most important criterion that makes it unlikely that our ordering would be changed if we looked at the next most important criterion, and so on. But the underlying logic of evaluation here is the logic of trade-offs, simplified in a rule-of-thumb way to a sort of lexicography. It is misleading to think of it as a true example of lexicographic ordering. It is in fact one of the simplifying devices we use to cope with the intractable difficulties of trading off criteria against one another.

It is to a review of these methods of simplification that we now turn.

## SECTION V: COPING WITH COMPLEXITY

We have suggested that no single criterion will do for evaluation. Nevertheless, all the various proposed single criteria that were discussed were on the right general lines, as we interpreted them, in that they were concerned with human well-being and nothing else, and they differed only in the way they attributed value to different features of the amount and distribution of well-being. And we have suggested that, in the absence of religious or particularistic values with no hope of general acceptance, human well-being is the only possible foundation of political evaluation. However, there are many reasons why two people, both committed to human well-being as the only basis of evaluation, might disagree over the preferability of two situations. First, they may differ in the relative weight they give to the amount as against the distribution of well-being, and second, they may actually have different criteria for the right distribution of well-being.

In addition, there is the point which for convenience we left over from the previous section: Conceptions of well-being may themselves differ. "Happiness," "pleasure," "interest," "welfare," "good," and "satisfaction," for example, are no mere synonyms, and all emphasize different facets of the end-state which we are referring to generically as "well-being," though we should allow further that each of these words itself allows infinite scope for argument about its precise signification. We could try the maneuver of saying that there is an overriding concept (often in the past taken to be "happiness") with a number of subsidiary components. But this does nothing really to resolve the problem because the argument simply shifts to one about the relative importance of the components. It is a somewhat depressing thought that most of the possible moves were made by Aristotle and that subsequent scholars have not only advanced little on Aristotle but even failed to agree about the answers he himself gave. Moreover, the "amount" of well-being is itself a pretty formidable factual question—so formidable that some have argued that it is not a factual question at all. We do not accept this contention but do recognize that, even if all possible information is available, two people may still in some cases disagree about whether, say, the total of well-being was greater before or after some social change. Finally, as we have already observed, the move from states of affairs to policy choices may involve predictions about causal sequences which in the nature of the case can often be hardly better than guesses.

In the light of all this, we might wonder whether the fundamental premises of political evaluation set any limits to what can be justified. Could not a government always defend itself without repudiating our fundamental basis of evaluation? The answer, surely, is that a government can indeed always put forward a justification but that it will not always be very plausible.

Several observations are in order here. It is significant that when the spokesmen of regimes appeal to the "decent opinion of mankind," it is normally to considerations of human well-being in some form that they attempt to relate their actions. We find that apologists of even the most barbarous regimes do not simply repudiate these considerations. Further, although no regime is without its apologists, some apologetics manifestly fail to impose on well-informed people whose interests or passions are not already engaged. The two techniques by which the indefensible is defended are always the same: causal assertions and selection of effects.[9] First, it is claimed unjustifiably that the actions in question were necessary to bring about—or to prevent from coming about—such-and-such a state of affairs. Second, of the effects attributed to the action, those which are favorable are pointed out and the rest silently passed over. There is absolutely no reason why a well-informed person should not be able to say that defenses of this kind are simply unacceptable. We can draw consolation from the fact that even at the time something is happening, those whose interests or passions are not directly involved can sometimes reach something approaching consensus. Recent examples are the condemnation by a sort of world public opinion of the Soviet invasion of Czechoslovakia, the United States bombing of North Vietnam, the seizure of power by the Greek colonels, and the suppression of the Bangla Desh movement in East Pakistan. If we extend our view to the past, where interests and passions are less immediately involved, we find an even more striking tendency to consensus. Few Roman Catholics can now be found to defend the torturing and burning of the Inquisition, few Communists the Stalin purges, and few Southerners the institution of slavery. It would be foolish to build too much hope on this tendency, but it would also be mistaken, we suggest, to be carried away by the difficulties to the point of believing nothing can ever be settled.

Nevertheless, the fact remains that political evaluation is obviously a formidable undertaking. How can people do it? One answer often given is that, for most people most of the time, the formulation and expression of apparent political evaluations is not a rational activity. Stated another way, what pose as political evaluations are only to a minor extent oriented toward reality. They may be formed to satisfy personal needs; for example, a sense of personal failure may be relieved if it is attributed to the machinations of some group (scapegoating). Or the exchange of political evaluations may serve purely social functions of expressing friendship and solidarity with some people and hostility to others.

The large element of truth in this view should be borne in mind as a qualification to everything that follows, but we shall not pursue this line any further. Instead we shall look at the ways in which the evaluative process may be simplified to bring it within the compass of human capabilities. Unfortunately, the work of social psychologists does not seem to be of much help here. True, they have noticed the problem:

> Problems calling for good judgement can be extremely complex: there can be a large number of alternatives, each with many factors, the factors can have many levels, or even be continuous; and they can interact. It seems likely that when the problem becomes complicated enough, people simplify it in one way or another. (Yntema and Torgerson, 1967, p. 312)

But the methods of simplification these authors go on to mention, though no doubt reducing "cognitive strain," would be obviously irrational from an instrumental point of view. And most experimental studies seem to be devoted to providing yet more evidence for the adage "there's nowt so queer as folks." (See the various reviews in Edwards and Tversky, 1967.)

In one experiment, subjects had to evaluate ellipses whose "worth was [arbitrarily] defined in such a way that it always increases with size, thinness and brownness and was a reasonably smooth function of those three factors (Yntema and Torgerson, 1967, p. 309). It was found that most subjects took some very rough short cuts. But political evaluation, though inherently more complex than evaluating ellipses, has three mitigating features. First, the underlying values are not given arbitrarily by an experimenter but are familiar bits of one's mental furniture. Second, evaluations of the main features of one's political universe can be made over many years; it is not necessary to start from scratch each time. Finally and most important of all, we are not forced (as the laboratory subjects were) to invent our own ways of dealing with the difficulties of multiple criteria. Political evaluation has been around for a long time, and a lot of intelligent people have put their minds to it. Or in more resonant language, there is no need for men to "trade each on his own private stock of reason" when they can "avail themselves of the general bank and capital of nations and of ages" (Burke, 1910, p. 84).

The best way to develop the last point is to turn from political evaluation to the evaluation of private conduct. In the sphere of private conduct it is essential to the peaceful coordination of different people's actions that some fairly specific guidelines for action should supervene between the individual decision-maker and the ultimate criteria such as are given by utilitarianism.[10]

How, then, is moral judgment possible? To this Kantian-sounding question we return the Durkheimian answer that it is made possible by society. We single out in particular three simplifying mechanisms, which we call focal descriptions, duties and obligations, and partial goods. Needless to say, we claim no originality for these features of moral evaluation; at most, we claim only to have put them in a slightly different perspective.

The first device, that of focal descriptions, is socially derived in that the term refers to conventions for the proper and adequate description of acts themselves. D'Arcy (1963) has called attention to the fact that, although there are many ways in which a given sequence of events involving a human agent can be described, we do not have carte blanche to pick and choose among them to suit the moral conclusions we want to arrive at. There are some act-descriptions with a sort of privileged status, such that if one of them applies to a certain situation, we cannot omit it from the description of the act without being properly accused of misleading our listener, unless the context is a very special one. D'Arcy calls these act-descriptions "non-elidable." For example, if among the possible descriptions of what happened is that one man killed another, we cannot "elide" it by referring only to his contracting a muscle, causing a shot to be fired, or starting a war. These focal descriptions, as we shall call them, refer to characteristics that are always relevant to the evaluation of actions. Of the theoretically indefinite number of things that a man might be said to be doing at any time, certain features have been picked out by experience as always important. Anyone, as D'Arcy points out, whatever general principles he professed, would feel that he had been denied adequate information on which to judge an act if it turned out that it was covered by the description "He killed a man" and this description had been withheld.

Duties and obligations as simplifying devices are closely connected with focal descriptions. In fact, they may usefully be regarded as a class of focal descriptions. Focal descriptions draw our attention to features of action which are important for evaluation; such features are usually enough by themselves to determine the verdict, whatever else might be said about the case. Duties and obligations have the same property. Neglecting our duty or failing to keep our obligations is in itself prima facie evidence that we have acted wrongly, though rebuttal is possible, by showing that the neglect or failure was the means to some greater good. Duties arise from jobs, families, and so on; obligations are essentially contractual. Neither would be very felicitously employed in ordinary speech to describe why we ought not to kill other people: Murder is a focal concept on the same level as breach of duty or obligation although philosophers have usually inflated the concept of "breach of duty" (or obligation) to cover all the act-descriptions which lead, almost irrespective of anything else, to condemnation.

The third simplifying device, which we call "partial goods," is in effect the recognition of a division of labor in the production of good and the prevention of evil. It has a naturally close connection with the "common sense" notion of duty we have just described. Indeed, the notion that it is more important to do your duty than to go hell-for-leather after the greatest happiness of the greatest number really depends for its plausibility on the idea that the world will be better in the long run if everyone cultivates his own garden rather than giving a dig here and a hoe there. Underlying the notion of "partial goods" is the idea that each man should (at any rate most of the time) concentrate his efforts on those in some special relationship to him, and that this pursuit of partial goods will get mankind nearer the general good than will any alternative overall strategy. We shall not inquire further into the soundness of these simplifying devices in individual morality; but, to the extent that these devices can themselves be modified by political action, they are obviously within the sphere of political evaluation, and some of what we say below will in fact be relevant to them.

In politics we cannot expect to find things as relatively straightforward as in individual morality, but the previous discussion can serve as a guiding thread. The things to be evaluated are heterogeneous. As we saw in Section II, they include the acts of those with political authority and of those seeking to replace them, of those voting for them or appointing them and of those seeking to influence their decisions; policies pursued over time by political authorities; "policy outcomes," by which we understand states of affairs which are claimed to be to some degree the result of action or inaction by political authorities; political institutions as they actually operate; rules, laws, and constitutions. In each case, of course, not only what exists can be evaluated but what might exist instead. Indeed, what exists cannot be evaluated except with reference (even if implicitly) to what might exist in its place—if the world as it exists is the only possible one, it is, trivially, both the best of all possible worlds and the worst of all possible worlds.

Taking into account this diversity in the objects of evaluation, we should perhaps not be surprised that we find in politics a less clear-cut situation with respect to focal descriptions than we did in individual morality. It is still true that, of all the ways in which an object of evaluation might be described, some would be thought of as always having too trivial a relation to any significant human concern to be acceptable as *the* description. But at the other end of the scale, if we ask where the privileged, non-elidable descriptions in politics are, we seem to finish up with much the same list as before. The difference is that, relatively speaking, this list covers less ground in politics. Thus euphemisms for killing people, such as "saving souls" (the Inquisition), "liquidating class enemies" (the Bolsheviks) or "the Final Solution" (the Nazis) are recognizable as tendentious attempts to lose a morally relevant feature of a policy in a more general description of it. Similarly, any description of the British government's Commonwealth Immigrants Act of 1968 which failed to mention that it broke a promise made by the British government at the time of Kenyan independence to those who chose to retain British nationality would be an incomplete description.

As we have already suggested, descriptions of this kind seem to play a smaller part in political evaluation than in the evaluation of individual conduct outside a political context. This comes about because an act falling under the same description can have a larger variance of relative moral significance when it is a political act than when it can be viewed realistically as simply an individual act within a fixed social context. For laws and institutions it is even clearer that there are not descriptions with built-in prima facie evaluation. Evaluation consists in characterizing the thing to be evaluated or in pointing to its consequences and evaluating those. If the description does not itself carry an evaluation, the way in which individual acts are evaluated is normally the same: We either say that an act can be characterized as generous, disinterested, unfair, cowardly, etc., or we draw attention to its consequences and argue that they were good or bad. (This can be done either by characterizing the consequences or by relating them directly to the general ground of evaluation in terms of suffering, health, etc.)

For individual acts, the most important characterizations are called virtues and vices—at least, that is what they have traditionally been called. In political evaluation, the most important characterizations may be called political principles, though a tinge of the same embarrassment hangs about "political principles" as about "virtues and vices"—somehow the terms are considered a little pompous or priggish. We shall not be deterred by these semantic qualms.

As with individual acts, an object of political evaluation may be characterized in terms of a political principle, or its consequences may be described and either related directly to the general ground of evaluation or characterized in terms of a political principle. Thus, a law withdrawing the protection of habeas corpus might be characterized as a reduction of personal liberty, whereas a speech whipping up public feeling on the "law and order" issue might be said to have brought about consequences which themselves could be characterized as constituting a reduction in personal liberty.

The role played by characterizations in practical political evaluation is crucial. It is these standard foci of attention which help to fill in the gap between what we have called the general basis of evaluation in terms of human well-being and the ever-changing welter of political phenomena to be evaluated. Explaining how the most important of these political principles—democracy, justice, freedom, the public interest, and so on—work is a large part of the study of political evaluation, and we shall take it up in Section VI. In broad terms, however, we suggest that the reason why these are able to function as standard foci lies in the fact that these concepts succeed in capturing features of objects of evaluation which are important to people who nevertheless differ in their interpretations of well-being and proper distribution.

But even if these characterizing concepts are of some help, there is still the problem that there is more than one of them. As we saw, an important simplifying device found in the ordinary moral evaluation of individual behavior is the idea of duties. In political terms, the equivalent would be a list of things which political authorities must do or must not do, such that failure to comply would be prima facie evidence of culpability so strong that only highly exceptional circumstances could overcome it. The most obvious attempts to supply such a list are the various declarations of the rights of man or of human rights that have been produced in the past two hundred years.

Like duties in relation to individual conduct, these codes are powerful weapons in the struggle to simplify evaluation. They provide, we suggest, standards of government performance failure to meet which can widely be agreed to constitute prima facie grounds for censure. Like duties in the evaluation of individual conduct, rights against the state, then, are things that anyone, whatever his ultimate evaluations, can agree are important. Freedom of movement, assembly, and speech, freedom from detention except after trial under a preexisting law—these are the kinds of thing that form a component of the good life on almost any interpretation, and they do not seem liable to offend any reasonable distributive criterion.

So-called social rights, such as those incorporated in the United Nations Declaration of Human Rights (1948), have been criticized, not as undesirable in themselves, but as lacking the same absolute priority as the more traditional civil rights. (See the articles by Cranston and Raphael in Raphael, 1967. This criticism may indeed be correctly applied to the article about holidays with pay seized on by critics.[11] However, it does seem compatible with almost any conception of human well-being and any plausible criterion for the distribution of this well-being to say that states should give a high priority to the relief of destitution relatively to any other and perhaps grander aims that they might pursue.

Unfortunately, although the ravages of war have been a constant threat to life and well-being, only a tiny fraction of the energy that has gone into the improvement of domestic conditions has been applied to the prevention of war. This obtuseness about priorities—plus, of course, the genuine difficulties of prescription for a Hobbesian world—results in a lack of generally accepted constraints on the warlike action of states. The requirement that states should not commit aggression is a precept of very limited usefulness since, as Hobbes pointed out, the distinction between aggression and self-defense is logically unclear in a condition of anarchy; and "genocide" appears to be condemned unequivocally only when it is pursued as an end in itself, not when it comes about as a by-product of military strategy. It would take us too far afield to do more here than point out this great, perhaps ultimately disastrous, lacuna in the commonly conceived duties of states.

Before leaving the subject of "duties" for states, we must note that they play an important part in structuring decision-making at a more humble level. Governments lay upon themselves, their successors, and their subordinate bodies "statutory duties," which have precisely the function of defining priorities: If a body has to choose between carrying out its duties and doing other desirable things, the understanding is that it should opt for the duties. Thus the city of Glasgow was recently deciding between building an opera house and treating the sewage which it now discharges raw into the Clyde. It is relevant to the decision that the latter is, whereas the former is not, a statutory duty of the corporation.

The foregoing leads to the third simplifying device, which we called "partial goods." As we saw before, there is a close connection with duties, since some duties at least make sense only in the context of a division of labor. This is true in politics as well. A municipal fire service, say, is expected to provide as much service in preventing and putting out fires as its budget will allow—not to spend its money on books for the public libraries because those in charge of the fire service regard that as a better way of employing the marginal penny of taxpayers' money. But this division of labor obviously makes sense only if funds are in fact being allocated to other purposes.

This example illustrates division of labor by fiat. As is well known from academic study, not to mention personal experience, the goals set for an organization are usually "displaced" to some degree, since they will tend to be pursued only insofar as the pursuit serves the interests and ambitions of those in the organization. But outsiders obviously can evaluate more easily the performance of an organization if it has relatively clear-cut goals than if it is simply in business to improve human welfare, as is, for example, an exclusively philanthropic foundation.

Division of labor can also, needless to say, come about nonbureaucratically. The example already given in connection with the moral evaluation of individual conduct can be used to illustrate this point. If parents look after their own children, most children will be looked after without the need for any overall plan to assign people to look after children. The archetype of this sort of "division of labor" occurs in classical economic theory. Adam Smith argued that a "hidden hand" would bring about results that, taken as a whole, would be generally regarded as desirable even if nobody (except the government—a deus ex machina introduced to fill the logical gaps) was doing any more than pursuing his own or his family's self-interest. "It is not from the benevolence of the butcher, the brewer, or the baker, that we expect our dinner, but from their regard to their own interest" (Smith, 1961, Vol. 1, p. 18). In a further development, political competition is seen as performing the same alchemy where collective decisions are unavoidable.

It is plain that, although these institutions may simplify the decision-making problem for most of the actors, they do not get rid of the problem of multiple criteria of evaluation. The outcome still has to be evaluated, and it is of course notorious that these evaluations—of such institutions as the family, the free-market economy, and representative government—have been among the most controverted in the past two centuries. What price independent decision-making when cultivating one's own garden means killing the fish and birds with insecticide? But the point remains that the problem of evaluation is more feasible if we focus on institutions rather than on millions of individual acts. Thus, if one is trying to apply the criterion that people should get the goods they want, it would be absurd to try to find out what all people want and then see whether they are getting it. A price system provides a much more feasible basis for talking about want satisfaction. As a first move, one can make the assumption that people are choosing, within the limits of their income, the combination of goods they prefer. This presumption can be challenged in various ways, and it may well be necessary to make big adjustments to allow for ignorance or misinformation. But even this process, rough and ready as it may be, leaves us in a much better position to estimate want satisfaction than we would be if we had to study each person's tastes and then match them up with his purchases.

## SECTION VI: FIVE POLITICAL PRINCIPLES

We are now at last in a position to say something about the "big words"—democracy, freedom, and the like—which are thought, rightly, to form an important part of the subject matter of an article on political evaluation. We hope that what has gone before serves to put into context the role which we conceive these political principles as playing in political evaluation. We argued that political evaluation requires practical aids if it is to be possible. There must be simplifying devices standing between what we have called the general ground of evaluation and evaluations of particular actions, policies, institutions, etc. Among these simplifying devices, the most important are political principles, criteria of evaluation derived from different interpretations of the general ground of evaluation, and emphasis on different aspects of it, plus factual beliefs about human behavior and society.

Note that the term "political principles" covers prescriptions for choice of almost any degree of specificity. For example, Sir Anthony Eden learned at Munich (and misapplied at Suez) the principle "Do not give in to threats from dictators." This principle fits our formula well enough. It is derived from factual beliefs concerning the insatiable appetites of dictators, the effect of appeasement on the perceptions of the threatening party about the appeasing party, and so on. By way of such factual beliefs, the principle can be connected to the general ground of evaluation if one holds further that successful aggression by dictators allowed to go unchecked leads in the long run to a bigger war and greater suffering and death than would have occurred had the aggression been stopped earlier.

It is clear that we cannot hope to discuss, even in a similarly sketchy fashion, other principles at that level of specificity. We have to concentrate on the most general principles of all—and that, of course, brings us back to the "big words." Strictly speaking, a word is not itself a principle, and the word "principle" is perhaps most happily applied to maxims governing conduct in a fairly specific way. But it is certainly not a freak usage to say, for example, "The party is dedicated to the principle of equality (social justice, or whatever)." If we want to spell the "principle" out in a plonking manner, we might say that the principle corresponding to "equality" is "When evaluating, give great weight to equality" or more succinctly, "Equality is important." However, we shall follow the common habit of treating the key words as themselves embodying principles.

The study of the way in which political principles are marshaled in arguments about evaluation—the study of political rhetoric—is one of the most potentially rewarding fields of inquiry, we believe. It is a field with surprisingly little systematic work in it. Stevenson (1944) gave interesting invented illustrations of arguments centering on the application of concepts, but his discussion of them is vitiated by his general theory, according to which words act directly on people's feelings as a result of conditioning—an implication of which is that any method of persuasion has an equally rational basis or lack of it, the only criterion being success. The best treatments, we suggest, concern themselves with legal reasoning, such as those of Hart (1961, Chapter 7) and Levi (1949). Legal arguments, especially in the higher courts, turn on the question whether such-and-such a concept should be deemed to cover such-and-such an admitted state of affairs. This obviously has something in common with political casuistry, though one should beware of moving too incautiously from the enclosed legal world to the inherently more open-ended world of politics, where it is always a possible move (though one with ramifying implications) to say, "Well, if that's what that principle commits me to, I'll forswear the principle."

Arguments over the definitions of words have consequences when the words are "freedom" or "equality," even if this fact is less immediately clear than that it may make a difference for someone between going to jail or not whether a court accepts a certain definition of "public road" or "vehicle." If you can convince people that some principle they accept (say, equal opportunity) covers some matter they hadn't applied it to before (say, opening jobs to women) you may thereby change their behavior.

It might appear that every strong adherent of a principle has a simple enough strategy in seeking to extend the application of the principle as far as possible. But there is a counterstrategy, akin to that practiced by the Russians against Napoleon, of weakening a concept by encouraging its overextension. In most controversies, as Harris (1971) remarks, "at least one side finds it useful to redefine the other side's basic demands so that they become unobjectionable" (p. 24).

Thus the waxing and waning of evaluative concepts requires careful interpretation. The rise of a principle to prominence may mean a genuinely increased acceptance of it in its original form, or it may be a sign that it has achieved popularity at the price of losing content. Conversely, the same object may be pursued in two superficially opposed ways. Suppose, for example, that you were concerned about reducing the impact of the idea of equality. You might try to absorb it by suggesting, say, that all defensible uses of it make it merely a special case of justice. Or alternatively, you might blow it up so that it subsumes all distributive criteria, by arguing, for example, that the essence of the idea of equality is that equals (however defined) are to be treated equally. Both kinds of move have been made by conservative liberals anxious to rob the idea of equality of its dangerous potential but unwilling to appear as overt partisans of inequality.

If we consider the last two centuries, we find a remarkable degree of stability in the basic concepts employed. All the main counters of debate found today—freedom (or liberty), justice, equality, the public interest, democracy—are to be found in the *Declaration of the Rights of Man* drawn up in the early stages of the French Revolution. Nor is this a matter of stability in the words covering a transformation in the sense. We find that most of the subsequent connotations of these key words (with their characteristic equivocations) may be found in the *Declaration*. Such variation in the uses of the words as we find over time and from one place to another may be accounted for by recognizing that there can be changes in the emphasis placed on alternative interpretations of the words that were current all along. Now it seems fair to say that the *Declaration of the Rights of Man* is one of those documents referred to a thousand or ten thousand times for every one it is read; but to such an extent are we still living on the intellectual capital of the French Revolution that it will be useful to quote its first six articles.[12]

> I. Men are born, and always continue, free and equal in respect of their rights. Civil distinctions, therefore, can be founded only on public utility.
>
> II. The end of all political associations is the preservation of the natural and imprescriptible rights of man; and these rights are Liberty, Property, Security, and Resistance of Oppression.
>
> III. The Nation is essentially the source of all sovereignty; nor can any individual, or any body of men, be entitled to any authority which is not expressly derived from it.
>
> IV. Political Liberty consists in the power of doing whatever does not injure another. The exercise of the natural rights of man, has no other limits than those which are necessary to secure to every *other* man the free exercise of the same rights; and these limits are determinable only by the law.
>
> V. The law ought to prohibit only actions hurtful to society. What is not prohibited by the law should not be hindered; nor should any one be compelled to that which the law does not require.
>
> VI. The law is an expression of the will of the community. All citizens have a right to concur, either personally or by their representatives, in its formation. It should be the same to all, whether it protects or punishes; and all being equal in its sight, are equally eligible to all honours, places, and employments, according to their different abilities, without any other distinction than that created by their virtues and talents.

To say that "we" are still living on the intellectual capital of the French Revolution may appear a highly culture-bound (or "Natocentric") judgment. Who are "we" in this context, anyway? Of course, qualifications to this sweeping statement are in order, but not so many as might at first blush be supposed. The main exceptions to be noted are first the nineteenth-century reactionaries, who hated everything the Revolution had stood for, and second the twentieth-century Fascists and Nazis—the two streams being linked, as Nolte (1965) has shown, by Maurras and his circle. On the other hand, Marxism is, in evaluative terms, no more than a variant on the ideals of the French Revolution. Those nineteenth-century conservatives, such as Mosca, who linked Rousseau and Marx displayed a sure instinct for the political jugular.

Considered as an evaluative system, Marxism is partly an attack on the pretensions of capitalist societies to provide for all citizens the rights set out in the *Declaration* and partly a vision (of a form quite common among nineteenth-century thinkers as different as Bakunin and Herbert Spencer) of a society in which liberty, equality, and fraternity would be realized without the necessity for the coercive apparatus of the state. In practical terms, Marx can be said to have made two claims, both of which are consistent with the principles already mentioned. First, he suggested that a capitalist society is a power system which makes a mockery of democracy, and second, he pointed out that the rule of the employer over the wage earner during working hours is in itself a serious infringement of liberty.

Had we been writing a few years ago, it would have been true to say that Marxism had contributed nothing distinctive to the *vocabulary* of evaluation. The recent vogue of the concept of "alienation" requires an amendment, though it must be said that the desire to trace the concept to Marx (rather than Hegel or Feuerbach) is a strategic exigency of radical politics. *Economic and Philosophical Manuscripts of 1844* (Marx, 1959), in which the concept occurs extensively, are largely derivative of Adam Smith and Feuerbach (Althusser, 1969). If Marx, instead of leaving these exercise books to the "gnawing criticism of the rats," had published them and then died, it is doubtful that anyone today would call himself a Marxist, or that his name would be known to more than a handful of scholars. Moreover, even after all the effort that has been expended in recent years, there still does not seem to have emerged any interpretation of "alienation" which is not more clearly expressed either as liberty, equality, or fraternity.

If we take an alternative tack and look at the evaluative criteria by which political parties and governments claim to be guided and in virtue of which they make demands on others, we again find an extensive common element, which again can be derived directly from the ideas of the French Revolution. We can illustrate this contention by looking briefly at the Soviet Union and the eastern European regimes on the one hand and the so-called Third

World on the other. Now the Communists, whatever their practice, apparently do not avow distinctive criteria of evaluation. Thus we get the so-called German Democratic Republic and the phenomenon of a Soviet academician gravely assuring an international conference (IPSA, 1964) that all the human rights referred to in the United Nations Declaration of Human Rights (of which the Soviet Union is, of course, a signatory) are cherished faithfully in Russia. Nor is this, as some zealous apologists of the Soviets have suggested, a matter of the use of the same word (e.g., democracy) with a different meaning (see Macpherson, 1958). Stalin's constitution of 1936 is a document that satisfies all the demands of late-nineteenth-century Western liberalism. It not only specifies all kinds of safeguards for individual liberty, but it also provides for the right of the constituent states of the federal republic to secede and for the autonomy of ethnic groups within these states. Such innovations as there have been seem to be ways of stating traditional Western ideas in ideologically acceptable ways: "Socialist legality" is simply "legality," and the substitution of the "interests of the toiling masses" for the "public interest" does not amount to much, since officially everybody is a member of the "toiling masses"—except those who actually deserve the name, the inhabitants of the labor camps. In eastern Europe, too, the official aims are not (as, for example, they were in Nazi Germany) in any way novel, and the various movements of reform that have occurred in most of those countries have been based essentially on the demand that the regime should actually live up to its professed aims. In the West, we might remark, the process of clothes-stealing is very far advanced: In 1970 one could see in France Communist Party posters calling for proportional representation to break the grip of the "totalitarian" Gaullists.

Any generalization about the heterogeneous collection of countries known as the Third World is obviously perilous, but it does in fact seem true to say that their independence movements (whether early, as in Latin America, or later as in Asia and Africa) made their demands in the name of such principles of the French Revolution as national self-determination and popular sovereignty and that their postindependence elites are almost invariably committed, at least formally, to similar criteria of evaluation in relation to their domestic policies. The two exceptions, which we have already noted, are significantly enough both explicitly opposed to the ideas of the French Revolution: politico-religious reaction running from, say, de Maistre to the *Syllabus of Errors,* and the more activist creeds of fascism and Nazism. Although by 1942 these traditional and novel movements of antiliberal, antidemocratic, antiegalitarian thought, in various mixtures and combinations, underlay almost every regime in Europe between Britain and Russia, they are now very much in decline, even within their strongholds of the Iberian peninsula and the Vatican. Their one area of growth is in the regimes of the white minorities of South Africa and Rhodesia. Let us say again that we do not regard this as accidental: Such doctrines are inherently less satisfactory than those of the *Declaration of the Rights of Man.* The ideas of reaction and fascism are not likely in the long run to appeal to a group wider than the specific beneficiaries. Authoritarianism (with or without religious underpinning) cannot allow the open expression of the wishes of most people; and ideas of racial purity or bellicose national destiny are bound to create a self-defensive coalition of those outside the charmed circle.

---

In the remainder of this section we shall discuss five principles which play a central role in political evaluation: the public interest, justice, freedom, equality, and democracy. We shall try to show how each connects to the general ground of evaluation and a little about the interrelationships among them.

## *1. The Public Interest*

In broad terms, the connection between "the public interest" and the general ground of evaluation is manifest in that interest, along with happiness and the satisfaction of wants, was introduced as one of the conceptions of the ultimate stuff whose amount and distribution constitute the raw material of evaluation. But what is "interest" exactly, and what does the qualification "public" do?

Briefly, "interest," used without further specification, always appears to have carried an emphasis on material advantage and thus to find its home especially in economic and quasi-economic discourse. "Public" is a familiar enough word (as in public parks, public transport, public performances, and so on), and it is of course the antonym of "private." Thus the public interest is the material advantage of a broad and undefined group of people, as opposed to private interests, which are material advantages confined to particular and specifiable people. We can illustrate this usage with a famous passage from *The Wealth of Nations* (Smith, 1961).

> [An individual] generally, indeed, neither intends to promote the public interest, nor knows how much he is promoting it. By preferring the support of domestic to that of foreign industry, he intends only his own security; and by directing that industry in such a manner as its produce may be of the greatest value, he intends only his own gain, and he is in this, as in many other cases, led by an invisible hand to promote an end which was no part of his intention. Nor is it always the worse for the society that it was no part of it. By pursuing his own interest he frequently promotes that of the society more effectually than when he really intends to promote it. I have never known much good done by those who affected to trade for the public good. (Vol. 1, pp. 477–8)

Thanks to Gunn's (1969) study, we can trace the development of the concept in seventeenth-century England. From the start it was used to emphasize the importance of material considerations in state policy, as against the much more inclusive concept of the "common good," the pursuit of which for medieval writers such as Dante and Aquinas had tended to sum up the duties of princes. In particular, it was used by the opponents of the Stuarts to insist that state policies should be defensible by showing that tangible advantages would accrue to actual people. As a consequence of this origin, there was a tendency to get confused about the relation between public interest and private interests: If the public interest is defined in contradistinction to a mistrusted *raison d'état*, is it not simply made up of private interests? Indeed, it was declared a virtue of members of Parliament that they had substantial private interests, on the grounds that they would therefore have a strong incentive to pursue the public interest. However, this does not mean that public and private interest were identical, though Gunn sometimes suggests that they were. The public interest was seen mainly as consisting in the trimming of state expenditures; therefore the biggest property-owners would have the biggest stake in pursuing it. In any case, by the middle of the century Harrington (1924) had analyzed the logic of the concept faultlessly by arguing that the members of any group have some common interests and some opposed ones. Harrington drew the inference that the nearest practical approximation to the public interest is the interest of a majority and thus arrived at a case for taking communal decisions by majority vote, an idea we shall take up below when discussing democracy.

Nowadays, the "public interest" can still be used, as it was in the time of the Stuarts, to advance the interests of the citizens at large against the state—certain taxes or policies may be said to be against the public interest—but it has also inherited something of the old *raison d'etat*. The claim is sometimes made that it is in the public interest to spend billions of dollars to put a man on the moon or millions of pounds to build supersonic airliners. Yet those planes may never be allowed to fly or, if they do, will make life very unpleasant for people below. But the claim, however specious, is that these achievements will produce tangible benefits for people other than the contractors and their employees. Thus the concept of "public interest" still maintains its connection with the idea of broadly diffused material advantages.

As we said, the connection between the public interest and the general basis of evaluation is clear enough. It is also however, clear that the concept of the public interest falls short of being equivalent in scope to the general basis of evaluation. First, "interest" is one component of the possible valued states but does not encompass the whole of either want-satisfaction or happiness. Second, "the public interest" is not simply the aggregate of all interests lumped together, however utilitarians may have defined it so officially. When I scratch my back in the bath, I benefit and nobody else loses, so there is a net gain in human welfare, but I am not advancing the public interest thereby. And third, public interest does not include any reference to distributive considerations, though some of the quotations in Gunn's book reveal that even in the seventeenth century the usual expansionist forces were at work, and some people were saying that the public interest consisted in the protection of "just rights."

## 2. Justice

We now have an appropriate cue for turning to the broadest of the distributive concepts, that of justice. The notion of justice is rooted in that of a judicial decision, and we may surmise that some word roughly translatable as "justice" will be found in the vocabulary of any society with some form of judicial mechanism for settling disputes. In tracing the descent of the Greek word *dike*, indeed, we can go back to a time when decisions were taken by arbitrary means (i.e., methods not involving reference to any arguments but involving such things as the use of scales), and *dike* referred to these outcomes. Later, the more refined conception that decisions themselves should correspond to an external standard was incorporated into *dike* (Huizinga, 1970, pp. 101–2). By the time that Aristotle wrote, in Book V of the *Ethics*, what is still the best discussion of the concept, it had acquired the sense of an external criterion by which not merely judicial decisions could be assessed as just or unjust (depending on whether they were right or wrong) but also any decision concerning the distribution of goods, privileges, and penalties could be criticized. Although conservative writers have unsurprisingly been drawn to the idea that justice should be understood to mean only conformity with positive law, the word "justice" today carries both a reference to judicial outcomes and a broader reference to any social arrangement from washing dishes in a family to the existence of private property in a nation. Although the demand for justice is one of the most potent in the political arsenal, the concept, in its broader sense, is almost devoid of substantive content. As Aristotle observed, justice is a kind of equality or, more exactly, proportionality. In its most simple form it is a matter of seeing that what A gets and the degree to which he has some relevant attribute is in the same ratio as that between what B gets and the degree to which he has the same attribute. (See Perelman, 1963 and Nathan, 1971). The substantive question, of course, is what characteristics are to count as relevant. And again as Aristotle noted, different social groups tend to want different lists. All we can say here is that there seems to have been a fairly well-established trend over several centuries, which still continues, toward accepting as relevant only actions and achievements as against such things as skin color (or other "racial" characteristics), age, or sex.

Abstracting from the actual properties on the basis of which it is claimed that benefits, burdens, and sanctions should be assigned, we are left with the formal principle of justice: Differences in treatment must be justified by reference to some property or other of the people involved. This may appear to be a pretty toothless principle, but in fact it has a surprising amount of bite. A strict utilitarian would be obliged to look only at the total sum of well-being, but from the point of view of justice a situation would be defective in which one person was very well-off and another very badly-off although their personal characteristics were similar—even if no alternative arrangement would produce as great a sum total of well-being.

The insistence that there be a reason (and not simply a utilitarian one) for differences in people's lots makes the principle of justice a potentially explosive one. It makes an immense difference to the way one looks at the world how far one is prepared to go in asking the question: Is this just? At one extreme are the conservatives, who wish to confine the question of justice to the application of the law: Justice is done provided that people whose characteristics differ in ways specified by law are treated differently according to the legal specification. At the other extreme are what might be called cosmic questioners, who indict God (or Nature) for injustice in visiting the innocent with suffering and death—and do not find the counterquestion "Where wast thou when I laid the foundations of the earth?" (Job 38:4) very satisfying. In between fall those who wish to challenge various social arrangements in the name of justice.

Let us suppose that someone asks in any society having private property whether the distribution of property is just. The answer to this question is not really in doubt. Most gross differences in wealth are the result of inheritance and cannot conceivably be related to personal characteristics. This illustrates vividly the point that the primary dispute about justice is its sphere of application. The sensible conservative will not try to show that the distribution of property is just. He will argue that an unequal distribution of property is desirable for various reasons, and that this is incompatible with any attempt to ask why the particular people who are rich should be rich, and so on. Perhaps, though, it is really surprising how relatively seldom the conservative finds himself called on to argue in these terms. Most people most of the time accept the main features of their social institutions as beyond question. How often, to take the most far-reaching example, do people anywhere see as raising an issue of justice the fact that the biggest determinant of one's life chances is the country one is born in.

The ultimate basis of evaluation we have described as concerned with the amount and distribution of well-being. The present discussion should make clearer the contention that sharp differences of evaluation can arise not only from differences in the conception of well-being or appropriate distribution but also in the relative importance given to, say, distribution against other things. Nothing further needs to be said about the relation of "justice" to the ultimate basis of evaluation, since justice is itself the most general distributive concept. But we shall have to discuss its relations to the other concepts, the closest of which is equality.

## 3. Equality

"Justice" is acknowledged as desirable on all hands, and the biggest question concerns its proper sphere of application. Equality has no such privileged position. You can be against equality as well as for it. We can explain this in crude and general terms by pointing out that two people might agree that A should be treated justly with respect to B while one thinks this entails equal treatment whereas the other (because of different criteria for just differentiation) thinks it entails unequal treatment; but there can be no such equivocation if they argue in terms of equality. More precisely, whereas "justice" is used only to claim that outcomes of certain kinds should be related to the possession of relevant characteristics, "equality" is used to rebut the idea that possession of some specific characteristic or characteristics should be related to outcomes of certain kinds.

Note that it does not follow from this definition that equality between possessors of property $x$ and nonpossessors of property $x$ will result in the members of both categories being treated identically. What the definition does mean is that if they are treated differently, it will be on the basis of the possession or nonpossession of some property other than $x$. We can illustrate this by going back to the call for equality as it was expressed in the French Revolution. The essence of this was a demand for "equality before the law—in other words, a demand for the cessation of the practice under which the nobility were treated more favorably by the legal system than others. Equality in this sense, then, means that any two men who have committed the same offense should be dealt with in the same way, even if one is a noble and one a commoner. But it does not mean there should be no legal penalties or that the legal penalties for all offenses should be the same.

A similar analysis can be made of equality between the sexes, racial equality, equality among ethnic or religious groups, etc. In this context, for example, "equal pay" means simply that persons differing in sex or race but doing the same job are paid the same; it has no implications for the differentials in pay between jobs. Indeed, to the extent that, say, racial groups occupy different segments of the stratification hierarchy, any reduction in the importance of race as a determinant of position in the hierarchy will, other things being equal, result in a greater spread of positions for the numbers of each group. In the United States, for example, blacks enjoy (if that is the word) a fair degree of homogeneity in occupational prestige and income (Blau and Duncan, 1967, pp. 238–41), whereas whites, except for real down-and-outs, are kept off the bottom of the ladder by blacks. Racial equality would mean a much greater social dispersion for blacks and a somewhat greater one for whites. Not surprisingly, the strongest pressure for racial equality (as against a straight improvement in conditions) comes from blacks who are in the best position to benefit (Wilson, 1960) and the most violent resistance from whites whose only advantage is the color of their skin.

There are, of course, broader claims that can be made in terms of equality, and it is with reference to these that people are called egalitarians or antiegalitarians. We have so far discussed claims that *some* feature or features should not be bases for treating people differently in certain respects; but it may be maintained that *no* features should be bases for treating people differently in certain respects. The most abstract claim of this kind is that people should be equal as potential bearers of rights (see Vlastos, 1962; Williams, 1962). This means in the last analysis only that *some* reason has to be given for treating people differently, and thus it comes to much the same as the claim that the criterion of justice should actually be applied. More concrete, though closely related, is the demand for "social equality." Although this notion has a range of interpretations, its core might be expressed as a rejection of Disraeli's "two nations," a demand that everyone should be treated as equal in dignity—as an "end in himself," to use Kantian terminology. Political equality and economic equality, at least in principle, are fairly straightforward demands for similarly unconditional equality. In practice, the former tends to be identified with one-man-one-vote representative democracy, the latter with a move toward equalization of earned incomes and a reduction of property-derived incomes.

Once again, we should ask briefly how equality ties in with the grounds of evaluation. Since it is concerned with the distribution of things that people want, there is, as with justice, a direct connection. In addition, equality can be supported as increasing the total amount of well-being. The simplest argument on these lines depends on the idea of the diminishing marginal utility of money: if a penny were transferred from a millionaire to someone without enough to eat, the gain to the latter would be greater than the loss to the former; this would also be true of a second penny, a third, and so on for quite a lot of pennies.

### 4. Freedom

The term "freedom" is so potent that one is hardly surprised to find its definition extended in all kinds of ways (Cranston, 1953). The fundamental idea, we suggest, is that to be free is to be left alone to do what you want to do. It is easy to see how this links with the general ground of evaluation, since the absence of restrictions on doing what you want must in general increase the chance of doing what you want, and "doing what you want" is one formulation of the stuff whose amount and distribution are the concern of political evaluation. Freedom is also argued to be an essential condition of happiness, both because people need to be able to explore ways of living for themselves and because they can learn from the experiences of others.

In contrast to the concepts we have so far examined, that of freedom does not provide any criterion for adjudicating between the claims of different persons. What happens when somebody exercises his freedom in a way that is damaging to the interests or welfare of somebody else? Giving people freedom means simply not preventing them from doing what they want. But then freedom for everybody, as Hobbes pointed out, means a condition of total anarchy. Every law, as Bentham put it, is an infraction of liberty. It does not help, as some have supposed, to introduce an explicit distributive criterion at this point and speak of the maximum liberty compatible with an equal liberty for others. For the maximum liberty is still simply an absence of all constraints.

This conclusion of course follows from the definition we have posed in terms of an absence of constraints. One possible way out is to expand the meaning of "freedom" so that it provides a criterion for adjudicating between conflicting interests. This involves redefining a "constraint" so that somebody else doing something you don't like counts as a constraint on your action. Such a definition, however, destroys the distinction between being free to act and being pleased with what happens to you. In fact, if the advantages of constraints on oneself and constraints on others are to be compared, it is necessary to reduce the two sides of the equation to a common measure, which can be only want-satisfaction. Freedom will then be maximized on a basis of equality when one achieves a uniform set of legal or other obligations such that the marginal constraint just produces a net benefit—in other words, where any additional constraint would cause more hardship to those constrained from doing what they would like to do than it generates satisfaction among those who would suffer the consequences of the others' doing what they wanted. This, however, is simply utilitarianism, interpreted in the "liberal" way, with wants as the raw material of aggregation, and expressed in a rather obscure form, which conceals all the difficulties about distribution associated with the utilitarian position. It should perhaps be pointed out parenthetically that, even if the rules apply equally to everyone, they do not necessarily bear on everyone with equal severity. Some may want very much to do things that are prohibited and may be adversely affected by things that are allowed; others may be more fortunate on both counts.

If freedom is inflated so that it comes to the same as getting what you want and not getting what you don't want, it follows, of course, that the distinctive feature of freedom as absence of constraints is lost. This burying of freedom as a distinctive value can be defended in relation to the general basis of evaluation by the argument, sometimes made, that being left alone is of no use if one is starving. Rich and poor alike are free to sleep under bridges. It does not in fact follow that absence of constraint is not to be valued in its own right; it is simply not very valuable unless other conditions are also met (Berlin, 1969, pp. 124–5). But one can say that the extent to which it is valuable is purely the extent to which it does satisfy wants.

This, however, could be said of any principle—that its fulfillment is desirable only to the extent that it can be justified with reference to the general ground of evaluation. The point of each of the principles we are discussing is to highlight certain features which actions, policies, constitutions may or may not exhibit. These features are ones of which it is widely believed that, when they are present, then (other things being equal) the action, policy, constitution, or whatever will tend toward a better amount and distribution of well-being than exist if they are not present. Thus the point of making freedom a principle is to emphasize the importance of not being constrained. To say it is important is not of course to say that it is the only valuable thing. It is inevitable that absence of constraint will clash with other principles and that in some situations it will be thought better on balance not to do the thing that would maximize freedom. It is quite illuminating to think in this way of "freedom" as a counterweight to the "public interest" in particular. "The public interest" is used in the formulation of demands that people should be stopped from doing things they might otherwise do: It is "contrary to the public interest" to build a house here, publish that piece of information, and so on. "Freedom" embodies exactly the opposite claim—that people should be allowed to do what they want to do. Similarly, though less centrally, freedom may conflict with the claims of justice and equality, since the achievement of distributive ends may well entail preventing people from doing what they would otherwise have done.

As a coda, but an important one, we should notice that freedom can be claimed not only for individuals but for groups of any size. "Freedom" here means the absence of constraints on the action of the collectivity; freedom for a group is of course compatible with the oppression of members of that group by the collectivity. If we are concerned to include in our analysis the leading ideas of the past two centuries, the idea of group freedom is crucial, because it underlies the notion of national sovereignty, which first redrew the map of Europe and then, especially in the period after 1945, more than doubled the number of nominally sovereign states while reducing formally dependent colonial regimes to a few scattered relics. Indeed, if we apply the harsh but realistic test of an idea's potency which consists in asking how many people have died for it, the answer is very clear. In the last two hundred years the number of people who have died in the service of nationalist movements or in wars perceived as necessary to defend a sovereign state must outnumber those who died in the cause of individual liberty by tens or even hundreds of thousands to one. We do not wish to suggest that this should be given too much credence as an index of the significance of ideas, but it is nevertheless thought-provoking.

Since we have insisted that the ultimate ground of evaluation lies in the well-being of individual human beings, the relation to it of group freedom must necessarily be indirect. It cannot, however, be doubted that the desire to be governed with and by people who are thought of as similar in some respect is an immensely strong one. In general, it is quite rational to wish to be in a state with other people who are as similar to oneself as possible. Since any state has a more or less extensive set of uniform, enforced rules, there is a greater possibility (whether it is exploited or not) of having rules that satisfy people as those subject to the rules are more similar in outlook and preference.

### 5. Democracy

The argument can be further extended by connecting the idea of national self-determination with that of democracy. This connection was made explicitly in the *Declaration of the Rights of Man,* and the whole complex of ideas surely reached the peak of its influence in the Versailles Peace Treaty, which followed the First World War. If one starts from the argument of the previous paragraph that uniformity in the population makes satisfactory uniform rules a possibility, the extension to democracy involves simply the claim that if the rules are such as are approved by a majority of this uniform population, they should be satisfactory to all. (This might be taken as a crude statement of one strand in Rousseau, 1947.)

This theory, which assumes a uniformity of aspirations and interests among "the people" and regards the object of politics as the service of this "general will," has been dubbed "populistic democracy" (Dahl, 1956), the "radical theory of representation" (Beer, 1965), and even "totalitarian democracy" (Talmon, 1960). (See also Shils, 1956.) It is not, indeed, the only argument in favor of democratic government. At the same time, although other arguments may be able to take account of a certain diversity of aspirations and interests in the population, they cannot deal with the problem posed by a minority sharply differentiated from the rest. The resort to nationalism to paper over the cracks, in other words, is a response (though often a lethal one) to a genuinely insoluble difficulty in democratic politics.

We have been running ahead and need to go back and prepare the ground for more detailed analysis. Democracy, then, means "rule by the people"—a "pure" condition of democracy would be one in which (by whatever means) it occurred that every state-imposed rule were such as a majority of the citizens wished. In practice, "democracy" means what the *Declaration* stated, the right of every citizen to share in the election of the legislature, plus (it is now understood) either direct election of the head of the executive or indirect influence over the executive via its responsibility to the legislature. A separate article would be required to investigate how far the machinery of representative democracy produces the coincidence in policy preferences by which we defined the pure concept. (For some preliminary remarks, see Barry, 1970, Chapters 5–7.) All we can do is state the arguments for representative democracy and note without discussing the empirical assumptions they require. The most general argument, then, might be expressed by saying that the rulers of a country will at least have an incentive to deal with complaints shared by large numbers of people, since they are otherwise liable to be voted out at the next election. This argument—that the voters know "where the shoe pinches"—can be found back in seventeenth-century England. "Can any man tell better than yourselves, where your shoe pinches you, and what is most expedient for you to do?" (Anonymous, 1647).

To the extent that we are prepared to assume that representative institutions do result in majority preferences for policies being put into effect as collective decisions, we can adopt a stronger argument to this effect: If the policy preferred by the majority is always chosen, the average number of people satisfied by each collective decision will be higher than under any alternative decision rule. But, to return to our theme, neither this argument nor the vaguer preceding one rules out the possibility of a distinct permanent minority, whose pinching shoes are a matter of indifference if not actual pleasure to a majority, and whose policy preferences are consistently voted down.

This is a distressing and sometimes disastrous feature of democratic politics, but the difficulty is inherent in the hypothesized set of preferences. It can at least be shown that, in a pure majoritarian democracy, the maximum possible proportion of the electorate who can lose is smaller than under any other system. Thus, if just under half of a society can "lose out" under a purely democratic regime, a larger number may lose out under any alternative (Rae, 1971).

One common form of magical thinking leads a number of authors to suppose that decision by unanimity escapes this difficulty. This leads Wolff (1970), for example, to say that only practical considerations prevent unanimous decision from resolving this central problem of the defeated (and therefore "non-autonomous") minority. Calhoun's doctrine of "concurrent majorities" is a similar example (Calhoun, 1953), and so, too, are a number of works which defend the prevalence of veto-points in the contemporary operation of the U.S. federal government. In every case, the argument is fixed myopically on defeats arising from the positive action of governments. This is, of course, well and good if everyone is satisfied with the status quo and the society is so static that this satisfaction is never disturbed. In such a case, no group can suffer a significant defeat, since it necessarily is able to block the imposition of policies to which its members object and will therefore permit only the imposition of advantageous policies. What all this ignores is the resistance of government policy to the desire for change. If the status quo works to the disadvantage of certain groups and a very restrictive regime prevents their changing policies, a serious disadvantage has been encountered. Most significant of all is the fact that regimes of this type make it possible for changes favored by nearly everyone to be rejected. In terms of our discussion of "forced choice" in Section II, this conception of decision-making gives a logically special place to the status quo.

Democracy, defined in terms of the conformity of collective decisions to majority preferences, is pretty clearly not acceptable as a sole political principle. It is easy enough to think of ways in which what a majority wants would not, if enacted, bring about a better amount and distribution of well-being than would some alternative (including the alternative of not doing anything). One possibility is that those making up the majority may have preferences which run counter to their own interests, out of ignorance, miscalculation, shortsightedness, or passion. Another possibility is that those making up the majority may be genuinely advancing their own interests but at the expense of those in the minority, the outcome being an inequitable distribution or an avoidable loss of overall well-being. And a third possibility is that the policy preferred by a majority may be evaluatively acceptable if one looks only at the group bound by the collective decision but unacceptable because of its effects on those outside the group.

Thus there are severe problems facing the inventor of constitutions, since it is one thing to show that democracy is capable of producing bad outcomes and another to find institutions that are not vulnerable to the same fault. But it is not a theoretical difficulty; all we have to do is allow for competing principles. In doing that, we implicitly acknowledge that on some occasions what is most democratic may not, on balance, be the best thing that could happen.

The doctrine that our cherished principles are good only on the whole and may sometimes need to be overridden requires a certain sophistication to appreciate, however. In the rough and tumble of political debate, how often does one hear some principle ridiculed because, if it were followed inflexibly, it would sometimes have bad consequences? Intellectuals, in a more systematic way, often start from the same assumptions. Berlin (1969), after referring to

> the natural tendency of all but a very few thinkers to believe that all the things they hold good must be intimately connected, or at least compatible, with one another

continues:

> The history of thought, like the history of nations, is strewn with examples of inconsistent, or at least disparate, elements artificially yoked

together in a despotic system, or held together by the danger of some common enemy. (p. 128n)

It is therefore hardly surprising that adherents of democracy have tried to anticipate attacks by reformulating the concept of democracy so as to draw their sting. There are two routes. One is to build into the concept of democracy the presence of various devices (an entrenched bill of rights, etc.) that in terms of our original definition are antidemocratic.[13] The other route—word-magic, pure and simple—is to make desirable ends part of the definition of democracy.

> In common parlance, we would speak of . . . a democratic aim in the pursuit of social justice or, to quote a famous document, of happiness. They are aims which, again in common parlance, are called democratic *ends*, to be achieved by democratic *means*. (Meisel, 1962, pp. 352–3)

This obviously opens up a rich vein of potential confusion since "democratic means" may not lead to "democratic ends," and "democratic ends" may be achieved by other than "democratic means." And it destroys any distinctive meaning for "democratic": If justice and happiness are part of the connotation of "democratic," there is not much difference between saying some policy is democratic and saying that it is good—saying, in other words, that it is evaluated highly on the basis of the general ground of evaluation. There is no point in having a principle of democracy because it no longer draws attention to any special features.

The first route is subject to the same objection, though in a modified form. Tailoring the principle so that it corresponds precisely to the institutions of particular societies—the so-called Western democracies—weakens the force of the evaluation. Satisfying majority preferences is a virtue, and so is safeguarding the rights of minorities, but they are distinct and potentially opposed virtues.[14] Calling a society democratic, if one means that its institutions in some way or another balance these two virtues, is admittedly more precise than saying it scores high on the basis of the general ground of evaluation; but it still conceals a crucial part of the process of evaluation, which concerns the weighting that *should* be given to the two features of majority will and individual or minority rights.

The result of fudging together these two potentially incompatible features in one principle is to inhibit serious discussion of the relative importance of majority rule and limits on its scope, since it is almost impossible to find the concepts in which to pose the issue. This result may not inspire universally shared regret. We noted at the beginning of this section the possibility that opponents of some principle may seek to debilitate it by extending its range so that it loses its original bite. The incorporation of an antagonistic principle within the original concept might be regarded as a more subtle form of subversion. At least in the United States there seems today to be a quite common tendency to associate the principle of democracy primarily with restraints on the majority—a curious reversal, presumably gratifying to those who benefit most from the status quo and therefore stand to lose most if the "sleeping giant" were ever to stir.

---

Before closing this section, let us look briefly at relations among the five concepts that have been examined and their use in argument. The relations, as we have noted in particular cases already, are both complementary and competitive. Thus, to pick up examples already mentioned *en passant*, democracy is related to public interest via the notion that the interest of the majority is a reasonable, practical approximation; and it is also directly related to the notion of political equality, even though universal suffrage may seem to the sophisticated a rather attenuated form of equal power. Competitive relations, as we saw, exist between the public interest and freedom in particular, but also between the public interest and justice or equality. Justice and equality themselves may be either complementary or competitive, while both (as we saw) may conflict with freedom. Finally, democracy in any given instance may produce outcomes conflicting with any or all of the rest.

Given this complexity, it would be understandable to wonder whether these concepts really simplify political discourse. Would it not be simpler, someone might ask, to cut out the middle-men and argue directly from the amount and distribution of well-being? We do not think this would help. These concepts have developed to express important, though diverse, considerations that have to be weighted before one says that a state of affairs embodies a desirable amount and distribution of well-being. If these criteria did not exist, they or something quite like them would have to be invented.

## SECTION VII: CONCLUSION

"It seems obvious that, in order to judge how well a system performs, one needs three elements: criteria of value, worth, goodness, excellence, desirability; data about the behavior of the system; and ways of applying the criteria to the behavior of the system in order to measure the degree of value, worth, goodness, excellence, desirability" (Dahl, 1967, pp. 169–70). Dahl's remark can be extended as follows. If we wish to ask whether a given political institution of form A in a certain society would be improved by being modified to form B, we have to perform three tasks. First, we need to set up some criteria of evaluation which will enable us to say that one set of consequences is preferable to some other set of consequences. Second, we need to develop a theory which will tell us the likely consequences of having form A of the institution rather than form B in a society with such-and-such relevant characteristics. And third, we have to bring these two together by asking whether the consequences of A are likely to be better or worse than the consequences of B on the basis of our criteria of evaluation.

This chapter has been addressed to the first of these tasks only. The second task is, of course, the subject of political science whenever it extends beyond description, and a number of the other entries in this *Handbook* may be regarded as reports on the "state of the art" with respect to various institutions, while the chapter by Michael Taylor in Volume 3 contains a generally relevant discussion at a high level of abstraction. We wish here only to repeat a point we made at the beginning of this chapter. A political scientist, having focused his attention on some political phenomenon, may analyze its consequences in any terms he chooses. But he can have little hope that anyone else will take an interest in his conclusions unless he focuses his attention on consequences that have some direct bearing on the amount and distribution of human well-being—in other words, consequences that have some evaluative import. Thus the second task cannot be carried out effectively unless there is at least tacit awareness of the first.

It should be made clear, if it has not become clear already, that no analysis of evaluation can hope to be uncontroversial. Perhaps the most disputable feature of this account is its ultimately "consequentialist" commitment. That is to say, although we acknowledge the possibility of judging political acts by "characterizing" them rather than by referring to their consequences, we suggest that attaching evaluative implications to such "characterizations" can be defended in terms of the usual effects on the amount and distribution of well-being of acts so characterized. Our analysis therefore does not fit the moral belief systems of those who claim that the rightness or wrongness of kinds of acts may be derived from a knowledge of the will of a supernatural being or may be discovered by "intuition." However, we should like to repeat here the observation that, when people with differing religious convictions or differing moral intuitions confront one another, they are not likely to find a common basis for argument unless they are prepared to go behind their beliefs about the rightness and wrongness of kinds of acts to some more general premises, which, we suggest, can scarcely be other than the amount and distribution of human well-being.

The discussion in this chapter leads up to our setting out and describing briefly a number of principles that are widely used in the evaluation of states of affairs and thus (given a "consequentialist" approach) in the evaluation of alternative institutions or policies. We have suggested that these principles operate as mediators between the most general basis of evaluation—the amount and distribution of human well-being—and decisions or recommendations to be made in particular cases. By concentrating attention on aspects of well-being and its distribution that have been found important in making evaluations, these principles help to solve the difficulties which, we pointed out earlier in the article, are inherent in any attempt to apply very abstract criteria of evaluation directly to complex phenomena.

Our conception of the place of political principles in political argument has implications which run counter to two opposite and, we believe, equally incorrect ideas. It is sometimes suggested (on the basis of a variety of philosophical positions, ranging from "moral sentiment" through "contractualism" to "natural law") that, but for the contaminating effect of the special interests which arise from different positions in society, etc., all human beings (or all "rational" human beings) would be able to reach agreement on political principles. At the other extreme is the idea that political principles are merely a matter of taste—and *de gustibus non est disputandum*. Sometimes it is tacitly assumed that these two positions exhaust the range of possibilities. Thus Weldon (1956) says of political principles that "if they are made precise, it can no longer be claimed with much plausibility that they are, or even might be, generally acceptable to all human beings" (p. 30) and moves straight from this to the assertion that "Everyone can decide what are his own political principles" (p. 33) and the conclusion that political principles are stop signs, like "Keep off the grass" notices, which do not have to be set up anywhere in particular (p. 34).

Our position avoids these extremes, though our claim for it rests not on its being a compromise but on its being correct. In our analysis, complete agreement on political principles and the appropriate trade-off among them would require that everyone share (1) the same view of the precise constituents of human well-being and the relative importance of these constituents, (2) the same criteria (with the same weightings) for adjudicating between the well-being of different people, and (3) the same causal generalizations connecting well-being to the features of situations picked out by the principles. We do not see any likelihood that these conditions will ever be met, and we therefore anticipate that political principles and the priorities to be observed among them will always be matters of controversy. But at the same time we suggest that any theory must stand condemned which cannot make sense of the phenomenon of *argument* about political principles. If principles were simply "Keep off the grass" notices which each person was free to place where he chose, all that anyone could do would be to note that somebody else had placed his notices in a different place from his own. In our view, however, a principle embodies an implicit connection with the ultimate basis of evaluation, and it is this which provides the possibility of argument.

More significant, it is this implicit claim which sets limits to what can (logically) be advanced as a principle, since it must be possible to see how the fulfillment of the principle might conceivably be taken to contribute to a desirable amount and distribution of human well-being. If someone puts a "Keep off the grass" notice on or near some grass, we can argue about the propriety of his doing so. Now there is, of course, nothing that physically prevents someone from erecting such a notice in the middle of an asphalt parking lot, just as there is no physical impossibility in enunciating any prescription as a political principle, even one which is completely arbitrary. But a "Keep off the grass" notice in the middle of a parking lot will not fulfill the function of a notice, nor will a principle with no connection to any conception of human well-being. The one will not keep anyone off any grass; the other will not convince anyone that the principle should be observed. Both are out of place.

## NOTES

1. Two policies are mutually exclusive when they are incompatible in some respect, not necessarily in every respect. Thus a parliamentary bill to which ten separate amendments are moved gives rise to $2^{10}$ alternative policies plus the alternative of defeating the bill in any form, in other words, retaining the status quo. It may be objected that our definition makes the number of alternative policies in a given matter potentially infinite. We regard this not as an objection to our definition but as a real problem. In practice, of course, the number of alternatives considered has to be reduced to manageable proportions, but this is often a pretty rough and ready affair, and we think our definition of an alternative is useful in emphasizing that most alternatives are never considered.

2. Our definition of an alternative entailed that there was a potentially infinite number of alternatives conceivable at any time; now our definition of a decision entails that the choice among them is taken at every instant. Having committed ourselves to one infinity, we see no great reason to draw back from multiplying it by another. The practical position in relation to both is exactly the same: Attention must be restricted in some more or less arbitrary way to some alternatives on any question and some questions at any time. But it is useful for our conceptual scheme to emphasize that there is an enormous, if implicit, process of selection going on.

3. It is not possible within the scope of this chapter to discuss the alternative ideas that have been proposed about the ultimate basis of evaluation. A good collection of the traditional theories is Sellars and Hospers (1952). For recent developments see Warnock (1967).

4. This is the meaning of a commitment to lexicographic hierarchy as a principle of decision. However, if we knew in a given case what the alternative policies were, we might be able to sum up our preferences by using lexicography, even if we in fact gave some independent weight to each of several criteria. The possibility of doing so depends, roughly speaking, on there being a finite minimum distance between any two alternatives in terms of the higher-order criterion and a finite maximum distance between the best and worst alternatives in terms of the lower-order criterion.

5. Indifference curves cannot intersect because we mean by a criterion of evaluation that, other things being equal, more fulfillment of it is better than less.

6. This criterion has a certain similarity to one discussed by Sen (1970, pp. 150–1 and 154–6). But the notion there presented of each person deciding whether he would prefer to be himself with his own tastes or other people with their tastes seems to us

to amount to a complicated way of talking about estimates of comparative utility.

7.  When the number of people in the two situations is different, the best-off people in the situation with more people should be eliminated from consideration until numbers are equal in the two situations, and the comparison of pairs then carried out. As already noted, this move maintains the link with minimax in both forms, though for utilitarianism (in both total and average utility forms) the link is severed. The most we can say is that if $x$ is the situation with more people, then $x$ R $y$ and $x$ P $y$ on dominance entail $x$ R $y$ and $x$ P $y$ on utilitarianism; but $y$ R $x$ and $y$ P $x$ on dominance do not entail anything about utilitarianism. We shall not further consider dominance with unequal numbers of people.

8.  It is perhaps worth repeating here that, while dominance entails utilitarianism and minimax, it is in turn entailed by Pareto optimality. Hence Pareto optimality also entails utilitarianism and minimax.

9.  These strategies are, in the logic of our conditions for evaluation, made available by the difficulties arising from risk and uncertainty. That is, one can seldom be sure about connections between policies and resultant conditions ($A_i$ to $C_i$), and it is therefore possible to call attention to the more desirable conditions which occur simultaneously with the application of a policy (for any two conditions $C_i$ and $C_j$, one can associate the policy with the more highly valued of the two).

10.  See Hodgson, 1967; and for an unintentionally hilarious account of the difficulties facing a conscientious utilitarian, see Book 4, Chapter 5, of Sidgwick (1907).

11.  Article 24: "Everyone has the right to rest and leisure, including reasonable limitation of working hours and periodic holidays with pay."

12.  Translation is that in Paine (1906), pp. 95–6.

13.  A nice example, drawn from the discussion of "democracy" in an American textbook on contemporary ideologies (Christenson et al., 1972) is the following: "There are limits to what the majority can do. It cannot oppress the minority: expropriate their property, diminish their citizenship, infringe their rights, or deny them the freedom to oppose and seek to become the majority" (p. 186). Although the last point merely specifies the continuation of majority control, the first rules the achievement of a socialist economy as incompatible with democracy. The second and third are too vague to comment on usefully (they are not spelled out), but presumably they are also intended to cover limits on the majority other than those on actions inconsistent with the maintenance of majority rule.

14.  "Everything is what it is: liberty is liberty, not equality or fairness or justice or culture, or human happiness or a quiet conscience" (Berlin, 1969, p. 125).

# REFERENCES

Althusser, Louis (1969). *For Marx.* London: Penguin.

Anonymous (1647). *A New-found Strategem Framed in the Old Forge of Machivilisme.*

Arrow, Kenneth (1951). *Social Choice and Individual Values.* New York: Wiley.

Barry, Brian (1965). *Political Argument.* London: Routledge.

——— (1970). *Sociologists, Economists and Democracy.* London: Collier-Macmillan.

Beer, Samuel H. (1965). *Modern British Politics.* London: Faber.

Bell, Daniel (1960). *The End of Ideology.* Glencoe, Ill.: Free Press.

Bennett, Jonathan (1968). "Whatever the consequences." In Judith J. Thomson and Gerald Dworkin (eds.), *Ethics.* New York: Harper and Row. Pp. 211–36.

Bentham, Jeremy (1948). *An Introduction to the Principles of Morals and Legislation.* New York: Hafner.

Berlin, Isaiah (1969). "Two concepts of liberty." *Four Essays on Liberty.* London: Oxford University Press. Pp. 118–72.

Black, Duncan (1958). *The Theory of Committees and Elections.* Cambridge: Cambridge University Press.

Blau, Peter M., and Otis D. Duncan (1967). *The American Occupational Structure.* New York: Wiley.

Buchanan, James M., and Gordon Tullock (1962). *The Calculus of Consent.* Ann Arbor: University of Michigan Press.

Burke, Edmund (1910). *Reflections on the Revolution in France.* London: Dent.

Calhoun, John C. (1953). *A Disquisition on Government.* Indianapolis: Bobbs-Merrill.

Christensen, Reo M., A. S. Engel, D. N. Jacobs, M. Rejai, and H. Waltzer (1972). *Ideologies and Modern Politics.* London: Nelson.

Cohn, Norman (1970). *The Pursuit of the Millenium.* London: Paladin.

Condorcet, M. J. A. N. C. (1785). *Essai sur l'Application de l'Analyse à la Probabilité des Décisions Rendues à la Pluralité des Voix.* Paris.

Cranston, Maurice (1953). *Freedom: A New Analysis.* London: Longmans.

Dahl, Robert A. (1956). *Preface to Democratic Theory.* Chicago: University of Chicago Press.

———— (1967). "The evaluation of political systems." In Ithiel de Sola Pool (ed.), *Contemporary Political Science.* New York: McGraw-Hill.

———— (1970). *After the Revolution.* New Haven: Yale University Press.

Dahl, Robert A., and Charles E. Lindblom (1953). *Politics, Economics and Welfare.* New York: Harper.

D'Arcy, Eric (1963). *Human Acts: An Essay in Their Moral Evaluation.* Oxford: Clarendon Press.

Downs, Anthony (1956). *An Economic Theory of Democracy.* New York: Harper.

Edwards, Ward, and Amos Tversky, eds. (1967). *Decision Making: Selected Readings.* Harmondsworth: Penguin.

Gunn, J. A. (1969). *Politics and the Public Interest in the Seventeenth Century.* London: Routledge.

Harrington, James (1924). *Oceana.* Heidelberg: Skrifter Vetenskaps-Societeten I.

Harris, Nigel (1971). *Beliefs in Society.* Harmondsworth: Penguin.

Hart, Herbert L. A. (1961). *The Concept of Law.* Oxford: Clarendon Press.

Hodgson, David H. (1967). *Consequences of Utilitariansim.* Oxford: Clarendon Press.

Huizinga, Johan (1970). *Homo Ludens: A Study of the Play Element in Culture.* London: Paladin.

Huntington, Samuel P. (1968). *Political Order in Changing Societies.* New Haven: Yale University Press.

Landes, David S. (1969). *The Unbound Prometheus.* Cambridge: Cambridge University Press.

Laslett, Peter (1965). *The World We Have Lost.* New York: Scribner.

Levi, Edward H. (1949). *An Introduction to Legal Reasoning.* Chicago: University of Chicago Press.

Lindblom, Charles (1968). *The Policy-making Process,* Englewood Cliffs, N.J.: Prentice-Hall.

Lipset, Seymour M. (1963). *The First New Nation.* New York: Basic Books.

Luce, Robert D., and Howard Raiffa (1957). *Fights, Games and Decisions.* New York: Wiley.

Macpherson, Crawford B. (1958). *The Real World of Democracy.* Toronto: University of Toronto Press.

March, James G., and Herbert A. Simon (1958). *Organizations.* New York: Wiley.

Marx, Karl (1959). *Economic and Philosophic Manuscripts of 1844.* Moscow: Progress Publishers.

May, K. O. (1952). "A set of independent necessary and sufficient conditions for simple majority decisions." *Econometrica* 20: 680–4.

Meisel, James H. (1962). *The Myth of the Ruling Class: Gaetano Mosca and the Elite.* Ann Arbor: University of Michigan Press.

Moore, Barrington, Jr. (1972). *Reflections on the Causes of Human Misery.* London: Allen Lane, Penguin.

Myrdal, Gunnar (1958). *Value in Social Theory.* London: Routledge.

Nathan, N. M. L. (1971). *The Concept of Justice.* London: Macmillan.

Nolte, Ernst (1965). *Three Faces of Fascism.* London: Weidenfeld.

Paine, Thomas (1906). *The Rights of Man.* London: Dent.

Perelman, Chaim (1963). *The Idea of Justice and the Problem of Argument.* London: Routledge.

Rae, Douglas W. (1971). "Political democracy as a property of political institutions." *American Political Science Review* 65:111–9.

Raphael, David D., ed. (1967). *Political Theory and the Rights of Man.* London: Macmillan.

Rawls, John (1958). "Justice as fairness." *Philosophical Review* 67:164–94.

——— (1971). *A Theory of Justice.* Cambridge, Mass.: Belknap Press.

Rescher, Nicholas (1966). *Distributive Justice.* Indianapolis: Bobbs-Merrill.

Rousseau, Jean-Jacques (1947). *The Social Contract.* In Ernest Barker (ed.), *Social Contract: Essays by Locke, Hume and Rousseau.* London: Oxford University Press.

Sellars, Wilfrid, and John Hospers, eds. (1952). *Readings in Ethical Theory.* New York: Appleton-Century-Crofts.

Sen, Amartya K. (1970). *Collective Choice and Social Welfare.* San Francisco: Holden-Day.

Shils, Edward (1956). *The Torment of Secrecy.* Glencoe, Ill.: Free Press.

Sidgwick, Henry (1907). *The Methods of Ethics.* London: Macmillan.

Simon, Herbert A. (1955). "A behavioral model of rational choice." *Quarterly Journal of Economics* 68:99–118.

Smith, Adam (1961). *The Wealth of Nations.* London: Methuen.

Stevenson, Charles L. (1944). *Ethics and Language.* New Haven: Yale University Press.

Talmon, J. L. (1960). *The Origins of Totalitarian Democracy.* New York: Praeger.

Taylor, Michael (1970). "The problem of salience in the theory of collective decision-making." *Behavioral Science* 15.

Vlastos, Greogry (1962). "Justice and equality." In Richard B. Brandt (ed.), *Social Justice.* Englewood Cliffs, N. J.: Prentice-Hall.

Warnock, Geoffrey (1967). *Contemporary Moral Philosophy.* London: Macmillan.

Weber, Max (1949). *The Methodology of the Social Sciences.* Glencoe, Ill.: Free Press.

Weldon, Thomas D. (1956). "Political principles." In Peter Laslett and Walter G. Runciman (eds.), *Philosophy, Politics and Society.* Oxford: Basil Blackwell.

Williams, Bernard (1962). "The idea of equality." In Peter Laslett and Walter G. Runciman (eds.), *Philosophy, Politics and Society,* 2nd series. Oxford: Basil Blackwell.

Wilson, James Q. (1960). *Negro Politics.* Glencoe, Ill.: Free Press.

Wolff, Robert P. (1970). *In Defense of Anarchism.* New York: Harper.

Yntema, D. B., and W. S. Torgerson (1967). "Man-computer cooperation in decisions requiring common sense." In Ward Edwards and Amos Tversky (eds.), *Decision Making: Selected Readings.* Harmondsworth: Penguin. Pp. 300–14. Originally published in *IRE Transactions on Human Factors in Electronics,* HFE-2 (1961), 20–6.

# *INDEX*

# *INDEX*

Abel, Theodore, 217
Absolutism, strategic, 351
Achinstein, Peter, 216, 218
Act-descriptions, 371
Action vs. movement, 161, 164
Almond, Gabriel, 134, 141, 170, 194 309, 310
*Agathon*, 239
Alienation, 380
Alston, William P., 295, 314
American Political Science Association, 34, 35, 42, 54
"Amoral familism," 173
Anarchy, 388
Anderson, William, 4
Anscombe, G.E.M., 166
Anthropomorphism, 179, 182
Apel, Karl-Otto, 217
Appraisals, 315-316, 317
Arendt, Hannah, 212, 272
Aristotle, 9, 162, 206, 230, 233-234, 237, 240, 244, 245, 248, 249, 252, 253, 259, 260, 263, 323, 326
Arros, Kenneth, 341
Ashby, R.W., 292
Austin, John, 307, 309
Authority, 192, 287, 303, 304
Averini, Shlomo, 15, 229
Axiom of choice, 197
Axiom of transitivity, 197

Bachrach, Peter, 307
Baier, Kurt, 318
Bakunin, Mikhail, 12
Banfield, Edward C., 171, 172-173, 174, 181, 219
Banks, Arthur, 312
Barnes, Harry E., 46
Barry, Brian, 131, 214, 215, 220, 221, 284, 391
Bay, Christian, 325
Bedau, Hugo A., 287
Beer, Samual H., 176-177, 181, 219, 390
Behavioralism, 58-62
Behavioralists, 258
Behaviorism, 292-293, 294, 295, 297, 299
Benda, Julien, 255
Benn, S.I., 284, 289, 308
Bennett, Jonathan, 351
Bentham, Jeremy, 12, 14, 220, 326, 360
Berelson, Bernard, 293
Berger, Peter L., 216
Bergson, Henri, 233, 261
Berlin, Isaiah, 292, 389, 392, 398
Bernstein, Richard J., 220
Bigongiari, Dino, 264
*Bios theōretikos*, 240, 245, 259
Black, Duncan, 341
Blalock, Hubert M., Jr., 216
Blau, Peter M., 386
Bodin, 12, 13

Brandt, Richard, 217, 321
Braybrooke, David, 306, 308
Breines, Paul, 274, 275
Brodbeck, May, 216, 217, 286, 299, 330
Brody, Richard A., 186
Brown, Norman O., 250, 274
Brown, Robert, 313
Buchanan, James M., 205, 220
Burke, Edmund, 247, 371

Calhoun, John C., 391
Calvin, John, 230, 234
Campbell, Norman, 216
Capitalism, 247
Care, Norman S., 293
Carey, George W., 114, 276
Cassinelli, C.W., 289, 330
Casvistry, 378
Catlin, George E.G., 8, 46, 49
Causal structure, 135, 136
Causation, 300-301, 305
Childe, V. Gordon, 5
Chomsky, Noam, 274
Christensen, Reo M., 398
Christianity, 232, 240, 241, 245
  medieval, 242
Civilizations, 232, 235, 242, 246, 247, 250
Classification, 309-310
Clement of Alexandria, 241
Cnudde, Charles F., 313
Coercion, 299
Cohen, Robert S., 219
Collectivities, 298-299
Collingwood, R.G., 180
Columbia University School of Political Science, 27
Communism, 244
Concepts
  categorical, 309-311
  comparative, 311-314
  extreme-type, 311
  quantitative, 313-314
Conceptual frameworks, 140
Concurrent majorities, 391
Condorcet, M.J.A.N.C., 247, 341

Conflict, 191
Connolly, William, 286, 318
Consensus, 170, 193
Consequentialism, 395
Conservatism, 247
Conservative party, 177
Constitution, 20, 21
Constitutive meanings, 168-171, 173, 176, 178, 181, 206, 208, 209
Constitutive norms, 167, 207
Control, 300, 301, 305
Conventions, 133, 167-168, 178, 208
*Cosmopolis*, 245
Cox, Richard, 275
Crane, William W., 38
Cranston, Maurice, 387
Crick, Bernard, 38, 252
Criteria, aggregation of, 342-344
  conflicts among, 349-357
  interpretability of, 342
Croce, Benedetto, 258, 260
"Cumulative knowledge," 3

Dahl, Robert A., 156-160, 285, 287, 290, 291, 301, 304, 306, 311, 312, 313, 363, 390, 394
Dahrendorf, Ralf, 191, 192, 193
Dallmayr, Fred R., 276
Dante, 10, 262
D'Arcy, Eric, 371
Davidson, Donald, 217, 297
Decision-making, 203
Declaration of Independence, 21
Definitions, 290-291
  explicative, 290-291, 308
  persuasive, 323-327
  reportative, 291, 308
  stipulative, 290
de Grazia, Sebastian, 274
de Jouvenel, Bertrand, 212, 273
Democracy, 306-307, 313, 386, 390-394
  as maximin consent, 390
Dentler, Robert A., 132
d' Entrèves, Alexander Passerin, 264, 277, 321
de Tocqueville, Alexis, 14

Deutsch, Karl W., 140, 141, 277, 297, 305
Dexter, Lewis, 231
Diminishing marginal utility, 387
Dispositional concepts, 301
Dispositional practices, 294
Dominance, 365-368
Donnellan, Keith S., 296
Douglas, Mary, 216
Downs, Anthony, 141, 195-197, 198-199, 200, 201
Duncan, Otis D., 386
Duties, 371
Duverger, Maurice, 138

Easton, David, 1, 70, 114, 118, 141, 276, 285, 293, 298, 304, 318
Eaton, Dorman B., 33
Eckstein, Harry, 190, 191
École Libre des Sciences Politiques, 33
Ecumenicism, attempted, 3
Edwards, Ward, 371
Efficiency, 343, 362
Egalitarianism, 286, 309, 311, 313
Elliott, William Y., 49, 50
Ellul, Jacques, 274
Emmet, Dorothy, 217
Empiricism, 291-292, 294, 297
Enlightenment, 252
Equality, 287-288, 310, 343, 361-362, 378, 386-387
  before the law, 386
  political, 387
  racial, 387
  sexual, 386
  social, 387
Essentialism, 290
Etzioni, Amitai, 274
Eulau, Heinz, 231, 285, 293, 298, 302
"Exchange theory," 195
Explanation of action, interpretative, 161-167, 174, 204, 206
  limitation of, 182-186
Explanation of action, naturalist, 156-161
Explanation, quasi-causal, 186-191, 192, 204, 208

Explanation, scientific, 135-140
  "covering-law model," 136-137, 157
  "explanation-sketch," 157
  "nomological explanation," 136-137, 18

Falco, Mario J., 134
Fallacy of reification, 286, 322
Fay, Brian C., 131, 212, 219
*Federalist* papers, 21
Feierabend, Ivo, 190
Feierabend, R., 190
Feigl, Herbert, 142, 218, 219
Ferejohn, John, 202-203
Ferkiss, Victor, 274
Fetscher, Irving, 235
Feyerabend, Paul K., 147, 148, 218, 219, 220
Filmer, Sir Robert, 264
Fiorina, Morris, 202-203
Flathman, Richard E., 274, 284, 293
Foot, Philippa, 301, 318
Forced choice, 344-345
Formalism, 290
Fourth Republic, 136
Frankena, William K., 319, 326, 330
Franklin, Julian H., 14
Freedom, 287, 288-289, 304, 305, 378, 387-390
  of choice, 288
  feeling free, 288-289
  free actions, 289
  social or political, 288
  of speech, 288
  from want, 288
Friedrich, Carl J., 264, 272, 277, 288
Functionalism, 192

Garfinkel, H., 216
Geertz, Clifford, 180
Gellner, Ernest, 179, 297
General possibility theorem, 341
Germino, Dante, 131, 209, 251, 272, 275, 276
Gibson, Quinton, 216, 323
Gilbert, Allan, 264

Ginsberg, Morris, 327
Goldberg, Arthur, 131, 146, 298
Goldenweiser, Alexander, 46
Goldman, Alvin L., 217, 297
Goodman, Paul, 274
Goodnow, Frank J., 39, 91
Gosnell, Harold F., 47
Government, 246
Graham, George J., 114, 276
Gramsci, Antonio, 235, 243, 256, 260
Great Dialogue, 8–11
Greenstein, Fred, 131
Gregor, A. James, 134, 284, 289, 309, 310
Gross, Bertram M., 285
Grotius, Hugo, 230
Grumm, John G., 138
Gunn, J.A., 383
Gurr, Ted Robert, 190, 220

Haas, Michael, 312
Habermas, Jürgen, 134, 217, 219
Hacker, Andrew, 307
Haddow, Anna, 24
Hanson, Norwood Russell, 147, 216
Hare, R.M., 318, 319, 322, 330
Harre, Ron, 216
Harrington, James, 383
Harris, Nigel, 378
Hart, H.L.A., 160, 212, 284, 302, 303, 320, 378
Hartz, Louis, 252
Hayek, F.A., 326
Hegel, Georg, 230, 231, 234, 235, 239, 243, 248, 252, 254, 255, 260, 262, 264
Hempel, Carl G., 132, 138, 142, 145, 155, 158, 159–160, 173, 216, 218, 285, 290, 291, 294, 301, 310, 313
Hermeneutical or interpretative circle, 172–173, 208
Herring, E. Pendleton, 47
Hesse, Mary B., 216
History, 248–250, 255
    philosophy of, 248
Hobbes, Thomas, 12, 13, 134, 135, 209, 231, 236, 239, 241, 246, 248, 249, 252, 260, 264, 288
Hodgson, David H., 398
Holcombe, Arthur N., 47
Holsti, Ole R., 186
Holt, Robert T., 220
Homans, George Caspar, 195, 216
Honoré, A.M., 160
Hook, Sidney, 307
Hooker, Richard, 241, 255
Hospers, John, 397
Huizinga, Johan, 384
Humanism, 242, 250, 261
    anthropocentric, 238, 241, 243, 246, 249, 261
    metastatic, 238, 243, 247, 250, 261
    theocentric, 238, 241, 243, 245, 246, 249–250, 261
Hume, David, 134, 288
Huntington, Samuel P., 347
Hyneman, Charles S., 307

Ideal-types, 176
Incrementalism, 346
Indifference curves, 354
Individual relevance, 347–348
Individualism, 252
Influence, 170, 299, 300, 301
Institutional fact, 318
Instrumental rationality, 210
Intentional action, 133, 155, 161, 164, 178
Intentions and inner states, 165
Interest, 382
Internal consistency, 341
International relations, theories of, 235–236
Interpretations, testing of, 171–177
Introspection, 165
Intuitionism, 319
Ions, Edmund S., 31

Jay, Martin, 217
Johns Hopkins University, 27
Johnson, Chalmers, 193, 314
Judaism, 232, 240
Justice, 322–323, 364, 384–386

Kalleberg, Arthur L., 310
Kant, Immanuel, 230
Kaplan, Abraham, 172, 284, 285, 292, 299, 309
Kariel, Henry, S., 114
Kaufman, Arnold S., 292
Kaufman, Herbert, 80
Kelley, Harold H., 195
Kim, Jaegwon, 217
Knowledge, 253, 254
   practical, 253
   productive, 253
   theoretical, 253
Korner, Stephan, 216
Kropotkin, Prince, 12
Kuhn, Thomas S., 141, 195, 218, 219

Labour Party, 177
Lakatos, Imre, 141, 148, 150, 151, 152, 153, 154, 194, 207
Landau, Martin, 39
Landes, David S., 345
Landesman, Charles, 293
Languages of politics, 16-18
Lasch, Christopher, 274
Lasswell, Harold D., 46, 66, 252, 284, 285
Laws, 132, 133, 134
   "accidental" generalizations, 138
   counterfactual conditionals, 138, 139, 189
   vs. general statements, 137
   generalizations, 133, 136-138
   "necessity" of, 138, 139
   subjunctive conditional, 138, 139, 189
   unrestricted universal statement, 138
Legal institutions, 301-303
   legal concepts, 303
   legal system, 303, 322
Legitimacy, 287, 321-322
Lenski, Gerhard, 285
Levi, Carlo, 174
Levi, Edward H., 378
Lexicographic hierarchy, 351-352
Liberalism, 246, 261
Liberty, 379

Lichtheim, George, 15
Lieber, Francis, 25-26
Lindblom, Charles E., 347, 363
Lipset, Seymour M., 337
Locke, Don, 166
Locke, John, 12, 230, 231, 241, 246, 248, 249, 252, 260, 264, 316
Logical empiricism, 141
Lonergan, Bernard J., 260
Louch, A.R., 295, 296
Luce, Robert D., 346
Luckman, Thomas, 216
Luther, Martin, 234

Machiavelli, 12, 13, 230, 231, 236, 241, 246, 248, 249, 252, 254, 260, 261 264, 316
MacIntyre, Alasdair, 175, 217
Mackenzie, William J.M., 4, 38
Macpherson, Crawford B., 381
Madden, E.H., 216
Majority rule, 363-364, 383
Man, 238, 239-243, 245, 246, 248, 249, 253, 255, 257
   mature man, 240, 245
   political man, 242
Mandelbaum, Maurice, 299, 302
March, James G., 285, 344
Marcuse, Herbert, 250, 259, 274, 327
Marginal rates of substitution, 353
Marini, Frank, 114
Maritain, Jacques, 249
Martin, Jane R., 217
Marx, Karl, 12, 14-15, 230, 234, 235, 236, 239, 243, 247, 248, 250, 252, 254, 260, 261, 265, 275, 276, 381
Marxism, 380
Masterman, Margaret, 141, 216
Maxwell, Grover, 216
May, K.O., 341
Mayer, Jacob P., 14
McCoy, Charles A., 114
McNeill, William H., 5
Meaning, openness of, 309
Meaning of action, 178, 180, 191, 207
Meehan, Eugene J., 276-277

Meehl, Paul E., 220
Meisel, James H., 393
Mental states, 299–300
Merriam, Charles E., 47, 48–49, 252
Merry, Henry J., 14
*metastasis*, 243, 250
Methodological holism, 299
Methodological individualism, 299
Methodology
    hermeneutical model, 133
    interpretative model of inquiry, 132, 133, 135, 155, 175, 177, 206, 207
    model of political and social inquiry, 132
    "naturalist" model, 132, 133, 155, 175, 206, 207
    and political philosophy, 211–212
    "positivist" model, 132
    scientific model of inquiry, 134, 135
Mill, John Stuart, 12, 14, 135
Miller, Warren E., 231
Minimax, 364–365
Mitchell, Edward J., 187
Models of man, 192–195, 204, 208, 209, 210
Montegranesi society, 173
Montesquieu, 13, 14, 230, 325
Moore, Barrington, Jr., 274, 345
Moral principles, 315, 316
More, Sir Thomas, 244
Morgenthau, Hans J., 252
Moses, Bernard, 38
Myrdal, Gunnar, 338
Myth, 234, 248

Nagel, Ernest, 138, 139, 140, 216, 284, 315
Natanson, Maurice, 216
Nathan, N.M.L., 384
Naturalism, 319
Neubauer, Deane E., 313
Neurath, Otto, 174
New Deal, 50–51
Noetic thought, 256
Nolte, Ernst, 380
Normative political inquiry, 314–328
North, Robert C., 186

Northrop, F.S.C., 262
Nozick, Robert, 212

Oakeshott, Michael, 236, 273
Obligations, 371
Observation terms, 298
Odegard, Peter H., 47
Ogburn, William F., 46
Olson, Mancur, Jr., 195, 200
Open society, 233, 256, 258
Operationalism, 293–294, 297–298, 299, 311–313
Operative ideals, 176
Oppenheim, Felix E., 212, 217, 218, 273, 284, 287, 290, 300, 311, 314, 317, 319
Ordeshook, Peter C., 202

Paci, Enzo, 250
Paine, Thomas, 398
Pap, Arthur, 290
Paradigmatic society, 243–248, 258
Paranzino, Dennis, 187
Pareto optimality, 362–363, 365
Parkinson, G.H.R., 289
Partial goods, 371, 375
Pegis, Anton C., 264
Perelman, Chaim, 384
*periagogē*, 239
Peters, R.S., 167, 284
Philosophers, 236, 238, 239, 241, 242, 244, 248, 254, 255, 257
Philosophy, 235, 236, 248, 249, 250–256, 258, 261
    classical, 240
    Greek, 241
    history of, 235, 260
    meaning of, 235
    practical, 234–235
    study of, 256, 257
    uses of, 235
Pi Sigma Alpha, 55
Pitkin, Hannah F., 212, 322
Plato, 9, 210, 231, 233–234, 235, 237, 239–240, 243, 244, 245, 248, 249, 252, 255, 258, 260, 261, 262, 263, 322

Playford, John, 114
Polanyi, Michael, 169
*Polis*, 241, 244, 245, 252, 261
Political evaluation, 209, 213-214
Political institutions, 4-7
   ancient empires, 5
   Greek experience, 5
   medieval influence, 6-7
   modern state system, 7
   neolithic revolution, 5
   Roman experience, 6
Political phenomena, explanation of, 131
Political philosophers, 230, 231, 233
Political philosophy, 209, 233, 235, 236, 241, 248, 251, 252-253, 254, 255, 257, 258, 260, 262
   analytic, 317, 321
   classics of, 229-230, 231, 237, 248, 252, 254, 257, 259-260, 261
   Greek, 232
   history of, 233, 236-237, 252-253
   relevance of, 256-262
   uses of, 230, 233-236, 256
Political reality, 231, 232, 236, 253, 257, 261
Political science, Americanization of, 30-32, 44-45
Political science, definition of, 1-2
   by David Easton, 1
Political science, development of in the United States, 18-23
   American political experience, 20
   citizen literature, 20-21
   industrialization, 21-22
   political knowledge, codification of, 19
   specialization, 21-22
   urbanization, 21-22
   university, rise of, 22-23
Political science, as discipline, 117-118
Political science, as enterprise, 123-124
Political science, as profession, 118-122
Political science, rise of university-based, 26-29
Political science, as science, 122-123
Political science, tradition of, 4-18, 116-117
   political institutions, 4-7

   political thought, 7-16
   politics, languages of, 16-18
Political science, before World War I, 23-41
   academic political science before 1880, 24-25
   historical-comparative method, decline of, 29-30
   Lieber, Francis, 25-26
   reformism, 32-34
   rise of university-based political science, 26-29
Political science, from World War I to World War II, 41-50
   Americanization and "re-Europeanization," 44-45
   interwar matrix, 41-42
   quantitative and organizational factors, 42-44
   scientism, 47-50
Political science, since World War II, 50-73
   behavioral movement, 58-62
   comparative method, expansion of, 68-69
   historical factors, 50-54
   professional-disciplinary developments, 54-58
   public-oriented activities and responsibilities, 62-67
   scientific philosophy and methodology, rise of, 71-73
   theory, revitalization of, 70-71
   voting and opinion studies, expansion of, 69-70
*Political Science Quarterly*, 27
Political scientists, 37-38, 231, 232, 254, 255, 258
Political society, 233
Political thought, 7-16
   Athenian thinkers, 8-9
   categorization, problems of, 15-16
   Christian church, rise of, 11
   experiment with democracy, Athenian, 9
   feudalism, influence of, 11
   Great Dialogue, 8-11

during medieval period, 10-11
modern period, 11-15
"natural law," 10
Roman contribution to, 10
"state of nature," 10
Stoics, 9-10
Politics, 245, 252-254, 257
American, 230
electoral, 230
history of, 230
international, 230
Pollock, Frederick, 4
Polsby, Nelson, 131, 132
Polyarchy, 306
Popper, Karl R., 218
Powell, G. Bingham, Jr., 141, 194
Power, 285, 287, 288, 289, 304, 305, 308
Practical inference, 163, 164, 166, 184-185, 189, 191, 192, 208
Practical syllogism, 162
Practices, interpretation of, 168-171, 172
Preference ordering, 197
constraints on, 198
Prescriptions, 314-315
Progress, 252
Property, private, 385
Property concepts, 286-287
Przeworski, Adam, 175
Public administration, 230
Public interest, 347, 382-384, 389, 394
Punishment, 299

Quine, Willard van Orman, 147

Radicalism, 235
Radnitzky, Gerard, 171, 217
Rae, Douglas W., 138, 205, 214, 215, 221, 391
Raiffa, Howard, 346
Raphael, David D., 375
Rapoport, Anatol, 200, 305
Rational choice paradigm, 195-204, 206
Rational choice research program
negative heuristic, 202
positive heuristic, 198-200, 202

"Rationale" explanations, 166
Rationalism, 252
Rationality, of action, 158, 192
as dispositional concept, 158
Rationality, of science, 207
Rawls, John, 273, 276, 323, 364
Raz, Joseph, 303, 308, 321
Reagan, Michael D., 307
Reason, 249
Reasons for action, 156, 160, 163, 165, 207
Reed, Thomas H., 48-49
Rees, W.J. 212
Reformism, 32-34
Reich, Charles A., 274
Relativism, 350
Representation, 170, 176-177, 231, 232
elemental, 231
existential, 231
transcendental, 231
Relational concepts, 287
Representation, 390
proportional, 381
"Reproductive fallacy," 179
Revelation, 249
Revolution, French, 379
Rice, Stuart, 46, 47
Richardson, John M., Jr., 220
Richardson, Lewis F., 184, 186
Rieselbach, Leroy N., 277
Rights, 320-321, 379
minority, 393
Riker, William H., 195, 202, 285
Risk, 345-347
Rokkan, Stein, 183
Role expectations, 192
Role of laws and generalizations in explaining actions, 156-161, 166
Roman law, 10
Rorty, Richard, 218
Rousseau, Jean-Jacques, 215, 230, 242-243, 247, 252, 254, 260, 264, 324, 390
Rudner, Richard S., 179, 181, 218
Rule-following, 169
Russell, Bertrand, 288
Russett, Bruce M., 187

Sabin, George H., 8, 11, 47
Satisficing, 344
Scarrow, Harold A., 311, 312, 315
Schattschneider, Elmer E., 47
Scheffler, Israel, 218
Scheler, Max, 257
Schlesinger, G., 293, 294
Schlick, Moritz, 291
Schutz, Alfred, 216, 295
"Scientific" ideal, 134-154
   explanation, scientific, 135-140
   theories, choice and testing of, 145-153
   theories, scientific, 140-145
Scientific progress, 195, 200-204
Scientific research programs, 151-153, 194-195, 196, 208
   positive heuristic, 198-200
Scientism, 47-50
Scriven, Michael, 218
Searle, John R., 167-168, 180, 301, 318, 319
Self-understandings, 132
Sellars, W.F., 220, 397
Sen, Amartya K., 341, 397
Shackleton, Robert, 14
Shaffer, Jerome A., 297, 300
Shapere, Dudley, 218
Shils, Edward, 390
Sibley, Mulford Q., 293
Sidgwick, Henry, 398
Simon, Herbert A., 216, 284, 285, 305, 344
Simon, Yves, 274
Skinner, B.F., 277
Smart, J.J.C., 218
Smith, Adam, 382
Smith, Paul E., 132
Smith, T.V., 252
Social change, 175, 183, 191, 210
Social sciences, 251
   behavioral, 251
Society, 243, 244, 247, 255
   class, 248
   closed, 245, 258, 262
   communist, 248
Socrates, 9, 232, 244, 261, 263

Somit, Albert, 27, 35, 38, 39, 42, 48, 67, 72, 124
Spector, Marshall, 144, 145, 216
St. Augustine, 11, 230, 231, 241, 245, 248, 252, 260, 263
St. Thomas Aquinas, 10, 241, 260, 263
"State," 230, 248
Statements
   descriptive, 316
   metaethical, 316
   normative, 316
Stevenson, Charles L., 319, 324, 378
Stoicism, 245
Stoics, 9-10
Stokes, Donald E., 231
Strauss, Leo, 273, 275
Surkin, Marvin, 114
Symbols, 251

Talmon, J.L., 390
Tanenhaus, Joseph, 27, 35, 38, 39, 42, 48, 67, 72, 124
Taylor, Charles, 168, 170, 220, 318
Taylor, Michael, 351, 395
Taylor, Paul, 315, 316, 317, 330
Teune, Henry, 175
Textor, Robert, 312
Theocentric humanism, 239, 241, 245, 246, 248-249
Theoretical adjustment, 202
Theoretical concepts, 298
Theories, 133, 134, 140-145, 204, 210, 251
   "correspondence" rules, 143
   empirically interpreted terms, 143
   falsification of, 145-148
   hypothetico-deductive system, 143
   and interpretative explanations, 186
   "orthodox" view, 141-145
   primitive terms, 142
   semantical rules, 142
   testing of, 145-153
   theoretical terms, 143
   uninterpreted postulate system, 142
   uses of the term, 141
Thibaut, John W., 195

Thompson, Kenneth W., 236
Thorson, Stuart, 131
Thucydides, 236
Torgerson, W.S., 370
Toulmin, Stephen, 216, 218
Tradition, 4
Tullock, Gordon, 205, 220
Tversky, Amos, 371

Unanimity, 391
Uncertainty, 345–347
Unfreedom, 287, 288, 301, 305
Unintended consequences of action, 182, 184, 208
Urmson, J.O., 320
Utilitarianism, 360–361, 388
Utility function, 197, 203
Utopia, 244

Value cognitivism vs. value noncognitivism, 319
Value judgments, 315, 317
  instrumental, 316
Values of science, 134
Van Dyke, Vernon, 140
Verba, Sidney, 170, 306
*Verstehen*, 180, 184, 294–297
Veysey, Laurence, 22
Vlastos, Gregory, 387
Voegelin, Eric, 231, 232–233, 245, 249, 256, 273, 275, 276
Von Leyden, W., 325
Von Wright, Georg Henrik, 163, 164, 165, 166, 184–185, 216, 218, 219, 300, 302, 330

Voting, 164–165, 169, 199

Wahlke, John C., 231
Waismann, Friedrich, 309
Waldo, Dwight, 80, 83

Waismann, Friedrich, 309
Waldo, Dwight, 80, 83
Want-satisfaction, 388
Warnock, Geoffrey, 397
Wartofsky, Marx W., 219
Weber, Max, 161, 219, 220, 234, 338
Weinstein, W.L., 289
Weldon, Thomas D., 284, 396
Wellmer, Albrecht, 167, 217
White, Alan, 293
Williams, Bernard, 387
Willoughby, Westel W., 36, 39
Wilson, Bryan, 217
Wilson, James Q., 387
Wilson, Woodrow, 31, 33, 91
Winch, Peter, 295, 296
Winch, Peter, 167, 168, 169, 170, 178, 180–181, 184, 217
Wittgenstein, Ludwig, 216, 289
Wolfe, Alan, 114
Wolff, Robert Paul, 274, 325, 326, 391
Wolin, Sheldon, 8, 254, 255
Wood, Ellen Meiksins, 213
Woolsey, Theodore, 39

Yntema, D.B., 370

Zagoria, Donald S., 187, 188, 190

JA
71
.P63